Power
and
Purpose

Power
and
Purpose

*U.S. Policy toward Russia
after the Cold War*

James M. Goldgeier

Michael McFaul

Brookings Institution Press
Washington, D.C.

Copyright © 2003
THE BROOKINGS INSTITUTION
1775 Massachusetts Avenue, N.W., Washington, D.C. 20036
www.brookings.edu

Library of Congress Cataloging-in-Publication data
Goldgeier, James M.
  Power and purpose: U.S. policy toward Russia after the Cold War/
James M. Goldgeier and Michael McFaul.
    p. cm.
Includes bibliographical references and index.
  ISBN 0-8157-3174-4 (cloth : alk. paper) —
  ISBN 0-8157-3173-6 (pbk. : alk. paper)
  1. United States—Foreign relations—Russia (Federation) 2. Russia
(Federation)—Foreign relations—United States. 3. United
States—Foreign relations—1989- 4. United States—Officials and
employees—Interviews. 5. Russia (Federation)—Officials and
employees—Interviews. I. McFaul, Michael, 1963- II. Title.

  E183.8.R9G626 2004
  327.73047'09'049—dc22   2003019079

                    9 8 7 6 5 4 3 2 1

Typeset in Minion

Composition by OSP
Arlington, Virginia

Printed by R. R. Donnelley
Harrisonburg, Virginia

Contents

Acknowledgments

Our first debt of gratitude goes to Richard Haass, former vice president and director of Foreign Policy Studies at Brookings, and Michael Armacost, former president of Brookings, who provided the initial backing for this project. We are grateful to their successors, James Steinberg and Strobe Talbott, for continuing this support.

The project depended heavily on the willingness of those interviewed to speak with us and to be quoted in this book. These individuals are listed in the appendix.

Participants who attended daylong manuscript review workshops at Brookings and Stanford gave us invaluable advice. Andrew Bennett, Toby Gati, Fiona Hill, George Kolt, Andrew Kuchins, Robert Legvold, Sarah Mendelson, Bruce Parrott, Dennis Ross, Stephen Sestanovich, and James Steinberg attended at Brookings. Herb Abrams, David Bernstein, Coit Blacker, John Dunlop, Lynn Eden, James Fearon, David Holloway, Gail Lapidus, Alex Montgomery, Richard Morningstar, Scott Sagan, Todd Sechser, and Steve Stedman attended the workshop at Stanford. In addition, Mikhail Alexeev, Ashton Carter, Derek Chollet, Adam Elstein, Timothy Frye, Joel Hellman, Pavel Khokhryakov, Eugene Rumer, Elizabeth Sherwood-Randall, Alex Sokolowski, and Andrew Weiss provided comments on various draft chapters, and Michael McFaul's students at Stanford read and commented on the entire book. The three anonymous reviewers for the Brookings Press provided extremely detailed reports, and James Lindsay gave the manuscript a thorough, final review for Brookings. We are particularly grateful to the late Andrew Carpendale, who helped us get the project started and who was instrumental in explaining issues in American foreign policy associated with the collapse of the Soviet Union.

The National Security Archive at George Washington University filed the Freedom of Information Act requests and collected the documents received. The editors of *Current History* provided input into an earlier version of chapter 13, which appeared in their journal in October 2002. Eric Bahn, Rachel Dubin, Jeanette Leeney, Catherine Nielsen, Mistelle Olsen, Angela Sheets, Kathryn Dornbush, Tatyana Krasnopevtseva, Caroline McGregor, Laura Bailey, and Elina Treyger provided research assistance, and Toula Papanicolas provided excellent administrative support. The Institute for European, Russian and Eurasian Studies at George Washington University provided support for James Goldgeier, and the Carnegie Endowment for International Peace, the Earhart Foundation, and the Hoover Institution supported Michael McFaul.

Brookings Foreign Policy staff Monique Principi, Tara Miller, Bethany Hase, and Stacy Rosenberg helped in innumerable ways, and Becky Clark, Janet Walker, and Theresa Walker at the Brookings Press helped bring the project to fruition. Carlotta Ribar proofread the book, and Robert Elwood prepared the index.

This book would not have been possible without the extraordinary support of our families, and we are most grateful to them.

Power
and
Purpose

1

Power and Purpose

For four decades after World War II, two superpowers leading antagonistic political and socioeconomic blocs dominated global affairs. Conflict between the United States and the Soviet Union, capitalism and communism, defined the central drama within the international system. During this period, each superpower possessed armies and arsenals unmatched by others. The two superpowers were organized internally in radically different ways. The United States had a democratic polity and a market economy, while the Soviet Union had a totalitarian polity and a command economy. Because each country believed its system was superior, it actively promoted the replication of these political and socioeconomic systems in other countries while also resisting the expansion of the other's system. This ideological divide drove the competition between them. In other words, the Soviet Union and the United States were rivals not only because they were the two greatest powers in the international system, but because they were two powers with antithetical visions about how political, social, and economic life should be organized.

At the end of 1991, one pole in this bipolar, ideologically divided system collapsed. For the first time in the history of the modern world, the international balance of power changed without a major war. For leaders in Russia and the United States, these were heady times. Giddy talk abounded on both sides about the new task of transforming Russia into a market economy, a democratic polity, and a new partner with the West, erasing the cold war in an instant.

By the end of the 1990s, however, the mood in U.S.-Russian relations had more affinity with the old cold war era than with the more optimistic times in 1991. Journalists, academics, members of Congress, and the emerging George

W. Bush campaign for president derided the policies that President Bill Clinton and Vice President Al Gore had pursued toward Boris Yeltsin's Russia. "Who lost Russia?" they asked. They charged the Clinton administration with failure on every conceivable issue: too much meddling into Russia's internal affairs, overpersonalizing the relationship with President Yeltsin, ignoring or even aiding corruption of leading Russian officials, turning a blind eye toward Russian atrocities in the breakaway Republic of Chechnya, and not stopping Russian assistance to the Iranian nuclear weapons program. To listen to the experts and to the Republicans, it would seem that everything that could go wrong did go wrong inside Russia and in U.S.-Russian relations.

What happened in the intervening years between the euphoria of Soviet collapse and the Who Lost Russia witch-hunt less than a decade later? Some argued that it was the first Bush administration's fault for not providing enough assistance to Yeltsin's fledgling regime in 1992, others that the Clinton administration after 1993 had provided all the wrong kinds of assistance or had pursued "anti-Russian" policies such as the enlargement of NATO or the war on Kosovo that increased Russian resentment of the West.

Less than a year after George W. Bush became president, in the aftermath of the September 11, 2001, terrorist attack on the United States, U.S.-Russian relations seemed to take a decisive turn for the better again. Russian president Putin moved quickly to show sympathy for the United States and pledged his support for a united front against worldwide terrorism. Optimism emerged that Russia had decided that it truly belonged in the West. On the domestic front, Russia's economy was no longer the object of pity, the state seemed to be consolidating after a decade of decline, and a majority of Russians gave positive job approval marks for President Putin. U.S.-Russian relations appeared better than they had in years, at least until the American-led war with Iraq.

In explaining the course of these events, we are primarily interested in what U.S. policymakers believed they were trying to accomplish and how they understood what was occurring and what was at stake. In 1991, did they recognize that a transition was occurring in the Soviet Union, and what did they believe they could do about it? Once the USSR had broken up, did they believe the old enemy was really gone and that the United States should provide massive assistance, or did they largely cheer on the revolution from the sidelines? Throughout, how did American decisionmakers calculate U.S. interests, in relation to Russia, in a post–cold war world?

A New World Order

The fall of the Berlin Wall in 1989 and the dissolution of the Soviet Union in 1991 were the most transformative events in world affairs since the period immediately following World War II. Before 1989–91, containing the threat posed by the USSR had been the overarching purpose of U.S. foreign policy since the late 1940s. For American officials from the late 1940s to the late 1980s, every issue in the world—the defense of Europe, peace in the Middle East, civil war in Africa, or even the development of resources on the ocean floor—was seen through the prism of the cold war struggle with the Soviet Union.[1] Thus the collapse of the USSR was both exhilarating and disorienting for U.S. foreign policymakers. Now that the main American enemy had been defeated, what would replace containment as the new defining tenet of American foreign policy?[2] Henry Kissinger, America's most famous diplomat, even felt compelled to write a book answering those who questioned whether the United States needed a foreign policy.[3]

The intellectual and organizational challenge of reorienting foreign policy away from forty years of cold war and toward a new relationship between the United States and Russia was enormous. As American leaders pieced together a new foreign policy, they confronted an age-old question: to what extent was the United States a traditional great power playing the global game of balance of power politics, and to what extent was the United States a special "city on the hill" pursuing a mission of helping others develop market and democratic institutions? As American foreign policymakers sought to balance power and purpose in the 1990s, they did so in a world in which American supremacy in global affairs only grew larger and Russia's status as a major power dropped precipitously as the decade wore on. American leaders also had to define U.S. interests within Russia, where officials and the public were in the midst of one of the most profound revolutions in the modern era.

American leaders had not faced such challenges in conceptualizing foreign policy since 1945. That new world order had been full of uncertainties. Soviet intentions were unclear to many in 1945, and a Europe of two blocs only emerged after the communist coup in Czechoslovakia and the Berlin blockade in 1948. Many of the institutional innovations proposed immediately after World War II—including Franklin D. Roosevelt's "Four Policemen" and even the U.N. Security Council—looked in retrospect naively inappropriate for addressing the real fundamental issues of the international system that only became clear with time.[4] The transformation of the U.S.-Soviet standoff in Europe into a global struggle of titanic proportions only really began five years after World War II with the onset of the Korean War.

In important ways, however, the global environment of 1945 was less uncertain than that of 1991. Although it would take time for Americans to embrace Germans and Japanese as partners and integrate those two former adversaries into Western security structures, what was certain in 1945 was the total defeat of these authoritarian regimes. Not only had the United States and its allies defeated those two nations militarily, but Germany and Japan had been occupied and their leaders put on trial. An American general, Douglas MacArthur, and his staff wrote the postwar Japanese constitution. Furthermore, the rise of the new threat from Moscow had helped to clarify the importance of a close relationship between the United States and its former enemies. By the early 1950s, the communist threat made it imperative that Japan and West Germany be transformed into democracies integrated into Western security and economic structures.

The world of 1991 and after was more ambiguous about America's former enemy. The USSR had lost the cold war since communist ideology as a force in the world had withered away, and the Soviet Union no longer existed as a country. Yet the defeat of the enemy was not as complete in 1991 as in 1945. Although the Soviet Union ceased to exist, post-Soviet Russia did not suffer defeat in war and still had tens of thousands of nuclear weapons that could destroy the United States. The United States did not occupy post-Soviet Russia, making the trajectory of political and economic change more of a Russian affair than it had been in Germany and Japan after World War II. The president of the newly independent Russia, Boris Yeltsin, seemed prodemocracy, promarket, and pro-Western, but others in his entourage seemed less inclined to transform Russia internally and integrate with the West. His enemies, some of whom seemed to have real popular support in the country, were categorically against these changes. In 1945, U.S. occupying forces suppressed anti-Western forces in Germany and Japan. In 1991, by contrast, Yeltsin could not call on his allies in the West to suppress his foes. Nor did he have the power to do so alone. In the first years of independence, Yeltsin's hold on power remained extremely tenuous, as communist and nationalist forces within and outside government structures challenged the Russian president and his policies. If Russia's ability to integrate seemed more tenuous after the cold war than the probability for effective integration of occupied West Germany, the imperative of integration in 1991 was diminished compared with the 1940s. Above all else, there was no threat to American security interests to the east of Russia. And consequently, there was also little domestic support in the United States for a large-scale transformation agenda at the end of the cold war.[5]

In searching for a new grand strategy for American foreign policy after the cold war, everyone seemed to agree on two propositions: the Unites States was now the dominant global military power, and a democratic and market-oriented Russia firmly ensconced in the Western camp would serve American national interests. But could U.S. power be channeled to foster the latter? Could or should the all-powerful United States become engaged in promoting regime change and market transformation inside Russia? If so, how proactive should the United States be, how much money should be spent on this endeavor, and who should spend it, and how? Should American foreign policymakers simply state their desire for Russia to join the community of Western democracies while focusing primarily on the reduction of the nuclear threat and the permanence of Russia's new borders? Or should the United States be more ambitious and create something akin to the Marshall Plan that had helped rebuild western Europe after World War II? In other words, what priority should be given to the promotion of Russian transformation and integration versus the preservation of the balance of power in the world that favored the United States?

"Regime Transformers" and "Power Balancers"

Policymakers and those seeking to influence them responded to the post–cold war era by advocating two different (and sometimes opposing) strategies for American foreign policy. In one camp were the *regime transformers*. These people believed that American leaders had to use the full arsenal of American nonmilitary power to help bring about the internal transformation of Russia. They believed that a democratic Russia would no longer threaten the United States, because history has shown that democracies do not go to war with one another. They argued that a market-oriented Russia would seek foreign investment, trade, and eventually membership in multilateral institutions such as the World Trade Organization (WTO). If Russia could consolidate democratic and market institutions at home, then it would not matter how many nuclear weapons Russia still possessed.

A second school warned against missionary zeal. Instead, these *power balancers* argued that the nature of the regime inside Russia did not dictate Russian international behavior. And besides, even if regime type did matter, the United States did not have the capacity to influence Russia's internal affairs anyway. Instead, what mattered most was the balance of power between the United States and Russia. These power balancers argued that American leaders had to take advantage of Russian weakness to lock into place a balance of power in favor of the United States. This meant moving aggressively to help destroy Russia's nuclear arsenal as well as ensuring the independence of the new states on Russia's borders. These power balancers recognized that a Russia too weak to defend its borders or control its nuclear stockpile might eventually create new threats to the United States. However, most power balancers believed that the weaker this former foe, the better. Some even hoped for the breakup of Russia itself.

These two strategic responses to the end of the cold war were not novel ideas. Rather, they reflected two deep traditions in the making of American foreign policy. Regime transformers echoed a tradition as old as the United States itself. Since the creation of the United States, some American leaders have believed that the American democratic system of government made the

United States unique. Many American leaders championed the democratic United States, in contrast to the power-hungry European nations, as a new moral force in international politics. The more countries that embraced freedom and the democratic way of life domestically, the more peaceful relations among states would be internationally. In the nineteenth century, American foreign policymakers who embraced this tradition had limited means and limited horizons. The American missionary impulse rarely extended outside of the American hemisphere. Only after the United States entered World War I did President Woodrow Wilson attempt to introduce American moralism onto the global stage. As he explained to a joint session of Congress in January 1918 when he was outlining his fourteen points for a new world order, "What we demand in this war . . . is nothing peculiar to ourselves. It is that the world be made fit and safe to live in; and particularly that it be made safe for every peace-loving nation."[6] In Wilson's view, the best way to achieve American security was not to defend the United States against the outside world but to change fundamentally the outside world. In policy circles, this tradition became known as Wilsonianism.[7] Although Wilson was a Democrat, this philosophy about international affairs crossed partisan lines. During the cold war, one of the staunchest Wilsonians in foreign policy was Republican president Ronald Reagan, who also believed in regime change as a means of enhancing American national security. In academic circles, this approach to foreign policy and theory about international politics has been labeled "liberalism" (somewhat misleadingly given how the term is used in U.S. domestic politics).[8]

Wilson's attempt to make the world safe for democracy failed. The Republican-controlled Senate blocked American membership in his League of Nations. The rise of Nazi Germany and communist Russia in Europe and the onset of World War II stimulated the emergence of yet another group in American foreign policy thinking—the power balancers or the realists.[9] In response to Wilson's "naive idealism," realists countered that the United States had to pay greater attention to the power capabilities of states and the balance of power between them. How states were organized internally—that is, whether they were democratic or autocratic—mattered much less. This school rose to prominence during the cold war, when the chief imperative for American foreign policymakers became the containment of Soviet power.

During the cold war, the impulse to promote regime change abroad did not disappear. On the contrary, American politicians invented all sorts of new tools of foreign policy—including the Agency for International Development (AID), the Peace Corps, the Alliance for Progress, Radio Free Europe, and the National Endowment for Democracy—to facilitate regime change in other countries. Moreover, realist and liberal impulses (or regime transformers and power balancers) have been present in every American administration's foreign policy since 1945; different administrations simply accentuated one approach over the other.[10] Swings between liberal and realist tendencies in American foreign policy did not follow neatly with changes in presidential party affiliations. For instance, Republican President Richard Nixon and his chief foreign policy adviser, Henry Kissinger, were classic realists or power balancers. They focused on the balance of power as the crucial ingredient of the international system and pursued policies that sought to preserve America's position in the world, for example, by reaching out to China to balance against a rising Soviet power.[11] While in office, Nixon and Kissinger cared little about the internal politics of the USSR or China. They were ready to reach out to dictatorships such as China if it helped to balance the power of the Soviet Union. As Nixon once told Chinese leader Mao Zedong, "What is important is not a nation's internal political philosophy. What is important is its policy toward the rest of the world and toward us."[12]

In contrast, fellow Republican Ronald Reagan devoted more attention to domestic regimes and crafted policies to undermine autocratic regimes, including most prominently (but not only) communist systems.[13] Reagan was selective about where he promoted regime change, concerned more about communist dictatorships in eastern Europe than capitalist dictatorships in Africa or Latin America. Nonetheless, Reagan's approach to international politics had more in common with Democrats Wilson and Harry Truman than Republican Nixon.

The Centrality of Individuals and Ideas in America's Russia Policy

Few administrations promoted regime change with the vigor of Wilson or Reagan or championed power balancing with the energy of Nixon and Kissinger. Most presidents have pursued some combination of both. As Bill Clinton's national security adviser Anthony Lake wrote nearly a decade before assuming his high-level position, "In foreign policy, [Americans] have constantly been torn between a heritage of hardheaded realism and an idealistic belief in America's mission to promote democracy and individual freedoms.... The latter pushes Americans toward an expansive belief in their power; the former toward a recognition of the limits of that power."[14] No matter what their stripe, presidents prone to power balancing will always be pressured by America's identity as the leader of the community of democracies to infuse power politics with a liberal purpose, and regime transformers will find that when America needs allies, a blind eye is easily turned to violations of liberal values. Throughout the first decade of the post–cold war era, both of these frameworks influenced American foreign policy toward Russia.

Yet at different periods in the post–cold war era, these two philosophical approaches influenced American policy in distinct, identifiable ways.[15] It is a central claim of this book that ideas do matter in the making of foreign policy. Individual actors—not states, structures, or bureaucracies—make choices about what foreign policy to pursue. People with names and faces, not "the United States" or "Russia" or "globalization" or "the international balance of power," make foreign policy. When making foreign policy, ideas about the nature of international politics shape the choices of these actors in profound, observable ways.[16] Policy entrepreneurs armed with and passionate about a particular set of ideas can push the policy of the entire government in a particular direction. In our story, James Baker and his ideas about denuclearization, Anthony Lake and his ideas about NATO enlargement, William Perry and his ideas about Cooperative Threat Reduction, or Lawrence Summers and David Lipton and their ideas about macroeconomic stabilization are a few of the most salient examples in which the fusion of effective policy entrepreneurs and novel ideas had a major impact on the formation of U.S. policy toward Russia in the 1990s. The potential causal weight of ideas grows especially during times of rapid change like the end of the cold war, when old institutions, norms, and practices have been challenged or broken down but new rules of the game (domestically and internationally) shaping foreign policy have not consolidated.[17]

To be sure, the balance of power in the international system defined the parameters of the possible for American foreign policymakers. U.S. foreign policymakers were confronted with decisions about the promotion of regime change in Russia or the destruction of nuclear weapons inside Russia because the United States had the power to consider such policies.[18] Nonetheless, the balance of power in the international system does not by itself *determine* the foreign policy of states.[19] Structural or systemic factors—be they the balance of power or international institutions—are least constraining for the most powerful state in the system, the United States.[20] Nor in this case did a particular geostrategic concern such as oil or the security of a vital ally trump all other foreign policy concerns. Worries over nuclear proliferation came closest, but even this concern did not determine what American policy toward Russia would be. In the crafting of post-Soviet Russia policy, U.S. policymakers had choices to make, and these choices were influenced to a great extent by their ideas about international politics.

Nor, looking inside the United States, did domestic forces play a major constraining role on the executive branch in the making of American policy toward Russia after 1991. In other foreign policy areas, corporate lobbies, congressional actors, and ethnic interest groups played an important part in shaping American policy during this period (and others).[21] But on Russia policy after 1991, these other kinds of actors were less consequential.[22] Rather, it was the philosophical approach embraced by the president and his key advisers that had the greatest impact on defining American policy toward Russia after the cold war. Ideas about the nature of the international system, the nature of

Russia, and definition of the American national security interests changed across administrations in ways that had consequences for the formulation of American foreign policy toward post-Soviet Russia.

George H.W. Bush and Prudent Realism

President George H. W. Bush was a power balancer. He leaned toward Nixonian realism (not surprising given that he and his national security adviser, Brent Scowcroft, served in high-level positions in the Nixon administration). As the Soviet Union waned, Bush was most concerned with maintaining global stability and less concerned with promoting freedom within the Soviet Union or Russia. Given Republican support for free markets and democracy, the first Bush administration also spoke about the importance of the Western zone of peace and prosperity and the possibility of a new Russia finding its place in that order. The last cold war president just was not prepared to spend significant resources on such an endeavor.

For George H.W. Bush, the fundamental challenge was how to manage a peaceful transition from the world we knew to the new world order. As the world transformed, the Bush administration's primary goal was to ensure that the transition was peaceful, and a fundamental security goal was to ensure that in a post-Soviet world, no rival power to American hegemony emerged. As articulated in a Pentagon paper overseen by Secretary of Defense Dick Cheney, "Simply put, it is the intent of the new Regional Defense Strategy to enable the U.S. to lead in shaping an uncertain future so as to preserve and enhance this strategic depth won at such great pains."[23]

It was not just with respect to the Soviet Union and then Russia where realism rather than Wilsonianism generally prevailed in the first Bush administration. The Bush team might have spoken about a commitment to a Europe whole and free (thus evoking Wilsonian ideals), but in the Balkans, the administration made clear it would not get involved in preventing ethnic cleansing because the United States—in Secretary of State James A. Baker III's words—had "no dog in that fight."[24] Yugoslavia would be a problem only if the conflict spread and involved other major powers, and so the Bush administration put a small U.S. force in Macedonia to deter the conflict from spreading but not to put the fire out. Similarly, the United States led a coalition to expel Iraq from Kuwait but did not seek to overthrow Saddam Hussein or dismember Iraq because the primary concern was to preserve the balance of power in the region.[25]

Bush did little to *promote* regime change in the Soviet Union. Although Bush and his foreign policy team welcomed the internal changes initiated by President Mikhail Gorbachev within the Soviet Union, they never pursued activist policies that might accelerate the process of internal change or push it in a particular direction. Reform, in Bush's view, was an internal matter for the

Soviet leadership to which the United States should only react and not try to shape or stimulate. Bush and his team were fundamentally nervous about radical regime change. Yugoslavia's breakup in 1991 became a stark reminder of how badly things could go in multiethnic countries when different constituent elements started to seek independence. In foreign policy, George H. W. Bush sought to obtain Soviet support for American foreign policy initiatives such as ensuring that a unified Germany remained in NATO and conducting the Persian Gulf War. For Soviet domestic policy, Bush wanted above all else to help avoid creating a Yugoslav scenario of civil war in a country that stretched eleven time zones and possessed thousands of nuclear weapons, and thus freedom of the constituent republics was not high on the list of foreign policy priorities for most of the team.[26]

For most of their time in office, Bush and National Security Adviser Brent Scowcroft hoped that Gorbachev could stay in power. After all, Gorbachev had offered concession after concession to the United States, and Bush and Scowcroft feared what might follow. But the events of the fall of 1991 were not subject to outside influence, and a team trained to fight the cold war now had to retool to respond to the drama of fifteen new post-Soviet and postcommunist states as they began the new year of 1992.

After the Soviet breakup, the Bush team did seek to foster Russia's integration into the West, but the emphasis remained on Russia's foreign policy and not its internal transformation. In the nuclear realm, this meant working with Russia and the other newly independent republics to consolidate the Soviet nuclear arsenal and ensure singular command and control. In economics, the focus was on ensuring that Russia avoid defaulting on its debt rather than on generating massive assistance for building a market economy.

In the aftermath of Soviet dissolution, four countries had strategic nuclear weapons stationed on their territory (Russia, Ukraine, Belarus, and Kazakhstan). Secretary of State James A. Baker III spent the winter and spring of 1992 cajoling the new countries of Belarus, Kazakhstan, and Ukraine to commit to the withdrawal of the vast nuclear arsenals on their soil to Russia. The ultimate transfer of the warheads, which was completed at the end of the Clinton administration's first term, was one of the most important and least noticed successes of American policy toward the region in the 1990s.

But in 1991–92, the Bush administration's efforts to reduce this clear and present danger were pursued without active involvement in the internal transformation of Russia. Thus, on the economic side, the policy was far less ambitious. Candidate Bill Clinton and former president Richard Nixon (in a dramatic turnaround from his days in office when he ignored other countries' internal philosophies) exhorted the Bush team in the spring of 1992 to provide massive financial assistance to the new Russian reform team. But that assistance was not forthcoming. Instead, the Bush Treasury Department under Secretary Nicholas Brady focused primarily on ensuring that Russia would assume the debt incurred by the previous regime.

The overarching message of the Bush team to Russia and the other republics emerging from the ashes of the Soviet Union was, "If you want acceptance into the West, you have to do X, Y, and Z." Get the nuclear situation under control. Commit to paying your debt. Although many in the West called for the Bush administration to give more aid, devote more attention, and generally engage more comprehensively in helping to guide Russia's transformation, Bush and his team put the onus of action on Russia. If Russia successfully transformed, then it would be welcomed into the Western club.

Bill Clinton and Democratic Enlargement

Bush's successor, Bill Clinton, was a regime transformer—a Wilsonian liberal. In the aftermath of the cold war, he believed that active promotion of the enlargement of the community of market democracies was a fundamental national security objective of the United States. Clinton's 1994 national security strategy stated, "Our national security strategy is based on enlarging the community of market democracies while deterring and containing a range of threats to our nation, our allies and our interests. The more that democracy and political and economic liberalization take hold in the world, particularly in countries of geo-strategic importance to us, the safer our nation is likely to be and the more our people are likely to prosper."[27] Clinton believed that democratic regime change in Russia would lead to a new security relationship, thereby allowing for lower U.S. defense budgets, which would in turn free resources for Clinton's cherished domestic programs. Only with Russia's transformation would a true peace dividend be possible. Unlike the Bush administration, Clinton and his team were determined to pursue policies designed to assist democratic and market reform in Russia as the key means of integrating Russia into the Western community of democratic states.

But promoting economic assistance and championing democracy were not so straightforward. As one of its first foreign policy initiatives, the Clinton team did put together an enormous aid package for Russia, but this turned out to be a one-shot deal. American statesmen emphasized the importance of the democratic process, but in practice, Clinton made the decision to stand by Yeltsin no matter what his friend in Moscow did, most dramatically during the Russian president's assault on his own parliament in October 1993 and Yeltsin's military intervention into Chechnya a year later. For the Clinton team, Yeltsin the man *was* reform, while his enemies represented regression and the possible return of communism.

Clinton did not abandon power-balancing policies initiated by his predecessor. Clinton's administration brought to successful conclusions the removal of strategic nuclear weapons from the non-Russian republics (which required that Russia be a good neighbor) and the withdrawal of Russian troops from the Baltic nations of Estonia, Latvia, and Lithuania. Even these policies of power balancing, however, had a new Wilsonian tinge in the Clinton era. Achieving these security goals was critical for Clinton's pursuit of Russia's acceptance into the Western club of democracies and market economies. To speed the process and encourage Russia to join, Clinton offered financial assistance, diplomatic support, and sometimes even a bending of the rules for admission. It was not the Bush message of "transform yourself and then you can join the club." Clinton offered assistance toward membership because he believed that if Russia were welcomed into the club, it would help promote internal transformation, which would foster even better relations with the West. The Clinton message emphasized the causal connection between transformation and integration and the U.S. role in promoting both objectives.

Clinton's team even deployed the language of engagement and integration to frame issues such as the 1995 Dayton Peace Accords that brought peace to Bosnia and the enlargement of NATO that appeared to the Russian elite to threaten its country's interests. In each case, the United States set the agenda, in the first by forcing an end to the war in Bosnia and Herzegovina on U.S. terms and in the second by paving the way for the former Warsaw Pact nations of Poland, Hungary, and the Czech Republic to join NATO. But these were not pure power plays for a Wilsonian administration; the United States actively sought to offer Russian counterparts something in return for their acceptance of the U.S. agenda. In the case of Bosnia, the Clinton administration helped Russia find a place in the Implementation Force sent to keep the peace so that it would not look as if Russian forces were directly under NATO command. In the case of NATO enlargement, Clinton offered a big ceremony in Paris in May 1997 so that Yeltsin could sign a new accord on NATO-Russian relations with all of the alliance's leaders. Not coincidentally, Clinton that summer granted Russia an equal place in what had been the G-7 (Group of Seven advanced industrialized democracies) and was now "the Eight." (The following summer at their annual meeting in Birmingham, the G-7 formally became the G-8.)

Despite this commitment to foster Russia's internal transformation, Clinton felt free to act in defense of U.S. national interests even when Russia objected strenuously. He and his administration enlarged NATO and led that organization's military campaign against Serbia because the new balance of power within the international system allowed them to do so. But he did come into office emphasizing the need actively to use American money and expertise to help Russia build capitalism and democracy, and it was that emphasis on traditional Wilsonianism that came under such fire as Russia's political and economic evolution seemed to sputter and fail by the late 1990s.

In Clinton and Yeltsin's second term, shocks in three major policy areas—democracy promotion, economic assistance, and security integration—led to the collapse of the ambitious American agenda and the low point of post–cold war U.S.-Russian relations. First came the Russian financial crisis of August 1998, which led to disillusionment for the U.S. economic team and compelled them to disengage from the effort to help transform the Russian economy. The Who Lost Russia debate soon absorbed the Western community of Russia watchers.

Then in March 1999, NATO launched its air war over Kosovo. Although the Russians played a significant role in the endgame that led to Yugoslav president Slobodan Milosevic's surrender, the war essentially chilled NATO-Russian relations for the rest of the Clinton presidency. American and Russian officials perceived the war through opposite analytical frameworks. Clinton officials believed they were spreading liberty to an oppressed people. Yeltsin's team believed that the American military was spreading its power into Russia's traditional sphere of influence. Any notion that the United States and Russia could work together within NATO was dead (and only the events of September 11, 2001, could bring it back).

Months later, Russia renewed its war in Chechnya, which led to mass atrocities and human rights violations. A media clampdown followed, further eroding Russia's already fragile democratic institutions, and it now seemed that hopes for economic and democratic transformation and security integration were all lost.

By the fall of 1999, Clinton's Russia policy had stalled completely. Clinton's chief Russia expert, Strobe Talbott, called for strategic patience, but patience had run out. The security team grew frustrated that Russia was not halting sales of nuclear technology to Iran. Nor would the new Russian president, Vladimir Putin, conclude a major arms control deal to reduce strategic offensive warheads while allowing the United States to pursue the development of limited missile defense under a revised Anti-Ballistic Missile Treaty. With President Clinton trying to make peace in the Middle East and seeking a breakthrough on the Korean peninsula in his final months in office, Russia became a distant concern. It was a far cry from the serious focus on Russia at the beginning of the Clinton presidency in 1993.

George W. Bush: From Realism to Selective Liberalism

By the time of the 2000 American presidential campaign, therefore, the talk was not about how Russia had been transformed and integrated but rather how Russia had been lost. If Clinton complained that Bush Sr. had done too little, the new George Bush and his advisers derided Clinton and Vice President Al Gore for trying to do too much in Russia's domestic affairs, arguing instead that America's true interests lay not in Wilsonianism but in a return to realpolitik. And since power was all that mattered, the Bush team entered office not with a Russia focus, as had its two predecessors, but arguing instead for a policy that reached out first to allies in North America, Asia, and Europe, and only then focused on dealing with Russia. Although it was a policy far different from where the Clinton team had started, it was in substance not that different from where the Clinton team had left things in January 2001. For U.S. foreign policy, Russia had clearly fallen from the core of U.S. interests to the periphery.

The new Bush team had derided Clinton and Gore during the 2000 campaign for believing that U.S. policy should be centered on a close personal relationship with President Boris Yeltsin and his prime ministers, in particular Viktor Chernomyrdin. Ironically, Bush Sr. had been accused of just such an obsession with President Mikhail Gorbachev. But try as they might to make policy about states and not individuals, the Bush team could not ignore internal politics and individuals in Russia. At his first meeting with Putin in Slovenia in June 2001, Bush made a special effort to establish a personal bond with his Russian counterpart.

After the attacks against the United States on September 11, President Bush suddenly and dramatically embraced a new set of ideas about foreign policy, which had more in common with the philosophies of Ronald Reagan and Woodrow Wilson than with those of his father or Richard Nixon. In several important speeches, Bush has made clear that he believes in the revision of the international system, not its preservation.[28] Bush's national security strategy, released in the fall of 2002, makes the promotion of individual liberty around the world an explicit U.S. national security interest. In many parts of the world, the president has explained, the promotion of individual liberty can only occur through regime change. At least rhetorically, Bush moved after September 11 closer to the regime transformers and away from the power balancers.[29]

To date, however, Bush has decided to promote Wilsonian ideals selectively. If he and the regime transformers in his administration have seemed determined to promote democracy in the Middle East even if it means using force, they have not demonstrated a similar enthusiasm for the same strategy for Russia. After September 11, Bush moved even further to embrace Putin as an ally in the war against terrorism. The Bush team was more than happy to move from a policy of neglect to a new embrace as long as Russia was not undermining U.S. efforts such as the establishment of American military bases in Central Asia. The rapprochement, however, was not a complete return to the early years of the Clinton presidency in that Russia's domestic transformation was not a part of the bilateral agenda. Instead, after September 11, Russia's international role once again became the primary focus of attention. The Bush administration focused heavily on a new strategic nuclear agenda (including abolition of the Anti-Ballistic Missile Treaty) and on the war on terrorism, and devoted less attention to Russian domestic issues such as the conduct of the Russian army in Chechnya or Putin's crackdown on media independence.

Shifting Parameters of Power and Threat

Ideas about the importance of regime transformation versus power balancing played a direct causal role in shaping American policy toward Russia after 1991. Over the decade, however, two other factors beyond American borders became increasingly important in U.S. policymaking. Most significantly, the asymmetry of power between the United States and Russia grew and became better understood. In the early part of the decade, Russia's power was difficult to gauge. Since Russia had not been defeated militarily, many Russian foreign policymakers still viewed their country as a major world power, and many Americans were slow to recognize how fast the world was changing.[30] This ambiguity about the real balance of power in the world initially constrained a cautious Clinton administration.[31] Perceptions of this power asymmetry changed more slowly than the actual power balance, but over time, the true distribution of power became clearer. By the end of the 1990s, decisionmakers in Washington correctly believed that Russia had little capacity to influence American foreign policy, even in traditional spheres of Russian influence such as the Balkans. This updating emboldened Clinton officials. They pursued foreign policies such as NATO expansion and the war against Serbia that a decade earlier would have been perceived as sure to spark conflict between the two great powers.

Second, uncertainty about the course of Russia's revolution also changed over time. At the beginning of the decade, the endpoint of Russia's transition from communism was highly uncertain. Those who believed that regime type mattered—and that the United States was better off with a democratic Russia than with a communist or fascist Russia—had the daunting challenge of devising policies that promoted democracy and markets in the largest country in the world with an unbroken history of autocratic rule and a seventy-year experiment with a command economy. Trying to assist a transition from that system to a market economy and democratic polity that could trade with the West and join Western institutions was simply unprecedented.

By the end of the decade, worst-case scenarios for Russia's domestic transformation seemed unlikely.[32] Imperfect capitalism and an even more imperfect democracy emerged in Russia in the 1990s, an outcome that left the regime transformers in the Clinton team frustrated. At the same time, the specter of fascism or the return to communism had disappeared, an outcome that allowed George W. Bush officials to worry less about the negative implications of domestic developments inside Russia for American national security interests. The emergence of these two factors over time would become influential in the formulation of American foreign policy even if worldview continued to shape the general approach. Recognition of the growing asymmetry of power between the United States and Russia enabled American officials to pursue foreign policy initiatives unilaterally with less regard for Russian reactions. Recognition of the end of revolution inside Russia allowed U.S. officials to focus less on internal developments inside Russia. At the same time, the growing asymmetry of power between these former equals and a mixed record of transformation inside Russia influenced the bilateral relationship, mostly in a negative way. Russian leaders grew tired of American arrogance in international affairs and wary of American intentions inside Russia. Only the combination of a new ideological orientation inside the White House and a shock to the international system as momentous as September 11 could change the mood in U.S.-Russian relations.

The Focus of Analysis

This book is predominantly about how the president and his top advisers in the executive branch formulated and carried out America's Russia policy. Our intent is not to deny the role that Congress or other actors play in the conduct of American foreign policy, but our focus is the overall U.S. approach to Russia in this period, which was set by the executive branch. There are moments when Congress is quite important, for example, in the case of Russia policy in the 1990s when senators Sam Nunn (D-Ga.) and Richard Lugar (R-Ind.) pushed the first Bush administration to provide assistance for Russian denuclearization or when congressional Republicans constrained the Clinton administration's ability to allocate funds for assistance or balked at removing the cold war era–restrictions in trade with Russia. We discuss these actors and these issues, but the book is chiefly about how three administrations conceptualized and managed Russia policy, and about the relative intensity of their efforts to transform and integrate Russia.

In analyzing American foreign policy toward Russia, we also write about the ebb and flow of U.S.-Russian relations after the cold war. Major figures from the Russian side naturally appear in central roles, not only in the context of their internal policy but also in their effect on American decisionmakers. We try to describe the Russian context and incorporate Russian influence on the U.S. policy process. Nonetheless, the book's main focus is the making of American foreign policy toward Russia.

Our goal is not to provide a blow-by-blow account of the evolution of America's post-Soviet Russia policy. Instead, we paint a picture of the principal themes, trade-offs, challenges, and opportunities as American foreign policymakers grappled with the extraordinarily historic transition from a world in which Russia was America's main enemy to a world in which the United

States hoped Russia would stand with it as Americans dealt with new (or, in some cases, old but neglected) challenges. The United States developed many other foreign policy objectives during this period , but the evolution of policy toward Russia was one of the most frustrating, challenging, and controversial American foreign policies of all.

To tell our story, we rely heavily on the recollections of the top U.S. decisionmakers as well as others involved in the issues. Often, individuals interviewed were still serving in an official capacity or hoped to serve in office in the future. Sometimes, they were being asked to recall events that took place five or more years earlier. We have sought to verify information by interviewing as many individuals as we could, by combing the available public record, and by using the Freedom of Information Act to get government documents declassified. Most of our document requests were denied, but several important records were released and provide further information for the story. In the end, though, even if information from interviews needs to be taken with a grain of salt, the ways in which policymakers describe and justify what they were doing is a critical part of the narrative and of our assessment.

In analyzing each administration's Russia policy, we focus on the three general policy areas raised above: democracy promotion (broadly defined), economic assistance, and security cooperation. For the first Bush administration and first Clinton term, the chapters discuss how policy was developed in each area. For the second Clinton term, we discuss the major setbacks to policy in these areas: the August 1998 financial collapse, the 1999 war on Kosovo, the 1999 resumption of war in Chechnya along with the clampdown on media freedom, and the failure in 2000 to put an end to Russia's sales of sensitive technologies to Iran or to conclude an arms control deal. For the second Bush administration, we examine the new team's initial approach in these three areas and the effect of September 11 on earlier assumptions.

The final chapter of the book attempts a broad assessment of the successes and failures of American foreign policy toward Russia in the first decade after the Soviet collapse. Throughout, we consider how power and purpose shaped U.S. foreign policy, and how different understandings not only across but *within* administrations on power and purpose changed over time.

2

George H. W. Bush and Soviet Regime Change

Although the Soviet collapse shocked the world, the process of regime change in the Soviet Union had been under way for several years before the aborted coup attempt in August 1991 and subsequent dissolution of the USSR in December 1991.[1] Selected by his colleagues on the Soviet Politburo as the general secretary of the Communist Party of the Soviet Union (CPSU) in March 1985, Mikhail Gorbachev had launched these political reforms. At the time, the authoritarian nature of the regime meant that reform could only originate at the top. Gorbachev's main focus was the revival of an economy that had stagnated under central planning. He did call for competitive elections at the 1987 Central Committee plenum, but during his first three years in power, he attempted to introduce economic reform using the existing set of political institutions. Eventually, he came to realize that he could proceed with his program of economic restructuring (perestroika) only by changing the institutions of governance, which would undermine his opponents entrenched within the existing CPSU and state structures and would strengthen new proponents of reform within the state and throughout society.[2]

To stimulate new allies for perestroika, Gorbachev initiated sweeping reform measures aimed at liberalizing political society. Gorbachev's policy of glasnost, or openness, allowed for the publication and discussion of previously taboo subjects, while changes in the Soviet criminal code no longer punished political assembly and demonstration; the goal was to put pressure on entrenched interests. At the Nineteenth Party Conference in 1988, Gorbachev outlined a plan for fundamental institutional change by announcing that partially competitive elections for the USSR's legislature, the Congress of People's

Deputies, would be held in the spring of 1989. These elections were followed by elections for legislatures at the republic, *oblast'* (region), and city level during the spring of 1990. Having decided that destroying the Communist Party of the Soviet Union (CPSU) governing apparatus was too dangerous, Gorbachev hoped to resurrect a set of state institutions that could gradually wrest governing power away from the Communist Party.

During the first stages of liberalization, Gorbachev's plan seemed to work. The 1989 elections produced an unprecedented whirl of new political mobilization in Soviet society. Media criticism exploded, electoral clubs sprouted, and noncommunist, pro-perestroika organizations convened. Reformers elected to the USSR Congress of People's Deputies still represented a very small minority, but the holding of elections and the subsequent live broadcast of the Congress's proceedings stimulated significant non-Party mobilization in society for the first time in decades. Mobilization from below grew even stronger during and immediately after the 1990 elections, when a newly organized opposition movement, Democratic Russia, won hundreds of seats in the Russian Congress of People's Deputies and controlled majorities in the Moscow and Leningrad city soviets (councils).[3] Boris Yeltsin, the leader of the democratic opposition, then won election as the chairman of the Russian Congress of People's Deputies in the spring of 1990. The following year, in June 1991, Yeltsin won a landslide victory in the election of Russia's first president.

Initially, these forces from below were Gorbachev's allies against the conservative midlevel bureaucracy of the Communist Party. Quickly however, the kind, extent, and pace of change demanded from below overtook Gorbachev's reform agenda. Beginning first with the Interregional Group of Deputies in the Soviet Congress, political actors bent on truly radical change began to organize against the traditional ruling institutions of the Soviet regime. Led by Boris Yeltsin, this new political force rapidly organized as a revolutionary opposition to the evolutionary reforms proposed by Gorbachev.[4] Although initially vague in their demands, these challengers eventually developed several antisystemic themes in direct opposition to Gorbachev's now *ancien régime.*

First, they demanded independence from the USSR. After elections for soviets on the republican level in the spring of 1990, opposition to the Soviet communist system was expressed most vividly as a demand for national sovereignty, first in the Baltic Republics of Estonia, Latvia, and Lithuania and then in Russia. By 1990, a "war of laws" erupted between the Soviet and Russian congresses, with each one using its legislative mandate to assert sovereignty over the other.[5] A second, but significantly less developed concept of the opposition, was the call for market reforms. If Gorbachev's perestroika sought to reform and revitalize the old socialist system, Yeltsin, Democratic Russia, and their allies eventually called for the destruction of socialism altogether.[6] Democracy was a third component of the ideology of opposition, and to make clear their differences with the old system, opposition forces carried out the election of their leader, Boris Yeltsin, to the newly created post of president of Russia in June 1991. Yeltsin's election in June 1991 was his third landslide victory in as many years, whereas the leader of the Soviet Union, Mikhail Gorbachev, had never obtained a mandate directly from the people.

During this same period, the nationalist movements consolidating in the non-Russian republics of the Soviet Union mustered an additional challenge to Gorbachev's grip on power. Gorbachev admits in his memoirs that he grossly underestimated the "national question" as interethnic conflicts within the Soviet Union were euphemistically called.[7] He did not anticipate the ethnic violence in Kazakhstan in December 1986, when Kazakh students protested the replacement of ethnic Kazakh Dinmukhammed Kunaev (removed as part of Gorbachev's anticorruption campaign) as CPSU first secretary in Kazakhstan with an ethnic Russian. In 1988, an even more violent conflict exploded between Armenians and Azeris over the disputed territory of Nagorno-Karabakh. These protests were followed by demands for independence in the Baltic republics and Georgia. A Georgian demonstration in 1989 ended in slaughter, when Soviet troops opened fire on unarmed protesters in Tbilisi, the Georgian capital. Two years later, in January 1991, Soviet soldiers took control of media outlets in Riga, Latvia, and Vilnius, Lithuania. Nearly two dozen people died during these raids, and hundreds more were injured. Gorbachev claimed no responsibility for the attacks, a statement that President George H. W. Bush believed. Increasingly, however, Gorbachev's regime sounded and acted reactionary, not reformist.[8] It also seemed to be losing its grip.

American Reactions to Yeltsin and Other Anti-Soviet Forces

Yeltsin and his supporters claimed to be more Western and more pro-American than Gorbachev. Gorbachev advocated reformed socialism; Yeltsin and his allies pledged allegiance to neoliberal market capitalism. Gorbachev allowed for elections of limited competition; Yeltsin called for multiparty elections and institutionalized a direct election for the Russian presidency. Gorbachev wanted to create a new Soviet federation; Yeltsin pushed for complete independence for Russia and the other republics. Soon after declaring Russia a sovereign state in the summer of 1990, Yeltsin created the Russian Ministry of Foreign Affairs and named a midlevel diplomat at the Soviet Foreign Ministry, Andrei Kozyrev, as Russia's first foreign minister. Gorbachev called for a Common European Home; Yeltsin and his allies wanted (at this moment) to join NATO. Gorbachev looked for a way to keep the Baltic "republics" in the Union; Yeltsin and his government recognized the independence of the Baltic "states" and labeled their annexation by the Soviet Union in 1940 as illegal.[9] Equally important were the ideas and ideological tenets absent from Yeltsin's rhetoric. Above all else, Russian opposition leaders avoided language that could be associated with ethnic nationalism. Eager to distinguish their cause from the independence movements in Yugoslavia, their quest for sovereignty was consciously devoid of an ethnic dimension, and their tactics were peaceful. Russia's opposition refrained from using violence as a means for seizing power because of the fear that violence would discredit the movement domestically as well as internationally.

The rise of Yeltsin, his more revolutionary approach to regime change, and his more pro-Western policy in foreign affairs presented a real dilemma for the Bush administration. Upon assuming power in 1989, Bush's foreign policy team was initially skeptical of Gorbachev's true intentions. The new administration slowed the process of rapprochement initiated by Gorbachev and U.S. president Ronald Reagan and instead undertook a lengthy policy review. By the end of 1989, however, Gorbachev's acceptance of free elections in eastern Europe and the fall of the Berlin Wall, coupled with Soviet troop withdrawal from Afghanistan and a general pullback from the third world, won him high praise from President Bush and his immediate circle of foreign policy advisers. Gorbachev's decision in 1990 not to block German unification followed by his support for the American-led military campaign against Iraq further endeared him to the Bush administration. In foreign affairs, Gorbachev and his foreign minister, Eduard Shevardnadze, agreed to almost every major policy preference of the Bush administration.[10]

Unsurprisingly, the Bush administration did not want to do anything that might weaken or undermine America's trusted friend in the Kremlin. Had their struggle for power been waged against a leader such as Josef Stalin or even Leonid Brezhnev, Russia's opposition forces might have had an easier time gaining recognition and support from the Bush administration. Instead, Yeltsin's challenge to Gorbachev was extremely inconvenient for U.S. national security interests. Gorbachev was delivering on things that mattered to President Bush and his national security team. Why, therefore, would these U.S. officials do anything to undermine the Soviet leader?

Moreover, for many in the Bush administration, the alternatives did not look appealing. At the time, many predicted a conservative swing should Gorbachev fall. And the so-called progressive option did not look terribly appealing to the Bush team. Yeltsin, for many in the Bush administration, was a drunken, undiplomatic demagogue who could not be trusted. He made a terrible impression on White House officials on his first visit to Washington in September 1989.[11] Yeltsin was scheduled to meet with National Security Adviser Brent Scowcroft, with a "drop by" from the president scripted into the program.[12] Yeltsin was furious that Bush did not have formal plans to meet with him, and he was not familiar with the tradition of presidential drop bys as a way to finesse awkward meetings. For a while, Yeltsin stood in the driveway of the West Wing, offended that he was not entering the White House through the main entrance and disgruntled that his appointment was with Scowcroft, and not the president.[13]

Yeltsin's boorish behavior made a particularly unfavorable impression on Scowcroft, who saw not just a drunk and an egomaniac but an autocrat and a demagogue. Scowcroft recalls, "The first time he came in he was all bombast. He didn't even have a job. When he came down to my office, I just asked him one question: 'why are you here?' And he launched into this Alice-in-Wonderland story. Yeltsin was a pure opportunist. He was a democrat because that was the way to get out. He was fundamentally after power, and unlike Gorbachev, he [was] a populist and knew what appealed and loved that part and did it very well."[14] Yeltsin allegedly arrived drunk and unprepared for many of his appointments during this same Washington visit, creating the strong impression at the White House that he was a man who could not be trusted.

Yeltsin's call for Russian sovereignty, declared in 1990 with the support of the Russian Congress of People's Deputies, made him particularly radioactive for many Bush administration officials. He did not appear to be a prudent leader. In sharp contrast to many revolutionary movements, Russia's opposition did not reject the existing international community but sought instead to integrate fully into it. By challenging the sovereignty of the USSR, however, Russia's opposition effectively breached one of the principal rules of the game of the international system in which states recognize one another's right to exist.

Yeltsin and his entourage upset the status quo. Although decolonization from imperial domination was a norm recognized by the international community of states, secession did not have a similar standing. As most international actors did not perceive Russia as a colony, Yeltsin's call for Russian sovereignty sounded illegitimate. As Mark Beissinger observed in 1993, "If we discount the case of Yugoslavia, which is still running its course, until the dissolution of the USSR, the only unambiguous case of a successful secession since the end of World War II is Bangladesh—a fact often pointed to by those who believed that the dissolution of the USSR was unlikely."[15] Yeltsin's call for Russian sovereignty was also frightening to other states that feared that he and his allies might instigate a civil war in a country with thousands of nuclear weapons.

Consequently, even as Yeltsin grew in strength, President Bush maintained a firm policy of noninterference in the internal affairs of the Soviet Union. Bush and Scowcroft discerned no strategic advantage in pushing the political change under way in the USSR. As for the battle between the Soviet Union and Russia and the very personalized contests between Gorbachev and Yeltsin, the

White House firmly sided with the internationally recognized leader of the USSR. For President George H. W. Bush and his national security adviser, Brent Scowcroft, the paramount importance of stability in the U.S.-Soviet relationship and the sense that Gorbachev could deliver for them on matters of importance to the United States led them to stand by their man. Scowcroft recommended that the United States "avoid involvement in Soviet domestic political wars."[16]

Not everyone in the administration shared Scowcroft's view. On the opposite end of the spectrum were analysts at the Central Intelligence Agency and leading officials in the Office of the Secretary of Defense. Key agency analysts, including the director of the Office of Soviet Analysis, George Kolt, and the National Intelligence Council chairman, Fritz Ermarth, had been touting Boris Yeltsin as the true democrat in Moscow for months before Yeltsin became the elected president of Russia. Secretary of Defense Dick Cheney and his top advisers saw the devolution of power and potential independence for the Soviet Republic of Ukraine as significantly advantageous for the geostrategic interests of the United States. Because Yeltsin was the main catalyst for dissolution, the Pentagon embraced him.[17] Stephen J. Hadley, Cheney's assistant secretary of defense for international security policy, recalls:

> The Pentagon earlier than most concluded that Gorbachev didn't have a plan; didn't have a clue how to do what he wanted to do. The Pentagon saw potential for Yeltsin much earlier than did the administration. Gorbachev was a communist reformer, and Yeltsin was clearly a democrat who was prepared to put communism behind. Yeltsin's view was that they had to break up the Soviet Union and kill communism to save Russia. So we began to feel that transition to Yeltsin was a good thing. That was not the view of everyone in the administration. To say we wanted to encourage the breakup of the Soviet Union misses the point. The point was that Gorbachev seemed not to be going anywhere and [Yeltsin] seemed to have the right agenda. And so the right question was did you have any fear of breakup and the answer was no. The emergence of Yeltsin might be a good thing.[18]

Adds then deputy undersecretary of defense Lewis "Scooter" Libby, "There were those who thought Yeltsin was drunk and not substantive. We never thought this at the Pentagon. Others thought he was a hidden autocrat. We didn't. Our view was that we should give him the chance to push democratic reform and undermine party rule in the main, and that at the margin his agenda could be shaped. And what mattered was that he was moving in the right direction."[19]

The advocates of regime change and Yeltsin at the Pentagon also had an ally in Jack Matlock, American ambassador to the Soviet Union. Matlock believed that the administration had established a false dichotomy between Gorbachev and Yeltsin. He believed that the United States could still preserve its relationship with Gorbachev and at the same time pursue a more active engagement with Yeltsin and the other leaders of the republics:

> The Soviet Constitution explicitly gave the union republics the right to maintain diplomatic relations with other countries, and each had its own ministry of foreign affairs. Thus, the heads of union republics theoretically had greater authority than American state governors to deal with foreign governments—and our governors never hesitate to travel around the world and to meet with foreign leaders in pursuit of trade and investment, the very topics Yeltsin was most interested in talking to us about. For these reasons, I could not understand why the White House staff felt we had to make a choice between Gorbachev and Yeltsin.[20]

Secretary of State James A. Baker III and his advisers stood somewhere in between the cautious voices at the White House and the more proactive regime transformers at the Pentagon. Baker recognized the importance of Boris Yeltsin and the leaders of the other republics sooner than did his colleagues at the White House, but he also feared that the breakup of the Soviet Union might present the worst of all nightmares: a Yugoslavia with nuclear weapons.[21] Baker and his top adviser on Soviet affairs, Dennis Ross, had spent a great deal of time with Shevardnadze, who made a big impact on their thinking. Recalls Ross, "I was always of the mind that we had to do more with the republics. It wasn't because I was more far-thinking than others, but I had been so heavily influenced by my discussions with Shevardnadze, who put such a premium on the ethnic issues and his own personal commitment to find a way in his eyes to reconcile the changes in relationship between center and republics. He knew clearly in a way that Gorbachev never did understand."[22]

Like Matlock, some in the intelligence community argued to Baker that more attention to Yeltsin did not mean that the administration had to frame this as an either-or situation. Baker has written that after hearing presentations by CIA Soviet specialists Robert Blackwell and George Kolt at a White House session in late January 1991, he responded by essentially saying, "What you're telling us, fellas, is that the stock market is heading south. We need to sell." But Kolt recalls that when asked by Baker for his views on how to deal with the Soviet Union, he replied, "First, you have to work with Gorbachev because he's the president of the country, you have to maintain relations. Secondly, I think you can lay out the kind of relationships that can come about depending on how the Soviet Union transforms; and third, one should treat the Soviet Union now as more pluralistic and deal with various forces, including Yeltsin."[23]

Despite voices in the administration in support of Yeltsin, the policy embraced by the president remained one of caution—endorsement of the status quo rather than a broader outreach to promote democratization or devolution. President Bush's diary entry of March 17, 1991, could have been written anytime that year: "My view is, you dance with who is on the dance floor—you don't try to influence this succession, and you especially don't do something that would [give the] blatant appearance [of encouraging] destabilization. We meet with the republic leaders but we don't over do it."[24] In Bush's view, Gorbachev was on the dance floor, and the others, including Yeltsin, were not. As he explained to a journalist who asked him about the triangle of 'Washington, Soviet central government, and the Republics,' "I don't think we've got a triangle. In other words, I view that the President of the United States primarily deals with the President of the Soviet Union."[25]

This policy explicitly meant support for Gorbachev. As Scowcroft stated on May 31, 1991, in an Oval Office national security briefing, "Our goal is to keep Gorby in power for as long as possible, while doing what we can to help head them in the right direction—and doing what is best for us in foreign policy." "Scowcroft," writes former deputy national security adviser and later director of Central Intelligence Robert Gates, "tended to write off CIA as hopelessly pro-Yeltsin and did not take seriously any CIA assessment of the Yeltsin-Gorbachev relationship."[26]

Even so, Scowcroft has written that he was always less confident of Gorbachev's democratic credentials than Shevardnadze's, whom he believed genuinely democratic.[27] Shevardnadze's resignation from Gorbachev's government in December 1990 and his warning of an impending coup gave cause for concern about Gorbachev's ability to press forward with reform. Gorbachev's government in 1991 was profoundly more conservative than his earlier teams. Nonetheless, Scowcroft still believed that Gorbachev was their best bet:

> First, Gorbachev was doing what we wanted him to do. We had few complaints. He slowed down on the reforms, but he was going in the right direction. Secondly, how do you withdraw support especially in a system like that and what does it mean to give it to somebody else? Thirdly at least was my own take on Yeltsin which was that fundamentally he was not an improvement anyway, and I think that had Gorbachev left a year earlier, for example, Russia might even be worse off. I don't think there's merit to the view [that we should have done more to support Yeltsin earlier] and there were a lot of people who felt that; there were a lot of people at the Agency who gave Yeltsin a quality that I didn't think Yeltsin had.[28]

Over time, however, it became increasingly awkward to ignore Yeltsin. To the annoyance of Yeltsin and his government, Baker managed to avoid a one-on-one meeting with the Russian leader while he was visiting Moscow in March 1991. Yet after Yeltsin became the elected president of Russia in June 1991, Bush administration officials believed that they had to engage the Russian leader. During a visit to Moscow in July 1991—amazingly, his first trip to Moscow since March 1985 when as vice president he represented the United States at the funeral for Soviet leader Konstantin Chernenko— Bush met separately with Yeltsin one-on-one, becoming the first head of state to meet with Yeltsin in such a manner. Yeltsin urged the American president to develop direct ties with the Russian Republic.[29] Bush refused. Instead, Bush was careful not to offend his friend Gorbachev. Though Bush called Yeltsin's most recent trip to Washington a "big hit," the Bush-Yeltsin meeting was short, and Bush's remarks after the meeting were brief and content free. On this same trip, however, he went out of his way to praise Gorbachev as a leader who "has earned our respect and admiration for his uncommon vision and courage in replacing old orthodoxy with glasnost and perestroika."[30] Yeltsin never received such praise from Bush on this visit. In his memoirs, Bush states clearly that he wanted to use this summit to bolster Gorbachev: "I thought a summit would take some of the pressure off him at home."[31] His show of solidarity did not help much. The following month, members of Gorbachev's government arrested the Soviet president and attempted to seize power.

The Other Republics

Consistent with its policy on the Russia versus USSR drama, the Bush administration maintained a similar policy of supporting the status quo in reacting to sovereignty claims from other republics. The only exception was the bolder language reserved for calling on the Soviet government to recognize the independence of Estonia, Latvia, and Lithuania, whose incorporation in the Soviet Union had never been recognized by the United States. Yet, even with the Baltic countries, the Bush administration never jumped ahead of events on the ground. *New York Times* reporter Thomas L. Friedman captured the Bush approach best when he noted in June 1991, "The Bush administration after nearly three years has established a consistent pattern in responding to changes in the Eastern bloc; it rarely catches the first train, but it rarely misses the last one."[32] Again, Bush was reluctant to get ahead of history. As he explained to the Ukrainian Supreme Soviet in August 1991, "We will not try to pick winners and losers in political competitions between Republics or between Republics and the center. That is your business; that's not the business of the United States of America."[33]

Germany's recognition of Slovenia's and Croatia's independence had helped to catalyze the collapse of Yugoslavia, whose consequences the Bush administration considered disastrous.[34] No one wanted a replay of the Yugoslav scenario in the Soviet Union. The United States did not recognize the independence of any Soviet republic other than the three Baltic nations until after the Belovezhskaya Accord effectively dissolved the USSR in December 1991.[35] Until the coup attempt in August 1991, the Bush administration did not pass judgment on the Soviet Union's internal matters. Nor did Bush ever label the USSR an empire or characterize the Soviet regime as illegitimate. Because the United States had never formally recognized the incorporation of the Baltic states into the Soviet Union in 1940, Bush did call on the new Soviet leadership "to repudiate one of the darkest legacies of the Stalin era" and "find a way to extend freedom to the Baltic peoples."[36] Bush, however, never used the same language to call for the freedom of the Armenian, Ukrainian, or Russian peoples. He was not a Wilsonian champion of self-determination; rather he was a realist seeking to manage the end of the cold war.

By working hard to maintain a policy of noninterference, Bush was supporting Gorbachev and the status quo, as he concedes in his memoirs: "Whatever the course, however long the process took, and whatever its outcome, I wanted to see stable, and above all peaceful, change. I believed the key to this would be a politically strong Gorbachev and an effectively working central structure. The outcome depended on what Gorbachev was willing to do."[37] Bush tried to emphasize that the United States was not taking sides. Yet, he expected the course of reform to be dictated by Gorbachev and not his opponents. Moreover, to those on the barricades fighting for independence and democratization, neutrality meant support for the center, the USSR, and Gorbachev.

In January 1991, President Bush did condemn the Soviet military incursions into Latvia and Lithuania. He sent a letter of condemnation to Gorbachev and mentioned the events in his State of the Union address. Bush refrained, however, from engaging directly with the local governments and instead found reassurance in Gorbachev's promise to "move away from violence." In other words, Bush was still dancing with Gorbachev, and not the embattled democratic movements in the Baltic republics. Bush did not heed the recommendation of Congress and publicly "review all economic benefits" provided by the United States to the Soviet Union. Privately, Bush did warn Gorbachev that he would freeze economic ties with the Soviet Union and not support the Soviet Union's quest for affiliation with the World Bank and the IMF if the violence continued. The president stated clearly that he was "disappointed in the Soviet actions in the Baltics because use of force is not the way to resolve that problem." Yet he also added, "We have a lot of common ground still with the Soviet Union as a country that has been strongly supportive of our objectives in the Persian Gulf."[38]

The Soviet military incursions into Latvia and Lithuania had occurred exactly when Bush needed Gorbachev's acquiescence to the American plan for conducting the war against Iraq. Bush therefore did not want to be too critical of his Soviet counterpart. More generally, Bush even took the occasion of the Baltic crisis to reaffirm his support for the Soviet leader: "I have not lost sight of the fact that Mr. Gorbachev was the catalyst, really, for much of the change that has taken place in Eastern Europe; had a lot to do with the reunification of Germany, which is obviously in the German interest, and I think in the interest of the United States; a lot to do with common ground in the Persian Gulf." In his memoirs, Bush retrospectively speculated that Gorbachev was not behind the orders to use military force, believing what Gorbachev told him.[39]

Throughout 1991, Bush officials avoided any speculation about the possible breakup of the Soviet Union. Bush never implied that breakup was inevitable. Asked to speculate about the Soviet Union's future in July 1991, Bush replied, "I'm an optimist about all that because I think you'll see a Soviet Union that has sorted out its internal relations with the Republics. I'm not saying you have to do it the way we do—50 States and a central government. But there may be some pattern, how we sort these relationships on taxation or power to regulate between State and Federal. But that will be sorted out on a Soviet Union scale, Soviet Union model; not a U.S. model; not a French model."[40]

In meetings with leaders from the republics, the Bush administration urged caution, not revolutionary action. Perhaps most infamously, Bush warned of the dangers of ethnic conflict fueled by state collapse in a speech in the Ukrainian capital, Kiev, in August 1991, just weeks before the coup attempt. In his "chicken Kiev" speech, Bush did proclaim, "We support the struggle in this great country for democracy and economic reform." At the same time, he warned advocates of Ukrainian independence, "Freedom cannot survive if we let despots flourish or permit seemingly minor restrictions to multiply until they form chains, until they form shackles. . . . Yet freedom is not the same as independence. America will not support those who seek independence in order to replace a far-off tyranny with a local despotism. They will not aid those who promote a suicidal nationalism based upon ethnic hatred. We will support those who want to build democracy."[41]

According to New Yorker diplomatic correspondent John Newhouse, Bush had inserted the phrase "suicidal nationalism" into the speech drafted by his staff.[42] Bush warned the Ukrainians about suicidal nationalism so that the multiethnic Soviet Union might avoid the fate of Yugoslavia.[43] According to Gorbachev, Bush also declined an invitation from Vytautas Lansbergis, the head of the Lithuanian parliament, to stop over in the Lithuanian capital, Vilnius, on his way out of the region. "Naturally," Gorbachev writes in his memoirs, "Bush assured me, they were not about to do that," though Bush privately urged Gorbachev during their July summit to let the Baltic states go.[44]

In other words, Bush still sought to influence regime change in the USSR by working with the center, and not the republics or the democratic movements in the Soviet Union. On this same trip, Bush praised Gorbachev as a leader who has "achieved astonishing things," and he even compared the Soviet president to Abraham Lincoln.[45]

By the time Bush had arrived in Ukraine, radical nationalists dressed up as democrats had sparked ethnic conflict in fractured republics such as Georgia and Moldova. The combustible combination of a large Russian minority, the rise of Ukrainian nationalist parties, and the presence of nuclear weapons made U.S. officials nervous about the future of Ukraine. Nonetheless, many inside of the Soviet Union as well as Western commentators interpreted Bush's words of caution as de facto support for the Soviet Union and its leader, Mikhail Gorbachev. As Ivan Drach, the chairman of the Ukrainian movement, Rukh, remarked, "Bush came here in effect as a messenger for Gorbachev. In many ways, he sounded less radical than our own Communist politicians on the issue of state sovereignty for Ukraine."[46]

Given a position of neutrality on "federal issues," Bush and his associates steered clear of offering advice or prodding about democratization in the Soviet Union. Administration officials were realists for whom regime type was not a subject for U.S. policy. Bush was wary of preaching to other foreign leaders. Instead, Bush stated, "We cannot tell you how to reform your society."[47]

The Role of American Nongovernmental Actors in Promoting Regime Change

If Bush and the top officials in his administration did not speak about or actively promote democracy in the Soviet Union, other U.S. actors did. Less constrained by the international regime respecting state sovereignty, American nongovernmental organizations were more aggressive in recognizing and supporting Russia's opposition movement. For instance, American groups such as the National Endowment for Democracy (NED), the National Democratic Institute (NDI), the International Republican Institute (IRI), and the AFL-CIO established working relationships with and provided limited financial assistance to leaders and organizations of Russia's opposition well before international recognition of Russia. The AFL-CIO gave assistance to striking coal miners in 1989 and again in 1991 and later helped to establish the Independent Miners Union in Russia.[48] During the same period, grants from the NED provided fax machines, computers, and advisers to the Russian Constitutional Commission. And while President Bush issued warnings about the dangers of nationalism, the NED was offering assistance to national democratic movements in the Baltics, Ukraine, Azerbaijan, Armenia, and Georgia.[49] In 1991, the NED approved a major grant to fund a printing press for the Democratic Russia movement. Similarly, the NDI initially directed "its efforts towards the institutions which are spearheading democratic reform—the city soviets and the republics of Russia and Ukraine."[50] This focus was directly counter to the Bush administration's policy of supporting the center and the Union. The NDI avoided direct financial transfers to Russian organizations at the time but did provide technical assistance, training, and limited equipment to Democratic Russia during this period. The NDI also provided recognition to Russia's democrats by working closely with Russia's foreign minister, Andrei Kozyrev, and by giving its prestigious international democracy award to St. Petersburg mayor Anatoly Sobchak in 1991. The International Republican Institute—called the National Republican Institute at the time—became deeply engaged in party building programs with Russian counterparts well before the Soviet Union collapsed.

At the time, all of these nongovernmental organizations received the bulk of their funding from government sources.[51] Indirectly, therefore, one could argue that the U.S. government was using a dual-track strategy to promote democratization within the Soviet Union and Russia indirectly. At times, however, officials from the U.S. government and representatives from the nongovernment organizations clashed regarding appropriate engagement with Russia's "revolutionaries." These American NGOs vigorously defended their independence from the U.S. government and occasionally engaged in domestic "meddling" inside the USSR that contradicted Bush's pledge of noninterference. Most of the time, under the steady stewardship of Ambassador Matlock, these nongovernmental actors worked closely with local U.S. officials. Matlock himself was an active promoter of engagement with Russia's revolutionaries.[52] He hosted dinners and discussion groups with these anti-Soviet leaders and groups at Spaso House, the ambassador's residence in Moscow, including a luncheon with human rights activists and Ronald Reagan in May 1988.[53] These events gave symbolic but important recognition to these new political leaders.

Reacting to the Coup

On August 19, 1991, while Soviet president Mikhail Gorbachev was on vacation and out of Moscow, a newly formed State Committee for the State of Emergency (GKChP) announced that it had assumed responsibility for governing the country. Gorbachev, the group claimed, was ill and would return to head the Emergency Committee after he recovered. Eight top Soviet officials orchestrated the coup—Vice President Gennady Yanayev, the formal head of the State Emergency Committee; Oleg Baklanov, first deputy chairman of the USSR Defense Council; Vladimir Kryuchkov, KGB chairman; Valentin Pavlov, prime minister; Boris Pugo, internal affairs minister; Vasily Starodubtsov, chairman of the Union of Peasants; Aleksandr Tizyakov, president of the Association of USSR State Industries; and Dmitri Yazov, defense minister.

Though they were not formally members of the Emergency Committee, USSR Supreme Soviet Chairman Anatoly Lukyanov, CPSU Politburo member Oleg Sheinin, Gorbachev's chief of staff, Valery Boldin, and General Valentin Varennikov, the commander of the Soviet ground forces, also were key conspirators. In other words, most of the coup leaders were already members of the Soviet government. They were also the ministers who controlled the guns. Gorbachev was the only person directly removed from power.[54]

Yeltsin and his allies immediately denounced the actions of the coup plotters as unconstitutional and vowed to resist. Yeltsin rushed to the White House (home of the Russian Congress of People's Deputies) and began to organize a "national"—that is, Russian—resistance effort. Yeltsin's strategy of resistance was simple. As the elected president of Russia, he called on Russian citizens—civilian and military alike—to obey his decrees and not those of the GKChP.[55] In Russia, two independent governments each claimed sovereign authority over the same territory. The Russian Supreme Soviet convened an emergency session to approve Yeltsin's decrees. This legal alternative to the coup leaders' decrees gave military commanders the necessary excuse not to fulfill orders. A situation of dual sovereignty ensued.

Which government would the United States recognize? Initial signals from the American White House were ambiguous. Because it was August, most senior Bush administration officials were on vacation. Scowcroft recalls, "I turned on CNN about midnight and called the CIA. They didn't know a thing. We couldn't get through to the embassy. So, we didn't know what to do."[56]

The newly appointed American ambassador to the Soviet Union, Robert Strauss, had not yet arrived in Moscow, making the deputy chief of mission, James F. Collins, the chief representative of the United States in the country during these confusing days. In the early morning of the first day of the coup, Collins and his staff made the decision—without guidance from Washington—that they were not going to take any actions that might appear to legitimate the coup. As Collins recalled, "We were not going to have anything to do with this crowd." Collins and his staff did not make contact with the Emergency Committee and decided only to deal with the "new" Soviet government on issues regarding the safety of American citizens in the Soviet Union at the time.[57] Collins did send embassy officials to the White House, just a few blocks away from the American embassy, to assess the strength of the resistance movement.

On the first day of the coup, the Bush administration maintained its policy of responding cautiously to events on the ground rather than trying to influence them. In speaking to reporters for the first time from his vacation home in Kennebunkport, Maine, Bush criticized the coup but not too harshly. He stated, "It seems clearer all the time that contrary to official statements coming out of Moscow that this move was extra-constitutional; outside of the constitutional provisions for constitutional change. Clearly, it's a disturbing development, there's no question about that. And it could have serious consequences for Soviet society, and in Soviet relations with other countries, including the United States." He also hinted that "we will not support economic aid programs, for example, if adherence to extra-constitutional means goes forward."[58]

Yet, even in this statement, Bush hinted that the United States might be ready to work with the new Soviet government as long as the Soviet Union would "live up fully to its international obligations." What they did internally evidently was of secondary concern. He made clear that the United States would not interrupt the adoption of the START I Treaty (strategic arms reduction talks) reducing strategic nuclear weapons, which he declared was in the U.S. interest no matter who controlled the Kremlin. Significantly, Bush recognized the act as extraconstitutional, but he did not forcefully condemn the coup plotters. On the contrary, in response to a question about the new acting president, Gennady Yanayev, Bush unfortunately responded, "My gut instinct was that he has a certain commitment to reform." When asked if he supported Yeltsin's countermeasures, such as the Russian president's call for a general strike or his defiance of the Soviet decrees, Bush equivocated.[59]

Bush stressed, "There's very little we can do right now." Bush did not try to contact Gorbachev on this first day, nor did he use the hotline to call the Kremlin, explaining, "We're not going to overexcite the American people or the world. And so, we will conduct our diplomacy in a prudent fashion, not driven by excess, not driven by extreme."[60] While Bush expressed the hope that the will of the people would prevail and thwart the coup, he also recognized that he might have to be dealing sometime soon with a new Soviet government.[61]

By the second day of the coup, tens of thousands of Russian citizens had mobilized to defend the Yeltsin government at Russia's White House.[62] President Bush had reminded reporters the day before that coups sometimes fail. Already by the second day, this one seemed to be unraveling. On the second day of the coup, therefore, Bush used harsher language to denounce what had occurred and expressed a more firm commitment to supporting those resisting the coup. As Scowcroft says, "We increasingly got more negative as we saw it wasn't a fait accompli."[63] The president told reporters outside his summer home in Maine that "the events of the Soviet Union continue to deeply concern the whole world. The unconstitutional seizure of power is an affront to the goals and aspirations that the Soviet peoples have been nurturing over the past years. This action puts the Soviet Union at odds with the world community and undermines the positive steps that have been undertaken to make the Soviet Union an integral and positive force in the world affairs." By this time, Bush had made a phone call to Yeltsin, whom Bush described as "the freely elected leader of the Russian Republic." Bush reassured Yeltsin that the United States continued to support "the restoration of Mr. Gorbachev as the constitutionally chosen leader." On the question of Baltic independence, Bush did not use the opportunity of the coup to move toward formal recognition but instead reiterated, "We are not giving up on the restoration of the constitutional government in the Soviet Union itself. And so we'll leave that matter right here."[64] By the end of the year, the August 1991 events had helped to trigger Gorbachev's ouster from the Kremlin once the Soviet Union ceased to exist. In the middle of the August 1991 coup attempt, however, Bush wanted to see Gorbachev return to power.

By the third day, the coup was over, sparing Bush the hard decision about how to deal with a new illegitimate government in Moscow. On this third day, Bush spoke with Gorbachev for the first time and reported to journalists that the Soviet president was on his way back to Moscow to resume his responsibilities as the head of state. Bush characterized the outcome a real victory for democracy and reform. The American president labeled "ridiculous" the speculations that Gorbachev might have been in cahoots with the coup plotters.[65] In Bush's view, this standoff was between the forces of good and evil, and Gorbachev, the "winner," was firmly in the former camp.

Bush's stance during the coup, although inconsistent with the Russian president's interpretation of events, did not seem to alienate Yeltsin. In a memoir just a few years later, Yeltsin described the American president's actions in August 1991 in the following terms: "George Bush not only called me but also immediately organized international support for Russia, talked with the leaders of NATO countries, issued political statements, and so on. George Bush unquestionably displayed himself first and foremost as a moral politician. . . . His support was invaluable and meant a great deal personally."[66]

History Speeds Up

For some both inside and outside the Bush administration, the failed August coup attempt represented the final shock to the Soviet system that would now finally break it apart. Boris Yeltsin, not Gorbachev, was calling the shots in Moscow, and the Russian president seemed eager to push for Soviet dissolution. Within the administration, the Pentagon team embraced Yeltsin and his agenda. Secretary of Defense Dick Cheney publicly expressed his views only a week after the coup had failed. In an address to the American Political Science Association on August 29, Cheney had stated his support for four core principles, "democracy, voluntary association, economic reform and demilitarization." And he added, "If you look at Boris Yeltsin's agenda, I think you'll find it's very close to the one I've just laid out." He also noted that with the coup having discredited the KGB, the CPSU, and the military, it was natural "that the bonds that have held together the Soviet Union for nearly 70 years should be weakened, and that the break-up of the Soviet empire as we've known it for so long should occur."[67]

Even after the coup attempt, however, Cheney remained the minority voice in the administration. As former CIA director Robert Gates recalls in his memoirs, "It was still Cheney against the field."[68] Cheney argued against supporting the center, in his view the obstacle to real reform.

But at a meeting of Bush's top advisers on October 11, 1991, Baker stated, "To say that support for the center makes you against reform is too simplistic. The guys in the center *are* reformers." He then added, "We should not establish a policy of supporting the breakup of the Soviet Union into twelve republics. We should support what they want, subject to our principles."[69]

Bush remained convinced that Gorbachev and the center could still play a role and that the United States should remain supportive. On November 7, more than two months after the failed coup attempt (and only a short time before the end of the USSR), he met in Rome with German chancellor Helmut Kohl during a NATO summit. Kohl asked point blank: "Tell me, George, is the U.S. position on the Soviet Union still the same?" Bush responded, "I support the Center and I support Gorbachev even though I am criticized in the United States for doing so. We have and we will continue to have contact with Yeltsin, [Ukrainian president Leonid] Kravchuk, [Kazakh president Nursultan] Nazarbayev and others. Some people have said that the place is coming apart, but this is not my position. But we do have to deal with the Republics. . . . But, my answer to your question is yes. We support the Center, or at least we support Gorbachev. Otherwise we could have anarchy." And he added, "I will give you the George Bush theory. Gorbachev and Yeltsin are not really getting along that well."[70]

As for the aspirations of the republics, Bush, Baker, and the rest of the administration did speak differently about the Baltic states after the August coup, calling on Gorbachev and Yeltsin to recognize their independence in early September. But the Baltic states were in a special category because their incorporation into the USSR was never legally recognized by the United States. Bush did not deliver the same message for the rest of the republics during the months after the coup.

As events progressed in 1991, the main focus of attention in the Bush administration on democracy in the Soviet Union was not Gorbachev versus Yeltsin but what to do about the upcoming December 1 referendum on independence in Ukraine. Without Ukraine, the largest republic after Russia, there would be no Union. Without Ukraine, the Soviet Union would lose a significant economic base, 50 million people from a republic crucial to the balance among Slavs and Muslims in the empire, and a geostrategic position in the heart of central and eastern Europe. Even Yeltsin—while telling Bush that if Ukraine voted for independence, Russia would recognize the new country immediately—said that he wanted some means to tie the two together: "Our relations with Ukraine are more significant than those with the Central Asian republics, which we feed all the time."[71]

As the referendum approached, Secretary of Defense Cheney and his aides favored being as forward leaning as possible. Pentagon officials wanted a bold statement from the president immediately following the referendum and argued that Ukrainian commitments to date were sufficient grounds to extend recognition. One official said publicly that the United States should grant diplomatic recognition of Ukraine "sooner rather than later," and the United States should "get in on the ground floor" in order "not to sour our relations with such an important state."[72]

Meanwhile, the State Department and White House were holding back. One State Department official said in response to the Pentagon position: "We want to see what Gorbachev and Yeltsin do. You should let them play it out. The question is, do we get more leverage if we recognize the Ukraine, or if we say we plan to do it and need certain assurances? It's crazy to do it until you know what kind of government is going to be running" an independent Ukraine.[73]

As had been the case all fall, Cheney was pushing for the breakup of the Soviet Union, whereas for Baker, it was more important that the Soviet Union break up peacefully, which meant avoiding a conflict between Russia and Ukraine. The State Department favored sending to Kiev after the referendum a career Foreign Service officer as an emissary, not at ambassadorial rank. State Department officials did not want the United States to be seen as accelerating the disintegration of the Soviet Union and did not want to make it more difficult to get commitments from all the republics to sign up to principles on issues like democracy and human rights that the United States was establishing as a precursor to recognition. Baker writes in his memoirs that on November 26, the president sided with the State Department's "delayed recognition" option, which he adds was understood at the time as meaning "weeks, not months."[74]

Domestic politics intervened to help shape U.S. policy on this issue. On November 28, Bush met with a group of Ukrainian Americans, who in turn leaked a U.S. position that sounded more like the Pentagon view. Gorbachev was furious, as were Baker and Scowcroft.[75] Ross told Baker, "This is what happens when the political side of the White House starts to take over." And Scowcroft agrees, "Yes, domestic politics came in. While it didn't make any difference, it turned out it was a humiliation for Gorbachev, and given where we were, we shouldn't have done that."[76]

But with the Ukrainian vote in favor of independence, the Soviet Union's collapse was going to accelerate regardless of what anyone outside the country did or did not do. On December 8, 1991, Yeltsin flew to Minsk, the capital of Belarus, to meet with Belarusian president Stanislav Shushkevich and Ukrainian president Leonid Kravchuk to form the Commonwealth of Independent States (CIS), an ill-defined grouping of newly independent states that would replace the Soviet Union. Yeltsin called Bush before he bothered to let Gorbachev know. Baker recalls, "I remember Minsk coming as a big surprise to us. And I think, frankly, that we were as surprised as some within the Soviet Union at the speed with which it broke up and I don't recall having seen any intelligence or having any prior knowledge that Minsk was going to happen, that Yeltsin was going to go there. Whether those other guys were going to show up and in effect, dissolve the Soviet Union right there." On the CBS show *Face the Nation* that day, Baker told host Bob Schieffer, "I think the Soviet Union, as we've known it, no longer exists."[77]

Democracy: A Nonagenda Item

At the dawn of a newly independent Russia, Yeltsin and his government believed that their most pressing problems were to secure the new borders of the Commonwealth of Independent States and to jump-start economic reform.[78] In August 1991, Yeltsin controlled no sovereign borders, no currency, and no army, and he sat atop weak, ill-defined state institutions. Even after the December 1991 agreement to create the Commonwealth of Independent States, Russia's political and territorial definition, its very identity, was still uncertain. Overnight, millions of ethnic Russians living in the non-Russian republics became expatriates at the same time that ethnic minorities within the Russian Federation pushed for their own autonomy. Soon after Soviet dissolution, major political groups inside Russia denounced the Belovezhkaya Accord signed in Belarus as illegitimate and unfortunate, a view shared widely within the Russian population. And foreshadowing what would become a bloody and intractable issue, the regime in power in the Chechen Republic at the time declared independence from the Russian Federation. The question "what and where is Russia" was not trivial.

Of equal magnitude and complexity was the Russian economy. The Soviet economy had been in rapid decline for years before its final collapse in 1991. The new Russian government inherited a mess. Soviet gold and hard currency reserves were depleted, the budget deficit had ballooned to 20 percent of GDP, money was abundant but goods were scarce, production had stopped, and trade had all but collapsed.[79] During the winter of 1991, experts predicted starvation throughout the Soviet Union.

Yeltsin and his new government, therefore, were focused immediately on these economic issues, and after that on border questions. At the time, they devoted little attention to democratic reform. Of the three issue areas—borders, market reform, and political reform—Russia's new democratic regime seemed at the time to be the most secure. Yeltsin had just been elected president in June 1991, and the institutions and organizations required to consolidate democracy, such as parties, civil society, and independent media, seemed to be budding. Yeltsin and his team also believed that Gorbachev had made a critical mistake in focusing too much on political change to the neglect of economic reform. They did not want to repeat this perceived mistake.

Yeltsin did take some important first steps toward transforming the Soviet political system when he banned the CPSU, subordinated Soviet ministries to the Russian state, and most dramatically, in December 1991, dissolved the USSR. Equally striking, however, are the steps that were not taken. He did not push for ratification of a new constitution though a draft was already in hand; he refrained from convoking a postcommunist "founding election"; he refused to create his own political party as a way to institutionalize support for his reforms in society; and he did not dismantle many Soviet-era governmental institutions, including most importantly, the Congress of People's Deputies and the KGB. Over time, each of these nondecisions critically impeded the emergence of new democratic practices.[80] In January 1992, however, the consequences to come were poorly understood.

No senior official in the Bush administration saw the priorities facing Russia in a different order than Yeltsin and his new government. As discussed in the next chapter, Baker and his advisers worried about the fate of strategic nuclear weapons now scattered among four countries rather than one. But overall, the Bush administration concurred with Yeltsin that the most pressing problem was the economy and avoiding conflict brought about as a result of new borders. The American definition of priorities was reflected in the kind and amount of assistance transferred to Russia in that first year of independence. The bulk of U.S. bilateral aid to Russia was food aid. Only a small fraction was earmarked for democratization assistance. Bush stayed true to his principle of noninterference. He did not offer Yeltsin advice about how to write a new constitution. The idea would not even have crossed his mind. Nor did he more generally stress the need to design new democratic institutions to rule independent Russia. A set of principles that included commitments to democracy were enunciated by Baker after the coup, but a U.S. role in the development of new political institutions was not.

As before the collapse of the USSR, American nongovernmental organizations, most funded by the U.S. Congress, did continue and then expand their democracy assistance programs in Russia. The National Democratic Institute opened an office in Moscow in June 1992. The International Republican Institute soon followed. The National Endowment for Democracy provided direct grants to Russian democratic organizations, which now had even greater freedoms and more power. None of these organizations took their cues from the Bush administration, in part because this was not their mandate and in part because the Bush administration had no cues to give. Although funded by government money, these groups at this stage of their work in Russia were acting independently of government policy.

In this first year of independence, many of these Western NGOs focused on facilitating the transfer of ideas about institutional design at a time when a vacuum of expertise, knowledge, and texts on democracy existed in the Soviet Union and then Russia. American assistance programs helped to translate constitutional practices in the West into the Russian experience, through direct grants to the Constitutional Commission of the Congress of People's Deputies, training exchanges and seminars with key constitutional drafters, or the translation into Russian of Western constitutions and constitutional debates like the *Federalist Papers*. After the 1990 elections for *oblast'* and city soviets, U.S.-funded assistance programs also injected Western models and ideas about the separation of power between the executive and legislative branches at the local level through a similar mix of seminars, exchanges, and translations.[81]

These kinds of programs continued after the Soviet collapse. In more technical fields such as electoral law design, Western assistance helped introduce Russian politicians to the effects of different types of voting systems. In 1992, the NDI convened a series of working group meetings on the relationship between electoral systems and parties, which included electoral experts on the American single-mandate system as well as the Portuguese, German, and Hungarian electoral regimes.[82] All of Russia's key decisionmakers on the electoral law at the time participated in these meetings, including People's Deputies Viktor Balala and Viktor Sheinis—the two leading authors of competing electoral law drafts at the time—and senior officials from the presidential administration. Of course, Russian politicians had other sources of information about electoral systems, but most of the sources drew on the Western experience.

Besides these constitutional design issues, Western NGOs provided ideas and convened meetings on the entire range of institutional issues facing Russia's new democracy, from elections and parties to the development of independent media, from the role of advocacy groups in democracy to the importance of civic education in developing democratic practice. Western groups were instrumental in providing Russian activists with specific technical information on how to monitor elections, organize electoral campaigns and political parties, develop media watchdog groups, and use the Internet to bring networks together.

None of these American organizations, however, played a central role in pivotal decisions about democratic consolidation in Russia in the first year of independence. In the fall of 1991, NDI officials did try to push the idea of having new elections and adopting a new constitution as soon as possible.[83] Their

Russian interlocutors politely listened to this advice but did not act on it. Their minds were focused on what they considered more pressing issues.

Conclusion

Promoting democracy in the Soviet Union and Russia was not an issue to which President Bush or his senior advisers devoted much attention. Nor did they pay much more than lip service to it. They were not passionate advocates of regime change. Of course, they all wanted to see the development of democracy in the Soviet Union. Some in the administration wanted to see democratic consolidation in Russia, even if the advent of Russian democracy also meant the destruction of the Soviet Union, the latter being the preferred outcome of top Pentagon officials. To facilitate democratization, however, Bush was not prepared to intervene in the domestic affairs of the Soviet Union or Russia. Rather than attempt to influence or shape events in the USSR and Russia, Bush preferred to react to historical processes under way there.

At the time, critics of the Bush administration claimed that U.S. officials acted too slowly in embracing Yeltsin or recognizing the Baltic states. The criticism that the administration had stuck with Gorbachev too long came not just from outside observers but from those inside who chafed in the fall of 1991 at the administration's reluctance to reach out to Yeltsin or even to promote Soviet breakup. Undersecretary of State and Secretary of State Baker's counselor Robert B. Zoellick argues, "There was a view held by some at CIA and DOD that continuation of President Bush's close relationship with Gorbachev would lead to a more antagonistic relationship with Yeltsin, which turned out not to be true." The CIA director of the Office of Soviet Analysis, George Kolt, replied, "This was not the issue; the issue was dealing with all the forces in the Soviet Union."[84]

Was there any harm in the Bush strategy? Zoellick says of his thinking at the time: "My view was that we should work with both leaders and could do so. There was still work to do with Gorbachev. Yeltsin would need the United States as much or more [than] we needed him." He adds, "If we treated him with respect, he'd respond in kind."[85] Even Robert Gates, who had urged the administration much earlier than it did to recognize that Boris Yeltsin was worthy of support, argues in hindsight that with Gorbachev making decisions on all the principal issues of concern to the United States, it did not make sense to abandon the Soviet leader too soon.[86] Secretary of State James Baker was blunter in his response to critics' complaints about the Bush administration's closeness to Gorbachev: "The minute Yeltsin took over, he couldn't wait [to get close to the United States]. So that's [the criticism that the Bush administration was too close to Gorbachev] just total crap."[87]

Yeltsin, in fact, did not adopt an anti-American foreign policy owing to any lack of respect that he felt he deserved when the Soviet Union was still in place. Instead, Yeltsin adopted a radically pro-Western—or more accurately— pro-American foreign policy once Russia became an independent state.

The United States did not seem to suffer much in its foreign policy by adopting a hands-off approach to Soviet dissolution, mainly because the USSR did implode. When officials say that there was little cost associated with a policy of caution, this is because they know how the story ended. But Bush, Scowcroft, Baker, and Zoellick could not and did not know how things would turn out at the time. If August 1991 had gone differently, and the opposition had been locked up, we would not be arguing that a standoffish policy toward Yeltsin was without consequence.

Did the Bush administration miss an opportunity in the fall of 1991 to help institutionalize democracy in Russia? In retrospect, it is clear that the decisions or nondecisions made in the fall of 1991 had significant consequences for the prospects for democratic consolidation in Russia thereafter. It is hard to imagine, however, what interventions by an American president might have helped to ensure further democratic consolidation in Russia at the time. And counterfactuals aside, it was not going to be George H. W. Bush doing the intervening. He was a realist who stayed committed to his philosophical orientation on foreign affairs until the end of his term in office. The United States could cheer democracy building from the sidelines, but foreign policy for this American president meant dealing with the foreign policies of the other leaders who populated the international system, not interfering in their internal affairs. A more robust policy of American support for Russia's transformation would not appear until Bush's Wilsonian successor took office.

3

Controlling the Nukes

After August 1991 the most significant question that the Bush administration had to address from the standpoint of U.S. national security interests was how to manage the potential shift from one country (the USSR) possessing strategic nuclear weapons that could destroy the United States to four countries with significant nuclear arsenals: Russia, Ukraine, Belarus (called Byelorussia at the time), and Kazakhstan. Ukraine had 130 six-warhead land-based SS-19s, 46 ten-warhead land-based SS-24s, and 30 long-range bombers located on its territory—in total, more than 1,600 strategic warheads. Kazakhstan had 104 ten-warhead land-based SS-18s and 40 nuclear-capable long-range bombers, giving it 1,400 strategic warheads on its territory. There were 81 single-warhead SS-25s located in Belarus. These nuclear weapons were controlled from Moscow during the cold war, so questions now arose about whether the republics would have joint control or whether these potentially independent countries would seek to take control of the nuclear weapons on their territory if the Soviet Union broke apart.[1]

Everyone in the Bush administration acted within the realist perspective to deal with this problem. Every senior official believed that it was in the interests of the United States to help "reorganize" the Soviet nuclear weapons systems in a way that enhanced American national security. But a realist worldview could point to two very different policy prescriptions. One school argued that it was in the American security interests to balance Russia with nuclear powers on its borders. Another school argued that American security was best served by maintaining order. If there was one nuclear power before, there should be one after. For this school, the specter of a "Yugoslavia with nukes" demanded greater attention than the potential of a Ukrainian deterrent.

The key proponent of this second school of thinking was Secretary of State James Baker, and his arguments had the greatest and most immediate impact on Bush policymaking at the time. Immediately after the Soviet collapse, Baker pushed hard to make the removal of nuclear weapons from Ukraine, Belarus, and Kazakhstan a top priority. In hindsight, the decision to push for the denuking of Ukraine, Belarus, and Kazakhstan seems obvious, and the completion of this effort in 1996 was one of the great success stories of both the Bush and Clinton administrations. Had it not been for Baker's single-minded efforts, however, it may never have happened. It was not that other senior Bush advisers opposed vigorously what Baker was doing, but officials at the White House and Pentagon did raise doubts about its wisdom, and they were not as energetic about the need to act, as was true for the Bush administration on issues of democracy promotion and economic assistance. And thus in the absence of a major Bush adviser making this objective a central priority, as Baker did from his first post-coup trip to the region in September 1991 all the way through his meeting with the new countries to seal the deal in Lisbon, Portugal, in May 1992, it is likely that nuclear-free non-Russian republics would not have become a reality.

Why were others more sanguine about the possibility of a nuclear Ukraine or Belarus? Partly it was the view that the fewer nuclear weapons in Russia's hands, the better. Moscow had been the enemy capital during the cold war. In the zero-sum calculus of realism, power balancers in the Bush administration argued that the weaker Russia became the more secure the U.S. became. And supporting this policy position was an argument made by some academic realists that nuclear weapons could stabilize potential conflicts through the workings of cold war–style mutual deterrence.[2] Many feared that a new independent Russia might with time resurrect imperial designs on the region. A prominent Russia watcher, Dimitri Simes, warned, "The collapse of the Communist establishment does not mean that the imperial, autocratic Russian tradition has come to an end. It only implies that, next time, it may have to reappear in a different form, with different slogans and different leaders."[3]

Nor was there consensus in the West about Russia's long-term democratic prospects. Just weeks after the coup, some began to speculate again about Yeltsin's populist and autocratic tendencies. In November 1991, two close observers of Soviet politics wrote, "As a hard winter descends, even reformers are turning from democracy to authoritarianism."[4] A new tsar in the Kremlin might mean renewed Russian expansionism. To check Russian imperial proclivities, therefore, some policymakers pushed for the balancing by other regional powers against the local hegemon. Pentagon officials in particular were keen to secure Ukrainian independence. To some, nuclear weapons might give Ukraine a needed deterrent force should Russia regress. Ironically, the same crowd at the Pentagon that embraced regime change and Yeltsin as its catalyst in the waning days of the Soviet Union also championed the logic of power balancing against Russia as a hedge against the possible failure of democratic transformation inside Russia after the Soviet collapse.

On this debate, Scowcroft has written, "I was perhaps the least worried. I thought there was positive benefit in the breakup of command and control over strategic nuclear weapons in the Soviet Union to several republics. Anything which would serve to dilute the size of an attack we might have to face was, in my view, a benefit well worth the deterioration of unified control over the weapons."[5] Later he clarified his differences with Baker: "[The nukes] didn't bother me at all. They bothered Baker. He was worried about the loss of command and control. That didn't bother me because there would be that many fewer aimed at us. We didn't really come to an agreement [on the issue of unified command and control]. The decision was that we wouldn't try to affect the course. We'd let it happen. I simply didn't agree with Jim Baker. That was not a monumental problem, the issue of nuclear weapons. That was Jim Baker. I wouldn't have been so frantic about it. They were not run by nuts. Especially Belarus then. They were all sensible people. To me it was not a big issue."[6]

Asked about the Pentagon debate over Ukrainian nuclear weapons, Stephen Hadley, Secretary Cheney's assistant secretary of defense for international security policy, recalls, "I don't know where Cheney came down at the end of the day. There was a view at the Pentagon that a Ukraine with nuclear weapons was the best way to safeguard that Russia would not try to reassert its control; there was another view that a Ukraine with nuclear weapons would be such a problem for Russia that you would ensure that it would not develop a good relationship with Russia. We had that debate in front of Cheney. I don't know where he came out. The politician in him must have not believed that the weapons would come out, because as a politician, one would want to have that option, but when it became clear that Jim Baker was going to push for Ukraine, Belarus and Kazakhstan to give them up, Cheney did not stand in the way." While Pentagon officials did debate what was best for Ukraine as well as what the Ukrainians were likely to do, at the end of the day, as Hadley says, they did not stand in Baker's way. But they also did seek to ensure that Ukraine's path to independence was not disrupted. From Deputy Undersecretary Scooter Libby's perspective, "The interagency process was determined to denuclearize Ukraine. The Pentagon view was to get the nuclear weapons out of Ukraine safely but not in a way that was adverse for Ukrainian independence. We viewed Ukrainian independence as important in its own right, first and foremost for Ukrainians, but also for us."[7]

Baker does not recall anyone at the White House making an argument that he should *not* push forward on denuking, and he is incredulous that his former colleagues could fail to see the importance of the efforts he undertook. As he puts it, "What the hell were we trying to do? Stir up a nuclear rivalry in the heart of Eurasia?" But he does remember that at the regular Wednesday morning breakfasts in Scowcroft's office, Secretary of Defense Dick Cheney raised the idea that perhaps it was not in U.S. interests to withdraw all of the nuclear weapons to Russia.[8]

Baker disagreed. In fact, he and his team at the State Department had pushed a nuclear weapons policy on unified command and control even before the Soviet collapse. Baker wanted only one nuclear power to emerge if the USSR broke apart. Initially on all sides, some thought was given to the idea of joint control over the weapons by the new states. But given its size and the international community's acceptance of its status on treaties and international organizations as the legal successor, if one nuclear country emerged, it would be Russia. And although Scowcroft says that the administration's policy was that the United States would not try to influence the course of events on strategic nuclear control (as we also saw for democratic institution building), Baker acted as if a decision to push for denuking had been taken. He prevailed because none of the skeptics made any effort to stop him.

The Tactical Nuclear Initiative

Strategic nuclear weapons were not the only nuclear weapons in the arsenals of these newly independent countries. At the urging of President Bush, the administration began to push for changes in the deployment of tactical nuclear weapons, the shorter-range weapons that the superpowers had deployed in Europe during the cold war for potential battlefield use. Chairman of the Joint Chiefs of Staff Colin Powell had first raised this issue with Cheney earlier in 1991, telling him that his staff was in favor of getting rid of artillery-launched nuclear weapons, no longer a necessity in a world in which the United States possessed much more accurate conventional weapons. But, Powell writes in his memoirs, "The report went to the Pentagon policy staff, a refuge of Reagan-era hard-liners, who stomped all over it, from [Undersecretary of Defense] Paul Wolfowitz on down." Powell tried again with Cheney later on a plane ride back to Washington from the Persian Gulf, acknowledging that the service chiefs would be opposed. Cheney knew his advisers were against the idea and did not support him. But on September 5, 1991, in a cabinet meeting to discuss how to proceed after the August coup in Moscow, Bush demanded that his team generate new ideas on arms control. And this time, there was no resistance. "The chiefs," Powell writes, "now responding to a radically changing world, signed on, as did Paul Wolfowitz and his hard liners. Cheney was ready to move with the winds of change."[9]

Besides these new Pentagon assessments about the utility of tactical nuclear weapons, there was a new concern about Russia that pushed this initiative within the administration—loose nukes. With the disappearance of the Soviet Union, many U.S. officials now worried about the new Russian state's ability to maintain control over its nuclear inheritance. Because of the size and mobility, loose tactical nukes presented a special threat. The Bush administration, therefore, had an interest in destroying as many of these weapons as possible, before they fell into the wrong hands inside the former Soviet Union or were smuggled to places such as Iran or Iraq.

The response to these new realities was President Bush's September 27, 1991, speech to the nation outlining a wide-ranging unilateral American arms control initiative and calling on the Soviet Union to respond. Given the new environment, the president announced, "I am therefore directing that the United States eliminate its entire worldwide inventory of ground-launched short-range, that is, theater nuclear weapons. We will bring home and destroy all of our nuclear artillery shells and short-range ballistic missile warheads." Bush said that the United States would remove tactical nuclear weapons from U.S. Navy ships, attack submarines, and land-based naval aircraft. On the strategic front, the president proposed de-alerting strategic bombers and all intercontinental ballistic missiles (ICBMs) scheduled to be de-activated under the START I agreement. He also called on both sides to field only single-warhead land-based ICBMs; the land-based Soviet ICBMs with in some cases ten multiple independently targetable re-entry vehicles (MIRVs) had long been the main U.S. concern about the Soviet Union's ability to launch a nuclear first strike. Bush also asked "the Soviet leadership to join us in taking immediate concrete steps to permit the limited deployment of non-nuclear defenses to protect against limited ballistic missile strikes, whatever their source, without undermining the credibility of existing deterrent forces."[10]

The president had called Mikhail Gorbachev ahead of time to preview the steps the United States was prepared to take (and for the first time on arms control, he also had called Yeltsin). Within a week, Gorbachev responded, proposing to destroy sea-based tactical nuclear weapons, offering among other things to reduce the Soviet strategic arsenal below START I levels (to 5,000 warheads), and announcing a one-year moratorium on nuclear testing.[11]

What about Ukraine?

In this period, the debate in the administration over how to manage the breakup of the Soviet Union, and in particular Ukrainian independence and possession of nuclear weapons, continued. On October 10, 1991, in preparation for a meeting of the president's top foreign policy advisers, the National Security Council senior director for Russian affairs, Ed Hewett, and Baker's top adviser for Soviet affairs, Dennis Ross, wrote a joint memo for Scowcroft and Baker. In it, they argued that while the administration had hoped that a "voluntary" union could continue in order to ensure economic and nuclear stability and had feared what a rapid disintegration might mean in a country with 27,000 nuclear weapons, that outcome seemed increasingly unlikely. They argued for using U.S. leverage to ensure that the republics, including Russia, acted responsibly during this period.[12]

That leverage was based on a set of principles developed right after the coup. The idea of a set of guiding principles had been proposed to Baker back on August 27 by two members of his Policy Planning Staff, Andrew Carpendale and John Hannah. Carpendale and Hannah borrowed the idea from their colleague John Fox, who had first developed the idea of delineating principles for the Yugoslav case. But the principles were never used for the republics of the former Yugoslavia because the message to them had been much simpler: "don't break up." Ross had argued to Baker back in August and early September that the president should give a major speech enunciating these principles for the Soviet republics. Baker apparently tried to persuade Bush to do this, but Bush and Scowcroft felt that it was too soon for a major defining speech by the president. Bush did agree that Baker could outline the principles (and the secretary of state did so in a Rose Garden press briefing on September 4); these five principles—peaceful self-determination, respect for existing borders, respect for democracy and the rule of law, guarantee of human rights, and respect for international law and obligations—had been used by Baker and his advisers since then as a way of encouraging the republics and the center to take steps that would help them join the West (even if not providing major assistance for them to do so, as we have seen). Hewett and Ross now urged a sixth principle dealing with control over nuclear weapons. Consistent with the more standoffish White House approach, Scowcroft wrote later that the principles did not amount to a "tight administration policy on the potential breakup of the Union."[13]

The debate between the Pentagon and the rest of the administration over Ukraine was now bubbling to a head. Baker recalls, "It was the only time I can remember during the Bush administration when a real policy dispute in which I was involved was aired in the press before we could resolve it among the principals."[14] NSC staffer Nicholas Burns agrees: "The big issue was not so much in working with Moscow, but in working out differences within the Administration on how to handle Ukraine."[15]

Unlike officials at the State Department or NSC, leading officials at the Pentagon like Paul Wolfowitz, Scooter Libby, Stephen Hadley, and Eric Edelman had no hesitation about the United States hitting the accelerator. In their minds, if Ukraine were independent, the entire geostrategic landscape in Europe would be altered in a fundamental way that favored U.S. interests. As

Hadley recalls, "We had a view that without Ukraine, a retrograde Russia would never reconstitute the Soviet Union. It would never become the threat posed by the old Soviet Union because of the enormous resources, population and geography of Ukraine. So that would become an important element of U.S. policy—putting aside all the principles that were all important—from a strategic standpoint, an independent Ukraine became an insurance policy."[16]

Despite the passion of these debates, they quickly became irrelevant after the Ukrainian referendum on December 1, 1991, which was followed only a week later by the Belovezhskaya Accord establishing the Commonwealth of Independent States. The discussion about Soviet collapse quickly turned from the hypothetical to the actual. The new focus was not whether Ukraine should be independent, but whether Ukraine should be independent and nuclear.

The Transition Begins

No administration official had given a major speech providing any conceptual underpinnings to U.S. foreign policy in this new era since George Bush's September 27, 1991, remarks on nuclear weapons. Bush was too fearful of being tagged a foreign policy president, particularly after the special election for U.S. senator from Pennsylvania in which Democrat Harris Wofford upset Bush's former attorney general Richard Thornburgh on November 5. Baker was preoccupied in October with Middle East issues, culminating in a major conference in Madrid at the end of the month. And all fall, the fence sitting over whether to support Gorbachev or Yeltsin had precluded a major address. But once the Ukrainian referendum had taken place on December 1, someone had to give a speech or, as Ross told Baker, the United States ran the "risk of losing control over this."[17]

Thus, to prepare the ground for U.S. policy in the post-Soviet era, Baker traveled on December 12 to his alma mater, Princeton University, to speak before a crowd that included legendary U.S. elder statesman George F. Kennan, the father of the containment doctrine that could now be officially put to rest. Even as he prepared his speech, Baker could not be certain what the new entity within the former Soviet space would look like. During the two days before the speech, Gorbachev and Yeltsin were each meeting with the Soviet military to gain support, "the stuff," Baker wrote in his memoirs, "of a geopolitical nightmare." And he still did not even know how to refer to the place. The speech draft mentioned U.S. relations with "Russia, Ukraine, and other republics." But since no one knew what the CIS might become, the final version read, "Russia, Ukraine, the other republics, and any common entities." What Baker and his team did know is that the United States needed to remain engaged with the former Soviet Union rather than choose isolationism now that the cold war was over, an approach he pushed for several days before the speech to provide some context.[18]

The speech had two major themes. One was to announce the start of an international effort to provide financial support for the newly independent states. The second was to remind the new countries about the U.S. position on the control of nuclear weapons. Baker reiterated that the United States wanted to ensure that no additional nuclear weapons states emerged from the wreckage, that the START Treaty be ratified and implemented, that all nuclear weapons be under a "single unified authority" (how was up to the new leaders to determine), that Ukraine, Belarus, and Kazakhstan adhere to the Non-Proliferation Treaty as non-nuclear weapons states, and that countries put into place effective controls on the export of technology that might be sought by other states with nuclear aspirations.[19]

Baker followed the speech with a trip to the region. In Moscow on December 16, he met separately with both Yeltsin and Gorbachev. Besides the question of humanitarian assistance Baker and his team had several major security concerns. Was the CIS an entity that might conduct foreign and security policy? Who had made what commitments on nuclear weapons? And did the Russians have positions yet on foreign policy? After a one-on-one with Yeltsin, Baker brought in his team for an expanded bilateral meeting. Everyone, writes Baker, had questions: "Ambassador Strauss asked whether Russia intended to recognize the other members of the Commonwealth, and exchange ambassadors. Dennis Ross asked about the Middle East peace process. [State Department arms control expert] Reggie Bartholomew asked what would happen with conventional arms transfers. [NSC staffer] Ed Hewett asked about shipping fees on grain shipments, and Tom Niles, the new assistant secretary of state for European affairs, asked about what was happening to hard-currency revenues from oil and gas." Russian foreign minister Kozyrev of course had no answers, but he did present a request for recognition of Russia by the United States; as Baker cabled the president later, "Recognition alone isn't going to solve this problem."[20]

One question was answered for Baker when Marshal Yevgeny Shaposhnikov, the new *Soviet* minister of defense who replaced one of the coup plotters, appeared at Baker's meeting with *Russian* president Yeltsin. Significantly, the meeting took place in St. Catherine's Hall in the Kremlin, the usual venue for meetings with Soviet leaders. On addressing the perceived food crisis in Russia at the time, Yeltsin agreed to allow U.S. military personnel to help provide food and medicine, an unprecedented invitation for American military personnel to work in the former enemy's territory. Yeltsin made clear his hope that the CIS military would have close ties to the former enemy, the North Atlantic Treaty Organization: "It would be an important part of Russia's security to associate with the only military alliance in Europe."[21]

About nuclear weapons, Baker could say afterward, "I personally feel very reassured. I have heard nothing that causes me any more concern."[22] Yeltsin affirmed that Russia, Ukraine, Belarus, and Kazakhstan would each join the Non-Proliferation Treaty, the latter three as nonnuclear states.[23] He told Baker that his government also agreed to strict export controls for nuclear weapons and technology. And he added that Ukraine and Belarus had already agreed that their nuclear weapons would be eliminated, rather than redeployed in Russia, though Yeltsin admitted that he had not yet spoken to Kazakh president Nursultan Nazarbayev about this point.[24]

Later that afternoon, Baker met with Gorbachev and asked the Soviet leader for his thoughts on how to avoid a disaster. He told Gorbachev that the United States would stay out of Soviet internal affairs, and that they saw him not only as a partner but as a friend. He told Gorbachev that the United States was comfortable with him and uneasy at seeing him treated badly, and he asked Gorbachev how best to deter "disintegration to the lowest common denominator."[25] Baker, however, also realized that the "train had left the station," and Gorbachev and his Soviet Union were left standing at the platform.[26]

From Moscow, therefore, Baker traveled to Kyrgyzstan, Kazakhstan, and Ukraine. He was struck by the power of the United States to shape attitudes in the region. As he has written, "In all my meetings that week, one theme had been uniform: the intense desire to satisfy the United States. Nazarbayev had told me he kept the five principles in his desk, and Kravchuk asked us to send experts to assure the Ukrainians' implementation of the principles."[27] This wholesale yearning for approval from the world's sole remaining superpower in order to become part of the West would not last forever. Less than three years later, after all, an anti-American dictator was ruling Belarus. But Baker took advantage of this unique moment in world history to push hard for denuclearization.

Ukrainian president Kravchuk stated clearly: "Ukraine has every intention to stick to and initiate whatever processes [are] geared toward the complete destruction of strategic and nuclear weapons. . . . We have addressed the United States with a request that U.S. experts should come to the Ukraine to help solve our problems concerning the destruction of nuclear weapons, not in the seven-year period as was envisioned earlier, but preferably in a somewhat shorter time." In fact Kravchuk told one reporter that the only hold-up for Ukraine was the lack of a facility to destroy the weapons—saying that if the United States helped, "we will destroy them tomorrow." But although Kazakh president Nazarbayev conveyed to Baker a willingness to join the Non-Proliferation Treaty as a non-nuclear state in return for recognition, publicly it was reported that he had spoken to Yeltsin about some nuclear weapons remaining on Kazakh soil even if there was unified control.[28]

After the USSR

In 1990–91, Bush tried to avoid doing anything that might accelerate the process of disintegration of the Soviet Union. In early 1992, the pace of American foreign policy abruptly changed, as U.S. officials moved quickly on several fronts to institutionalize the collapse of the Soviet Union that had just occurred. Baker pushed for opening embassies in the new countries to help shore up their independence. The United States convened a major multilateral conference in Washington to begin the process of generating economic assistance to the region. And the team began thinking about measures to deal with the core issues on the nuclear front: reductions in offensive nuclear systems, prevention of the so-called brain drain of Russian, Ukrainian, and other former Soviet nuclear scientists selling their know-how to states like Iraq and North Korea, and export controls on leakage of sensitive technologies. Even the idea of a joint U.S. and Russian effort to develop missile defenses began to percolate. In Russia's first year of independence, the U.S. Ballistic Missile Defense Organization opened discussions with its Russian counterparts about an experimental joint project on early warning and missile defense, which produced the Russian American Observation Satellite program (RAMOS), the first ever cooperation between the United States and Russia in this highly sensitive field. Despite his poor treatment by American officials when he was a challenger to Gorbachev, Yeltsin moved quickly on the security front to demonstrate Russia's willingness to cooperate with the United States. Expectations about the new possibilities for cooperation in military matters soared.

Senators Sam Nunn and Richard Lugar

To help address the concern about uncontrolled nuclear weapons, the administration had at its disposal $400 million available under the Cooperative Threat Reduction program, better known as Nunn-Lugar. Back in August 1991, Congressman Les Aspin (D-Wisc.) and Senator Sam Nunn (D-Ga.) had proposed a $1 billion program to be drawn from the Pentagon budget for humanitarian assistance and nuclear assistance. Aspin argued that the Pentagon budget was the only source of fungible money that could be used in this monumental transition. But he also argued that this was "another form of defense spending. . . . During the Cold War, the threat was deliberate Soviet attack. Now the bigger threat seems to be chaos in a nation with 30,000 nuclear weapons. If we can reduce that threat by spending less than one half of one percent of our defense budget on humanitarian aid, we're defending ourselves and democracy too."[29]

Secretary of Defense Cheney knocked down Aspin's proposal immediately. He argued first that violating budget agreements was bad policy. And he added, "I would suggest that instead of looking for ways to cut the defense budget further, Les ought to be looking for ways to find money in the budget to restore the unwarranted cuts that his committee made in the Strategic Defense Initiative."[30]

Nunn tried again. On November 19, 1991, in a meeting arranged by Carnegie Corporation president David Hamburg, Nunn and his Republican Senate colleague Richard Lugar brainstormed with Harvard nuclear expert Ashton Carter, Stanford professor William Perry, and Brookings Institution scholar John Steinbruner on strategies for dealing with nuclear weapons disposition in the Soviet Union.[31] At this meeting, the idea of Cooperative Threat Reduction was born. Two days later, Nunn and Lugar convened a breakfast session with other senators to win approval for their idea. By the end of the month, Nunn and Lugar secured eighty-six votes in the U.S. Senate to win overwhelming approval for their amendment to the annual defense bill, establishing the Cooperative Threat Reduction (or Nunn-Lugar) program, which authorized $500 million from the Pentagon budget for assistance to the Soviet Union, with $400 million earmarked for dismantling Soviet nuclear and chemical weapons.[32]

Bush did sign the legislation on December 12, but neither he nor his staff had done much to promote it. There were several reasons why the Bush team did not push earlier or put more money into a program clearly in America's interest. One is what Baker adviser Dennis Ross calls the "intellectual fatigue after the Gulf War." Ross argues that in the spring of 1991, his team at the State Department began pushing the idea of needing to think about the loose nukes problem. But he argued that after the draining experience of the Gulf War, "there wasn't intellectual energy to take on new challenges."[33] Second, the origins of the idea—Capitol Hill—made it suspect for executive branch officials. Scowcroft recalls, "We didn't really think of it before Nunn and Lugar did. And I don't think there was any enthusiasm about it."[34] Finally, bureaucratic politics affected the design, development, and momentum of the program. When Baker first became aware of Nunn-Lugar, he thought the idea had merit, but he wanted the State Department to have a larger role. Unfortunately, the program needed money, and that meant drawing from the existing Defense Department budget. But to draw money from existing Pentagon sources meant taking money away from other cherished Pentagon programs. And using American dollars to get rid of someone else's nuclear weapons did not appeal to the Pentagon intellectually or bureaucratically. This method for securing American defense was novel.[35]

Still, by late December the State Department was thinking about ways to press ahead and lock in any gains that might be made with the new Yeltsin team. Ross had written to Baker just before the formal collapse of the USSR on the next steps in the security relationship with the Russians. He warned Baker that Yeltsin had made clear he needed some political cover to move forward since conservatives in Russia were not happy with the efforts to reduce the Russian military and nuclear capacity. And Ross did not want domestic critics in Russia to be able to argue later that the United States had taken advantage of them. Responding to this need to move forward with concrete steps, Baker sent his leading arms control expert, Reginald Bartholomew, to Moscow in mid-January to discuss the issues.[36]

An Even More Cooperative Friend in the Kremlin—Boris Yeltsin

When he was visiting Moscow on January 29, 1992, for talks on the Middle East, Baker met with Yeltsin. In part as a result of this meeting, Baker once again began to speculate that the administration's conventional wisdom might be wrong. Back in 1989, it had been Baker who realized most quickly that Gorbachev and Shevardnadze were serious about ending the cold war because he had met with them before his White House colleagues did.[37] Now, Baker found a Boris Yeltsin who not only was not a drunken fool but was instead "impressive. . . . [H]e spoke at great length, with no notes, about highly technical issues."[38]

In his State of the Union address the day before, Bush had stated that the United States would lower its nuclear forces to 4,700 warheads, eliminating its Peacekeeper multiple warhead ICBMs, reducing the number of warheads on Minuteman missiles to one, and cutting its sea-based force by one-third, if Russia and the other former Soviet Republics made a commitment to eliminate all land-based MIRVs. Yeltsin countered by proposing the elimination of all MIRVs and reductions to 2,000–2,500 warheads. In fact, Yeltsin had written Bush on January 27 (that is, the day before the State of the Union) to inform him that Russia was "without any conditions or linkages" discontinuing production of TU-160 and TU-95MS heavy bombers, long-range air-launched cruise missiles, and long-range nuclear sea-launched cruise missiles.[39]

In reporting to Bush after his meeting with Yeltsin, Baker laid out the radical proposals made by the new Kremlin occupant. The Russian leader wanted major cuts in nuclear forces, a joint project for pursuing global missile defense (while wanting reaffirmation of the importance in the meantime of the Anti-Ballistic Missile Treaty), and a joint declaration to be issued at the upcoming presidential summit that would herald a new era in relations. Yeltsin also told Baker that the Soviet Union had built a secret biological weapons program that he would order dismantled within a month. Baker told Bush that the United States had a real opportunity to change the military threat that the United States had faced for decades, and he cautioned his boss that Yeltsin could not appear as if he was the one making all the concessions.[40]

After the failed coup attempt and the subsequent dissolution of the USSR, Yeltsin and his new government were reaching out to the Bush administration as well as other governments of the Western world. Yeltsin had forgotten about his so-called snub at the White House in 1989 and held no grudges against Bush for supporting his rival, Mikhail Gorbachev, for so long.[41] Yeltsin was even careful to make sure that Gorbachev could retire without facing retribution given the Soviet leader's status in the West. More generally, Yeltsin's new regime tried to make the transition as peaceful as possible. The Communist Party of the Soviet Union was put on trial, but individual party members were not held personally accountable. Nor did Yeltsin's government undertake a national purge of party officials from government bureaucracies. During the initial period of seizing power, Yeltsin and his revolutionary allies wanted to demonstrate to the outside world that they were not radicals but were instead reliable and cooperative partners of the West.

As Bush prepared for a February 1, 1992, summit with Yeltsin at Camp David, he and his team thought about how they might help shore up Yeltsin's position. The idea that the fate of Russian reform depended on Boris Yeltsin the individual did not originate with the Clinton administration after 1993; it had begun already in early 1992. One administration official said at the time, "The only alternative to Yeltsin is Stalin—and authoritarian regimes." And U.S. ambassador to Moscow Robert Strauss was warning Baker that there was no "better alternative" than Boris Yeltsin. The view in Washington was that Yeltsin was looking for acceptance from the West because that helped him in his battle with the communists, and there was a growing realization that the West needed to give it to him.[42]

But when Yeltsin came to Camp David, there was still a lot of doubt about who he was and what he wanted. Baker had seen that Yeltsin could perform, but others still held lingering doubts from the first trip that Yeltsin had taken to Washington in 1989. After Camp David, however, there were almost no doubters (save perhaps Vice President Dan Quayle).[43] Russian deputy foreign minister Georgy Mamedov later told his American counterparts that Yeltsin had rehearsed for two or three days for what he realized was his big exam. And he was ready. Sitting down with President Bush, Yeltsin gave a half-hour presentation without any notes, ticking off eight strategic priorities. And for the Americans, this new Russian leader was saying all the right things. NSC staffer Nicholas Burns, who was the notetaker at the meeting, recalls that Yeltsin talked about having vacationed in Latvia for many years, and he knew the Latvian leadership and wanted the Baltic republics to be independent and successful. He also said that Ukraine was a great country and had a right to be independent. And finally he said that he wanted to remove all the blank pages from Soviet history. Burns remembers Yeltsin telling Bush, "When the Soviet army conquered Poland and the Eastern part of Germany, we liberated a lot of POW camps where your people were held. [Yeltsin adviser, General Dmitri] Volkogonov has discovered that we isolated the American pilots with Russian and Jewish surnames. We didn't return to you 320 American officers who were Jews and who had Slavic surnames. Because it was a time of paranoia, and we executed them. And we lied to American authorities. Volkogonov is going to work with you where you have concerns."[44]

Most important (and not for the last time), Yeltsin warned U.S. officials that other potential Russian leaders could be dangerous for U.S. national security. He told Bush that if reform failed, the world could expect a police state and a resumption of the arms race. He then asked for food aid. He stated his hope that Russia would be a full member of the International Monetary Fund by April. On the security front, he called for reducing strategic warheads to 2,500 and again reiterated the need for cooperation on global defense, noting that Russia had a couple thousand experts who could help. He wanted to use the $400 million available in Nunn-Lugar funds for safe storage of dismantled nuclear warheads, and he wanted to go even further by selling highly enriched uranium to the United States.[45]

Finally, Yeltsin had one more matter he wanted to discuss. He asked Bush whether or not the two countries were still adversaries. And Bush replied no. But Yeltsin pressed him, asking why the proposed joint statement did not say that the two countries were allies. Baker pointed out that the statement did say "friendship and partnership." But Yeltsin wanted more; he wanted the two leaders to say that the two countries were moving from being adversaries to allies. But Bush wasn't ready, arguing, "We are using this transitional language because we don't want to act like all our problems are solved."[46] This "transitional language" would last a long time.

The Road to Lisbon

From February through May 1992, Baker was a whirlwind of activity as he pursued his nonproliferation objectives. In mid-February, he traveled to one of the Soviet Union's most famous secret labs, Chelyabinsk-70, to discuss a new scientific center that the United States and Germany were supporting in order to encourage Russian nuclear scientists to devote their intellectual energy to commercial pursuits and to discourage them from selling their know-how to other states. In a tripartite statement released on February 17, Baker, Germany's foreign minister, Hans-Dietrich Genscher, and Russia's foreign minister, Andrei Kozyrev, announced the venture and called on foundations and other nongovernmental organizations to provide support. The financier George Soros had already started providing money for these purposes back in December.[47]

On the nuclear weapons front, things seemed to be going smoothly, although Senator Nunn bemoaned at a congressional hearing in early February that "not one penny" had been used for nuclear threat reduction.[48] Then in mid-March, Ukrainian president Leonid Kravchuk announced that he was suspending the transport of tactical nuclear weapons to Russia, saying he had no guarantee that these weapons would be stored safely or destroyed. (The Russian military continued the process anyway, and all the tactical nuclear weapons were withdrawn in short order.) Only a few months before, Ukraine had seemed eager to get rid of its nuclear weapons given the high degree of antinuclear sentiment that had existed ever since the 1986 explosion at the Chernobyl nuclear power plant. On December 30, 1991, Ukraine had promised to get rid of all its nuclear weapons within three years. But Ukrainian elites began to worry that they had been rushed into these decisions, and particularly in parliament the feeling grew that Russia would receive all the compensation for withdrawn and dismantled nuclear weapons.[49]

The Ukrainians then decided that as a sovereign state, their country should formally be party to the START Treaty. On April 7, Baker called Russia's foreign minister, Kozyrev, and explained the need to get all four nuclear states to sign on to the START Treaty. The following week, the two men spoke again, and Baker told Kozyrev that the United States wanted a commitment from Yeltsin on the Russian position on the treaty before he called Kravchuk. Meanwhile, Scowcroft was growing worried that START ratification would be jeopardized if the United States continued to insist on requiring all three states to accede to the NPT as non-nuclear states because of Kazakhstan's intransigence and was willing to drop reference to the Non-Proliferation Treaty from the START protocol.[50]

But having received commitments from Russia, State Department officials wanted to hold firm. An intensive U.S.-Ukrainian dialogue on the disposition of the nuclear weapons began soon after. From April 28 to May 4, Baker spoke to Ukrainian foreign minister Anatoly Zlenko eight times. Zlenko expressed concerns about parliamentary support, the need for security guarantees, and international oversight of any reductions. The United States refused the last point because it wanted the Ukrainian government to take responsibility; furthermore, START had no international oversight component.[51]

Although the Kazakh situation was also unsettled, Baker and his team were more worried about Ukraine. Kazakh president Nazarbayev had more control over his domestic situation than did Kravchuk, who really did have a parliament to worry about that was pushing him to take a more nationalist stand.

And the United States also felt Nazarbayev was more diplomatically skilled than his Ukrainian counterpart. Finally, Ukraine and Russia had already had conflicts over issues like the disposition of the Black Sea Fleet, and tensions were running higher.[52] Nazarbayev announced on a May 19, 1992, visit to Washington that Kazakhstan would sign up to the U.S. proposal.

On May 23-24, Baker and the foreign ministers of Belarus, Ukraine, Kazakhstan, and Russia met in Lisbon to sign the START protocols, which stated that the non-Russian states would become non-nuclear "in the shortest possible time" and "immediately take all necessary actions to this end in accordance with their constitutional practices." In a side letter, Kravchuk committed Ukraine to getting rid of its strategic nuclear weapons within seven years of START's entry into force. But even at the signing ceremony, the American delegation was not sure what ultimately would happen. Baker had gotten so mad at Ukrainian foreign minister Zlenko over apparent Ukrainian backsliding just before the meeting in Lisbon that he had hung up the phone on him. And just before the ceremony, Zlenko said he was not sure he was going to sign. Baker screamed at him, telling Zlenko that if Ukraine did not sign, it would have no U.S. support. Baker argued that Ukraine's relationship with Russia would be better if it gave up its nuclear weapons, and he made clear that if Ukraine did not relinquish these weapons, then relations with the West would sour immediately. But Baker was so unsure of the outcome that he decided not to let anyone make a statement at the ceremony for fear someone would walk back on his commitments. Finally, the four came out, and "six minutes later" Baker had achieved what he wanted, a commitment that only one nuclear power would emerge from the wreckage of the Soviet Union.[53]

Going to Lower Numbers

Also at Lisbon, Foreign Minister Kozyrev proposed that the United States and Russia commit to drastically lowering the numbers of strategic nuclear weapons. He suggested a first phase in which the sides would go to 4,500–4,700 in seven years and then take the much more radical step of going to 2,500 warheads by no later than 2005, with elimination of all land-based MIRVed ICBMs. As Baker writes, the offer had one significant downside—it was "far lower than [the U.S.] Defense Department was willing to go." The Russians' main concern was that they would not be able to afford to carry out the reductions. And for the first time, they seemed to delink the land-based MIRV issue from their concerns about U.S. sea-based weapons.[54]

Baker's negotiations in the ensuing weeks were not with the Russians but with his fellow Americans. As he says of the arms control bureaucracy at DOD, "They don't like arms control. Talk to the Chiefs about cutting the numbers of our warheads, and it's like pulling teeth."[55]

On June 4, Baker met with Scowcroft, Cheney, and Powell, and he argued, "They have offered us what we want, and what no one else has ever come close to: zero MIRVed ICBMs, and without eliminating MIRVed SLBMs. We can't let this slip through our fingers because we think we need a *higher* total number. That is not sustainable with the public or the Congress."[56] Cheney's focus was different; he wanted to make joint missile defense the centerpiece of the summit and tie the de-MIRVing proposals to progress on defensive systems. Baker's position was that the United States had worked for years to delink the offensive and defensive parts of the equation (dating back to Gorbachev's efforts to tie offensive reductions to Reagan's willingness to concede on the Strategic Defense Initiative) and should not reverse this arrangement now. The State Department also believed that Yeltsin could only agree to de-MIRV if the United States could agree to go below 4,000.[57]

Baker then met with Kozyrev in Washington on June 8–9 and in London on June 12 to move the negotiations forward. In London, the U.S. side tentatively agreed to a 3,500-limit on nuclear weapons for phase two but also pushed for de-MIRVing land-based ICBMs by 2003. In turn, Kozyrev made clear that Yeltsin could not agree to any deal that imposed an economic burden on Russia by having to reduce too many weapons too quickly.[58]

On June 15, Yeltsin came to Washington for a state visit. One item of business was the signing of a Charter for American-Russian Partnership and Friendship. At the White House, Yeltsin proposed a phased withdrawal down to 3,000-3,500 warheads on both sides under START II. Yeltsin several days before had complained that the United States was trying to take advantage of him by pushing for the elimination of the Russian SS-18s without being willing to cut enough in the American sea-based arsenal. But by the summit, he was focused on the idea of a 3,000–3,500 range in order to allow Russia for economic reasons to go lower than the United States might be willing to go.[59] He said publicly what should have been obvious to both countries years earlier, "Each country will elect a figure that it will consider appropriate to ensure its defense and security. Thus we are departing from the ominous parity where each country was exerting every effort to stay in line, which has led Russia, for instance, [to] having half of its population living below the poverty line."[60] (Cheney was worried that the U.S. Congress would push the American side to go to 3,000 if the Russians did, and the Pentagon believed that 3,500 was as low as the United States could go.)

Baker called Bush after the meeting and said, "I hope you're going to accept Yeltsin's proposal. I think this will be a significant achievement for your presidency, but you're going to have to tell the arms control theologians you want it to happen. I've done all I can trying to roll this rock uphill." Bush concurred. And the next day, the two sides announced that within seven years following the entry into force of START I, they would reduce their strategic forces to between 3,800 and 4,250, and by 2003 they would go down to a maximum level of 3,000 to 3,500 and eliminate all MIRVed land-based ICBMs.[61] On January 3, 1993, just weeks before leaving office, President Bush met Yeltsin in Moscow to sign START II, with the full support of President-elect William Jefferson Clinton, who was happy not to be burdened with having to sign a treaty that might bring him criticism from the right.

Conclusion

Up until the final moments of the Soviet demise, President Bush and his administration remained reluctant to meddle in the internal affairs of the Soviet Union. At a time of revolutionary change inside the Soviet Union, the Bush team supported the status quo. This policy of noninterference translated into support of Gorbachev, their man in Moscow.

On the nuclear front, however, once the Soviet Union had collapsed, Secretary of State Baker moved rapidly—without much support from his colleagues—to achieve one main policy outcome—the denuclearization of Belarus, Kazakhstan, and Ukraine. To accomplish this objective, he developed ties with the new leaders in the new countries and moved aggressively and proactively to offer recognition, cooperation, and pledges of assistance in return for denuclearization. Had Baker not pressed so hard, the treatment of nuclear weapons might have followed the same path as the one for democratization and been viewed as an internal affair. That was Scowcroft's preference, and this position had many backers in the Pentagon. For these realists, balancing Russia with a nuclear Ukraine was also discussed as a possible strategy for enhancing American national security. But Baker believed he had a mandate from Bush to push ahead on unified command and control, which he argued best served U.S. national security interests. Baker almost single-handedly pushed the issue, making sure that the United States capitalized on the reservoir of desperation in the region to join the West in order to gain the commitments he sought not only from Russia but also from Ukraine, Belarus, and Kazakhstan. Under the rubric of the Nunn-Lugar program, the United States also became engaged in the denuclearization of Russia as well, but it was the Clinton administration that expanded that program as part of its overall Wilsonian foray into Russia's internal affairs.

4

Limited Assistance for Economic Reform

Few in the West anticipated the collapse of the Soviet Union. Even fewer correctly calculated the speed of this monumental event. And still fewer predicted the degree to which the new government leaders in now independent Russia would embrace Western economic and political institutions and aspire to replicate them on Russian soil. After seventy years of fearing Soviet Russia and forty years of seeking to contain (if not destroy) Soviet communism, Western leaders suddenly faced an opposite task—how to aid the development of a market economy and a democratic polity in Russia. Western governments, including the Bush administration, were not prepared for the task.

In the immediate wake of communist collapse in December 1991, Russian authorities granted Western governments huge opportunities to intervene in the sovereign affairs of Russia. Western advisers were invited to "occupy" virtually every branch of the Russian government; IMF officials were asked to prepare comprehensive economic plans; American military personnel were allowed to subsidize and oversee the destruction of Russian nuclear weapons. With this opportunity, however, came a tremendous responsibility as the transformation of the Soviet command system into a market economy and the Soviet authoritarian regime into a democratic polity constituted the greatest *peaceful* revolutionary agenda ever attempted in the history of the modern world. Many believed the West's challenge comparable to that faced by the architects of the Marshall Plan, the American program for rebuilding western Europe after World War II.

In several critical respects, however, the task was even greater than after World War II. Different from west European countries, market and demo-

cratic institutions could not be resurrected in Russia. They had to be constructed from scratch while old Soviet institutions were being dismantled at
the same time in a peaceful process.[1] Independent Russia also inherited from
the Soviet Union an economy in free fall, including a massive balance of payments crisis, a huge monetary overhang, depleted hard currency reserves, and
a panicked society. During the winter of 1991–92, even starvation loomed.
Before pursuing long-term reforms to nurture a healthy market economy,
Russian leaders had to ensure that the patient did not die.[2] Moreover, in contrast to Germany or Japan in 1945, Russia had not been defeated in a major
war at the time of reconstruction, so many Russian political forces resented
and resisted Western interference. Complicating matters, the urgency and
need to rebuild Russia were neither recognized nor shared by all in the West
to the same degree that Western leaders saw the urgent need to rebuild western Europe after World War II to save those countries from communist
takeover and prevent another European war. If Russia had an enemy that
threatened not only Russia but the Western powers, then the importance
assigned to aiding Russia would have been much greater. However, this geopolitical condition did not exist.

There is a final difference between postwar Europe and post–cold war
Russia. U.S. officials in 1945 welcomed the end of Nazi Germany and imperial
Japan. In contrast, the collapse of the Soviet Union in 1991 was considered a
mixed blessing by some in Western capitals. For many officials in the Bush
administration, the collapse of the Soviet Union presented not so much an
opportunity as a danger, a danger that everything the administration had
achieved with Mikhail Gorbachev would go up in a puff of smoke (or worse,
a nuclear cloud). Gorbachev, after all, had not stood in the way of Germany's
unification within NATO or the American-led war against Iraq in Desert
Storm. He had ended Soviet assistance to anti-Western regimes, and he had
allowed eastern Europe to go its own way.

In the security arena, the fear of instability led to Baker's push to ensure
that no new nuclear states emerge from the wreckage, and then to the efforts
to go to lower (but not radically lower) numbers of nuclear weapons. Belarus,
Ukraine, and Kazakhstan did start down the path of non-nuclear status in the
spring of 1992 (although, as we shall see, the browbeating strategy employed
by Baker was no longer working by 1993 in the case of Ukraine and had to be
replaced by incentives and engagement). And Bush and Yeltsin signed START
II in January 1993, paving the way for at least some reductions in the heavy
weaponry that had been of such concern to Western military planners during
the cold war.

But whereas on the security side, the Bush administration demonstrated
aggressive, innovative policies and subsequent achievements, the economic
story is more ambiguous. The Bush administration did not show much imag-

ination in dealing with Russia's troubled transition to the market. Because no one in the Bush foreign policy team was a dedicated "regime transformer," a policy of massive intervention into Russian domestic affairs to help build cap-italism had no champion in this administration. Instead, smaller issues trumped the larger agenda of economic transformation. In the fall of 1991, the number one priority of the Bush Treasury Department was to gain agree-ment from the soon-to-be independent republics that they would accept all financial obligations incurred by the Soviet Union. Thus, precisely when the new regime in Russia might have been freed from the burdens of the past, the West, led by the United States, ensured that the Russians would continue to be saddled with a large financial burden amassed by Soviet communists. Nor did the Bush administration couple these demands of debt payment with signifi-cant offers of new economic assistance. Many in the administration were skeptical about Russia's ability to use effectively massive inflows of Western economic assistance; as Brent Scowcroft says, "We didn't give them economic aid because we just couldn't see how to do it without putting money down a rathole."[3]

Domestic politics in the United States helped to sustain the arguments of these skeptics. The combination of American economic recession and the Republican campaign challenge from isolationist Patrick Buchanan made the Bush team cautious about proposing a large-scale assistance package for Russia. Ironically, it was only criticism from another presidential hopeful, Bill Clinton, that compelled Bush to pledge a serious aid package in April 1992. Yet, even this package did not contain the needed ingredients that might help guide Russia's transition from a command system to a market economy. And by April 1992, few in the Bush administration had the energy or vision to think strategically about Russia's economic woes. They were focused instead on Bush's electoral woes.

Aiding the Enemy?

For forty years after World War II, American foreign policy decisionmakers embraced containment of Soviet communism as the overarching framework for defining American foreign policy. The appearance of a pro-Western reformer in the Kremlin, Mikhail Gorbachev, began to challenge the logic of and rationale for containment, but not immediately. Even after the Soviet col-lapse, many feared a return of a hostile, anti-Western regime in Moscow and the prospect of renewed confrontation between the United States and Russia. Others argued that Russia was imperialist and had been imperialist long before becoming a communist regime. This state, therefore, should not be assisted in any way, since the Soviet Union or Russia might one day again rise up to threaten Western interests. As conservative economist Martin Feldstein argued, "The idea of giving our former enemies aid without asking them to lay down their arms is a mistake." For this camp of power balancers, giving aid to Russia was irrational.[4]

Isolationists advanced a different set of arguments to oppose active engagement with and assistance to the new Soviet and Russian governments. These voices in both the Republican and Democratic parties called for American disengagement in world affairs now that the central threat to American security—Soviet communism—had been destroyed. Patrick Buchanan was the most outspoken isolationist opponent of aid, but the left wing of the Democratic Party also pushed an isolationist line. For instance, in response to President Bush's proposal for a $24 billion aid package to Russia, Representative David Bonior (D-Mich.) sent a letter to the White House signed by one hundred fellow representatives that stated, among other things, that American "jobs must come first."[5]

A third school cautioned against aid on the grounds that it would not work. As New York Times columnist Leslie Gelb wrote early in the Clinton administration, "Throwing money at a trillion-dollar economy that's sinking in political anarchy, waste and corruption is not a brilliant idea."[6] Although Gelb was writing about Russia, many analysts had made the same point about the Soviet Union before its collapse.

The Grand Bargain

While American politicians methodically were debating the merits of assisting economic reforms in the Soviet Union and Russia, change within the Soviet Union accelerated exponentially. During this period, U.S.-Soviet relations had never been more cordial. Building on the close personal relations forged between both President Ronald Reagan and General Secretary Mikhail Gorbachev and Secretary of State George Shultz and Foreign Minister Eduard Shevardnadze, President Bush and his administration developed close and cooperative relations with their Soviet counterparts. Bush and Gorbachev worked together successfully on arms reductions, the peaceful dismantlement of the Warsaw Pact, and the reunification of Germany. Given these amicable ties, built in large measure by Soviet concessions to U.S. interests, Mikhail Gorbachev and his government expected that the United States would play an instrumental role in assisting economic reforms in the Soviet Union.[7] (Western assistance with political reforms was not requested by the Soviet government at the time.) Officials in both countries believed that the West could play a positive role in guiding Soviet economic reform. As former U.S. ambassador to the Soviet Union Jack Matlock writes in his memoirs, "When I reviewed the situation at the beginning of the year [1989], I came to the conclusion that 1989 could be a year of opportunity for the United States to bring its influence to bear on the evolving Soviet system. Our policies had already helped set the Soviet agenda on such matters as human rights and the free flow of information; now was the time to bring our economic might to bear, not as we had done during the cold war, with sanctions and punitive measures, but by supporting steps to bring the Soviet Union into the community of states."[8]

In 1990, these discussions became more serious, because Gorbachev was prepared to introduce more radical reforms and because the Soviet economy was on the edge of collapse. Early in the following year, Gorbachev asked economic adviser Grigory Yavlinsky to develop a comprehensive aid program in partnership with Western governments. In the spring of 1991, Yavlinsky teamed with Harvard professors Graham Allison (who in 1993 would join the Clinton Pentagon) and Robert Blackwill (who had only recently left the Bush National Security Council staff) to propose a "Grand Bargain."

The Grand Bargain had two central themes. One was the idea that the West needed to come up with billions of dollars in assistance, a sum of Marshall Plan proportions, for a reforming Soviet Union. The second was the notion that the money would flow after the Soviet Union had taken certain steps to ensure that the institutions necessary for the transformation to a market economy were being established. Allison and Blackwill argued that Gorbachev had helped the West tremendously and that "America has no preeminent interest in the rapid disintegration of the Soviet Union." Since avoiding nuclear war remained the number one priority of U.S. national security and since breakup was a real possibility, the Harvard academics argued that the G-7 summit scheduled for July 1991 was the perfect opportunity for the West to pony up real money "*conditional* on continuing political pluralization and a coherent economic program for moving rapidly to a market economy." If the Soviet Union cut defense spending and subsidies to state enterprises, legalized private ownership, and liberalized prices, then the United States, Europe and Japan should provide $15 billion to $20 billion in grants each year for three years to provide balance of payments support, develop infrastructure projects, and ensure a social safety net.[9]

Allison had taken Yavlinsky to meet with State Department officials Robert Zoellick and Dennis Ross on May 21, 1991. Zoellick believed Yavlinsky understood well how to integrate micro- and macroeconomics, but unfortunately Soviet society did not yet have the microeconomic foundations required to develop a market economy. The Grand Bargain, argued Zoellick, assumed "that money from the outside can compensate for a lack of basic property and contract rights and even a crude rule of law for market exchange in society." He warned Yavlinsky that the Grand Bargain risked creating a backlash in Russia because nationalists and communists would charge that reformers were following a Western plan. Zoellick suggested that Yavlinsky state that his plan was designed to serve Russia's interests and that Russia would need to take these steps under any circumstance, but it would be easier to do so if the United States or Europe provided support. Yavlinsky in turn let Zoellick know that he felt strongly that the USSR should not get any money up front, but only after taking the necessary steps; otherwise, he said, "You'd only be putting my children in debt. You have to use the promise of money in the future to make us do what we must do now."[10]

There were three major problems with providing assistance on the scale that Yavlinsky, Allison, and Blackwill were proposing. One was that the recipient was still the Soviet Union, which continued to spend significant sums of money on weapons aimed at the United States. As the world would find out in August 1991, hardliners remained in place at the top levels of the Soviet government. Thus, those individuals in the U.S. government who favored further devolution and even breakup had no desire to support the Gorbachev regime with a massive infusion of money. They had an ally in Boris Yeltsin, who also did not want Western countries to subsidize and thereby prolong the existence of the Soviet regime.

Russian leaders took a series of steps to counter the Soviet Grand Bargain. In response to Harvard University's involvement with the Soviet government, Yeltsin's government signed up its own group of American advisers from the Hoover Institution and then used these alliances with Western economists to discredit the Soviet plan. Well before the collapse of the Soviet Union, Russian leaders also established contacts with the World Bank and the International Monetary Fund to ensure that no programs were negotiated with the Soviet government alone. Although Russian leaders understood that these international financial institutions would only sign agreements with them after Russia had obtained international recognition and joined these institutions, they wanted to thwart financial transfers to the Soviet Union. Given this dynamic context of multiple sovereignty within the Soviet Union, Western engagement with economic reform stalled.[11]

A second problem was the difficulty of putting together a credible program that could facilitate macroeconomic stability and structural change in a country that had paid little attention to deficits, inflation, or property rights for nearly a century. Compared with eastern Europe, the scale of change needed in the Soviet Union was much greater. Western economists were particularly in the dark when measuring, let alone recommending, policies to promote institutional change.

As Stanley Fischer, then an MIT economist and adviser to Yavlinsky and Allison and who would later become first deputy managing director at the IMF, muses, "You read these critiques of how we didn't understand the need for institutional reform. That's wrong. What can be fairly said is that nobody understood how difficult institutional reform would be in light of the bureau-cratic and other interest groups that were operating in Russia. So I would say the need wasn't underestimated, but the difficulty of changing institutions was underestimated."[12] Nor did American policymakers have much faith in Gorbachev's understanding or commitment to radical economic reform. The U.S. position stated categorically that Gorbachev had to initiate genuine mar-ket reforms *before* assistance would be pledged. Yet, even in the spring of 1991, U.S. officials were not convinced that Gorbachev had wholeheartedly embraced market principles, and therefore they remained skeptical about the feasibility of the Grand Bargain with Gorbachev.[13]

Finally, of course, was the question, who would provide the cash? The Japanese remained unwilling to offer massive assistance to the Soviet Union until territorial disputes lingering since World War II over the Kurile Islands had been resolved. The Germans already had provided huge sums to Gorbachev as a quid pro quo for unification and Soviet troop withdrawal, and unification itself was an enormous financial drain for the government in Bonn. George Bush was preparing to run for re-election at a time when the American economy was in recession and the government continued to run a huge budget deficit. Thus the political downsides of proposing a major infu-sion of cash to the Soviet Union of all places seemed to the administration rather steep.

During the spring and summer of 1991, Yavlinsky and Allison lobbied vig-orously for this aid package throughout the capitals of western Europe and Washington. In London in July, Gorbachev made history by becoming the first Soviet leader to attend a G-7 summit meeting, at which he made his case for massive Western aid for the Soviet Union.[14] The G-7 assistance or American aid, however, was not forthcoming. Aside from minor pledges of assistance for troop resettlement negotiated during talks over German unification, American officials resisted pleas for assistance. The August 1991 coup attempt derailed the Grand Bargain idea for good.

Soviet Collapse and a New Window of Opportunity

Opportunities for engaging in Russia's economic transformation changed radically after the collapse of the Soviet Union in December 1991. In the fall of 1991, Russian president Boris Yeltsin appointed Yegor Gaidar as deputy prime minister in charge of economic reform. Gaidar brought into the Russian government a group of young, radical reformers who were deter-mined to introduce sweeping market reforms as fast as possible. Because they predicted (quite rightly) that their tenure in office would be short, Gaidar's team tried to implement a comprehensive economic package all at once—a strategy that acquired the unfortunate label of "shock therapy."[15] Gaidar's strategy called for immediate liberalization of prices and trade. At the same time, the government had to control spending and the printing of money to achieve macroeconomic stabilization as soon as possible. Once prices were free and a stable macroeconomic environment was in place, full-scale privatization would follow. In Gaidar's view, this plan to reduce rapidly the role of the state in the economy also fit what was possible for Russian reformers. The Russian state—an entity that did not exist just weeks earlier—simply did not have the capacity to implement economic reform through administrative means.[16] Policies that required a strong state, such as gradual price liberalization or state-run competitive auctions of enterprises, were simply untenable at the time. Because Gaidar and his team believed that they would be in power for a very short time, they also wanted to do as much as they could as fast as possible.

To implement a sweeping reform package, Gaidar initially held out little prospect of aid from the West. He plunged ahead with his price liberalization and macroeconomic stabilization programs without any guarantee of assistance from the West. His achievements in closing the budget deficit and bringing down inflation—from over 240 percent in January 1992 to roughly 8 percent in August 1992—occurred before substantial aid from the West to Russia began to flow. He and his new government associates did not believe that the United States would put money into a country that was just recently the number one enemy of the West. His initial interaction with International Monetary Fund (IMF) officials also made him and his colleagues in the Russian government skeptical of the Fund's ability to intervene in a timely and positive manner. Conservative IMF bureaucrats moved slowly in making Russia a new member. Moreover, one of the Fund's first recommendations to Russia was to preserve the ruble zone within the former Soviet Union, a policy that Gaidar considered disastrous for Russia. Aid and advice from governments or international financial institutions simply seemed to move at a slower pace than the revolutionary events unfolding in Russia.

It was the announcement in April 1992 by President Bush and Chancellor Helmut Kohl that large assistance would be forthcoming that made Gaidar excited about the possible benefits of foreign aid.[17] First, he and his associates reasoned that the West could provide immediate and major balance-of-payments support to close the budget deficit and thereby help Russia control inflation.[18] Russian reformers also hoped that Western governments might offer Russia a stabilization fund to support a convertible ruble similar to the one put in place in Poland in 1990. Many experts agreed that such external funds were necessary for Russia to have any chance of achieving stabilization in the short term. Writing in the spring of 1992, Fischer and economist Jacob Frenkel argued, "General financial assistance, balance-of-payments support, has not yet been provided. Such aid, especially in the form of a currency-stabilization fund for Russia, will be needed if the reform momentum is to develop and be maintained."[19] The scale, of course, had to be different. If Poland needed $1 billion to stabilize its currency, Russian officials and their advocates in the West lobbied for a $6 billion pot of hard currency.

Given this set of circumstances in the fall of 1991 and early in 1992, the door for Western engagement and influence in remaking the Russian economy and polity was wide open. Issues of sovereignty that often emerge as major sources of tension between donors and recipients in other countries were simply not an issue for Russian reformers at this early stage. Because the task of transforming the Soviet command system into a Russian market economy was arguably the most ambitious economic "reform" ever attempted, Russian reformers welcomed intellectual support from foreigners. Gaidar and his team needed the West to provide ideas and knowledge about economic reform. Because Gaidar and his team were political unknowns in Russia, they also relied on Western support for domestic legitimization, both before their detractors within the Russian parliament as well as before their president, Boris Yeltsin. If authoritative figures from the World Bank, the International Monetary Fund, or the White House told Yeltsin that his young reform team was pursuing the correct policies, Yeltsin might be persuaded to stay the course. During this period, therefore, Western economists Anders Åslund, David Lipton, and Jeffrey Sachs played a direct and intimate role in providing advice to the new Russian government on macroeconomic issues. At the State Property Committee (GKI) headed at the time by Anatoly Chubais, a team of Western advisers led by Harvard economist Andrei Shleifer and American lawyer Jonathan Hay worked closely with their Russian counterparts to draft laws and regulations on privatization.[20] Although the presence of these (mostly American) advisers at GKI eventually elicited a strong visceral reaction from Russian nationalists and communists, this external intervention in the internal affairs of Russia lasted for several years. Later, through programs sponsored by the Agency for International Development, American consultants worked directly for or developed contractual arrangements with virtually every Russian government agency involved in the economic reform process, including the Central Bank, the Ministry of Finance, the Ministry of the Economy, and the Federal Securities Commission.

Gaidar and his team had champions in the United States, who argued that the West had a historic opportunity that could not be squandered to bury communism forever. Harvard professor Jeffrey Sachs, one of the most outspoken proponents of engagement at the time, asserted forcefully that international assistance was a *necessary* condition for economic reform in Russia: "Countries cannot be transformed without the generous and farsighted involvement of the international community." Having helped Poland make the jump to a market economy through a comprehensive and simultaneous set of reforms, Sachs believed that the same could be done in Russia.[21] The scale of aid, however, would be greater. Sachs estimated that "a comprehensive package, including a stabilization fund, balance-of-payments supports and food aid, should cost $15 billion-20 billion in 1992."[22]

The World Bank estimated that "Russia's financing requirements for 1992 are on the order of $23 billion," most of which was not available from domestic sources. Former president Nixon became an unexpected ally of the Sachs strategy. By comparing the situation with Russia and the West to earlier debates about China and the West in the 1950s, Nixon warned policymakers that historians would ask "Who lost Russia?" if reform in Russia failed while the West stood on the sidelines. Chancellor Helmut Kohl was also active and visible in persuading the United States to be more assertive in assisting Russian reforms. Other advocates of engagement and aid to Russia deployed the historical analogy of the Marshall Plan to highlight the gravity of the situation and scale of the task.[23]

Not everyone at the time endorsed a bold approach. Some, such as economists Charles Wolf of Rand, Martin Feldstein of the National Bureau of Economic Research, and Judy Shelton of the Hoover Institution, urged the United States to send technical assistance teams to Russia but warned against government transfers. They believed these funds would be wasted in Russia because Russia at the time lacked the basic market institutions. Without basic rules of the game in place on property rights, a commercial code, or sound monetary policy, these conservative economists believed that aid to Russia would simply fuel corruption and delay reforms.[24]

Others pushed the importance of Russian initiatives, not Western aid. Germany's finance minister Theo Waigel implored his fellow finance ministers during a meeting with Gaidar in Washington in April 1992, "Our message must be for self-help. . . . We want to signal to them that we want to help, but a major responsibility must be theirs." Others argued that Russian membership in the IMF and World Bank would be disastrous for Russian reform. In the spring of 1992, Craig Roberts of the Center for Strategic and International Studies stated categorically, "I don't think any advice the IMF could give the former Soviet Union would be worth 2 cents."[25]

The Debt

Ironically, the most animating economic issue for the Bush administration in the aftermath of Soviet dissolution was not how much the United States should give to help rebuild Russia but how and how much the Russians should pay to honor Soviet debts. After the Bolshevik revolution in 1917, the new Soviet regime had renounced its responsibility for debt incurred by the Tsarist government. The West was going to make sure that the Russian revolution of 1991 produced no such renunciation.[26]

When Secretary of State Baker traveled to Moscow in September 1991, he impressed on Gorbachev the link between future Western assistance and the fulfillment of obligations toward the previous Soviet debt. In his meeting with the Soviet leader on September 11, Baker laid out the U.S. position: first, the Soviet government needed to approach debt restructuring cautiously since the West would be unable to provide even emergency food and medicine if the Soviets could not maintain creditworthiness. Second, the Soviet government had to be transparent to the G-7 about its gold reserve holdings. Finally, if economic power did devolve to the republics, they had to take responsibility for the debts incurred by the Soviet Union.[27]

As fall wore on, Baker's advisers did not believe the debt issue was the primary concern (Counselor Robert Zoellick believed the chief strategic issue was getting the microeconomic foundations in place to build a market economy; Policy Planning Staff Director Dennis Ross argued strongly for taking advantage of the historical moment and providing significant assistance to support the new democrats), but for the first time since the Bush administration had taken office in 1989, the Baker State Department lost authority over a major issue of Soviet affairs, in this case to the Treasury Department, which was not interested in activism on the assistance front. As Dennis Ross recalls, "No one could prevent Baker from achieving what he wanted to achieve with Bush. Not Scowcroft, not Cheney. But [Treasury Secretary Nicholas] Brady could. There were a lot of contests there, and Bush didn't want to be put in a position of playing favorites. He didn't want to have to decide. Baker knew not to push it." But he adds, "By not deciding, Bush was deciding for Brady." And while Zoellick continued to work on these issues sporadically, he was losing touch with his Russian counterparts. He had built close contacts with Gorbachev adviser Grigory Yavlinsky but had no ties to Yegor Gaidar and the new economic team that was being developed around Boris Yeltsin.[28]

Undersecretary of the Treasury David Mulford took the lead on economic policy toward Russia. Mulford had served in the Treasury Department since 1984. Besides Russia policy, he was also responsible for coordinating policy among the G-7. He had a deep background on debt issues, and as Mulford saw it, "Debt issues are rather clean cut. They work according to certain financial realities." Furthermore, according to a State Department official who worked with Treasury Department officials, "At the time the argument was that it wasn't a poor country. It had energy exports. And if it chooses to spend on defense, that's its choice. It can pay its foreign debts and it should."[29]

Before the annual meeting of the World Bank and International Monetary Fund in Bangkok, Thailand, in October 1991, the G-7 finance ministers heard from Yavlinsky (serving at the time in an interim government commission for economic policymaking established after the coup) that the Soviet Union would be unable to meet its foreign debt payments after November 10, which, as Mulford recalls, "was big news to all of us." The G-7 deputies were sent immediately to Moscow since neither the United States nor its partners would be able to provide new credit to a country that was no longer current on its existing debts. This meant, as Baker had told Gorbachev in September, that humanitarian aid would be impossible, and the West feared an eruption of violence during the coming winter if emergency assistance was not delivered. Only if the Soviet government reached an understanding with Western governments on debt restructuring would new credit flows be possible.[30]

So the G-7 deputies went to Moscow for several days of meetings at the Oktyabrskaya Hotel. As Mulford remembers, "The seven of us explained to them how all this stuff worked and what would happen if there was a suspension of payments and what a Paris Club was and how it worked. There were huge differences of views and a lot of hostility around the table between, for example, Ukraine and some of the others and Russia. They all said maybe the Soviet Union contracted all this debt, but we never saw any money from it and so we're not responsible for any share of that debt because we never got anything."[31]

As a group, the G-7 decided that Russia and the other republics should enter what is known as a joint and several agreement. Under such an arrangement, not only are the partners jointly responsible, but each one is individually responsible for the entire body of debt. As Mulford says about such an accord, "It is perfectly ideal if you want to tie somebody up or a group up, but if the group has widely different capacity then you can argue that the most important benefit is that the strongest country is on the hook for everything, that is, Russia. But if Russia doesn't pay and neither does anyone else, then the smallest guy is on the hook, which is totally impractical. So I was a little nervous about a joint and several agreement for that reason, but we decided that we would try to negotiate that."[32]

The resulting negotiations were extremely difficult because the republics insisted that they should not be responsible for a debt that had not benefited them. And the Russians understood that they would have to assume all of it, which they eventually did in exchange for an agreement with the other republics that Russia would get Soviet foreign assets (for example, embassies and other properties).

Mulford and Assistant Secretary of the Treasury for International Affairs Olin Wethington were convinced that it was premature to consider an economic assistance program, even one based on Moscow fulfilling the basic conditions required for the creation of a market economy. They were fundamentally concerned that international markets had to have confidence in Russia, and that meant Russia had to avoid default. In their view, it was the only way to get Russia into the IMF and the World Bank, which was the key to gaining access to Western credit. And given Russia's natural resources, in particular oil and natural gas, there was skepticism about its lack of ability to pay, and certainly Russia could always shift funds out of its defense sector if necessary.[33]

Treasury Department officials not only maintained that the Soviets and then Russians had to agree to service the debt to remain creditworthy, but they also argued that the Russians never asked for forgiveness.[34] Partly this was because of the desire of Russian officials to be accepted as the successor state to the Soviet Union. But they also may have been afraid to ask. Gaidar recounts how Mulford "threatened that if the agreement was not signed as written, he would stop delivery of American grain." In fact, Gaidar reports that the new Russian government first joined the negotiations when the Western officials came to Moscow in November 1991, and the Soviet government had already made a commitment to export one hundred tons of gold. In exchange for Russia's willingness to sign the joint and several agreement, the Western creditors dropped their demand for the gold, whose export would have been, as Gaidar puts it, a "financial Brest-Litovsk."[35]

Although it is true that a default might have caused serious damage to Russia's international reputation, critics like Sachs argue that the need to service the debt (even on a restructured basis) helped contribute "to Russia's financial destabilization at the critical period of early 1992."[36] It also begs the question of what might have happened had the G-7 taken the lead to offer Russia forgiveness on at least part of the Soviet debt, especially after the Soviet Union's collapse in December 1991. Russia's creditworthiness would have been damaged, but, as we now know, Russia's creditworthiness sank anyway. Moreover, Russia would not have been saddled with a burden incurred by the horrific regime that had ruled Russia for the previous seventy years. As conservative Richard Perle argued at the time, "We should find a way to wipe the books clear and give Yeltsin a fighting chance. The least we can do is cancel the IOUs of his undemocratic predecessors."[37] It is true that Germany had far greater debt exposure, and it would have been difficult for the United States to push its allies hard given that in December 1991, it held only $2.8 billion of a total Soviet debt of roughly $65 billion.[38] And yet, just imagine the effect on Russian public opinion for the entire 1990s had the United States at the end of 1991 offered to forgive even that $2.8 billion to help the new Russia get on its feet.

But imagination was not forthcoming. State Department official Dennis Ross argues that part of the problem was that Egypt had been offered debt forgiveness in return for participating in the Persian Gulf War coalition, and this made it harder for the Treasury Department to offer to forgive more debt yet again. But he also complains, "The problem wasn't just Treasury's attitude toward the debt, it was their attitude toward assistance. They were just against it. They took a green eye-shade view of the stuff. We'd be making the case, look at the strategic reality here. It was like pulling a wagon loaded with rocks up a hill. They resisted every step of the way. Brady could always go to Bush and make a case on narrow economic grounds, and Bush would find it hard to overrule him. Bush would say, I want to do something. And it was all profoundly limited because of [Treasury's] criteria."³⁹

The Half-Hearted Bilateral Assistance Effort

Bilateral assistance was limited and would remain so through the end of the Bush presidency. Besides the attitude just cited by Ross, there were two other reasons for the limited help. One was the fear and uncertainty about what would happen to the money, especially since no one seemed to know what had happened with the money that had already been sent to Moscow. Second was the concern about the politics of foreign assistance. After Harris Wofford's November 1991 U.S. Senate victory in Pennsylvania, the president was extremely nervous about major economic assistance since polls showed the public's increasing doubts about his ability to manage the nation's economy.

Bush's timidity is clear from his own memoirs. Describing the cabinet meeting on September 4, 1991, the day after he returned from his vacation in Kennebunkport and following the August coup, Bush recalls, "The more I listened to the discussion in the Cabinet Room, the more I was convinced we simply did not know enough to design any detailed aid programs. We did not want the Soviets to starve, or to lack medicine. Yet, as far as I was concerned, the broad program of technical assistance that we set out at the G-7 meeting was still the best approach. . . . We had to see what relationship survived between the republics and the center before we offered any major financial support."⁴⁰

A small interagency group was established to deal with assistance issues. Led by Chairman of the Council of Economic Advisers Michael Boskin, it included officials from the White House, Department of State, and Department of Agriculture. Given the lack of enthusiasm for assistance designed to promote a transition to a market economy, the group quickly focused on short-term needs. On November 20, 1991, the United States announced $1.5 billion in food assistance (largely agricultural credit guarantees). And a week later, Congress voted an additional $100 million for emergency assistance as part of the package of Nunn-Lugar money. At this point, however, the administration had yet to articulate a framework or strategy for assistance.⁴¹

Publicly, State Department Counselor Zoellick was putting the onus on the Soviet Union: until it adopted reforms pressed by the major international financial institutions, money would have no effect. As he told a congressional subcommittee in early October 1991, "The critical fact is that given the size of the Soviet economy, even large infusions of funds from Western governments would be insufficient to make a difference on the fundamental question of economic growth. We don't do the new reform leaders any favor by obscuring the fact that only private capital flows will enable them to create growth and jobs."[42] Direct aid to Russia and the other republics was still not on the agenda.

Although it is true that the Soviet Union was unable to begin laying the foundation for a market economy, a major problem for what was to follow was the U.S. failure to work closely enough with the Yeltsin team. Victoria Nuland, who was serving in the U.S. embassy in Moscow during the fall of 1991, believes that if there was a cost to "sticking with Gorbachev too long," this was it: the delay until early 1992 in working with Yeltsin's team.[43] It was not that the Bush team was hostile to the Yeltsin government. Rather, American officials were not completely focused on the new Russian government's concerns and needs. Until the Soviet Union collapsed formally in December 1991, the Bush team delayed in engaging the Russian government, meaning that more than four months were lost at a moment when time was moving very rapidly.[44] Contacts between Gaidar's team and the Bush administration were sporadic. Most amazingly, the $24 billion aid package announced in April 1992 by Bush and Kohl was not negotiated or even discussed with the Gaidar government. Gaidar himself learned of the package only hours before it was announced.[45]

This failure is not only attributable to the continued gridlock at the highest levels over when and how to reach out to Yeltsin but also to the State Department's reduced role in economic affairs. Because the Treasury Department took over and focused on the debt issues, there was a real vacuum on assistance discussions for months after the coup. As Zoellick recalls, "There was discontinuity for me when Gaidar replaced Yavlinsky and Treasury stated it would take over. I was concerned that Treasury was preoccupied with the debt question, which while important was only one element of a comprehensive macro and micro economic challenge. The channel for action shifted to the G-7 Finance Ministers and their deputies, which added another bias toward budgets and debts instead of the basic economic building blocks." But Zoellick also felt that the public focus on the dollar size of assistance created a mistaken bias, believing that critics tested the administration's commitment by counting the dollars it was willing to give Russia even though the money would be wasted if Russia did not establish basic private property and contract rights, competitive markets, and transparent rules for markets. He also felt they were caught in a bind since he believed that the Russians had to work the microeconomic side first. Although he acknowledges that to gain any credibility in this area the administration may have had to offer a great deal more money, he argues that if Bush had said that microeconomic building blocks were essential first steps, the president's critics would have said he was "missing a great historical moment."[46]After months of standing on the sidelines, both conceptually and in practical terms on economic assistance, the

State Department finally made an effort to get out in front again. The venue was the speech at Princeton University that Baker delivered on December 12, just two weeks before the Soviet Union officially expired. The State Department was so eager to take the lead on a U.S. approach that it kept drafts of the speech out of the hands of officials at the Treasury Department. Ross stopped returning their calls. Because Bush's approval ratings had dropped to 47 percent by December, the president wanted to avoid foreign policy issues, giving Baker wide latitude to seize the moment.[47]

The roots of the Princeton speech go back to the immediate post-coup environment and the "What Has to Be Done" memo done for Baker by his staff. Proposed in the memo were several initiatives that served as the core of the December 1991 address: a donor's conference to provide humanitarian assistance, money for defense conversion and other technical assistance, as well as Peace Corps presence in Russia and the other republics.[48]

When Baker went to Russia in September, he wrote Bush from St. Petersburg laying out the stakes involved in supporting the new democrats, citing the analogy of the postwar recovery of Germany and Japan. He reiterated that Moscow would have to put together a "credible program for moving to a market economy" by working with the international financial institutions, but if they did so, "the onus will be on us, especially if we hang back."[49] In December, he finally had the opportunity to put some ideas forward. The major piece of the economic package was the announcement of a "coordinating conference" (for political reasons, it was not going to be called a donor's conference, as had been planned initially) that would bring together, as Baker said, "Our NATO allies, Japan, South Korea, the other OECD states, our Gulf coalition partners and international institutions," particularly to meet humanitarian emergencies. Beyond that, Baker said that the three most important tasks were demilitarization, democracy promotion, and assisting free market forces.[50]

Baker announced in his speech that he was designating Deputy Secretary of State Lawrence Eagleburger to head the assistance effort. And picking up the threads of the earlier internal State Department proposals, the secretary proposed an expanded Peace Corps presence, a Commerce Department business training program, and a G-7 offer to defer some of the interest payments on the Soviet debt.[51]

Although the speech had been kept away from the Treasury Department, the drafts put together by the State Department Policy Planning staff had been run past Ed Hewett at the National Security Council and Paul Wolfowitz from the Pentagon, who had come over to Ross's office at the State Department and added their suggestions. The State Department European Bureau had gone over the remarks, but no one noticed its most glaring error: the European Union was not mentioned (which State Department officials say was an oversight on their part). The Europeans were furious, not only because they believed they had already been doing so much more than the Americans but also because at this time the Maastricht Treaty was about to be signed, giving rise to a new union that was going well beyond its European Community predecessor in promoting political and economic unity on the continent. Baker tried to make amends the following week in Brussels by telling the Europeans that it was a mistake not to have included them on the invitation to the coordinating conference, but the French were so annoyed that they refused to lend their support to the January gathering. In the end, Eagleburger aide and conference organizer Kenneth Juster proposed that the January conference in Washington be the first of three, with the EU to host the second (as it did in Lisbon in May), and Japan the third.[52]

The fact that Baker, not Bush, was laying out a U.S. framework for assistance did not go unnoticed. The day after the Princeton address, *Washington Post* columnist Charles Krauthammer wrote, "As Truman understood, massive engagement in the reconstruction of faraway former enemies is an enterprise too large and alien to Americans to be led by anyone other than the president. The president must emerge from his Rose Garden cocoon, confront the isolationist tide, and explain to the country on national television that nothing on the American agenda is as important to our future as the demilitarization, democratization, and pacification of the old Soviet Union. Election year or not, it is no time for political timidity and complaints that the whole thing is just too difficult to figure out. Those who can't figure it out shouldn't temporize. They should resign." Or as scholar Leon Sigal wrote years later, "When the Soviet Union came to an end in 1991, so did the struggle over whom to aid, Gorbachev or Yeltsin. The answer was neither."[53]

The Coordinating Conference and Beyond

As the State Department prepared for the January 1992 coordinating conference in Washington, Baker sought to ensure high-level participation from other countries while also maintaining control over the process internally. Baker told Eagleburger that while he agreed with the need to set up interagency task forces because the State Department would be relying heavily on the Department of Agriculture, the Agency for International Development, the Department of Energy, the Defense Department, and the Joint Chiefs of Staff, the deputy secretary had to maintain firm control, since, Baker argued, they did not have time for an "interagency debating society."[54]

In late December, Dennis Ross and Acting Assistant Secretary of State for European Affairs Ralph Johnson had written a strategy paper to Baker and Eagleburger in which they laid out further the objectives of the conference beyond showing U.S. leadership. One was to provide a "message of hope" from the world to the democrats in Russia and the other newly independent states; another was to serve as a means for building domestic support for sustained U.S. involvement in the post-Soviet transformation. Ross and Johnson warned that in the run-up to the conference, the administration had to make a strong case to the public for why money for this purpose made Americans more secure, more free, and more prosperous.[55]

But Ross had for months been more focused on the transformative agenda than other White House and State Department colleagues. Internal skeptics of the conference feared that the United States would not be able to come up with any money and thus that the administration would look foolish for calling the conference. Treasury Department officials firmly opposed providing new money. Even at the State Department, Robert Zoellick came on board only because the conference "was responding to the public mood that things must be done . . . and it became an organizing device for the West at large to demonstrate a stake in Russia's transformation." But since Zoellick did not believe that material support would do much good until Russia had engaged in structural transformation, he was not enthusiastic about the venture.[56]

Ross, who had proposed holding a "donor's conference" only days after the coup, remained the most enthusiastic. He acknowledges, "I didn't come at it through an economic lens. I came at it from the standpoint of the historical moment, driven by a sense of the historic stakes, the historic opportunity, the historic losses if we didn't do anything. We would let them down if all we did was offer them rhetorical support." He adds that it was clear that their needs "were so great that they had to have help from the outside." But he also notes that in retrospect, there was "an excessive degree of hubris about what could be done from outside. What [Zoellick] brought to bear was a more hard-headed calculus of an understanding of what will work and won't work."[57]

The coordinating conference created five working groups: food, medicine, shelter, energy, and technical assistance. State Department officials debated whether recipient countries should be invited, but they feared that if they came, an unseemly bidding war would ensue (a team was dispatched to Minsk, Belarus, to brief representatives from the newly independent states a few days after the conference). There was also a parallel conference of nongovernmental organizations established to discuss what role the private and nongovernmental sectors might play.[58]

As for the U.S. dollar contribution, Baker writes that he "shook down" the Office of Management and Budget Director Richard Darman for $645 million, a figure the president announced at the coordinating conference. On January 22, 1992, the conference brought together representatives from forty-seven countries and seven international organizations.[59] It was not a lot of money, but in defending what they did, Baker argued years later to Russian officials, "I got $5 billion for you from the Saudis, if you remember. . . . It's not

$15 billion but it's 33 percent of it, and it's a nice piece of change. . . . It would have been impossible for us to cobble together $20 billion given particularly the legislative restraints we were under. But in the absence of real fundamental reform and evidence that that was going forward, it wouldn't have worked anyway."[60]

Critics at the time were not impressed. *New York Times* columnist William Safire wrote, "Baker arranged this week's diplomatic extravaganza to dramatize our interest in acting like a superpower—while, in an election year, passing the tab to Japan and the Saudis." Safire argued that while there was a huge potential downside for not helping Russia, the risk in providing real help was insubstantial. So, he argued, "The prudent hard line is to help, and the President's $645 million pledge yesterday is not much help." To put the assistance to the former Soviet Union in perspective, one report noted, the European Union had provided 71 percent of aid to the region while the U.S. total stood at only 6 percent.[61]

The most concrete U.S. action at the conference was setting up Operation Provide Hope, an effort to deliver immediate humanitarian assistance to the Soviet Union. It had been difficult for U.S. officials to gauge the seriousness of the threat of famine and civil unrest that winter. National Intelligence Estimates provided by the CIA were not particularly clear. In November, CIA analysts argued that on the one hand, "Severe economic conditions, the fragmentation of the armed forces, and ongoing interethnic conflict this winter will combine to produce the most significant civil disorder in the former USSR since the Bolsheviks consolidated power." On the other, they stated only a few pages later, "On balance, however, Yeltsin's statements and actions give grounds for modest optimism that the Russian government will not be destabilized."[62]

Under the direction of State Department official Richard Armitage, the United States flew fifty-four sorties by C-5 and C-141 cargo planes in February 1992. By the end of the year, sixty-five flights and 311 surface containers had delivered $189 million in humanitarian assistance (using food and medicine left over from Desert Storm the year before) to Russia. Baker back in December had proposed to Yeltsin that the U.S. military work with the Soviet military to deliver emergency assistance, and Yeltsin agreed.[63]

And while Operation Provide Hope was an important symbolic gesture to Russia and the other former Soviet republics and did provide real food and real medicine, it was not completely altruistic. Baker has written that Joint Chiefs of Staff military planners and Defense Department officials worked with State Department officials to choose the assistance targets. "Five years before," he writes, "the targeters would have been identifying sites to be hit by ICBMs and the OSIA staff would have been chasing Soviet missiles. It was yet another indicator that the Cold War had been turned on its head."[64] Not quite.

What Baker does not add is that when the targeters got out their map of the Soviet Union to pick cities, they looked at it not only for purposes of logistics but also to take a closer look at the targets in the U.S. strategic nuclear plan.[65]

Strange Bedfellows: The Clinton and Nixon Alliance against Bush

Neither Russia nor representatives from the other newly independent states had been invited to the coordinating conference, but they were certainly expressing their desires for more assistance. During the conference, Gennady Burbulis, Russia's first deputy prime minister, expressed gratitude at the humanitarian assistance but asked for more, including, at a minimum, $6 billion to help finance hard currency imports; $7 billion to create a fund to stabilize the ruble during currency conversion; and $6 billion more for emergency food and medicine. He also asked for deferral of interest payments in 1992.

At the end of January, Yeltsin's chief of administration, Yuri Petrov, met with Thomas Niles, assistant secretary of state for European affairs, and told him that Russia's reform program had a fifty-fifty chance of succeeding in the absence of real assistance. "The time for rhetoric has ended," said Petrov. "Humanitarian aid won't save us. Russians need to see improvement tomorrow, not in 1995. We are now at a breaking point." But the day before, in a meeting with Foreign Minister Andrei Kozyrev, Secretary of State Baker said that even the planned airlift was not easy "in the middle of a recession and a presidential election." He also worried that continued Russian arms sales to Iran and Libya would adversely affect public support in the United States.[66]

At Camp David, President Boris Yeltsin countered with his own threat, warning that if his government failed, the arms race and the cold war would resume, and "again this will be the same regime that we have just recently rid ourselves." A briefing done for American allies suggested that in these meetings, Yeltsin asked for more food aid "but made no specific requests for broader economic assistance." The press reported, however, that Yeltsin was so frustrated at Camp David about the lack of concrete help that when he went to Canada afterward, he complained about countries that "talk and talk" but would not respond to Russian pleas for help.[67]

Administration officials needed prodding, since in general, they took the approach that Mulford articulated in early February 1992 in response to the Russian requests: "Nobody is going—and I'm speaking now for the whole G-7—nobody is going to sit down tomorrow morning and write a $12 billion check."[68] Just as the Bush team had cautiously avoided intervening in the political transformation of the Soviet Union and Russia, they were now seeking to avoid real American involvement in the economic transformation under way inside Russia.

But political pressure started coming from two sources. One was Bill Clinton, governor of Arkansas and Democratic candidate for president, who was scheduled to make a major address on foreign policy on April 1 in advance of the New York primary. For most of the 1992 campaign, candidate Clinton focused on domestic issues, implicitly criticizing President Bush for spending too much time on foreign affairs to the neglect of domestic issues. "It's the economy, stupid" was the battle cry of the Clinton campaign. However, under the guidance of the Progressive Policy Institute (a think tank associated with the Democratic Leadership Council that Clinton chaired before he became a candidate), Clinton's team did develop a foreign policy program that included a call for increased and more rapid assistance for Russia's reforms.

As Bush had a solid record on other foreign policies issues, his lethargy about aid to Russia gave Clinton an issue in foreign affairs on which to criticize his opponent. In his April 1 remarks, the leading Democratic candidate chided the incumbent, "The present administration has been overly cautious on the issue of aid to Russia. Not for policy considerations, but out of political calculations. Now, prodded by Democrats in Congress, rebuked by Richard Nixon, and realizing that I have been raising this issue in the campaign since December, the president is finally, even now as we meet here, putting forward a plan of assistance to Russia and the other new republics." The triumph of democracy in Russia, he added, would be a tremendous boon to the United States and the world, ensuring "lower defense spending, a reduced nuclear threat, a diminished risk of environmental disasters, fewer arms exports and less proliferation, access to Russia's vast resources through peaceful commerce, and the creation of a new, major market for American goods and services."[69]

As he alluded to in his speech, Clinton was riding the coattails of a second Bush critic, Richard M. Nixon. Evoking the memory of the "Who lost China?" debate in the 1950s that was so instrumental to his early career, the former president warned that losing Russia would be "an infinitely more devastating issue in the 1990s" in a "secret" memo of March 1992 titled "How to Lose the Cold War" that he leaked to every journalist and interested party in Washington, D.C. The memo was a blistering attack on the Bush administration and its failure to support Yeltsin, "the most pro-Western leader of Russia in history." If Yeltsin failed, wrote Nixon, "the prospects for the next fifty years will turn grim." And what had the Bush administration done? "We have provided credits for the purchase of agricultural products. We have held a photo-opportunity international conference . . . that was long on rhetoric but short on action. We are sending sixty cargo-planes of surplus food and medical supplies leftover from the Persian Gulf War. We have decided to send two hundred Peace Corps volunteers—a generous action if the target of our aid were a small country like Upper Volta but mere tokenism if applied to Russia. . . . This is a pathetically inadequate response."[70]

Nixon proposed providing humanitarian assistance, sending "thousands of managers" to teach the Russians and others how to build private enterprise, rescheduling the Soviet-era debt and deferring interest payments, opening Western markets to Russian exports, putting together a multilateral currency stabilization fund of "tens of billions of dollars" once Russia had reined in its money supply, and establishing one Western organization to manage and coordinate these efforts. "The stakes are high," wrote the former president, "and we are playing as if it were a penny ante game."[71]

To get his points across, Nixon went on an all-out media blitz. He appeared on ABC's *Nightline* and CNN's *Larry King Live*. He worked the leading reporters and columnists to write about the memo, and they did, including Thomas Friedman at the *New York Times* and Strobe Talbott at *Time* magazine. All of these efforts led to a major conference at the Four Seasons Hotel in Washington on March 11-12, where Nixon was the lunch speaker and Bush the dinner speaker.[72]

Bush and his top advisers still remained cautious. They were focused primarily on the American economic recession and the Republican primary campaign challenge from isolationist Patrick Buchanan (who had been hammering away at Bush's devotion to foreign policy). They also continued to worry about the money already provided to Moscow that proved difficult to account for. The day of the conference, Deputy Secretary of State Lawrence Eagleburger went before a House appropriations subcommittee to warn that America's resources were not unlimited. The administration was proposing a little more than $600 million in 1992 and 1993 for the former Soviet republics in addition to $860 million from existing legislation. Finally, when he was asked at a news conference about Nixon's exhortations, President Bush refused to lean forward, saying, "There isn't a lot of money around. We are spending too much as it already is. So to do the things I would really like to do—I don't have a blank check for all of that." And he added in a major understatement, "And so in that area, there may be a slight difference."[73]

But even Congress was putting pressure on the president to do more. On the day of the Nixon conference, U.S. ambassador to Moscow Robert Strauss had gone before the Senate Foreign Relations Committee and echoed Nixon's concerns, "This isn't beanbag we're playing. These are big-time issues, this is life or death, this is the future of nations." Senator Jesse Helms (R-N.C.), not known for his charity toward international causes, wrote the ambassador, "You lead and I'll follow. Tell me what we need to do, Bob."[74]

The $24 Billion Pledge

Although Bush's leading advisers do acknowledge feeling the heat from Congress to do more, they deny that either Nixon or Clinton pressured the president into making his first major announcement on assistance on April 1, 1992. Scowcroft notes that the administration had to do something given political pressure but argues that it took some time to figure out what kind of package made sense under the circumstances and adds, "Nixon was annoying but had no impact on what we did." Meanwhile, Baker writes that Bush had to make the announcement after March 31 (the deadline in Congress for a continuing resolution on foreign assistance over which the administration wanted to avoid having money for Russia debated) but before April 6, when the Russian Congress of People's Deputies would take place at which Gaidar and his reformist team would have to fight for their political survival. Yeltsin had mentioned the need for a show of support before this meeting to Bush several times in phone calls and letters, and Foreign Minister Kozyrev had raised the issue with Baker in Brussels in March. Since April 3-5 were a Friday through Sunday, Baker argues that any announcement had to come on April 1 or 2.[75]

And yet it hardly seems an accident that Bush's news conference at the White House to announce a major Western package was convened at 11:04 a.m. Governor Bill Clinton's address to the Foreign Policy Association of New York began approximately twenty minutes later. At his news conference, Bush proposed a $24 billion package that sounded like real money: $4.5 billion would come from the IMF and the World Bank; $11 billion would be in the form of bilateral assistance from the G-7 countries, of which $2 billion would come from the United States (mostly in grants and credits to buy U.S. food products); $6 billion would be set aside for a ruble stabilization fund; and $2.5 billion in non-U.S. debt would be rescheduled.[76] The total U.S. contribution to the package would theoretically come to about $5 billion and included a legislative proposal known as the Freedom for Russian and Emerging Eurasian Democracies and Open Markets (FREEDOM) Support Act. In addition, President Bush also promised to ask Congress to supply $15 billion in additional funds to international lending institutions to assist the new countries of the former Soviet Union.[77]

Although merely one speech in a long campaign for both candidates in the American presidential race, this number—$24 billion—heightened expectations in Russia about America's engagement in Russia's transition. As already mentioned, this announcement sparked real optimism in the Gaidar team that the West might be able to play a pivotal role in helping to sustain the difficult stabilization program that he was busy fighting to save at the time. In Gaidar's view, price liberalization in January had gone off better than expected. People were not rioting in the streets in response to astronomic price increases overnight. And after January, the rate of monthly inflation was moving in the right direction. Yet, by April, pressures from the industrial lobbies for more subsidies were mounting at the same time that populist politicians were beginning to cite the lack of results from reform as evidence that reform was not succeeding. Gaidar and his associates believed that a massive, one-time infusion of external financing for the federal government would be the perfect anti-inflationary way to help with Russia's balance of payments woes. The timing of the announcement also had an impact on Russia's domestic political struggles. At the time, opponents of Gaidar's formula for economic transformation were mobilizing votes in the Congress of People's Deputies to oust him and his team of young reformers. In their defense, Gaidar and his associates cited this pledge of $24 billion as the fruits of their work, warning that if they were removed from government, such offers of assistance would be withdrawn. After threatening to resign, Gaidar and his economic reform team survived the attacks at the April Congress. In this round, American rhetoric helped to rescue Russia's reformers.

The rhetoric, however, was not followed by real assistance. The G-7 had not even been consulted about the announcement. The Japanese had not agreed to the numbers in the package, and Prime Minister Kiichi Miyazawa was only given six hours' notice of the Bush remarks. A British Treasury Official stated after the announcement, "If you take a snapshot, at the moment we are in mid-air, about three-quarters through our double spin." And a German official derisively called the Bush statement "pure campaigning."[78]

Elements of the package had been the subject of much debate during the previous months. Yeltsin had asked Baker in Moscow back in February for a stabilization fund for the ruble, as had been provided for Poland earlier. Baker told him that he would push for it, and he did, despite the initial resistance of the Treasury Department. Even his top economic adviser, Robert Zoellick, was highly skeptical, believing that "the prospects of a stable currency in Russia [were] highly unlikely; moreover, the Fund would require tying up a huge sum of money that could be better used elsewhere. The Fund became another symptom of support out of proportion to its relative usefulness." And while the proposed IMF quota increase had been in front of the Congress for some time, it was only in April that President Bush was signaling that he really wanted it.[79]

Bush acknowledged on April 1 that the package did not represent "a lot of new money." Undersecretary of the Treasury David Mulford adds, "The $24 billion was made up substantially of previous commitments. The United States position was that we were not putting new money into Russia." Bush himself said the week after announcing the package in response to a general question about foreign aid, "Let me tell you something, it is going to be impossible to get anything through the Congress this year, in terms of foreign aid, beyond what we have suggested. We would be unrealistic to think that there might be more."[80]

The money needed most immediately—support for Russia macroeconomic stabilization—was to come from the IMF, not the United States directly.[81] The

IMF eventually made its first $1 billion loan to Russia in August 1992, but this infusion of money came well after Gaidar's strategy for stabilization was falling apart. By the time the money reached Russian government accounts, Gaidar had lost control of the reform agenda.[82] More damagingly, the $6 billion stabilization fund promised by Bush on April 1 was never established by the IMF or anyone else. When those assigned to assessing the feasibility of creating such a fund made their recommendations, Russia's first attempt at stabilization had already failed. The first attempt at multilateral assistance for the purposes of achieving macroeconomic stabilization was too little, too late.

The U.S. bilateral package for Russia announced in April did not aim to assist Russia with stabilization. On the contrary, a substantial portion of this money—the $1.1 billion of "tied credits" that could only be used to purchase American food—was given to increase American exports. Perhaps useful in December 1991 or January 1992 had they been delivered then, these credits for food seemed less timely in April 1992 after the scare of starvation had subsided.

The most substantial and innovative element of the bilateral package was the Freedom Support Act. To provide assistance, the United States had to lift the myriad of legislative restrictions that had been in place during the cold war. Baker had first proposed this effort in December 1991 in his speech at Princeton, and after months of work within the department, the president had a legislative proposal ready to transmit to Congress.[83] During the next decade, this program contributed to Russia's internal development on a wide range of issues. In 1992, however, the strategic objective of the act was not clear. While the administration was pointing fingers at Congress, senators on both sides of the aisle complained that they could not even understand exactly what the Freedom Support Act entailed. The administration, after working for months on a program, had rushed its announcement on April 1 without consultation. When State Department official Richard Armitage testified before Congress, Senator Robert L. Kasten (R-Wisc.) declared that the Freedom Support Act was "mirrors, paper clips and smoke."[84]

When Yeltsin came to Washington in June 1992, Bush quietly urged him to make a strong statement on accounting for American prisoners of war in order to gain strong congressional support for the legislation. The president wrote a note to Baker during the summit suggesting language for Yeltsin to use: "Yeltsin needs to tell Congress something like this. I do not know if one single American POW/MIA is alive in Russia or anywhere in the former Soviet Union. But I will tell you this. We will go through every record in every archive in order to shed light on the fate of Americans unaccounted for. I can assure you if any American has been held and can be found I will find him. I will bring him to his family."[85]

On June 17, 1992, Yeltsin spoke before a rare joint session of Congress and said, "I promise you that each and every document in each and every archive will be examined in order to investigate the fate of every American unaccounted for. As President of Russia, I assure you that even if one American has been detained in my country and can still be found, I will find him. I will get him back to his family."[86]

Yeltsin then chided his audience for not doing more to support him: "I thank you for the applause. I see everybody rise. Some of you who have just risen here to applaud me have also written in the press that until Yeltsin gets things done and gets all of the job done, there should be no Freedom Support Act passing through the Congress. Well, I don't really quite understand you, ladies and gentlemen. . . . So now you are telling me, first do the job, and then we shall support you in passing that act. I don't quite understand you."[87]

By summer, everyone in the Bush administration believed that without Yeltsin, any chance of reform in Russia would fail. Even Mulford said at a conference in June, "[U.S. ambassador to Moscow] Bob Strauss told us. . . that when Yeltsin is in Moscow he is number one, two, three, four, five, and six, and that there is no other. He makes all the decisions and those close to him in fact are reliant upon his physical presence, really to do it."[88] But whereas Bill Clinton's similar assessment led to a huge package a year later, Bush was too constrained politically, too uncertain about Russia, and too cautious by nature to do more. The Freedom Support Act was passed in the fall and provided for around $400 million in humanitarian and technical assistance. At the end of 1992, however, while the United States was about to change administrations, Russia's Congress of People's Deputies ousted Gaidar, replacing him with Viktor Chernomyrdin, an experienced Soviet *apparatchik* and former minister in the Gorbachev government. The best moment for assisting Russia's reform effort had passed.

Conclusion

In addressing issues of economic assistance to the Soviet Union and Russia, President George H. W. Bush remained true to his basic ideological orientation on international affairs. In his view, managing relations between states was the business of world statesmen. Trying to influence the affairs within other states was not. Just as Bush had little inclination to push democratization within the Soviet Union and then Russia, he aspired to play only a limited role in Russia's transformation from a command economy to a market system. As a result, the United States moved slowly and cautiously to assist in Russia's economic transformation.

This policy was not determined by the distribution of power in the international system or domestic politics in the United States. To be sure, both played a contributing role. Russia, of course, was still the country in the world most capable of destroying the United States with nuclear weapons. Realist theorists have cited this fact as the reason why the United States could not assist this rival power. However, the specter of economic chaos inside Russia had the potential to be more threatening to the United States than a reforming Russia. The balance of power in the world did not provide obvious guidance for how the United States should respond to Russia's internal challenges. Domestic politics, as already discussed, also influenced policy. Bush was reluctant to give money to those living in Moscow when those living in Manchester, New Hampshire, wanted more from him as well. Again, however, American economic woes may have limited options but did not determine them. More forceful pressure on the IMF to deliver bigger aid faster, for instance, would have entailed little direct or immediate expense to Americana taxpayers.

That some in the Bush administration were making the case for a different strategy suggests that the policy that resulted was not inevitable. Some in his administration, such as Dennis Ross at the State Department, gravitated toward a policy of more aggressive intervention after the collapse of the Soviet Union. Anders Åslund recalls that Zoellick told him at the time that one could put up $25 billion if the cause was right, but one had to be prepared to lose the money, and if the chance of success was not great enough, it just did not make sense. Zoellick was not convinced it was. Ross was more willing to think about serious assistance, but in the end there was complete resistance from the Treasury Department. Ross recalls, "I was focused on one big deal. We are seeing one of the most extraordinary strategic changes of the twentieth century. The undoing of the Russian revolution. The first priority for me was that we've got guys who want to be democrats in Russia and we have an unbelievable stake in wanting to make sure they succeed. And they feel they need the money. We ought to find ways to help them. Give them $60 billion a year." But as Scowcroft, who was much more skeptical than Ross and perhaps even Zoellick about what could be achieved, reminds us, "Treasury wasn't enthusiastic about anything."[89] In other words, the Bush strategy for aiding Russian economic reform resulted from political battles among individuals with different ideas about U.S. priorities from within the executive branch. At the end of the day, the president did not share Ross's view. Nor did many others in the Bush administration hold this view, including, most crucially, those at Treasury at the time.

Of course, it is impossible to know if a major assistance package would have made a real difference. And even if the United States and its Western partners could have devised in the winter of 1991–92 a program in which they provided much greater sums in return for concrete steps, would the politics in Washington and Moscow have sustained the effort? Political scientist Peter Reddaway argues that the Yeltsin government could not have applied Polish-style shock therapy in the early 1990s because it would have been thrown out of office, and one could not expect it to have put in place a rigorous program given that "governments do not deliberately commit suicide."[90] (In December 1992, Yeltsin removed Gaidar from the government.) Sachs, Åslund, and others contend that an infusion of real money at the right time might have helped Russia achieve stabilization in 1992. Few argue with the claim that early stabilization is better for economic growth than a prolonged struggle.[91]

There is no way to know what more money might have meant in that first year of Yeltsin's regime and the last year of the Bush presidency, or whether Russia could even have absorbed large sums of money given the lack of government and private infrastructure. What we do know is that a major attempt to help Russia achieve stabilization in the first, critical year of reform was never tried.

5

Bill Clinton's Assistance Policy

B y the time President Bill Clinton and his new administration took office in January 1993, the first window of opportunity for fundamental Russian economic reform had already closed, while the moment for genuine political reform was quickly passing as well. When they assumed responsibility for economic policymaking within the Russian government in the fall of 1991, Deputy Prime Minister Yegor Gaidar and his team of young reformers aimed to achieve rapid transformation to the market by following a so-called big bang strategy.[1] As discussed in chapter 4, this plan called for immediate price and trade liberalization, accompanied by decreased state spending and tight control over the monetary supply. Once liberalization and stabilization had been achieved, mass privatization was to follow quickly thereafter.

In January 1992, when Gaidar launched this plan by beginning with partial price liberalization, few interest groups inside Russia openly supported his program.[2] Already in the spring of 1992, Yeltsin was succumbing to political pressure from antireform forces in the Russian parliament and reconsidering his reform policies. Only months after "shock therapy" began, Yeltsin diluted Gaidar's reformist team with three deputy prime ministers known at the time as conservative "red" directors, including Viktor Chernomyrdin, the former director of a giant Russian gas conglomerate, Gazprom. Instead of shock therapy, the coalition government pursued a "mixed plan" of reform.[3] This mixed plan resulted in a postponement of liberalization of oil and gas prices, renewed state subsidies for enterprises, and concessions to enterprise directors on the government's privatization program. The expansion of state subsidies quickly undermined stabilization and increased monthly inflationary rates back to double digits. Yeltsin's appointment of Viktor Gerashchenko to head the Central Bank in July 1992 exacerbated inflationary pressures as Gerashchenko quickly approved the printing of new money and the transfer of government credits to enterprises. (Additionally, the central banks of other former Soviet republics exacerbated the problems by issuing ruble credits of their own.) By the end of the year, inflation had skyrocketed and Central Bank credits amounted to 31 percent of GDP.[4]

When Gaidar attempted to rein in Gerashchenko and the Central Bank, the new chairman claimed that he answered to the Congress of People's Deputies and not the government.[5] These disastrous economic outcomes—produced not by shock therapy but by half measures and muddled reforms—undermined Yeltsin's confidence in his young reform team. By the end of 1992, at the Seventh Congress of People's Deputies, Yeltsin gave up on Gaidar altogether, and instead nominated Chernomyrdin as prime minister, who pledged to adopt a more "pragmatic" approach to economic policymaking, which Russian liberals interpreted as the end of true reform.

Besides these reversals on the economic reform agenda, Russia was also midstream in a constitutional crisis by the time that Clinton was sworn into office. After the failed August 1991 *putsch* attempt, Yeltsin seized the moment to push forward several important political changes, including most dramatically the dissolution of the Soviet Union. Yet, he also refrained from implementing other important reforms. He did not call for new elections, he did not create a new political party, and he did not try to ratify a new constitution. By the fall of 1992, the absence of clearly defined political rules of the game had produced a polarized standoff between the Russian president and the Congress of People's Deputies.[6] This conflict raged throughout the spring and summer of 1993, ending only tragically in October 1993 when the two opposing sides used military forces against each other to resolve the impasse.

Kantian Ideals

Much of the drama of economic and political reform in Russia was over before the Clinton administration assumed the reins of executive power in Washington. By January 1993, the first attempt at stabilization had already failed, the Russian privatization program was six months old, and Yeltsin and the Congress of People's Deputies were already threatening each other with impeachment and disbandment respectively. It was in the context of stalling economic reforms and political polarization in Russia and not the euphoric moment of communism's collapse that Clinton and his team were compelled to devise a strategy for dealing with Russia. As campaign adviser and soon-to-be National Security Council staffer Toby Gati correctly noted in a December 1992 transition team memo, "It is probably too late for the U.S. to make a big difference in the general direction of the reform process. The leverage we had a year ago is gone and Yeltsin of August 1991 is not the Yeltsin President-elect Clinton will meet in 1993."[7]

The American context was important. American voters had elected Clinton to address a vast array of American domestic ills. (It was the economy, stupid, not Russia's internal transformation.) As promised during the campaign, the substantive focus and important policy innovations of the Clinton administration in the first years revolved around domestic reforms in the United States. Many of Clinton's closest political advisers, such as George Stephanopoulos, wanted to keep this domestic focus and avoid distracting international issues.[8]

In general, Clinton sought to keep foreign policy off his early agenda. Nonetheless, despite his reputation as a new president uninterested and inexperienced in foreign affairs, and despite the seemingly downward spiral in Russian market and democratic reforms, Clinton and his foreign policy team made Russia a top priority. At the time, aides estimated that he spent "about 50 percent of his foreign policy day cramming to understand the place."[9] And in sharp contrast to Bush and his advisers, it was Russia's internal transformation that became the central focus of Clinton and his team in the first years of their administration.

Perhaps the attraction was the nature of the subject: economic and political transformation on a scale and scope unprecedented in world history. Toby Gati recalls, "When I watched Clinton in the White House, I thought yes, it was a foreign policy issue but it was also an economic issue. He likes this kind of stuff. He was going to do for Russia what he had promised he was going to do for the U.S., even though he knew it would take a long time."[10] But even more than that, assisting economic and political change in Russia fit Clinton's Wilsonian liberal philosophy about international relations. The intellectual roots of this approach to foreign policy date back to the German philosopher Immanuel Kant.[11] Clinton and many of the senior members of his foreign policy team embraced Kant's idea about a democratic peace.[12] Democracies, Kant argued, do not fight one another, and thus the consolidation of democracy in Russia would help keep the peace between Russia and the United States. Rather than simply waiting for democracy in Russia to take hold, officials in the Clinton administration believed that the United States could assist the reform process. Clinton officials firmly believed that market reform would facilitate the emergence of democracy in Russia and help tie Russia to the West. Clinton firmly identified himself as a "liberal internationalist."[13]

Writing about George H. W. Bush in 1992, Clinton's old friend and former Oxford University housemate and soon-to-be top Russia expert Strobe Talbott argued, "While unquestionably an internationalist, [Bush] saw himself as a pragmatist; he never had his heart in the cause, or in the concept, of inter-vention on behalf of democratic and humanitarian principles." In contrast, Anthony Lake, Clinton's national security adviser, explains how democracy promotion as a general theme fit an ideological and political agenda for the new team. "During the course of the campaign, I helped develop the impor-tance of democracy as an issue both because I believed it and also because that emphasis on the idea of democracy helped us bring together wings of the Democratic Party that hadn't been the case since Vietnam. And that carried over in 1993 into a series of speeches we gave on democracy."[14]

For the Clinton administration, the United States had a national interest in promoting democracy and markets, especially in the ideological and institu-tional vacuum left by the collapse of communism. The ultimate aim was to enlarge the community of democracies in Europe. If Secretary of State James Baker made passing references to this theory of international relations in the wake of communism's demise. Clinton and his administration made the dem-ocratic peace thesis a mantra of U.S. foreign policy pronouncements in the 1990s.[15] In a spring 1996 address, Talbott paraphrased philosopher Isaiah Berlin to remind his listeners that the fox knows many things, but the hedge-hog knows just one big thing, and in American foreign policy that one big thing was democracy promotion. "There is still a place for the hedgehog in the terrain of U.S. foreign policy. We will advance all the objectives I just enumer-ated, and others as well, if we also strengthen associations among established democracies and support the transition to democracy in states that are emerg-ing from dictatorship or civil strife. Democracy, in short, is the one big thing that we must defend, sustain, and promote wherever possible, even as we deal with the many other tasks that face us."[16]

Wilsonian ideals infused President Clinton's thinking about Russia. In an address devoted to U.S.-Russia relations on the eve of his first trip abroad as president to meet Russian president Boris Yeltsin in Vancouver in April 1993, Clinton argued, "Think of it—land wars in Europe cost hundreds of thou-sands of American lives in the twentieth century. The rise of a democratic Russia, satisfied within its own boundaries, bordered by other peaceful democracies, could ensure that our nation never needs to pay that kind of price again. I know and you know that, ultimately, the history of Russia will be written by Russians and the future of Russia must be charted by Russians. But I would argue that we must do what we can and we must act now. Not out of charity but because it is a wise investment. . . . While our efforts will entail new costs, we can reap even larger dividends for our safety and our prosper-ity if we act now." He also argued that spending on aid for Russian reform in the short term would save Americans trillions of dollars that the United States would otherwise have to spend on defense should authoritarianism win out in Russia, and he added that a reformed Russia would provide new economic opportunities for American businesses, including 150 million new market consumers.[17]

Aid to Russia was never packaged as altruism but rather as a policy that served American security interests. Clinton officials shied away from the "idealist" or "liberal" labels but instead tried to recast "*idealpolitik* as *realpolitik*."[18] Strobe Talbott explained in defending the U.S. assistance program before the U.S. Senate, "Our foreign policy is rooted in American self interest. Just as the Nunn-Lugar program is defense by other means, so the Freedom Support Act is an investment in a safer future. It is an instrument for promoting those geopolitical and economic trends that will reinforce our nation's well-being." And he added later, "What we needed to do to increase the chances that the integrationist, Westernizing influences prevailed was to identify the various loci throughout the former Soviet Union and throughout the systems and polities and societies that came out of the Soviet Union and try to find ways to plug into them and to help them. We weren't in the business of saving Russia or losing Russia; we were in the business of trying to create an environment that was conducive for Russia finally making it."[19] A democratic and market-oriented Russia firmly embedded in Western international institutions would be a more cooperative partner of the United States, thereby enhancing U.S. national security. A Russia that did not succeed in transformation would become a threat to American national security interests yet again. As Thomas Dine explained to the Senate Foreign Relations Committee during his nomination hearings to become assistant administrator for Europe and the new independent states at the Agency for International Development, "The Cold War is over but the failure of reform in Eurasia would saddle America with unwelcome challenges and new, crippling costs. Action now is a preventive measure, indeed far less expensive than the consequences of inaction."[20]

Expanding the Mission of American Aid

As a realist, President George H.W. Bush believed that the United States could do little to promote transformation in Russia, even if the United States would ultimately benefit from such internal changes. In contrast, Clinton and his aides believed that they could make a difference. They were regime transformers who were not content to be observers of history—Russia's history. They wanted to be makers of history as well.

To promote transformation in Russia, the first policy change between Bush and Clinton was to provide more money. During the 1992 campaign, Clinton had chastised the Bush administration for doing too little to support Russian reform. The Bush administration had developed new aid programs for Russia and the newly independent states, supporting at least rhetorically the Nunn-Lugar program to dismantle nuclear weapons and more emphatically by gaining congressional approval for the Freedom Support Act. Clinton endorsed these programs but wanted to expand the U.S. effort immediately and dramatically.

Three days after Clinton took office, Yeltsin called the president with a request to meet as soon as possible. National Security Council staffer Nicholas Burns recalls, "President Clinton said that relations with Russia would be his top foreign policy priority in his first year in office." Against the advice of some on his domestic policy team, Clinton soon agreed to Yeltsin's request and proposed a meeting in Vancouver in April. Preparing for this meeting with Yeltsin became the central focus of Clinton's new foreign policy team.[21]

The new president wanted to announce something big in this first meeting with Yeltsin. Clinton personally rejected the first aid package cobbled together by his staff as "not bold enough." When aides reminded the president that Congress must ultimately approve his proposals, he countered, "You guys tell me what you think needs to be done on the merits. Don't worry about how Congress will react to the price tag. I'll deal with those guys."[22]

In his first budget submitted for congressional approval in April 1993, the Clinton administration increased bilateral assistance to Russia and the other newly independent states to $704 million, almost double the $417 million proposed by the Bush administration the year before.[23] At the Vancouver summit, Clinton then announced that U.S. bilateral assistance to Russia and the other newly independent states would increase to $ 2.5 billion for 1994 (some money was technically included as a "supplemental" to the fiscal year 1993 budget), a sixfold increase over similar funds earmarked in the last Bush budget. Of this total, $1.6 billion would go to Russia.

Even bigger numbers announced at Vancouver were multilateral commitments, not U.S. funds. First made public by the G-7 finance ministers in April and then formally agreed to at the G-7 summit in Japan in July 1993, Clinton and his partners raised the ante of aid to Russia to $43 billion. These figures nearly doubled those pledged by Bush and his partners the previous year, though like the 1992 pledge, the content and implementation of this aid package were left vague.[24]

The scale and the scope of pledges announced at the Vancouver summit marked a major turning point in U.S. aid to Russia. The United States had agreed not only to provide significant amounts of assistance; it also promised to assist reforms in virtually every sphere of public and private life in Russia. From environmental policy to the development of women's organizations, from the restructuring of the coal industry to the reorganization of political parties, from the dismantlement of nuclear weapons to the opening of business schools, the United States (and other Western countries) initiated a massive and comprehensive program aimed at transforming almost every aspect of Russian economic, political, and social life. As Talbott describes,

The whole venture was not "foreign aid" of the kind that we had devoted over the years to helping countries in Asia, Africa, and Latin America pull themselves out of poverty and attain "sustainable development." It was also different in concept (not to mention magnitude) from the Marshall Plan, which was intended to help Western Europe rebuild the economic base and political structures that had been devastated by World War II. The Vancouver package was not aimed at the recovery of what had been lost. Rather it was intended to help in the creation of what did not exist; it was an investment in a revolution, an attempt to help Russia complete the destruction of one system and the building, virtually de novo, of a new one.[25]

Clinton could pledge and Talbott could conceptualize, but Congress had to appropriate funds for these new programs. In his first year in office, therefore, Clinton devoted considerable time and energy to passing his new $2.5 billion bilateral assistance package for the newly independent states (NIS). It should have been a hard sell. Little in the American economy had changed between the last year of Bush and the first year of Clinton. The economy was still stalled and so too were Clinton's remedies for jump-starting it. At the time he introduced his new aid package on Capitol Hill, his first major legislative initiative, a $16 billion stimulus package, was being blocked by a Republican filibuster in the Senate. Public opinion polls at the time also showed little enthusiasm for more money to Russia. A March 1993 Gallup poll showed that only 18 percent of respondents favored more aid to Russia while 35 percent endorsed decreasing funds.[26]

Nonetheless, aid to Russia enjoyed strong bipartisan support built through a series of dinners at the White House, and with the help of Republican leaders on Capitol Hill, including Newt Gingrich (Ga.) and Robert Michel (Ill.), as well as leading Democrats such as David Obey (Wisc.). However, even these backers of aid to Russia warned that the $2.5 billion package was a one-time budgetary increase that could not be sustained on an annual basis. That is how the package was sold to Congress.[27] In fact, that is what it ended up being—a one-time spike in assistance. After 1994, funding for Russian reform steadily decreased for the rest of the decade (table 5-1).

Was $2.5 billion a big number? For advocates of aid, the answer was no. Writing in 1995, Harvard economist Jeffrey Sachs argued that "Yes, Clinton promoted more aid than Bush, but still in amounts too small to be consequential."[28] For those involved in securing congressional support, however, this figure seemed like a huge accomplishment and a dramatic improvement over what the Bush administration had accomplished.[29] Given the weak American economy, this procurement of new funds may have been the highest that could have been expected. After all, the American public seemed to be turning inward and could be forgiven for believing that with the cold war

Table 5-1. U.S. Bilateral Assistance to the New Independent States under the Freedom Support Act

Millions of dollars unless noted otherwise

Year	Total	Russia
1993	417	86.6
1994	2.5 billion	1.6 billion
1995	850	379
1996	641	100
1997	625	95
1998	770	152
1999	847	167.9
2000	839	168.1
2001	808	159
2002	958	157.08
2003*	755	148
2004*	576	73

Source: Office of the Coordinator of U.S. Assistance to the NIS, *Government Assistance to and Cooperative Activities with the New Independent States (FY 1994–1999)*, annual reports (Department of State)(www.fpa.org); for 2000 and 2001 reports (www.state.gov/p/eur/ace); for fiscal years 2002–2004 international affairs budget requests (www.state.gov/m/rm/rls/iab) [July 2003 for all sites].

Note: The sharp increase in total numbers for 2002 is due to increased funds for central Asia.

* These are the requested numbers for 2003 and 2004.

over, America no longer needed to worry about what happened in Russia. Clinton was willing to invest his political capital in convincing Congress and the American people of the need for greater sacrifice to support Russian domestic reform, but only once, in his first year as president.

Clinton's decision to forge a "strategic alliance with Russian reform" (as he put it in his April 1, 1993, address at the Naval Academy) signaled not only a change in the quantity of aid to Russia but also a qualitative change in the kind of engagement that the U.S. government would undertake in promoting domestic reform in Russia. Clinton did not announce a strategic alliance with *Russia* but with Russian *reform*. To signal the new kind of relationship that he planned to embark upon with Russia, Clinton had created a new position at the State Department: special adviser to the secretary of state and ambassador-at-large for the new independent states (S/NIS). To further emphasize the importance of this new position, Clinton asked Strobe Talbott to fill the slot. Talbott recalls a lot of discussion about whether the new position should "report to the Undersecretary for Political Affairs like the other Assistant Secretaries. I was quite adamant that it should report directly to the Secretary, and that's how it came about." But it was even more than that. National Security Adviser Tony Lake deferred to Talbott's knowledge of Russia and relationship with the president, and he knew that the Russia policy was Talbott's to run. Secretary of State Warren Christopher also understood the importance of Talbott's direct ties to the president in the making of Clinton's Russia policy.[30]

The coordinator of U.S. assistance to the NIS, a position and office that had been created by the Freedom Support Act, now reported directly to Talbott. (Eventually, Clinton elevated this coordinator position by giving the office-holder the added title of "special adviser to the president and to the secretary of state on assistance to the new independent states" and ambassadorial rank. But even so, the coordinator knew that as a practical matter his boss was Talbott.)[31]

Microeconomics and Bilateral Assistance

If the State Department coordinated bilateral aid to Russia, the U.S. Agency for International Development (AID) assumed primary responsibility as the main provider of funds to contractors who provided assistance. U.S. aid to the Soviet Union and then Russia went quickly from zero in 1990 to $400 million in 1991 to its peak in 1994 of $1.6 billion. The central focus of most AID-funded projects at the time was "technical assistance" (TA) and training. AID contracted with private American companies and nonprofit organizations to provide advice, knowledge, and expertise to their Russian partners as they attempted to implement reform.The agency almost never gave direct assistance to Russian people or organizations. For instance, AID contracted with the Harvard Institute for International Development (HIID) to provide technical assistance to the Russian Committee for State Property as it devised and implemented privatization. AID underwrote the work of numerous American consulting companies and accounting firms that were assisting Russian companies restructure. Eventually, AID was funding technical assistance programs in nearly every sector of reform. Besides technical assistance, AID also funded the development of Russian expertise, through training programs in the United States, the direct funding of Russian think tanks, or financial support for institutions such as the Eurasia Foundation, which provided direct grants to Russian organizations involved in fostering the reform process.[32] AID and other U.S. governmental agencies also became involved in programs to support trade and investment.

AID had growing pains in learning how to deal with and operate in Russia. During the Soviet era, AID did not have an office in Moscow. Just establishing a presence in the country proved to be a major and difficult endeavor. Clinton AID administrator Brian Atwood recalls, "We didn't actually have a mission there until 1995. We tried to run everything out of Washington and it was extraordinarily difficult. I think if you look at the evolution of the program, you'll see how much more complex and in-depth the program became in terms of strategy after AID put a mission on the ground and had people contacting Russians [to] know which ones they could work with and which ones they couldn't work with."[33]

Nor did AID have the proper staff to run a major operation in Russia. Not surprisingly since AID had never had a mission in the Soviet Union, the bureaucracy had very few Russian speakers in its ranks.[34] Nor did AID have many specialists on board who had addressed the problem of transforming a command system into a market economy. AID's personnel had acquired field experience in Africa, Latin America, and Asia, and were schooled and trained in developmental economics. Some of this knowledge and experience could transfer into the Russian context, but much of it did not. For instance, Russia's high level of urbanization, literacy, and industrialization contrasted sharply with the profile of a typical AID client state in which large segments of the population lived in a village, did not read and write, and worked in the fields. A special Newly Independent States (NIS) Task Force was created within AID to which the best and brightest from other divisions were recruited. Nonetheless, the process of training these recruits *on the job* as well as setting up a multibillion dollar assistance program—one of the largest in AID history—took time.

AID also faced a series of conflicting pressures in Washington. On the one hand, the agency was under siege for alleged incompetence. As the Clinton administration took over, AID already was under fire after a series of journalistic exposés charged the organization with corruption, inefficiency, and exporting American jobs. Many at the time predicted that AID would be dissolved, and its activities collapsed into the State Department, a development that eventually did occur as the result of congressional insistence. The political battle over merger undoubtedly distracted senior AID officials at a time when they should have been devoting their time and energy to assisting reform in the postcommunist world.

On the other hand, at the same time that AID was defending its programs and existence and therefore moving cautiously into new areas, political appointees in the Clinton administration teamed with congressional leaders to insist that AID deploy its newly secured resources for Russia as fast as possible. Russia was in crisis, and the United States needed to help immediately. As Atwood argues, "The people in Congress have a much different time frame in mind, especially members in the House who run every two years. . . . They expect that what we are doing should create that transformation overnight."[35]

These time pressures created some perverse effects. As the fastest way to get money into the field, AID relied on its traditional partners—so-called Washington beltway bandits—to provide assistance to Russia.[36] AID, in fact, was required to give its money to these American contractors rather than providing money directly to Russian organizations. These aid contractors had zero knowledge of Russia but intimate knowledge about the intricacies of applying for and winning AID contracts.[37] In their proposals, these organizations decorated their teams with fancy institutions having expertise in the former Soviet Union, but once actual spending began, these smaller institutions less accustomed to the ways of living off AID grants received little if any money. Instead, most of the funds earmarked for technical assistance were spent in Washington, not Moscow. And the contracts were big, because AID needed to spend money fast and did not have the administrative capacity to distribute smaller grants to more grantees.[38] Grantees were rewarded for spending money quickly, not wisely. Mary Louise Vitelli, the project director of an AID-funded project to assist coal miners, stated candidly, "This is the system. If you don't spend it this year, you lose it next year."[39] Mark Medish, an AID and Treasury official during this period, says, "There was too little money initially (1991–92). Then by 1994, the assistance budget was too big. It was more than AID could handle. More than the coordinator could get through the system. Also the need to hype and overadvertise for congressional and public relations purposes was a problem."[40]

The game, in many ways, began to resemble Soviet Five-Year Plan practices. There was a plan. To fulfill the plan, people had to spend a certain amount of money by a specified deadline. What they produced with this spending was less important than spending the money on time. For those contractors working to develop the Russian private sector, there were few market incentives attached to grant money. For instance, a grantee working on privatization or restructuring received no reward for helping to make a company successful. AID simply did not have the time to develop contracts that provided incentives to the grantees. Ironically, then, those Western organizations hired to promote the market in Russia did not operate according to market principles themselves.

The pressure to produce quick results had other negative consequences on AID procedures. Perhaps most important, AID (and its grantees) had to invent success in a highly superficial and politicized context. For AID officials working in Moscow, the flurry of congressional delegations ("Codels") provided intense pressure to highlight projects that had already produced results. With little analytic grounding or scientific method, AID contractors were compelled to invent "quantitative" measurements of success. AID even hired creative writers to canvass Russia and write up individual success stories.

The AID administrators and the staff of their grantees had to forgo training and preparation because of the pressures to get to the field and begin assisting Russia's transition. This lack of preparation was most apparent for language training as few AID officials could communicate in Russian. This problem also hampered the work of many American providers of direct assistance that were funded by AID grants and contracts.

In the early years, the mad rush to spend also undermined AID's ability to develop a comprehensive strategy for assisting reform. To discern post facto a comprehensive game plan and sequence of Western aid programs designed to foster economic reform would do injustice to history. Once Clinton made the political decision to aid economic reform in Russia, American government officials crafted an array of programs and projects that were pursued simultaneously on a range of policy issues and economic sectors. Midlevel bureaucrats within AID—not senior officials in the Clinton foreign policy team—made most of these decisions about how to spend money.

It was only after Richard Morningstar became the assistance coordinator in 1995 that priorities changed and a coordinated strategy from above was attempted. Carlos Pascual, who had served earlier at AID and then became a member of Clinton's NSC staff, argues, "For the White House, the key [had been] the speed in getting the money out. Morningstar understood that speed was not the issue, but the real question was 'Is it working?'" Even Atwood says that "[Morningstar's] challenging AID people . . . produced a greater awareness of whether we were getting the most for the taxpayer dollar. In that period, it was like working with a GAO [General Accounting Office] person at State."[41] In his most important strategic initiative, Morningstar announced in 1996 a new approach called Partnership for Freedom, under which funds for those assisting the Russian federal government decreased and those working with nongovernmental actors and regional government increased.[42]

Macroeconomics and Multilateral Assistance

Besides new bilateral aid, the Clinton team made it clear from the outset that it would pursue a more coordinated and activist policy with international financial institutions in supporting Russian reform. The Bush Treasury Department had been concerned first and foremost with making sure that Russia honored debts incurred by the USSR. Clinton's team at Treasury had a different priority—to promote market reform in Russia. As Clinton Treasury Department official David Lipton argues, "The wisdom is in realizing that part of the solution is that you don't make people pay if paying cripples the country from going down the road to reform success. The problem with the [Bush administration's] approach was that there was no roadmap for economic revival to go along with the debt deal, and that the joint and several debt agreement locked countries into repayment obligations they could not sustain."[43]

In contrast to their predecessors, Undersecretary of the Treasury Lawrence Summers, a professor of economics at Harvard and former chief economist for the World Bank, and Lipton, his deputy and a former IMF official who had worked with Sachs in providing advice to Poland, Russia, and other postcommunist governments about market reform, came to Washington with a coherent set of ideas about how to pursue reform.[44] The duo also had a mandate and authority within the administration. As Talbott recalls, Secretary of the Treasury Lloyd Bentsen "had delegated aid to Russia almost entirely to

Summers." Talbott in turn deferred to this team at Treasury as the chief policymakers for the administration's economic assistance program to Russia.[45]

By the time Summers and Lipton came to the Treasury Department, Russia's first attempt at macroeconomic stabilization was already unraveling. In the early part of 1992, as discussed earlier, Gaidar had implemented price liberalization in most sectors of the economy (except crucially oil and gas).[46] Gaidar's unsuccessful attempt to achieve macroeconomic stabilization, however, had helped to produce his ouster just one month before the Clinton team took the reins. Still, the new team at the Treasury Department believed that a massive influx of Western capital might be able to nudge stabilization back on track. Russia's monetary policy at the time was the main culprit in derailing stabilization, but control of the Russian money supply was an issue over which outsiders had weak and indirect influence.[47] The budget was a more direct target for external intervention.

Initially, few officials on the new Clinton team supported this approach. Their predecessors in the Bush administration had resisted supplying large levels of direct assistance to the Russian government, partly because the necessary outlays were expensive and partly because they were suspicious of the Russian government's intentions and ability to deliver. Initial drafts of the aid program developed by the new Clinton team for the Vancouver summit focused almost exclusively on aid to small-scale bilateral assistance programs and not macroeconomic assistance to the Russian government.[48] David Lipton recalls, "Many in the U.S. government focused on programs that were for civic society, not government to government. This approach had a lot of support in Congress. Our view was that the U.S. approach also needed support for economic reform, what you might call the –tions [liberalization, stabilization, privatization]. These were all things that were necessary conditions for creating capitalization and its institutions and could only be carried out by the government. And certainly if those reforms were managed badly [they] would doom the many creative efforts we were supporting in civic society."[49]

This kind of direct support for the Russian government, however, was expensive. Even if the administration's entire bilateral package were devoted solely to budgetary support for the Russian government, Clinton's $1.6 billion bilateral assistance plan would not be enough to do much good. No one directly questioned the wisdom of Lipton and Summers, but the political wing of the White House staff argued that Clinton could not make a multibillion-dollar request to Congress for aid to Russia at the same time he was trying to pass his new economic stimulus package.

The solution, therefore, was to secure financial support for stabilization from multilateral institutions. Lipton says, "We found out quickly we couldn't get financing from the U.S. Congress that was government to government so we turned to the international financial institutions for multilateral support.

This became the $43 billion package announced at the G-7 summit in Tokyo."[50] In essence, the Clinton administration transferred the responsibility for assisting Russia's economic transformation from the United States to the International Monetary Fund (IMF).

The IMF had established a working relationship with the Russian government well before Summers and Lipton took over at the Treasury Department. The IMF and the new Russian government, however, did not get off to a good start.[51] During the last year of the Bush administration, IMF economists had helped Gaidar and his team to develop some fundamental concepts about reform through a shadow program, codified as government policy on February 27, 1992. [52] As discussed in chapter 4, the IMF also provided a $1 billion loan in 1992. The loan was secured in August 1992, however, well after Gaidar and his reformist colleagues were no longer secure in their jobs. A $6 billion currency stabilization fund—modeled after the highly successful fund for Poland—was pledged in April 1992 but never established. In 1993, talk of a ruble fund fueled expectations about the imminent arrival of the $6 billion. Speaking soon after the April 1993 Vancouver summit meeting, Finance Minister Boris Fyodorov anticipated the fund's creation in the summer of 1993, but he also warned of the dangerous consequences of unmet promises; "If this (1993) is another year in which there is a lot of noise or just confirmation of aid promised earlier it would be catastrophic."[53] However, the IMF did not establish the stabilization fund in 1993 or any other year.

In its early engagement with Russian government officials, the IMF urged the Russian government to do more, while providing little by way of financial assistance. In these early days, assistance was cast as a reward for progress on the economic reform agenda, not a facilitator of progress on the reform agenda. This coercive approach to financial assistance led many Russian government officials, including some of the most ardent reformers, to question the true intentions and competence of these multilateral lending institutions. The IMF's institutional fit for the task of transforming the Russian economy was less than perfect since it was not designed to make policy based on political calculations.[54] In 1993, the IMF had little experience working in postcommunist countries, where the task of stabilization was much more complicated than in capitalist economies. IMF officials had to improvise to address the new issues associated with assisting the transition to capitalism from communism. Moreover, as bankers, IMF officials make loans, not grants, which they expect to be repaid. This form of assistance is very different from the grant-driven orientation of the Marshall Plan.[55] When faced with high levels of uncertainty, bankers err on the side of caution.

Upon coming to power, the Clinton administration tried to infuse a new sense of urgency for IMF engagement in Russia. Treasury Department officials worked quietly with their IMF counterparts to ease IMF conditions for lending to Russia. In the run-up to the Vancouver summit, Clinton even publicly called for relaxation of IMF conditions to allow for loans to Russia of $13.5 billion a year.[56] On April 10, 1993, the IMF acquiesced and announced that it would adopt a new approach to Russia and offer up to $4.5 billion under more lenient conditions regarding inflation targets and budget deficits.[57] The director of the IMF, Michel Camdessus, stated that the IMF planned to loan Russia $30 billion in the next four to five years. That same spring, the IMF introduced a new lending instrument, the Systemic Transformation Fund (STF), as a way to provide funds to Russia even when Russia did not meet IMF targets on monthly inflation rates or deficit limits.

The intellectual force behind the STF was not an IMF official, but Summers. As Lipton describes, "Larry [Summers] came up with the key insight. Larry said to me one day, you know if people can't jump over a high hurdle, you just have to build a step ladder with a number of steps. So Larry invented a new IMF facility that had lesser conditionality and lesser money, a fixed period of time, and was only for transition economies. By being available for all transition economies, it was designed to be compatible with the IMF's rule that you have to treat all members the same. It was open to the East Europeans, some of whom participated." He adds, "The idea was in essence get Russia to take a significant step in the right direction, but to recognize that the first step would not be 'total reform.' We knew they couldn't achieve zero inflation or a zero budget deficit in the course of the STF. The idea was that Russia would take a step in that direction and finish it off later with a more rigorous IMF program when they were able to do so. We had to reckon with the fact that during this period the central bank was still in the hands of people who were not on board with the reform program. You can't overstate the importance of that problem."[58]

Formally, of course, the IMF was an independent institution that answered to all of its board members. In reality, however, the United States had a special say in IMF operations, and the United States during the Clinton administration had specific messages it wanted to convey to the Fund when speaking about Russia. Lower-level economists in the Fund complained about the "politicization" of their mission, but their protests fell on deaf ears at the highest levels of the Fund.[59] Camdessus, and his deputy, Stanley Fischer, became intimately involved in the Russian portfolio. Camdessus in particular relished his geopolitical mission.

The IMF played the leading role in Russia on stabilization issues, but other international financial institutions also established active programs in Russia in the early 1990s.[60] The European Bank for Reconstruction and Development launched a major lending program to Russia aimed at stimulating enterprise restructuring. The World Bank provided some supplemental loans to the IMF disbursements to assist in macroeconomic stabilization. The main focus of the

Bank in Russia, however, was a series of large sectoral restructuring programs, first in agriculture, then later in transportation, coal, oil, and social protection. The International Finance Corporation (IFC), the arm of the World Bank responsible for financing private sector development, also established major programs on privatization and the development of capital markets. In the first two years of engagement with Russia, the World Bank approved ten loans worth roughly $3 billion, making Russia one of the Bank's biggest clients almost overnight.

These early years, however, were not good ones for the Bank in Russia. Agriculture, one of the Bank's first targets, was one of the sectors slowest to change in Russia. The billions spent in trying to restructure the coal industry were tainted by corruption and poor economic performance. While Russia soon grew in the mid-1990s to become the Bank's third largest recipient, the record of achievement was mixed. As a World Bank press release candidly admitted, "By 1995, the Russian portfolio of projects was one of the most troubled in the Bank."[61]

Assisting Russian Reformers (and Those Who Talked Like Them)

When making decisions about microeconomic and macroeconomic assistance to Russia, Clinton officials always tried to identify and work with individuals in the Russian government most closely associated with reform. Given the extreme volatility of Russian institutions during this period, the crafters of American aid to Russia made the decision early on to back *individuals* who advocated reforms, believing that there could be no reforms without reformers. At the highest levels, this strategy meant supporting Boris Yeltsin. Throughout the volatile political period in 1992 and 1993, when the political rules of the game in Russia were uncertain and Yeltsin's hold on power precarious, the U.S. government attempted to use pledges of aid as a way to help Yeltsin and his team remain in power.[62]

Bush gave his big assistance speech, and the IMF had announced its first major program to Russia in April 1992 during the volatile days of the Sixth Congress of People's Deputies when Yegor Gaidar, the deputy prime minister in charge of economic reform, was fighting for his political life. Clinton signed into law his $2.5 billion assistance package to Russia and the newly independent states during the September 1993 standoff between Yeltsin and the Russian parliament, signaling unequivocally that this aid was earmarked to assist Yeltsin and his side of the barricade. Yeltsin played this game as well, urging Western governments during the spring of 1993 to provide aid before it was "too late."[63] In response, Ruslan Khasbulatov, the speaker of the Congress of People's Deputies at the time and one of Yeltsin's chief foes, warned Western governments and the United States in particular to stop taking sides in Russian internal affairs.[64] Critics of the Clinton administration in the West argued that the United States had identified too closely with one personality and not a policy. Throughout several difficult periods, however, American foreign policymakers kept to this strategy.

Besides supporting Yeltsin, American government officials also targeted special assistance to those identified as reformers in the Russian government. In his capacity first as head of the State Committee on Property (GKI) and later as first deputy prime minister, Anatoly Chubais became a favorite partner for American assistance programs. Chubais had established a very effective technical assistance program, initially funded by the Ford Foundation, with his American counterparts, Andrei Shleifer and Jonathan Hay, well before the Clinton team came to office or AID set up shop in Russia. Shleifer, a Harvard microeconomist and Russian émigré, provided ideas for Chubais' first privatization program, while Hay, a young lawyer working directly in the GKI offices, acted as the main conduit of these ideas into the Russian bureaucracy.

Contrary to popular myth, Russia never adopted the "American" model for privatization. Shleifer, Chubais, and their colleagues had wanted to implement a program under which outsiders would own a majority share of privatized enterprises, because only outsiders could then discipline enterprise managers in order to fulfill their "fiduciary responsibility to maximize the wealth of shareholders."[65] This scheme later became codified as option one of the 1992 privatization program. The Congress of People's Deputies pushed an alternative formula whereby insiders (and enterprise directors especially) would acquire majority ownership. This became known as option two in the 1992 privatization program. Three-quarters of the nearly 100,000 companies undergoing privatization between 1992 and 1994 selected option two, and not the more American model of ownership embodied in option one.[66] On arguably the most important reform design in this early period, American advice was not heeded. Nonetheless, on other aspects of the program, such as the need to give away, rather than sell, properties, and the need to privatize assets as quickly as possible, Americans did have influence.[67] A shared ideological vision, generous financial backing from the Ford Foundation, and close personal relationships between Chubais, and his deputies, Dmitri Vasiliev and Maksim Boyko on the one hand and Shleifer and Hay on the other, made this effort at the GKI the most successful technical assistance program in Russia at the time.[68]

When AID eventually began to fund programs in Russia (and replaced the Ford Foundation as the leading funder of technical assistance for the GKI), it sought to replicate the GKI successes and adhered to the idea that supporting individual reformers was the best strategy for supporting reform. If Chubais backed a proposal, then it received generous funding with little to no oversight. Years later, several observers lambasted AID's support for Chubais.[69] In retrospect, however, Clinton officials still defended the strategy of seeking out reformers and supporting them. Brian Atwood argues, "Economic policy on a national level was really being run by one man and his colleagues. If you didn't have a relationship with him, then you wouldn't have been able to influence his thinking as much as happened."[70] State Department Coordinator Richard Morningstar adds, "Did we all think Chubais was someone we could work with? Obviously. He was our apparent best hope to get the kinds of changes we were looking for. It wasn't a question of supporting him as an individual. It was supporting what he and others were trying to do. With all my criticisms of some programs, I wouldn't second-guess that for a minute. You're dealt a hand; he looked like the high card, and we did our best with it."[71]

At the peak of AID's operations in Russia in the mid-1990s, American consultants worked in virtually every Russian government office that had something to do with economic reform. A close personal relationship with a "reformer" in the bureaucracy was considered the key to success. The Ministry of Finance under radical reformer Boris Fyodorov, for instance, was considered a successful aid target, while technical assistance missions to the Ministry of Agriculture—a bureaucracy where a reformer could not be identified— were considered less fruitful and therefore less of a priority.[72]

On this strategic decision to help reformers, there was little controversy among senior officials in the Clinton team. For example at the State Department, those more skeptical and cautious about Russia, such as Secretary of State Warren Christopher's Chief of Staff Thomas Donilon and Policy Planning Staff Director James Steinberg, were much more active in trying to alter policy on security issues such as Bosnia and NATO enlargement than on the economic issues. Steinberg says, "There was nobody in the school of 'it's hopeless, never had a democracy,' that whole line of thinking. People all thought it was possible. There were maybe some differences on how long it would take. But there were no serious differences on the need to try to make it go faster if we could. And [there was] also a strong consensus that you needed to make sure that the break [with the past] was as irreversible as possible."[73] At lower levels in the bureaucracies and within the American embassy in Moscow, some did question the wisdom of focusing solely on the "reformers" especially when the reform content of their actions became questionable.[74] At the highest levels, however, there was no serious debate about the strategy, since supporting "nonreformers" or working with those not committed to democracy, markets, and a pro-Western orientation did not seem like a policy in the U.S. national interest.

This strategy of bolstering reformers, however, became difficult to sustain over time, since the reformers had a difficult time staying in positions of power. Gaidar was out of power before Clinton became president. Chubais at the GKI, Fyodorov at the Finance Ministry, and a handful of others in lesser positions remained in the government throughout 1993 and were boosted briefly in the fall of 1993 when Gaidar rejoined the government as minister of the economy. However, soon after the 1993 parliamentary elections, Gaidar and Fyodorov were forced to resign from public office again, leaving Chubais as the only reformer of stature left in the government. In solidarity with Gaidar and Fyodorov, economists Jeffrey Sachs and Anders Åslund also resigned from their positions as Western advisers to the Russian government.[75]

Clinton administration officials, therefore, faced a dilemma. Should they try to engage Prime Minister Viktor Chernomyrdin and others with dubious commitments to economic reform, or should they wait until the reformers came back to power? Policymakers serving in limited-term governments gen-erally are not very good at following a policy of patience, and the Clinton team was no different. Vice President Al Gore gradually established a close personal relationship with Chernomyrdin, making the vice president and his staff a pro-Chernomyrdin lobby within the administration.

Treasury Department officials, after some initial hesitation, agreed that they could not limit their contacts only to the small group of young reform-ers that rotated in and out of government. Nor, in sharp contrast to the pre-decessors in the Bush administration, were they prepared to sit on the sidelines and watch reform—especially macroeconomic reform—fail. Instead, they adopted an activist and engaged strategy. Former professor Summers delivered several lectures on macroeconomics to the Russian prime minister, sessions Talbott describes as "Gore deliberately exposing Chernomyrdin to the full Summers."[76] Chernomyrdin eventually earned, but only after years of pur-suing partial reforms, a degree in economics that Russian liberal reformers called the most expensive education in history.

Trade and Investment

Besides technical assistance for the reformers implementing economic reform and multilateral aid to help the Russian government curb inflation and obtain stabilization, the promotion of trade and investment emerged as another major component of aid to Russia as early as 1993 and then more earnestly the following year. In this "second" phase of aid, traditional organizations designed to promote American investment in risky markets such as the Overseas Private Investment Corporation (OPIC), the U.S. Export-Import (Ex-Im) Bank, and the U.S. Trade and Development Agency (TDA) played an increasingly larger role in the aid program.[77] New programs designed for Russia and the post-communist world were created and expanded during this period, including the U.S. Department of Commerce's Business Information Service for the NIS (BISNIS) and AID programs aimed at fostering business development.

American trade and investment, Clinton officials argued, would help con-solidate market reforms in Russia.[78] This idea of aiding American companies fit well with Clinton's focus on stimulating the American economy.

Proponents of these programs claimed that OPIC, TDA, and the Ex-Im Bank served a key American national interest by helping to "level the playing field" for U.S. exporters whose foreign competitors receive subsidies from their governments. Congressional representatives were especially keen to increase these kinds of programs. As Senator Mitch McConnell (R-Ky.), the chairman of the Senate Appropriations Subcommittee on Foreign Operations, argued, "We can strengthen popular support for foreign aid by making it more clearly serve American business interests."[79] By the mid-1990s, the high-risk markets of the former Soviet Union accounted for nearly 20 percent of OPIC's portfolio.[80] The Ex-Im Bank and TDA also had active portfolios in Russia.

A key institutional innovation for promoting trade and investment was the U.S.-Russian Bi-national Commission on Economic and Technological Cooperation. Cochaired by Vice President Al Gore and Prime Minister Viktor Chernomyrdin, this government-to-government commission (known as the Gore-Chernomyrdin Commission) met once every six months. Privately, Foreign Minister Andrei Kozyrev first suggested the idea to Strobe Talbott in the run-up to the April 1993 Vancouver summit as a way of helping to build the Russian government interagency process, and Clinton proposed it to Yeltsin at that first meeting. Yeltsin accepted the proposal once he understood that Gore's counterpart would be Chernomyrdin, and not his vice president and enemy Aleksandr Rutskoi.[81]

This commission made the development of trade and investment a top priority, focusing at first on space and energy cooperation and later becoming a major forum for managing all sorts of contentious issues, from Russian exports of nuclear technologies to Iran to American chicken imports into Russia. Gore-Chernomyrdin was erected "to ensure that there was momentum in the relationship because there would be regular meetings."[82] Lipton says of the commission's work, "It's novel in the history of the U.S. government to have such an intense interaction between two governments. Given Russia's problems, it seemed extremely clever. I didn't know at the time that it was Kozyrev's idea. The Commission provided a way of helping them see how government runs by watching ours. It was also a way of getting to know much of the Russian elite. They'd cycle through for preparatory meetings. You'd meet the new minister of whatever. And it gave us a way of solving particular problems that came up through these governmental contacts, and a way of encouraging particular trends."[83]

As the emphasis on investment grew, U.S. government money also established several investment funds in Russia and elsewhere in the former Soviet Union. At the end of the 1997 fiscal year, U.S. AID had earmarked $440 million to the U.S.-Russian Investment Fund (TUSRIF), and $50 million to support two funds cosponsored by the European Bank for Reconstruction and Development.[84]

Neglected Economic Issues

Some economic policies and sectors received less attention from American aid providers. In the early moments of their brief tenure in power, Gaidar and his government had planned to maintain a minimum level of social support for those hit hardest by the shock of price liberalization. Several Western advisers, including Jeffrey Sachs, also underscored the necessity of Western assistance in this crucial area of institutional reform.[85] In preparation for the U.S.-Russia Vancouver summit, Finance Minister Boris Fyodorov proposed a $3–4 billion dollar fund to finance social welfare.[86] The Russian government, however, did not have the funds to provide a more robust social safety net, and Western actors did not step in to fill the gap. In fact, Western countries and international financial institutions provided only modest assistance for the creation of a new social welfare system in Russia. Clinton believed that he could not ask the American people to pay for a social safety net in Russia, when many Americans needed more support. Only in April 1997 did the World Bank sign a major loan agreement with the Russian government earmarked primarily for restructuring of the social spending sector. Western governments also spent few resources explaining the economic reform process. Education was another sector that received little attention in the early years of assistance.[87]

Sustaining Cooperative Threat Reduction and Other "Security" Assistance

Clinton and his team used major speeches on Russia to explain the importance of Russia's domestic transformation for American national security interests. And in hindsight, analysts have devoted most of their (usually critical) attention to Clinton administration efforts to support economic reform in Russia.[88] In official statements on American aid to Russia, however, U.S. government officials always emphasized three components to their assistance strategy—democracy promotion, market assistance, and cooperative threat reduction. In his report on U.S. assistance to the newly independent states in 1996, the coordinator of these programs, Richard Morningstar, listed three core objectives (not one or ten) of the policy: "Objective 1: Promote democratic institution-building, the rule-of-law, and the development of civil society; Objective 2: Help establish open and competitive market economies and expand the opportunities for trade and investment; Objective 3: Enhance U.S., NIS [newly independent states] and international security through cooperative threat reduction and non-proliferation efforts."[89]

The Cooperative Threat Reduction (CTR) program, established by the Nunn-Lugar Amendment to the Defense Appropriation Bill of 1992, did not seek to promote domestic change within Russia. Although a small portion of the funds was devoted to promoting defense conversion in Russia, most of this assistance was dedicated to the withdrawal of nuclear weapons from Ukraine, Kazakhstan, and Belarus, and then the destruction of those nuclear weapons in Russia. Senators Nunn and Lugar as well as Deputy Secretary (and later Secretary) of Defense William Perry championed the project as preventive defense that could and should be pursued no matter the regime type and economic system in Russia, although the Pentagon team believed that any cooperative work that could be done in a framework of reforming the Russian military would benefit the overall societal trends toward democratization.[90]

The ordering in Morningstar's report did not reflect the priority of budgetary spending in these three areas. On the contrary, many in the Clinton administration and especially those on the Perry team at the Defense Department considered Cooperative Threat Reduction the most important aid program toward Russia. Perry called these programs "defense by other means" and promoted their continued support during the first Clinton term. Perry emphasized in particular the imperative of denuclearization in Ukraine.[91] His views prevailed. In the early 1990s, spending on the CTR program for Russia was roughly half of the sum devoted to economic assistance, but six times the level devoted to democratic assistance. Gradually, economic assistance to Russia declined in the 1990s, but the CTR budget remained robust, though increasingly controversial, throughout the Clinton administration, always hovering in the neighborhood of $400 million per year.[92] By the end of the Clinton administration, the Defense Department had allocated $ 2.6 billion to the CTR program and spent nearly $2 billion of these funds on executing these programs.[93] In fiscal year 2001, the Department of Defense still had a $385.7 million budget for assistance to Russia. Comparatively, USAID's fiscal year 2001 budget was $9 million for economic restructuring, $10.4 million for private sector development, and $16 million for democratic reform.[94]

Initially, CTR programs in Russia focused primarily on the dismantling of nuclear weapons. In fiscal year 1997, Senators Sam Nunn, Richard Lugar, and Pete Domenici (R-N.M.) successfully introduced an amendment to the legislation to provide an additional $94 million to Department of Defense and Department of Energy budgets to expand U.S. efforts to help Russia and other post-Soviet states safely store their nuclear, chemical, and biological weapons. Under the rubric of CTR, the Bush administration had established International Science and Technology Centers (ISTC) in Moscow and Kiev. These centers aimed to keep nuclear scientists employed, so that they would not be tempted to emigrate to work for rogue states. Eventually, the State Department assumed financial responsibility from the Defense Department for these centers. At the height of the program, the U.S. State Department estimated the ISTC and its sister organization in Kiev had provided employment opportunities to 11,500 former Soviet nuclear scientists.[95]

In parallel to these efforts, the Clinton administration's Department of Energy (DOE) also operated a number of programs that promoted security reforms in Russia. In 1994, American nuclear laboratories initiated contacts with their counterparts in the formerly closed Russian cities of Arzamas-16 and Chelyabinsk-70. Eventually these lab-to-lab exchanges, in parallel to government-to-government partnerships between the Department of Energy and the Ministry of Atomic Energy, evolved into the Material Protection, Control, and Accounting (MPC&A) program. The MPC&A aimed to secure and take account of Russian nuclear stockpiles. The MPC&A started slowly, since no one wanted to divert attention from denuclearization efforts, especially in Ukraine, Belarus, and Kazakhstan.[96] After beginning with a modest $3 million program in 1993, however, the program grew dramatically under the Clinton administration, to $145 million by 2001.[97]

Under the Clinton administration, Energy Department officials also started the Initiative for Proliferation Prevention. Similar to ITSC, this program was designed to provide funds to nuclear scientists who sought to explore nonmilitary applications of their technologies and know-how. In 1994, Congress provided $35 million for this program, and incrementally smaller budgets following this peak. In 1998, the Department of Energy began a similar project called the Nuclear Cities Initiative, funded at $23 million in 2000.[98] By fiscal year 2001, the Department of Energy had a total budget of $335.5 million for assistance to Russia, making this bureaucracy the largest provider of aid to Russia, second only to the Department of Defense. By contrast, the total U.S. AID budget for Russia in fiscal year 2001 was $91.4 million, while the entire 2001 budget under the Freedom Support Act was $159.4, less than half of the Department of Energy's budget.[99]

In the early years of the program, no one in the Clinton administration doubted the need to continue Cooperative Threat Reduction. Debates, however, did arise about the priority of these programs in the overall Pentagon budget. William Perry and his staff pushed hard for maximum funding and sacrificed other Defense Department projects to this endeavor. Perry recalls, "I had to go out and put together an executing program and go out and find the source of funding for it and then go over to Congress and say, 'These six programs that you wanted to get done, we aren't going to do. Instead we are going to put the money into Nunn-Lugar.' Now, we got that done, but . . . Sam Nunn fronted for me on that to a great extent and helped me pull through the opposition."[100]

Perry's staff also believed that the program should be pursued regardless of political and economic developments in Russia because the reduction of nuclear weapons enhanced American national security no matter who controlled the Kremlin. Assistant Secretary of Defense Ashton Carter was known to be particularly protective of these programs and dismissive of those who wanted to divert funds into economic and political reform. As he explained,

"My focus at least was on security not on reform, and I felt that assisting reform in a comprehensive way was beyond the scope of the instruments of U.S. foreign policy. Maybe it was a good idea but it was not something that the government was going to be capable of pulling off. And so I know there were others who thought that [assisting reform] was the key or that that was possible, but I did not."[101] In a speech on Russia, in March 1994, Perry also noted, "As the secretary of defense, I have a more narrow portfolio of interests. My principal priority is the protection and advancement of United States national security interests."[102]

Conversely, those concerned primarily with Russia's economic transformation were promoting greater assistance for economic stabilization and privatization programs. If Russia became a robust market economy, these economists argued, then the Russian government would be able to pay for its own denuclearization program. Moreover, if Russia succeeded in consolidating a robust market economy and democratic polity and integrated fully into the Western community of democracies, then the United States would not have to worry about how many nuclear weapons Russia possessed. Those most concerned with Russia's internal transformation, therefore, believed the balance of assistance was too skewed to security programs. As Talbott's successor as ambassador-at-large for the newly independent states and later ambassador to Russia, James F. Collins argues, "Throughout the 1990s, [we] never got off the old cold war pie chart. If you looked at where the big money, the big programs, the big effort [went], it's all in security and the rest of it always was playing catch-up. Talk about missed opportunities; I always felt that one of the big missed opportunities of the 1990s . . . was that we never got that pie chart to be more balanced. Almost all, I'd say close to 80 percent of that was security, you know Nunn-Lugar and DOE programs, some aspect of that."[103]

Monies for Russian aid, however, were not fungible even in the Clinton administration. Because Nunn-Lugar funds came out of the Defense Department budget, officials at the Department of Treasury or AID officials could not divert this money easily for other purposes. Instead, the Defense Department assistance programs operated and were financed independently of other assistance programs. Even the State Department's coordinator of the U.S. assistance to the newly independent states, whose job was oversight and coordination of all aid to Russia, had little oversight control, let alone programmatic impact on, these programs.[104]

Democracy Assistance: The Third and Weakest Leg

The Cooperative Threat Reduction program was established during the Bush administration and enhanced during the Clinton administration. The focus on food aid established by the Bush administration continued under Clinton.

In 1992, the humanitarian disaster predicted for the former Soviet Union on the covers of American newsmagazines never occurred. Yet, once in place, the powerful agricultural lobby in the U.S. Congress made sure that these programs were not cut, despite reports of corruption, waste, and the lack of need. Even at the 1993 Vancouver summit, almost half of the total assistance package proposed by the Clinton administration was earmarked for food transfers. Of the $1.6 billion bilateral assistance promised to Russia, grant food assistance accounted for $194 million and concessional food sales (that is, credit assistance to purchase American food products) was $700 million of the total aid package. By contrast, the Clinton administration pledged an additional $148.4 million for private sector development and only $48 million for democratic assistance at the Vancouver meeting. Nearly a decade later, the assistance budget still included $60.5 million in food assistance delivered by the Department of Agriculture, a budget four times the size of AID's democracy assistance budget for that same year.[105]

The Primacy of Economics

If somewhat locked into CTR and food aid, the new Clinton team did have the opportunity to make strategic decisions about the relative importance of economic versus political assistance. Under the Bush administration, the funds allocated for aid to Russia were small, while the strategy for distributing these funds was ill defined. As Brian Atwood, Clinton's AID administrator recalls, "If you go back to the early days, when we came into office, I thought the former Soviet program was an absolute scattershot; it was [Bush State Department official] Dick Armitage basically like a kid in a candy shop throwing money in a number of different directions hoping that something will stick. There was no strategy behind it and there were a lot of people at AID who didn't want anything to do with the program."[106] As budgets for assistance grew, the new team had to decide about priorities.

Beginning with a first meeting on February 6, 1993, a senior group in the new administration met for three months to devise an overall strategy toward Russia and the other newly independent states (NIS). Participants included Clinton; National Security Adviser Anthony Lake and his deputy, Samuel Berger; Vice President Gore and his national security adviser, Leon Fuerth; senior NSC staffers for this region, Toby Gati and Nicholas Burns; Ambassador-at-Large for the NIS Strobe Talbott; and presidential adviser George Stephanopoulos.[107]

At this early stage, officials at the Treasury Department and on the NSC staff had different priorities, and despite Talbott's overall status, the State Department was relatively less important in this area, primarily because Talbott by all accounts (including his own) had little expertise in economic matters. During his tenure, he focused primarily on traditionally defined strategic issues in the U.S.-Russian relationship, which had been the subject of many of the books he had written earlier in his career. Many former Clinton officials reported that Talbott was not engaged in the technical issues of privatization, stabilization, or social policy reform. As Brian Atwood reflected, "He was bored by that kind of thing. He's a brilliant analyst, reporter and writer. I've seen some private things after returning from trips and he was so clear. But on the economic side, very weak. [Secretary of State Warren] Christopher, [UN Ambassador and later Secretary of State] Madeleine [Albright], Strobe really didn't pay attention to the economic side."[108]

Is the design of aid programs a technical issue best handled by specialists, not senior policymakers? Recall that the last great assistance program to Europe was not named after an undersecretary or an assistant secretary but still is remembered as the Marshall Plan, after the secretary of state who announced the program and oversaw its implementation. In retrospect, former acting prime minister Yegor Gaidar believed that the absence of a major political figure behind the aid effort had negative consequences: "I don't think that the leaders of the major Western powers were unaware of the magnitude of the choices they faced. The trouble, in my view, was that there was no leader capable of filling the sort of organizing and coordinating role that Harry Truman and George C. Marshall played in the postwar restoration of Europe."[109]

Instead of a Christopher plan or a Clinton plan, Russia got a Summers-Lipton plan. In the early years, Summers and Lipton provided the guiding intellectual principles for assistance to Russia in the Clinton administration. They prevailed in large part because they had a plan for reform, a theory behind it, and a clear idea of the tools needed to implement their blueprint, in contrast to others with different concerns (such as democratization), but with no coherent game plans or tools to pursue them. These two new Treasury officials believed in the imperative of economic reform that would create a better setting for political reform. As Lipton recalls, "Our view was that America should make clear its support for reform in Russia. We thought that U.S. support for reform in Russia with Yeltsin, with the elites, with the public would be helpful to people who wanted to carry out reform."[110] If Russia could not stabilize its economy, then democracy would have no chance. Summers and Lipton outlined a comprehensive approach for achieving stabilization that would then establish the permissive context for other kinds of microeconomic reforms and political change.

Although many in the administration may not have understood the technical details of stabilization or privatization assistance, the more general idea of economic reforms first, other reforms later, did have wide appeal. Academic theories about modernization informed this strategy. Forty years ago, distinguished scholar Seymour Martin Lipset wrote that "the more well-to-do a nation, the greater the chances that it will sustain democracy."[111] Many in the administration took this hypothesis to be a statement of fact, citing the pattern of economic development and then pressure for democracy in such successful countries as South Korea and Taiwan as recent evidence for why Russia should follow the same sequence.[112] Even China's delays in adopting democratic reforms to pursue economic reform seemed a more desirable transition model to many than the mess of simultaneity initiated by President Mikhail Gorbachev.

Russia's underdeveloped civil society offered another reason for sequencing. From this perspective, Russia had to develop a middle class before it would be ready for democracy.[113] At the time of transition, some argued, Russia had no well-defined social groups favoring capitalism. Voters needed to develop interests—interests redefined in the context of a new capitalist system—before they made meaningful votes. The analysis ironically echoed Marxist theory—Russians needed class consciousness before they could act politically.[114]

A third argument for sequencing and the primacy of economic assistance had to do with the dangers of simultaneity. In the short run, most economists argued that the majority of society would have to endure economic dislocation associated with the costs of economic transition. If, however, this majority controlled the government as majorities are supposed to do in democracies, then they would be tempted to vote the reformers out of office before reforms had produced new growth.[115] In the transition period, therefore, proponents of this logic suggested that reformers had to be insulated from populist pressures. Some even advocated an interim dictatorship until the process of economic transformation was complete.

Fourth, U.S. advocates of delaying democratic reform in the name of economic reform had another convincing argument, and their counterparts in Russia shared this view. Russian reformers also believed that economic and political reform had to be sequenced, with economic reform coming first.[116] After the failed *putsch* in August 1991 and the subsequent dissolution of the USSR in December 1991, there was a consensus within the Russian government that Yeltsin had a popular mandate to initiate radical economic reform. Yeltsin told the Congress of People's Deputies in October 1991, "We fought for political freedom, now we must provide for economic [freedom]."[117] Russia's reformers also endorsed this new focus on economics. As Vladimir Mau, an adviser to Gaidar at the time, recalled, "At this moment [the end of 1991]— whether consciously or subconsciously—there is a principal decision made— the reforms of the political system are halted. If in 1988–89 political reform was a first priority for Gorbachev and his close associates, now Yeltsin decides to freeze the situation, to preserve the status quo regarding the organization of state power."[118] Even those who later criticized the pace and scope of

Yeltsin's economic reform efforts agreed on the sequencing strategy. Organizations like Democratic Russia, which had previously been devoted to promoting political reform, now accepted the primacy of economic reform.[119] It is not surprising, therefore, that their supporters in the United States endorsed this idea as well.

Finally, Russian economic reformers believed that they had a finite reserve of time before trust in Yeltsin and support for reform would wane. [120] Gaidar, after all, was already out of power by the end of 1992. Driven by this perceived time constraint, Russia's reformers wanted to transform the economy as fast as possible and make their reforms irreversible before leaving office.[121] Anything that detracted from this overriding objective of "locking in" market reform was considered superfluous. Their American counterparts, especially at the Treasury Department, shared their view. When Yeltsin's commitment to democratic practices came under question during the October 1993 shelling of the parliament and especially after the invasion of Chechnya in December 1994, advocates of economic reform in the U.S. government could still persuasively argue for continued support of Yeltsin and his government because there was a limited amount of time before the Russian public would turn against the reform agenda.[122]

The budgets reflected these priorities. The IMF, which focused almost exclusively on economic reform, played the central role in aiding Russia in the beginning of the 1990s and throughout the decade.[123] U.S. bilateral assistance—the package of aid handled directly by the U.S. government and not by the multilateral financial institutions—also reflected the "economics first" strategy. Especially in the early years of aid to Russia, the lion's share of Western assistance was devoted not to political reform but to economic reform. The cumulative budget of AID in 1995 illustrates this priority assigned to economic versus political reform.[124] In table 5-2 the programs are listed in order of budget size.

Of the $5.45 billion in direct U.S. assistance to Russia between 1992 and 1998, only $130 million or 2.3 percent was devoted to programs involved directly in democratic reform.[125] When U.S. government expenditures channeled through the Department of Commerce, the Overseas Private Investment Corporation, the U.S. Export-Import Bank, and the U.S. Trade and Development Agency are added to the equation, the primacy of economic reform becomes even clearer.

In the years of debate that followed in response to Russia's mixed record of economic reform, analysts, nongovernmental actors, and government officials have stressed the negative consequences of these reform priorities championed by Lipton and Summers and accepted generally as policy within the Clinton administration. Some have argued that not enough attention was given to institutional reform earlier on.[126] Others have emphasized the neglect

Table 5-2. U.S. AID Assistance to Russia as of September 30, 1995

Category	Millions of dollars (cumulative)
Private sector initiatives	445.91
Enterprise funds	274.00
Housing sector reform	203.60
Democratic reform	99.50
Heath care improvement	98.70
Energy and environmental CIP	90.00
NIS exchanges and training projects	88.17
Energy efficiency and market reform	75.83
Environmental policy and technology	62.60
Economic restructuring/financial reform	59.60
Food systems restructuring	49.70
NIS special humanitarian initiatives	38.46
Eurasia Foundation	12.90
Total	1,598.97

Source: Office of the Coordinator of the U.S. Assistance to the NIS, *U.S. Government Assistance to and Cooperative Activities with the New Independent States of the Former Soviet Union* (Department of State, 1996), p. 200 (www.fpa.org [July 2003]).

of social safety issues. To these criticisms, Clinton and other Western officials responded at the time and in retrospect that they were always sensitive to institutional reform issues, they just did not believe that they could wait for these institutions to take hold before undertaking other reforms. Recall the earlier quote from Stanley Fischer: "You read these critiques of how we didn't understand the need for institutional reform. That's wrong. What can be fairly said is that nobody understood how difficult institutional reform would be in light of the bureaucratic and other interest groups that were operating in Russia. So I would say the need wasn't underestimated but the difficulty of changing institutions was underestimated."[127] Moreover, the Russian government had already initiated (though partially and with mixed results) many of the reforms typically associated with the attempt at shock therapy in Russia. The Clinton team's mandate, as American officials understood it, was to assist in advancing these reforms and not attempt to rewrite or reverse a course already plotted.

Another critical school has highlighted the lack of democratic reform as a principal cause of economic ills in transitional countries, including Russia.[128] For instance, the National Democratic Institute (NDI) report to the U.S. State Department in 1994 stated, "Economic development without political freedom is a contradiction and ultimately doomed to failure. Democratic political systems and free-market economics are two parts of the same process, sustaining each other."[129] In hindsight, the record of reform in the postcommunist world has demonstrated that the fastest democratizers are also the best performers in economic reform.[130] Decisions about sequencing, however, had to be made without the benefit of hindsight. Conventional wisdom in 1993 was still the exact opposite—democratic reform would impede economic reform. Moreover, in January 1993, these criticisms had not ripened, and their advocates were not part of the inner circle in the Clinton administration on aid policy.[131] Clinton advisers on Russia believed that democratic consolidation in Russia was a vital U.S. security interest.[132] They also believed that economic reform would help aid democratic consolidation, not the other way around.

Everyone, therefore, deferred to the "real economists" in the room, Summers and Lipton, when making decisions about assistance priorities. And for these real economists, the immediate focus was the health of the macroeconomy.

Continuing Democratic Assistance at the Grass Roots

Rhetorically, the Clinton administration was dedicated to the mission of promoting democracy in Russia. American dollars, however, did not follow American rhetoric. For instance, the United States and Russia established joint commissions on defense conversion, the environment, and trade at the 1993 Vancouver summit but did not create a similar working group for political reform. AID did join with the National Endowment for Democracy to fund the operations of the International Republican Institute, the National Democratic Institute, the Free Trade Union Institute (AFL-CIO), and the Center for International Private Enterprise (CIPE) in Russia. AID also supported democratic assistance programs run by ABA-CEELI, ARD-Checchi, the International Foundation for Electoral Systems (IFES), Internews, the Eurasia Foundation, and a host of other nongovernmental organizations.[133] These groups focused on fostering the development of political parties, business associations, trade unions, civic organizations, as well as promoting electoral reform, the rule of law, and an independent press. Their budgets were only shadows of the amounts spent on economic technical assistance. In fiscal year 1994—the peak year of assistance when Russia received $1.6 billion from the Freedom Support Act—support for political freedom was only $99.5 million. By the time of the last Clinton aid budget for Russia, democracy assistance had increased as a percentage of Freedom Support Act funds, but the budget was only a paltry $16.1 million. This figure was less than 2 percent of all U.S. assistance to Russia in 2001.[134]

Given the strong rhetoric from senior U.S. officials about the importance of Russian democracy, the relatively small amount of aid for democracy and rule of law assistance is curious. Promoting democratic reform is a difficult and poorly understood undertaking, compelling some to argue that the United States should not be involved in such endeavors. In contrast, for instance, to the well-understood programs for achieving macroeconomic stabilization, Western officials— American and European alike—lack clear blueprints for how to promote democracy effectively from abroad.[135] Others have cautioned that democracy promotion is politically too sensitive, though one wonders why advocating free elections would be more controversial than providing advice about how to distribute property. A third and perhaps most compelling argument relates to the already discussed primacy of economic reform. If U.S. officials pushed too aggressively for democratic reforms, they might undermine their objectives for the transformation of Russia's economy. A fourth argument frequently championed by Clinton officials was that democracy assistance did not need as much money because this kind of aid was cheaper to provide than economic assistance. As Brian Atwood explains, "Democracy programs don't cost that much money. Even if it's a case of running a successful election, you may spend $15-20 million on the mechanical equipment and ballots; that's not a lot of money."[136]

Just as the United States devoted few funds to democratic assistance, the reform of the Russian state also has received little attention. Markets need market-preserving states to thrive, and yet American assistance for reconstructing Russian state institutions was minimal. AID did fund rule of law technical assistance projects, but these programs were largely ineffective in the early 1990s.[137] Programs designed to decrease the size of the state—a priority emphasized by many outside analysts—did not exist.[138] Small projects provided technical assistance for reforms of local self-government, but again these programs represented only a fraction of the total aid package. For instance, the Eurasia Foundation has provided some assistance in this area, but of the foundation's $20 million annual budget in 1996, only 23 percent was devoted to public administration and local government reform.[139]

Russia versus the Other Newly Independent States

In the first years of the aid program, Russia received the bulk of U.S. aid distributed in the former Soviet Union. During the peak year of assistance in 1994, when the region received $2.5 billion, Russia accounted for 65 percent of all these funds. In part, this distribution reflected the size of the countries involved. In part, it reflected a strategic calculation. If Russia made the market and democratic transitions successfully, then the rest of the region would have a better chance of making a similar kind of transition. If Russia did not make the transition, none of the surrounding states would have a chance at consolidating market and democratic institutions. In economic matters, Russia was still the linchpin for the region. Economic growth in Russia would benefit the entire region, while economic stagnation also would reverberate throughout the rest of the former Soviet Union.

Already by 1995, however, the total pie decreased to $850 million and Russia's share of this smaller pie also fell to 45 percent.[140] In 1995, Deputy Secretary of State Talbott (he had been promoted from ambassador-at-large in early 1994) reported that the United States had a concerted policy to shift aid to the other non-Russian states of the former Soviet Union, and projected that a full two-thirds of Freedom Support Act funds would go to the other eleven states of the Commonwealth of Independent States.[141] In part, strategic considerations—including the desire to fortify the security and independence of Ukraine and Uzbekistan and the goal of establishing better relations with the oil-rich states of the Caspian region—pushed aid in this non-Russian direction.[142] Pressure from Congress also continued to move the distribution of aid away from Russia. By 1997, Ukraine emerged as the largest recipient of U.S. aid in the region, ranking behind Egypt and Israel as the third largest recipient of American aid in the world. Armenia became the largest recipient of American per capita assistance, while Azerbaijan—Armenia's enemy—was prohibited from receiving direct American assistance owing to section 907 of the Freedom Support Act.[143] These disbursements had little to do with strategic calculations or need and everything to do with American domestic politics, particularly the preferences of the Armenian-American community in the important state of California. By 1998, Russia received only 17 percent of assistance funds earmarked for the newly independent states.[144] (After all, there is no Russian-American lobby in the United States as there is for the Baltic states, Ukraine, and Armenia.)

Conclusion

The Clinton administration made the internal transformation of Russia a much greater foreign policy priority than had the previous Bush administration. Philosophically, the key decisionmakers in the Clinton foreign policy team were Wilsonians. They believed and articulated a sound rationale for why the consolidation of democracy and capitalism in Russia mattered and could be considered a national security interest of the United States. They then followed up this rhetoric with concrete policy changes, including greater bilateral assistance and a more concerted effort to push for more multilateral assistance for Russia.

Lawrence Summers in his confirmation hearings had said, "The task of rebuilding the Russian economy is the greatest economic restructuring job since the Marshall Plan."[145] It had thus been nearly half a century since an American administration had attempted such a gigantic mission of "nation building" in a country as large and important as Russia. The team began this mission full of optimism about the capacity of the United States to assist and guide domestic reforms in a foreign land. After all, the cold war had just ended. Compared to containing communism, this was supposed to be the easy part.

But the mission to contain communism received orders of magnitude more funds than the mission to dismantle communism and replace it with capitalism and democracy in Russia. The Clinton administration did increase the funds to pursue this rebuilding objective, but nonetheless, even a billion dollars a year was a small fraction of money in a country as large and with as many problems as postcommunist Russia. These levels of assistance meant that Clinton officials had to make strategic choices about what to fund and how to fund, with the obvious implication that many sectors in desperate need of help—that is, social welfare or education—received almost no funding at all. Looking back, Talbott says, "It seemed to me that the Bush people didn't have much of a plan for economic assistance. They just grabbed what they could off the shelf. My criticism of us is that we had a plan, but it didn't conform as much with reality as in hindsight we wished it had. [Treasury officials Lawrence Summers and David Lipton] deserve a lot of credit for having quite a sophisticated analysis and strategy but reality didn't cooperate and the Russians didn't cooperate."[146]

At the end of 1991, Yeltsin estimated that the transitional period of economic difficulty for Russia would be six to eight months.[147] Regrettably, many American observers, funders, and providers of assistance to Russia made this same erroneous assumption. Under pressure to show results from their spending, U.S. policymakers had incentives to exaggerate the speed and extent of reforms in Russia. A combination of limited budgets but great expectations created a difficult, if not dangerous, context within which to try to assist in the transformation of a country that had endured seventy years of a command economy and centuries of authoritarian rule.

Privately, Talbott wrote to Christopher in early 1995 that they were dealing with what he called "the rickety, leaky, oversized cannon-laden Good Ship Russia, with its erratic autocratic captain, semi-mutinous crew and stinking bilge (complete with black eye patches and peg legs)."[148] The more the regime transformers in the Clinton team learned about the Russian regime, the more daunting their mission seemed. And their Russian partner at the top in this endeavor, as Talbott's imagery suggests, was also being increasingly understood as a flawed and limited regime transformer. It wasn't a ringing endorsement of Boris Yeltsin, but given how the United States viewed the crew and the bilge, it is no wonder that in their first term in office, Clinton and his aides did everything they could to help the captain stay in charge.

6

Our Man in Moscow

As Clinton administration officials followed a strategy of providing moral, economic, and some political assistance to those in Russia they believed to be reformers, at the top of the list was President Boris Yeltsin. To Bill Clinton, Yeltsin was the indispensable leader of Russia's market and democratic revolution. If Yeltsin fell, Clinton believed, reform would fail.

Some in the new administration worried about developing a policy around one individual, as Bush had done with Mikhail Gorbachev. Even before becoming Clinton's first senior director for Russia, Ukraine, and Eurasia affairs at the National Security Council, Toby Gati was advising the transition team, "We should also avoid the most common (and mistaken) feature of past U.S. policy toward Russia—the personalization of the reform process around one man. For the United States, the important thing is the continuation of Yeltsin's reform, not Yeltsin's presidency."[1] Others in the new team were suspicious of Yeltsin's true orientation. Brian Atwood recalled a meeting that he and former vice president Walter Mondale had with Yeltsin in 1991 in which Yeltsin lectured without engaging in dialogue. According to Atwood, "He did not convey the bearing of a democrat."[2] Among the top policymakers in Clinton's first term, Anthony Lake, national security adviser, was most suspicious of the Russian president, and especially doubtful of his democratic proclivities. In fact, Lake says, "The time the president got angriest at me was over Russia policy. I think he had more confidence in Yeltsin than I did." Coit D. Blacker, who served as the National Security Council's senior director for Russia, Ukraine, and Eurasia Affairs in 1995–96, adds that Lake's view on Russia was "pretty dark. He thought that Strobe, that the whole Russia crowd had a romantic view of these guys, that they were thugs, that they were reforming thugs, which was good, but they were basically communists who had changed their suits from red to blue."[3]

Lake aside, and even among many who were cautious about Russia (except for some analysts at the CIA and in the U.S. embassy in Moscow), there was a firm belief that without Yeltsin, reform would die. Strobe Talbott recalls, "We had a lot of discussion among ourselves about whether Boris Yeltsin was the reformer-in-chief of Russia. And slicing through the caveats, the answer we came up with was, yes." National Security Adviser to the Vice President Leon Fuerth adds, "There was never a time when it was possible to figure out who, if you were interested in Russian reform, you would be rooting for other than Yeltsin." James Steinberg, the State Department's Policy Planning director and later deputy national security adviser, argues, "I believe now as I believed in 1993 that for all his flaws, Yeltsin was a democrat and much more so than others. In some ways, he was the better bet than the Western-type reformers because he was a Russian [populist]." For Clinton, there was never any wavering; Samuel R. "Sandy" Berger, Lake's deputy and later national security adviser, says that Clinton "believed Yeltsin was the best hope for preserving Russia's democracy."[4] Throughout the Clinton presidency, Boris Yeltsin was our man in Moscow.

Between 1993 and 1996, antidemocratic acts as well as threats of transgression against the democratic process challenged Clinton's hypothesis about the causal relationship between Yeltsin and reform. Yeltsin ordered the Russian parliament to disband in September 1993, used armed force to oust recalcitrant parliamentary deputies from power in October 1993, and invaded the breakaway Russian republic of Chechnya in December 1994. The challenges to democracy culminated in the spring of 1996 when top Yeltsin advisers hinted at plans to cancel the scheduled 1996 presidential elections. Throughout this period, Yeltsin's hold on power appeared increasingly under siege, especially after stunning parliamentary election victories by ultranationalist Vladimir Zhirinovsky and his Liberal Democratic Party of Russia in December 1993 and a Communist Party comeback in December 1995.

Despite or perhaps because of these challenges, Clinton and his administration remained firmly committed to Yeltsin, and in the margins, tried to do what they could to keep him in power. Their primary fear was that the communists would return to power. And even Yeltsin skeptic Lake argued retrospectively, "We were right to want Yeltsin to win. He was running against Communist party leader Gennady Zyuganov, hardly a committed democrat or economic reformer."[5]

Throughout this period, the administration never conducted a major reappraisal of the policy. Some officials have argued that Lake at certain moments wanted to reassess what the administration was doing, but he denies it, saying,

"There was never a call for an agonizing reappraisal of our policy toward Russia. It would be more accurate that I was occasionally skeptical and not happy with where we were. . . . There were issues on which I disagreed with the State Department: Haiti, Bosnia, etc., where I really fought. One of the reasons I didn't push for a review on Russia and a full-scale bureaucratic war was because of Strobe, whom I had a deep admiration for and still do. I had a lot of confidence in him. That's why I didn't fight too hard on the issue." But he also says that the team was focused in a "particularistic way" on economics, Yeltsin, nuclear issues, and so on and that "We should have had a more general review of our strategy." In retrospect, Lake has written that his administration did not see how destructive "our nearly exclusive focus on economic reforms" and inattention to democratic reforms would be in the long run. In 1995, Lake hired Stanford professor Coit D. Blacker to be his top Russia hand at the NSC in part because, says Lake, Blacker "was more skeptical" about trends in Russia. But Talbott had firm control over the policy and was not going to open up the process to a major review. As he remembers, "There were a couple of times, Tony in particular, talked about . . . Russia's really going bad, we ought to have a Cabinet or Principals level meeting. I tended to resist that. Not because I wanted to keep the Principals out of Russia policy, but because the way this town works, you immediately get a news story saying that the Cabinet has met to reappraise and presumably to redirect the policy. Agonizing reappraisals are associated with policy failures, and you never want to admit or entertain the possibility of a policy failure."[6]

Constitutional Crisis and Civil War

The first challenge to the our-man-in-Moscow strategy came in the first month of the Clinton administration. By the time Bill Clinton became president on January 20, 1993, his Russian counterpart, Boris Yeltsin, was already struggling to remain president of Russia. During Russia's first year of independence, Yeltsin's economic reform agenda and his reform team headed by Yegor Gaidar had come under vicious attack. Some political forces resisted reform altogether. Communist parties and factions of various stripes called for new price controls, import restrictions, collective ownership, and a "planned-market economy."[7] The more serious challenges came from those who wanted partial reform. In particular, Soviet-era managers of state-owned enterprises, the so-called red directors, had mobilized to resist Gaidar's plans for privatization and undermine the reformist team's stringent monetary and fiscal policies. The political voice of these enterprise directors could be heard and seen through the actions and words of regional heads of administration, parliamentary factions such as the Industrial Union and Agricultural Union, and, by June 1992, in the form of a new political movement, Civic Union.[8] Led by Arkady Volsky, the chairman of the Union of Industrialists and Entrepreneurs, Vice President Aleksandr Rutskoi, and parliamentary leader and Democratic Party chairman, Nikolai Travkin, Civic Union proposed a slower, more moderate recipe for economic reform in contrast to so-called shock therapy ideas advocated by Gaidar and his associates. They called for wage and price indexing, insider privatization, subsidies and credits to strategic industries, and greater restrictions on imports and foreign investment. Civic Union leaders claimed that the International Monetary Fund, the World Bank, and other Western institutions had duped Gaidar's government into destroying Russia's industrial base. Civic Union statements had a distinctly anti-Western tone.[9]

Civic Union's proposals served the interests of Soviet directors and their trade union allies, the Federation of Independent Trade Unions (FNPR in Russian), but also had a populist ring to them. Who could be against less painful reforms? At the Seventh Congress of People's Deputies in December 1992, Civic Union and their parliamentary supporters won a major victory by forcing Yeltsin to abandon his acting prime minister, Yegor Gaidar, in favor of one of their own, Viktor Chernomyrdin.

Yet Russia's Congress and especially its chairman—Yeltsin's former protégé turned enemy, Ruslan Khasbulatov—were not satisfied with these personnel victories. At this same December Congress, Khasbulatov and his allies—now a majority in the legislative body—curtailed the president's power to rule by decree and passed several constitutional amendments further limiting the president's power. At the time, Russia had no post-Soviet constitution. Instead parliamentary deputies and the presidential administration took their cues about who governs from a heavily amended constitution drafted under Leonid Brezhnev, former general secretary of the Communist Party of the Soviet Union (CPSU). A constitutional commission in the Congress had drafted a new basic law, but the draft had yet to be voted on by the Congress. Some interpreted these constitutional amendments and the government reshuffling as major victories for the Russian Congress and steps toward greater parliamentary authority and constitutional clarity.[10]

Yeltsin did not share this view. He denounced the constitutional changes approved by the Congress of People's Deputies, since he believed that these new constraints on his power would impede economic reforms and exacerbate political instability. In response, he threatened to hold a referendum the following month to decide, "Who do you entrust to take the country out of economic and political crisis [and] restore the Russian Federation: the present composition of the Congress and the Supreme Soviet or the President?"[11] According to Yeltsin's formulation, the referendum's winner would stay in power with a mandate to articulate the reform agenda, while the loser would be compelled to face new elections in April 1993. Yeltsin's plan did not fly, since the Constitutional Court declared the referendum scheme unconstitutional. What emerged from the discussions, however, was an agreement to hold a referendum in early April on the basic principles of a new constitution, including first and foremost a clarification on the division of power between Congress and the president.

The compromise negotiated in December 1992 between Yeltsin, Khasbulatov, and Constitutional Court chief justice Valery Zorkin did not hold, as opposing sides could not agree on a general set of questions for the referendum. Yeltsin threatened to hold the referendum without the approval of Congress, arguing that "an attempt to restore the Communist regime of the Soviets is now emerging."[12] The Russian president eventually called for a state of emergency and the creation of a new interim government that would rule the country until after a new constitution had been ratified. Vice President Rutskoi and Security Council head Yuri Skokov refused to sign the emergency decree. A furious Congress reconvened, denounced Yeltsin's "coup attempt," and began impeachment proceedings.[13] Yeltsin's opponents barely failed to garner the necessary two-thirds votes to remove the president.

The spring constitutional crisis was still in full swing when Yeltsin boarded his plane for Vancouver. In making preparations for the Clinton-Yeltsin summit, Clinton's Russia team was committed to supporting Yeltsin. For Clinton personally, Yeltsin's domestic battles made increased economic expenditures for Russia even more important.

Some American embassy officials in Moscow questioned this public endorsement of Yeltsin.[14] These diplomats worried that Yeltsin might lose this constitutional battle. The United States, therefore, had to build relationships with other political figures to hedge its bets. At a dinner meeting with Russia experts in preparation for the Vancouver summit, Clinton also heard warnings about having a Russia policy too closely identified with Yeltsin.[15] In these first months of the Clinton administration, however, the notion of abandoning Yeltsin was not seriously entertained. The same constitutional ambiguity that fueled polarization in Russia also made it difficult for American officials to identify the "correct" democratic process to champion. Khasbulatov and the Congress deputies were challenging Yeltsin's authority under the auspices of a Soviet-era constitution. Yeltsin's threat of emergency rule seemed confrontational, yet this same president had just agreed to Congress's demands for a new government.

For Clinton officials like David Lipton and Lawrence Summers at the Treasury Department, Yeltsin's abandonment of Gaidar signaled a major setback for reform. Others, however, could point to this action as indicative of Yeltsin's willingness to compromise. Congress deputies had an electoral mandate from the spring of 1990, but Yeltsin secured his democratic mandate in a national election in June 1991. Yeltsin's election as Russia's first president was also his third electoral victory in as many years. At this stage, therefore, it was not a stretch to argue that backing Yeltsin meant backing democracy. As Clinton watched Yeltsin's speech on CNN during the March 1993 crisis with his top advisers, Talbott argued that Yeltsin was "the only horse the forces of reform had." Clinton, writes presidential adviser George Stephanopoulos, agreed, but asked, "What if Yeltsin turned into a tyrant and we got tagged with a 'who lost Russia' challenge two months into the job?"[16]

At the Vancouver summit, Clinton went out of his way to praise Yeltsin as Russia's democratic leader and used the meeting to announce the $1.6 billion bilateral aid program as well as the $43 billion multilateral program slated for approval by the G-7 in Tokyo that summer. Yeltsin welcomed the pledges but stressed that "it would be good if we could receive $500 million before April 25," the date of the national referendum on Yeltsin and his reforms.[17] Clinton let everyone know where he stood, saying to Yeltsin in front of the press, "Mr. President, our nation will not stand on the sidelines when it comes to democracy in Russia. We know where we stand. . . . We actively support reform and reformers and you in Russia." After saying good-bye to Yeltsin, he added, "Win! Win!"[18]

Yeltsin returned to Moscow from Vancouver to wage his battle. In a final compromise, Yeltsin allowed the Congress to draft four questions for the referendum:

—Do you trust Russian president Yeltsin?

—Do you approve of the socioeconomic policy conducted by the Russian president and by the Russian government since 1992?

—Should the new presidential election be conducted ahead of time?

—Should the new parliamentary election be conducted ahead of time?

As specified in the agreement between Yeltsin and the Congress, the outcome of the first two questions had no obvious consequences, while the third and fourth questions needed a majority of all eligible voters (and not just a majority of those voting) to be considered binding.

Russia experts in the U.S. government, both in the Moscow embassy and back in Washington, predicted that Yeltsin would lose this referendum.[19] Given the sharp downward turn in real incomes, skyrocketing inflation, and extreme uncertainty about Russia's economic future, most predicted that Russian voters would cast their ballots against the reform policies on question two and probably also vote against Yeltsin on question one. At the Vancouver summit, Clinton and his team did not respond directly to Yeltsin's $500 million advance request. To help Yeltsin, however, the U.S. Agency for International Development (AID) tacitly allowed an American public relations firm, Sawyer Miller, working at the time for the State Property Committee (GKI), to assist in the Yeltsin campaign. The American company helped to script Russia's first political jingle, a television spot that urged voters in a rhyme to vote, "da, da, nyet, da." Beyond this intervention, however, Clinton officials just waited for the results.

Clinton, writes Talbott, "followed the referendum as though it were an American election."[20] Clinton and his foreign policy team breathed a huge sigh of relief when a majority of Russian voters reaffirmed their trust in Yeltsin and their support in his reform policies. On the first question, 58.7 percent of the voters affirmed their trust in Yeltsin, compared with 39.3 percent who voted against. Even more amazingly, 53.0 percent expressed their approval of Yeltsin's socioeconomic policy, while 44.5 percent disapproved. On questions three and four a plurality (49.5 percent) supported early presidential elections, while a solid majority (67.2 percent) called for new parliamentary elections. The referendum victory defused the constitutional crisis in Russia and seemed to affirm the validity of continuing to support Yeltsin and his approach to reform. At the G-7 summit in Tokyo a few months later, Clinton argued even more emphatically for increased support for Yeltsin.

The euphoria sparked by the April referendum victory was short-lived. Over the summer of 1993, Yeltsin's administration convened a Constitutional Conference to draft a new constitution. Everyone, including Yeltsin's greatest detractors, was invited to attend. Yeltsin and his aides hoped that the Constitutional Conference could ratify a political pact that might guide Russia into a new political era. These hopes went unrealized. Instead, Congress chairman Khasbulatov and other opposition leaders soon abandoned the conference and began making preparations for passing their own constitutional draft at the next meeting of the Congress of People's Deputies in October 1993. Believing that Khasbulatov planned to propose a constitutional draft that would eliminate the office of the president altogether, Yeltsin made a preemptive strike the month before. On September 21, 1993, he issued Presidential Decree 1400, calling for the dissolution of the Congress of People's Deputies, as well as the popular ratification of a new constitution and elections to a new bicameral parliament in December 1993. As a conciliatory gesture, Yeltsin stated that he would hold an early presidential election in March 1994.[21]

Russian parliamentarians denounced Presidential Decree 1400 as unconstitutional, an interpretation that a majority on the Russian Constitutional Court shared. When Yeltsin refused to rescind the decree, the Supreme Soviet declared Yeltsin no longer fit to govern. The full Congress convened on September 23, 1993, and approved Rutskoi as Russia's new president, who in turn, named a new government. In a replay of August 1991, Moscow had two chief executives, one in the Kremlin and one in the White House (the home of the Congress of People's Deputies), each claiming to be the head of state. To mobilize popular resistance to Yeltsin and his government, opposition leaders in Congress refused to leave their parliamentary offices in the White House and encouraged supporters to defend their building in the name of democracy and the existing constitution.[22]

Decree 1400 was a serious affront to the Clinton assumption about the intertwined relationship between Yeltsin and democratic reform. The decree was unconstitutional. Endorsing Yeltsin's actions, therefore, might look like—and very well be—an abandonment of the policy of supporting democratization in Russia. Nor was it clear in the first days of the standoff which side would win. Thousands turned out to defend the White House, and Vice President-President Rutskoi was a general who commanded respect in some parts of the armed forces. An early American endorsement of Yeltsin might complicate the process of establishing new relations with a Rutskoi government if his side prevailed. Moreover, influential Russia analysts in Washington outside the government such as Dimitri Simes and Jerry Hough had praised Rutskoi as a popular, charismatic leader who offered a legitimate alternative to the "failed" policies of Yeltsin's shock therapy.[23] An unambiguous Yeltsin victory also worried some in the West. Would a full-blown dictatorship follow?

Although political advisers like Stephanopoulos urged the president to distance himself from Yeltsin, Clinton and his foreign policy team believed that they had to back Yeltsin and live with the consequences. As Nicholas Burns, who had succeeded Toby Gati as the NSC's senior director for Russia, recalls of Yeltsin's moves to disband the Russian parliament, "On September 21, Strobe Talbott and I went to talk to the president to advise that he call Yeltsin and support his efforts. We had determined that Yeltsin's survival was critical for the survival of Russian democracy."[24]

Although surprised by the turn of events in Moscow, Clinton never doubted on which side of the barricade he stood. After speaking to Yeltsin for seventeen minutes, Clinton affirmed, "I support him fully," in his first public reaction to Yeltsin's dissolution of the parliament.[25] Clinton echoed Yeltsin's rationale for his actions. Yeltsin explained to the Russian people that "the fruitless, senseless and destructive struggle" and the consequent "decline of state power . . . make it impossible not only to implement difficult reforms but to maintain elementary order." Yeltsin lamented that he had no other choice but to break the stalemate through decisive action. Clinton in turn explained to the American people that "there is no question that President Yeltsin acted in response to a constitutional crisis that had reached a critical impasse and had paralyzed the political process." Vice President Al Gore echoed that Yeltsin was still "the best hope for democracy in Russia" and pledged that the administration would "continue to urge the international community to be supportive of the reform efforts that are under way." Clinton officials said Yeltsin's precarious hold on power was a reason for the U.S. Congress to support with even greater speed the administration's $2.5 billion aid package for the region.[26]

As the standoff continued, Clinton officials stressed compromise and a peaceful resolution. Secretary of State Warren Christopher said that Yeltsin assured Clinton in their first phone call after the crisis began that he would hold new parliamentary elections in December to be followed soon thereafter by a new presidential vote. As the crisis developed, Christopher became the senior Clinton official most worried about bloodshed and therefore persisted in securing assurance from his Russian counterpart, Andrei Kozyrev, that there would be no military action. Clinton was less worried and became even more supportive of Yeltsin as the crisis progressed. He explained that "the United States has to be on the side of reform and democracy in Russia. And President Yeltsin represents that." A week into the standoff, Kozyrev met with Clinton at the White House to present him a letter from Yeltsin that assured Clinton that there would be no use of military force. In response to Yeltsin's letter of gratitude for Clinton's support, Clinton remarked that Yeltsin was "on the right side of history."[27]

As events unfolded, Clinton's support for Yeltsin became easier to justify. Rutskoi, Khasbulatov, and the other leaders holed up in the Russian White House began to invite all sorts of unsavory characters to carry weapons in their cause, including proto-fascist paramilitary groups. At the same time that the number of paramilitary units inside the White House multiplied, the more moderate defenders inside the White House, including most Congress deputies, gradually left the building. Rutskoi's side suffered a serious blow on October 2, when Communist Party chief Gennady Zyuganov called on his followers to quit the defense and avoid violent confrontation. The next day, on October 3, Rutskoi's forces went on the offensive, first attacking the adjacent mayor's office and then moving across town to seize the Ostankino television tower. A serious gunfight at the television tower ensued, compelling Yeltsin to use military force to counter the attack. By the following day, a combination of tank shelling and a special forces raid subdued the White House occupants. Estimates are that 147 people had died in the fighting.[28]

In explaining why he reneged on his promise of no bloodshed, Yeltsin invoked self-defense. Clinton endorsed Yeltsin's move and Yeltsin's interpretation of events, blaming opposition forces for the armed conflict. On October 3, Clinton explained, "It is clear that the violence was perpetrated by the Rutskoy-Khasbulatov forces. . . . It is also clear that Yeltsin bent over backwards to avoid the use of force . . . and I am still convinced that the United States must support President Yeltsin and the process of bringing about free and fair elections. We cannot afford to be in a position of wavering at this moment or backing off or giving any encouragement to people who clearly want to derail the election process and are not committed to reform." Talbott added that Rutskoi and Khasbulatov "had sent mobs into the streets to attack people," clearly assigning the blame for the conflict to them.[29] On October 4, after Russian special forces had seized control of the White House, Clinton called the military action a defense of democracy. Yeltsin, in Clinton's view, had "no other alternative but to try to restore order."[30]

Speaking on October 4, Clinton noted that Yeltsin had committed to new elections for his own office, a positive democratic step. "As long as he goes forward with the new constitution, genuinely democratic elections for the Parliament, genuinely democratic elections for the president, then he is doing what he said he would do [and that] is all that we can ask."[31] Soon, however, Clinton had to withdraw this line of argumentation in defense of Yeltsin's democratic instincts after the Russian president quietly reneged on his pledge for early presidential elections.

Throughout the standoff, no senior official in the Clinton administration publicly advocated abandonment of Yeltsin or recognition of Rutskoi. The general-turned-politician might have impressed some in Washington, but no one in the upper ranks of the Clinton foreign policy team held Rutskoi or Khasbulatov in high regard. Senior officials in the Clinton administration interpreted Russian politics through the eyes of their interlocutors. Clinton's main source for political insight about Russia came from Yeltsin. Talbott's main source was Deputy Foreign Minister Georgy Mamedov. Summers and Lipton relied on Gaidar and Chubais. Perry called on his old friend and counterpart Deputy Defense Minister Andrei Kokoshin. All these Russians shared the same view on the "October events," the euphemism eventually coined to camouflage the tragic mini–civil war that gripped Moscow that fall. They cast the standoff as the final battle between communism and reform, and their Western counterparts echoed this framing of the crisis (even if no senior leaders from the Communist Party of the Russian Federation participated in the final military conflict). As NSC staffer Nicholas Burns remembered the deliberations about the October events, "The extra-constitutional acts [Yeltsin] took in September/October 1993 were meant to preserve democracy from a resurgent authoritarianism. And we very much agreed with that." Christopher aide Thomas Donilon adds, "There was no flinching at this point because the U.S. analysis was that he was resisting the forces of the dark. There was expressly in the minds of policymakers in the fall of 1993 the Bush administration's performance with respect to Yeltsin in the streets of Moscow in August 1991. There was a high premium on not flinching, not delaying, not missing it in terms of support."[32]

The mood among Clinton's Russia team, however, was not triumphant. Talbott called the events of October "a tragic moment in Russian history."[33] Yet there was also a sense of relief. Clinton and his aides wanted Yeltsin to prevail, and he did, even if the costs of his victory were much greater than anyone had expected.

In Washington, it was not just the U.S. president who backed Yeltsin. American congressional leaders did not side with their institutional counterparts in the Russian Congress. Before becoming Speaker of the House, Newt Gingrich (R-Ga.) was an outspoken supporter of Russia's reforms who helped build congressional backing for Clinton's Russia policy. During the constitutional crisis in Moscow, Gingrich firmly supported Yeltsin. In the fall of 1993, Yeltsin's opponents had few friends in Washington. A high-powered congressional delegation cochaired by Majority Leader Richard Gephardt (D-Mo.) and Minority Leader Robert Michel (R-Ill.) called on Rutskoi during a visit to Russia in April 1993, and he had made a terrible impression. No one on Capitol Hill was prepared to make the argument that Russia would be better off with Rutskoi as president and Khasbulatov as the head of parliament.

The crisis, in fact, speeded the approval of Clinton's aid package to Russia. Congressman Michel called the aid package "the single most important move this country could make for generations."[34] Senator Patrick Leahy explicitly linked congressional deliberations about Russia aid to the turmoil in Russia. "I met with the President last night and told him that I have every intention of forging forward [with the foreign aid bill]. I wanted to send a clear signal that the U.S. is moving ahead with this aid so there won't be any questions in Moscow as to whether the United States is supporting a move towards democracy and a move toward a market economy. I don't want Yeltsin's opponents to think there is any slackening off." Congressman Lee Hamilton, chairman of the House Foreign Affairs Committee, added, "With regard to our aid, I think the choice here is really very stark: Yeltsin favors democracy, the Parliament does not. Yeltsin favors market reform, the Parliament does not. Yeltsin favors an open society, the Parliament is pushing back toward the centralized state. We want to see Russia move in the direction of democracy and market reform. The purpose is to foster that, and as long as Russia is moving in that general direction, even with some bumps along the way, that is what we ought to do."[35]

Two days after Yeltsin's decree dissolving the Congress, the U.S. Senate overwhelmingly passed the 1994 foreign aid bill, 88-10, which included the $2.5 billion for the former Soviet Union, of which $1.6 billion was earmarked for Russia.[36] Clinton signed the bill into law at the end of the month. Years later, congressional leaders would chastise Clinton for standing too close to Yeltsin.[37] At the very moment when Yeltsin was acting most undemocratically, however, only a few lone voices on Capitol Hill questioned the wisdom of backing Yeltsin.[38] Most in Congress stood firm with President Clinton in backing the Russian president.

The Fascist Flare and the Beginning of Doubts

For many Clinton administration officials, backing Yeltsin's bombing of the parliament was troubling and unpleasant, even as they believed that the United States had to stand behind Yeltsin against the "communists" because without Yeltsin, reform could not move forward. Rutskoi and Khasbulatov were retrograde figures who had to be pushed aside. Years later, most senior officials involved with Russia policy still believed these arguments. At the same time, the bombing blackened not only the Russian White House but also the spirits of some within the Clinton team. After all, this was the same building that gave birth to Russian democracy after the 1990 parliamentary elections and then was defended in the name of democracy during the August 1991 coup. And Rutskoi and Khasbulatov, the evil leaders of the nationalist-communist cabal, were just months earlier part of Yeltsin's entourage.

These uneasy feelings about the October 1993 conflict were eventually off-set that fall by new optimism about the prospects for further economic reform and political stability that might follow now that the final battle between the "communists" and "reformers" was over. Although retracting his promise to hold an early presidential election, Yeltsin did keep his commitment to new parliamentary elections slated for December. Early polls suggested that the pro-reform coalition, Democratic Choice, headed by Yegor Gaidar, would win the largest number of seats in the new parliament, thereby changing the confrontational dynamics of executive-legislative relations that had plagued Russia throughout its first two years of independence. While visiting Moscow only weeks after the October events, Secretary of State Warren Christopher gave a public address about the upcoming elections at Gaidar's institute, tacitly demonstrating American preferences in the upcoming vote. U.S. officials were optimistic about the election outcome. As one unnamed State Department official stated, only days from the vote, "There's just a real upbeat feel around here, a real sense that the reformers will do well."[39]

American government and nongovernment officials also applauded the electoral process—the first national election in Russia since the collapse of the Soviet Union—and offered assistance in making it as free and fair as possible. American electoral observers participated in an international delegation of poll watchers. The International Foundation for Electoral Systems (IFES) worked with Russia's Central Election Committee to provide technical assistance in organizing the vote, while the National Democratic Institute and International Republican Institute collaborated with parties and nongovernmental organizations to organize domestic monitoring of the historic vote. For outsiders observing and facilitating the election process, it was a moment of hope and optimism about Russia's democratic future.[40]

Equally important to the parliamentary vote, Yeltsin announced a referendum for a new constitution to be held on the same day. Yeltsin's draft constitution gave the president far-reaching powers. If ratified by the people, Russia's reformers and their backers in the West would finally have the kind of executive power that they deemed necessary for executing painful but necessary economic reforms.

These reformers did not have to wait for the new constitution to be ratified to jump-start their agenda. They saw the October-December period with no parliament as a real opportunity to implement reforms. That fall, Gaidar had rejoined the government as minister of the economy, while Boris Fyodorov was still deputy prime minister and finance minister. In this interregnum, the Russian government used decrees to abolish subsidized credits to enterprises, deregulated some aspects of agriculture, liberalized prices of bread, grain, and baby food, and kept the planned budget deficit to 9.5 percent of GDP, an effort at expenditure control praised by the IMF.[41] For those in the West most concerned about Russian economic reform, the fall of 1993 was a period of progress and hope.

Electoral Shock

At the end of November 1993, U.S. embassy official Wayne Merry wrote a cable home from Moscow countering the prevailing wisdom and warning that the election would be a disaster. Merry says that his original subject line was "Russian electoral countdown: looming disaster," but Ambassador Thomas Pickering changed it to the less dramatic "watch for surprises."[42]

What a surprise it was. The Liberal Democratic Party of Russia, headed by Vladimir Zhirinovsky, captured almost a quarter of the popular vote on the party list ballot, while Gaidar's Russia's Choice won a disappointing 15 percent. In the aggregate, the final distribution of votes cast for and against reformers did not differ dramatically from previous elections.[43] Yet Zhirinovsky's message made his unexpected capture of the opposition vote (in contrast to other opposition parties) especially frightening. Zhirinovsky openly espoused militant, racist, imperialist, and nationalist goals and threatened to overthrow the system to achieve them. His rhetoric and style drew immediate comparisons to Hitler, an analogy that Zhirinovsky did nothing to discourage. Zhirinovsky was also stridently anti-American at the time. Suddenly, after one election, Russia's experiment with democracy was beginning to resemble 1920s Weimar Germany.[44] Many Western observers agreed with scholar Charles Fairbanks who wrote in the spring of 1994 that "many of the preconditions of fascism are or will soon be present in Russia."[45] After Zhirinovsky's startling victory, many predicted a return to the institutional standoff between parliament and president of the previous year. Some even predicted civil war, with former Russian parliamentarian Oleg Rumyantsev warning that the "downtrodden" would rise up against Yeltsin and his reforms. Liberal Grigory Yavlinsky even speculated that Yeltsin would dissolve Russia's nascent democratic order and install an authoritarian regime.[46]

These shocking electoral results fueled real doubts in the Clinton administration about the wisdom of the "shock therapy" economic reform course espoused by Gaidar and his associates and also raised suspicions about the long-term viability of Russian democracy. In reality, shock therapy in Russia had ended long before the December 1993 elections. Yeltsin already had appointed a mixed government by the spring of 1992 and replaced Gaidar and his reformist government a full year before Zhirinovsky's victory. The economic policies being pursued by Prime Minister Chernomyrdin at the time were hardly radical. On the contrary, they represented only partial reform, a situation that helped to undermine financial stabilization, impede price liberalization in the energy sector, and slow enterprise restructuring. Nonetheless, senior Clinton officials interpreted Zhirinovsky's victory and Gaidar's poor showing as a popular rejection of radical reform. Many in the administration entertained the analogy of Russia to Weimar Germany.

As election results from Siberia began to trickle in, Strobe Talbott and Vice President Gore were flying to Russia from Kazakhstan. Gore was coming to Moscow for a meeting of his joint commission with Prime Minister Chernomyrdin and to prepare the way for Clinton's first visit to Russia the following month. The very timing of the commission meeting demonstrated how unexpected these election results were for the Clinton team. As they landed in Moscow, they—like their Russian counterparts—had to scramble to write new talking points, as they "were left dazed and largely speechless by the weekend balloting." As Talbott remembers on hearing the results, "We were focused on the communist, the red threat, and even though Zhirinovsky was a character and we all knew that, I don't think we fully appreciated the Liberal Democratic Party as an electoral force, and we certainly underestimated the extent to which it would score high in the December 1993 election."[47]

Talbott and his aides, like Gaidar and his team, took solace in the constitution's ratification. The day after the vote, some U.S. officials even underplayed the significance of the Zhirinovsky victory. Victoria Nuland, Talbott's top assistant, expressed confidence that Zhirinovsky's win was a protest vote that would not translate into sustained support for his extremist agenda.[48] Time proved Nuland right in her assessment of Zhirinovsky's staying power. But in the tense and uncertain atmosphere that immediately followed Zhirinovsky's victory, the Clinton team publicly backtracked on the policies it had been supporting.

At the time, Clinton officials attributed Zhirinovsky's rise to the economic hardship that Russia had endured under "shock therapy." This electoral theory had many flaws. Russia had never really attempted shock therapy as a reform package; the lack of reform or the persistence of partial reform was the real cause of many people's economic woes.[49] In addition, polls showed that Zhirinovsky's voters were not motivated primarily by economic concerns but attracted to the charismatic orator because of other, more nationalistic features of his campaign message.[50] In the heat of the moment, however, Clinton officials had neither the time nor the data to understand the causal factors that propelled Zhirinovsky to power. The coincidence of their presence in Moscow also compelled them to say something.

What they did say sounded at first like a reversal of American policy toward Russia. Gore echoed the sentiments of his commission counterpart when he suggested that Russia's reform strategy had been too harsh and too fast.[51] Chernomyrdin did not support any party in the parliamentary election and therefore quickly distanced himself from Gaidar and the other reformist parties after the election. He called for an "end to market romanticism" and pledged to reintroduce price controls, implement greater state regulation of markets, and provide increased state support for ailing enterprises. To the dismay of Russian liberals and their allies at the U.S. Treasury Department, Gore seemed to sympathize with Chernomyrdin's interpretation of Russian politics. The vice president accused the IMF of recommending economic measures that were too rigorous for Russia at this time, criticized the Fund for withholding money too often when Russia did not meet targets, and called on the IMF's board to be more sensitive to the hardship of the Russian people. Gore's embrace of Chernomyrdin and his economic policy statements fueled a real division between the Office of the Vice President and the Treasury Department over how the Clinton administration should publicly speak about Russian reform.[52]

Treasury Department officials were shocked by Gore's comments but had to endure more distress upon returning home. In a press conference in Washington, Talbott echoed the vice president's message, suggesting that it was time for "less shock and more therapy for the Russian people." Warren Christopher communicated a similar message, stressing that Russia's reformers had to pay greater attention to the suffering of the people.[53] For a brief period, the White House and State Department seemed to be turning against the Treasury Department and, in the opinion of the Treasury team, against "real economic reform" in Russia.

The Clinton foreign policy team met in order to give the Treasury Department a chance to make the case for the soundness of the policy they had been advocating and pursuing. Lipton recalls, "We made our case and at the end of the day, I think we convinced Strobe and the others that the approach wasn't fundamentally wrong, it was fundamentally right, but I think Strobe forevermore felt you had to have more therapy along with the shock. But I think we convinced others that without strong reforms there could be no economic revival."[54] In fact, in an interview he gave to Newsweek just after leaving office in 2001, Talbott argued, "I don't think [Yeltsin] or his leadership ever came up with the right answer to the problem of what ratio of shock to therapy to have. I don't think that the United States and the international financial institutions ever came up with the perfect recipe for them either."[55]

In retrospect, Talbott acknowledged that his "less shock, more therapy" utterance was a "dumb thing for me to do and say."[56] He was right. Unfortunately, his statement served to undermine the embattled reformers within the Russian government. As Fyodorov stated bluntly, recalling Talbott's phrase, "It was a betrayal, a stabbing in the back. Clearly it was nasty. I remembered the name Strobe Talbott ever after. A big political gaffe."[57]

Talbott's utterance emboldened those in the administration who had questioned the "go fast" approach to reform. In not-for-attribution comments to the press, senior officials in the Clinton administration admitted to being "startled and shaken" by Zhirinovsky's victory. Others suggested Clinton's Russia policy now would have to be rethought.[58] Although no "B team" had penned an alternative strategy for aiding reform and backing reformers, quiet criticism began to fester. Department of State Policy Planning Director James Steinberg and Christopher Chief of Staff Thomas Donilon (known by the Russia team as "Steinilon" for together representing a more skeptical approach) questioned whether U.S. policy should rely so heavily on a group of politicians in Russia who were so unpopular. Backing the charismatic, politically savvy Yeltsin was one thing; remaining loyal to Gaidar was another. Steinberg also argued that if the United States were "too close to them, [we] might undermine them."[59] Skeptical analysts on the outside of government buoyed these internal skeptics with a new flurry of op-ed pieces and longer essays about Clinton's misguided Russia policy.

But what was the obvious alternative policy? Some administration officials leaked that American diplomats might have to establish some kind of working relationship with Zhirinovsky. Yet Zhirinovsky's racist statements about minority ethnic groups in Russia, promises to blow nuclear waste into the Baltic states, and neoimperialist claims to Alaska made him a very unattractive partner. Consequently, senior Clinton officials decided early on to denounce Zhirinovsky and his movement.[60] State Department press spokesman Mike McCurry stated that Zhirinovsky's utterances "embody views that are obviously completely an anathema to the principles of democracy, to our own views on issues like human rights and the democratic process, economic reform and relations among sovereign states."[61] After briefly mulling over alternative policies for a few days after the election, Clinton officials cited the specter of Zhirinovsky's "reprehensible" message as a reason to bolster aid to Zhirinovsky's opponents even further. Clinton emphasized that more Western assistance should be earmarked for a Russian "social safety net" to relieve the common person's suffering.[62] AID and other agencies responded to the president's idea with a flurry of working groups and meetings on social safety issues, though with few concrete initiatives or new substantial outlays.

The Clinton team did take some solace in the constitution's ratification and the positive implication of this institutional change for economic reform. In the long run, the passage of the new constitution did help to clarify responsibilities for economic policymaking. Most important, the Russian Central Bank eventually became more accountable to the president and pursued less inflationary monetary policies. (Sound fiscal policy, however, took much longer to achieve.) In the short run, however, the results of the elections served to derail economic reformers and their policies. After their poor electoral showing, Gaidar and his electoral bloc partner, Boris Fyodorov, resigned from the government in January 1994. Following the cues of their Russian comrades, Anders Åslund and Jeffrey Sachs—two of the biggest Western backers of radical reform—quit their unpaid positions as advisers of the Russian government. Sachs predicted the worst for Russian economic reform. His intellectual partners in Russia shared his pessimism.[63]

Some of those in the Clinton administration responsible for aid policy began to question the appropriateness of continued Western assistance, especially an IMF program that required a disciplined government in Moscow to work. However, the converse policy—doing less or withdrawing IMF support—seemed even more problematic. Less than a year since taking office, was the Clinton administration going to abandon its Russia policy after trumpeting so loudly for many months the historic proportions of Russia's reforms? No. The one person most decisively still committed to sticking it out was also the boss—Bill Clinton.

Chechnya and a Crescendo of Doubts

An even greater challenge to Clinton's "stand by our man" policy erupted just a year later. On December 2, 1994, Russian aircraft began striking targets inside the breakaway Republic of Chechnya in the Northern Caucasus. On December 11, three columns of Russian armed forces crossed into Chechnya.[64] A full-scale ground invasion soon followed. For the second time in as many years, Yeltsin had ordered the deployment of Russian military forces against his own people, this time in a brutal fashion with little regard for civilian casualties. Both in Washington and Moscow, one-time supporters of Yeltsin began to doubt their original assumptions about the man and his regime. Russian "reform" looked neither progressive nor stable.

Yeltsin's decision to invade Chechnya represented not only a setback for democratic consolidation but in several respects resulted from the weakness of democratic institutions and democratic forces in Russia. The new constitution ratified in December 1993 strengthened executive power. Pro-market technocrats celebrated the creation of this superpresidency, which was more insulated from societal pressures, unconstrained by checks and balances, and therefore in theory more able to implement economic reforms. These same institutions could be deployed for illiberal missions if liberals lost their privileged position in the Kremlin and the government. And they did after their poor electoral performance in December 1993.[65] In their place, a new group—labeled the "party of war" by Russia's liberal press after the invasion—gained power and influence. Composed of several key Kremlin officials within or closely affiliated with the security ministries, this group included Defense Minister Pavel Grachev, First Deputy Prime Minister Oleg Soskovets, Deputy Prime Minister Nikolai Yegorov, Security Council chief Oleg Lobov, and Aleksandr Korzhakov, Yeltsin's personal bodyguard.[66]

Although several of these officials had been in Yeltsin's government from the beginning, the influence of this hawkish coalition grew while the influence of liberals and liberal interest groups declined throughout 1994. To "save Russia" from collapse and win the upcoming presidential election, this group urged Yeltsin to adopt a more muscular position toward Chechnya.[67] For this group of politicians and the interest groups behind them, a military victory in Chechnya would reaffirm their importance to the Russian state.[68]

Russian society had very different views. From the start, roughly two-thirds of all Russians opposed the war, a figure that grew steadily over the next two years. Had their interests been represented in the state through the usual pluralist institutions found in stable, liberal democracies, the decision to attack may not have been made.

The Chechen crisis had simmered for years. In August 1991, Chechen president Dzokhar Dudayev and his government in Chechnya had declared Chechnya's independence. For the next three years, Chechnya enjoyed or endured de facto independence. In this interval, the Russian state was too weak and too distracted to exercise its sovereignty over the breakaway republic. By the fall of 1994, however, Yeltsin and his party-of-war cabal were feeling more emboldened, in part because their foes in the Congress had been defeated, in part because the new constitution gave the Moscow regime more legitimacy, and in part because Chechnya after the ratification of the 1993 constitution looked more radical compared with the other autonomous republics. By the spring of 1994, every other republic, including independent-minded Tatarstan, was abiding by the new Russian constitution, leaving "Chechnya as the sole secessionist holdout in Russia."[69]

After a series of insults from Dudayev regarding Russian sovereignty during negotiations over the Federal Treaty in the spring and a spate of bus highjackings that summer in the region, Yeltsin decided on a military solution. A failed coup attempt orchestrated by Russia's Federal Security Service (FSB), one of the successor organizations to the KGB, was then followed by a full-scale air attack and ground invasion. On the eve of attack, Defense Minister Grachev predicted that the military action would be over within hours. He was radically mistaken. By the time Russia finally sued for peace in the summer of 1996, an estimated 45–50,000 Russian citizens had lost their lives.[70]

Yeltsin's decision to invade Chechnya came as a surprise to Clinton's Russian team.[71] Before the Russian military intervention, the Clinton administration had not even developed a policy on Chechnya. As Talbott recalls, "It's not a good story. Real late and it was on the periphery of the radar screen. I don't know the answer. I think if you could do a word search and you plugged in Chechnya to the hard drive, I don't know about incoming cables but certainly memos we were writing you wouldn't get many hits. It was in every sense of the word an exotic, peripheral issue."[72]

The only time that senior Clinton officials discussed Chechnya was in April 1993, when intelligence sources passed along Dudayev's claim of possessing a nuclear bomb. A subsequent investigation revealed that the boast was not true, but the event confirmed for several Clinton officials that Dudayev was a dangerous, unstable leader.[73] Clinton officials had begun to worry about Russia's projection of force in the Caucasus in 1994, when intelligence reports revealed a heavy Russian involvement in the Abkhaz independence movement in the Republic of Georgia. The issue was so important to the administration that a Principals Committee meeting was convened, rather than the more typical meeting of Talbott's small interagency "rump group." The administration was not prepared, however, for a full-scale military invasion of one of Russia's own republics. Even so, their view of Chechnya was not positive. As Talbott writes, "During the Russian Revolution in 1991, Chechnya declared itself a separate country. Had Chechnya attained the independence it claimed, it would have immediately qualified as a failed if not rogue state. Kidnapping, drug trafficking, money-laundering, gun-running, counterfeiting, trafficking in women and children were rampant. It was an anarchist's utopia and any government's nightmare."[74]

The Chechen ruler (or nonruler) over this anarchy, in Talbott's view, was an especially unsavory character. "Instead of being hailed as a founding father," Talbott argues, "Dudayev was regarded—insofar as the outside world paid any attention to him at all—as a renegade. Had the world given him more notice, it would have had even less reason to tolerate him, since he routinely slaughtered demonstrators and used his bodyguards to assassinate his political adversaries." In recalling the nuclear bomb scare, Talbott stated bluntly, "He was whacko." In addition, U.S. intelligence sources suggested that international supporters of Chechens were enemies of the United States as would become better known after September 11, 2001.[75]

Consequently, the Clinton administration did not rally to Dudayev's defense when Russian forces invaded. Compared with the nearly unanimous support for Yeltsin's bombing of parliament in October 1993, however, debate internally on Chechnya was more pronounced. Everyone on the team agreed that the United States had to respect Russia's territorial integrity; no one advocated recognition of Chechnya. But different from October 1993, some wanted to send a signal of discontent about Yeltsin's methods for preserving the Russian Federation. Talbott aide Victoria Nuland recalls, "In Chechnya, it was different. Many people were arguing inside, myself among them, that there ought to be a way to make it hurt and there needed to be a way to make it hurt. Because it seemed to us such an unnecessary response to the threat."[76]

Christopher had become increasingly wary of the trajectory of Russian reform and articulated these views in a March 1995 speech in Bloomington, Indiana. But his caution was a reaction to general Russian developments and not a specific response to Chechnya. Lake, the senior official in the Clinton administration most concerned about the conflict and least enamoured with Yeltsin personally, became increasingly suspicious of his administration's pro-Yeltsin stance. He brought in a new senior director for Russian affairs at the NSC from outside the government, Stanford professor Coit D. Blacker, as a way to balance Talbott and the overly pro-Yeltsin voices in the administration, but Blacker shared the view of Chechnya as an internal Russian issue. And as Gore adviser Leon Fuerth says, "Throughout the remainder of the administration, the underlying policy toward Chechnya never wavered."[77]

The center of gravity in the administration remained where it was before the war. Treasury Department officials opposed the use of economic sanctions as a response to Chechnya. Pentagon officials did not want their Cooperative Threat Reduction (CTR) programs and military-to-military programs to be scaled back, even though these programs indirectly subsidized the Russian military. Bigger security issues, in their view, had to be addressed even if it made for some awkward moments, including a dramatic one recalled by Ashton Carter, assistant secretary of defense for international policy, "When [JCS director of policy and plans, Gen.] Wes Clark and I hosted staff talks in the Pentagon, the Russian general staff gave us a briefing on artillery tactics in urban areas. Wes and I looked at each other—we couldn't believe it. This is a topic that we didn't think about very much."[78]

The United States was developing a larger foreign policy agenda with Russia that State Department officials did not want derailed by Chechnya. On the traditional security front, for instance, Christopher in March 1995 called talks with the Russians "the most ambitious arms control agenda in our history."[79] Some U.S. officials believed Chechnya enhanced American leverage in these other issue areas such as NATO enlargement, CTR, and Bosnia, because Yeltsin needed Clinton's support more than ever. As Ashton Carter recalls, "On the one hand, he [Yeltsin] becomes a figure in Russia under attack. But it means that he needs some compensating act of internationally legitimate statesmanship all the more because he's doing something the international community abhors."[80]

Perhaps as a corrective to his own wavering remarks after the December 1993 elections, Talbott emphasized that the United States should not "zigzag" in its policy, since Russia's revolution would be a long and difficult one, full of ups and downs. U.S. support for reform therefore had to act as ballast to help keep Russia on track. No one liked what Russia was doing, but no one had an alternative policy as even Lake, one of the policy's chief skeptics, admits:

> I'm sure a lot of folks will want to say that we wanted to be tougher but that Strobe was in the way, but I don't think that's true. . . . There were sometimes specific issues on Chechnya you could address, but the hard fact was that the United States did not have the leverage to make the Russians reverse course. . . .
>
> It was a heaven sent issue for those who wanted to use it to destroy American relations with Russia for other reasons or to take shots at the administration not for powerlessness but for not caring about it when it was an issue of what you can do and what you can't do.[81]

In addressing the Chechen problem, Clinton administration officials constructed their policy by first affirming respect for Russia's territorial integrity. U.S. officials insistently stated, "We support the territorial integrity of Russia, and we oppose attempts to change international borders through the use of force." In his first reaction to the Russian military intervention, Clinton emphasized, "It is an internal Russian affair. And we hope that order can be restored with a minimum amount of bloodshed and violence. And that's what we have counseled and encouraged." Even after several months of fighting, Clinton accepted the definition of the "problem" as an "internal affair," implying that the United States had no moral authority to try to intervene and influence the situation in Russia.[82] Nicholas Burns, who in 1995 replaced Mike McCurry as State Department press spokesman, argues, "Chechyna was a rude awakening for the administration but most saw it in its early stages in 1995 as a largely internal problem for the Russian Federation." The administration was not about to make the conflict an international crisis.[83]

U.S. officials also accepted Yeltsin's argument about dominoes. If Chechnya quit the Russian Federation, Yeltsin explained, the other republics would follow. Even before the intervention, Russian officials constantly underscored this threat. In explaining their lack of criticism of Yeltsin's military action, U.S. government officials echoed these fears about disintegration, an outcome that would not be in the American national interest. As one anonymous senior official explained to Washington Post correspondent Jeffrey Smith, "I accept Yeltsin's argument that if Chechnya is able to break away from Moscow, other republics may be tempted to do the same." To avoid disintegration, Christopher suggested that Yeltsin had "probably done what he had to do to prevent this republic from breaking away." Years later, Talbott recalled that one of the worst nightmares was a Russia too weak to defend its borders; "Chechnya seemed to illustrate rather than the brutality of Russian power, it seemed to illustrate the danger of continuing dissolution."[84] More generally and in contrast to thinking about the Soviet Union a decade earlier, a weaker Russia—that is, a Russia not able to exercise sovereignty within its borders—was considered a problem for and threat to the United States.[85]

Clinton, however, did not confine his policy on Chechnya to a respect for Russian sovereignty. Instead, the American president went out of his way to rationalize and defend Yeltsin's military campaign, comparing Russia's struggles with southern defectors to the American Civil War and thereby suggesting that Yeltsin was Lincoln. In January 1995, soon-to-be presidential press secretary Mike McCurry made the first public allusion to the American Civil War. "We have a long history as a democracy that includes an episode in the history of our country where we dealt with a secessionist movement through armed conflict called the Civil War." [86] Had the analogy never been mentioned again, McCurry's quip could have been interpreted as his own off-the-cuff remark. More than a year later, however, while in Moscow, Clinton repeated the analogy. Having traveled to Moscow in April 1996 primarily to assist Yeltsin's re-election campaign, Clinton gave a short American history lesson to the journalists attending their joint press conference, "I would remind you that we once had a civil war in our country in which we lost, on a per capita basis, far more people than we lost in any of the wars of the 20th century, over the proposition that Abraham Lincoln gave his life for, that no state had a right to withdraw from our union."[87]

Standing behind their boss while he made these remarks, Clinton administration officials, and Talbott in particular, were appalled by the comparison. Clinton, however, was unapologetic. Talbott recalls Clinton trying out the line in private ahead of time and says, "I should have pounced on the line the minute it came out of Clinton's mouth and told him never to use it again. I didn't. There was hell to pay back home. Clinton's response was, 'If Yeltsin wins, then nobody will remember what the Republicans said about backing off from supporting him. But if he loses, they'll blame me. I want this guy to win so bad it hurts.'"[88]

Some did try to counter Clinton's unqualified endorsement of Yeltsin's Chechen war. Lake called on Russia to seek a peaceful resolution to the conflict and criticized Russia's conduct of the war. As he argued just months before the Russian presidential vote (and to a crowd very pro-Yeltsin and pro-Russian), "We oppose terrorism in all forms. But we also oppose strongly the means the Russians have been using [in Chechnya]. Widespread and indiscriminate use of force has spilled far too much innocent blood and eroded support for Russia. The cycle of violence must end." Talbott also stated that the invasion violated international standards on human rights spelled out in the Helsinki Act and other Organization for Security and Cooperation in Europe (OSCE) and UN documents. Christopher noted that a prolonged conflict in the Caucasus would delay Russia's reform process at home and therefore its progress toward Western integration. "We want to see a stable, democratic Russia being integrated into the international community. What we do not want to see is a Russia mired in a military quagmire that erodes reform and tends to isolate it in the international community."[89]

At the same time, U.S. officials including Christopher and Talbott argued that the Chechen conflict did not signal the end of reform in Russia. Talbott said at the time, "We believe that Russia must end the violence and killing, urgently seek a peaceful solution, and reach out for a reconciliation with the people of Chechnya. At the same time, we believe it is premature to interpret the debacle in Chechnya as the death of democracy, freedom, and reform all across Russia." And Christopher even praised the Russian armed forces for showing restraint.[90]

Above all else, the Clinton team remained determined to not let Chechnya define their Russia policy or derail the linchpin to their Russia policy in Moscow, Boris Yeltsin. Chechnya in their view was a hiccup in a difficult and long transition, but the transition was still moving—and had to be moved—in the right direction. The Clinton administration also underscored that other issues in the U.S.-Russia relationship were more important. As McCurry said, "I again stress it [Chechnya] by no means defines this very important bilateral relationship. It is a broad expansive relationship that has many elements on the agenda, of which this is no doubt one but is by no means the most significant."[91]

Clinton followed up his rhetorical support for Yeltsin in the military campaign with policy support. When the Russians violated the Conventional Forces in Europe Treaty (CFE) by moving more military equipment near the conflict in the Caucasus, the United States tried to help Russia amend the original treaty provisions. Despite Talbott's citation of possible human rights atrocities that might violate international treaties, the Clinton administration never called on the international community to hold Russia accountable. Clinton officials also rejected the idea of Russian expulsion from international organizations as punishment for the Chechen war. Instead, the Clinton administration pushed forward with plans for transforming the G-7 into the Group of Eight (G-8). Discussions about Chechnya were never institutionalized as a working group within the Gore-Chernomyrdin Commission.[92]

Nor did the Clinton administration cut assistance to Russia at any point during the first Chechen war. Instead, officials flatly rejected the idea. As Christopher argued, "Some people would say that we should end these programs to punish Russia when it does something that we oppose. Now, I am all for maximizing our leverage in every way we can, but I personally reviewed all of our assistance programs, and I have come to the conclusion that cutting them back at the present time simply would not make sense, is not in the interest of the American people."[93] Talbott adds in retrospect, "I'm a big skeptic of punitive sanctions, but particularly to load those on the back of this beast of burden called Russia policy struck me as absolutely out of the question."[94] In response to the first Chechen war, the United States was much more muted in its criticisms of Russia than European countries and the Council of Europe in particular.

In comparison to the October 1993 crisis, voices outside of the administration were much more critical of Clinton's support for Yeltsin on this issue. Republican critics on Capitol Hill threatened to cut aid to Russia in response to the war, and some Democratic voices joined the chorus. Tim Roemer (D-Ind.), for instance, had urged Clinton to cancel his trip to Moscow in May 1995 to celebrate the fiftieth anniversary of the defeat of Nazi Germany. "We think that it is bad policy, symbolically and substantively, for the president to meet, and be seen in Moscow, with the Russian military at a time when the Russians are brutally killing Chechens in their terrible war."[95] Not surprisingly, Senate Majority Leader and 1996 Republican presidential candidate Robert Dole repeatedly criticized Clinton's response to the Chechen war, saying that he would not have extended IMF assistance and would not have compared the conflict between Russia and Chechnya to the American Civil War. Nongovernmental organizations such as Amnesty International, Human Rights Watch, Physicians for Human Rights, and Doctors without Borders also were animated by the Chechen war. The International Commission of Jurists even called for suspension of IMF loans.[96] Zbigniew Brzezinski, the former national security adviser to President Carter, emerged as the most vocal critic of Clinton inaction on Chechnya, and argued for a more conditional policy of support for Yeltsin. "I do feel that the administration, while correct in helping him and supporting him, has been too timid in not criticizing him when he does things which he shouldn't have done. I have particularly in mind the massive killings of the Chechens. That's inexcusable. It's immoral. It's politically bad because it weakens the forces of democracy in Russia."[97]

Liberal opponents of the war in Russia bolstered the voice and moral position of these American-based critics. Important human rights advocates such as Yelena Bonner (Andrei Sakharov's widow) denounced the war as immoral and chastised those Western leaders who continued to support Yeltsin. Grigory Yavlinsky, the leader of the liberal opposition party, Yabloko, called the administration's continued support for Yeltsin shortsighted and wrong. "By supporting the Yeltsin Government, you are alienating the average Russian."[98] Even Yegor Gaidar, a favorite among Clinton officials, openly and repeatedly criticized the war, a principled stance that caused a split in his own political party.[99]

The first Chechen war, however, never became a major foreign policy problem for the Clinton administration. Clinton officials admit that congressional pressure helped to change their language about Chechnya and moved the issue higher up the list during public briefings.[100] But this was the extent of domestic influences on the policy. The Chechens had no important backers in Washington. There is only a minuscule Chechen diaspora in the United States. Chechnya did not have oil or diamonds or some major economic interest that might attract American business support. On the contrary, the American business community firmly supported Russia in this conflict.

As just mentioned, several nongovernmental organizations took an interest in the war, but they never articulated a united policy alternative to the Clinton administration's approach. Human Rights Watch, arguably one of the most important human rights organizations in the United States, focused primarily on gathering data about human rights atrocities in Chechnya and did not lobby directly to change policy. Other democracy-promoting organizations working in Russia did not focus on Chechnya, since they wanted to continue their work in other areas such as party building, rule of law, trade union development, and promotion of civil society more generally. To stay in business, these kinds of groups needed to maintain a friendly relationship with the Yeltsin government in Moscow and continue to receive funds from Capitol Hill in Washington. Among these democratic assistance organizations, only the National Endowment for Democracy spoke out openly against the war and actively supported those groups in Russia that opposed the war. Congressional threats to cut aid to Russia never gained steam since most members of Congress accepted Clinton's argument that the U.S.-Russian relationship was too big and important to be held hostage to one issue. Finally, Chechnya never became a campaign issue in the 1996 presidential election despite Bob Dole's criticisms. International press access to the conflict was limited, and Dole never mustered an effective threat to Clinton to make the Clinton foreign policy record a major campaign topic. At this stage in U.S.-Russian relations, keeping the communists out of the Kremlin trumped all other concerns. Even most of Clinton's critics accepted this set of priorities.

The Red Scare and the Specter of Dictatorship during Russia's 1996 Presidential Election

In the very first days of his presidency, Clinton had made the strategic decision that Yeltsin was Russia's best bet for reform and therefore America's best bet as a partner in Russia. Clinton never firmly defined the meaning of "reform." In speeches, Clinton and his aides often used the term in reference to democracy and democracy building. Oftentimes, Clinton officials conflated rather different processes of reform, using the dreaded phrase "market democracy" to refer to all that was unfolding in Russia.[101] Clinton never seemed to look too deeply into the details of how well his statements about democracy corresponded with political practices in Russia or how consistent his aid policies in Russia were with his prescriptions at home for economic and social policies. Instead, Clinton saw the drama of Russia's second revolution through the personal aspirations and shortcomings of one historical figure—Yeltsin. If Yeltsin was on top, then "reform" was proceeding. If Yeltsin was faltering, then reform was in trouble.

After the bombing of the parliament and the invasion of Chechnya, this "Yeltsin-is-reform" strategy needed to be defended and could no longer be assumed as self-evident. With the advantage of hindsight, the pro-Yeltsin position staked out by Clinton and his associates seems less wise. After his re-election in the summer of 1996, Yeltsin was often incapacitated by illness or alcoholism. His inability to govern allowed others—the oligarchs and the "family" (a group of Kremlin insiders that included Yeltsin's daughter)—to fill the vacuum. Yeltsin also presided over a catastrophic financial meltdown and another invasion of Chechnya in his second term. In retrospect, even many of Yeltsin's staunchest backers have questioned the wisdom of his serving a second term.[102]

So why did the Clinton administration support him so vigorously? They stayed with their policy because in the run-up to the Russian 1996 presidential election, all the alternatives to Yeltsin seemed much worse.[103] Gennady Zyuganov, the communist candidate, promised to undermine most market reforms that had been put in place in the last four years. General Aleksandr Lebed, another presidential hopeful, looked and talked like a leader who might institute martial law. If they could vote, many in the Clinton administration (and U.S. embassy in Moscow) might have supported Grigory Yavlinsky as the next president of Russia. But the Russian people would not, making support for his candidacy seem irrational.[104] Of the viable candidates, Yeltsin was considered the best of the bunch.

They also believed that their investment in Yeltsin would begin to produce dividends in other foreign policy arenas should Yeltsin win re-election. In particular, the Clinton administration was setting the stage in 1995 for moving forward on NATO enlargement the following year. With Yeltsin in the Kremlin, U.S. officials believed that they could enlarge NATO and still maintain a productive relationship with Russia. If Zyuganov or Lebed won, all bets were off.

The good news resulting from Russia's parliamentary elections in December 1995 was that they occurred on time and under law, and that Zhirinovsky won only 11 percent of the popular vote, less than half of his total in 1993. The bad news was that the Communist Party of the Russian Federation headed by Gennady Zyuganov doubled its total from 1993 and captured almost a quarter of the vote. In 1993, communism appeared to have died as an ideology and political movement. In 1995, communism seemed to be back. In contrast to east European leftist parties, Russia's post-Soviet strain of communism was not pink or social democratic. On the contrary, Zyuganov still preached openly about the need for a reversal of "illegal" privatization, greater state control of prices, and a renationalization of key Russian economic sectors, including foreign trade. Zyuganov also sounded like a militant nationalist who trumpeted strong anti-American themes in his stump speeches. He often ridiculed Yeltsin as a puppet of the United States and vowed to repel American imperialism upon coming to power. It was not difficult to understand why the Clinton administration believed that U.S. interests would not be served well by a Zyuganov victory. American business groups also expressed extreme anxieties about a communist return to the Kremlin.[105]

Zyuganov looked like he might have the votes to win the presidency through democratic means. History seemed to be on his side. Throughout eastern Europe, several anticommunist leaders who won electoral victories in first elections lost to former communist leaders in second elections. Russia seemed poised to follow a similar trajectory. After all, Russia's economic reform had produced more hardship than any of the east European countries, and no east European incumbent had initiated an unpopular civil war as Yeltsin had in Chechnya. Moreover, because communism came to Russia through revolution and not on the turrets of the Red Army, many analysts assumed that communists enjoyed more legitimacy in Russia than in the rest of eastern Europe.

The CPRF won only 22 percent of the popular vote in 1995, but communist and nationalist parties altogether won roughly 50 percent of the popular vote. At the same time, the party headed by Yeltsin's own prime minister, Chernomyrdin, won a pathetic 10 percent of this parliamentary vote, despite enjoying tremendous financial advantages. Gaidar's newly reconstituted reformist party, Democratic Choice of Russia, won less than 4 percent of the vote. As the presidential campaign kicked off in January 1996, Yeltsin's approval rating was in the single digits.

Many Western observers predicted a Zyuganov victory in a free and fair election, and some Western businesspeople began to hedge their bets.[106] That winter, Zyuganov even received an invitation to the world's most elite gathering of capitalists, the World Economic Forum at Davos, Switzerland. Even Clinton met with the communist leader that spring during a visit to Moscow at a roundtable of political party leaders.[107]

Some in Yeltsin's entourage shared these assessments of Zyuganov's prospects for victory. Aleksandr Korzhakov, Yeltsin's bodyguard and informal adviser, allegedly argued with Yeltsin at the time, "It is senseless to struggle when you have a 3-percent approval rating." To avoid defeat, Korzhakov proposed a novel solution—postponement of the presidential vote indefinitely. To convince Yeltsin of its proposal, Korzhakov's analytical center fed the president deflated polling numbers. By March 1996, the specter of postponement seemed credible enough that Korzhakov deputies floated trial balloons to Westerners to assess what the reaction would be, while Russian liberals called on their allies in the West to warn them of this possible antidemocratic action.[108] In retrospect, Yeltsin admits that he inched very close to following Korzhakov's advice and canceling the election.[109]

Backing Yeltsin or the Democratic Process?

In the spring and summer of 1996, the Clinton administration faced two serious challenges to its Russia policy: on the one hand, how to avoid Yeltsin's electoral defeat and how to respond if he did lose; and on the other hand, how to deter a cancellation of the election and how to respond if it were canceled. On both accounts, the Clinton administration had few effective instruments to influence the outcomes.

Well before the presidential campaign in Russia began, Clinton and his administration already had committed to several policy positions that were undertaken chiefly as a strategy for helping to keep the communists from coming back to power. U.S. criticism of Yeltsin concerning Chechnya was muted because Clinton did not want to damage Yeltsin's chances of winning the presidential vote. Clinton also made clear to Yeltsin in their meetings that he would keep NATO enlargement from happening until after the Russian presidential vote.[110]

In a major sin of silence that later came back to haunt the Clinton administration, U.S. officials refrained from criticizing the massive insider sell-off of valuable state properties to friends of the Kremlin. Called "loans-for-shares," this program aimed to buy oligarchic support for the re-election campaign. Presidential aide Anatoly Chubais designed the program so that the oligarchs buying these oil and mineral companies could only gain complete control after the 1996 vote.[111]

Upon hearing about the scheme, both Lawrence Summers and David Lipton did not like the plan, preferring instead another round of voucher privatization. But at this stage in Russian reform, their ability to dictate terms had waned. Russia's bankers had a greater voice than the Americans, especially as the presidential election approached. Treasury officials were not going to threaten to cut off money, which would not stop the loans-for-shares scheme from moving forward but could produce bigger budget deficits, higher inflation rates, and a volatile ruble. And at the State Department, issues like Bosnia loomed much larger than whether some oligarchs were getting too much power. Lake admits, "Maybe the crucial moment is the loans-for-shares because that had huge political consequences, and I don't recall the political implications having our attention. I remember thinking, that's an interesting way to privatize."[112]

Others were appalled at the program's unfairness and lack of economic rationality, since companies soon to be worth billions were being sold off through noncompetitive auctions for millions. Brian Atwood, the head of AID at the time, stated emphatically that his agency criticized the program and "every major donor opposed it." In retrospect, Talbott called the program "bad economics, bad civics, and bad politics."[113] But because the program bought support for the re-election effort and transferred these assets into private hands in the event of a possible communist return to power, Clinton officials did not criticize the program or publicly try to stop it from moving forward.

As the election drew nearer and Yeltsin's electoral prospects seemed dimmer, some on Clinton's team, including Talbott, urged caution in identifying too closely with Yeltsin. Before Clinton's April 1996 trip to Russia, Talbott told Clinton to give Yeltsin "another firm warm handshake but not an embrace," since too much American support might hurt Yeltsin's re-election chances. Talbott's assessment was based on his reading of Russian electoral moods. "I urged him to be careful lest he do damage both to Yeltsin and to himself. Too conspicuous a display of American support for Yeltsin could be a kiss of death, I said, given all the anti-Americanism in Russia." Talbott also argued that "we shouldn't bet the ranch on what was still a long-shot Yeltsin victory." Many senior officials in the Clinton administration as well as lower-level Russia analysts at the CIA and the State Department shared this assessment very late into the campaign. As James Collins, Talbott's successor as ambassador-at-large for the new independent states, proclaimed, "Nobody—believe me, nobody— can tell you what is going to happen in this vote." Talbott did not want Yeltsin's electoral defeat to become a stigma for his boss. "We had to be careful not to let a Yeltsin defeat be seen as a Clinton defeat."[114]

Most important foreign policy issues in the Clinton administration were discussed among the "principals" or cabinet-level officials. Generally in the Clinton administration's first term, Russia policy was dealt with not by the Principals Committee but by the interagency group meetings run by Talbott. But a formal Principals Committee meeting was called to discuss Russia policy in early March 1996, ostensibly to talk about the upcoming April summit in Moscow. The meeting was set up to give the Russia team an opportunity to talk generally about the election with Clinton and Gore. The team's goal going into the meeting, and Talbott's primary objective, was to stress to Clinton the necessity of supporting the process rather than Yeltsin as an individual. As the session began, Talbott laid out the rationale for not sticking too close to Yeltsin as the campaign went into high gear because it might backfire.[115] Gore, who along with his national security adviser Leon Fuerth had not been briefed in advance of the meeting, countered Talbott's logic, stressing the high stakes and lack of alternatives. While many in the administration admired Grigory Yavlinsky, the liberal opposition leader of the Yabloko party, no one believed he had a serious chance of winning the presidential vote. The senior director for Russia affairs at the National Security Council, Coit D. Blacker, recalls Gore saying, "Strobe, no one in this country has more respect for your point of view and your expertise on Russia than I do, but I just have to say that I think that that is exactly the wrong advice. This is Russia's one chance. Boris Yeltsin is its one chance. We made this investment and if we stand by as this communist guy, Zyuganov, runs and he wins, we're not going to have a policy. We're going to take a huge hit. Russia's going to go down the drain, and we can't afford that at this time." Or as Fuerth puts it, "The Vice President was asking, you have maybe another candidate who is likely to advance democracy?"[116]

Clinton clearly agreed that Yeltsin had to win. As Clinton remarked, "I know the Russian people have to pick a president, and I know that means we've got to stop short of giving a nominating speech for the guy. But we've got to go all the way in helping in every other respect. I appreciate that some of you are worried about avoiding any embarrassment for me if Zyuganov ends up winning. Don't worry about that. I'll handle that part of it."[117]

Dick Morris, one of Clinton's campaign advisers at the time, also helped to cast Yeltsin's victory as a component of Clinton's 1996 re-election effort. Morris has written that for Clinton, Russia was the California of international politics in the 1996 election, "the one place he couldn't afford to lose." Morris adds, "The State Department types were saying, we'll have to deal with who-ever wins. Don't get that involved. Clinton said, to hell with you, I'm going to put all my eggs in the Yeltsin basket and make it work. Gore as well. The for-eign policy establishment was play it cautiously, intervene modestly, we have to deal with whoever wins. Clinton's concept was to throw caution to the wind. Be aggressive, deeply involved, heavily partisan, bet it all on red. And since Yeltsin was at 9 percent [in the polls], it was like, bet it all on twelve." Even then Deputy National Security Adviser Sandy Berger says, "Did [Clinton] do as much as he could in 1996 to help Yeltsin short of where he thought it would backfire? Absolutely."[118]

Even Russian critics of the administration found it hard to disagree with Clinton's attitude on the election. Former Russian finance minister Boris Fyodorov has said, "In '96, I can't really blame the West, because clearly the choice in '96 was between Yeltsin and Zyuganov, the communist party leader, and at that time we were selecting between the worst and just very bad. It was not a choice between good and bad. And at that time, I think it was quite nat-ural that anybody with any brains would support Yeltsin in principle, even looking at all those dirty things happening."[119]

Rhetorical and Symbolic Support

During the campaign itself, Clinton spoke often about the importance of the democratic process, without mentioning the significance of the outcome. In addition, the Clinton administration also undertook several initiatives to support Yeltsin. Rhetorically, Clinton said everything just short of outright endorsement. In his public speeches about Russia during the campaign period, Clinton praised Yeltsin as a historic figure whom Russia still needed at the helm. Only weeks before the first round of voting Clinton affirmed that Yeltsin and his allies for reform "represent the future—and we hope the Russian people will vote for the future."[120] The statement was short of a full endorsement, but just barely.

Clinton also demonstrated his support for his friend Boris by agreeing to attend a meeting of the G-7 plus Russia, now called "The Political Eight," in Moscow in April 1996. Yeltsin himself had requested the summit at the G-7 meeting the previous year in Halifax. The formal agenda of the summit of world leaders was nuclear safety, but the real mission was to underscore Western support for Yeltsin, demonstrating to Russian voters that Yeltsin was now a member of this elite club, even if the formal designation of the G-8 as such would have to wait.[121]

Besides the public support, and to an extent not realized by the foreign policy team, Bill Clinton was offering Boris Yeltsin his own personal advice on how to win an election. Presidential adviser Dick Morris says,

> Clinton was constantly talking to Yeltsin and giving him over the phone advice coming out of Yeltsin's polling. The central piece of advice was that the Russian people felt strongly that a communist victory would automatically bring a war, whether an expansion of the war in Chechnya or war with the U.S. was ambiguous, but they were sure that if you voted for the communists it would cause a war. So the central role that Yeltsin was keeping the peace and American statements that he was essential to keeping the peace would reinforce that view that the Russian people had. So Clinton went out of his way to stress his personal relationship with Yeltsin, their close collaboration, their mutual commitment to the goals of peace, etc.[122]

Requests for Cash

Yeltsin wanted more than pats on the back and campaign cues. He wanted money. In the spring of 1996, Yeltsin made repeated requests to his friends in the West to provide financial support to his re-election effort. Both Germany and France provided credits to Russia, totaling $2.4 billion, which helped to create the impression in Russia that the West was helping to finance Yeltsin's re-election campaign.[123]

Yeltsin asked Clinton directly for a large loan to Russia in order to win re-election. Clinton initially told Yeltsin he would see what he could do but was noncommittal. His advisers argued against considering any direct bilateral assistance from the United States. Clinton eventually agreed, realizing that a bilateral direct bailout of Russia, coming just after the controversial bailout of Mexico, was not possible, and Summers was sent to Moscow to deliver the news. Nonetheless, Clinton did publicly urge the IMF to provide new funds to Russia during this period. He also apparently asked the Saudi government to forgive some of its Soviet-era debt to free up resources for Yeltsin.[124]

Senior officials within the Fund argued that a new program was the next logical step after the one-year 1995 standby agreement, which Russia had completed successfully. Not everyone agreed with this assessment of these earlier programs. Boris Fyodorov believed that "The IMF deals in 1994 on were big disasters, I was always on the record as criticizing, but nobody was listening." Economist Anders Åslund has provided a more complex assessment of IMF programs in the region, including in Russia. In his view, one-year standby agreements that sought to reduce inflation and help countries achieve stabilization were relatively successful, while the three-year programs that tried to stimulate structural reforms, such as the program signed between Russia and the IMF in 1996, proved less successful.[125] Lower-level IMF officials did not think that Russia's progress on economic reform justified new money. "By the mid-1990s," according to Augusto Lopez-Claros, the IMF's resident representative in Russia from 1992 to 1995, "IMF lending to Russia was less driven by policy content and the associated conditionality than by geopolitical considerations defined by the Fund's largest shareholders."[126] The United States is the largest shareholder.

In December 1995, the State Duma, Russia's lower and most powerful house of parliament, had succeeded in passing a 1996 budget, an accomplishment that "set the stage" for the negotiation of the Extended Fund Facility (EFF)—a larger and more comprehensive IMF loan program—the following year. Stanley Fischer characterized the new program as simply good economics. "There was a lot of controversy over our March 1996 EFF. The decision was not a close call. Russia had done exceptionally well in meeting the conditions—month-by-month—in its 1995 standby program. Now they proposed going on to implement a serious program of structural reforms."[127] The IMF believed it had enough reasons of its own as an economic institution to support the package.

In January, Gore argued that the administration was considering support because Russia's "performance during the previous twelve months has been extraordinary, given the circumstances and given the challenges faced by Russia."[128] But was it really just economics? After all, the announcement was made in March 1996, in the midst of the Russian presidential campaign, when

Yeltsin's prospects looked bleak. Some officials say that there was a timing question—the United States was going to support a package on economic grounds in 1996, but why give it after the election when it would be of no help politically for Yeltsin? Lipton learned later that the Germans pushed the IMF hard to proceed. And Berger says of the United States, "We did lean forward with the IMF."[129]

And go ahead they did. In March 1994, the IMF had initialed a new major agreement with the Russian government to provide $1.5 billion. The following year, the IMF increased its exposure considerably by pledging $6.8 billion. Now, in March 1996—three months before the Russian presidential elections—the IMF agreed to provide $10.2 billion to the Russian government over a three-year period, including $4 billion in the first year. The sum was $1.2 billion more than figures being discussed just a month earlier. At the time, Russia became the second largest recipient of IMF assistance after Mexico. A month before its final approval, Clinton had publicly endorsed the loan, arguing, "I believe the loan will go through, and I believe that it should. I do support it strongly." Yeltsin himself urged American intervention in the IMF program. "We had to involve Clinton, Jacques Chirac, Helmut Kohl, and [John] Major," Yeltsin said, to get the IMF to commit these new loans. The Clinton administration wanted to use the IMF to support Yeltsin in his time of need; the IMF obliged, although U.S. and IMF officials say that the question of whether money would be disbursed was left entirely to the IMF.[130]

IMF managing director Michel Camdessus explicitly tied these funds to Yeltsin's course of reform, warning that the loans would be terminated if a different course [that is, communist course] were adopted.[131] The former finance minister, Boris Fyodorov, a one-time proponent of massive aid to Russia when he was in power, criticized the agreement, arguing that "this money corrupts the system. . . . The moment you get a billion dollars you delay necessary measures."[132] Yeltsin and his campaign team, however, welcomed the financial infusion with great enthusiasm.

In retrospect, U.S. and IMF officials still argued that Russia was performing well on its commitments to the 1995 standby agreement.[133] After the October 1994 ruble crash, the new Russian government, under the leadership of Deputy Prime Minster Anatoly Chubais, had undertaken drastic measures to achieve stabilization in 1995. The IMF believed that given what had been accomplished, a bolder program like the EFF was the natural next step. The IMF officials also saw the advantages of signing a multiyear deal before the elections as a way to lock in the program no matter who won the vote. In the event of a communist victory, Zyuganov would have to take the difficult step of canceling the program.[134] Maintaining the IMF relationship, especially when Zyuganov would be trying to prove his competency to the outside world, would require much less political will. However, if no agreement was signed before the vote, it would have been much more difficult for Zyuganov to take the proactive initiative of signing a new agreement.

Deterring Cancellation

On March 18, 1996, Ambassador Pickering communicated to Washington a warning from Yegor Gaidar about Yeltsin's plans to postpone the election for two years.[135] Another well-connected Russian official approached Blacker, NSC senior director, to test his reaction to postponement. The Clinton team met to discuss scenarios and U.S. preemptive and responsive policy options. As Talbott recalled, "The best [outcome for the Clinton administration] was a Yeltsin victory, the worst a Zyuganov one, but the trickiest was what we called a 'Yeltsin cheat or steal.'" Although very worried about this third plot, the Clinton officials recognized that they had few policy tools to deter such a plan. They opted to refrain from making any public threats about sanctions should the election be postponed. Instead, they used quiet but urgent diplomacy. At the urging of Pickering and Talbott, Clinton sent Yeltsin a private message that registered his "strongest disapproval of any violation of the constitution." As Talbott explains, "He [Clinton] felt we had no choice. He'd backed Yeltsin through thick and thin, always on the grounds that the U.S. was supporting not just the man but the principle, that Russia would work its way out of its crisis through elections, referendums and constitutional rule." And Berger says that "Clinton was always very tough with Yeltsin on this."[136]

By the end of the day on March 18, Yeltsin appeared to have decided against postponement. The idea, however, lingered, in part because Korzhakov wanted it to linger. Clinton repeatedly pushed the importance of holding the presidential vote in phone calls he had with Yeltsin that spring. During a call on May 7, Yeltsin explained to Clinton that those in his Kremlin pushing for postponement were expressing their "personal opinions" and hinted that he might fire such people. And during one call, Yeltsin reassured Clinton by saying that he was the "guarantor of the Russia constitution."[137] Yeltsin's message had an upside and a downside. On the upside, he sounded like he rejected the idea of postponement. On the downside, his admission made clear that someone close to the president was whispering such ideas into Yeltsin's ear.

The Advisers

Independent of the Clinton administration, a Russian émigré living in the United States helped to recruit a team of campaign consultants based in California. Ironically, these consultants ended up working for the same faction in the Kremlin campaign that was pushing hard for postponement. They had little contact with the reformist wing of the re-election campaign headed by Anatoly Chubais that eventually assumed full control of the campaign effort in March 1996 and pushed to the sidelines Korzhakov and his campaign team.[138] Unaware of these internal battles within the Yeltsin entourage, the American campaign consultants nonetheless did what they could to support their marginalized clients. They did succeed in meeting with Yeltsin's daughter and played a useful role in educating her in campaign techniques, but they never had a personal meeting with their candidate or anyone in the leadership ranks of the campaign headquarters.[139]

No senior members of Clinton's foreign policy team were informed of the American operation in Moscow other than Al Gore and Sandy Berger. Paradoxically, the president that benefited most from their work was in Washington, not Moscow. Richard Dresner, the head of the American consulting team in Moscow, was a close associate of Dick Morris (and a Republican). Morris began feeding to Clinton on a regular basis polling data obtained by and strategy memos written by the American team in Moscow. Morris had strict orders never to "advise [the president] on foreign policy in front of any other person." Although Morris also talked to Gore and Berger, he stayed away from National Security Adviser Tony Lake, who found this intervention by Morris into foreign policy appalling and dangerous, as did Talbott. Nonetheless, Clinton was a political junkie, who could not help but become wrapped up in Yeltsin's re-election effort.[140] Using the data provided by Morris, Clinton then gave Yeltsin campaign advice, something Morris says he loved to do:

> Clinton came to realize there were two things he was good at. One was winning an election. The other was charming people and making them feel close to him. He decided that through those two strengths he would fashion his own foreign policy. The latter skill was in evidence in Northern Ireland. The former skill was in evidence in getting Yeltsin re-elected and in developing a sense of trust with Yeltsin. What that really amounted to was a view on Clinton's part that he would transcend the notion of national interest and replace it with personal partisan political interest on the part of the foreign leader. That in a sense he would help Boris Yeltsin meet his political goals in Russia by being his political consultant.[141]

Senior foreign policy officials in the Clinton administration detested these direct forms of intervention in the Russian electoral process. For some, it was morally wrong. For others, it was strategically unwise, since any hint of American involvement might taint the very candidate that the United States wanted to win. When given the chance to scale back American involvement in Russia's electoral process, U.S. State Department officials usually did.[142]

Indirectly, however, American democracy assistance programs did contribute to Yeltsin's re-election effort. As dicussed earlier, both the International Republican Institute and National Democratic Institute initiated programs in the Soviet Union in 1990 and opened offices in Russia in 1992. In these early years, both institutions focused their efforts on party building, which included training programs on how to win elections.[143] Dozens of active participants in NDI and IRI programs worked on Yeltsin's re-election campaign.[144] Tracing the causal relationship between these training programs and the effectiveness of the campaign, of course, is fraught with complexity.[145] Yet, many of the campaign technologies deployed in this campaign, such as direct mail projects or door-to-door campaigns, were all "made in America."

Still on the Sidelines

Did any of these American initiatives help Yeltsin win re-election? Probably not. Russian voters did not cast their ballots in these elections based on rec-ommendations from Clinton. At its core, the 1996 presidential vote was a choice between two opposite political and socioeconomic systems. It was a referendum about Russia's future, not a vote about specific issues, foreign or domestic.[146] In this kind of vote, it is difficult to trace the impact of the IMF program, let alone the importance of Clinton's trip to Moscow in April. In the margins, the IMF loans may have contributed to the government's ability to make transfers to regional heads of administration, but these new funds only began to arrive in Moscow just before the vote. Moreover, these funds went directly to the Central Bank, not the government. Compared with funds raised by the Finance Ministry through bonds, the IMF money constituted a small sum. These outside sources were also only a very small fraction of the resources that Russia's oligarchs claimed to provide to the campaign. David Hoffman's careful investigation of contributions from the oligarchs reveals that their support was grossly exaggerated. Finally, Yeltsin promised a lot more pork than he delivered. After the election was over, Yeltsin's government sim-ply refused to pay for many of the promises that he made on the campaign trail.[147]

More indirectly, Clinton's unequivocal support for Yeltsin may have helped the Russian president establish his reputation as the keeper of stability. Especially in the latter stages of the campaign, Yeltsin campaign organizers sought to contrast the guarantee of stability under Yeltsin with the likelihood of instability under Zyuganov. The return of confrontation with the West should the communists win was part of this campaign message. Measuring the causal relevance of American gestures to this electoral goal, however, is very difficult.[148]

Did Clinton's note and phone requests to Yeltsin help dissuade the Russian president from postponing the election? This intervention is also difficult to judge. In his final memoir, Yeltsin recalls his flirtation with postponement, but he gives his daughter, Tatyana Dyachenko, and Chubais, not Clinton, the credit for dissuading him from executing the antidemocratic plan.[149] At the same time, Yeltsin strongly valued his relationship with Clinton. Clinton offi-cials believe that the prospect of losing face with his buddies in the West played a role in Yeltsin's thinking.

Conclusion

After many tense weeks of uncertainty, cancellation of Russia's 1996 presiden-tial election was yet another disastrous dog that did not bark. Nor did the pre-dicted and feared tragedy of communist restoration occur. Yeltsin's second-round victory in July 1996 was a huge relief. As Clinton told Russian deputy foreign minister Mamedov in the Oval Office after the election, "We were dancing in the White House after the results came in."[150]

Yeltsin won despite suffering a heart attack between election rounds. Some worried that Yeltsin's heart problems were the sign of bad times to come. Most, however, had the opposite reaction. With communism now defeated and Yeltsin reaffirmed as president for another four years, Clinton officials expressed optimism that their man in Moscow might be able to finally press ahead with delayed economic reforms. Yeltsin's dismissal of Korzhakov and his "party of war" allies between rounds and the reemergence of Anatoly Chubais as a Kremlin insider (he eventually became Yeltsin's chief of staff) were grounds for even more optimism about the market and democratic reform agenda. The regime transformers in the Clinton team suddenly had newly strengthened allies in Moscow. Now that Russia's revolution seemed on track again, the Clinton administration was eager to press ahead with its arms control agenda and NATO enlargement, two issues that had been delayed in part by the uncertainty of Russia's first post-Soviet presidential election. After Clinton wrapped up his re-election bid that November, those planning to stay on for the second term had ambitious plans and high aspirations for U.S.-Russian relations. They would be deeply disappointed.

7

Security Partners?

Since Bill Clinton strongly believed that assisting Russia's internal transformation to a democracy and a market economy was a core U.S. national interest, he also believed that thorny foreign policy issues carried over from the previous administration had to get resolved. In part this was because the outcomes were significant for U.S. interests, but even more important, because he and his team worried that not resolving them would derail the larger effort to assist Russia's economic and political transformation. It seemed a vicious circle: if Russia stalled its withdrawal of troops from the Baltic states of Estonia, Latvia, and Lithuania, for example, the U.S. Congress would withhold democracy and market assistance. But if aid were withheld, the administration feared that the transformation necessary to make Russia a full partner in the West would never take place. Above all, the Clinton administration wanted to help ensure the irreversibility of Russia's transition away from its communist, imperial, and anti-Western past.

The administration knew that it was asking the Russian government, and especially the Russian military, to "eat a lot of spinach" in trying to resolve a range of security issues, and the new team looked for ways to make this as easy as possible.[1] If absolutely necessary, the Clinton administration would get tough, but it preferred to find ways to cajole, coopt, and bribe Yeltsin and his government. This thinking was not new. In its final year in power, Secretary James Baker's team at the State Department had made the argument that the United States had to reciprocate Russian cooperative behavior or it would engender a backlash in Russia. What did change was that the Clinton team was much more active in finding carrots that could induce the desired Russian behavior.

From the start of the Clinton administration, the United States also worked to foster a bureaucratic process on the Russian side that could manage the problems that arose. Ambassador-at-Large for the New Independent States Strobe Talbott created a Strategic Stability Group with Deputy Foreign Minister Georgy Mamedov that allowed both sides to develop an interagency process that would be led by the diplomats in the U.S. State Department and in the Russian Foreign Ministry. As mentioned earlier, Presidents Clinton and Yeltsin also created a Bi-National Commission chaired by Vice President Al Gore and Prime Minister Viktor Chernomyrdin, which was established in part to try to rein in some of Russia's more independent and less cooperative government actors, particularly those responsible for the sale of sensitive technologies to states like Iran. At first the commission dealt mainly with energy and space issues, but it grew to encompass a broad range of bilateral issues that were not being solved in other venues.

The early efforts on the security side were in part necessary because of several core unresolved issues that remained after the collapse of the Soviet Union. First on the list was ensuring that nuclear weapons in Ukraine, Kazakhstan, and Belarus inherited after the breakup of the Soviet Union be shipped to Russia for dismantlement. Russian cooperation was critical for keeping a balky Ukraine on track and committed to achieving this goal as soon as possible since any tension in Russian-Ukrainian relations made Ukraine more hesitant about eliminating its potential nuclear deterrent (although it never had independent command and control over the weapons). The other major security issue was keeping Russia on a tight schedule to remove troops from the Baltic nations of Lithuania, Latvia, and Estonia, whose sovereignty and independence could not be secure if Russian troops remained entrenched.

Besides these lingering issues from the Soviet collapse, a new postcommunist issue came to the fore early in the Clinton administration that officials feared could undermine the effort to assist Russia's internal transformation: the obscure problem of Russia's provision of cryogenic technology to the India Space Rocket Organization (ISRO). The Russian sale of this technology violated the Missile Technology Control Regime, which had been created to prevent new states from acquiring the capacity of delivering weapons of mass destruction. This Russian technology transfer threatened to bring U.S. sanctions down on the Yeltsin government's head in the summer of 1993 at the precise moment when Clinton was pushing his major assistance package. By 1995, a second Russian activity developed that had even more potential to thwart efforts to create a new U.S.-Russian security partnership for addressing threats of mutual concern: Russian sales of nuclear technology to Iran.

Russian and American disagreements about this trade with India and Iran highlighted a potential problem in the Wilsonian vision of international politics. Even if Russia were to become a full-fledged democracy and market economy, would Russia really stop pursuing these lucrative contracts? The benefits of Russia's regime change for American national security interests were real, but even under the best of circumstances, regime change was not going to be some magic silver bullet that would eliminate every conflict between the United States and Russia.

Finally, some policies that the United States and its Western partners began pushing elsewhere in Europe and Eurasia antagonized Russia and threatened a domestic backlash against Boris Yeltsin, and thus became contentious issues in the overall U.S.-Russia agenda. First and foremost from the fall of 1994 (through the summer of 1997) was the U.S. effort to design a path for prospective membership for those central and eastern European nations that wished to join NATO. Second was the need by early 1995 for the United States to do something about the horrific conflict that raged in Bosnia; officials in Washington understood that any solution brought about by the United States would be viewed as humiliating to Russia's military and political elite given their strong ties to the Serbian government. Third, the Russians felt straitjacketed by a Conventional Forces in Europe (CFE) Treaty scheduled for implementation in November 1995 that limited their ability to station more military equipment in the Caucasus as they were trying to quell the secessionist movement in Chechnya with massive military force. At a lower level of intensity (at least in the first part of the decade), American and Russian officials also had to manage several issues in which their national interests seemed to clash in the former Soviet Union. For instance, American oil companies, supported by their government, became increasingly active in exploring new opportunities for expansion in countries surrounding the Caspian Sea. Russian officials perceived these American initiatives not as win-win market transactions but as encroachments on Russian geostrategic interests.[2] American and Russian diplomats had different interpretations of American military-to-military contacts with countries bordering Russia.[3] For Americans, these relationships helped to facilitate integration of the region into the West and ensured the independence of the non-Russian new independent states. For Russians, this kind of cooperation looked like encirclement.

In the first term of the Clinton administration, U.S. decisions reflected a general policy of creating incentives for Russian cooperation as part of the larger effort to assist Russia's domestic transformation, strengthen Yeltsin, and generally avoid "losing Russia." The administration offered Russia a chance at substantial cooperation in the launching of commercial satellites and partnership in a joint International Space Station if Russia would abandon its support for the India rocket deal. In Vancouver in April 1993, Clinton offered Yeltsin financial assistance to pay for new housing in Russia for Russian officers in order to make troop withdrawal from the Baltics easier for Yeltsin to carry out. The new U.S. administration switched from the Bush administration's approach of merely threatening Ukraine that it would be isolated internationally if it failed to denuclearize to a strategy of cooperation. Clinton's administration offered Ukraine Nunn-Lugar assistance and participation in a deal with Russia that provided compensation for the highly enriched uranium (HEU) processed from the dismantled warheads (while still making clear that the threat of isolation remained). The administration also kept NATO enlargement from becoming a reality until after Boris Yeltsin's re-election in July 1996, ensured that Russia had a place in the implementation force that was created to keep peace in Bosnia at the end of 1995, offered relief on the CFE Treaty, and tried to find the right incentives to keep Russia from helping Iran build a nuclear weapons program.

The administration officials responsible for Russia policy always worked feverishly to keep any one issue from undermining Yeltsin and contributing to the return of the communists or the victory of Vladimir Zhirinovsky and his fascist allies. This fear for Yeltsin's hold on power lasted until the Russian president's re-election in July 1996. As Talbott aide Victoria Nuland recalls, "The whole first Clinton term in my memory is about helping democrats survive and about buyout on tough Westernizer decisions. And every strand that's pursued is one of those two things. It's very easy with 20-20 hindsight to forget how absolutely fragile it felt at the time . . . all the way through [July] 1996." Every issue discussed in the following paragraphs, according to Nuland, "was hard. None was a foregone conclusion, and every one was a litmus test for our saying they are still on the right track."[4]

Although a real partnership seemed to be emerging in 1993–94, tensions in the security relationship would grow over time because the United States had other foreign policy interests in the world besides Russia. Since Russia was weak, the United States pursued those interests and expected Boris Yeltsin, after all his bombastic complaining, to go along with the American approach. In the case of NATO enlargement and NATO's actions in the Balkans, the United States could largely set the agenda unilaterally, and so Russia was forced to accede to the American approach. But on Iran, where the United States needed Russia to alter its behavior, the policy eventually failed.

Because the relationship would sour in the security field as it did in the other areas of the relationship as the 1990s wore on, the resolution of the three relatively obscure but potentially explosive problems of Russia's relationship with India, Ukrainian nuclear weapons, and Russian troops in the Baltics became a critical piece of the puzzle of U.S.-Russian relations after the cold war. In 1993–94, the policy of inducing Russia to accept the U.S. objectives was working even in areas where the United States needed Russia's cooperation to be successful. By the second half of the 1990s, on issues like arms control and Russian-Iranian relations, the strategy produced fewer results.

India and the Immediate Threat of Sanctions

The first thorny security issue to confront the Clinton administration as it embarked on its task of assisting Russia's transition to a market economy and democracy and of creating a security partner for the United States was Russian sales of cryogenic rocket engines and technology to the Indian Space Research Organization (ISRO). The United States contended that Russia's actions constituted a violation of American and international prohibitions against the sale of technologies that might facilitate the proliferation of weapons of mass destruction (and development of the vehicles to launch them) and automatically according to U.S. law carried the threat of American sanctions. If Russia refused to change its behavior, then the strategy of supporting Boris Yeltsin and the effort to establish a working relationship between Vice President Gore and Prime Minister Chernomyrdin would be derailed.

In this first instance of clearing away a potentially troublesome issue, the Clinton administration embarked on a path that it would repeat many times in succeeding years: offer Russia serious incentives to abandon its old ways in favor of joining the Western club. The Clinton team offered new kinds of carrots that could only be put on the table for a new market-oriented, Western-friendly Russia. In these early years of the Clinton-Yeltsin relationship, Russia was receiving something tangible and responded as the United States hoped it would.

Al Gore: Sanctions Man

Ironically, the reason that the Clinton administration faced the legal problem of having to sanction Russia was largely because of the efforts of Senator Al Gore, who was a major force in Congress behind the Missile Technology Control Act, passed in 1990 as part of the defense authorization bill. In July 1989, Gore and Senator John McCain (R-Ariz.) had introduced an act that would fill gaps in an informal agreement among the Group of Seven (G-7) industrial powers established in April 1987 known as the Missile Technology Control Regime (MTCR).[5]

The United States had promoted the MTCR as a way of getting international agreement among its major allies for adherence to the U.S. approach on technology transfer. As communist regimes began to fall after 1989, countries that were previously part of the proliferation problem joined the MTCR. But the two major suppliers, China and the Soviet Union, could take advantage of restraint on the part of the G-7 and others in order to establish sales to countries like India and Pakistan, which were in the process of developing the capability of building weapons of mass destruction and the systems to deliver them.

In stepped Gore and McCain, with strong support in the House from Congressman Howard Berman (D-Calif.). The Gore-McCain Missile and Proliferation Control Act in the summer of 1989 would, as Senator Gore said, "impose sanctions on companies and nations that engage in the trade or development of long-range missile systems capable of delivering weapons of mass destruction."[6] In 1993, now Vice President Gore and the rest of the Clinton administration were confronted with a major test of the legislation from the Russian sales to India.

In the spring of 1992, the Bush administration first threatened to impose sanctions on both India and Russia over the deal that had been struck between the Russian space agency, Glavkosmos, and ISRO. Russia argued that the engines and technology it contracted to sell did not violate the MTCR because they were being used for peaceful purposes, and the government invited an international team to inspect their adherence to MTCR guidelines. First Deputy Minister of Foreign Economic Relations Sergei Glazyev also demanded a carrot in exchange for Russia formally joining the MTCR regime: an elimination of the trade barriers erected during the cold war to Russian exports still imposed by the United States. From the U.S. perspective, Russia was violating the MTCR, and the Bush administration threat turned to reality. The United States announced it was sanctioning ISRO and Glavkosmos for two years.[7]

By the fall of 1992, however, President Bush had to certify that Russia was not violating the MTCR in order to be able to provide assistance under the newly passed Freedom Support Act. Assistant Secretary of State for European and Canadian Affairs Thomas M.T. Niles and Assistance Coordinator Richard Armitage wrote in an unclassified memorandum to Secretary of State Lawrence Eagleburger that before October 24, 1992, the United States had imposed sanctions on Glavkosmos but had also established a dialogue to resolve the problems that had arisen. In order to allow assistance to move forward, the memo stated, "The President has not determined that after October 24, 1992, the Government of Russia knowingly transferred to another country . . . missiles or missile technology inconsistent with the guidelines and parameters of the Missile Technology Control Regime."[8] In fact, the problem of sanctionable activity had not disappeared, and the new Clinton administration found itself face to face with the problem at precisely the moment that the president was exhorting his team to think big on Russian assistance.

The Clinton Administration and Proliferation

During the transition, the Clinton team in Little Rock, Arkansas, made the decision to make combating the proliferation of weapons of mass destruction a major priority. As the transition team worked to organize the National Security Council, it decided to promote Daniel Poneman, formerly a director in the Defense Policy directorate in the Bush administration, into a newly created slot as a senior director at the National Security Council (NSC) for nonproliferation. In addition, arms control expert Rose Gottemoeller, who was seeking a position in the Clinton administration to work on the Nunn-Lugar programs and denuclearization issues, was given a job in the Russia directorate at the NSC. Her presence would enable the Russia team and the nonproliferation team to work closely together from the start.[9]

Because of Vice President Gore's work on nonproliferation in the U.S. Senate, NSC staffers wasted no time in meeting with National Security Adviser to the Vice President Leon Fuerth to figure out how Gore was likely to react to the Russian sales. Meanwhile, Clinton's national security adviser, Anthony Lake, had told Poneman that the test of the new administration's nonproliferation policy would be the extent to which it was "woven into the fabric of our bilateral relationships." Poneman knew that the Russian assistance to India could trigger sanctions under the U.S. missile sanctions law, and he felt that at the time, the State Department experts were simply giving the White House "warmed over options dusted off from December [1992]." When these were presented to Fuerth, the vice president's right-hand man responded, "We will be tested many times, so we can't just roll over on this one." The White House directed Poneman and Gottemoeller to get an interagency team together to come up with a creative solution.[10]

That creative solution was to pose a stark choice to the Russian space agency and by implication, the Russian government as a whole: did Russian officials want to spend their time on small deals worth millions of dollars with countries U.S. officials called "bottom feeders," or did they want to be part of something the big boys in the G-7 did and join deals worth billions of dollars? To offer something tangible in order to help Russia make the right choice, the Clinton team looked out into space. Not only could the United States remove some of the constraints on allowing the Russians to compete for commercial space launches, but it could offer Russia the chance to participate in the International Space Station, which until then was a consortium effort with the Europeans and Japanese. Publicly, the United States did not state that it was offering a quid pro quo, and it merely declared that it looked forward to more cooperation with countries that abided by nonproliferation norms. But privately, the deal to Yeltsin's government was clear: give up the sale to ISRO and you can be our partners in space.[11]

Those who worked on space issues were not being altruistic. The National Aeronautics and Space Administration (NASA) appreciated that the Russians had experience in long-duration manned flight, and given the technology developed in the Mir space program, they could help the United

States and its partners complete the space station earlier and at less cost than the United States expected. Space was one of the few issue areas in the post–cold war world where the two countries had something significant to offer each other.

Enter Gore-Chernomyrdin

As discussed earlier, in advance of the Vancouver summit between Clinton and Yeltsin in April 1993, Foreign Minister Andrei Kozyrev suggested to Strobe Talbott that Clinton propose to the Russian president the creation of a commission that would be chaired by Vice President Gore and Prime Minister Chernomyrdin. Kozyrev hoped that the commission would force the creation of a more organized interagency process on the Russian side. But as Leon Fuerth recalls, "[Gore] didn't leap at this. There had to be a strong call from the president, and I had to argue the case that he should accept this. [But] he could have had no idea what the 'this' was, since it began from a clean sheet of paper in a discussion between Strobe and me."[12]

Given the vice president's policy interests, the initial focus of the Gore-Chernomydin Commission (GCC) was space and energy. Yeltsin agreed to the idea of a commission, but the ISRO problem remained. Russia wanted the launching of commercial satellites and the space station on the agenda of the first meeting of the GCC to be scheduled for Washington in the summer of 1993. The United States said that the ISRO deal had to be canceled first.[13]

For the United States, overcoming this early problem could satisfy a number of the administration's goals. It would show that the United States could work with Russia to establish a real partnership on an issue of importance to members of the Clinton-Gore team. It would also show the benefits of establishing a commission between Gore and Chernomyrdin to work through problems. And it would establish for many at the NSC and State Department that they could integrate Russia into the West by getting Russian officials to believe that choosing a path that ran counter to Western interests was simply not in Russia's strategic or economic interest—that is, to let them see that cooperation with the West was more fruitful than proliferating to countries like India.

In late June, 1993, however, the deal still had not been struck. On June 20, Deputy Prime Minster Alexander Shokhin met with Undersecretary of State Lynn Davis and told her that Chernomyrdin would come for the GCC meeting in July only if space was on the agenda. Davis suggested that the meeting be postponed until September. Several days later, the United States announced that it was imposing sanctions against two Russian companies for violating the MTCR. The United States did, however, agree to waive the sanctions until July 15, five days after the leaders of the G-7 were scheduled to meet with Yeltsin in Tokyo.[14]

Yeltsin was concerned that the summit might turn sour, and Mamedov called Talbott to ask him to come to Moscow in advance of the Tokyo meetings. On July 3, 1993, Talbott and his team (which included Leon Fuerth and Lynn Davis) met with the Russian president and got what Talbott calls "the full Boris." Yeltsin said it was "totally unacceptable" to sanction Russian companies for the ISRO deal. Yeltsin proposed allowing Russia to continue with the deal until January 1994, "a transitional period." Talbott countered that by that time, Russia would have fulfilled the contract.[15]

Later that evening, Deputy Foreign Minister Mamedov laid out what was for the United States an acceptable proposal: the Russians would freeze the ISRO contract, and then Moscow would have a transition period in which Russia would pull out of the deal. Since there would be no sanctionable Russian activity, there was no need for U.S. sanctions.[16]

In Tokyo, Yeltsin told Clinton that he was sending a new team led by Russia's Space Agency director, Yuri Koptev, to Washington to clinch the deal because, he argued, "Friends don't sanction each other, Bill." Koptev met with Davis on July 14. At 10 p.m., two hours before the sanctions waiver was set to expire, Koptev and Davis reached final agreement. Russia agreed to conform to the MTCR and cancel the transfer of cryogenic rocket engine technology to India (although it would fulfill the contract to supply the engines, a deal worth about $300 to $400 million).[17]

Not everyone in Moscow, however, accepted that a deal was done. On July 21, the Russian parliament passed a resolution saying that it had authority and responsibility to ratify any deal on the ISRO contract that the Yeltsin government had agreed to with the United States. (Russia, as discussed earlier, was in the throes of constitutional crisis between the legislative and executive branches.) The following day, Glavkosmos officials stated that until the Russian Congress had ratified the agreement, the deal with ISRO was still on.[18]

Fortunately for the U.S. position on proliferation, even as American officials were championing democracy, they were benefiting from Yeltsin's growing strength vis-à-vis his parliamentary opposition. The first GCC meeting was held in Washington as planned in September 1993, and it produced a Memorandum of Understanding that Russia would adhere to the MTCR, and the United States would cooperate in space. The United States agreed to spend $400 million dollars over the next three years for the use of Mir modules in U.S. experiments and also agreed conditionally to allow Russians to compete with American companies in the launch of domestic satellites.[19]

A few weeks later, Fuerth, Gottemoeller, and NASA head Daniel Goldin arrived in Moscow for talks on space cooperation. During their stay in Moscow, Yeltsin's forces assaulted the Russian parliament. For the deal on India and cooperation in space, Yeltsin's victory over the parliament would have immediate and positive implications for U.S. foreign policy interests.

Goldin told his counterparts, "We feel for the Russian people, but we're here to talk about the future." And by the time of the next GCC session in Moscow in December 1993, all the elements of the deal were in place. Russia agreed to adhere to the MTCR provisions, the sanctionable activity had been canceled, and space cooperation was real. What had been achieved fulfilled what Talbott viewed as key to the U.S.-Russia agenda. "We have to find ways of making concrete this talk about partnership. We can't just keep mouthing the words."[20]

Ukraine's Nuclear Weapons

Ukraine had agreed to the protocol at Lisbon in April 1992 that made it party to the START Treaty while ensuring that it joined the Non-Proliferation Treaty (NPT) as a non-nuclear power, but there were enormous pressures inside Ukraine not to give up its newfound nuclear deterrent so quickly.[21] In 1992, Secretary of State James Baker had browbeaten the Ukrainian leadership to commit to eliminating all non-Russian strategic nuclear weapons, but he could not browbeat them into actual implementation or get them to stay on the agreed-upon schedule. During the first few months of 1993, it became increasingly clear that Ukrainian backtracking on the non-nuclear commitment was a serious possibility, particularly because in February, the Ukrainian parliament, or Rada, had voted to postpone consideration of the START Treaty.[22] Talbott recalls that Deputy Secretary (and later Secretary) of Defense William J. Perry viewed "Ukraine's reluctance to give up the missiles . . . [as] the single biggest threat to international peace and security that we faced anywhere in the world."[23]

During the U.S.-Russia summit in Vancouver in April 1993, a group of Ukrainian-Americans asked senior U.S. government officials why they were paying attention only to Russia. Talbott asked NSC staffer Rose Gottemoeller to pull together an interagency group to figure out how the United States could keep the process moving whereby the warheads would first be taken out of operational deployment and then transferred out of the country to the Russian Federation for dismantlement.[24]

As the Clinton administration began its policy review in May 1993, it turned to consideration of the sweeteners available to induce the Ukrainian government to move in the right direction.[25] It was no longer enough to threaten Ukraine, as Baker had done in April 1992 to ensure the signing of the Lisbon protocol. To get the Rada to ratify the Lisbon protocol meant finding the right carrot. One of the breakthroughs was deciding that the United States would not insist on moving the weapons out of Ukraine immediately but rather would focus first on getting them off their missiles and into a Ukrainian storage facility pending final resolution. In other words, aid would not be conditioned on parliamentary ratification of START but rather moving to denuclearize with concrete steps and the promise of ratification. And the other was determining that Nunn-Lugar funds for safe and secure dismantlement could be offered if Ukraine made clear that it would get this job done.[26]

As Perry and Assistant Secretary of Defense for International Security Policy Ashton Carter wrote after leaving government, implementing the Nunn-Lugar program was initially quite difficult because of the way the Pentagon staff and budget were structured. Carter has noted that when he came into office in 1993, he had staff responsible for nuclear targeting, and he had staff responsible for pursuing arms control, but he had no staff set up to provide assistance to the new independent republics of the former Soviet Union. He proceeded to create such a structure. But the legislation that was passed in 1991 only authorized the secretary of defense to take money from other existing Pentagon programs and "reprogram" that money to Nunn-Lugar projects, which guaranteed a lack of enthusiasm elsewhere in the building.[27] As the interagency group of officials geared up in May 1993 in advance of Secretary of Defense Les Aspin's trip to Ukraine in July, and as they considered the tools available to ensure denuclearization in Ukraine, they realized that the new democratization in the former Soviet Union was a double-edged sword. On the one hand, the United States wanted to do everything it could to promote free, prosperous, stable, democratic states in what had been Russian imperial space for centuries.[28] On the other hand, the United States could not be sure that a deal struck with Ukraine would be agreed to domestically, as it would also find out over time in Russia as well. An even bigger fear was that Ukrainian governance would become so ineffective that implementation would falter. As Ashton Carter recalls, "I don't think there was a camp [in Ukraine] per se saying that they needed to be a nuclear power. It wasn't so much a bargaining issue; my fear was that they would dither and dawdle so long that this would turn into a fact, or that other facts would intervene that would make this more difficult. For example, I worried that Ukraine would undergo further disaggregation of authority and it would be impossible to reach a deal. Time didn't seem to be on our side and therefore it was urgent to get a deal done on a short timetable."[29]

Ambassador-at-Large Talbott flew to Kiev in May 1993 with a mission to expand the portfolio of activities in the bilateral relationship and to assess what the Ukrainian government wanted.[30] President Leonid Kravchuk was seeking billions of dollars in assistance and a U.S. security guarantee similar to the one provided by NATO allies to one another. Thus began a process whereby Talbott would go to Ukrainian deputy foreign minister Boris Tarasyuk and then to Russian deputy foreign minister Mamedov (and vice versa) to try to work a deal among the parties for removing the Ukrainian nuclear weapons. Russia would be receiving financial compensation as part of its denuclearization efforts, because the United States was creating a mechanism to pay for the highly enriched uranium (HEU) that was coming off the warheads. Since Ukrainian warheads were being transferred to Russia, the regime in Kiev wanted its share of the proceeds. And thus any deal was going to involve all three parties. But as Mamedov told Talbott in May, "Remember, anything between us and the Ukrainians is a family matter, and any disagreement we have is a family feud. Don't expect Russian gratitude if you butt in, however virtuous you may think your intentions are."[31]

Talbott's trip was then followed by a visit from Aspin to Ukraine. In a meeting with Ukrainian parliamentarians, the secretary of defense fueled Russian suspicions about U.S. intentions when he stated, "A non-nuclear Ukraine is a better ally for us. Ukraine is a small country with a big enemy, and we should show that it also has a big friend. Any arrangement that keeps the Russians farther to the East is a good thing." Pavel Grachev, Russia's defense minister, who had just spent time with Aspin in Garmisch, Germany, inaugurating a new center for East-West military consultations, was visibly unhappy.[32]

But in 1993, Yeltsin was still looking to curry favor. At the same G-7 meeting in July in Tokyo at which he made the decision to get the ISRO problem off the agenda, President Yeltsin also suggested that he, Clinton, and President Kravchuk of Ukraine come together to sign a trilateral accord. Clinton, says Talbott, agreed to it "on the spot."[33] For the time being, however, negotiations took place bilaterally: between the United States and Ukraine, between the United States and Russia, and between Russia and Ukraine. And those negotiations were not going smoothly.

In September, Yeltsin and Kravchuk met to resolve a growing dispute over whether Ukraine or Russia owned the former Soviet fleet based out of Ukrainian territory on the Black Sea, as well as discuss the disposition of the nuclear weapons. Yeltsin publicly announced that the two had agreed that if Ukraine transferred strategic nuclear warheads to Russia during the next two years, Russia would compensate Ukraine by providing it with nuclear fuel rods for its nuclear power stations. But the domestic reaction in Ukraine against the Black Sea fleet discussions was so furious that Kravchuk quickly disavowed Yeltsin's statement.[34]

In October, Secretary of State Warren Christopher took his first trip to Ukraine. Just before he left, Kravchuk started to back away from the commitment he had made to James Baker in Lisbon in 1992 to remove all nuclear weapons within the seven-year timetable established for START, and he demanded $2.8 billion in Nunn-Lugar funds and $5 billion in HEU compensation.[35]

On October 25, Christopher met with Kravchuk in Kiev. Kravchuk stated that Ukraine was committed to fulfilling the Lisbon protocol, but the Rada would only ratify START if Ukraine received sufficient compensation. Ukraine was also asking for legally binding security guarantees from the major powers before it proceeded; the United States was insisting on START ratification and accession to the Non-Proliferation Treaty before providing guarantees of any kind (and then presumably only those provided for by the NPT).[36] Kravchuk told Christopher that while he was confident about START ratification, he was much less sure about NPT accession, and he added that the Rada was "part Bolshevik, part nationalist, and part Trotskyite. No one knew what the Rada wanted." Kravchuk also complained that the Russian media "had said that the Secretary had come to Moscow to support Yeltsin, democracy and reform, while he had come to Ukraine to force ratification of START."[37]

Christopher offered $175 million in funds for the safe and secure dismantlement of the nuclear weapons plus $155 million in economic assistance.[38] A month later, the Rada ratified START I, though still claiming that START ceilings did not cover all of the launchers and warheads located on Ukrainian territory, and that the section of the Lisbon protocol calling for joining the NPT as a non-nuclear weapons state in the shortest possible time was not binding. On November 29, Clinton called Kravchuk to get the process back on track. Kravchuk responded that he would resubmit the START and NPT ratification protocols to a new Rada, which would be formed after the March 1994 elections.[39]

By the time of the second Gore-Chernomyrdin Commission (GCC) meeting in mid-December 1993, several outstanding issues still remained, in particular the compensation that Ukraine would be provided for both the tactical nuclear warheads that had already been transferred and the strategic nuclear warheads still needing to come out, and in addition the nature of the security guarantee that the United States would offer. At a GCC lunch, Talbott suggested to Russian foreign minister Kozyrev that the United States would provide the money to ensure the exchange of Russian fuel rods for Ukrainian warheads. But in the aftermath of the strong showing by Vladimir Zhirinvosky in the Russian parliamentary elections only days before, Kozyrev was unwilling to make any commitments.[40]

Sensing it was time to get the three parties together to come to an agreement, Talbott suggested that he and Mamedov fly immediately to Kiev. Gore and Chernomyrdin agreed, and the vice president suggested that Deputy Secretary of Defense William Perry join them.[41] With Perry present, the United States agreed to pay for a transfer of Russian fuel rods to Ukraine in exchange for the withdrawal of the strategic nuclear warheads. The Russians were unwilling to agree publicly to compensation for the tactical nuclear warheads since they had already been withdrawn, but the United States prevailed, saying that a confidential side agreement could be put together that would ensure that Ukraine received something. The United States was willing to offer the standard NPT language on security assurances, but nothing that approached the NATO Article V guarantee.[42] Talbott says the sweetener that clinched the deal was the promise that Clinton would stop in Kiev on his January 1994 trip to Europe, and $100 million in Nunn-Lugar would be released immediately after the accord was signed.[43]

A Ukrainian delegation arrived in Washington in early January to finalize the deal. Vice Premier Valery Shmarov said later, "We had very intense negotiations, during which the American and Russian sides were constantly pressing us to withdraw our conditions and just sign the agreement. We almost walked out of the meeting, [Deputy Foreign Minister] Tarasyuk and I; we practically slammed the door behind us because we just couldn't have a good conversation." The next day, Shmarov and Tarasyuk met with Clinton and Lake at the White House. Lake said the United States was committed to the agreement reached in Kiev. Shmarov asked Clinton not only to stop in Kiev on his upcoming trip but to get Kravchuk invited to Moscow. The president agreed. On January 13, Clinton met Kravchuk at the Kiev airport and invited him to Moscow. On January 14, the three presidents signed the Trilateral Accord in Moscow, which committed Ukraine to the "elimination of all nuclear weapons, including strategic offensive arms, located in its territory." They promised to deactivate all SS-24s (10 warhead monsters) within ten months, when they would also transfer at least 200 strategic nuclear warheads to Russia. And in a private letter to Clinton, Kravchuk promised that Ukraine would be nuclear free by June 1996.[44]

The United States for its part agreed to pay Russia $60 million in order to ship 100 tons of nuclear fuel to Ukraine; this money would come from the U.S. purchases of highly enriched uranium from Russia. The United States and Russia would reaffirm Ukrainian territorial integrity in line with the provisions of the 1975 Helsinki Final Act (which sought to ensure that any border changes in Europe occurred peacefully), and in a secret side letter, would establish a commission to determine the value of the HEU already transferred by Ukraine. Russia also agreed to forgive some of the Ukrainian debt that was owed to Russia for energy supplies. The Rada then ratified START I without any conditions, and when Kravchuk visited Washington in March, Clinton announced that Ukraine's aid package would grow to $750 million. Later that year, the United States, Great Britain, and Russia provided Ukraine with stronger security guarantees, and Ukraine formally acceded to the Non-Proliferation Treaty as a non-nuclear weapons state. And in June 1996, although fingers stayed crossed until the last moment, Ukraine completed the transfer of its final nuclear weapons to Russia.[45]

In its first year in office, the Clinton administration had taken two difficult issues left over from the previous administration and resolved them. In getting the Russians to give up their deal with the India Space Rocket Organization and in getting the Ukrainians to implement the Lisbon protocol (which could not happen without Russian cooperation), the administration had made clear what the penalties would be for failing to accede to U.S. demands, but it had also offered new and attractive carrots. In both cases, substantial assistance had to be put forward to resolve what otherwise would have been thorny problems that could threaten the entire assistance agenda. This pattern would continue in 1994 as the United States and Russia dealt with a third unresolved security issue that threatened to get in the way of the larger U.S. efforts to assist Russia's transformation and integration: ensuring that Russian troops completed their withdrawal from the Baltic states.

Russian Troops in the Baltic States

When the Soviet Union collapsed, well over 100,000 Red Army troops were stationed in Estonia, Latvia, and Lithuania. These three Baltic nations had been forcibly brought into the Soviet empire in 1940, and the United States had never legally recognized their incorporation in the USSR. After the Soviet Union dissolved, the Baltic states wanted all of these occupying troops out in order clearly to establish their newly achieved independence. They also wanted the Russians to abandon their radar site at Skrunda, Latvia, and their nuclear submarine facility in Paldiski, Estonia. Yeltsin responded to these American requests unenthusiastically, since the new Russian government had no place for returning troops to live, and the military valued its facilities in Skrunda and Paldiski. Tied up more generally with the humiliation of retreating from strategic and imperial positions in the aftermath of the Soviet breakup, this issue was yet another irritant for U.S.-Russian relations that would either get resolved or would threaten to unravel the efforts to assist Russia's economic and political transition.[46]

The Bush administration had made some progress on troop withdrawal in 1992. At the 1992 G-7 summit meeting, Yeltsin had stated that "a political decision has been made to withdraw the troops completely." Later that summer, the Russians committed to the "early, orderly and complete withdrawal" of the troops. At the same time, Foreign Minister Andrei Kozyrev outlined the conditions that Russia would impose in order to fulfill that commitment, which included money to build housing for those troops returning to Russia and greater protection of human rights for ethnic Russians still living in the Baltic countries. Russian officials also made clear that they planned to maintain the radar site and nuclear training facility. For the newly independent Baltic leaders, however, an illegal occupation meant that no discussion of conditions was justified.[47]

When the Clinton administration came into office, the Russians had only agreed to an August 31, 1993, deadline for withdrawal of troops from Lithuania, the Baltic country with the smallest ethnic Russian population and no key Russian military facilities. Estonia and Latvia posed more significant problems for Russia because they had large ethnic Russian populations (and the valued military facilities); of the 1.6 million people living in Estonia, for example, roughly 300,000 were ethnic Russians. Most contentious were the 10,000 retired Soviet military officers wishing to gain Estonian residency, who were not welcomed by Estonian officials.

U.S. National Security Adviser Anthony Lake personally believed in the intrinsic importance of Baltic independence, and the Balts had tremendous political support on Capitol Hill stemming from the efforts during the cold war to support the rights of these "captive nations." If Russian troops did not leave, Congress would try to hold the rest of the U.S. agenda for Russia hostage and would limit American dollars to assist Russia's transformation. Talbott recalled later, "There was a meeting with the President very early on . . . where we talked about the Baltics. And we identified getting the Russian troops out of the Baltics as exceedingly important, comparable to the goal of getting Russian nuclear weapons out of Ukraine while bolstering Ukraine's security and independence."[48]

At their April 1993 summit in Vancouver, Clinton raised with Yeltsin the need for clear commitments and follow-through on troop withdrawal from all three Baltic countries. Yeltsin responded that he needed money for officer housing. Clinton initially offered $6 million to build 450 housing units for returning Russian officers, and Yeltsin made an impassioned plea for more. By the time the G-7 met with Yeltsin in Tokyo in July, the United States had increased the offer by another 5,000 housing units; total proposed assistance for this project had reached $165 million.[49]

Some in Congress objected to using American taxpayers' dollars to build new condos for Russian officers. As Talbott recalls, "We discovered with [Alabama Republican Congressman] Sonny Callahan and [Louisiana Republican Congressman] Bob Livingston that officer housing was an absolute killer. Livingston and others kept lists of American officers who didn't have housing or who weren't satisfied with their housing." But the administration had a trump card to play: the Baltic-American lobby. NSC staffer Nicholas Burns had served as White House liaison with that group since 1990 and was able to use these lobbying groups to push Congress to finance officers' housing not as a way of supporting the Russian military but in order to get them out of Latvia and Estonia.[50]

A major problem for Estonia and Latvia was the deterioration in the Russian political scene during 1993. As Yeltsin was battling his nationalist and pro-Soviet foes in the Russian Supreme Soviet and at the same time trying to keep his military loyal (in case they were needed in the showdown with the parliament, as they eventually were), it was difficult for him politically to do what the West and the Balts wanted on troop withdrawal. Yeltsin looked even more vulnerable after Zhirinovsky's surprising performance in the December 1993 parliamentary elections. During his campaign, Zhirinovsky stridently chastised Yeltsin for not doing enough to defend ethnic Russians in the "near abroad." But in part as a result of this electoral outcome and the threat to the Baltic states that Zhirinovsky raised, in the aftermath of those elections, the U.S. Congress was even more eager to tie American assistance for Russian reform to Russian troop withdrawal from the Baltic states. Burns recalled later that the administration had "served notice that progress in the Baltics was something of a litmus test of Yeltsin's commitment to change. . . . The President raised it in every phone call and letter to Yeltsin during that period."[51]

The Clinton team used the president's upcoming trip to Europe in January 1994 to try to get some resolution on this issue. The United States proposed to Latvia a deal by which Russia would be allowed to operate the Skrunda radar site for four years after the completed troop withdrawal and then have another eighteen months to complete the dismantlement of the site. (U.S. defense officials were nervous about shutting down Skrunda since it provided early warning to Russia in the event of nuclear attack, and its absence might put Russian strategic rocket forces on hair trigger alert.) Latvia's president, Guntis Ulmanis, agreed, and when Clinton went to Moscow in January, he proposed the new deal. Yeltsin accepted. Ulmanis was still nervous about his political opposition at home, and to help him, Clinton invited opposition parliamentarians to Washington to gain their acceptance later in the month, where they met with the president, Vice President Gore, and National Security Adviser Lake. The United States and Sweden also offered financial assistance for the Skrunda dismantlement process, a sum that eventually reached $7 million.[52]

In late April 1994, Yeltsin and Ulmanis met in Moscow and sealed their deal. The Russians committed to troop withdrawal by August 31, 1994; the Latvians agreed to the proposed arrangement for Skrunda and permanent residence for Russian military pensioners who had retired in Latvia before the collapse of the Soviet Union. Two countries down; one to go. But the last one was Estonia, the most difficult because of the high number of Russians living there, including the 10,000 retired Soviet military personnel, and the questions that had been raised about whether Estonia would allow those retired personnel to remain in Estonia as civilian pensioners.[53]

Clinton was scheduled to meet Yeltsin in Naples, Italy, during a G-7 meeting in July 1994, a gathering that would be preceded by the first ever visit by a sitting U.S. president to the Baltic states. The day before Clinton left for Europe, Yeltsin called to say that there had been some progress in the Russian-Estonian talks, but Russia was unlikely to meet the August 31 deadline. Clinton stressed to Yeltsin the importance of staying on track. And he said to his team (using a phrase that he would often repeat in various forms to express his philosophy in dealing with Yeltsin): "It's a pretty simple deal. We get 'em into the G-7 and they get out of the Baltics. If they're part of the big boys' club, they've got less reason to beat up on the little guys."[54]

In Latvia, Clinton met with Estonian president Lennart Meri. The United States had been working through U.S. ambassador Robert Frasure to craft a proposal in advance of the Clinton-Meri meeting. According to Nicholas Burns, Clinton said to Meri at their meeting, "How would it be if I offered to take a very realistic proposal from you on the troop withdrawal personally to President Yeltsin?" Meri replied, "Mr. President, I accept your offer, and I will communicate my proposal to you in Naples through your Ambassador, Mr. Frasure." Burns recalled later, "[Frasure] cabled [the proposal] to us from Tallinn to Naples, and . . . we had it typed up, and the President handed it to Yeltsin. And the President was able to say, 'I've been able to work out with President Meri, on the basis of my July 6 meeting with him in Riga, the following offer. And I can vouch for its good offices and its integrity and sincerity.'"[55]

Clinton and his advisers thought Yeltsin's response in the meeting was positive. And Clinton at the press conference gave Yeltsin what he wanted, saying, "As you know, this was a very important day in which President Yeltsin joined us as a full partner in the G-8 for political discussions."[56] (U.S. Treasury Department officials continued to resist formally recasting the G-7 as a G-8 owing to the G-7's role in managing the global economy.)

Yeltsin went second. First he made clear that he was not asking for "preferential conditions" for full membership in a G-8, but rather simply seeking that the West finally "take that red jacket off the President of Russia." But then came the bombshell. Longtime White House correspondent Helen Thomas asked the Russian president whether he would meet the August 31 deadline for troop withdrawal. And Yeltsin, who often surprised the Americans with his public remarks, replied, "I like the question, because I can say no. We took [soldiers] out of Lithuania...and we're going to take . . . that last soldier from Latvia. Now Estonia [is a] somewhat more difficult relationship since there in Estonia, there are very crude violations of human rights, vis-à-vis the Russian speaking population, especially toward military pensioners. . . . I promised Bill that I will meet with . . . the President of Estonia. We're going to discuss these issues, and after, we're going to try to find a solution to this question."[57]

Because of Talbott's promotion to Deputy Secretary earlier in the year, the president's top Russia expert was no longer exclusively working on Russia and the other former Soviet republics. Talbott had not been on the trip to Latvia and Naples because he was at home managing the crisis brewing in Haiti, and he blames himself for failing to ensure a better outcome in Naples.[58] But in general, regardless of how these summits went (and Yeltsin's press conferences became notorious for color and spontaneity), Clinton often used meetings with Yeltsin to create the sense that the two leaders had made commitments to each other. He would then follow up with a phone call or letter that reminded Yeltsin of things he had said privately and needed to accomplish. Yeltsin would do the same with Clinton. Thus, their summits were important to Clinton as a means of getting his man in Moscow to resolve thorny issues. And so it was in this instance. Clinton wrote a letter after Naples urging Yeltsin to meet with Meri as soon as possible and fulfill his commitments; the Germans and Swedes sent similar letters. It was critical for Clinton's overall efforts toward Russia that the deadline be met; Congress was making clear that if Russian troops remained in the Baltics past August 31, the administration's economic assistance program would be suspended.[59]

Just before Meri's scheduled visit to Moscow on July 26, Talbott was in Bangkok for the Association of Southeast Asian Nations' (ASEAN) regional forum (ARF). Meeting with Kozyrev, Talbott told the Russian foreign minister that the United States would no longer be able to support Russian participation in the ARF, the Political Eight (that is, the G-7 plus Russia), or the Balkans Contact Group if Russia did not get its troops out on schedule. Kozyrev was extremely pessimistic.[60]

To the surprise of many, at their meeting on July 26, Yeltsin and Meri agreed to complete the troop withdrawal process by the end of the following month. In his public comments on the deal, Yeltsin cited the letters from Clinton and Kohl. But he also made clear to his domestic audience that Russia had bargained hard for the rights of ethnic Russians in Estonia. Clinton told Talbott over dinner at the latter's house, "I knew he'd do the right thing in the end."[61]

The Thorniest of All: The Bushehr Nuclear Reactor

For the first two years of the Clinton administration, dealing with security issues meant managing issues that had little public visibility—the India rocket deal, the denuclearization of Ukraine, the withdrawal of troops from the Baltics—but that could upset the overall policy of attempting to transform and integrate Russia had they not been dealt with effectively. There had been major sighs of relief within the U.S. government at the end of the summer of 1994, both because the domestic Russian situation finally seemed stable and because these nagging security issues had been resolved. As Victoria Nuland recalls, "We were feeling stable for the first time . . . less like every month was an emergency."[62]

Before long, however, two enormous foreign policy issues threatened to throw the U.S.-Russian relationship completely off the tracks. The U.S. push to enlarge NATO into central Europe led to a blistering Russian reaction; and the continued Russian sales of technologies that could be used by Iran to develop nuclear weapons frustrated the Clinton administration and led to calls from Congress to end assistance programs to Russia.

No issue dominated U.S.-Russian relations more in the Clinton administration's first term than NATO enlargement, but enlargement, as chapter 8 discusses, was ultimately managed successfully. Iran, however, was a very different story. Like the other issues discussed in this chapter, the United States needed Russia to do something in order to achieve a policy success (unlike other policies, for example, NATO enlargement, on which the United States could forge ahead regardless of Russia). And through 1995, the issue seemed to be moving toward resolution. In the end, however, the United States failed to stem Russian assistance to Iran, and the Clinton administration's second term was marked by sanctions against Russian entities and revelations of secret deals reneged on by the Russians.

In part the failure to solve the problem more satisfactorily was because of the dominance on this issue in Russia by Minister of Atomic Energy Viktor Mikhailov, who was no fan of the United States and who was not easily controlled by either Yeltsin or Chernomyrdin.[63] Second, it may have been in part a reaction to growing Russian frustrations with NATO enlargement. Russia could not stop the United States in central Europe. But it could gain satisfaction by stymieing the United States in Iran. Perhaps most fundamentally, however, Russian officials stated publicly that democratizing Russia had the right to seek exports for its technologies just as democratic America vigorously sought new markets for its products, civilian and military alike. In particular, Russian officials claimed that the type of light water nuclear power technology that they were supplying to the Bushehr reactor in Iran was very similar to the nuclear technology that the United States had agreed to supply to North Korea in 1994 and could not be used to develop a nuclear weapon. U.S. officials disagreed. Radically different interpretations in Moscow and Washington of this Russian trade to Iran lingered like a dark cloud about to burst over U.S.-Russian relations for the entire decade.

The building of the Bushehr nuclear reactor had begun originally through a deal between then–West Germany and the shah's government in Iran, but the Germans had ended their role at U.S. request after the 1979 Iranian revolution. The Soviets and then Russians stepped into the breach. More ominous than the decision by Russia to step up construction of nuclear reactors at Bushehr were the reports that the Russian Ministry of Atomic Energy (Minatom) had secretly agreed to sell gas centrifuge equipment, which would enable the Iranians to enrich uranium for nuclear weapons use.[64]

The Bushehr problem was not a new one for the United States. The earlier Bush administration had first confronted this deal back in the spring of 1992, and Undersecretary of State Lynn Davis had been pursuing this issue with Mikhailov since the onset of the Clinton administration in January 1993. As Talbott reports about Mikhailov's demeanor at the first Clinton-Yeltsin summit in Vancouver, "Mikhailov was the only member of the Russian delegation who seemed not in the least deferential to Yeltsin himself."[65] On this particular issue as with other proliferation problems, U.S. officials were never sure if Russian behavior was being carried out with the full knowledge of the Yeltsin administration, or if Mikhailov and company were free agents who were not controlled by the Kremlin.

In Washington for a summit with Clinton in September 1994, Yeltsin had stated that while Russia would fulfill a 1988 arms contract with Iran, "no other new contracts, no other new supplies, no other new shipments of weapons and weapons goods will be shipped." Clinton was guarded in his public comments saying that the two sides had "reached a conceptual agreement in principle" but had not "resolved" the problem. The U.S. side did not know how far into the future the 1988 arms contract was intended to run nor what the agreement actually covered.[66]

The United States was growing increasingly concerned that Russia was playing with fire. While Russian officials argued that Iran was complying with the Nuclear Non-Proliferation Treaty, allowing International Atomic Energy Agency inspections, and doing no more than what the United States had contracted to do to turn North Korea away from nuclear weapons development, the United States believed that with Russian help, Iran would be able to develop nuclear weapons capability. As one Western diplomat put it at the time, "The Russians are right to say that these reactors are the same as North Korea's. But the difference is that the North Koreans were already well along towards nuclear weapons. Giving them light-water reactors was the best you could do to slow them down, under the circumstances. Iran, on the other hand, is just starting out on its program. We can still try to stop it from getting off the ground."[67]

Tough Voices

In a speech at Harvard on January 20, 1995, just days before public announcements of the Bushehr deal, U.S. Secretary of State Christopher hit the Russians hard: "Today, Iran is engaged in a crash effort to develop nuclear weapons. We are deeply concerned that some nations are prepared to cooperate with Iran in the nuclear field. I will not mince words: These efforts risk the security of the entire Middle East. The United States places the highest priority on denying Iran a nuclear weapons capability. We expect the members of the Security Council, who have special responsibilities in this area, to join with us." One aide made clear afterward that the remarks were intended as "a shot at the Russians."[68]

From Capitol Hill, the voices of concern were even more confrontational. The new Speaker of the House of Representatives, Georgia Republican Newt Gingrich, threatened to cut off all U.S. assistance to Russia if the nuclear deal with Iran was not halted. Only two years earlier, Gingrich had applauded

Clinton for his first big aid package to Russia. But Russian officials were not impressed with the new threats. Deputy Foreign Minister Mamedov on a visit to Washington at that time made clear that the Russian position was unchanged. Senator Patrick Leahy (D-Vt.) responded, "The Russians could try the patience of a saint."[69]

Given the Russian actions in Iran as well as in Chechnya, leading Republicans were calling on the president not to go to Moscow in May 1995 to help Yeltsin celebrate the fiftieth anniversary of the defeat of Nazi Germany. For the Russians, there was no bigger event than the commemoration of the millions of Soviet citizens who lost their lives fighting the Great Patriotic War, and Talbott and Gore were pushing hard that Clinton needed to make the trip to stay engaged with Russia. But domestic political advisers George Stephanopoulos and Leon Panetta were advising against a trip, partly on the grounds that the president would see Yeltsin at the next G-7 meeting in Halifax in July, partly because they did not want the president out of the country on V-E day.[70]

To help the president discern the domestic political fallout from making the trip, Clinton turned to political strategist Dick Morris. As Stephanopoulos has written, "From December 1994 through August 1996, Leon Panetta managed the official White House staff, the Joint Chiefs commanded the military, the cabinet administered the government, but no single person more influenced the president of the United States than Dick Morris."[71]

Morris recalls, "Sometime around March (1995), in our strategy meetings, somebody raised the issue of Clinton's trip to Russia and the Iranian reactor issue. I did a fair amount of polling on that to assess how the American people felt. Clinton clearly did not want to have a big confrontation with Yeltsin over it. He wanted to help Yeltsin survive; he was much more interested in Yeltsin's survival than in the reactor sale. On the other hand, he understood that if he dealt lightly with the reactor sale, he could be in big political trouble himself."[72]

Morris posed the questions on the reactor sale in a variety of ways, including asking whether or not the public would agree to a slower approach to NATO enlargement in return for Russia not helping Iran build a reactor. Morris says of the results: "[The American people] saw it basically the way Clinton did. They were much more worried about a cold war starting again with Russia than they were about Iran having the reactor. We tested a cutoff in aid, and people were against it. Not only were people not going to force Clinton to cut off aid, they didn't want him to cut off aid. It was close, but they were against it. [And] if you ask, do you favor not including Poland, Hungary, and the Czech Republic in NATO in return for Russia not selling the reactors to Iran, they would vote no, because it sounded really seamy. But when you asked them, how important is it that we expand NATO quickly, or should we consider deferring it if we feel it will antagonize the Russians, and perhaps start a new cold war, people said, yeah, let's delay." He has written of that polling, "People were not willing to put our relations with Russia on thin ice just to kill the reactor deal, but they would demand that aid to Russia be cut off if the Iranian deal ultimately went through."[73]

The administration believed strongly that Iran was seeking to build a bomb. Iran, after all, had vast supplies of oil and did not need nuclear power. As the NSC senior director for nonproliferation, Daniel Poneman, recalls, "The Bushehr deal as an energy deal makes no sense. So it only made sense as a stalking horse for a weapons effort. We thought that the only reason the Iranians would consider shelling out a billion dollars for this reactor was to get their hands on the ancillary fuel capabilities to enhance their nuclear weapons program." The hope was that between Clinton's efforts at the May summit and Gore's work with Chernomyrdin, the Russians would give up enough of the program that "the Bushehr part would fall of its own weight."[74]

Part of the effort involved giving U.S. intelligence information to the Russians to convince them that the Iranian program was not a peaceful one. Secretary of Defense Perry called on Russia to cancel the deal when he was in Moscow a little more than a month before the May summit, but he also said that U.S. assistance for denuclearization should not be halted over Bushehr. Meanwhile the United States also tried the buyout track: Christopher promised Kozyrev $100 million for Minatom to build more modern reactors in Russia and suggested Russia might be cut in on the North Korea deal. But was $100 million going to look that tempting in the face of a nearly $1 billion arrangement Minatom had with Iran?[75]

Christopher's aides were trying to make clear that their boss no longer viewed Russia through rose-colored glasses. In Bloomington, Indiana, in late March, the secretary of state gave his first speech on Russia since 1993. Besides outlining the skeptical views on Russian domestic politics that his advisers James Steinberg and Thomas Donilon had held for some time, Christopher delivered an even tougher message on Russia's relationship with Iran. "Because of the importance we attach to fighting the spread of nuclear weapons, we are firmly opposed to Russia's nuclear cooperation with Iran. . . . Russia should take note that no major industrial democracy cooperates with Iran on nuclear matters."[76]

Meeting in Moscow

In the end, the president did decide he should go to Moscow, but on the flight to Russia, he was concerned about his ability to resolve the dispute over Iran. He gave a speech at Arlington national cemetery just before leaving, and several veterans told him, "Don't let those bastards do that reactor deal with Iran." Presumably reflecting those concerns, which were also appearing in Morris' polls, the president told his staff, "I'm going to Russia because of the dogs we have in this hunt, but we've got to do something on Iran. Joe Lunchbucket out there in Ames, Iowa, doesn't care about NATO enlargement. He cares about whether this ol' boy is going over there to Russia and let those people give the new ayatollah an A-bomb."[77]

As the president arrived in Moscow, he and the team had low expectations about what the May 1995 Moscow summit would achieve. It was important to Clinton and Yeltsin that the U.S. president show up and help the Russians celebrate the historic anniversary, but the U.S. team had had no illusions about resolving differences on either Iran or NATO enlargement. After a phone call between the two presidents just before the summit, Coit D. Blacker, the NSC senior director for Russia affairs, was asked about the progress being made. He answered by saying that Clinton had raised a number of issues and had again described their importance to Yeltsin. When asked if that meant no progress was being made, Blacker replied, "You can characterize it as you choose."[78]

The United States did make some minimal progress, although not enough to trumpet the results. Yeltsin agreed not to sell the centrifuges to Iran, and he consented to sending the other issues in the Russia-Iran relationship for review by the Gore-Chernomyrdin Commission.[79] Although the worst of the Iran deal had apparently been nixed, the Russians would not concede that completing the reactor deal was of concern to anyone. Administration officials exhibited "palpable disappointment" over the meeting. The joint press conference made the differences pretty clear, and the president did take a beating at home as expected from congressional Republicans. Said Senator Mitch McConnell (R-Ky.), chairman of the subcommittee through which all aid legislation went, "The summit was a failure. Nothing was achieved, nothing at all. It is an embarrassment for the administration that the president went to Moscow to watch a parade at Yeltsin's behest, and brought nothing home."[80]

A Private Deal

As foreshadowed by the Clinton-Yeltsin summit in May, a deal on Iran was struck in the summer of 1995 between Gore and Chernomyrdin, and once again, it seemed that the pattern that had developed during the management of the earlier contentious security issues was repeating itself. At the time of their meeting, Gore said publicly that he and Chernomyrdin had concluded a "very significant" arrangement that meant the issue "has been resolved in a specific, mutually agreed fashion that does not leave any uncertainty or open ends that would create problems in the future."[81]

The details of the Gore-Chernomyrdin discussions remained private until the 2000 campaign, when it was revealed that the two men had signed a deal in June 1995 that would allow Russia to fulfill existing contracts for sales of *conventional* weapons by December 31, 1999. All sales were to stop at that date. Systems to be sold included a diesel-powered submarine, T-72 tanks, armored personnel carriers, and a variety of mines and munitions. Then in December 1995, Chernomyrdin wrote Gore a letter that appeared to end Russian efforts to assist Iran's nuclear fuel cycle program and limited the Bushehr project to only one reactor.[82]

Unfortunately for Al Gore's 2000 presidential campaign, Russia did not end up halting sales by the agreed-upon date.[83] In 1995, however, the Clinton administration was cautiously optimistic that Russia seemed to be making a firm commitment to ending what was becoming a serious threat to U.S.-Russian relations. Certainly, enough had been done to keep the administration's transformation and integration agenda alive. It was only in the second Clinton term that the problems stemming from Russia's relationship with Iran would escalate dramatically.

Conclusion

In its first years on the job, the Clinton foreign policy team could feel good about how it had managed security issues with the Yeltsin government. The Clinton policy of offering Russia financial inducements, memberships in international clubs, and status as an important global power seemed to be working. The Clinton team had stopped unwanted Russian proliferation to India, ensured troop withdrawals from the Baltic countries, and gotten Ukraine and Russia to work together in the nuclear sphere. Even the Russia-Iran arrangements seemed within range of a shift in policy that would satisfy the core U.S. concerns. All of these developments helped confirm for the Clinton team that Boris Yeltsin's hold on power was vital to the American agenda, further strengthening the need to support America's man in Moscow. More abstractly, Russia's internal transformation and desire to integrate into the West seemed to be making Russia a more cooperative partner on these difficult security concerns. It is hard to imagine the Soviet Union reneging on export contracts with the Indians, and Russian troops might still be in the Baltic states if a militant nationalist leader like Zhirinovsky had come to power in Moscow.

Even with Yeltsin in the Kremlin, Russia making progress on market and democratic reforms, and Russia seeking to move closer to the West, one contentious issue came to dominate the U.S.-Russian security agenda at the end of the first Clinton-Yeltsin terms and the start of the second: NATO enlargement. The Western alliance's enlargement into central Europe raised questions in Russia about the true U.S. desire to integrate Russia (as opposed to a renewal of a policy of containment). Russia's complaints about enlargement in turn left many in the West unsure about Russia's ability to adapt to a new Europe and a new NATO. No U.S. policy infuriated Boris Yeltsin more, and none kept Strobe Talbott busier for the moment, than the U.S. effort to enlarge NATO onto territory formerly belonging to the Warsaw Pact.

8

NATO Is a Four-Letter Word

The North Atlantic Treaty Organization had been the West's collective defense effort against the threat posed by the Soviet Union. With the cold war over and Russia on a path of democratic and market change at home and integration with the West abroad, Russians wondered why this organization was not only still standing but growing even larger. Almost nothing underscored Russia's decline as a major power as much as NATO enlargement. As with the other security issues, Bill Clinton did try to make Boris Yeltsin feel better about the process, in this case through the creation of the NATO-Russia Founding Act and the formal invitation to Russia to join the G-7 and thereby make it the G-8.[1] But the process was always rocky. The key foreign policy officials responsible for enlargement, National Security Adviser Anthony Lake and Assistant Secretary of State Richard C. Holbrooke, were determined to not let concern with Russia's feelings get in the way of their effort to enlarge NATO as a means for reintegrating central Europe into the West and stabilizing the Balkans. But the Russians' bitterness over their failure to stop the alliance was strong, and Clinton and Strobe Talbott would spend an inordinate amount of time trying to assuage Russia's concerns.

Why the Russians Felt Betrayed

Until December 1994, Boris Yeltsin and company felt that they had dodged a bullet on NATO enlargement since the United States appeared not to have the alliance on a concrete path for taking in new members. So when it became clear that NATO was setting the stage for taking in new members with an enlargement "study" in 1995, Yeltsin became enraged. What fueled the Russian reaction was a belief that the United States had promised several times over the previous years that no enlargement was in the offing. The Russian understanding of enlargement was a reasonable one, partly because of the ambiguity in the Clinton administration's internal deliberations and partly because of public Clinton administration statements on the course that enlargement might take, which seemed to stress the eventuality of the policy without specific target dates. Russian reformers, and Yeltsin in particular, could not understand why the Americans considered a democratic Russia a threat. NATO, in their view, was a military alliance designed to protect members from nonmember aggressors. If NATO was expanding toward Russia's borders, this meant for many in Russia that the Americans did not believe in the probabilities of success of Russia's internal transformation. As Russian reformer Anatoly Chubais explained in 1997, "Frankly, the politicians who support this decision [to enlarge NATO] believe that Russia is a country that should be put aside, a country that should not be included in the civilized world—ever. That is a major mistake."[2]

Chubais, as discussed earlier, was a friend of the West and an advocate of Russia's internal transformation. His resistance to NATO enlargement stemmed not from his worries about a NATO attack on Russia but from the problems created by the enlargement debate for liberal reformers in Russia. Russian nationalists and communists labeled Foreign Minister Andrei Kozyrev a traitor for signing the Partnership for Peace agreement; communist leader Gennady Zyuganov drew a parallel between Partnership for Peace and Hitler's Barbarossa plan for invading Russia. When the Russia-NATO charter was finally signed in 1997, Zyuganov and his comrades called it treason.[3] NATO enlargement, therefore, created real political problems for America's allies—that is, the regime transformers—in Russia. These supporters of reform in Russia had helped to make Russian foreign policy more Western friendly.[4] For those fighting for market and democratic reforms in Russia, therefore, it was difficult to understand how Clinton could champion and assist their cause with one set of policies and at the same time frustrate their agenda by pursuing another policy, the policy of NATO enlargement.[5]

Russians had good reason to be confused about America's real intentions. Many in Russia charged that enlargement violated promises made in 1990 when President George H. W. Bush, Chancellor Helmut Kohl, President Mikhail Gorbachev, and their foreign ministers negotiated the terms of Germany's unification and status in NATO. The first statements on NATO and the East that had been made by leading German and U.S. officials in January and February 1990 as they grappled with the fast-moving events that were leading to Germany's unification seemed to support this interpretation. On January 31, 1990, West German Foreign Minister Hans-Dietrich Genscher had declared, "What NATO must do is state unequivocally that whatever happens in the Warsaw Pact, there will be no expansion of NATO territory eastwards, that is to say closer to the borders of the Soviet Union."[6]

Following a session with Secretary of State James A. Baker III in Washington soon after, Genscher reiterated, "What I said is, there is no intention of extending the NATO area to the East."[7] Baker then repeated this language in Moscow a short time later in meetings with Gorbachev and his foreign minister, Eduard Shevardnadze. Baker told Gorbachev that "there would be no extension of NATO's jurisdiction for forces of NATO one inch to the east." When Gorbachev later argued that "any extension of the zone of NATO is unacceptable," Baker replied, "I agree."[8]

For the Russian security experts in 1994, those comments were sufficient to argue that NATO was now breaking old promises, but the German unification story did not end in February 1990, when the Soviets might have received this pledge in writing had they been willing to cut a deal at that time. Once American officials had realized the implications of Baker's remarks for the alliance's defense commitments to the eastern zones of Germany, they started to back away from them and before long had adopted NATO secretary general Manfred Woerner's idea of a "special military status" for what was then East Germany rather than a notion of no extension of NATO.

The final deal on German unification signed in September 1990 did not include the language on enlargement that had been put forward verbally earlier in the year. And whatever Baker and Genscher had discussed in January and February 1990 in relation to the unification process could only concern Germany's status in NATO; after all, neither official was in any position to make decisions for countries to the east.[9]

While the Bush administration left the issue of further NATO enlargement unresolved, several members of the Clinton administration, in particular, National Security Adviser Anthony Lake, began to argue by late summer and early fall of 1993 that the president should propose at the NATO summit of January 1994 a set of criteria and a timetable for NATO's enlargement into central Europe and even perhaps the notion of associate membership status for leading candidates.[10]

Lake believed in enlargement as a vehicle for extending the community of market democracies eastward by providing an incentive for central and eastern Europeans to carry out the political, economic, and military reform necessary to become members, not as a mechanism for shutting Russia out of Europe. At the same time, he took a tough view on Russia's objections, believing that the United States should simply stick to its guns on a policy that he viewed as squarely in American interests. As he recalls, "I was always of the view that we musn't mislead [the Russians] on NATO enlargement into believing that there was any chance that they could prevent it. We were doing reformers no favor by allowing them a hope they could influence our decision; they would thereby nail their political flags to the mast of preventing this and then lose when they couldn't. I remember a number of hair raising arguments I had with Russian friends about this."[11]

The Russians were not the only ones whose hair was standing on end. The notion of enlarging NATO was hugely controversial in the Clinton administration and was of particular concern in two places: Strobe Talbott's office in the State Department and the Office of the Secretary of Defense at the Pentagon. At the State Department, the Russia team in the fall of 1993 had just worked out the India rocket deal and was preparing to conclude the Trilateral Accord to remove the nuclear weapons from Ukraine. That was their number one priority—and they did not want NATO enlargement to get in the way of what they were achieving with Russia.

The Clinton administration's Russia team supported a program being pushed from the Pentagon known as the Partnership for Peace (PFP). The PFP was open to all states of Europe and the former Soviet Union and provided for the development of ties to the alliance without any guarantees of membership. For Pentagon officials, the goal of integrating Russia into the West and the continuing efforts to denuclearize the former Soviet Union far outweighed any benefits of enlarging NATO. In their view, the PFP was the best way to work with central and eastern European countries while not antagonizing Russia.[12]

The president's top foreign policy advisers (at the cabinet level, they were referred to as the Principals) met in mid-October 1993 to decide on a strategy for Clinton's January 1994 trip to the NATO summit in Brussels, and most in this group favored emphasizing PFP and not NATO enlargement. It was decided that some statement on NATO's eventual enlargement would be made in January, but those worried about Russia's reaction seemed at this moment to have carried the day in the administration.

Most important to Secretary of State Warren Christopher's position had been a memo written to him by Talbott shortly before the Principals Committee meeting in which Talbott argued against concrete steps on enlargement at a time of such uncertainty in Russia. Talbott wrote of the integration of central European countries into the West, "We must not advance that goal at the expense of our support for reform further East, especially in Russia—which, after all, the President keeps saying is our No. 1 priority."[13]

A few days after the Principals Committee meeting, Christopher met Yeltsin in Moscow to explain the administration's policy. The secretary of state described the PFP program to Yelstin and said, "There would be no step taken at this time to push anyone ahead of others." Yeltsin asked for clarification that partnership did not mean membership. Christopher reiterated, "Yes, that is the case, there would not be even an associate status." Yeltsin replied, "This is a brilliant idea, it is a stroke of genius." Christopher then added that the policy that had been decided upon in the United States meant that "we will in due course be looking at the question of membership as a longer term eventuality. There will be an evolution, based on the development of a habit of cooperation, but over time. And this too will be based on participation in the partnership. Those who wish to can pursue the idea over time, but that will come later." But he again made clear that the policy would not exclude anyone; all would be treated equally, and Russia should be satisfied with where things stood. In Moscow in January 1994, Clinton too emphasized that while NATO "plainly contemplated an expansion," the Partnership for Peace was "the real thing now."[14] Clinton's comments in Moscow in January 1994 would make the following year's developments that much more difficult for the Russian government to comprehend. In the spring and summer of 1994, however, NATO-Russia relations still seemed to be moving on track. In March, after meeting with his counterpart William Perry, Russian secretary of defense Pavel Grachev announced that "at the end of this month we will be ready [to join the PFP]."[15] On June 22, 1994 (the anniversary of Hitler's invasion of the Soviet Union in 1941), Kozyrev signed the Partnership for Peace Framework Document, and Russia officially became a PFP member.

The Winds of Enlargement Begin to Blow

Despite Russian hopes, the development of PFP did not eclipse the enlargement of NATO.[16] On a visit to Prague to see the central European leaders after his meetings in Brussels in January 1994, President Clinton, at Lake's urging, remarked that "the question is no longer whether NATO will take on new members but when and how." Given that very few people inside the administration were actively seeking to move the process forward, however, Russian foreign minister Andrei Kozyrev could be forgiven for believing at mid-year that "the greatest achievement of Russian foreign policy in 1993 was to prevent NATO's expansion eastward to our borders."[17]

But the policy began to pick up steam in July 1994. On a visit to Warsaw (a trip made to pacify Polish president Lech Walesa who had been apoplectic earlier in the year about "only" getting membership in the PFP and not NATO), Clinton reiterated his line about the question no longer being whether but when. And he added that the alliance partners needed to get together "to discuss what the next steps should be."[18]

In early September, Vice President Al Gore spoke by videoconference to a gathering in Berlin. Having a major hand in his remarks was Richard C. Holbrooke, on his way back to Washington to become assistant secretary of state for European affairs after a brief stint as U.S. ambassador to Germany. Talbott recalls that in the run-up to the speech, there were arguments in favor of including a timetable to give the leading candidates for membership some hope of acceptance into the alliance the following year, but he declares, "I threw my body in front of this idea. The alliance was already under severe strain over what to do in Bosnia. . . . We didn't need an additional debate over enlargement. Even if the alliance had been in total harmony, 1996 would be the worst imaginable time to bring new members into NATO, given what would be happening in Russia that year: Yeltsin's uphill campaign for re-election against some sort of red-brown coalition."[19]

Even so, a number of high-level officials in the administration were upset with the Gore speech. Gore had advanced Clinton's line in Warsaw by stating, "Beyond Partnership for Peace and [the North Atlantic Cooperation Council], several countries have already expressed a desire to become full members of the alliance. We will begin our discussions on this important question this fall." General Wesley Clark, then head of strategic plans and policy at the Joint Chiefs of Staff, and his boss, General John Shalikashvili, had complained about the drafts of the speech to no avail.[20]

Meanwhile, Talbott was in Moscow during the Gore speech, meeting with Deputy Foreign Minister Georgy Mamedov in advance of Yeltsin's upcoming trip to Washington, D.C., in September 1994. Mamedov expressed concern about enlargement and the possibility of new members joining in 1996. Talbott told him that he thought they would "get through 1996 without the first new members being admitted or even formally designated, but if so, we were just buying time." On the flight home, Talbott wrote Christopher that he was "concerned" that the Warsaw and Berlin remarks "may have re-started the NATO expansion juggernaut without really intending to and without sufficient consideration of the consequences." He added, "We must not let PFP become a passing fad or OBE [overtaken by events]. The [central and east European] states have joined PFP not for its own sake, but because they see it as an anteroom to NATO. Russia has joined mainly because it doesn't want there to be any new security structures from which it is excluded. If we were to declare ourselves in a rush to expand NATO now, it would vindicate the cynicism of both sides. The Poles would pay zero attention to PFP and concentrate entirely on getting into NATO, while the Russians would feel sucker-punched, and their refusal to participate in PFP would vitiate its genuine promise." He then wrote a memo the following day for wider distribution proposing that PFP govern for another year or so, and then in 1996, NATO could start pushing a two-track process of enlargement and a NATO-Russia accord.[21]

The key for the Russia team was that enlargement could not be allowed to undermine the policy of supporting Boris Yeltsin, their man in Moscow, especially as he entered an election season. But despite all of the efforts to reassure Yeltsin as enlargement moved forward, Yeltsin still felt that Clinton was undercutting him. Yeltsin in August 1993 had signed a communiqué with

President Lech Walesa in Warsaw giving a green light to Poland joining NATO, but the Russian president only a few weeks later sent a strident letter against expansion to NATO heads of state after he was pressured by officials at Russia's foreign and defense ministries.[22] Given his belief that he would pay domestic political costs if he could not postpone NATO's move east, Yeltsin by the end of 1994 could not contain his growing anger at the emerging U.S. policy to promote enlargement.

The Road to Budapest: Did the Mamedov Channel Fail?

Yeltsin arrived in Washington in late September 1994 for a summit meeting with Clinton. At a private lunch, Clinton told Yeltsin that Russia was eligible for NATO membership, and he reassured his Russian counterpart that while NATO was going to expand, there was no timetable. "We're going to move forward on this," Clinton told Yeltsin, "But I'd never spring this on you." Clinton offered "three no's," which meant "no surprises, no rush, and no exclusion." And he added, "As I see it, NATO expansion is not anti-Russian. . . . I don't want you to believe that I wake up every morning thinking only about how to make the Warsaw Pact countries a part of NATO—that's not the way I look at it. What I do think about is how to use NATO expansion to advance the broader, higher goal of European security, unity and integration—a goal I know you share."[23]

Later in the day, Yeltsin asked Clinton in turn to come to the Conference on Security and Cooperation in Europe (CSCE) summit in Budapest in December. Clinton replied that if it was important to Yeltsin that he participate in that meeting, he would.[24]

The CSCE had been established in Helsinki in 1975 primarily as a mechanism to stabilize the standoff between NATO and the Warsaw Pact and dampen tensions between the two blocs. Remarkably, the most important feature of the CSCE had turned out to be not the security and economic "baskets" but rather the human rights basket, which enabled dissidents in eastern Europe and the Soviet Union to pressure their governments with greater effect.[25] Because of the continentwide membership of the organization, Russia was looking to make it a more important institution in the post–cold war environment at NATO's expense (although Russia would soon learn that one of the organization's tasks would be trying to prevent human rights violations in Chechnya). The major new item of the Budapest summit was the upgrading of the CSCE to the OSCE, with O standing for "Organization," which sounded more important than "Conference." The United States had no intention of letting the OSCE undercut NATO, but the Russia team in Washington saw the new name as something to give the Russians during the NATO enlargement process.

Given Clinton's domestic troubles in the fall of 1994, culminating in the shock of the Republican sweep of both Houses of Congress in November, White House domestic political advisers were not eager to have the president go to Budapest—there were no voters in Hungary. Getting word of this preference, Talbott, Christopher, and Lake all pressed for the president to keep his commitment. Talbott reported that he wrote to the president, "Chief, believe me, this is an absolute, total, no-question-about-it MUST. You gotta go. If you go, it'll do a lot of good, diplomatically and politically; if you don't it'll cause big problems on both fronts. . . . If you give Budapest a miss, you'd appear to be abandoning the field to Yeltsin, Kohl and others; we'd miss the chance to establish a CSCE 'second track' that must parallel the NATO expansion track. Yeltsin (who's under huge pressure to come out against NATO expansion) would feel vulnerable at home and, frankly, let down by you, since you agreed when he was here that you'd meet in Budapest 'if there's serious work to be done,' which there sure is." Talbottt wrote that if Clinton went, it would "vindicate this appeal and the trouble we're putting you to."[26]

On November 8, Clinton met with Finnish president Martti Ahtisaari, who asked him if he was going to Budapest. Clinton replied that he had not decided. With the devastating and historic Republican sweep of Congress that was under way, his chief of staff Leon Panetta and domestic adviser George Stephanopoulos argued that a scheduled congressional reception the night of the Budapest summit (scheduled by the White House precisely to prevent Clinton from going to Budapest) was more important for the president politically than the OSCE summit. But Gore, Lake, Holbrooke, and Talbott pressed for Clinton to commit to go to Budapest, thus setting the stage for a quick trip that would enable the president to fulfill his promise to Yeltsin while getting him back in time for the congressional reception.[27]

The trip was a disaster. The American side tried to choreograph events leading up to the Budapest summit that would produce a happy ending. First would come an announcement on December 1 from the NATO foreign ministers that NATO could conduct a study to be completed by December 1995 of "how NATO will enlarge, the principles to guide this process, and the implications of membership."[28] Second would come a meeting of the foreign ministers with Russian foreign minister Andrei Kozyrev, who was scheduled to meet his NATO colleagues to sign Russia's Individual Partnership Program (a document all PFP participants signed to make concrete their participation) and another document that would have established a NATO-Russia dialogue.

The dance did not develop as planned. When Yeltsin heard that NATO was going to examine how the alliance would enlarge, he was furious.[29] He called Kozyrev, who had already left for the Brussels meeting, and told him not to sign. The resulting press conference by Kozyrev, held during the NATO Ministerial (meeting of foreign ministers) in Brussels, caught the Americans completely off guard. But since the NATO representatives had shown the Russian point man in Brussels, Vitaly Churkin, the draft communiqué, when Kozyrev showed up at 6:00 p.m. for a meeting he had asked for and then refused to sign the two documents, the Allied foreign ministers were also furious.[30]

There was still more choreography for the Russians to trash. From the U.S. side, the whole point of the upcoming summit in Budapest was to give Yeltsin a forum to tout how the CSCE would now become the OSCE. Clinton had tried to make clear, even before the North Atlantic Council meetings, that the forthcoming NATO communiqué was as much a delaying tactic as anything else. At a news conference in Washington with Ukrainian president Leonid Kuchma on November 22, Clinton had said, "I believe we will have discussions in Budapest about how we might go about expanding NATO but not about when and which particular countries would be let in; I think that is premature."[31]

Despite the ominous signs, the president and his team forged ahead to Budapest, leaving Washington around 9:00 p.m. on December 4, 1994, and flying overnight. Because the president would have only about five hours on the ground in Hungary, he was unable to schedule a private meeting with Yeltsin before the plenary session of the CSCE. At the plenary, Clinton stated much more strongly than he had in the November press conference with Kuchma that NATO was moving forward regardless of the concerns of other countries. "We must not allow the Iron Curtain to be replaced by a veil of indifference. We must not consign new democracies to a gray zone. . . . NATO will not automatically exclude any nation from joining. At the same time, no country outside will be allowed to veto expansion." Talbott says the remarks were drafted at the National Security Council (NSC)—not in his office—and represented the "most in your face" version of the administration's position on NATO expansion.[32]

Then it was Yeltsin's turn. In words that shocked President Clinton and his team, the Russian leader declared, "Europe, even before it has managed to shrug off the legacy of the Cold War, is risking encumbering itself with a cold peace." He added, "NATO was created in Cold War times. Today, it is trying to find its place in Europe, not without difficulty. It is important that this search not create new divisions, but promote European unity. We believe that the plans of expanding NATO are contrary to this logic. Why sow the seeds of distrust? After all, we are no longer adversaries, we are partners. Some explanations that we hear imply that this is 'expansion of stability,' just in case developments in Russia go the undesirable way. If this is the reason why some want to move the NATO area of responsibility closer to the Russian borders, let me say this: it is too early to give up on democracy in Russia!" Kozyrev said later that Yeltsin had rewritten the speech himself just before delivery in order to attack Clinton.[33]

Clinton and his advisers were stunned and angry, largely because of the surprising tone rather than being fearful of the substance (and the president would write Yeltsin to tell him this in the days after the summit—no surprises in their actions toward one another). But numerous questions were raised on the American side: what are Yeltsin's advisers telling him? How predictable is the relationship? Why were the Americans caught off guard? According to Nicholas Burns, then the president's top adviser for Russian affairs at the NSC, the president on the trip home called him and Anthony Lake to the front of the plane to ask how Budapest could have happened. Burns says that Yeltsin's speech "was a rude awakening for the U.S. The President and all of us were stunned by it as there had been no advance warning. Our reaction was to try to figure out if it was a long-term change or a brief interruption in what had been very close and friendly relations between Washington and Moscow." Clinton was so upset with his staff that Talbott recalls, "I wrote my wife a note at the time because she was out of town, saying I think this is it; you're about to get me back!" Talbott (who was not on the Brussels or Budapest trips because he was back home dealing with Haiti) knew he would bear the brunt of the blame for having stressed the importance of the trip and for having not been able to give anyone a heads up.[34]

Talbott knew he was partly to blame, because it was his special relationship with Deputy Foreign Minister Mamedov that was supposed to prevent such unscripted confrontations between Clinton and Yeltsin. The Talbott-Mamedov relationship began even before Talbott joined the government in large measure because of Dennis Ross, Baker's top Soviet adviser. Soon after Clinton won the November 1992 election, Ross called Talbott to brief him about his friend Mamedov. As Ross recalls, "I was afraid that there could be a break. I had developed a relationship with Mamedov that I'd had with [Soviet Foreign Minister Shevardnadze's key assistant Sergei] Tarasenko. I knew with that kind of connection, things would continue. . . . [I told Talbott] that if you want to get things done, this guy is a problem solver."[35]

In his initial discussions with Ross, Talbott was noncommittal about pursuing anything with Mamedov because he had yet to be named to a post in the new administration. But as soon as he was finally named to the Clinton team, Talbott moved to establish a special relationship with Mamedov. Mamedov asked Talbott to put together an interagency working group with Pentagon and CIA officials because this would help Mamedov do the same on his side. Thus was created the Strategic Stability Group. According to Victoria Nuland, the value for the United States was that it created some sense of stability on the Russian side, and it enabled Talbott to hear from Mamedov, "You want to get X done, here's what you have to do; here's who has to send a letter to whom; here's who has to call whom; here's my problem; or I can't get this or that agency on board."[36]

Until the fall of 1994, Mamedov appeared to deliver when called upon. But then came Yeltsin's behavior at the Budapest summit and the war in Chechnya, neither of which was foreshadowed for the U.S. side by Mamedov. Given the surprising Russian reaction at NATO and then in Budapest on issues that had been worked on by both sides throughout the fall, some began to wonder if Talbott relied too heavily on Mamedov. In retrospect, Talbott responded, "I suppose in one sense it's self-evidently true. So nolo contendere. But in another sense it's irrelevant. There's no question that I did rely . . . on the Mamedov channel. It's unique and it's almost unique in the history of U.S.-Russian diplomacy. . . . He was extraordinarily both honest and able in his handlings of the internals on the Russian side. Given how chaotic they were, how unpredictable, how contentious, I think if you score his perform-ance, you've got to give him an A+. We had some breakdowns, that was the worst [Budapest, December 1994], but he never ever deliberately misled or overstated. What other channels were we supposed to use? . . . Part of the problem was that Yeltsin was so erratic. He was erratic in his dealings with Clinton. . . . And he was equally erratic in the Russian government."[37]

The Budapest blowup could not be totally blamed on Talbott and Mamedov. A larger part of the problem for U.S.-Russian relations in the fall of 1994 was that the American side was still sending out ambiguous signals on where the United States stood on enlargement. And that was because there was not yet a unified position in the government. In the State Department Richard C. Holbrooke had taken charge of NATO enlargement, and he had pushed the process forward. Holbrooke was pressuring the bureaucracy to examine how NATO would go about adding new members. And with this new push, the United States and its Allies developed a plan to announce in December that NATO would spend 1995 studying the "how and why" of NATO enlargement. But the U.S. secretary of defense did not even believe NATO enlargement was administration policy until after a meeting with President Clinton and other top officials in late December 1994, that is, after the announcement of the NATO study.[38]

The administration was riding two difficult currents, which it kept trying to manage in parallel for the next two years. On the one hand, Clinton offi-cials wanted to reassure the central and eastern Europeans (and their sup-porters in the United States, especially the Polish American community) that NATO enlargement was going forward at a steady pace. The purpose was to assist these countries in their own postcommunist transformation and inte-gration; NATO membership would anchor in the West those countries that had made the necessary political, military, and economic reforms required of them to join.[39] At the same time, Clinton's foreign policy team wanted to reas-sure Yeltsin that no enlargement would take place before the Russian presi-dential election in the summer of 1996. Yeltsin was still hoping to stop expansion indefinitely, but at a minimum, he was desperate to freeze the process until after his election in July 1996. Clinton as Yeltsin's biggest supporter certainly did not want to undertake a policy that would cause his man in Moscow trouble in his re-election campaign. Pentagon officials feared that enlargement might undermine U.S. efforts to reduce Russia's nuclear capabilities. At the end of 1994, the paradox for the administration was that the central Europeans were not convinced that enlargement was on track, but the Russians were convinced it was. To add to the swirl of confusion, many of the Allies were still not on board the enlargement train Some of them interpreted Clinton's push for affirming the enlargment process now as a political response to the November 1994 elections (as did officials at the Pentagon).[40]

Aftershocks from Budapest

Less than two weeks after the Budapest summit, Vice President Gore, Defense Secretary Perry, and Deputy Secretary of State Talbott were in Moscow for the scheduled meetings of the bi-national commission with Prime Minister Viktor Chernomyrdin. Talbott argues, "The Gore thing saved [the relationship]."[41] Whatever the original purposes of the trip, now the vice president's immediate job was to get things back on track after Budapest. Vice President Gore met Yeltsin in a sanitarium, where the Russian leader was recovering from an operation on a deviated septum. Gore tried out a new idea on Yeltsin, which the Russian president apparently enjoyed. As his national security adviser Leon Fuerth recalls, "The metaphor was the prospective docking of the major components of the space programs in the joint work with Mir, and using his hands, Gore illustrated how two massive objects could approach each other in space with their trajectories and velocities aligned such that when they met, there would be no tremor in either one. So he said what we would aim to do was to align a meeting between NATO and Russia in such a way that there would be linkup rather than collision."[42]

Echoing Clinton's statement in September, Gore made clear that the enlargement process would be a gradual one. Yeltsin pressed for assurances that only the study of enlargement would happen in 1995. "Once again," responded the vice president, "I repeat our absolute assurances that in 1995, there will be only a study of the conception of a possible expansion of NATO." Yeltsin added his hopes that gradual would mean ten to fifteen years. Gore then again reminded Yeltsin that the enlargement process was open to eventual Russian membership. But Yeltsin responded, "Nyet, nyet, that doesn't make sense. Russia is very, very big and NATO is quite small." At least Gore was able to say publicly, "My impression is there is no 'cold peace,' but instead a warm relationship that's very much on track."[43]

Yeltsin wrote Clinton on December 29 to confirm Clinton's "promise" in their September summit that the NATO-Russia relationship would be agreed upon before NATO enlargement went forward. Although he seemed some-what reassured by his conversation with Gore, Yeltsin was still nervous about American intentions and timetables.[44] Yeltsin was not the only one fearful that the enlargement process was moving forward too quickly. Secretary of Defense William Perry told Talbott, Gore, and Fuerth in Moscow that the NATO foreign ministers' communiqué had come as a complete surprise to him. Perry wanted to put off the question of enlargement until later in the 1990s. From the Pentagon's view, Partnership for Peace was an ideal program that would allow NATO to develop ties with all states in the region while the alliance was resolving two big questions: finding a solution to the conflict in Bosnia and managing the relationship with Russia. When he returned from Moscow, Perry called for a meeting with the president on December 21 to get clarification of the policy.[45]

Perry believed that "NATO membership at that point would only seriously get in the way" of the Pentagon's priorities. Perry made his case with his col-leagues for allowing PFP to develop, for strengthening the NATO-Russia rela-tionship, and then later addressing expansion. Perry recalls that at the meeting, "The Vice President was chosen as the hit man. He explained to me why that was not going to be. Why, while all that [I said] was true, it was not a compelling enough argument in view of the other factors. Strobe was at the meeting and said nothing. Christopher was at the meeting and said nothing. Tony Lake was at the meeting and said nothing. The President said very little, but at the end explained to me what we were going to do. Now I had to think that that meeting was orchestrated before I went into it, but I don't know. They had to give me a chance to get it off my chest, I think that was seriously what the meeting was. Nobody was there seriously planning to change their views. [Talbott] could have at least said, 'Well I agree with that.' But, he said nothing."[46]

Talbott's recollection is somewhat different, and he argues that Gore assisted Perry's efforts to slow the process down at the meeting by gaining agreement that the study was the most that would be done in 1995. But enlargement proponents like Lake were concerned that if the United States followed Perry's plan, the administration would be charged with having given Russia a veto. Chief of Staff Leon Panetta recalled, "If you did Russia first, you would send a signal to the central and eastern Europeans that you are letting Russia call the play."[47]

For those opposed to enlargement at that stage, like Chairman of the Joint Chiefs of Staff Gen. John Shalikashvili, the short-term domestic political costs of a "Russia-first" policy were well worth the longer-term benefits of not re-dividing Europe. At the Pentagon, the overriding goal was to continue to reduce the threat Russia could pose to the United States in the future, which meant proceeding aggressively with Nunn-Lugar, not enlargement. But the basis had now been set within the administration for what became a two-track policy: enlarge NATO and at the same time create a new relationship between NATO and Russia. But given what had happened in Brussels and Budapest, getting the two tracks in line posed a real challenge.

Regaining Balance

Talbott writes that Clinton, fearing that Yeltsin would pull another Budapest, was never more concerned about a summit with Yeltsin than the one proposed for May 1995.[48] As for substance, trying to put a stop to Russia's assistance to the Iranian nuclear program was a major agenda item, but so too was getting Yeltsin back to where the United States and its allies thought he was before Kozyrev's December 1, 1994, appearance in Brussels: that is, ready for Russia to sign its documents on its concrete participation in the Partnership for Peace. In early January 1995, Mamedov had asked Talbott in Brussels to delay enlargement past the 1996 election season. Mamedov's request implied that some Russian officials might be getting used to the idea of *expansion* (as they preferred to call the policy). Exceeding instructions, Talbott told Mamedov that political pressure in the United States would not force enlargement in 1996. In his report of the meeting to Christopher, Talbott recommended that the president tell Yeltsin that no new members would be designated before the summer 1996 Russian presidential election. Even so, the two sides still appeared to be far apart on expansion. Russia wanted to make sure the NATO-Russia track was done before any new members were admitted, that NATO become more like the OSCE, and that Russia be part of the NATO decision-making process. The United States, however, insisted that enlargement not be held hostage to progress on the NATO-Russia front, that there be no changes from the 1949 Washington Treaty that established NATO, and that Russia not be given a veto over NATO decisions.[49]

And yet the outlines of a deal were emerging. In meetings with Mamedov, Talbott broached the idea of a charter, rather than a formal treaty, between NATO and Russia, and he proposed the idea of having a "standing commission" that would allow Russia to be involved in discussions with NATO short of having a direct say in the NATO decision process. As one official said at the time, "We fully understand that by the time NATO acquires a 17th member, there must be an agreed definition [of a NATO-Russian relationship]." Meanwhile, the Russians began seeking a pledge from NATO that it would neither deploy troops nor station nuclear weapons on the territory of new members. These would all be elements of the accord struck two years later.[50]

Two years, however, would be a long time. In March 1995, during a speech to the Russian military, Yeltsin blasted his Foreign Ministry team for committing "gross blunders" in addressing NATO expansion, in particular by arguing that Russia could accept expansion if NATO made the pledge on nuclear weapons and troops. Yeltsin said these proposals had not been cleared with him, and he reassured his military that the official Russian position was still "nyet" on NATO enlargement.[51]

Then, during their meetings in Moscow in May, Yeltsin pressed Clinton to pause the enlargement process until the year 2000. Clinton responded that the process would be gradual enough "not to cause you problems in 1996." He continued, "What I'm telling you is that this process will take a major portion of 1996 for further reflection. I'm mindful of political pressures on you as well as the substantive merits of what we're doing, and I have tried to structure the process with this in mind." But Yeltsin did not want to see any movement on expansion, noting with some understatement, "My position heading into the 1996 elections is not exactly brilliant." He added, "Let's postpone NATO expansion for a year and a half or two years. There's no need to rile the situation up before the elections."[52]

According to Talbott, Clinton pushed back, "Let me tell you about my situation. I face a difficult campaign, but I have a reasonable chance. The Republicans are pushing NATO expansion. Wisconsin, Illinois, and Ohio are key; they represented a big part of my majority last time—states where I won by a narrow margin. The Republicans think they can take away those states, which have a lot of Poles and others who like the idea of NATO expansion. Let me be clear, Boris: I'm not bargaining with you. I'm not saying, 'Do what I want or I'll change my position.' I've already met with those groups and told them I'm not speeding up NATO expansion. We're going to stay with our plan, with our decision—no speed-up, no slow-down; we're going to proceed in the steady, measured pace, according to the plan I just laid out for you. You can ask us not to speed up, since I've already told you we're not going to do that. But don't ask us to slow down either." And he added, "So here is what I want to do. I've made it clear I'll do nothing to accelerate NATO. I'm trying to give you now, in this conversation, the reassurance you need for '95 and '96. But we need to be careful that neither of us appears to capitulate. For you, that means you're not going to embrace expansion; for me, it means no talk about slowing the process down or putting it on hold or anything like that. If you can sign the PFP and begin the Russian-NATO dialogue, I can get you past the next elections with no discussion of 'who' or 'when.'"[53]

So, the two presidents agreed to disagree. Yeltsin could keep saying that he did not like expansion, but he did agree to get Russia back in a process with NATO. And Clinton could say that the enlargement process was moving forward, even though he had conceded that nothing concrete would be done until after his friend was safely re-elected. It was not much progress, but at least the two had put Budapest behind them.

Finally, a Real Success in Bosnia

Although the issues of NATO enlargement and Iran would continue to haunt the relationship during the political season in both nations, a more pressing issue loomed by the fall of 1995: could the United States get a deal to end the fighting in Bosnia, and would the Russians participate in the implementation force that would be set up to enforce it? In fact, the United States did strike a deal at Dayton in November 1995, thanks to the efforts of Assistant Secretary of State Holbrooke and his team. Equally remarkable, U.S. and Russian officials found a way to get Russia's participation in what was clearly a NATO-led operation. The hard work of Secretary of Defense William J. Perry and Defense Minister Pavel Grachev as well as the efforts of two generals, American George Joulwan and Russian Leontiy Shevtsov, made the collaboration possible.

Clinton and Yeltsin met in October 1995 at Hyde Park, home of Franklin Delano Roosevelt, in an effort to evoke memories of the Grand Alliance of World War II. Two major issues loomed for this meeting. One was Bosnia. The other was an obscure, but important, post–cold war issue: agreement on an adaptation of the 1990 Conventional Forces in Europe (CFE) Treaty that would respond to Russian concerns before November 1995, when the final treaty provisions were supposed to be met.

The CFE Treaty codified the end of the cold war in military terms. During the previous decades, U.S. military planners had feared a surprise conventional military attack from the East that would overwhelm NATO forces and lead to a need for a nuclear response. The two sides, by agreeing to severe limits in the quantity of key equipment (such as tanks and armored personnel carriers), made sure that the massing of major concentrations of military weaponry would no longer be possible in Europe.[54]

Negotiated in the Europe divided by blocs, the 1990 CFE Treaty was designed to limit equipment held by a Western group of countries (NATO members) and an Eastern group of countries (the soon-to-be defunct Warsaw Pact), and it limited equipment in different zones of Europe. With the fast-moving events of the 1990s, the Russians were faced with two problems: first, the equipment in countries like Poland, Hungary, and the Czech Republic that were seeking to join NATO still counted toward the Eastern group totals; second, and of greater immediate concern, the Russians were limited in terms of the equipment they could place in their North Caucasus Military District (part of the treaty's "flank" zone), which restricted their ability to project military force in Chechnya.

The United States wanted to preserve the treaty. One of its key Allies, Turkey, did not want to see a concentration of military equipment in the Russian Caucasus. But the Russian military did not want to be limited and was threatening to make a unilateral decision that certain territory be excluded from the treaty or simply to walk away from the treaty altogether.

At their May 1995 summit, Clinton had discussed Russia's concerns. At their press conference, Yeltsin could not have been happier with the public presentation. He stated, "On the question of flank restrictions, Bill was the first to bring this matter up. And he said that he will surely support us on this difficult issue because it is true we are sort of in a trap with that issue." Clinton publicly was more supportive than the private discussions between the two governments would indicate. "We believe some modifications are in order. We are supporting the Russian position there. What we want to do is to figure out a way for us to preserve the integrity of the treaty and compliance with it, but, in the end, respond to the legitimate security interests of Russia."[55] As October approached, however, CFE Treaty adaptation remained unresolved.

Meanwhile, on Bosnia, most officials in the U.S. government just did not want to have to worry about the Russian angle. Perry, cutting against the grain of conventional thinking in the administration, insisted that any solution to the most important European security problem of the 1990s had to include Russia. In his view, getting practical NATO-Russian cooperation was important for creating a NATO-Russian framework; in other words, if the United States and Russia could get the practice right, the theory would follow.[56] Nonetheless, as Assistant Secretary Ashton Carter recalls:

> It was very lonely. There was a very small group of people who recognized the importance of doing this, but almost no one among the allies, and almost no one in the U.S. government. Without Bill [Perry], it wouldn't have been possible. And the reason wasn't so much that people were anti-Russian as that Bosnia was a consuming obsession for a large fraction of the senior leadership of the U.S. government. So people felt our relations with allies were so strained, our relations with the Hill were so strained, and this was such a difficult thing to do, that nobody needed an additional complication. . . . We disagreed. . . . We wanted to make Bosnia an example of doing things right in the new Europe. Yes, that the implementation force would be NATO-led but it would not exclude Russia. Everybody else just looked at you like you were out of your mind, believing that this was hard enough without complicating it with the Russians.[57]

Perry and Defense Minister Grachev met on October 8, 1995, in Geneva. Grachev put his hands around his neck to demonstrate to Perry what the Americans were doing to him. Grachev said Russia needed its own sector in Bosnia. And he said that Russia was prepared to ignore the CFE flank limits. Meanwhile, the United States had to have unity of command in Bosnia. One idea circulating was that Russia could handle some civilian operations rather than performing a combat role.[58]

As Carter points out, Yeltsin had to find some way to join the Bosnia operation. Otherwise, he was faced with "a real conspicuous example of how he was not in the club; he didn't need that politically." And the U.S. team knew that if Grachev and the military could agree to a plan, then it did not matter what Russian diplomats thought about the arrangement, as was also the case on the American side.[59]

At Hyde Park, Yeltsin and Clinton agreed that the defense ministers would figure out how to make possible a NATO-led operation with Russian participation. And Grachev and Perry and Joulwan and Shevtsov did indeed figure out a plan. The Russians had agreed to serve under an American general but not in the NATO chain of command. Joulwan was the supreme allied commander (SACEUR) in Europe, but he was also the commander in chief (CINC) of U.S. forces in Europe. So for operational command, Joulwan would wear his American hat, and Shevtsov would be his deputy. As Carter and Perry have written, "Under the Joulwan-Shevtsov scheme, we got what we wanted; unity of command, under Joulwan, for all combat forces, including Russian forces. And the Russians got what they wanted: a role 'with, but not under' NATO."[60] Perry and Grachev also agreed to a CFE map alteration that would allow Russia more flexibility in where it could station its military equipment that would help ensure the continuation of a CFE Treaty regime. Some issues would still be unresolved until 1996–97, but the Russians no longer had to walk out of the treaty to maintain higher equipment levels in the Caucasus than outlined in the 1990 deal.

Acceleration of NATO Enlargement after Yeltsin's Re-election

True to his word, Clinton avoided explicit statements on "who" and "when" until after Yeltsin had been safely re-elected in July 1996. With the election behind them, Deputy Secretary of State Talbott began to reinvigorate efforts to create a NATO-Russia charter. In August, Talbott met with Deputy Foreign Minister Mamedov to talk about drafting a document, and he charged his executive assistant, Eric Edelman, with developing a three-page "non-paper" to share with the Russians.[61]

Many of the elements that would become part of a NATO-Russia accord had been discussed for some time. The Russians wanted assurances that neither nuclear weapons nor new conventional NATO forces would be stationed on the territory of the new members. The United States wanted to make sure that Russia was unable to disrupt the decisionmaking process within NATO and wanted to avoid any hint that new members were second-class citizens. None of these would prove particularly controversial in the end. One major unresolved sticking point was whether this new arrangement would be codified as a legally binding treaty (as the Russians wanted) or whether it would be a political document, not sent to parliaments for ratification (as the Americans wanted).[62] In Stuttgart in early September 1996, Secretary of State Warren Christopher offered a "formal charter" that could lead to "standing arrangements for consultation and joint action between Russia and the alliance."[63]

The problem for the United States was that having waited until after Boris Yeltsin's July 1996 election to move forward concretely on NATO enlargement, the Clinton administration then had to wait another six months finally to engage Russia on a formal charter. Yeltsin's health problems sidelined him for the entire second half of the year, and without Yeltsin, there could be no NATO-Russia agreement. No one else in the Russian government—and certainly not Foreign Minister Yevgeny Primakov, who had replaced Kozyrev during the 1996 presidential campaign to beef up Yeltsin's nationalist credentials—had the incentive or the bureaucratic authority to assent to an accord with NATO without the president's blessing.[64]

Primakov met with Christopher in New York later in September in a meeting that many U.S. officials have described as extremely unpleasant. Talbott writes that Primakov called NATO Secretary General Javier Solana a "stool pigeon," thus trying to discredit the idea of having Solana as NATO's negotiator with Russia on an accord. Edelman recalls, "They had a terrible meeting in New York. My assessment was that Primakov was not even close at that point to being ready to deal on NATO enlargement, and he still thought he could drive wedges [between the United States and its European Allies]; he was traveling to Germany and France to try to block it if he could."[65] The combination of Yeltsin's absence and Primakov's ascendance spelled new trouble for the NATO-Russia partnership.[66]

The Enlargement Track Goes Forward

Although Bill Clinton appears to have decided sometime in the spring or summer of 1994 to push to enlarge NATO at some point, he could not move too fast or he would risk jeopardizing his policy to assist reform in Russia, the single most important national security objective for his administration. Yeltsin's precarious position and Russian outbursts about enlargement had pushed the president to go more slowly; central Europeans and congressional Republicans had pushed him to go faster. The president could not be seen as holding central Europe hostage to Moscow, but neither could he afford to undermine his man in Moscow. And as long as Bosnia raged, the United States could not hope to press the alliance to enlarge. After all, how could one credibly argue that NATO enlargement could stabilize central and eastern Europe as long as *the* major conflict in Europe continued unabated?

By fall 1996, with several issues resolved, the Clinton administration could now move forward on enlargement. The communist threat faded after Yeltsin's re-election victory in July 1996. The Dayton accords had brought peace to Bosnia so it was no longer embarrassing to say that NATO enlargement could help prevent future Bosnias. In his speech in Stuttgart in September, Christopher had called for a summit of NATO heads of state in spring or early summer of 1997 to issue invitations. But despite this announcement, neither the president nor the secretary of state had said anything about a date for accession to NATO for the new members.

A debate ensued within the administration about how far to go in finally saying "when" NATO would enlarge. Talbott and others in the Russia team argued that the president should not name a date, but rather should simply state that NATO intended to take in new members sometime during the second term. Talbott always worried about one track getting ahead of the other, and he feared that providing a specific date would make negotiating a charter with the Russians more difficult. The administration had consistently opposed congressional attempts after 1994 to name names or set a date for enlargement. Why should it abandon this approach now?[67]

But National Security Adviser Anthony Lake, and his NSC staffers Daniel Fried and Alexander Vershbow, wanted to make sure enlargement happened. And the best way to do that was by being clear about a date. These advisers on the foreign policy side had allies on the political side. After all, a presidential announcement that enlargement was truly taking place could be helpful with certain ethnic constituencies, particularly since Republican presidential candidate Bob Dole had been chiding the administration for going too slowly on enlargement.[68]

Two weeks before the election, in a speech in a heavily Polish American area of Detroit, Clinton finally made enlargement concrete: "Today I want to state America's goal. By 1999, NATO's fiftieth anniversary and ten years after the fall of the Berlin Wall, the first group of countries we invite to join should be full-fledged members of NATO."[69] And in March 1999, Poland, Hungary, and the Czech Republic would indeed formally join the alliance.

Warming in Lisbon

The impending 1997 NATO summit and a firm date for accession turned out to be helpful for focusing Moscow's mind on the need to make a deal. So was Yeltsin's return to the world of the living at the end of 1996. In December, Vice President Al Gore and Prime Minister Viktor Chernomyrdin met in Lisbon for a meeting of the Organization for Security and Cooperation in Europe (OSCE) in place of Clinton and Yeltsin. This was a great opportunity for the United States to talk with someone other than Foreign Minister Primakov. The vice president carried a message from Clinton to Yeltsin; essentially, it was,

"Boris, we've got to do this." Publicly, Chernomyrdin repeated Russia's opposition to NATO enlargement; privately, his message from Yeltsin was that the Gore-Chernomyrdin channel was the right place to pursue the negotiations.[70]

In Lisbon, the United States signaled that it was moving toward one element of the Russian position in another area—the adaptation of the Conventional Forces in Europe (CFE) Treaty. The Russian military still felt straitjacketed by the terms of this treaty and was opposed to the continuing "group" basis for establishing limits for the military equipment covered by the accord. After all, by the terms of the treaty, the military equipment held by Poland, Hungary, and the Czech Republic would be counted against the Eastern group of forces even after they joined NATO.

The United States now agreed with Russia that these groupings no longer made sense, and the treaty should be adapted to place equipment limits nationally. Not only was this change logical, but it also allowed the United States to argue that any discussion of conventional force limits take place in the context of the negotiations to adapt the CFE Treaty rather than in discussions of the NATO-Russia accord.

Privately at Lisbon and then publicly at the subsequent NATO foreign ministers' meeting in Brussels, U.S. officials also made clear that Russia need not worry about the nuclear weapons issue. In Brussels on December 10, Secretary of State Warren Christopher declared "that in today's Europe, NATO has no intention, no plan, and no need to station nuclear weapons on the territory of any new members, and we are affirming that no NATO nuclear forces are presently on alert."[71] The United States was careful that this be a unilateral declaration from NATO rather than something that was negotiated with the Russians, in keeping with the desire not to create second-class members in NATO.

The following day, Foreign Minister Primakov announced that Russia had agreed to negotiate a charter. And U.S. officials in turn said that Javier Solana, NATO secretary general, would be the formal negotiator between NATO and Russia. What followed was what Talbott has described as a "Kabuki" process: Solana would have the lead role, but the United States would control the process from behind the scenes. The United States would also meet with key Allies to ensure that NATO had a unified position as Russian officials traveled to different capitals.[72]

To boost the prospects for success, the United States tried to reach Yeltsin through channels other than the Foreign Ministry. In January, 1997, Talbott and a large team of American officials met with Anatoly Chubais, Yeltsin's chief of administration. Chubais told Talbott that NATO enlargement was destroying the liberal camp. "This is the first time in my political life that I have the same position as [fascist Vladimir] Zhirinovsky and [Communist Party boss Gennady] Zyuganov." When Talbott then met alone with Chubais, Chubais emphasized that what Russia needed as enlargement went forward was membership in the Western clubs: a G-8, the World Trade Organization, the Paris Club group of Western creditors, and the group of advanced economies in the Organization for Economic Cooperation and Development.[73]

Some Wobbly Knees

The Russians were the least of Talbott's problems in January 1997. Much more troublesome was French president Jacques Chirac, who beginning in Lisbon the month before argued that NATO should not forge ahead with enlargement if it could not first come to agreement with Russia. If the Russians knew that they could hold up enlargement, then they would have no incentive to come to agreement. Chirac was trying to enlist the help of Chancellor Helmut Kohl in his effort to create a European position that differed from that of the Americans. When Kohl had gone to Moscow in early January, Yeltsin told him that enlargement was too much for Russia to handle and warned, "The security of all European countries depends on Russia feeling secure."[74]

On January 14, 1997, Talbott met with Chirac in Paris. The French president argued that the United States was managing the negotiations poorly and that responsibility should now devolve to France and Germany. "This problem has been poorly handled because the process started during the U.S. election campaign," Chirac complained. "My conviction is that the United States does not take full account of Russian sensitivities. Yeltsin needs a meeting with me and Helmut Kohl because Russia knows that France and Germany understand the situation better than the others."[75]

Fortunately for Talbott, Kohl sided with the United States. The chancellor argued that bringing Poland into the alliance was important for Germany's future as a country in the middle of Europe rather than on the border between East and West since with Poland's inclusion, NATO's eastern border would be that of Poland, not Germany. He believed that Yeltsin needed high-profile events to soothe his feelings, including at the G-7 meeting in June, but Kohl agreed that Russian officials needed to know that NATO was going to enlarge in order to convince them that they needed to sign the NATO-Russia charter.[76]

Talbott may have thought he was out of the woods, but he then had to face a jittery Bill Clinton, who at a cabinet meeting on January 17, 1997, asked his team why Russia should climb on board. After hearing the answer that Russia was going to get some kind of NATO-Russia mechanism and an adaptation of the CFE Treaty, Clinton replied, "So let me get this straight. What the Russians get out of this great deal we're offering them is a chance to sit in the same room with NATO and join us whenever we all agree to something, but they don't have any ability to stop us from doing something that they don't agree with. They can register their disapproval by walking out of the room. And for their second big benefit, they get our promise that we're not going to put our military stuff into their former allies who are now going to be our allies, unless we happen to wake up one morning and decide to change our mind?"[77]

Having reminded Clinton why the United States was moving forward on the president's own enlargement policy, Talbott then moved forward on producing a document. In mid-February 1997, he asked John Bass, a young Foreign Service officer, to take the materials that had been developed previously and draft the charter. Initially, Bass included a long section on how both NATO and Russia had changed, but the reaction from his colleagues was that the document should look forward rather than reminding everyone how NATO and Russia had arrived at this juncture. After Bass's rewriting along these lines, the NATO-Russia charter began to take shape.[78]

From a Russian perspective, however, Clinton had hit the nail on the head in his questions to his team. After all, whereas Russia had received tangible benefits in 1993–94 for doing what the United States asked on issues like sales to India (receiving cooperation on space projects) and Baltic troop withdrawal (receiving funds for officers' housing), Moscow was now getting symbols rather than substance. The difference was that the United States needed Russia to do something to stop the sales of missile technologies or to withdraw occupying troops out of the Baltics. By contrast, U.S. officials now understood that they did not need Russia in order to bring Poland into NATO.[79]

A Fourth No

In early March, Deputy Secretary Talbott and National Security Council Senior Director for European Affairs Alexander Vershbow met Solana in Brussels on his way to Moscow. As they were talking about troop deployments on the territory of new members, Vershbow scribbled some language on a piece of National Security Council note paper. With Solana's concurrence, Talbott took the piece of paper to Moscow and xeroxed it for review by his team there. He then brought it back to Washington for approval by the Interagency Committee of Deputy Secretaries, chaired by Deputy National Security Adviser James Steinberg. Vershbow's scribbles became NATO's second unilateral statement. Although Russia wanted a binding commitment that no foreign troops would be stationed on the territory of the new members, what it got was a pledge by NATO issued on March 14 that "in the current and foreseeable security environment, the Alliance will carry out its collective defense and other missions by ensuring the necessary interoperability, integration, and capability for reinforcement rather than by additional permanent stationing of substantial combat forces." In English, the statement meant that NATO had no intention, plan, or need to introduce substantial forces onto the territory of the new members.[80]

The statement was issued before Clinton and Yeltsin met in Helsinki later that month in order not to give the impression that NATO was selling out the central Europeans in private conversations with the Russians. But critics were not mollified. Former secretary of state Henry Kissinger complained, "I will hold my nose and support enlargement even though the conditions may be extremely dangerous. . . . Whoever heard of a military alliance begging with a weakened adversary? NATO should not be turned into an instrument to conciliate Russia or Russia will undermine it."[81] Docking NATO and Russia was not going to be easy. Important domestic voices in Russia and the United States remained skeptical. One of the most important was Senator Jesse Helms (R-N.C.), whose Foreign Relations Committee would be playing the lead role in the Senate's ratification of NATO enlargement and who, like Kissinger, feared that Clinton and Talbott were letting a weak Russia destroy a mighty NATO through this charter.

The Helsinki Summit

As he approached his next meeting with Yeltsin in Helsinki in March 1997, Clinton made clear to his team that it needed to respond to Russian requests for membership in key clubs to ease the pain. "It's real simple," the president said. "As we push ol' Boris to do the right but hard thing on NATO, I want him to feel the warm beckoning glow of doors that are opening to other institutions where he's welcome."[82] It was the same approach Clinton had taken from day one.

At Helsinki, Clinton offered Yeltsin several things to ease the pain of enlargement. One was agreement to move forward on the latest round of strategic arms reduction talks (START III) as soon as START II was ratified; START III would reduce the level of nuclear warheads on each side to between 2,000 and 2,500 by the end of the year 2007. The great disparity in each country's resources meant that the United States could maintain much higher levels of nuclear weapons than could Russia if there was no new arms control agreement. Since the Russian Duma was unhappy with certain provisions in START II (mainly on matters concerning multiple independently targetable reentry vehicles [MIRVs]), Washington viewed this proposal on START III as helpful to Yeltsin domestically.[83]

On NATO enlargement, Yeltsin told Clinton, "Our position has not changed. It remains a mistake for NATO to move eastward. But I need to take steps to alleviate the negative consequences of this for Russia. I am prepared to enter into an agreement with NATO, not because I want to but because it's a step I'm compelled to take. There is no other solution for today."[84]

Following the repeated requests for concrete offers of inclusion in the West to ease Russia's pain, Clinton in Helsinki publicly stated, "We will work with Russia to advance its membership in key international economic institutions like the W.T.O., the Paris Club, and the O.E.C.D. And I am pleased to announce, with the approval of the other G-7 nations, that we will substantially increase Russia's role in our annual meeting, now to be called the Summit of the Eight, in Denver this June." Yeltsin immediately announced to the Russian public that Clinton "promised me that at the next G-7 meeting, Russia will become a full-fledged member of that club. The G-7 will become the G-8." In Denver on June 20, negotiations would be completed between Russia and the Paris Club, and the United States went out of its way to emphasize what was being done now in the Eight.[85]

Bringing Russia into what would eventually become the G-8 (formally achieved the following year and reaffirmed by George W. Bush) was a real symbolic victory for the Russian president. Yeltsin valued dearly these memberships but none more than the G-8. As he wrote in his last memoir, "the Group of Eight was indeed a club. It was a club for informal meetings among the heads of the eight strongest industrial nations in the world. All the leaders tried strenuously to maintain the relaxed, friendly atmosphere."[86] And Yeltsin makes clear that he saw Russian membership in this prestigious club as compensation for his acquiescence to NATO expansion. As he remembers, "Paradoxically, I think our tough stance on the eastern expansion of NATO, a position I had elaborated at the Russian-U.S. meeting in Helsinki several months earlier, played a role in gaining us this new status [that is, G-8 membership]."[87]

The group's makeover was also a victory for Clinton, who, argues Sandy Berger, "would have gone to a G-8 two years earlier" than happened. Clinton wanted to give Yeltsin something for going along with the American agenda. But both National Security Adviser Lake and Treasury Secretary Robert Rubin opposed pretending that the Russians belonged in the leading group of advanced industrialized countries. Lake says, "The time the President got [most] angry with me was over the G-7 becoming the 8. And it seemed to me it was deluding them and us." Lipton adds that the discussions among the finance ministers were important to the Treasury Department, "and so we took an extremely hard line and [Secretary Robert] Rubin essentially said no."[88]

The two presidents did make clear in Helsinki that they disagreed on the wisdom of the U.S. policy on NATO, with Clinton acknowledging that Yeltsin felt enlargement was "a mistake" but saying that the "Madrid summit [for inviting new members to NATO] will proceed." Most significantly, Yeltsin was rebuffed in the private talks when he sought a "gentleman's agreement" that the Baltic nations of Estonia, Latvia, and Lithuania would never be allowed to join NATO. Clinton responded to this request, "If we made the agreement you're describing, it would be a terrible mistake. It would cause big problems for me and big problems for you. . . . I know what a terrible problem this is for you, but I can't make the specific commitment you are asking for. It would violate the whole spirit of NATO. . . . I don't want to do anything that makes it seem like the old Russia and the old NATO."[89]

As State Department official John Bass recalls, "Helsinki was important because it was where we got the real clear signal from Yeltsin that at the end of the day, after all the bluster, Boris wanted to be part of the club. The main obstacles [at that point] were all in the last section [of the proposed document] on military forces. They were trying to lock in in advance the best deal they could on CFE adaptation to try to limit enlargement's military impact and prevent further expansion in the future."[90]

Whatever leverage Primakov may have had was rapidly eroding. Yeltsin followed the discussions in Helsinki by stating on a trip to Germany in April that he was going to be in Paris on May 27 to sign an accord. As NATO press spokesman Jamie Shea argues, "Every time there was a problem, Primakov would phone Yeltsin and Yeltsin would say, 'do it.' Primakov was under more pressure from Yeltsin than NATO, because Russia wanted to get the best deal, and once the French put forward the prize of a summit in Paris, an agreement had to be done, and Yeltsin was prepared to give up things Primakov had started with and insisted on." In the end, whereas the Russians were trying to get a collective ceiling on NATO military equipment as well as the elimination of "flank" restrictions in a revised CFE Treaty, Primakov had to settle for a Western compromise on the flanks and on limited forces near Russia's borders. (There was a later agreement on subceilings for ground equipment that was stationed in central Europe.)[91]

The Founding Act

On May 27, 1997, Boris Yeltsin and the NATO heads of state met in Paris to sign what was formally known as the Founding Act on Mutual Relations, Cooperation and Security between the Russian Federation and the North Atlantic Treaty Organization. It was not a legal commitment, but Yeltsin did get "an enduring political commitment undertaken at the highest level." The two NATO unilateral statements of December and March were included. And the act stated that a Permanent Joint Council (PJC) was being established that would "provide a mechanism for consultations, coordination, and, to the maximum extent possible, where appropriate, for joint decisions and joint action with respect to security issues of common concern." It further stated that the sides envisioned that they would be engaged "once consensus has been reached in the course of consultation [in] making joint decisions and taking joint action on a case-by-case basis, including participation, on an equitable basis, in the planning and preparation of joint operations, including peacekeeping operations under the authority of the UN Security Council or the responsibility of the OSCE."[92]

At the ceremony, Clinton expanded on a theme that he had spelled out on his first presidential trip to Europe in January 1994. In 1994, he had said to his

Russian audience, "Once every generation or two all great nations must stop and think about where they are in time. They must regenerate themselves. They must imagine their future in a new way." Now, three and one-half years later, he stated, "The NATO-Russia Founding Act we have just signed joins a great nation and history's most successful alliance in common cause for a long-sought but never before realized goal—a peaceful, democratic, undivided Europe. . . . From now on, NATO and Russia will consult and coordinate and work together."[93]

Reaction in Russia was more mixed and less ebullient about the charter. Some, such as former acting prime minister Yegor Gaidar, congratulated Clinton for managing to "pull off the seemingly impossible: to implement NATO enlargement without causing irreparable damage either to democratic elements in Russia's political establishment or to U.S.-Russian relations." By contrast, nationalists and communists labeled the charter a sellout of Russian security interests.[94]

Conclusion

After the signing of the NATO-Russia Founding Act, the Clinton administration could be forgiven for believing that a pattern had been established in the U.S.-Russian security relationship during the previous four years that vindicated the emphasis on supporting Boris Yeltsin. It appeared that the Clinton team was adept enough to prod and assist regime transformation in Russia and at the same time pursue more realist policies in third areas and countries in which Russian and American interests appeared to clash. At the end of Clinton's first term, Russia's political and economic reform was still inching forward. At the same time, Russia had abandoned the India rocket deal and withdrawn its troops from Estonia, Latvia, and Lithuania. Russia also had done its part to assist the effort to ensure that Belarus, Kazakhstan, and Ukraine became nuclear free. Russia participated in the implementation force in Bosnia in a way that few thought would be possible for a NATO-led operation. A deal had been struck on adapting the CFE Treaty. A solution to the problem of Russian assistance to the Iranian nuclear program had not been found, and an arms control deal remained elusive, but on balance Russia, with Yeltsin driving it, was pursuing a path of integration and was extraordinarily accepting of the American foreign policy agenda.

From December 1994–May 1997, no issue had dominated the foreign policy scene quite like NATO enlargement. Russian and American officials had profound disagreements about the intentions behind enlargement. Clinton officials insisted that enlargement served Wilsonian goals of democracy promotion in central and eastern Europe, which was not detrimental but actually beneficial to Russia's long-term interests. Enlargement was "win-win." Yeltsin officials perceived expansion as a realist ploy for increasing American influence and power in Europe and thereby decreasing Russian influence and power. Expansion was "zero-sum." Nonetheless, after the summits in Paris and Madrid in 1997, the United States appeared to have managed the difficult balancing act between promoting its interests in central Europe's transformation and integration and its interests in assisting Russia's transformation and integration. Yeltsin had been re-elected in July 1996, and his clear role in the signing of the NATO-Russia Founding Act reaffirmed for U.S. officials his centrality in ensuring a productive and cooperative relationship.

The ceremony in Paris in May 1997 turned out to be not the beginning of a beautiful friendship but the high point of relations for the rest of the Clinton-Yeltsin years. In the next three years, a series of shocks in the relationship in the three major spheres—economic assistance, security partnership, and democratization—would send the relationship into a downward spiral. In short order, Russia experienced financial collapse in August 1998, walked out on its new relationship with NATO over the spring 1999 war on Kosovo, resumed its war in Chechnya, reneged on its agreement over arms sales to Iran, and rejected the Clinton team's efforts to amend the Anti-Ballistic Missile Treaty. These setbacks provided serious tests to just how far the new Russia and the new Russian-American partnership had come.

9

Things Fall Apart: August 1998

After Yeltsin's re-election victory in the summer of 1996, Clinton and his Russian team finally exhaled. For the entire time that they had been in office, the specter of Yeltsin's potential fall from power and a possible return to power of the communists had loomed like a dark cloud over the administration's Russia policy. Yeltsin seemed vulnerable until late in the 1996 campaign. His victory, therefore, sparked a real sense of optimism about Russia's internal transformation. Yeltsin had another four-year mandate. He could now move forward on the many market reforms that had been delayed by politics and campaign calculations in the previous years.[1] The United States could also move forward with its agenda in other areas such as NATO enlargement that were considered too dangerous to push while the trajectory of Russia's domestic transformation remained uncertain.

In a September 1997 speech delivered at Stanford University, Deputy Secretary of State Strobe Talbott quoted Winston Churchill to label this new era "the end of the beginning." Talbott contrasted this new era with the "beginning of the beginning" in Russia that had coincided with the first term of the Clinton administration. In this earlier era, "All of us came to work more than once with the bracing sense that everything in Russia was up for grabs, that Russia itself was teetering on the brink of regression or chaos." Yeltsin's re-election victory punctuated an end to this uncertain era and gave Talbott hope that the "latter-day Westernizers" could now prevail over the "latter-day Slavophiles." In a piece for the *Wall Street Journal* a few weeks later, Talbott cited not only Yeltsin's re-election but economic stabilization, the end of war in Chechnya, and the NATO-Russia Founding Act as reasons for "strategic optimism." He added, "The key concept is integration."[2]

Talbott and his colleagues still aspired to help the Westernizers succeed. The basic goal of Clinton administration policy had not changed: it was still to promote domestic change in Russia as a strategy for making Russia a more cooperative partner of the West in foreign affairs. As Talbott reaffirmed, "Like Britain in 1942, Russia in 1997 is still in the throes of a titanic struggle. We Americans have a huge stake in how that struggle turns out. Our goal, like that of many Russians, is to see Russia become a normal, modern state—democratic in its governance, abiding by its own constitution and by its own laws, market oriented and prosperous in its economic development, at peace with itself and with the rest of the world. That, in a nutshell, is what we mean—and more to the point, what many Russians mean—by the word reform."[3]

At the beginning of Clinton's second term, Talbott and other senior members of the foreign policy team had reason to be optimistic about the prospects for Russian reform. After hundreds of years of autocratic rule, Russia had just completed three national elections in as many years, all conducted on time and under law. After a rough start, the Russian constitution appeared to be functioning as the highest law of the land. Russia's retrograde communists had been defeated, and now many of Russia's reformers were back in power. As he stated at the meeting of "The Eight" in Denver in June 1997, Clinton believed that Russia was making real progress toward becoming a full-fledged partner of the West. "I'm pleased that for the first time Russia took part in our summit from the start and that this week we reached agreement on Russia's joining the Paris Club for creditor nations—evidence of Russia's emergence as a full member of the community of democracies."[4] The "transition" appeared to be over. Agency for International Development (AID) officials told American organizations working in Russia to promote democracy that their grants could soon end. The mission seemed accomplished.

There were positive signs on the economic front too. Anatoly Chubais, who had overseen Russia's privatization and had run Yeltsin's presidential campaign, became Yeltsin's chief of staff after the 1996 presidential vote. In March 1997, Yeltsin appointed Chubais deputy prime minister in charge of the economy, including the Finance Ministry, and named Boris Nemtsov, a young reformist from Nizhny Novgorod and a darling of Western aid programs, as another deputy prime minister. Lawrence Summers called the new government Russia's "dream team." A year later, when Yeltsin fired Viktor Chernomyrdin and named Sergei Kiriyenko as Russia's new prime minister, Clinton officials were even more bullish about the prospects for real economic reform in Russia. As Summers commented in May 1998, "The current economic team is more cohesive and more united in its commitment to economic reform than any other government Russia has had in the last five years."[5] Throughout this period, Chernomyrdin was still the prime minister but was almost invisible on economic reform issues.

Complementing these positive government reshuffles were optimistic data about economic recovery. Beginning in 1995, Russia had achieved a real degree of macroeconomic stabilization as inflation was tamed—dropping to 22 percent in 1996 and 11 percent in 1997—and the exchange rate on the ruble remained relatively stable.[6] Russia's economy continued to contract in 1995 or 1996, but in 1997, Russia recorded positive growth—though very small growth—for the first time in the decade.[7]

In addition, many basic economic indicators pointed to a brighter future. Clinton officials and Western business executives were especially encouraged by the booming Russian stock market. In 1996 and 1997, the new focus of American aid programs was the promotion of trade and investment, a policy change that implied the technical assistance phase of American aid policy was coming to an end. The joint statement released by Russia and the United States after the Helsinki summit in 1997 committed the U.S. government agencies to "maximize support under their programs to finance American investment in Russia. U.S. efforts will include intensified efforts for project finance, political risk insurance and investment funds through the Overseas Private Investment Corporation; expanding financing for transactions involving equipment exports through the Export-Import Bank that will result in capital investments in the Russian economy; and additional investments through the U.S.-Russia Investment Fund."[8]

In emphasizing the need for greater trade and investment, Vice President Al Gore could boast in 1997 that American companies accounted for a third of all foreign investment in Russia in 1997.[9] To increase these numbers, U.S. officials promised to make $4 billion available to American companies planning to invest in Russia in line with the joint statement that the two countries had issued at the March 1997 Helsinki summit. In 1997, the Clinton administration also announced that it intended to push for Russia's membership into the World Trade Organization (WTO) the following year. Ambitious plans for restructuring Russia's loans to developing countries (estimated to be worth roughly $120 billion) were also outlined.[10] The AID contractors working on economic reform, like those who were working on political reform, were told to write up exit strategies.

Russia also was performing admirably in meeting its obligations to the International Monetary Fund. At the end of 1994, Chubais had left the State Property Committee to become deputy prime minister responsible for macroeconomic policy and finance minister. Chubais assumed these new responsibilities during a government reshuffle that occurred in response to the ruble crash in October of 1994, sometimes called "Black Tuesday." IMF and Treasury officials credited Chubais for sticking to the 1995 IMF standby agreement and achieving at long last financial stabilization. Years later, IMF first managing director Stanley Fischer recalled, "I was first actively involved in Fund negotiations with Russia in the 1995 stand-by, during which inflation was stabilized. Russia's compliance with the terms of that loan was exemplary. There was monthly conditionality, and for 9 of the 12 months Russia essentially met all the conditions."[11]

To senior IMF officials, the programs seemed to be working. Looking back, Fischer wrote, "Russia joined the International Monetary Fund in 1992. Inflation that year was 2,500 percent, and output fell 15 percent. Under IMF programmes, inflation was tamed in 1996 and growth returned in 1997."[12] The progress was so impressive that Treasury official Lawrence Summers suggested in 1997 that it was time for the IMF to phase out of Russia and make way for the World Bank to provide increased funding for structural reforms, "It's time to pass the baton across Nineteenth Street [the street that separates the IMF and World Bank in Washington]. I call on the World Bank to now take the lead, and greatly increase its role in Russian reforms. The Bank is clearly ready. Through intense efforts it has nearly doubled its project execution and disbursement rate in Russia. The Bank should now greatly expand the scope of its activities, in areas of fiscal management and social protection, and in sectoral programs in areas such as agriculture and power, to provide $2 billion in additional loans this year."[13]

Deeper Economic and Political Woes

Beneath the surface, however, the Russian polity and economy still had many ills. On the political side, it was actual illness—Yeltsin's illness—that crippled the president's second term from the outset and thereby weakened political will at the top during the run-up to Russia's 1998 financial collapse.[14] Yeltsin spent the first months of his second term recovering from a multiple bypass heart surgery. After a brief appearance in the Kremlin in December, Yeltsin finally returned to active duty as president in the spring of 1997. Yeltsin's absence allowed Russia's oligarchs to assume greater responsibility for running the government. Two of them, Vladimir Potanin of Oneximbank and Boris Berezovsky of Logovaz actually served in the government. Besides his formal government job as deputy head of the Security Council, Berezovsky assumed an increasingly powerful role as a member of Yeltsin's inner circle in the Kremlin, sometimes referred to as the "family."

Anatoly Chubais, however, did not want to cede control of the state to Berezovsky and his allies. As head of the presidential administration—a job that made him de facto the president's regent during Yeltsin's long convalescence period—Chubais wanted to establish new rules of the game for Russian capitalism that would produce greater separation between the state and the oligarchs.[15] Chubais seemed to want to make amends for his sins in concocting the loans-for-shares program two years earlier.

The conflicting conceptions of state-society relations held by Berezovsky and Chubais clashed over the auction of Svyazinvest, a government telecommunications company. Like Gazprom, Svyazinvest had been created from hundreds of smaller entities to make it a viable private entity, and it became the largest telecommunications company in Russia. Vladimir Gusinsky, the head of Most Bank and the media empire, Media-Most, presumed that Svyazinvest was his for the taking. All the other major oligarchs had acquired lucrative oil and mineral companies through the loans-for-shares program. Now it was his turn. He teamed up with Berezovsky and the Alfa group to raise the capital to acquire the company. Chubais was willing to permit Gusinsky to purchase the firm, but only if he was the highest bidder in a "fair" auction.[16] Before Svyazinvest, competitive bidding had never occurred. Instead, every previous auction of a major company was an inside deal (that Chubais had sanctioned). Gusinsky was incensed that Chubais was now trying to change the rules but went ahead with his bid anyway. He lost. Vladimir Potanin and a consortium of Western investors, including George Soros, outbid Gusinsky and his partners by $160 million ($1.87 billion to $1.71 billion).

Chubais was elated with the process, because he believed that markets were working.[17] Gusinsky was furious and insinuated that Chubais had provided information about Gusinsky's bid to Potanin. Deploying his various media as his weapon, Gusinsky set out to destroy Chubais and his reformist government. Berezovsky joined the battle and put his ORT—Russia's largest national television network—into action to besmirch Chubais and his allies. Muckraking campaigns encouraged by Berezovsky and Gusinsky produced some embarrassing results for Chubais and his associates, including most damagingly a book contract for the Chubais group that paid five authors $90,000 each to write chapters for a book on privatization.[18] (The $450,000 was cash left over from the 1996 campaign. The book contracts were a way to launder the money back to those who had worked on the campaign.) As a result of the book scandal, three of Chubais's closest associates were forced to resign from their government posts. Chubais stayed on as deputy prime minister but was forced to give up his valuable Finance Ministry portfolio. He was damaged goods.

As Chubais and his comrades battled to stay in power, they set aside their ambitious plans for economic reform. Contrary to hopes in the West, Yeltsin's second term did not jump-start economic reform in Russia. Instead, political battles continued to delay real progress on the economic agenda.

Persisting Budget Deficits

Despite the oligarch wars and their consequences for the government reform team, Chubais still believed that the economy was stable and making progress toward recovery. He and his associates proudly boasted that they had finally conquered inflation and stabilized the exchange rate. To underscore their victory, the Central Bank issued new ruble notes on January 1, 1998, with three zeros removed. Instead of 6,000 to 1, the new dollar exchange rate was 6 to 1, and Chubais vowed to keep it that way.

Pressure on the ruble mounted, however, as a result of Russia's growing economic problems. Inflation had been tamed and a fixed exchange rate achieved through the deployment of novel fiscal and monetary instruments. After the passage of the 1993 constitution, Russia's executive branch gained control over the Central Bank, reined in its chairman, and thereby eliminated monetary expansion as a source of inflation. But fiscal policy was still abysmal. Budget deficits persisted throughout the 1990s as the government continually failed to pass balanced budgets through the parliament.[19] Last-minute deals needed to pass the budget, particularly with the agrarian lobby, consistently resulted in the proliferation of financial obligations that the government could never meet, which in turn necessitated the constant sequestering of expenditures. Persistently poor tax collection also undermined sound fiscal policy. By one estimate, companies paid less than 10 percent of money owed to the government in 1997. (The tax code was in need of reform. If a company paid all the taxes that it was officially obliged to pay, it would have given the government all of its profits.)

IMF officials responsible directly for Russia were becoming more worried about Russia's fiscal imbalance. In the fall of 1996, IMF officials debated what to do about the Russian government's failure to collect revenues, and this led to periodic halts of other disbursements scheduled as part of the 1996 Extended Fund Facility.[20] Russia's oligarchs were notorious for not paying taxes, and in 1997, the fiscal deficit was still 7 percent of GDP, almost 4 percentage points above the target of 3.2 percent.[21]

In the earlier part of the decade, the Central Bank simply printed new money and issued new credits to compensate for the deficit, a policy that fueled inflation and undermined the stability of the exchange rate. In the latter half of the decade, after the enactment of the constitution gave the executive branch control over the Central Bank, the government deployed a new set of noninflationary methods to deal with the deficit.

First, the Central Bank stopped printing money. The lack of liquidity in the economy in turn stimulated the use of barter, a highly inefficient method of transaction.[22] By 1998, experts estimated that over half of all industry transactions took place through barter. In addition, tight monetary policy exacerbated the accumulation of debt between enterprises. According to one study, interenterprise debts increased from 33.9 percent of GDP in 1993 to 54.2 percent of GDP by the end of 1997.[23] The absence of hard budget constraints on firms allowed in part by expansion of interenterprise debts allowed managers to focus on acquiring greater control of the companies rather than pushing ahead with restructuring and the attraction of investment.[24] Lack of restructuring at the enterprise level in turn stymied economic growth and, when compared to more successful reforms in east central Europe, helped to slow and stretch out Russia's economic recovery.[25]

A second novel method for achieving stabilization was simply not to pay money owed to state employees. The gap between the approved expenditures in the budget and actual expenditures was always significant. As the 1998 crisis grew, Yeltsin attempted to decrease expenditures even more, announcing on May 26 a new budget proposal that was supposed to cut $10 billion (or 12 percent) from the 1998 budget. This strategy of ignoring commitments resulted in an explosion of wage and pension arrears. Because workers and pensioners were not organized collectively to protest the state's nefarious behavior, the Russian government could get away with this method of "macroeconomic stabilization."[26]

Third, in addition to its debts to the IMF and World Bank, the Russian government began borrowing money from international markets. The Eurobond was the instrument of choice. The IMF and the Russian government liked the Eurobonds, but World Bank officials have asserted in retrospect that they did not, claiming that the dollar-denominated loans were based on an overvalued ruble. When the Russians eventually devalued the currency, the debt burden for the Russian government multiplied. These were long-term, dollar-denominated bonds that the Russian government sold to investors. By the summer of 1998, the Russian government had borrowed $4.25 billion through such medium- and long-term instruments.[27]

As a fourth new method for raising revenue, the Russian Finance Ministry introduced new debt instruments in 1995, a short-term bond called in Russian *gosudarstvenniye kratkosrochniye obligatzii*, or GKO, and the medium-term bond known by its acronym, OFZ. GKOs were denominated in rubles and matured after three or six months, making them especially attractive to those investors looking for quick turnaround on their money. Especially after new regulations allowed Western investors direct access to the GKO market, this debt instrument ballooned in the 1990s.

For a while, this mix of creative instruments worked. Many celebrated the GKOs as a particularly useful innovation since they brought money into the Russian state coffers in a noninflationary way, while at the same time giving investors a stake in low inflation rates and a stable currency. Earlier in the decade, bankers made enormous profits by obtaining credits from the government and then delaying the transfer of these funds to targeted recipients, making profits on the delay because of the high inflation rates. Now they had a new way to make money that was less harmful to macroeconomic stabilization.

The downside was that the lucrative GKO market helped to prop up an overvalued ruble (at six rubles to the dollar), making it difficult for Russian domestic producers to export or compete against cheap imports. Russian banks also had no incentive to make risky loans to untested, unprofitable domestic companies when they could receive amazing returns on their *government-guaranteed* GKOs.[28] The interest paid to investors on the GKOs was outrageously high, especially in 1998 when the Russian Ministry of Finance had to offer high interest rates as incentives to compel GKO holders to roll over their money every three months to avoid reducing the total amount of GKO debt. (In other words, the government was borrowing new money at a higher rate to pay for old debts at a lower rate.) Nonetheless, Russian government officials and their allies in the West anticipated that the skyrocketing interest rates for the short-term bonds would be temporary, lasting only until the government initiated the new tax policies and structural reforms necessary to balance the budget and stimulate growth. Foreign confidence could be measured by the clip at which investors purchased Eurobonds issued by the Russian government and eventually by regional Russian governments. In 1997 and 1998, they had scooped up $15 billion of Eurobond debt. Foreign banks at the time communicated their confidence in the Russian economy by issuing an explosion of private loans to Russian companies. In 1997, portfolio investment also exploded, reaching $46 billion, or 10 percent of Russia's GDP. Some estimated that foreigners owned nearly two-thirds of all stocks traded in Russia.[29]

The Role of Outsiders: Asia, Oil, and Hedge Funds

As a package, however, these schemes for maintaining stabilization were not sustainable over the long run. The GKO market grew exponentially. In 1994, the short- term bond market amounted to only $3 billion. By 1997, GKO debts outstanding totaled $64.7 billion, which then grew to $70 billion in the summer of 1998.[30] By one estimate, the GKO and OFZ market exploded to become 15.9 percent of GDP by July 1998.[31] Significantly, the foreign share of the GKO market also expanded faster than anyone anticipated, first through intermediaries and after January 1, 1998, directly when the Russian government liberalized the market. At the time, the IMF had been pushing for this liberalization of Russian capital markets, because Fund officials believed it was better for the private sector, rather than the IMF, to help finance Russia's budget deficit. The Clinton administration also had made the liberalization of capital markets a pillar of its policy toward emerging market countries. By the summer of 1998, foreigners owned roughly a third of the entire GKO market.[32] The expanded participation of foreigners in the GKO market added new pressure on the ruble, since these bonds would lose their value for these hard currency investors if the ruble fell. To hedge their bets, foreigners as well as Russians bought dollar-forward contracts with Russian banks. For a fee, these forward contracts guaranteed buyers a hard currency price on their GKO investments at a specified date in the future. The inability to pay these forward accounts was one of the main reasons that so many Russian banks collapsed after August 1998.

The Asian financial crisis made foreign investors in Russia's GKO market and foreign lenders to Russian banks increasingly twitchy. The root causes of the Asia and Russia crises were fundamentally different. Asia suffered from bad debts in the private sector, while Russia suffered from poor governmental fiscal policy.[33] But the same people who were losing money in South Korea had money tied up in Russia. As forward calls became due in other markets, these investors had to pull cash out of Russia. On October 28, 1997, for instance, in response to the market crash in Asia the previous day, foreign investors moved major amounts of capital out of Russia, causing a 20 percent decline in the stock market, the largest fall ever. The Central Bank had to spend more than $1 billion in reserves to save the ruble. To provide incentives for these investors to keep their money in Russia, the Finance Ministry, which had been resisting IMF advice to raise interest rates, eventually was compelled to raise the return rates on GKOs. A month before the crash, yields on these treasury bills had reached 113 percent.[34] The pullout of Western investors from Russia also decreased the price of Eurobonds through which Russian banks had borrowed heavily and used as collateral against other loans. As the value of their collateral decreased, Russian banks were compelled to raise new cash—dollars, not rubles—to pay their creditors in the West.[35] Many tried to raise this money by cashing out of the GKO market, which in turn put more pressure on GKO prices and the fixed ruble exchange rate.

Asia's meltdown had another indirect effect on the Russian economy— falling oil prices.[36] The fall in demand for energy in Asia sank the price of crude oil, which fell by 40 percent in the first six months of 1998 compared with prices during the same period in 1997.[37] The fall in oil prices decreased Russian export revenues, causing the Russian current account to go from a $3.9 billion surplus in 1997 to an estimated $4.5 billion deficit in 1998.[38] Russian tax receipts in turn fell dramatically, as did Central Bank reserves. The market began to doubt if the Central Bank would be able to continue to defend the ruble.

One possible solution was a gradual devaluation of the ruble. Early in the year, Russian economist Andrei Illarionov had suggested this option several times privately to the government and in print.[39] A gradual devaluation would displease the holders of GKOs and fuel inflation but might also help to pre-serve Central Bank reserves and gradually reduce the GKO debt. Over the long term, devaluation also would help Russian domestic producers, who could not compete with cheap imports especially in the food processing and textile sectors. Exporters and direct foreign investors would also benefit.

The Russian government and the leadership at the Central Bank, however, flatly rejected the idea of a slow devaluation. In their view, the defeat of inflation and a stable exchange rate were the crowning achievements of their reforms.[40] As Treasury official Mark Medish recalls, sharp devaluation was their worst nightmare. For the Russian Central Bank and government, beating hyperinflation was "like the Battle of Stalingrad. . . . The new ruble was ready January 1, 1998. This was a huge victory for a strong monetary policy. They were about to reap the maximum political benefits at the moment when they came under maximum external pressure on the strategy. Even if the ultimate goal was a graduated, controlled devaluation, they couldn't say it."[41] Unlike other reforms, a stable currency and low inflation were milestones that every Russian citizen could recognize and appreciate. To save these victories, Chubais and his government colleagues had another idea—call in the Americans.

U.S. Reengagement

In 1997, Clinton administration officials had accepted the basics of the positive story coming out of Russia. The government was stable, reformers were in charge, and the stock market was booming. Russia seemed to have turned the corner.

American efforts to assist this reform hit troubled water in the second Clinton term. Ironically, the same year that Russia first recorded modest growth in the decade, the American economic assistance program to Russia endured its worst scandal of the decade. As mentioned in chapter 5, a Harvard team of economists and lawyers had become deeply involved in providing technical assistance to the State Committee on Property at the beginning of the reform process. Most evaluators believed the program to be a huge success, especially compared with the many less successful technical assistance programs funded by the U.S. government. Their Russian partners also believed that the advice and technical support received was invaluable to the privatization program, postprivatization restructuring efforts, and the creation of the Russian Securities and Exchange Commission.[42]

However, the final manifestation of the Harvard effort, the multimillion-dollar program of assistance managed by the Harvard Institute for International Development (HIID) on behalf of the U.S. Agency for International Development, ended in complete disaster. The Agency for International Development accused HIID's director in Moscow, Jonathan Hay, and one of its chief advisers to the Russian government, Harvard economics professor Andrei Shleifer, of misusing government funds and insider information to help generate profits for investment companies run by Hay's girlfriend and Shleifer's spouse, respectively.[43] In a letter sent to Harvard, U.S. AID claimed that Shleifer and Hay "abused the trust of the United States government by using personal relationships, on occasion, for private gain."[44] Chubais, one of HIID's chief clients within the Russian government, eventually asked AID to terminate HIID's activities in Russia, contending that "continuation of these agreements is not consistent with Russian interests." Commenting on the scandal, Jeffrey Sachs, HIID director, remarked, "In 40 years of HIID activities this case is basically unparalleled."[45]

The Harvard institute left Russia, and eventually closed its offices in Cambridge. A civil suit filed by AID against Hay and Shleifer lingered in the Boston courts for years. But even if Hay and Shleifer did not commit crimes or misuse government funds, they were still guilty of terrible diplomacy and bad public relations. As the leaders of arguably the most important U.S. bilateral assistance program in Russia, they should have been extra careful to avoid even the slightest hint of impropriety. In not doing so, they tainted permanently the *entire* American effort to assist Russian economic reform. Brian Atwood, the head of AID at the time of the scandal, reflected, "It's a shame because they [HIID] did very good work. To make that kind of progress you had to have a degree of confidentiality. You could not have AID bureaucrats being involved in that relationship. No one should enter that kind of relationship assuming the worst. I do think that was the most healthy way to bring about change internally with Yeltsin's advisers. It makes me all the more angry that they did what they did because we lost a tremendous opportunity."[46]

The scandal, however, did not derail enthusiasm for market reform in Russia or the more general American effort to assist the transformation. Clinton and his international financial team had other worries at the time. Beginning with Thailand's currency devaluation in the summer of 1997, Summers and Lipton were devoting nearly full attention to the Asian financial crisis. In the early stages of the Asian meltdown, Russia seemed immune. Because the Russian economy had been disconnected from the world economy for so many decades, few Western financial analysts initially looked for a causal relationship between economic woes in Thailand and the health of the economy in Russia. Lipton, who now spent a lot of his time working as an international troubleshooter, acknowledges that he did not. In December 1997, Lipton and Summers met briefly with Chubais during the IMF annual meeting in Hong Kong to discuss Russia's economic situation. Chubais assured them that everything in Russia was fine. Consumed with more immediate crises, Lipton took his Russian colleague's assessment on good faith. Chubais had a reputation in Washington for being honest, to the point, and unafraid of giving or receiving bad news. If Chubais said that things in Russia were fine, then things in Russia must be fine.[47]

This time, however, Chubais was wrong. By spring of 1998, Clinton officials in Washington began to realize that Russia's fragile economy might collapse. By then, the Russian government's finances already were dire. Amidst the crisis, on March 23, Yeltsin unexpectedly named an unknown, 37-year-old oil minister and former banker from Nizhny Novgorod, Sergei Kiriyenko, as his new candidate for prime minister. Kiriyenko struggled to win parliamentary approval, needing five weeks and three votes before taking control of the government. By the time Kiriyenko and his ministers finally settled into their offices, the GKO market had ceased to raise money for the Russian government. Instead the short-term bond market became a liability for the government because the Finance Ministry had to pay out more each week for mature bonds than it took in from the sale of new bonds.[48] The government's reform package, so dear to the IMF, was also stalled in parliament. Something dramatic had to be done.

By the time U.S. Treasury officials saw Chubais again, in May of 1998 when he came to Washington begging for help, they realized the situation was serious, even more serious than the Russians understood. Summers had visited Moscow earlier in May and had been appalled by how poorly the Russian government grasped the magnitude of its predicament. Kiriyenko refused to see the deputy secretary, believing that the American official was too lowly to deserve an audience with the prime minister. Lipton recalls, "We were puzzled because it seemed to us that we had information about the Asian crisis and the economic climate in the outside world, and what was troubling was how unworried they were. They just didn't get that they had no forward momentum on reform and that the markets were getting concerned about Russia."[49]

By the time Chubais arrived in Washington later that month, Clinton officials wanted to help. But they also wanted to see a coherent Russian plan for getting out of the crisis. In May, not only did the Russians not have a strategy, they did not even seem to be thinking about one.

The Bailout Debate

In spite of all of their strategizing, U.S. officials had very few instruments available to influence domestic developments in Russia. This dilemma was becoming a recurrent and frustrating refrain. The debate in the administration boiled down to one big choice. Should the United States encourage the IMF to negotiate a new program and attempt to stave off financial collapse in Russia? An opinion required two sets of calculations. First, could the IMF provide new funds to Russia and still maintain its credibility as a bank that abided by and demanded adherence to performance standards? Second, even if the IMF could justify a new program to Russia, would new money make a difference? Furthermore, how much money was needed to make a difference?

On the first issue, there were real differences of opinion inside the IMF and the Clinton administration. At the Fund, midlevel bankers responsible for the Russia portfolio and in-country representatives had become increasingly frustrated with the politicization of their work.[50] In each new round of negotiations with their Russian counterparts, they would devote countless hours to specifying the exact economic conditions that Russia needed to meet in order to be awarded the next tranche of an existing program or new financial package. This was the method by which the Fund could push for reforms inside a country. With Russia, IMF officials felt compelled at times to do a monthly monitoring of Russian government promises and economic targets. Such a tight leash on a country was rare.[51] When Russia failed to meet monthly targets, the IMF delayed sending funds to Russia for that month. The IMF was micromanaging economic policy in Russia and in effect became a major actor in Russian politics. For instance, in his first speech ever to the Duma in December 1997, Yeltsin urged deputies to pass his budget by warning them that "the whole world" was watching how they voted. That whole world was IMF bureaucrats.

These efforts to push and nudge Russia in the right direction, however, were undermined when political decisions were taken to provide IMF funding to Russia irrespective of Russia's economic performance. According to Boris Fyodorov, former finance minister, the Americans prompted the IMF to pour funds into Russia even when the Russian government delivered on only a fraction of IMF conditions. Even in 1994, Fyodorov asserted, there were "15 points in the program, [but only] 2 implemented," and yet the money continued to flow.[52] The Fund's top officials, Michel Camdessus and Stanley Fischer, made these "political" decisions in consultation with senior officials in the Clinton administration and other G-7 countries. On crucial issues, the IMF did as the G-7 instructed. And the G-7 did as the Americans instructed.[53] Joseph Stiglitz, at the time the chief economist at the World Bank, argues, "In spite of strong opposition from its staff, the Bank was under enormous pressure from the Clinton administration to lend money to Russia [in 1998]."[54] When the final bailout package was announced, the Bank assumed a small chunk of the obligation.

Debates in the IMF about Russia were taking place when the Fund was overextended financially and under critical scrutiny from many different circles. At the time, the U.S. Congress was threatening to renege on a U.S. commitment to replenish IMF resources with an additional $18 billion. Many independent economists and government officials around the globe savaged the IMF's performance in handling the Asian financial crisis and South Korea in particular. Writing in February 1998, George Shultz, William Simon, and Walter Wriston called for the IMF to be abolished. Consequently, avoiding another perceived failure in Russia was considered paramount.[55]

Within the Clinton administration, the voice of caution came surprisingly from the Treasury Department. Usually, the Treasury Department called all the shots in discussions of international financial institutions, while the Department of State and the National Security Council staff listened.[56] Earlier in the decade, it was U.S. Treasury official Lawrence Summers who had invented a new IMF lending mechanism (the STF) to get Russia money on easier terms. This crisis was different. As Treasury Department and White House veteran Mark Medish says, "The dominant push to intervene came from the White House, OVP [the Office of the Vice President], and State. Treasury was almost always the brake."[57] In Lipton's view, the Fund already was overextended with new major commitments in Thailand, South Korea, and Indonesia. The threat of a Brazilian meltdown also loomed, and economic trouble in Brazil had more direct negative consequences for the American economy than did Russian financial failure. Treasury officials also worried about the Fund's reputation. If Russia were to be bailed out because it was "too big to fail," then the Fund's ability to enforce future economic conditionality in Russia and elsewhere would be very limited. More generally, Secretary of the Treasury Robert Rubin had grown increasingly worried about corruption in the Russian government and its ability to deliver on sound economy policies.

Gore, Talbott, Berger, and later Clinton himself argued robustly for a massive IMF bailout. They did believe that Russia was too big to fail. A financial meltdown in a country with thousands of nuclear weapons frightened everyone, so those who believed in the need to bail out Russia could always use the nuclear card to trump the economists from the Treasury Department. And while Rubin tended to take a hard line, even Summers was willing, in Ambassador-at-Large Stephen Sestanovich's words, to "pay ten or twenty billion dollars per year just for insurance" that Russia would not blow up the world.[58]

Supporters of a package also feared that a major financial meltdown in Russia would erase all of the economic reform achievements of the past decade—achievements that they too wanted to cite as part of their legacy some day. Recalls Leon Fuerth, "We thought it problematic but we thought it increasingly desperate, and I don't think we had a very clear fix on the consequences. We had discussions about what would happen if there would be a collapse of the ruble and Treasury was pursuing what the rest of us thought was a hard-line."[59] Madeleine Albright says of the Treasury Department: "They were doing economics in a vacuum and I think that we kept saying, now this is, never in the history of the world has one adversary managed the devolution of the other in a friendly way, and therefore you cannot just throw out the politics of this . . . This is not just an accounting activity." And for Clinton, Albright adds, "There definitely was this . . . sense of 'I can't let Boris down.'"[60]

The Timing and Expectations Game

To have a positive impact, however, the timing of new funds for Russia was critical. Already in January 1998, Western investors in Russia's GKO and stock market were losing faith in the Russian government and expressed their concern by triggering a speculative attack on the ruble. In response, those investors committed to Russia for the long haul began to clamor for an immediate and massive IMF program. Since their GKOs and shares were denominated in rubles, these investors worried first and foremost about devaluation. (Default was not even on their radar screens.) The Russian Central Bank, in their estimation, needed larger reserves to save the ruble from the pressures of skittish, fleeing investors. In their view, an infusion of IMF money into Russia would not have to be spent but could instead be used as a kind of stabilization fund that would deter currency speculators and stretch the time horizons of existing investors.

Officials at the IMF had a different set of priorities. Although Fund officials did not want to witness a major and sudden devaluation, they were still more concerned with Russia's fiscal woes. The Russian government claimed that the budget deficit was only 3.3 percent of GDP in 1997, yet the IMF had estimated the figure at 7.7 percent; the 1998 budget looked even farther out of balance. Besides falling oil prices and the subsequent declining tax receipts, budget balancers also had to deal with another unexpected shock, the government's failure to sell Rosneft (with an asking price of $2.1 billion), the last remaining major oil company to be privatized.[61] In reaction to these fiscal setbacks, IMF funding for Russia during this period was erratic and interrupted. The IMF delayed four disbursements: in June, September, and October 1996, and then another in November 1997. Russia received no funds between February and May 1997. The following year, the IMF provided no funds to Russia from January to June 1998.[62] In contrast to earlier years of sound performance, Russia was definitely considered a problem client by IMF officials in 1997–98.

To increase state revenues, the Fund urged the Russian government to pass through the Duma a new set of taxes. The proposal was wildly unpopular in the parliament and among many in the Russian government. Prime Minister Kiriyenko wanted to focus instead on cutting expenditures, a solution that the IMF deemed impossible. The dispute between the Russian government and the IMF became acrimonious. As Deputy Finance Minister Oleg Vyugin contended at the time, "We should have the right to decide what course we need. It should not be the job of the I.M.F."[63] But without the new taxes, the IMF threatened to delay future disbursements. To appease the IMF, Kiriyenko's government eventually drafted an emergency tax package to include increases in the value-added tax, the excise tax on gasoline, and import tariffs. The IMF officials also wanted to see genuine progress on the long list of structural reforms that Russia had committed to when it signed up for the IMF's $10.2 billion Extended Fund Facility (EFF) program in 1996. Besides tax reform, the list included restructuring of banks and industry, reform of agriculture, social safety net reform, efforts to eliminate barter, policies to increase transparency of the operations of both the government and private firms, and streamlined regulations for foreign direct investment. To stimulate progress on this long list, the World Bank approved two loans totaling $1.6 billion in December 1997, bringing the Bank's total investment in Russia in the 1990s to $10 billion. The size of these loans made Russia one of the Bank's largest recipients and demonstrated that the international financial institutions had not given up on Russia.

The additional World Bank money and the start-and-stop slow drip of new IMF funds were not enough for Russian government officials. In May 1998, one of Russia's largest banks, Tokobank, had collapsed, prompting many investors to fear a similar fate for the rest of the banking sector.[64] Another run on the ruble at the end of the month depleted the Central Bank's foreign reserves even further, fueling speculation in Moscow that the outstanding GKO debt already exceeded Russia's total liquid foreign reserves. In a desperate measure to keep hard currency in the country, the Central Bank raised interest rates to 150 percent.[65] Yields on GKOs skyrocketed to 80 percent for a three-month bond. By mid-summer, the stock market had dropped 78 percent from its peak in October 1997.[66] Something drastic had to be done.

On May 29, 1998, Chubais flew to the United States to persuade his American colleagues to pressure the IMF to provide new funds immediately. Chubais was officially no longer a member of the government and was now the CEO of United Energy Systems. However, Yeltsin, Kiriyenko, and Russia's oligarchs drafted Chubais to fly to Washington because they knew that Chubais was their best hope for securing new IMF assistance. He put his reputation on the line to obtain the new funds. In Washington, Chubais met with all the top officials of the Clinton administration as well as Stanley Fischer at the Fund and James Wolfensohn, the head of the World Bank. Although sympathetic to Chubais's mission, Treasury officials and Summers in particular warned that the Russian government had to enact a radical and credible economic reform package to win back the confidence of Western investors.[67]

In a highly unusual move, the president himself issued a supportive statement for Russia in response to Chubais' visit:

> I strongly welcome Russia's announcement today of its new economic program for 1998. This program, developed in consultation with the IMF, signals Russia's commitment to a bold economic reform agenda to strengthen financial stability and encourage investment and growth. The United States intends to support this program when it is reviewed by the IMF Board. . . . Russia's new economic plan puts in place a solid strategy for fiscal reform. It gives Russian officials the authority they need to collect taxes, crack down on companies that ignore their obligations to the Government, and control spending in line with revenues. What is now important is to carry out these reforms decisively and res-

olutely. The United States will continue to encourage strong IMF and World Bank engagement in support of reform.[68]

Chubais did not come home with a new package since the Americans, Lipton in particular, were still not confident that the Russian government had an effective plan for dealing with its crisis, but he did get promises of new money in the range of $10–15 billion.[69]

Amazingly, Russia managed to float a $2.5 billion Eurobond in early June, prompting some hope that Russia might be on the road to recovery. Chubais continued negotiations with the IMF throughout the summer. In June, IMF officials were making noises that they could not afford a multibillion-dollar bailout for Russia. In response to the $10–15 billion numbers floating in the press at the time as the amount needed to save Russia, Stanley Fischer replied, "It's a lot of money. . . . It's more than the IMF can give to one economy."[70] At the end of June, the IMF moved cautiously forward by approving the next scheduled disbursement due under the previous agreement (the 1996 EFF) of $670 million. A week later, after some pressure from the Clinton administration, a new deal of much larger proportions looked imminent. Michael Mussa, IMF's research director, said a "further support package" was being "actively discussed," because Russia was "too important to fail." Negotiations, nonetheless, between the Fund and the Russian government were difficult and tense. As late as July 12, Western reporters speculated that the deal might not be closed at all.[71]

Two days earlier, however, on July 10, Yeltsin called Clinton asking him to intervene personally with the IMF to prompt a new transfer of emergency loans to the Russian government immediately.[72] In Yeltsin's voice, according to Talbott, was "a tone of urgency we'd never heard before."[73] Russian markets were crashing and Central Bank reserves were disappearing, forcing the Russian Finance Ministry to offer annualized yields of over 100 percent for GKOs. Even before Yeltsin's phone call, the security team in the administration had trumped the economics team on the bailout debate. Deputy National Security Adviser James Steinberg recalled that the Asian crisis and eventually Russia became issues on which the diplomatic and military voices in the government gained a leading role given the potential consequences to U.S. interests:

In the very early parts of [the Asian financial crisis], May-July 1997, Treasury was handling it exclusively. By then Treasury failed to understand political and security implications. As we saw it, the Chinese were supporting the Thai *baht* and we aren't, and they are our ally! It was being handled by low-level people at State and NSC but at the highest levels of the Treasury. After that, there was a strong high level interagency team dealing with all dimensions of it; Asia, Turkey, Pakistan, Russia. So there were regular meetings at least at the senior director level. As the Russia situation began to unravel, it was not just a Treasury operation.[74]

Even the Treasury Department team came around to believe that while a new package was a calculated risk, with probabilities about the outcome that no one could calculate, it was nonetheless a risk worth taking. As Mark Medish recalls, "July was a gamble that didn't work. In late June or early July [we] were in Larry's office. Talked Russia for an hour and a half. Larry asked each of us for the odds of the ruble collapsing without and with support. We did probabilistic assessments. The consensus view was that it was a better than 50 percent chance that intervention could stave off disaster. Some said a 30-40 percent chance; others said [there was a] 90 percent chance of working. Everyone thought the stakes were high enough that intervention was worth a try, even if the odds of success were only 30 percent."[75]

Three days later, on July 13, 1998, and despite Stanley Fischer's earlier pronouncement that $9–10 billion was too much for one country, the IMF announced a $22.6 billion emergency financing package, which included $15.1 billion from the IMF, $6 billion from the World Bank, and an additional $1.5 billion from Japan. Of this total, creditors planned to transfer $14.8 billion in 1998 and the remainder in 1999. The initial disbursement was to be used to replenish the Central Bank's foreign currency reserves, which had dwindled officially to $13.7 billion as the Bank battled to defend the ruble.[76] In accepting the new program, the Russian government agreed to implement a 5 percent sales tax, increase the land tax, restructure the corporate tax, force companies to pay utility bills and taxes or face bankruptcy, and cut the budget deficit from 5.6 percent to 2.8 percent of GDP by the following year. The new program also included a massive debt swap, to be organized by U.S. investment firm Goldman Sachs, which aimed to transform $8 billion of ruble-denominated GKOs into longer-term, dollar-denominated Eurobonds. The combination of the debt swap and the new infusion of hard cash was designed to lessen the immediate pressures of the exploding GKO market and slow the outflow of hard currency out of the country.[77]

The first infusion of the new IMF loan was originally announced at $5.6 billion, to be composed of half from the 1996 Extended Fund Facility and half from a new Compensatory and Contingency Financing Facility—a program for countries that have suffered from the consequences of adverse balance of payments developments. As a punitive response to the Duma's failure to pass new tax laws, however, only $4.8 billion from the Fund (along with $0.3 billion from the World Bank and $0.4 billion from Japan) was actually delivered.[78]

Russian officials tried to hype the importance of the new external funding. Kiriyenko called the release of the first tranche an "absolute victory" for Russia, while Chubais, though less triumphant, said, "I don't think it's a great success, but I do think it's a historical moment."[79] Initially, the world reaction was positive. The *Economist* wrote, "At the very least, the IMF-led rescue has staved off the nightmarish possibility of Russia plunging into simultaneous financial meltdown and political crisis. But with coup rumours and industrial unrest still simmering, the prospect of a hot political autumn is still strong. Still, the IMF package may tilt the balance in the government's favour during any political showdown."[80]

At the same time, IMF director Camdessus asserted or hoped that "the strengthening of Russia's economic policies—both fiscal and structural—the large additional financial resources and the debt conversion scheme, should fundamentally improve the financial situation of the Russian government."[81] Even as late as July 28, Secretary of the Treasury Robert Rubin stated publicly, in a letter to skeptical Speaker of the House Newt Gingrich, the need to stay the course with Russia, "The new government in Russia has staked its credibility on getting Russia's fiscal house in order. . . . Equally important, the financial crisis has added a sense of urgency. This is the wrong time for the IMF to withdraw from this strategically critical country. We have a significant opportunity to use the leverage of IMF financing to help the Russian government finally take the myriad steps needed to put its finances on a sustainable path."[82]

Camdessus and Rubin had either flawed arguments or fleeting hopes. The first tranche was also the last tranche. Before the next installment of the IMF's new program could be delivered, all hell broke loose.

The Meltdown

In the first week of August, the IMF's second-in-command, Stanley Fischer, traveled to Moscow to discuss with Chubais the conditions under which the Russian government could secure the second $4.3 billion tranche of the IMF stabilization loan. As usual, the collection of federal budget revenues was the centerpiece of their deliberations, yet both sides "expressed satisfaction" with the progress made on raising new revenues in July.[83]

Investors, especially Western investors, could not wait for the second IMF infusion. For them, the announcement of the new IMF program came too late. Their confidence in the Russian government's ability to meet its debt commitments already had shattered as demonstrated by their unwillingness to purchase new GKOs offered after the announcement of the IMF package. In the week of August 10-14, three successive GKO auctions had to be canceled, because the market pushed the purchasing price to more than 200 percent on a three-month GKO, a price that the Russian government could not afford and that signaled zero confidence in the government's ability to pay its outstanding debts. The RTS—the main listing of Russian stocks—plunged 25 percent that same week.[84]

By July, most investors were in a mad rush to get their money out of the country before the Central Bank's hard currency reserves disappeared altogether. As businessman Boris Jordan reflected, "Everybody thought that the big announcement was going to solve Russia's big problems. But that's total hogwash, because all everybody used it for was an exit out."[85] Lipton, sensing disaster, flew to Moscow on August 11 and was shocked to learn that Chubais was on vacation in Ireland and Sergei Dubinin, the chairman of the Central Bank, was relaxing in Italy. He quickly realized there was little that he or the United States or the IMF could do. He came to the conclusion that the IMF had to pull the plug on the Russian bailout. A country with thousands of nuclear weapons was going to have to be allowed to fail. He urged Kiriyenko to face up to the gravity of the problem. Lipton recalls:

> Wherever I went, I heard the same story. They all said the same thing, that the GKO redemptions could be managed; they knew when they were maturing and how much money they had. And they said, we have enough money to service the GKOs until September 21 and the next IMF drawing is September 28, so if you guys advance the drawing by another seven days then we can go another three months. And I said, your Central Bank has been losing $300 million a day for eight days, $2.4 billion. You don't have enough foreign exchange reserves to get to September 21; in fact $300 million is not a stable path. Either you do something to restore confidence and the outflow decreases or it goes up to an unsustainable outflow.[86]

The following week, the Russian government responded with emergency measures. A precipitating event was an opinion piece written by financier George Soros in the *Financial Times* on Thursday, August 13, 1998, in which the billionaire warned that Russia's meltdown had reached its "terminal phase," a diagnosis that triggered panic in the international markets.[87] Before markets opened on Monday, Kiriyenko's government felt compelled to do something. Even though Yeltsin had promised as late as August 14 that there would be no devaluation, most financial analysts expected Kiriyenko to allow a soft float downward of the ruble. Devaluation, among other things, was supposed to decrease the value of the ruble-denominated debts relative to the dollar and thereby make it easier for the Russian government to meet its repayment commitments with the limited stock of hard currency available in reserves.

Holders of GKOs had braced themselves for such a possible gradual devaluation. But they were shocked to learn on August 17 that the government was devaluing the ruble (with a target of 9.5 instead of 6.2 rubles to the dollar) *and* defaulting on all its outstanding debts to private holders of Russian bonds.[88] At the time, outstanding GKOs were estimated to be worth $60 billion.[89] The government also announced a ninety-day moratorium on claims against Russian banks. This three-month grace period gave Russian banks a chance to restructure and protect their assets before they went bankrupt or had to face litigation charges from Western banks and investors.

Many of these Russian banks had provided Western investors with forward contracts that "guaranteed" the Western investors a future price—denominated in hard currencies—on their GKO investments. In a sense, these forward contracts were insurance against a financial collapse. Russian banks also had offered up their Eurobonds as collateral to these Western creditors. After devaluation, these Russian banks had no way of paying back these forward contracts or dollar-denominated bonds.[90] Most of these large Russian banks also held billions in GKOs. The combination of holding worthless government debt, dollar-denominated debt to outside lenders, and forward contracts that they could not repay meant that most of these banks went out of business. (Even if the banks closed, the well-connected bankers still did very well after the crash. Many have since become some of Russia's richest people.)

The Clinton administration and IMF officials did not support the package of emergency measures. The day before the program was announced, Treasury and IMF officials urged the Russian government to reconsider. As Summers reported during a congressional hearing a month later, "Russia's economic policy framework collapsed in the middle of last month as the Russian authorities—in the face of severe market pressures—decided on the enormously risky course of simultaneously devaluing the ruble, imposing a debt moratorium and restructuring government bonds. This was the Russian government's decision and not one which we supported."[91]

There was a frenzy of discussions among Western officials. IMF and Clinton administration officials were blindsided by the emergency measures. IMF officials were especially appalled by the ninety-day moratorium for Russia's banks, which was an obvious bailout for those most unworthy, in their estimation, of bailout. After hours of difficult conversations, the IMF and the Clinton administration eventually agreed to endorse publicly the emergency measures. Privately, however, they were not enthused.[92]

Kiriyenko's government hoped that these drastic measures would help stabilize the currency and Russia's fiscal balance. As agreed the day before, the IMF also issued its statement of support. In the final line of the IMF statement, Camdessus affirmed that "it is important that the international community as a whole, both public and private sectors, show solidarity for Russia at this difficult time."[93] Few did. Foreign investors were furious about their treatment and tried to cash out immediately, putting tremendous pressure on the ruble.[94] A week later, the ruble had lost two-thirds of its value vis-à-vis the dollar. In one day, the two purported economic achievements of the Boris Yeltsin era—control of inflation and a stable, convertible currency—were wiped out. The IMF's July transfer of $4.8 billion disappeared immediately, $3.8 spent by the Central Bank buying up rubles and another $1 billion by the finance minister in redeeming GKOs, though who actually secured these hard currency funds remains a mystery. Secretary of the Treasury Robert Rubin acknowledged that much of the final $4.8 billion IMF loan distributed to Russia in the summer of 1998 "may have been siphoned off improperly."[95] The stock market all but disappeared, the ruble continued to fall, banks closed, prices soared, and stores emptied. By the end of the year, the ruble had lost 71 percent of its value compared with the beginning of the year, while Russia's GDP had decreased by 5 percent compared with 1997. Western investors were left holding worthless pieces of paper, be they stock, GKOs, new bonds, or forward contracts signed with Russian banks. For the first time in a century, Russian economic woes also reverberated throughout the world economy, reaching even the American stock market. Adam Elstein, the head of Banker's Trust in Moscow at the time, captured the sentiment of the day when he told a *Financial Times* correspondent that investors "would probably rather eat nuclear waste" than put money in Russia again.[96]

Short-Term Consequences of the Crash for Russia

A week after announcing his emergency plan to avoid economic crash, Kiriyenko himself crashed. Yeltsin called for his resignation, and asked his former prime minister, Viktor Chernomyrdin, to reassume the reins. Yeltsin also pushed Sergei Dubinin out of his position as head of the Central Bank, even though the president did not have the constitutional authority to do so. He then nominated Viktor Gerashchenko to fill the slot, the same former central bank chairman who had spearheaded Russia's inflationary monetary policy earlier in the decade. Russia's communist opposition in the parliament, emboldened by the absolute failure of the last government and Yeltsin's own weakness, rejected Chernomyrdin twice. To avoid a third vote, which would have compelled Yeltsin to undertake the very risky measure of dissolving the Duma, Yeltsin acceded to the will of the parliament and nominated Foreign Minister Yevgeny Primakov to run the government. With strong backing from the Communist Party and its allies, Primakov's nomination as prime minister sailed through the parliament. Though not obligated constitutionally to consult the Duma on ministerial appointments, Primakov nonetheless cooperated with Duma leaders to form a coalition government. Primakov rejected candidates for ministerial posts who were too firmly identified with previous governments and instead cobbled together a new government of centrists, communists, liberals, and even one member from Vladimir Zhirinovsky's Liberal Democratic Party. He appointed Communist Party official and former Gosplan head Yuri Maslyukov as his deputy prime minister in charge of the economy.

Early in Primakov's tenure as prime minister, Russia appeared to be not at the "end of the beginning" as Talbott had described the country just a year earlier, but at the "beginning of the end." The reformers backed by the Clinton administration for the last five years were now out of power, and their ideas and policies seemed to have failed. As Russia analyst Arnold Horelick stated, "Washington now quite clearly, if somewhat reluctantly, sees Yeltsin as a spent political force. His decline, moreover, is accompanied by the departure of the liberal economists to whom Washington and the West generally have looked to lead Russia's reform. Along with them, this brand of liberal reform is gone."[97] Andrei Illarionov, a staunch neo-liberal, echoed Horelick's prediction.

> The most serious *ideological* consequence of the crisis was a powerful shift in public opinion. The words "democracy," "reforms," and "liberal" and the concepts and the people associated with them have been discredited. The ideas of the market economy, liberalism, and friendship with the West have been seriously undermined. The Russian population at large has become much more receptive to vigorous government intervention in economic and social life, theories of a Western conspiracy against Russia, and the idea of a unique "Russian way." . . . One can hardly avoid the painful conclusion that the repeated attempts to create a stable democratic society with an effective market economy in Russia have failed.[98]

A nonbinding resolution banning Kiriyenko, Nemtsov, Gaidar, and Chubais from political office forever passed both the Duma and Federal Council, without a court or legislative commission ever investigating their allegedly illegal activities let alone convicting them of illegal acts.

In the early stages of his rule, Primakov sounded like he planned to turn the clock backward on all reforms implemented in the 1990s. Proposals for nationalization of monopolies, increasing radically the monetary supply as well as pensions and wages, reprivatization of enterprises along more equitable lines, and price controls dominated discussion in the wake of the August financial crash. On foreign policy, U.S. officials braced for the worst. Primakov had always distrusted the West and the United States in particular. Now, he was running the Russian government.

At the time, Yeltsin—"our man in Moscow"—was a weak check on Primakov's power. In a January 1999 expert rating of influential figures, Primakov placed first, well above Yeltsin, who was a distant third to Moscow mayor Yuri Luzhkov.[99] Yeltsin appeared so physically weak and politically vulnerable that rumors of his resignation and even death sporadically swirled through Moscow.[100] Others speculated that regime meltdown would eventually follow economic meltdown, leading to some kind of praetorian or even fascist state. In an echo of December 1993, talk of "Weimar Russia" intensified, especially after the assassination of democratic leader Galina Starovoitova.[101] Even Yeltsin began talking of planned coups, warning potential conspirators, "We have enough forces in order to stop any plans for taking power."[102]

More concretely, Yeltsin's foes in the Duma tried to take advantage of the president's weakness to force his acquiescence to a power-sharing pact, which would have changed Russia's constitutional rules unconstitutionally.[103] After this idea fell apart, new proposals emerged to amend the constitution properly in order to scale back the powers of the president. Some draft amendments even called for the elimination of the presidential office. Gennady Zyuganov and his Communist Party spearheaded these suggestions for constitutional change, but the general idea had widespread appeal among political groups representing a wide political spectrum. After August 1998, several groups in the Duma drafted proposals for amending the constitution to give the parliament more power.[104]

Nightmare scenarios, however, never unfolded. The more Primakov learned on the job, the less retrograde he sounded. Primakov's government did not swell the budget but instead made serious expenditure cuts that Kiriyenko's government had wanted to undertake but had lacked the political will to accomplish. Finance Minister Mikhail Zadornov kept Primakov on track regarding fiscal policy and checked the influence of Maslyukov. Although some government sectors such as defense and intelligence did enjoy spending increases under Primakov, the budget submitted to the Duma allowed for only a 2.5 percent budget deficit as a percentage of GDP, a figure much smaller than the previous two years. The World Bank even criticized Primakov's cuts in the education budget as too drastic. Nor did the Central Bank print scads of new money. In the first days after the August meltdown, Primakov launched many diatribes against the neoimperial and ineffective policies of the IMF.[105] Nonetheless, after a temporary severing of ties, Primakov even reached out to this villainous institution.[106]

Radical changes did not occur in the way Russia was governed. All the proposals for constitutional change failed. None of the extraconstitutional plots were attempted. Later in the spring of 1999, the Duma tried to impeach Yeltsin but fell short of mustering the necessary votes needed to move the proceeding past the first stage. By that time, Yeltsin had recovered well enough politically that he removed Primakov as prime minister and replaced him with Sergei Stepashin, a Yeltsin loyalist who was much more sympathetic to the liberal reformist cause. The Duma approved Stepashin with little drama. Only weeks later, Yeltsin removed Stepashin in favor of an unknown Kremlin apparatchik, Vladimir Putin. In nominating Putin, Yeltsin stated explicitly that he planned for Putin to replace him as president the following year. The man who only a year earlier seemed marginal, if not finished, as a political force in Russia was now orchestrating the transition of power in the Kremlin precisely as he wanted it to happen.

Consequences of the Crash for the Clinton Team

Ironically, the August 1998 financial crash may have done more lasting damage to Clinton's policy toward Russia than it did to Russia itself. Although never an issue of national importance, the August meltdown triggered a major debate among American experts and policymakers about the wisdom and success of Clinton's approach. At that moment, many used the August crash to conclude that the policy was a resounding failure.

For one day, Russia's financial crash was the most important story in the United States. On the day of the crash, CNN repeatedly broadcast a scene of a minor brawl among frustrated depositors trying in vain to get their money out of a closed bank—the full extent of societal mobilization in response to the crash. On the second day of the crisis, Clinton's confession about his affair with Monica Lewinsky buried the Russia story for good for most of the American public. Clinton's foreign policy team, although also deeply disturbed by the unfolding Lewinsky scandal, became preoccupied with another major foreign policy decision—how to respond to the terrorist attacks against American embassies in Kenya and Tanzania. That week Russia fell back to a distant third consideration.[107]

For Osama bin Laden, the United States at least had some response: eighty cruise missiles fired at al Qaeda training camps in Afghanistan and at a factory thought to be producing chemical weapons in Sudan. For Russia, it was much more difficult to articulate a policy reaction. Days after the Russian government announced its ill-conceived crisis measures, the Russian economy seemed to be on an unstoppable, downward spiral. After economic collapse, several American analysts predicted political collapse would follow.

The Clinton team had first to decide if the president should travel to Russia to attend a scheduled summit with Yeltsin during the first week in September. The greatest fear for Clinton foreign policy officials was that Yeltsin might be forced out of power on the eve of a Clinton visit. Talbott traveled to Russia a week before the summit and received assurances from Yeltsin personally that he had no intention of resigning. Even if Yeltsin was ready to meet and greet the American president, Clinton's domestic advisers strongly opposed the trip, arguing that it would seem as though Clinton was running away from the Lewinsky scandal. Pundits and analysts in Washington ridiculed the planned summit as a meaningless meeting with no agenda, a metaphor for the new state of affairs in U.S.-Russian relations. As one observer wrote, "Unless 1,200 people accompany Clinton on his upcoming trip, as they did to China, and thus inject money into the Russian economy, there is little hope that anything positive will emerge from this summit."[108]

Talbott disagreed. He argued that Clinton had to go. To cancel the trip would create the appearance that the United States was giving up on Russia. The trip had been announced back on July 6, before the new IMF package had been put forward publicly. Talbott recalls that Yeltsin himself communicated such a message to the deputy secretary during his presummit visit to Moscow. "His [Yeltsin's] message was simple: if the summit went ahead, the two leaders would be able to steady the relationship; if he cancelled, everything they accomplished was in jeopardy."[109]

Treasury officials expressed little enthusiasm for the trip, but again, to the National Security Council, State Department, and the president, the costs of not going seemed too high. Mark Medish recalls, "When [Primakov] became Prime Minister, there was pressure from other agencies to reengage. But Treasury had been burned. Russians had acted so crudely in August. Rubin did not want to stake his reputation on Russia. From Treasury's perspective it was once burned, twice shy. Clinton did go in September, but Treasury didn't support the trip. Ultimately, it was Clinton, Berger, and Strobe, taking into account the larger U.S.-Russia relationship, who decided Clinton should go."[110]

Russian reform was not Clinton's top priority at the time, and it showed at the summit. To be sure, Clinton was in Moscow when the Russian government did not even have a prime minister; Yeltsin was still trying to get Chernomyrdin's nomination through the Duma. Yet the Clinton administration brought to the meeting no real agenda. Instead, the "new" agenda was the old one from its first years in office: how to keep Yeltsin in power. Much to Clinton's dismay, even this concern was not of interest to the American journalists traveling with him. At the joint press conference with Yeltsin and Clinton, two of the three questions from the American side concerned Lewinsky, and Clinton was embarrassed and angry.[111]

Clinton's frustration and lack of focus were a metaphor for the entire U.S. policy toward Russia at the time. On the one-year anniversary of the crash, a cover story written by John Lloyd for the *New York Times Magazine* would ask "Who Lost Russia?" launching a witch-hunt in Washington (not, curiously enough, in Moscow).[112] The question presumed that Russia was lost (and that it was America's to lose). Adding fuel to the fire was the exposure of a major money-laundering scheme in Russia involving the Bank of New York.[113] Some even asserted that IMF bailout funds had been diverted by the Russian government into Swiss bank accounts.[114]

After the Bank of New York scandal (and the continuing Lewinsky fiasco), Clinton's critics were unconstrained in their accusations. Most damagingly, some Clinton foes asserted U.S. complicity in Russian government corruption. For years, many had speculated that Prime Minister Chernomyrdin was a very wealthy man, who stashed away millions for himself and his family that were stolen assets from Gazprom.[115] Reports surfaced that Vice President Gore wrote "bullshit" on page one of a CIA report documenting Chernomyrdin's illegal activities.[116] Gore advisers refuted the claim then and later, but the public relations damage had already been done. Russian government officials were corrupt, criminal, and incapable of creating real capitalism, and the Clinton administration was in cahoots with them. To reaffirm the connection, Speaker of the House J. Dennis Hastert (R-Ill.) commissioned a study of American policy toward Russia, chaired by Congressman Christopher Cox (R-Calif.) and including no Democrats on the committee, which blamed Gore directly for complicity in Russian corruption.[117]

Although few accused the Clinton team of being outright criminals, many political pundits, Washington think tanks, and the Republican Party devoted much time and many resources in the next two years to the Who Lost Russia debate.[118] Especially as the 2000 U.S. presidential election heated up, critics assigned Clinton and Gore major credit for Russia's failures. During the election year, the Cox Report prodded some to blame Gore directly for Russia's troubles. For instance, the *New York Post* wrote, "America won the Cold War, defeating the Soviet Union. But who lost Russia? The list of suspects is long. But a compelling new study [the Cox Report] points a finger at a key culprit —Vice President Al Gore." The *New York Post* suggested that "Al Gore owes the American people an explanation as to who lost Russia."[119] Columnist David Ignatius even used the term "Russiagate."[120] Many commentators joined in to say that American aid to Russia had been useless, money poured down the drain. Former Reagan secretary of defense Caspar Weinberger went one step further to contend that American assistance was not just wasteful but harmful to American national security interests. "Billions of dollars in aid misused—and some of it disappeared entirely. . . . The aid vanished right off the radar screen—aid was supposed to go for industrial recovery but instead went in large part to support an extremely large program of regaining sophisticated military capabilities. . . . A great deal of the money from the IMF went directly into the acquisition of arms or the programs for acquiring them."[121]

The theories for failure were abundant and contradictory. For some analysts, the Clinton team did not understand Russia: it had adopted "a flawed conceptual approach" that was "based on an insufficiently complex appreciation of the effects of the Soviet legacy on the constellations of interests, institutions, and behaviors within these [postcommunist] countries."[122] American economic assistance, while perhaps well intentioned, "was inappropriate to Russian traditions and conditions."[123] Russia analyst Thomas Graham was even more direct in a 1999 condemnation. "The financial collapse of last August shattered all illusions about Russia's trajectory. It marked the failure of the Western policy of the past seven years, the end of the grand liberal project of rapidly transforming Russia into a normal market economy and democratic polity."[124] For others, the Clinton team did not understand economics and emerging markets; members had failed to push through the "right" economic reforms and then had failed to deliver the IMF bailout when it could have made a difference. On the IMF's role, one side said the IMF was too lenient.[125] Some even accused the Fund of prolonging Russia's economic woes rather than helping to solve them.[126] Others said the IMF was too strict.[127] Both of these camps, however, blamed American pressure on the IMF for the Fund's poor performance.

Critics charged that the Clinton administration encouraged Russia to attract "hot money" into the stock market without pushing Russia to create the propitious conditions for foreign direct investment. In retrospect, combatants on both sides of the Who Lost Russia debate cited the overflow of portfolio and bond money from abroad and the premature liberalization of the capital markets as one of the main causes of the August 1998 financial meltdown. Who is to blame for this inflow, however, is still hotly contested. Some blame the IMF for pressuring the Russian government to liberalize capital markets too quickly. Others blame the Western investors for offering Russian banks and governments too much money too quickly.[128] A third school blames the Russian government for having to rely so heavily on this kind of "hot money" to finance its budget. China, with foreign direct investment of $181 billion at the time compared with Russia's $8.7 billion, became the model case for emerging markets. Russia was the example to avoid.[129]

Others cast the debate in more general terms about the nature of international politics. One school argued that the policy had failed because the United States had pretended for too long that Russia was still a great power. "American engagement with Russia tended to perpetuate the bipolar imagery and discourse of the Cold War era, long after the growing disparity between American and Russian power had rendered it anachronistic."[130] Others countered that the policy failed because the United States did not treat Russia like the great power that it still was.[131] American aid policy was cited as a strategy that negatively (if not deliberately) exacerbated asymmetries in the bilateral relationship. As Dimitri Simes concluded, "There are now strong suspicions in Russia that Washington deliberately sought to keep it on its knees by forcing it to accept destructive economic policies. While there is no evidence that the Clinton administration was either capable or desirous of so Machiavellian a policy, senior administration officials certainly must be aware that, notwithstanding the rhetoric of partnership advanced by both sides, there could be no genuine equality in the relationship between a powerful donor and a beleaguered recipient."[132] In a similar vein, other critics argued that the United States did not understand Russian security interests. Policy recommendations ran the gamut, including a return to containment, disengagement, or renewed, more comprehensive engagement.[133]

Clinton's Russia team defended the policy by first rejecting the terms of this debate altogether. They argued that Russia was not lost but simply undergoing some difficult hiccups in its transition to capitalism and democracy. Clinton officials defended the gamble to try to bail Russia out in July, even if the effort did not succeed. As Lipton explained to skeptical members of Congress, "The rationale for the $22.6 billion additional multilateral financing package mobilized in July was to provide measured, conditional assistance to support these reform efforts and, by helping Russia withstand intense financial pressures, give it time to continue reform. . . . We supported this financing because we believed there was a reasonably good chance, not a certainty, but a reasonably good chance, that reform would move forward in the period ahead. This judgment was based on the fact that President Yeltsin and Prime Minister Kiriyenko had just taken some important steps, largely in the form of decrees, to cut Russia's federal deficit."[134]

In the immediate aftermath of the August crisis, Clinton officials publicly urged renewed and patient engagement of Russia, not abandonment.[135] Just as Clinton had decided that he needed to go to Russia in September to show his support, Treasury officials *publicly* called for a renewed commitment to support Russian reform:

> The United States thus has a strong stake in Russia successfully overcoming today's crisis and laying the grounds for a more stable future—by carrying out the kind of macroeconomic and structural reforms included in the IMF program. We will strongly support a Russian government that is determined to carry out these changes and continue the process of democratization. This is not about imposing "American" economic models or any other kind. Russia has its own unique history and traditions and it will plot its own path in the economic arena, as it will in every other respect. It will have to make its own decisions about specific institutions and market arrangements. Yet, as President Clinton said in Moscow last week, if the past year has taught anything it is that no country can escape the imperatives of the global marketplace.[136]

And even this beleaguered Russia was still cooperating with the United States on issues dear to American security interests such as denuclearization.

In response to the corruption charges, Clinton officials claimed that they were well aware of the problems but also incapable of doing much about them. Clinton and Yeltsin did not create corruption in Russia. Rather corruption was "not a new phenomenon—Soviet society was characterized by pervasive corruption." Nonetheless, the Clinton administration argued that it had been engaged in fighting corruption and promoting the rule of law for some time.[137] Testifying before the House International Relations Committee a month after the crash, Summers emphasized the following focal points of American policy toward Russia:

> Mr. Chairman, starting with the Vancouver Summit in 1993, President Clinton has made clear that the United States would take a leading role in international efforts to help Russia develop the institutions and policies of a functioning market economy. . . . On a bilateral level, legal reform and the battle against corruption have long been a central focus of Vice President Gore's work with the Russian Prime Minister and President Clinton's dialogue with President Yeltsin. To cite just one Treasury-related example, we are working with Russia to curb money laundering through promoting passage of legislation which criminalizes money laundering and consulting on the creation of a financial intelligence unit.[138]

Yet Clinton officials also admitted to the limitations of their programs because of Russia's own limitations. As AID administrator Brian Atwood reflected, "We eventually were under a great deal of pressure—why don't they have rule of law, why don't they have commercial codes, why don't they have all these things, why don't they have more help for the private sector—we put a lot of effort into that, but found we couldn't work with the central government. The people running those ministries were not the reformers."[139]

Clinton officials also emphasized the long-term nature of Russian reform and Russian—not American—ownership of the process. Speaking in Chicago soon after the crash, Secretary of State Albright, stated, "We cannot say that Russia has lost its way when in fact it has just begun its journey. Nor can we say that Russia is ours to lose. We can help Russia make tough choices, but in the end Russia must choose what kind of country it is going to be." She also declared, "They have to heal themselves."[140]

Albright, of course, was right. She also would have been right in the mid-1990s. Yet, back then, U.S. officials were all too eager to take partial credit for Russia's successes, be they the privatization program or the creation of a new securities and exchange commission. Just a year earlier, Summers had emphasized the crucial impact of U.S. efforts on Russian reform. In his last meeting with Prime Minister Viktor Chernomyrdin, Summers said that he was able to "highlight the very substantial efforts that the United States and the IMF are already making and will continue to make to provide technical assistance on tax reform. I don't think this effort is widely known. We have 20 advisors living in Russia and an additional 50 advisors, who visit regularly to provide advice and assistance. Since 1993, there have been more than 100 tax reform missions to Russia organized by the IMF, Treasury, and AID. A central objec-

tive of my March visit was to make the most senior levels of Russia's government fully aware of this effort and to improve cooperation between U.S. advisors and their Russian counterparts."[141] These were not claims Summers
highlighted after August 1998.

AID statements also claimed that the United States had helped to privatize
tens of thousands of firms in Russia. After August 1998, making such boasts
did not seem appropriate.

Despite these valiant public defenses, the August 1998 collapse and subsequent finger pointing took its toll on the Clinton administration. For the first
time, some veterans of the Russia policy team began to have doubts about
whether Russia could make it.[142] In her October 1998 Chicago address,
Albright warned, "We cannot say with confidence that Russia will emerge
from its difficulties any time soon."[143] A month later, Talbott delivered an
uncharacteristically gloomy speech about Russia's future, in which he called
for a policy of "strategic patience."[144] Although Talbott still made the case for
engagement with Russia, he implied that the administration's previous policy
objective of "strategic partnership" with Russia was premature.

Privately, even Clinton, always the most bullish member of his Russia team,
hinted that Russia might be lost.[145] Similar to its feeling of impotence concerning the Chechen war in the mid-1990s, the Clinton foreign policy team
found that there was little it could do to prevent Russia's economy from tank-
ing. The world's only superpower looked powerless in the face of Russia's
domestic problems.

In this new context, the administration rhetoric and policies did change in
the margins. Vice President Gore and his national security adviser, Leon
Fuerth, successfully pushed for increased efforts in denuclearization.
Secretary of the Treasury Rubin was more than happy to focus resources on
security concerns rather than financial rescue. The new Enhanced Threat
Reduction Initiative (ETRI) was a supplement to the Nunn-Lugar program.
Proponents of increasing Nunn-Lugar funds at the expense of economic
assistance projects contended that the threat of political instability as a result
of August 1998 made the acceleration of denuclearization programs more
immediate.

These advocates of Nunn-Lugar prevailed. The Cooperative Threat
Reduction budget increased from $382.2 million in 1998 to $440.4 million in
1999 and $475.5 million in 2000. In parallel, the Department of Energy's
Material Protection, Control, and Accounting (MPC&A) program, which was
designed to secure and take account of Russian nuclear stockpiles, saw
increases in its budgets as a response to August 1998, going from $137 million
in 1998 to $152 million in 1999. Congress tried to force the administration to
take these funds out of existing aid budgets for Russia by insisting on a 30 percent cut from the Freedom Support Act budget. Although this congressional

initiative for decreasing funds for Russia was eventually reversed, Congress did succeed in writing earmarks into the appropriation's legislation that limited funds available for the Russian central government.[146]

The administration made few changes in the bilateral assistance program to Russia after August 1998.[147] Well before the crash, AID had gradually decreased direct assistance to the Russian federal government, while at the same time increasing percentages (though often not actual dollars, since budgets were shrinking commensurately) of assistance earmarked for development of nongovernmental organizations and regional governments. But the talking points on assistance did change after August 1998. Before the meltdown, the Clinton administration emphasized Russia's economic reform achievements and the American role in assisting these reforms. U.S. officials placed special emphasis on Russian privatization, to which AID had devoted large resources. After August 1998, the new themes were denuclearization and democratization. White House briefing papers made little mention of economic reform successes but instead emphasized that "U.S. programs have deactivated over 1,500 nuclear warheads, destroyed 300 missile launchers in Russia, and ensured the denuclearization of Ukraine, Kazakhstan, and Belarus."[148] On democracy, Secretary of State Albright, who had not previously spoken much about Russia, assumed a bigger voice in explaining the importance of civil society development as a chief component of Clinton's Russia policy.[149] A year later, Deputy Secretary Talbott explained Clinton's veto of the 2000 appropriations bill in the following terms: "The funding levels proposed by the Congress would force us to make unacceptable trade-offs between our core economic and democracy programs and programs that prevent the proliferation of weapons of mass destruction. The President believes such cuts would be dangerously short-sighted, because the purposes of this assistance—from building an independent media to promoting small business—are fundamentally in our interests."[150] These kinds of issues, once relegated to the end of talking point lists, were now center stage, in part because there was little else left on stage. The Agency for International Development also launched new efforts on fighting corruption and money laundering, and administration officials made sure to include a large dose of tough language about the importance of the rule of law and fighting corruption when they were testifying on Capitol Hill.

Blaming the Russians for their own ills also appeared as a new theme in Clinton administration speeches. Clinton's team at the Treasury Department and IMF officials never liked Kiriyenko's emergency package. In the aftermath, Western officials placed the blame for the August 1998 crash squarely on the shoulders of the Russian government. Stanley Fischer captured the sentiment of many when he wrote, "The key lesson here is that it is the country—not the IMF or World Bank—that fundamentally determines whether a

programme succeeds or fails. The outside world can make a difference, sometimes a decisive one, by supporting good policies and opposing bad ones. But,
in the words of Lawrence Summers [who had been promoted to U.S. Treasury
secretary after Rubin's departure] 'We cannot want reform in Russia more
than Russia's government and people do'. . . . If Russia had implemented the
1996 reforms, its economy would now be stronger, incomes would be higher,
and it would have avoided the 1998 collapse."[151]

Some Clinton officials also accused (not without cause) Russian government officials of lying to them about Central Bank reserves during the critical
summer months before the crash. In floating these claims, Clinton officials
were suggesting that their policy advice might have worked had Russian officials had more integrity. Albright went out of her way to censure the Russian
government for failing to attract direct foreign investment. "Russia has
tremendous inherent wealth, yet it has only attracted a trickle of outside
investment where there should have been a bonanza. . . . Just think how much
could have been done if investment on this scale had been coming into Russia
from the very beginning of the '90s. Those who blocked it have a lot of
explaining to do to their people."[152] (There was potential for $50 billion to be
pumped into the oil and gas sector alone, but in 1997, energy investment only
reached $2 billion.)

Members of the Russia team in the Clinton administration were exasper-
ated with their counterparts in Moscow. American officials no longer had the
energy or conviction to defend them. At the same time, those who had always
been more skeptical about Russia's chances for success began to speak more
publicly.

On new money to Russia, there was really not much of a debate. Publicly,
the official line of the administration was to still support the already
announced IMF package until the dust had settled in Russia. As the dust settled, however, there was little enthusiasm for any new funds for Russia.
Summers adamantly opposed any financing from multilateral institutions
and made sure Clinton delivered a "tough love" message during his meeting
with Yeltsin in September. During the summit, Chernomyrdin pleaded for
softer IMF conditions but to no avail.[153]

Clinton even brought the tough love message to the Russian people during
his September 1998 visit in a speech to students at Moscow State University
when he urged them to "stay the course." To many in Moscow, the speech
seemed preachy, harsh, and unsympathetic about the severe conditions grip-
ping the country at the time. It was very un-Clinton.[154]

Privately, Clinton was deeply frustrated by the message he was told to
deliver. What the IMF had done to date, Clinton said (as remembered by
Talbott) was "a 40-watt bulb in a damned big darkness. We're giving them a
big, tough reform message but there ain't no dessert on the menu we're show-

ing them—hell, I'm not sure they can even see the main course. They've got to know that there's something worth waiting for after all this hardship. If they don't, they'll do what people do when they've got the vote: they'll throw the bums out. That's just Politics 101."[155]

Clinton always wanted to do more than the rest of his team. Treasury Department officials were arguing for the president to take a tough line when he delivered his conditionality and austerity talking points. This time around, the tough guys at the Treasury Department prevailed. After August 1998, Albright also spoke more prominently about the need for tough love. As she told the U.S.-Russia Business Council in October, "Foreign funds should continue to be used to help Russia pursue credible reforms, but not to help delay them."[156]

The new Russian government headed by Primakov quickly tired of the lectures.[157] Primakov blamed the American "darlings, the young reformers" for Russia's ills, indicting the Clinton administration and IMF experts as accomplices in the economic crimes executed against Russia.[158] Nonetheless, Primakov and his government still wanted new IMF financing and therefore refrained from implementing any of the spending programs that they had promised on first coming to power. In January 1999, Primakov sent his Communist Party deputy, Yuri Maslyukov, to Washington not to complain about Western evil schemes but instead to request a new IMF program. In accepting the "tough love" message or the "spinach" that the Clinton administration delivered, they still resented the Clinton administration. Talbott recalls that a meeting between Vice President Gore and Prime Minister Primakov at Davos in January 1999 "was the single worst high-level U.S.-Russian meeting in the eight years of the Clinton presidency."[159]

Primakov and his government never undertook any of the drastic antimarket measures that they had promised upon first coming to power. Instead, they maintained a tight monetary policy and instituted budget cuts. Over time, they also learned how to interact with international financial institutions. Nonetheless, they never managed to secure a major new IMF package. Instead, the IMF offered Russia just enough new money to help Russia avoid defaulting on IMF loans already outstanding. The "transferred" funds never left Washington. As Stanley Fischer reported a year later, "Relations [between Russia and the IMF] are very cordial, but there is no pressure to be in a program."[160]

Long-Term Consequences of the Crash for Russia and Clinton

In the immediate aftermath of the August 1998 financial crash, most analysts in the West assumed the worst. Riots and coups—responses to similar kinds of meltdowns in other countries—were two possibilities that were given high probabilities. Indonesia had just experienced a similar economic failure, which had produced a change in regime. The chaos and political turmoil experienced in Argentina in the winter of 2001–02 is another example of what people, not without reason, expected in Russia in 1998. Prolonged economic stagnation was another.

Negative effects of the crash were visible years later. Incomes took a long time to recover, foreign investment shied away for years, and the Russian banking system—not in great shape before the crash—never recovered. Offsetting these long-term economic scars, however, were some surprising positive economic developments that stemmed directly from the August 1998 crisis.

First and foremost, Russian domestic producers benefited immediately from the devalued ruble. Food producers found new markets in Russia. Exporters, particularly in the energy sector, saw huge volume increases in 1999 and 2000. Second, powerful financial oligarchs endured real economic losses in the August meltdown. The era of easy rents and bankers running the Kremlin effectively ended in August 1998. Third, the Russian government finally took cutting budget deficits seriously. After the 1999 parliamentary elections, the government succeeded in passing the first balanced budget in post-Soviet Russian history. Fourth, the post-August 1998 governments also succeeded in implementing serious economic reforms. As economist Anders Åslund argues, "The financial crash of August 1998 delivered the shock that the Russian elite needed, but the reformers had failed to impose. It altered the economic thinking of both the elite and the government. Reforms that were legislated just before the crash have only become effective in its aftermath."[161]

The reform agenda became especially accelerated after Putin was elected president in the spring of 2000. Putin's first major economic reform was the introduction of a flat income tax of 13 percent in the summer of 2000. Subsequently, Putin's government and the new pro-Putin Duma (which supported the president as it had never done when Yeltsin was in office) passed into law a series of fundamental reforms, including a new land code (making it possible to own commercial and residential land), a new legal code, a new regime to prevent money laundering, new legislation on currency liberalization, and a reduced profits tax (from 35 percent to 24 percent).[162]

Devaluation, rising oil prices, and momentum on economic reform have been positive for the economy. Russian GDP grew by 3.2 percent in 1999, and 7.7 percent in 2000.[163] Since 1999, the economy has grown every year. Russian industrial growth increased by 8.1 percent in 1999, with the biggest gains in food production and textiles.[164] Inflation also remained under control—dropping from 84.4 percent in 1998 to 36.5 percent in 1999, while the currency stayed relatively stable.[165] Analysts still disagree about the causes of the rebound and its long-term viability, but few dispute the data about Russia's real economic recovery in 1999 and economic growth since that time.[166]

As a consequence of these other economic achievements, IMF financing was removed as an issue in U.S.-Russia relations.[167] Since Putin became president, his government has welcomed IMF consultations but never asked for new financial assistance.[168] By the end of 2001, Russia's debt to the IMF had dropped to $7.69 billion, a level low enough to drop Russia from the IMF's list of major debtors.[169]

It may not be hyperbole to assert that the August 1998 financial collapse in Russia had more long-term negative consequences for American policy toward Russia than it did for the Russian economy. The Clinton administration's policy never really recovered from the crash. For the first six years of his time in office, Clinton had said Russia was his primary foreign policy concern. Prodding, assisting, and cheering for Russia's internal transformation—especially Russia's economic transformation—was one of the main objectives of Clinton's Russia policy. The dual blow of the August 1998 financial crisis in Russia and the Lewinsky scandal at home permanently altered the way in which Clinton engaged on Russia issues for the rest of his term. Optimism in Clinton's tenure as president diminished after the Lewinsky affair. In parallel, optimism about Russia also waned within the Clinton administration and the United States as a whole after the economic meltdown. The August collapse led the Treasury Department to wash its hands of Russia. The project of transformation seemed to be failing. The Wilsonians in the Clinton team began to wonder themselves if they were "idealists," who might suffer the same fate as Wilson himself.

The combination of the Lewinsky scandal and the August financial crisis also forced the Clinton administration to play defense on its Russia policy. Clinton was vulnerable, and Congress took advantage of the situation. Both the House and Senate convened dozens of hearings to investigate every aspect of U.S. policy toward Russia. For the rest of their time in office, Clinton administration officials would testify in order to defend their policies, not to lay out new strategic thinking about the future agenda of U.S.-Russia relations. And just when it looked like it could not get any worse, Russia nearly came to blows with the United States over Kosovo and then invaded Chechnya, again.

10

Kosovo

W hen the NATO heads of state gathered in Paris in May 1997 to sign the NATO-Russia Founding Act with President Boris Yeltsin, which heralded a new era of cooperation, few could have imagined that this ceremony would mark the end of good feelings, rather than the beginning. Yeltsin had acquiesced to NATO expansion because he had no choice, but the West had tried to reassure him that NATO was no longer an enemy of Russia and that NATO was more political than military in nature. The integration of Russia into the West seemed to be succeeding; after all, Russia was gaining a voice in the most important Western security organization on the continent.

Only two years later, NATO went to war for the first time in its history against Slobodan Milosevic's regime in Yugoslavia. This military campaign commenced just two weeks after Poland, Hungary, and the Czech Republic formally joined the alliance. Many in Russia were stunned that NATO took the unprecedented step of bypassing the UN Security Council to attack Yugoslavia not for actions it took against another sovereign state but rather for crimes the government was committing against ethnic Albanians inside the country. Many in the United States and Europe were stunned in turn at the extreme nature of Russia's reaction, since NATO's goal—as defined by NATO—was to stop genocide.[1] How could a country aspiring to join the West be against stopping genocide? Kosovo was, says Strobe Talbott, "a near death experience for them and for us."[2]

The gulf between the West and Russia never seemed larger after the end of the cold war than it did over Kosovo and highlighted how tenuous integration remained. In Russia, critics from both the left and right denounced the NATO campaign as a belligerent exercise of American imperial power. Conveniently forgetting the Soviet invasions of Hungary in 1956 and Czechoslovakia in 1968, Foreign Minister Igor Ivanov called the NATO bombing the worst aggression in Europe since World War II. Communist Party leader Gennady Zyuganov compared "NATO ideology" to "Hitlerism," while several members of his party called for a military response.[3]

Eventually, Russian policy became more accommodating to NATO interests. Russia even joined the diplomatic endgame that helped bring about Milosevic's surrender. Yet even while cooperating, Russia seemed to have a parallel agenda. Questions were raised about private assurances that Russian officials may have given the Yugoslav government about creating a Russian-patrolled sector in northern Kosovo in order to foster and protect a Serb enclave. Russian behavior in the war culminated in the movement of a small contingent of Russian troops from the Bosnia peacekeeping effort to the airport in Pristina, the Kosovo capital. This Russian deployment of armed forces in Kosovo, unauthorized by NATO, almost triggered combat between Russian and American troops. In 1999 on the tarmac in Pristina, no trace was left of the cooperative spirit of the May 1997 NATO-Russia summit in Paris.

What had happened? If good relations with Russia were so important to the Clinton administration, how was it that this U.S. foreign policy team inched the closest to exchanging blows with the Russians since the Kennedy administration in the Cuban missile crisis four decades earlier? The fallout between Russia and the United States is especially surprising when it is placed against the backdrop of institution building under way among Russia, the United States, and NATO before the start of the war. When the NATO air campaign against Serbia commenced, Russian and American troops were serving side by side in neighboring Bosnia. The Permanent Joint Council (PJC) created by the NATO-Russia Founding Act was designed precisely to defuse crises like Kosovo. Yet neither the goodwill generated from cooperation in Bosnia nor the existence of the PJC could offset the negative Russian reaction to the NATO campaign and the ensuing negative American response to Russian attitudes and behavior.

Having waited four years to intervene forcefully enough in Bosnia to stop the war there in 1995, the United States and NATO were not going to go through a similar experience in Kosovo. Bosnia had produced a debilitating effect on U.S. foreign policy for the first two years of Clinton's presidency, and officials on both sides of the Atlantic believed that NATO's credibility was on the line as violence escalated in Kosovo.

But Kosovo was not Bosnia. Kosovo was a constituent element of the Federal Republic of Yugoslavia, and no Western official was arguing that it should be considered otherwise. Thus while the intervention in Bosnia was on behalf of an internationally recognized state and thus squarely within the tradition of international law, intervention in Kosovo, without UN Security Council authorization and in violation of a state's sovereignty, was more ambiguous for international diplomacy.

The U.S.-Russian crisis over Kosovo focused attention on two problems that would continue to impede U.S.-Russian partnership well after the residue of Kosovo faded. First, Kosovo demonstrated the gulf between the Wilsonian liberals in the Clinton administration and the practitioners of realpolitik in Russia. Clinton and his advisers believed that they were using force for humanitarian purposes to protect the Kosovar Albanians, and they hoped eventually to foster liberty in Serbia.[4] In contrast, Yeltsin, his advisers, and most of the foreign policy community in Russia believed that the United States and NATO were using their military power to extend their sphere of influence into the Balkans, a region they considered Russia's turf.[5] This extension of power in southeastern Europe looked particularly ominous after NATO's inclusion of the three central European countries less than two weeks before and seemed to belie the notion that NATO had become a mere political organization. No amount of talk, negotiation, or massaging could reconcile these opposing frameworks.

Second, NATO's campaign against Yugoslavia brought Russia's international impotence into painfully sharp focus. NATO took action against Milosevic by bypassing the United Nations, the one international institution in which Russia could wield real power through its veto on the UN Security Council. As Yeltsin lamented in retrospect, "After the bombing of Belgrade, all the rules that had been established by the UN during the long postwar decades collapsed."[6] Unilaterally, Russia could do little. It remains unclear if Yeltsin—after all of his blustering was done—would have really wanted to try to balance against NATO in Serbia. If he did have the desire, however, he did not have the military or diplomatic means to pursue such a policy. Some Russian leaders even warned alarmingly that NATO intended to bomb Russia over Chechnya to protect Muslims trying to gain independence from a Slavic state as was happening in the Balkans. To Westerners that was an absurd claim, but the fact that Russians could believe it underscored how weak many in Russia perceived their country to be.[7] Many in Washington learned a similar lesson about Russian weakness from Moscow's military efforts during the war.

The Road to War

The United States and the United Nations had made some effort to stop the violence committed against Kosovar Albanians by the Yugoslav government during the year before war. In March 1998, the UN Security Council passed resolution 1160, which condemned the Serbs for excessive use of force and put in place an arms embargo against the Federal Republic of Yugoslavia. Clinton and Yeltsin discussed Kosovo briefly at their September 1998 summit in Moscow, and later that month the United Nations passed Security Council Resolution 1199, calling for a cease-fire and the withdrawal of Yugoslav security forces from the province, as well as access to Kosovo for nongovernmental and humanitarian organizations.[8]

While the Russians supported UN efforts to defuse the conflict, they also made clear their opposition to the use of force. On October 5, Yeltsin called Clinton to say that his foreign and defense ministers had been to Belgrade and received Milosevic's agreement to comply with all UN obligations. Any use of force, said Yeltsin, "was inadmissible and forbidden." According to Talbott, Yeltsin did not even let Clinton speak during the phone call but hung up on him after he had concluded his remarks.[9]

Milosevic had no intention of complying with the UN resolutions. Clinton dispatched Ambassador to the United Nations Richard C. Holbrooke, architect of the Dayton Accords, to Belgrade, and he gave NATO the authority to conduct air strikes against Yugoslavia if Milosevic did not cease and desist his military activities. NATO issued an action order, and in response, Milosevic agreed to put an end to hostilities, withdraw some but not all of his security forces from Kosovo and allow an Organization for Security and Cooperation in Europe (OSCE) ground verification mission as well as air verification. He also agreed to allow the entry of relief organizations into the province and to begin negotiations for greater autonomy for Kosovo within the Federal Republic of Yugoslavia.[10]

Before long, this "deal" was unraveling. In January 1999, after civilian bodies were discovered in Racak, Kosovo, NATO issued an ultimatum to Yugoslavia. Peace talks were called, and in February, those talks began in Rambouillet, France. When those failed, Holbrooke was dispatched again to Belgrade to deliver one last warning.

Did Russia Matter?

The details of the failures at Rambouillet and of the war on Kosovo that followed are well told elsewhere.[11] What is of particular interest to our story is the relative importance of the "Russia factor" in the decision to go to war. How did U.S. decisionmakers assess the importance of the U.S.-Russian relationship as they prepared to commence the NATO bombing campaign and as they then sought to win the war?

Many calculations had to be made as the bombing campaign began. First, the United States and its Allies had to estimate how important it was to use force to stop the conflict. They had to consider how much bombing would be needed to get Milosevic to stop his campaign of "ethnic cleansing." Second, the United States had to assess the extent to which Russia could be brought into deliberations about the military campaign. If Russia was allowed access to NATO decisionmaking to disrupt NATO war plans, or if Russia used information gained from contacts with NATO to provide valuable intelligence to the Serbs, then NATO would be shooting itself in the foot. However, even though the Pentagon did not want its military plans subject to Russian veto or review, Department of Defense officials had a stake in engaging their Russian counterparts since they continued to tout U.S.-Russian cooperation in Bosnia as one of the major success stories of the 1990s.[12]

At the White House, powerful voices argued that NATO could not let concerns over Russia dominate the decision to bomb Kosovo. Deputy National Security Adviser James Steinberg recalls, "For those of us who wanted to do something, the worst outcome would be not to do something because Russia didn't want us to do it. It would have been bad for us, bad for the Balkans, and bad for Russia. It would have been catastrophic. The whole security of Europe would be thrown into question if Russia's sense of its interest precluded the international community addressing this serious question." Leon Fuerth, Gore's national security adviser, adds, "There was a conscious decision made that the issue toward NATO was existential and we would have to proceed whether the Russians liked it, bought it, rejected it, whatever. But that we would make every effort to explain our purposes and to conduct ourselves in a way that would allow them to reconcile themselves to this."[13]

Some in the U.S. government hoped that Milosevic would back down quickly, and thus whatever damage was done to the U.S.-Russian relationship could be easily repaired. Ivo Daalder and Michael O'Hanlon report from their interviews in Washington, Brussels, and Allied capitals that "there was a widespread consensus that Milosevic would give in after just a few days of bombing but also that the likely upper bound on the duration of the air campaign was seen as two to three weeks." Similarly Alexander Vershbow, then the U.S. ambassador to NATO, recalls, "Everybody said we have to be prepared for the long haul, and it's a phased campaign, but everybody I think felt that there was a high probability that Milosevic would cave fast. We talked about bombing for 48 hours and then we'd pause so he could sue for peace." Senior Clinton officials also believed that any suggestion of a prolonged war would fracture alliance support for the commencement of the campaign.[14]

The more confidence one had that the war would be short, the less one had to worry about Russia. As State Department official John Bass argues, "Our ability to sustain the NATO-Russia relationship was predicated on the idea that it would be a short war. The judgment among many of us—erroneously, it turned out—was that we would be able to contain and manage Russian reaction. They'd bluster and be angry, but we would be able to get back to business relatively quickly, in part through follow-on peacekeeping, if we had a short conflict."[15]

The view that the war would be short has been attributed privately and publicly to Secretary of State Madeleine Albright, one of the leading proponents for using force to stop Milosevic's ethnic cleansing. In retrospect, Albright responded forcefully that this view is too simplistic. She contends that her view of "short" was in reference to concerns that the Balkans would become another Vietnam, and compared with Vietnam, the seventy-eight days of the Kosovo campaign were a short war: "Whenever we talked about the Balkans, there were people who always would say it's Vietnam, meaning it was long and endless. And those of us who were saying that it was not Vietnam were saying that it wouldn't be Vietnam, it would be shorter. . . . The night after the bombing began I went on [*The News Hour with*] *Jim Lehrer* and he said to me . . . 'will it be short or long?' and I said, 'it will be relatively short.' The word 'relatively' is very important because I was thinking Vietnam; he wasn't thinking Vietnam. I don't know what he was asking, but for me it all came out of this, so I said, 'relatively short.'"[16]

NATO at War

Even if one believed that Russia should not be allowed to stop a necessary use of force, and even if one believed that while doing so, the United States and NATO should make every effort to inform and not embarrass Moscow, there were still at least three issues related to Russia's reaction that the United States and NATO had to consider as the bombing campaign began. First, how should Clinton handle Yeltsin? Second, what should U.S. officials say to Russian prime minister Yevgeny Primakov, who was scheduled to arrive in Washington for meetings with Vice President Gore? Third, should NATO utilize the Permanent Joint Council (and would Russia even agree to be seen at NATO), which arguably had been set up precisely to allow for NATO-Russia consultations in this type of situation?

On March 24, Clinton and Yeltsin had a forty-five minute conversation before the onset of the bombing. Yeltsin strongly objected to NATO's prospective use of force. He told Clinton, "I am confident that if we had continued to work together, we would have toppled Milosevic."[17] As former National Security Council (NSC) staffer Andrew Weiss recalls, "Yeltsin beseeched him. He said, 'You must not launch an air campaign. You can't do this.' [Clinton] kept coming back to the facts. 'Look, he's driven people from their homes; driven the international monitors out.' Yeltsin wouldn't have it. Finally, he said 'I have failed to convince the President of the United States,' and he hung up." Yeltsin warned Clinton that he intended to respond, but he remained evasive about the nature of his response. The administration could still hope that the typical pattern—in which Yeltsin blustered but in the end went along—would prove the rule again.[18]

Dealing with Primakov was even more complicated since he was firmly against the war, had no close personal relationships with senior officials in the Clinton administration, and was en route to Washington. The Russians had asked that the United States hold off the bombing until after the prime minister had finished his trip. They feared that Primakov's presence would imply that Russia was showing approval for the mission or, in contrast, that it would highlight Russia's weakness.[19] The vice president knew he needed to give Primakov advance warning so that the Russian prime minister would have time to decide whether or not to proceed. But he could not call too soon. As Fuerth explains, "Gore said that in the spirit of making sure that he had all the information he needed for a decision, and with apologies for the shortness of time, he was authorized by his government to inform Primakov that we were going to commence operations. The balancing thing was that early notification of Primakov would have led to early notification of the Serbs. And so we delayed, and delayed, and delayed and essentially gave the guy a heads up but he was already airborne when he got it, and that was the only place we could find to strike the balance between letting him know when there was still time to change course or letting him know soon enough to possibly do us some damage in the conduct of the first operations."[20] Primakov turned his plane around and went home.[21]

Finally, what about the Permanent Joint Council? Recall Clinton's words in Paris two years earlier. "From now on, NATO and Russia will consult and coordinate and work together."[22] There was no consultation now. But as NATO press spokesman Jamie Shea argues, even without Russia storming out of the PJC and cutting off contact with NATO, the Allies had their own concerns, which were largely the same as those expressed above by Fuerth. "You could suggest the PJC was a place to give Russia a major role, in line with the Founding Act, [but] all of the analysis being done here was that it would make the situation more complicated rather than better."[23]

The deepest break in U.S.-Russian relations since the end of the cold war ensued. Even though Yeltsin resumed contact in late April, the negative effects of the war on U.S.-Russian relations and, for the first time, on Russian mass attitudes toward Americans, were overwhelming. In April 1999, polls demonstrated that 90 percent of the Russian population believed that the NATO bombing campaign was a mistake, while 65 percent believed that NATO was the aggressor in the conflict. Perhaps most disturbingly, even Russia's youth were turning against the United States in response to the war. According to the Foundation for Public Opinion's polls conducted soon after the war began, 67 percent of people between the ages of eighteen and thirty-five had a negative view of the United States compared with only 18 percent who had a positive view.[24] Yegor Gaidar told Talbott, "Oh Strobe, if only you knew what a disaster this war is for those of us in Russia who want for our country what you want."[25] American actions in Kosovo in the name of Wilsonian ideals were hurting their Wilsonian allies in Russia. Another Russian liberal, Duma deputy and Yabloko leader Aleksei Arbatov, called "NATO's action against Yugoslavia . . . the apex of Russian-U.S. relations in the last few years and to some extent, in the post–Cold War period."[26]

The magnitude of the break in the U.S.-Russian relationship came as a surprise to the Americans. Two years after the war was over, Clinton NSC official Andrew Weiss argued, "The Kosovo War provoked this moment of incredible rupture that I don't think any of us knew was coming. We all wanted Milosevic stopped, but did not anticipate just how bad, how piercing it would be. It was really ugly and well beyond what anyone had fathomed."[27]

Throughout the 1990s, Russia had made progress in building democratic and market institutions at home and moving closer to Western international institutions. These changes, however, did not alter the way Russian leaders saw the conflict over Kosovo. Most Russians did not perceive the NATO bombing campaign as a humanitarian effort to stop genocide and promote democracy. Instead, it was perceived as a power grab by the United States and its Allies. To the Russians, the American sphere of influence was moving into the Balkans because American power and Russian weakness made this expansion possible.

Would Russia Send Help to the Serbs?

In the days immediately following the onset of bombing, the worst-case scenario had to be contemplated: would Russia provide military assistance or intelligence that would impair NATO's chances of success? The hysterical rhetoric coming out of Moscow made this scenario seem plausible. A few days after the war began, Russian officials stated their intention to deploy warfighting vessels in the Mediterranean. NATO Supreme Allied Commander Wesley K. Clark was worried not that Russia was preparing for war but rather that the ships could and would provide the Serbs with intelligence about the American-led air campaign. Foreshadowing his tough attitude at the end of the war when Russia would send a small contingent of ground troops to Kosovo, Clark told his staff, "We're not going to let them come into the Adriatic, or through the Straits if I can help it. We're going to get this stopped, or pull in the forces to block them."[28] Even more dangerously, some right-wing radicals in Russia, including Vladimir Zhirinovsky, were threatening to send Russian volunteers into the theater. Even more mainstream political figures in Russia advocated a military response. For instance, Aleksandr Lebed, the popular retired general who was serving as the governor of Krasnoyarsk, advocated the transfer of antiaircraft weapons to Serbia. In the heat of the moment, the Duma voted to form a new Slavic nation by uniting Yugoslavia with Russia and Belarus.

U.S. officials, however, were most worried about Russian government actions. Gore called Primakov to elicit a promise that Russia would not provide military assistance to the Serbs, but the prime minister refused him. Then Yeltsin bombastically raised the specter of World War III. The American team only breathed a sign of relief when the Russian naval convoy finally positioned itself. As Steinberg recalls, "We got nervous when they started moving ships. But the actual response was very limited and sent us a clear signal. They didn't get close, and they didn't establish the intelligence links to make it useful. When they were in transit, we were nervous, but when we saw the operating posture, it was reassuring. After that, it was clear they needed to do a little to save face." Or as *New York Times* columnist Thomas Friedman argued, Yeltsin proved, by ensuring that his rhetoric was only hot air, that "this is why even a half-dead stone-cold-drunk Boris Yeltsin is still an enormous asset for the U.S."[29]

Russia Gets Back in the Game

During the first weeks of the military campaign, it seemed that any effort to repair the U.S.-Russian relationship would have to wait until the war was over. The Russians had no intention of using the NATO-Russia forum while NATO was engaged in hostilities. As the war dragged on, however, the United States began to believe that opening a diplomatic track with Moscow was important, not necessarily because it had any real chance of causing Milosevic to agree to NATO's terms but rather because U.S. officials believed it was necessary to keep nervous Allies on board while NATO pressed its military campaign.

At the fiftieth anniversary NATO summit in Washington in late April, the Allies demonstrated complete unity. They issued a clear statement of terms that would allow for a cessation of bombing. Milosevic would have to "ensure a verifiable stop to all military action and the immediate ending of violence and repression in Kosovo; withdraw from Kosovo his military, police and para-military forces; agree to the stationing in Kosovo of an international military presence; agree to the unconditional and safe return of all refugees and displaced persons, and unhindered access to them by humanitarian aid organizations; and provide credible assurance of his willingness to work for the establishment of a political framework agreement based on the Rambouillet accords." NATO added that the bombing would stop only after both the terms were accepted and the Serbs had begun withdrawing forces from Kosovo "according to a precise and rapid timetable."[30]

The unexpected strength of Alliance cohesion seemed to have an effect on officials in Moscow, who eventually feared a solution to the conflict that did not involve Russia. Yeltsin, who had been invited to the NATO summit but had not attended, called Clinton on Sunday, April 25, the final day of the gathering in order to inject himself into the proceedings. At this point, Russia was still trying to push for a strong UN role, a Russian troop presence, and even a Serb sector in Kosovo after the war ended.[31]

But what Russia was pushing for was less important than the call itself. As Steinberg argues, "Yeltsin's call was the most extraordinary thing, the first time since the beginning of the military campaign. I knew what that call was about. It was 'Bill, we've got to bring this to an end. I don't care how we do it.' I knew we'd been handed the card we needed. It gave us the diplomatic strategy to go with the military strategy. We'd always wanted to get the Russians to be part of the solution. That was the first time it was clear that Yeltsin and the Russians got it." Steinberg's boss, National Security Adviser Sandy Berger, adds, "Yeltsin's call to Clinton the day of the NATO summit was the call of a man who was distressed, hyperventilating. You can't do this. You've got to stop the bombing. He had no veto power over the big decisions, but it's also true that Clinton never really wavered on the notion that maybe we had to swing this guy over our shoulder and pull him down the field."[32] Yeltsin sensed that an important Western club was convening, and he was not at the event. He wanted to find a way to get back in.

Yeltsin proposed that Gore and former prime minister Viktor Chernomyrdin be charged with finding a solution. Yeltsin's decision to send Chernomyrdin was rooted in large part in his domestic political battles. Most important, he wanted to push prime minister (and former foreign minister) Yevgeny Primakov to the sidelines since Yeltsin despised Primakov. Primakov's allies in the Russian Duma were gearing up for impeachment, and many considered Primakov a strong opposition candidate for the 2000 presidential election.[33] From Washington's perspective, Chernomyrdin was a great choice: he was seen as someone who was independent of the bureaucracy and would answer only to Yeltsin. He also had six years of experience working directly with Al Gore. Clinton agreed that the Gore-Chernomyrdin channel should be revived.[34]

Yeltsin told Clinton that he was under tremendous pressure from his military, and he had managed to hold it off, but he wanted NATO to accept Milosevic's latest proposal and cease bombing. Clinton reiterated the NATO conditions that had to be met before bombing could stop, and he rejected Yeltsin's plea for a pause in the bombing. Yeltsin responded, "You know what Russia is! You know what it has at its disposal! Don't push Russia into this!"[35]

Clinton did agree to send Talbott immediately to Moscow to work out details with Chernomyrdin about how to proceed. Gore then called Chernomyrdin to suggest that they meet in Washington in early May. The new Russian envoy was adamant that a solution to the war was only possible if some Serb forces stayed behind in Kosovo.[36]

A Troika Is Born

The following Sunday, Yeltsin called again to say he wanted to send Chernomyrdin to Washington. Chernomyrdin arrived the next day and had a ninety-minute meeting with Clinton and Gore. The Russian envoy brought a letter from Yeltsin, and Clinton again explained the NATO conditions. At his meetings at the White House and later with the vice president, Chernomyrdin asked that "an international personage" be named to work with him since Russia could never be in a position of having to "accept the sword of surrender from Milosevic."[37]

After the meeting, Talbott suggested the name of Finnish president Martti Ahtisaari for this mission to national security adviser Sandy Berger. Ahtisaari offered several unique advantages. As a Finn, he knew the Russians well; as the president of a non-NATO country, he was not associated with the bombing campaign; and since Finland was about to assume the rotating presidency of the European Union, Ahtisaari could represent a Western organization that was much more palatable to Russia than NATO. Finally, Ahtisaari had a long and distinguished experience with peacekeeping and conflict resolution.[38]

For Talbott, an additional advantage was that serving as U.S. ambassador to Finland was his former executive assistant and close confidant, Eric Edelman. Edelman had been in town during the NATO summit the weekend before, and Ahtisaari had told him he would not be running for re-election, making it more likely that he would be willing to serve as a special mediator in the Kosovo endgame.[39]

Secretary of State Albright agreed that Ahtisaari should be proposed, and at a meeting the next morning at the vice president's residence, she suggested the idea to Chernomyrdin, who immediately accepted. Members of the U.S. team and Ahtisaari agree that the Russians likely miscalculated in thinking that Finland was a neutral country. The Finns were not members of NATO, but they were members of the EU, and the EU conditions were nearly identical to those of NATO.[40]

Talbott called Ahtisaari on May 5 to explain how his name had been proposed and what the plans for the mission would be. According to Ahtisaari, Talbott said that he did not have "much hope in the outcome of his exercise; it was important to carry on nevertheless because of U.S.-Russian relations." The goal was to help the war effort by keeping prodiplomatic voices content that an alternative to war was being pursued.[41]

In the meantime, Gore wrote Chernomyrdin to explain NATO's intentions on two core issues: "Two things—the total pullout of Serb forces from Kosovo and NATO at the core of the international force, preferably on the basis of a UNSC resolution—are for us take-it-or-leave-it issues. Failure would not serve anybody's interests, except Milosevic's. In fact, it would not even serve his interests. In the long run, the continuation of the hostilities will make it increasingly difficult for the international community to maintain Yugoslavia's unity because of the growing radicalization of the Kosovar Albanians."[42]

Russia was not yet on board. Officials in Moscow did not want to compel all Serb forces to leave Kosovo, pushing instead for some Serbian units to remain on patrol at key Serbian holy sites. NATO's position was that all Serb forces had to leave, and then some might be allowed back in after NATO had secured the area. The Russians continued to call for a pause in the bombing as soon as Milosevic said he was in agreement with the general principles, rather than after he committed fully to the NATO language and had offered a withdrawal on a precise timetable. Finally, the United States used the phrase "NATO at the core" to refer to a unified command under NATO for the peacekeeping effort to follow, while Russia was holding out for its own sector. When Chernomyrdin called Ahtisaari on May 6, he said that he thought a deal was possible once NATO accepted Milosevic's limits. The Russian envoy stressed that a UN role was vital, as was an end to the NATO air strikes.[43]

Talbott flew to Moscow for meetings with Chernomyrdin on May 12. While he was there, Yeltsin fired Primakov and nominated Sergei Stepashin as his replacement, a choice that the Duma eventually approved. Although Stepashin was decidedly more pro-Western than his predecessor, Talbott was not sure at the time who spoke for the Russian government.[44] Foreign Minister Igor Ivanov was a Primakov protégé who many thought would be fired, but he continued in his job. What did the reshuffling mean for Chernomyrdin, who was appointed in large measure as a counterweight to Primakov? With Primakov gone, would his services still be needed? This internal confusion suggested that Russia would be unable to perform as an effective diplomatic actor on the international stage.

On May 13, the troika of Talbott, Chernomyrdin and Ahtisaari met in Helsinki for their first meeting to discuss the endgame strategy together. By this time, Ahtisaari had formally been appointed the EU's envoy for the conflict, so he was wearing that hat as well as that of Finland's president.

Eric Edelman, U.S. ambassador to Finland, recalls how much more powerful the message to Russia was coming from Ahtisaari, whom the Russians expected to be more sympathetic to their demands for a UN-led operation. Instead, Ahtisaari said that he knew the UN well and thus would not consent to peacekeeping under the UN. "It has to be NATO at the core and a unified chain of command; that's the EU position and that's my position as president of Finland. I'm not going to put Finnish soldiers in harm's way in Kosovo if they're not under unified NATO command."[45]

According to Ahtisaari (and confirmed by Edelman and Talbott), Chernomyrdin seemed to accept that this formula was inevitable. "Russia agrees to the Bosnia model of an international force and united command structure," said Chernomyrdin. "We still have to define the scope of NATO's participation." He continued to argue that the "pullout of all Serb troops is a problem that needs to be discussed" yet also seemed to be open to the Western formula as the seven-hour conversation wound toward conclusion. In the morning, however, (and presumably after conferring with his team and officials in Moscow), Chernomyrdin was again raising objections to the notion that all Serb troops had to leave and with the formula of NATO at the core of the international force. Until the troika agreed, there was nothing to take to Milosevic.[46]

At Helsinki, Talbott and Ahtisaari pressed Chernomyrdin to have an agreement in writing that the Finn and the Russian could take with them when they went to Belgrade to see Milosevic. After phoning home, Chernomyrdin said that he could not go along with an ultimatum, and he went alone to Belgrade to talk to Milosevic.[47]

A week later, on May 20, Talbott and Ahtisaari flew to Moscow to be briefed by Chernomyrdin after his Belgrade visit. Chernomyrdin reported that Milosevic acquiesced to NATO's presence in Kosovo but not to a NATO command. Talbott pushed Chernomyrdin to agree publicly that the force had to be NATO-led, and again Chernomyrdin consented to make public what he had said in Helsinki two days earlier about NATO "at the core." But when Talbott went to see Foreign Minister Ivanov, Russia's top diplomat refuted what Chernomyrdin had said. Talbott shuttled back to see Chernomyrdin, who now had a new position: NATO could serve at the core, but the command would operate under a troika made up of NATO, Russia, and a neutral country, and that this command would serve under the UN.[48]

So the original sticking points remained. Would all Serb forces be required to leave, and would there be a unified command under NATO? One breakthrough, however, was that Ahtisaari convinced Chernomyrdin that the two of them could only go to Belgrade with one document laying out conditions for Milosevic. There could not and would not be a separate Russian document (at least that the West saw).[49]

On May 27, Chernomyrdin again traveled to Belgrade alone to see Milosevic. Chernomyrdin told the Serb leader that if he refused to accept NATO's conditions, he was likely going to face NATO ground troops, which Russia could not prevent from being deployed. Milosevic seemed to bend. Rather than rejecting any intervention out of hand, he countered that any NATO troops participating in a peacekeeping force (called KFOR) had to come from countries that had not taken part in the air campaign. No NATO forces could be deployed in northern Kosovo, and non-NATO forces would have to be under UN rather than NATO command.[50]

The United States had one enormous advantage as the end of May approached. Scheduled for June 18-20 was the next G-8 meeting in Cologne.

Yeltsin had worked too hard to join this club to have this meeting torn asunder by Russia's refusal to be in accord with the others on Kosovo, which is precisely why Clinton had pushed to make the G-7 the G-8. It was not because Russia belonged; it was to make Russia feel important and part of the West. This forum was much more important to Yeltsin than the Permanent Joint Council at NATO because at the G-8, Yeltsin could appear as one of the world's top leaders, whereas the PJC included all the countries of NATO—small and large.[51] Another "cold peace" performance along the lines of the 1994 OSCE Budapest summit was out of the question. To have a successful G-8 meant that Chernomyrdin had to come to closure with Talbott and Ahtisaari. On May 31, Prime Minister Stepashin called President Clinton (the Kremlin said Yeltsin was "indisposed") and said that Russia wanted a deal struck before Cologne. The end was near.[52]

Receiving the Sword

On June 1, Talbott, Ahtisaari, and Chernomyrdin met again at the Petersberg castle near Bonn. The troika's teams held lengthy discussions about whether the Serbs could keep a small force in Kosovo as a symbol of their sovereignty over the territory or whether all would have to leave, after which a few could be reintroduced; the U.S. delegation was pushing to get the word "all" into the document. Discussions continued until 4:00 a.m., and then the teams agreed to meet again at breakfast, at which point the Russians brought their text. Surprisingly, the word "all" was where the United States wanted it.[53]

Even so, disagreements remained. The Russians may have agreed to the word "all," but they still argued that the details of how, how many, and when Serb forces would return were to be negotiated later in a military-technical agreement. Back in Moscow, members of Russia's military brass were signaling that they were not prepared to serve under a NATO-led operation in Kosovo as they had in Bosnia.[54]

What really had NATO Supreme Allied Commander Gen. Wesley Clark worried was the wording on NATO's role. The document referred to "substantial NATO participation" and simply mentioned unified command and control. A footnote then explained that "substantial NATO participation" meant "NATO at the core." Russia's participation was left for later, as the negotiators decided that this issue was for NATO and Russia, not Milosevic, to decide. Talbott suggested moving the KFOR command issue to a footnote because this was not needed in order to put a stop to the bombing. But in Clark's view, this all added up to an agreement that provided for less than what was in the Dayton Accords for Bosnia.[55]

With the new Russian text that included the word "all," Chernomyrdin asked Talbott, "If Milosevic meets those conditions, can you absolutely and immediately guarantee me that the bombing will stop?" And Talbott responded, "Yes, once we've verified that he has indeed complied." At this point, Col. Gen. Leonid Ivashov, chief of the Russian General Staff's department for international cooperation, said that he was disassociating himself from the document that was on the table.[56] In effect, the Russian military was signaling that it was parting ways with the civilian authorities on this issue, an ominous sign of things to come.

Most, if not all, members of the U.S. team believed that the chances of Ahtisaari and Chernomydin gaining Milosevic's agreement to the document were slim. Ahtisaari recalls, "I shared those doubts, and I had warned Strobe that look, it may not be enough that you and I are around. You may have to produce higher echelons within your administration. Madeleine Albright, the Vice President or as high as you could. Because I thought had I been Milosevic, that's what I would have wanted. But to the surprise of all of us, they accepted."[57]

Funny Business?

With Ahtisaari reading the conditions and Chernomyrdin sitting stone-faced next to him, Milosevic had no reason to believe anyone would help him. Add to that the growing talk of U.S. ground troops sent to the war zone, and there were sufficient reasons for the surrender to take place. But given the Russian troop movements to the Pristina airport that followed, questions abound about what the Russians told Milosevic in advance about the possibility of creating a Russian-controlled sector in northern Kosovo.

Milosevic had agreed in general to NATO's conditions, but the military-technical talks that ensued quickly bogged down. Clark grew increasingly nervous about the U.S. position. He believed that Russia could have no independent sector because NATO would then have no control over what occurred inside that territory. But Chairman of the Joint Chiefs of Staff Henry Hugh Shelton and Secretary of Defense William Cohen seemed to have a different idea and called Clark on June 3 to ask if a Russian sector was possible. When Clark expressed his opposition, Cohen said that officials in Washington would consider his "recommendation." In a subsequent conversation, Shelton asked Clark how many sectors were included in the plan. When Clark said five, Shelton said perhaps NATO only needed three or four. And then when Clark went to a briefing for the North Atlantic Council conducted by Talbott and the military member of his team, Lt. Gen. Robert H. "Doc" Fogelsong, Talbott said he could not confirm that Milosevic accepted all the principles or that NATO's role was understood by all.[58]

Clark worried that his superiors would agree to a Russian sector. When the NATO military operation ended, the Russia issue still had not been solved.

Clinton called Clark to congratulate him, but Clark told the president that a possible Russian sector still loomed as a problem for the postwar environment. "I felt by his reaction that the issue was still open in his mind," recalls Clark. He then received a call from the team in Moscow saying Russia still wanted its own sector and perhaps NATO should consider giving it a small one.[59]

Talbott had earlier told the team in Moscow negotiating the military-technical agreement that the Russians should know, "The KFOR train has left the station and the Russians need to cooperate or they'll miss the train." On June 10, it was General Ivashov who said that Russia had decided "to take her own train."[60] What followed was part comedy, part tragedy, and potential disaster.

The Mad Dash to Pristina

On June 10, Talbott opened a bottle of champagne with Chernomyrdin to toast their success in ending the war. While he was in Moscow, however, reports came in that a small contingent of Russian troops in Bosnia was put on alert for possible redeployment, and CNN showed Russian armored personnel carriers being repainted with KFOR markings. (Under the terms of SFOR—the Stabilization Force, as the follow-on to the Implementation Force in Bosnia was called—any movement of troops from Bosnia was supposed to be done only with four months' notice.) While Talbott was with Chernomyrdin, others on the U.S. team were meeting with Russian military officials. As Talbott aide John Bass recalls, "There was a real dichotomy to our discussions. Strobe kept hearing unified command, no problem, everything's great. We kept hearing, 'don't come in here and think you are going to dictate what KFOR is going to look like; we have other ways of making sure that our interests are represented.' We kept feeding that back into Strobe's conversations, and Chernomyrdin, Ivanov and finally Putin [at the time, the head of the Federal Security Service, or FSB] kept telling him that the military guys did not represent the government's official views and would be reined in. But that turned out not to be the case."[61]

Having received assurances from Chernomyrdin, Ivanov, and Putin, Talbott and his team had left Moscow. While they were in the air, 200 Russian troops crossed into Serbia on their way to Kosovo. An official on Talbott's plane was calling in to the White House situation room to relay the assurances the Americans had received; he soon ran to the front of the plane to get Talbott after learning what was taking place. More and more of the leading U.S. officials were brought into the call. Finally, Berger told Talbott to turn around and head back to Moscow. John Bass recalls, "When we turned the plane around to go back to Moscow, I really felt like the whole policy construct had pretty much evaporated and we were on uncharted territory. There were two possibilities. One, the Russians were really double-dealing and we had a volatile situation in Kosovo. But the part that was really disconcerting was the possibility of a military operating without civilian control. That prospect was pretty daunting."[62]

Once Talbott and his team were back in Moscow, they had good reason to believe that the Russian military was out of control. According to the Americans, neither Foreign Minister Ivanov nor Defense Minister Igor Sergeyev seemed to have any real idea what was going on.[63] But unfortunately for those officers who were managing the Russian military operation, the balance of forces in that part of the world had changed. They had 200 troops in an exposed position needing reinforcements. Flying in reinforcements, as Moscow planned, meant obtaining airspace rights from Hungary, Bulgaria, and Romania, but these countries were no longer members of the Warsaw Pact. The United States worked hard to get them to deny the Russians the use of their airspace, and they did. Hungary was a new U.S. ally in NATO, and Bulgaria and Romania understood that their prospects for NATO membership rested on how well they supported NATO and particularly the United States in this crisis. Still, the situation was serious; Talbott told the Russians their request for airspace had "created the possible preconditions for a genuine confrontation," especially since there were reports that Romania had scrambled fighter jets in response.[64] Had the general in charge of NATO forces on the ground not been Michael Jackson, a three-star officer from the United Kingdom, who was not willing to do as much as Clark wanted to do, a genuine confrontation might have erupted. Clark had called Secretary General of NATO Javier Solana, who told him that the NATO action order gave Clark the authority to send a contingent to the airport as soon as possible. Back in Washington, Vice Chairman of the Joint Chiefs of Staff Joseph Ralston agreed that Clark could send "a small element; this shouldn't be a military confrontation, just explain that this is for coordination and information flow."[65] But Solana and Ralston agreed to allow Clark to use Apache helicopters to block the runways in Pristina. Jackson, however, was not prepared to go along. Clark describes their conversation:

Jackson: "Sir, I'm not taking any more orders from Washington."

Clark: "Mike, these aren't Washington's orders, they're coming from me."

Jackson: "By whose authority?"

Clark: "By my authority, as SACEUR [Supreme Allied Commander, Europe]."

Jackson: "You don't have that authority."

Clark: "I do have that authority. I have the Secretary General behind me on this."

Jackson: "Sir, I'm not starting World War III for you. . . . "

Clark: "Mike, I'm not asking you to start World War III. I'm asking you to block the runways so that we don't have to face an issue that could produce a crisis. . . . It doesn't have to be a confrontation. . . . You will have the position. . . . They will have to challenge you."

Jackson: "Sir, I'm a three-star general; you can't give me orders like this. . . . I have my judgment."

Clark: "Mike, I'm a four-star general, and I can tell you these things."[66]

Clark argues, "I saw the problem in strategic terms. This could be a defining moment for the future of NATO. Would we or would we not be able to conduct our own peacekeeping missions? Would Russia be coequal with NATO in this operation? Would Russia get its way by deception and bluff or by negotiation and compromise? Would we have an effective operation or another weak U.N.-type force?"[67]

In the end, Jackson prevailed. The British sealed off the roads that led to and from the airfield, and Jackson wrote a letter making clear that NATO did not accept Russia's claim to be in control of the airfield. Without reinforcements, Russia would not be able to control the airport anyway. In the end, the Russians were reduced to begging the British for food and water.[68]

Throughout this tense period, Yeltsin and Clinton spoke often. In one conversation, Yeltsin told Clinton that he had to do what he did and knew Clinton would forgive him. Finally, on June 14, after Yeltsin ranted incoherently, one of Clinton's staffers passed him a note with some language that pretended the two leaders had come to closure. Clinton told Yeltsin that he agreed with him and then told the Russian president the three points they had agreed upon: that they would resolve the Pristina issues on the Bosnia principles, that the long-term deployment would be done on Bosnia principles, and that Secretary of Defense William Cohen and Defense Minister Igor Sergeyev would work out the details in Helsinki. Yeltsin gave his assent.[69]

At the G-8 meeting in Cologne in June, Yeltsin reached out to Clinton. "Our relationship came to the very brink of collapse. If you and I hadn't kept in touch and dealt honestly and openly with each other, it would have gone over the brink. . . . There were a couple of points when we made pretty clear to each other that our friendship had just about reached its limit. But even at the toughest moment, we asked ourselves, 'Should we keep working together?' And we always answered, 'Yes! We're going to fix this problem this way or that way.' And we'd find a way of agreeing on whatever the question was. Why did we do that? Because everything depends on our two powerful countries, that's why?"[70] Writing in June 1999, Yeltsin's foreign minister, Igor Ivanov, also highlighted the importance of Cologne and the personal relationship between Clinton and Yeltsin. "The recent months were not the easiest in the relations between Russia and the U.S. At the same time given the safety margin built up over the years, as highlighted by the last meeting between Boris Nikolayevich Yeltsin and President Bill Clinton of the U.S. in Cologne, we can firmly count on overcoming the current problems."[71] Clinton must have believed that pushing for a G-8 was one of the smartest things he ever did.

At Cologne Clinton showered Yeltsin with praise for his help in ending the war. He told his staff he wanted to let Yeltsin get "all the credit he deserves and more, and he can rewrite history to his heart's content." Asked by the press if he trusted his counterpart, Clinton said of his man in Moscow, "Well, all I can tell you is, every time I've had an understanding with Boris Yeltsin, he's kept it."[72]

Enduring Effects

When Americans remember Kosovo, they likely think first about NATO's willingness to go to war for the first time in its history not to protect a member state but rather to prevent Milosevic from carrying out a campaign of genocide against the Albanian population in Kosovo. Some also focus on the miscalculations made on both sides as war approached, as well as after the bombing started.

But Kosovo also had important implications for U.S.-Russian relations. NATO's campaign to convince Moscow that it was no longer a military organization designed to protect others against Russia but rather a political organization eager to take account of Russia's interests now fell on deaf ears. Any notion that the Permanent Joint Council could operate in a major European crisis seemed absurd to the Russians. Moscow foreign policy elites—liberal, communist, and nationalist—rejected the Wilsonian explanation for NATO action, instead seeing the bombing campaign through a realist lens—that is, a lens that framed the outcome as a win for the United States and a loss for Russia.[73] At the same time, there was real suspicion in Washington about whether Russian leaders shared the values espoused by the Western community. Yeltsin and his team may have been frustrated by Milosevic and privately understanding of what NATO was doing, but publicly, they stood not with the victims of ethnic cleansing but with the butcher of Belgrade. This public position seemed to resonate with most Russians, who expressed real displeasure with the NATO-led campaign.[74]

There are also lingering questions about Russia's actual intentions and actions at the end of the war. President Ahtisaari, so convinced that the diplomatic mission would fail, has spent a great deal of time speaking with Russian officials about what occurred, and he is convinced that Milosevic surrendered because "it had been agreed between the Russian armed forces as well as intelligence services and the Yugoslav leadership that Russia would take control of Pristina and the northern part of Kosovo and form a sector of its own of them. If matters in Kosovo in two to three years proceed[ed] to the point where the

Albanians are declaring their country independent, Serbia [would] by means of Russian troops be able to keep a large part of it and fill it with Serbs only."[75]

Had the Russians been able to fly in reinforcements, they might have been able to secure part of Kosovo for the Serbs, thus creating havoc for NATO command and control. But they had not counted on defiance from former members of the Warsaw Pact who were now in NATO or trying to get in, and their plan failed. Ahtisaari's thesis is perfectly plausible (if unproven), however, given the events that unfolded, and his argument remains a cautionary tale for those who want to see NATO work more closely with the Russian military to deal with common threats. Because of Kosovo, the joint consultation and decisionmaking forum, the PJC, never was able to develop, and in 2002, NATO and Russia decided to replace it. But Kosovo reminded everyone that not allowing the Russians to veto NATO operations was critical to ensuring that NATO could act if it needed to do so.

Finally, Kosovo raised questions about the Kremlin's ability to manage obvious demonstrations of Russia's weakness. Yeltsin's handling of the Kosovo crisis suggested that he was no longer in full control of foreign and military policy at home. Curiously, in his State of the Federation address in April 1999, Yeltsin made "preventing schisms and discord within the country . . . our number one task" in *foreign* affairs.[76]

One of the major patterns of the 1990s was Yeltsin blustering about things he did not like but then going along with the U.S. position. We asked U.S. officials if they assumed that this pattern would continue in March 1999, and thus whether they discounted the danger that the war would be too much for the U.S.-Russian relationship. Leon Fuerth responded, "One of the things that worried us was whether the political resentments were cumulative. The model that says that they blustered before and bought it before works only if you believe that these experiences leave no residue. On the other hand, if they have progressively poisoned the atmosphere, then the next incident might be the one that really crosses the threshold. We couldn't know that either."[77]

Events did seem to be cumulative in one sense. Following the economic shock of August 1998, the NATO bombing provided another nail in the coffin of U.S.-Russia relations during the latter part of the 1990s. In the wake of Kosovo, Russian politicians began to champion the benefits of a Russian-Chinese alliance against the United States.[78] In 2001, a twenty-year friendship treaty between the two Asian giants was signed. In elite circles in Moscow, getting on the U.S. bandwagon was out; balancing against the United States was back in.[79] First internal economic transformation seemed to be failing, and now Russia's embrace of the West seemed to be faltering. Then, just a few months after Kosovo in the fall of 1999, a third shock hit when the Russian government renewed its war against the rebellious republic of Chechnya and followed that with a clampdown on media freedom at home.

11

Chechnya, Again

On August 2, 1999, Chechen commander Shamil Basayev led a group of roughly 2,000 armed rebels into the Russian republic of Dagestan with the stated purpose of liberating the republic from the Russian empire.[1] The group included the Arab commander Khattab, who had ties to al Qaeda, as well as Wahhabists originally from Dagestan.[2] In response, the Russian Security Council met and declared that Russia's armed forces would be used to restore order in the region. American officials, like those in most other countries in the world, condemned the rebel intervention into Russian sovereignty.[3] As State Department spokesperson Jamie Rubin stated on August 16, 1999, "It is our view that the action by armed groups from Chechnya against lawful authority and innocent civilians are condemnable."[4]

Russian armed forces launched a major counteroffensive against the Chechen and Arab units in Dagestan.[5] By the end of the month, they had pushed Basayev and his forces back into Chechnya. On August 27, 1999, Prime Minister Vladimir Putin visited Dagestan and pledged 300 million rubles for rehabilitation work. Many hoped that this might be the end of the conflict.

It was not. The following week, on September 1, an explosion on Manezh Square in downtown Moscow wounded forty-one people. Two days later, the Russian government reported that terrorists blew up an apartment building in Bunyaks, Dagestan, that housed families of Russian officers, killing several dozen people. On September 5, 2,000 Chechen fighters crossed back into Dagestan and occupied several villages in the Novolakskii region. Only three days later, another attack destroyed an apartment building in a residential neighborhood in Moscow, killing 21 people and wounding more than 150.

The attacks in the heart of Russia continued two days later when a bomb exploded in another apartment building in Moscow. Still another attack against civilians occurred on September 16, 1999, in Volgodonsk, Rostov, where a nine-story apartment was destroyed, killing 17 and injuring 300.[6] In one month, more than 300 Russian civilians had been killed.

Mystery still surrounds these attacks. Some have even suggested that the Russian intelligence services carried them out as a pretext to get Russia back into a war with Chechnya. Calculating that the war would be successful and popular, this scheme would then propel Prime Minister Putin to the top of the list of presidential candidates.[7] For most Russian citizens, however, there was no mystery. They understood these attacks to be acts of war committed by Chechen terrorists and their foreign supporters against innocent Russian civilians. Society demanded a response, and the Russian government responded. On September 17, 1999, Putin told the upper house of parliament that Chechnya is a subject of the Russian Federation and that a major counteroffensive would take place. In a subsequent statement, Putin emphasized that the new conflict "is not a civil war, but a war declared against Russia by international terrorism with the aim to seize some territories with rich natural resources. . . . [The] terrorists are prepared, financed and sent abroad."[8] Putin and official government news sources emphasized the role of Wahhabbists from Saudi Arabia in spearheading these latest attacks against Russia.

In October, Russian troops crossed into Chechen territory for the second time in a decade.[9] Some had hoped the Russian armed forces might occupy the northern half of Chechnya, stopping at the Terek River above which most ethnic Russians in Chechnya lived. Putin, however, opted for full-scale occupation of the republic using maximum force. Chechnya was to be liberated from the rebels by any means necessary. More than 100,000 troops were sent to the theater to accomplish this objective, more than double the amount deployed in the first war.

In contrast to the first war in 1994–96, Russian armed forces initially appeared to be more successful in this second campaign.[10] More methodical and relying to a greater extent on air power, Russian forces eventually recaptured Grozny and most of Chechnya's cities by the beginning of 2000, sending the Chechen fighters into the mountains. The severity and extent of human rights violations against noncombatants in this second war—including rape, torture, summary executions, bombings of villages, and the inhumane treatment of prisoners of war—also increased dramatically (or were better documented). Human Rights Watch titled its report on the war on prison conditions inside Chechnya, "Welcome to Hell."[11] Western experts estimate that 400,000 people have been displaced.[12] In his careful study of war crimes conducted in Chechnya, Matthew Evangelista concludes, "By any measure, the

Russian government has fallen short of its international obligation to pursue war criminals."[13] Chechen fighters also have carried out terrible abuses of Russian prisoners of war.

Russian victory has proved elusive. At the time of this writing, Russian troops are still in the republic fighting Chechen rebels.

The renewed and prolonged war in Chechnya represented the most serious setback to democratic practices in Russia during the last two years of the Clinton administration. Yet Putin's rise to power first as prime minister and then as president coincided with some additional challenges to Russia's already fragile and unconsolidated democracy. Also on Putin's watch, the Federal Security Service stepped up harassment of targeted human rights activists, investigative journalists, trade unionists, environmental leaders, and Western nongovernmental organizations and religious groups and their Russian affiliates.[14] New guidelines on foreign contacts for academics were published, and a few academics were charged with espionage.[15]

Putin also moved to weaken alternative power centers in the state. Putin's allies invented a new party, Unity, to compete in the 1999 parliamentary elections.[16] Its capture of almost a quarter of the popular vote helped to make the State Duma much more cooperative with the president. Subsequently, the Kremlin orchestrated a merger of Unity with Fatherland, its vehement foe during the 1999 parliamentary election.[17] The merger made the Duma even more of a rubber stamp for Putin's policies. Putin's so-called reform of the upper house of parliament, the Federation Council, weakened this once important check on presidential power—a body once elected and now appointed. Plans for reasserting Moscow's authority throughout the regions of Russia have been less successful, but there is an unmistakable tilt toward the center.[18]

On Clinton's watch, Putin's antidemocratic proclivities were most starkly exposed in his approach to the non-government-controlled media. The Russian state arrested, intimidated, and pushed into exile journalists Andrei Babitsky and Anna Politkovskaya for reporting the "wrong" news about Chechnya. The Russian government also introduced a new Information Security Doctrine, which threatened to control the free flow of information in and out of Russia. The government's campaign against Vladimir Gusinsky's Media-Most in 2000, at the time the biggest privately owned media group in Russia and owner of the NTV television network, most dramatically demonstrated Putin's intolerance of criticism. By the end of the Clinton administration's second term, the Russian government had succeeded in forcing the transfer of control of NTV and Media-Most's newsweekly *Itogi* to Kremlin-friendly hands, and helped to close down altogether Media-Most's daily newspaper, *Segodnya*.[19]

The U.S. Response: Words

For the veterans of the Russia team in the Clinton administration, "Chechnya Two" and the related antidemocratic developments inside Russia added yet one more blow following the loss of confidence in the economic and diplomatic spheres. Russia's financial crisis, followed by the Bank of New York scandal and the Who Lost Russia debate, combined to seriously dampen moods about Russia's prospects of becoming a normal country and a stable partner of the United States. Just months after the August 1998 financial meltdown and what seemed at the time to be the end of market reform in Russia, Clinton officials had to muster all their diplomatic talents to avoid a major blowup in U.S.-Russian relations over Kosovo. They were exhausted by the feat and still troubled at Russia's erratic behavior—that is, at the Pristina airport in June 1999—but still entertained the idea that the positive results of cooperation at the end of the Kosovo campaign might give the bilateral relationship a jump start. Above all else, Clinton officials hoped to use their final two years in power to secure a major arms control agreement with Russia, an objective that had eluded them in their first six years in power.

Russia's invasion of Chechnya in the summer of 1999 extinguished any twinkles of optimism about a START III (strategic arms reduction talks) accord. Instead, some officials began to worry privately that all of their accomplishments on the Russian account over the last six years were being washed away by this second war. The manner in which the Russians fought the second war also frustrated U.S. officials who might have otherwise been more sympathetic to their sovereignty challenges. As senior State Department official John Beyrle lamented, "Instead of fighting the war in a smart way, the Red Army went in like a sledgehammer."[20] This extreme disappointment with their Russian counterparts colored the American response to the second Chechen war.

Complementing these changes in attitude were other changes in the Clinton administration that shaped the policy response to Chechnya. Clinton was no longer vested in his Russia policy as he had been in his first term. For Clinton, Monica Lewinsky and impeachment proceedings had pushed all other concerns to the sidelines. Talbott writes, "The ensuing political mayhem took a heavy toll on the government and the nation. Policymaking suffered as institutions were diverted from nobler or at least more normal business, and officials were distracted and discouraged in the conduct of their duties."[21]

Both Clinton and Yeltsin were at the end of their long tenures in power. In contrast to 1994, they needed each other less in 1999. Nor did investments in the Russia policy seem likely to produce results. Some continued to believe that a major arms control agreement could be signed before the end of Clinton's term, but it was a long shot.

The personnel working on Russia issues also had changed between wars. The secretary of state during the second war had a reputation for being much more concerned about human rights than her predecessor. The ambassador-at-large for the new independent states during the second war, Stephen Sestanovich, also adopted a much more critical view of the Russian intervention than did his predecessors in the State Department (but note that he was brought into the government by one of those predecessors, Strobe Talbott). Sestanovich's reputation as a Russia expert sympathetic to Russia's reformers amplified his voice within the administration. The "pro-Russia guy" was nonetheless very critical of Russia's new military mission. Those groups within the administration who had previously opposed a tough line on Chechnya during the first war were now weakened or absent. The departure of Secretary of Defense William Perry and many of his team meant that the Pentagon was much less focused on Russia. The Treasury Department's voice on Russia was also vastly weakened after the August 1998 debacle, and in any event, its viewpoint on Russia had changed after August 1998. Treasury officials had been burned by their Russian counterparts, saw no prospects for reform in the immediate future, and therefore, played no role in muting criticism of Russia and its actions toward Chechnya.

Finally, some in the Clinton team, including most importantly Strobe Talbott, had deep regrets about the softness of their response to the first Chechen war and therefore crafted a different reaction this time around. As Talbott recalled, "I regret it [the U.S. response to the first war] not only for humanitarian reasons but I think that if we had been able to shake Yeltsin and use the Clinton-Yeltsin [relationship] in the way that we did successfully on other issues maybe he wouldn't have been susceptible to Stepashin or Kulikov, who got him to do it again in 1999. And Putin, of course, big time. . . . And second, if we had reacted more to the first war, then we might have disinclined Yeltsin to start the second."[22] Even if their tools to influence Russian behavior were just as limited in 1999 as they were in 1994, those Clinton officials still in the government for the second Chechen war were determined at least to say the right things about the war. They firmly believed that words mattered.[23]

Russia also had changed between wars. Most important, Yeltsin was not fighting for his political life during this second invasion, although the Russians tried to emphasize that the war was tied to domestic politics, arguing that Yeltsin's strong response was needed to keep Gen. Aleksandr Lebed out of power.[24] The threat of a communist comeback ended with the 1996 presidential election.[25] In positions of power after the August 1998 financial meltdown, communist leaders had demonstrated that they had no intention of trying to resurrect Soviet-style communism. The future of Russian reform was not tied to Yeltsin's survival anymore. In part, this was true because economic reform at the time was stalled. In part, this was true because the specter of a real reversal was no longer a threat. In addition, the threat of federal dissolution, if ever real, had seriously faded by 1999. Finally, in contrast to 1994, this military action was initially popular in Russian society, which saw the intervention into Chechnya this time as self-defense. Until the end of the Clinton administration, solid majorities in Russia supported the war effort.[26] Even some of America's closest friends in Russia, including Anatoly Chubais and his new coalition of liberals, the Union of Right Forces, supported the war.[27] Only liberal Grigory Yavlinsky publicly criticized the second war, a stance for which many believed he paid dearly at the polls in the parliamentary elections of December 1999.[28] This new set of circumstances in Russia made devising a policy response to the Chechen war even more difficult.

The U.S. policy response to the second war changed but only in the margins. Similar to the first war, the Clinton administration continued to respect Russia's territorial integrity. As Talbott explained, "Chechnya, Dagestan, Ingushetia—these are all republics on the territory of the Russian Federation. We recognize Russia's international boundaries and its obligations to protect all of its citizens against separatism and attacks on lawful authorities. We also acknowledge that the current outbreak of violence began when insurgents, based in Chechnya, launched an offensive in Dagestan. Russia also has been rocked by lethal bombings of apartment buildings deep in the Russian heartland, including in Moscow itself."[29] The Chechen invasion of Dagestan made it impossible for the United States or any other country to adopt a different position on sovereignty. Russian territory had been invaded. Russia, therefore, had the right to defend its borders.[30]

Also similar to the first war, the Chechens had no friends in the administration. To be sure, those that closely followed the conflict recognized that different Chechen fighters had different agendas. Some in the administration had sympathy for Aslan Maskhadov, the elected president of Chechnya, while everyone despised Shamil Basayev and his allies. Publicly for the Clinton administration, however, Basayev's nefarious activities tainted the entire Chechen cause. Even Maskhadov's actions complicated open support. For instance, Maskhadov's government of Ichkeria had condemned American counterattacks against Osama bin Laden's camps in Sudan and Afghanistan in 1998, while Chechen deputy prime minister Vakha Arsanov declared war against the United States in response to the U.S. counterattacks.[31] In testimony before Congress, Ambassador Sestanovich revealed, "Chechen rebels are receiving help from radical groups in other countries, including Usama Bin Laden's network and others who have attacked or threatened Americans and American interests."[32] Such allies and statements made it difficult for anyone in the administration to champion the Chechen cause. The attacks against

Russian civilians in Moscow and elsewhere, while never directly tied to Chechens, also dampened enthusiasm for the Chechen cause.

Some aspects of U.S. policy, however, did change. In affirming Russia's sovereignty in Chechnya, Clinton officials reversed their previous policy and refrained from calling the Chechen war an "internal affair." Clinton undermined the premise about "internal affairs" most dramatically at a speech at the meeting of the Organization for Security and Cooperation in Europe (OSCE) in Istanbul in November 1999. Clinton, speaking to Yeltsin directly across the table in front of dozens of European leaders, argued that he would not have wanted the international community to sit by idly if Yeltsin had been arrested during the coup in Moscow in August 1991.[33] Yeltsin hated the analogy, but Clinton made clear his intention of treating the Chechen crisis as an international issue. More bluntly, Secretary of State Madeleine Albright affirmed, "Russia could not consider this war simply an internal affair."[34] While attending a multilateral conference on the Middle East peace process held in Moscow, Albright hinted at the need for a similar kind of multilateral intervention in Chechnya: "Conflicts within states, as well as those between states, threaten our common security. . . . I believe there is a very important role that the OSCE can play in helping to resolve a variety of conflicts within countries."[35] In his initial dealings with Putin, Clinton also tried to emphasize the international consequences of the Chechen war, a framing of the problem that the Russian prime minister and soon-to-be president categorically rejected.[36] When Clinton brought up Chechnya, the Russian president became extremely annoyed. Putin was unwilling to listen to Clinton's criticisms. In part because of Chechnya, the two men never hit it off and endured a frosty relationship until the end of Clinton's second term.

Rhetorically, Clinton officials were more critical of Russia's conduct during the second war even though the tactics used were not that different from those used in the first war. In comparing tactics, Russian military expert Pavel Baev wrote, "Some Western experts have concluded that the Russians are following the NATO model from Kosovo, but in fact it is quite difficult to find much similarity between the two operations: NATO used massive airpower with high-precision strikes in order to avoid a ground campaign, while Russia has used limited airpower (with very little precision to speak of) in support of a ground campaign, relying primarily on the massive and indiscriminate use of artillery. There is nothing new about this 'firewall' Russian tactic."[37] Despite Baev's claim of continuity, U.S. officials tried to highlight differences, emphasizing that the "indiscriminate use of force" was a big problem that invited international attention and action. As Sestanovich described, "A relentless bombing and artillery campaign has been carried out in nearly all parts of the republic. This indiscriminate use of force against innocent civilians is indefensible, and we condemn it." Sestanovich came very close to calling Russian actions war crimes:

> Like other countries, Russia has assumed obligations under the Geneva Conventions and commitments under the OSCE Code on Political-Military Aspects of Security. Common Article 3 of the Geneva Convention states that "in armed conflicts not of an international character, persons taking no part in hostilities . . . shall be treated humanely." Article 36 of the OSCE Code of Conduct states that "if recourse to force cannot be avoided in performing internal security missions, each participating State will ensure that its use must be commensurate with the needs for enforcement. The armed forces will take care to avoid injury to civilians or their property." Russia's current campaign does not match these commitments.[38]

Talbott, in contrast to his statements about the first Chechen war, was much more critical of Russia's behavior this time around. "The violent secessionism and extremism of Chechen rebels, coupled with provocations in Dagestan and elsewhere were legitimate security concerns. We don't dispute Russia's rights, or indeed its responsibility, to fight terrorism on its soil. But none of that begins to justify the Russian government's decision to use massive force against civilians inside Chechnya. The numbers speak for themselves: 285,000 people displaced, thousands of innocent civilians dead or wounded, and thousands of homes and businesses destroyed since last September."[39]

Albright called the Russian bombing of a marketplace in Grozny "ominous and deplorable," emphasizing that the "Russian army's indiscriminate use of force was indefensible and we condemn it."[40] Such language was never used to describe the first war. As an alternative, Clinton officials said "that there must be a vigorous and conscientious effort to engage regional leaders in a political dialogue." The pleas for negotiations were aimed at both Russian and Chechen leaders.[41]

Clinton officials also developed a new theory about the relationship between Chechnya and democracy. In the first war, some in the Clinton administration cited the debate about the war in Russia as a sign that democracy was working. But too much criticism of Yeltsin during the first war was considered detrimental to democracy's long-term prospects in Russia. Now the argument was the exact opposite: the war in Chechnya threatened to undermine democracy.[42] Clinton officials also emphasized how the war was damaging to Russia's international reputation and "casts a shadow over the entire process of Russia's integration into the international community." As Talbott concluded in congressional testimony, "I would submit, Mr. Chairman, that no other development in the nine years since the collapse of the Soviet Union has raised such serious questions about Russia's commitments to international norms as the war in Chechnya."[43] Allusions to Lincoln and the American Civil War never surfaced during the second Chechen war. Rather than being praised for preserving democracy as Lincoln was, Yeltsin was charged with undermining it.

Despite the new critical edge to American statements about the Chechen war, the Clinton administration still did not want to go too far. American officials did not want to make Chechnya the only issue in U.S.-Russian relations. As Albright argued on returning from the very difficult 1999 OCSE meeting in Istanbul at which Chechnya was a major topic, "The last thing that we should be doing is trying to turn Russia back into an enemy."[44]

The one official in the Clinton administration who most hated discussing Chechnya was Clinton himself. He obliged his staff in adding Chechnya to the talking points during phone calls and meetings with Yeltsin and then Putin, but he never devoted serious attention to the problem. Clinton disliked the issue in part because he did not think it was a major problem and in part because his leverage for changing Russian behavior was extremely limited. In Clinton's mind, harping over a "small" issue like Chechnya should not be the central focus of American foreign policy toward Russia. In his farewell ode to Yeltsin published soon after the Russian president resigned, Clinton used the unfortunate phrase—"to liberate Grozny"—a euphemism for Yeltsin's war against Chechnya. After years of discussing Chechnya, Clinton's phraseology revealed that his sympathies lay with Moscow all along. His attitude severely constrained how far his advisers could push on this issue.[45]

The U.S. Response: Unstated Linkage

In addition to new language for describing the second Chechen war, the Clinton administration did make some policy changes designed to exercise what little leverage the U.S. had. In the first war, the Clinton administration had worked hard to keep the issue of Chechnya from dominating discussion at international forums. This time around, the United States pushed to have Chechnya discussed. The Americans, not the Europeans, pushed to make Chechnya the focus of the OSCE meeting in Istanbul in November 1999.[46] More generally, State Department officials repeatedly sent out talking points to American allies in Europe so that the West adopted a common approach to the Chechen conflict. Putin worked hard to develop special relationships with European leaders and pull them away from the U.S. position on Chechnya. In the end, State Department officials concede that Putin achieved partial success. At the November 1999 OSCE meeting in Istanbul, for instance, a paragraph criticizing the Russian policies in Chechnya in the joint communiqué was softened at the insistence of West European foreign ministers.[47]

Similar to their position on the previous war, Clinton administration officials refrained from cutting bilateral assistance programs to Russia. Using Nunn-Lugar funds to dismantle Russian nuclear weapons was still considered a national security interest no matter what the recipients of this program—the Russian military—did in other arenas. Other military-to-military cooperative projects were also considered sacrosanct because the cooperation was seen as important in its own right.

Nor was the Agency for International Development (AID) eager to cut its programs. By the fall of 1999, most nonmilitary American assistance to Russia did not go to the Russian federal government but was channeled instead to nongovernment organizations and regional governments.[48] Clinton officials argued therefore that cutting this assistance would only punish those not directly responsible for the war.[49]

Two aid programs, however, did suffer: IMF assistance to Russia and Export-Import Bank projects with Russian companies. Formally, the IMF is an independent institution not beholden to U.S. policy positions. Informally, as discussed in earlier chapters, the United States exerts considerable leverage over the Fund on highly sensitive portfolios such as Russia. Before the second Chechen war began, the Clinton administration and its allies in the IMF wanted to resume lending to Russia in the summer of 1999, in part because they considered engagement with Russia, even after the August 1998 financial crash, to still be important, and in part because they wanted to bolster Russia's new reformist-leaning prime minister, Sergei Stepashin, who had replaced Primakov in May 1999. During Stepashin's first visit as Russian prime minister to Washington in July 1999, the IMF announced a new program with Russia and delivered the first tranche of assistance that summer.[50] As part of this new program, a second tranche was due to Russia in the fall. Once the war began, however, Clinton administration officials signaled to the IMF that they did not want the lending program to continue business as usual. Treasury Secretary Summers framed his objections in economic terms—the war, in his view, would be too costly for the Russian government to finance and in turn would prove destabilizing. Others, including Talbott and Sestanovich, made the case in moral terms.[51] They argued that new money for Russia, coming immediately after the war began, would make it look as if the United States condoned Russia's military campaign. Clinton administration officials did not publicly link IMF assistance to the Russian war in Chechnya, since such an overt intervention in the affairs of the IMF would tarnish the Fund's reputation. However, they asked their colleagues at the Fund to be extraordinarily diligent in making sure that Russia met all the conditions for the second tranche. Russia did not meet these conditions, and so the second tranche was never delivered. To avoid embarrassment, the Russians were told privately that they would not meet the conditions for the second installment of the program. With this knowledge, the Russian government formally withdrew its request for the loan and has never asked to borrow money from the IMF since.

In these discussions about Chechnya and the IMF, Ambassador-at-Large Stephen Sestanovich was the most outspoken proponent of cutting IMF funds to punish Russia for its behavior in Chechnya. Eventually, the senior director for Russian Affairs at the National Security Council, Carlos Pascual, sided with Sestanovich. Strobe Talbott and Sandy Berger were less enthusiastic about leaning on the IMF, but in the end they went along. Even Lawrence Summers and David Lipton lobbied against new funds. Summers reportedly said at one meeting, "What level of violence would it take for you folks? Does a nuclear bomb have to go off?"[52]

Treasury officials still opposed any *public* linkage between the war in Chechnya and IMF programs, as formal and public linkage would set a dangerous precedent and destroy the integrity of the IMF, although the precedent of linkage between IMF programs and political behavior had been established when the IMF cut funding to Indonesia over the conflict in East Timor. At the same time, Summers was also opposed to any new IMF money to Russia for economic reasons. After August 1998, Summers had become so disappointed with Russia that he now became a principal anti-Russia voice in the administration. The IMF delayed a second tranche in 1999 and did not initiate any new discussions about a bigger program. When the Russians complained that the IMF was linking financial decisions to Chechnya, no one in the Clinton administration denied it.[53]

The postponement of Export-Import Bank loans also was linked indirectly to Chechnya. After months of delay and negotiation, the Ex-Im Bank was preparing to make a $500 million loan to Tyumen Oil Company. Ex-Im Bank chairman James Harmon was very enthusiastic about the loan as were U.S. embassy officials in Moscow. They hoped that the Tyumen Oil loan might help to instill renewed confidence among American investors in the Russian economy. Such confidence was in severe deficit after August 1998 and the Bank of New York scandal. Secretary of State Albright, however, had different concerns. In part, she and her staff worried about the U.S. government making a loan to a Russian company—Alfa Bank, the owner of Tyumen Oil that had just (allegedly) stomped on the property rights of BP-Amoco, a company with a strong lobbying presence in Washington. In the context of the times, loaning any money to Russians seemed like a bad idea, but loaning money to this particular firm looked like an especially bad idea. Chechnya made the deal look even worse. Albright wanted to signal to Russia that there would be consequences for the war; delaying this loan was something she could do. When the Ex-Im board refused to delay the loan, Albright sent a letter to board members outlining why she thought it was "in the national interest" to post-pone the loan.[54] According to a rarely invoked law, such a letter from the sec-retary of state overrode any Ex-Im board decision. Harmon was furious, arguing with some merit that Tyumen Oil was not fighting the war in Chechnya. But Albright argued, "We are not either in the banking or the accounting business, we are in [the business of] trying to have effective for-eign policy. . . . I always say that foreign policy is trying to get some other country to do what you want, that's all it is. . . . You can't do everything mili-tarily and diplomacy doesn't work unless you have a lot of sticks and carrots to go with it—if you just decide that something is pristine economics business and decide that it has no relevance to politics, then you have lost one arm basi-cally."[55] Over time, however, Tyumen Oil and the Russian government did take measures that partially alleviated BP-Amoco's concerns and the loans were allowed to move forward the following year even though little inside Chechnya had changed for the good. (After leaving office, Harmon joined the board of directors of the Tyumen Oil Company.)

In response to Chechnya two, Clinton administration officials also did more to try to help alter conditions on the ground in Chechnya. The United States provided $10 million to help address the problem of displaced persons. Clinton officials also pushed incessantly for international monitors to be allowed into Chechnya, which Clinton himself pushed with Prime Minister Putin in September 1999 in Auckland, New Zealand.[56] At the OSCE summit in Istanbul in November 1999, Putin agreed to allow the chairman of the OSCE, Norwegian foreign minister Knut Vollebaek, to visit Chechnya. Putin also agreed to meet with UN human rights commissioner Mary Robinson, though the results of the encounter were inconclusive. Sestanovich summed up the successes of these lobbying efforts in the following terms, "In response to persistent pressure from the U.S. and other western nations, Russia has agreed to grant the International Committee of the Red Cross (ICRC) access to detainees, agreed to establish an OSCE Assistance Group in Chechnya and agreed to add Council of Europe experts to the staff of Russia's new human rights ombudsman for Chechnya."[57] The Clinton administration also increased its assistance program to Georgia to beef up security at the Georgian-Russian border, so that Russia could not use the excuse of interven-ing in Georgia in the cause of "hot pursuit of terrorists."[58]

When all these policies are added up, the effort was still a small one. The rhetorical rebukes were sharper and IMF and Ex-Im loans were delayed, but little else changed. Clinton did not postpone planned bilateral meetings with his Russian counterparts; Russia was not kicked out of any major interna-tional club; and bilateral business in other arenas continued with no inter-ruption. As they had in the first war, Clinton administration officials felt helpless, believing they lacked the tools to influence positive change. Unlike the first war, however, they were more frustrated with their impotence and with the stupidity of both the Russians and Chechens for allowing this war to rekindle. As Talbott lamented in retrospect:

> The West had neither the desire nor the means to engage diplomatically in the Chechen conflict, much less intervene militarily. The U.S. and its allies had no leverage on the rebel leaders, nor did we have sympathy either with their goal of independence or the raids in Dagestan that had precipitated the conflict. They had indisputably—and, it seemed, deliberately—brought down the wrath of the Russian armed forces on their people. That meant there was little we could do but cite Russia's obligations under various international covenants to protect civilian life and call on Moscow to let representatives of the Organization for Security and Cooperation in Europe into Chechnya to help deal with the refugee crisis or monitor the behavior of Russian troops.[59]

Voices outside of the Administration

Critics of Clinton's policy on Chechnya were much more active and vocal during the second war than they had been in the first one. The rationale for Russia's second military intervention was arguably more plausible than the first move against Chechnya. The Russian government launched the first war with little or no prodding from the Chechen leadership, whereas it was responding to Basayev's invasion of Dagestan in the second war. It was the brutality of Russia's military campaign, not the actual precipitants of the second conflict, that critics of the war highlighted. By 1999, general disdain for both Clinton and Yeltsin helped to fuel the fires of criticism. For Republicans, the 2000 presidential election added incentives to discredit the policy.

Republicans in Congress led the charge. Senator Jesse Helms, the chairman of the Senate Foreign Relations Committee, and his staff, in particular Steven Biegun and Ian Brzezinski, were the most focused, dogged, and outspoken critics on Capitol Hill of Clinton's response to Russia's invasion of Chechnya. Helms convened several hearings to sustain attention. He constantly ridiculed the administration for its implicit support of genocide in Chechnya. He called on the United States to push for Russia's expulsion from the G-8. He tied up ambassadorial confirmations, in part as a tactic for punishing the administration. Clinton officials believed that Helms and his staff had a romanticized view of the freedom struggle in Chechnya. It was odd, they thought, that a conservative senator should be so sympathetic to a movement that was allied with Osama bin Laden. Nonetheless, they dreaded the idea of appearing before his committee, and they did all they could to soothe the senior senator from North Carolina.[60]

Helms did not work alone. Senator Mitch McConnell, an influential Republican from Kentucky, shared Helms's disdain for Clinton's Chechnya policy. His documented dislike of Clinton amplified his virulent indictment of the administration's response to the second Chechen war. In his opening statement before Strobe Talbott's appearance before the Foreign Operations Subcommittee, Senator McConnell stated bluntly:

> Now you [Talbott] and I can spend the next hour parsing syntax over the real intent behind U.S. policy pronouncements. Let's just stipulate that we disagree: you believe the Administration has been clear in objecting to the course Russia has pursued in Chechnya. I believe your message has been muddled, at best. At its worst, your failure to take decisive action invited contempt and a war against the Chechen people which reminded many local witnesses of the round-ups and forced deportations, famine and devastation of the Stalin era. Frankly, it reminds me of what Milosevic did to Kosovo, only with more firepower and speed. What I can't understand is why we supported war crimes indictments for ethnic cleansing in Kosovo, yet turn a blind eye to identical savagery against civilians in Chechnya.[61]

House Republicans tried to bring even greater attention to Clinton's failures on Chechnya by framing the problem in the context of a general policy failure toward Russia. Speaker of the House J. Dennis Hastert (R-Ill.) commissioned a study of American policy toward Russia, chaired by Republican congressman Christopher Cox. The "Cox Report" was called *Russia's Road to Corruption: How the Clinton Administration Exported Government Instead of Free Enterprise and Failed the Russian People.* It looked like a campaign document—slick, lots of pictures, and a provocative title—and was published in September 2000 just before the November presidential election. Though funded by Congress and distributed as a congressional study, the commission included no Democrats. These factors combined to limit the attention paid to the study, which was a good thing for Clinton and his administration given the conclusions.

The study reported, "The conduct of the first and second wars in Chechnya and the U.S. Administration's long quiescence concerning it, reveal the tragic cost of the overpersonalized Clinton Russia policy. Rather than acting forcefully to advance U.S. values and interests, the Clinton administration tacitly accepted Russia's agenda in Chechnya." The report even suggested that the "failure of the Clinton administration to apply pressure and diplomacy and to encourage a political solution in Chechnya may have actually encouraged Russia to broaden its war objectives in 1999." Like McConnell, the Cox Report was blaming the Clinton administration for the war itself. The Cox Report also drew a causal connection between Clinton complacency and Russia's intimidation of its neighbors.[62]

Democrats never went this far, but they too criticized the Clinton policy on Chechnya as weak, ineffective, and immoral. In February 2000, the Senate passed a resolution that called on the American president to "promote peace negotiations between the Government of the Russian Federation and the leadership of the Chechnya Government, including President Aslan Maskhadov, through third party mediations by the OSCE, United Nations, or other appropriate parties."[63] The same resolution also urged Clinton to endorse the recommendation of the UN high commissioner for human rights, which called for an investigation into alleged war crimes. The resolution denounced the detention of Radio Free Europe/Radio Liberty correspondent Andrei Babitsky, who was being held by Russian military authorities because of his alleged sympathetic reporting about the plight of the Chechens. This resolution, which won a majority in the Senate on February 25, 2000, was introduced by Paul Wellstone (D-Minn.), one of the most liberal democrats in the Senate. Congressman Tom Lantos (D-Calif.) was the author of the House resolution that called for Russia's expulsion from the G-8. (The resolution never won a majority in the Senate or the House.)

Congressional leaders backed up these rhetorical flurries and nonbinding resolutions with concrete actions. In the appropriations bill for 2000, U.S. legislators initially cut 30 percent from the President's Freedom Support Act budget. Talbott claimed that this was one of the many reasons Clinton vetoed the bill. "The funding levels proposed by the Congress would force us to make unacceptable trade-offs between our core economic and democracy programs and programs that prevent the proliferation of weapons of mass destruction. The President believes such cuts would be dangerously short-sighted, because the purposes of this assistance—from building an independent media to promoting small business—are fundamentally in our interests."[64] In part as a response to the Chechen war, as well as a more general reaction to Putin's antidemocratic policies, Congressman Tom Lantos introduced a new bill—the Russian Democracy Act of 2001—to earmark $50 million in new dollars in assistance targeted to democracy promotion in Russia.[65]

Eventually, Chechnya even emerged, however briefly and marginally, as a presidential election campaign issue. During the Democratic primaries, candidate Bill Bradley called for delays in Ex-Im bank loans (a policy the Clinton administration eventually pursued) saying, through spokesperson Eric Hauser, that "it is inappropriate to give assistance to Russia while it is engaged in the brutal war in Chechnya."[66] Republican candidate George Bush went further, calling for an end to both the Ex-Im Bank loan and IMF assistance to Russia.[67] Other issues dominated the 2000 presidential campaign, and

Clinton's critics never defined an alternative policy. What was clear by the end of Clinton's term, however, was how little enthusiasm there was for his Chechnya policy. This criticism in turn shaped in a negative way the assessments of his Russia policy as a whole.

Bush, Bradley, Helms, McConnell, Wellstone, Cox, and Lantos made a strange alliance on the Chechen issue. The coalition of critics in the policy community was even stranger. Zbigniew Brzezinski, the former national security adviser to President Jimmy Carter, constituted the most important lobby for the Chechen cause in and of himself. Though he had last served in government twenty years earlier, Brzezinski remained one of Washington's most important voices on foreign policy matters. He put the full force of his reputation, intellect, and acerbic tongue behind a campaign of pressure and ridicule of Clinton over Chechnya. His campaign was multifaceted. He defended the Chechens as freedom fighters and lambasted the Clinton administration for accepting the Russian interpretation of events in Chechnya. "What should be done? To start with, the U.S. should not fall for Russia's entreaty that 'we are allies against Osama bin Laden.' Reminiscent of the earlier Russian pitch that 'Yeltsin, like Lincoln, is saving the union,' which the Clinton administration bought hook, line, and sinker, this is a marginal issue intended as a distraction. Terrorism is neither the central geopolitical nor moral challenge here."[68] Brzezinski suggested that Clinton and his foreign policy team were guilty of contributing to genocide. "It is tragically the case that the Administration's indifference to what has been happening in Chechnya has probably contributed to the scale of the genocide inflicted on the Chechens. The Kremlin paused several times in the course of its military campaign in order to gauge the reaction of the West. Yet all they heard from the President were the words, 'I have no sympathy for the Chechen rebels'—which the Russians construed as a green light for their ruthless policy; and later the President in effect even endorsed their efforts to 'liberate Grozny.'"[69]

Brzezinski tried to increase attention to the Chechen cause by forming the American Committee for Peace in Chechnya, which he cochaired with Alexander Haig and Max Kampelman. In its founding declaration, the committee echoed longtime Russian human rights advocate Elena Bonner's characterization of the war as "genocide" and argued, "There is no excuse for inaction. The United States should immediately announce a comprehensive plan to deter Russian aggression, provide humanitarian relief to the Chechen people, and begin a process of bringing the war to a negotiated end."[70] Unlike many others, Brzezinski suggested alternatives for policy formation, including a discontinuation of high-level contacts between Russian and American officials and an elevation of American-Chechen interactions.[71] The American Committee for Peace in Chechnya also made recommendations: oppose the release of World Bank and IMF loans to Russia, initiate talks about Russian

G-8 suspension, call upon the UN Commission on Human Rights to appoint a special rapporteur on Chechnya, take the lead in providing humanitarian relief, call on the OSCE Assistance Group in Chechnya to "act upon its mandate ... to negotiate a political solution to the present crisis."[72] Brzezinski promoted direct American development assistance to Chechnya and the region.[73] Finally, Brzezinski helped to establish and finance Chechen representation in Washington headed by Lyoma Usmanov. Eventually, Chechen representatives opened offices in eleven countries.

Few devoted energy to the Chechen issue like Brzezinski. Yet his view on the war was shared by many. As already mentioned, Human Rights Watch devoted serious attention to documenting human rights violations inside Chechnya. The National Endowment for Democracy by law could not adopt a policy position on the war, but the foundation went out of its way to support financially critics of the war inside Russia, including Lev Ponomarev, Sergei Grigoryants, Elena Bonner, and the Russian-Chechen Friendship Society. Private foundations such as the Ford Foundation gave direct assistance to war critics such as the Russian human rights organization *Memorial*. The Jamestown Foundation tried to attract attention to the Chechen conflict by publishing a weekly digest on events in Chechnya penned by Hoover Institution senior fellow John Dunlop, one of the country's leading experts on the subject. Under the leadership of its new editor, Fred Hiatt, the *Washington Post* editorial page sustained attention on the war. In addition to Hiatt, editorial page deputy editor Jackson Diehl made the Chechen war one of his signature issues. Such editorial focus did not exist in any newspaper during the first Chechen war. American silence, some of these critics asserted, was not only morally reprehensible but also weakened civil society leaders in Russia who sought a peaceful solution in Chechnya.[74]

Less publicly, some friends of the administration urged a more critical approach. Talbott says that he listened more closely to criticism about Chechnya from colleagues and friends—including Richard Holbrooke, scholar Grigory Freiden, Russian journalist Masha Lipman, and novelist John Le Carre—than he did to partisan attacks.[75]

Outside analysts were not unanimous in their condemnation of Russia and Clinton's support of Russia. Especially in the early stages of the second war, Yeltsin and Putin had many more supporters in the West than during the first war. Anatol Lieven, a former journalist who had covered critically the first war and written a book about it, adopted a very different perspective on the second war, calling the Russian response justified and American moralizing about the intervention unwarranted.[76] Similarly, Dimitri Simes, the president of the Nixon Center, called Clinton's criticism of Russia unjustified:

> Clinton should get an award for hypocrisy. In 1994/96, he talked about Russian "civil war" and he compared Yeltsin to Lincoln. It was ridiculous

and preposterous. Now he is talking about the Russian war in Chechnya after the Russians were attacked by the Chechens and he tells them how they should [not] kill innocent civilians. Do we remember Kosovo? Do we remember the Branch Davidians? Can you imagine a major nation which allows a territory with fifty or sixty thousand people, unarmed, no control, no central government. . . . And the truth is that the Russians are learning from what the United States and NATO have done in Kosovo, but they do not have precision-guided munitions.[77]

Well before September 11, 2001, other critics of Clinton highlighted his administration's inability to understand the real security threats to Russia and the West posed by terrorist groups in Chechnya. As Robert Bruce Ware wrote soon after the war began, "Recent Chechen aggression has been financed by some of the same forces of international terrorism against which the West has long been struggling. The same forces that took American lives in Riyadh, Nairobi, and Dar es Salaam are taking Dagestani lives today."[78]

No one praised the Clinton approach to Chechnya two. For some, the Clinton response was too muted. For others, it was too loud. But no one believed that the Clinton team had a policy that was just right.

Rhetorical Support for Freedom of the Press

The Clinton administration, as it did in regard to war in Chechnya, believed that it had few effective tools available to influence the dramas of democratic rollback that gained steam in the new Putin era. The Clinton administration did complain and helped to secure the release of Andrei Babitsky, a journalist who was working for the American organization Radio Free Europe/Radio Liberty, but the administration did little to redress the violation of human rights of Igor Sutyagin, a Russian security expert accused of spying for the United States and held without trial for years. In cases like that of Sutyagin, some Clinton officials argued that the United States did not have the moral authority to be intervening in Russia's domestic affairs.

The government campaign against Media-Most, however, was simply too big to be ignored. Vladimir Gusinsky, the owner of Media-Most, hired one of Washington's most prestigious law firms, Akin, Gump, Strauss, Hauer, and Feld LLP, and one the best-known public relations companies in the United States, APCO Worldwide, to help keep his cause on the administration's radar screen. The National Conference on Soviet Jewry, which advocates on behalf of Jews in Russia, Ukraine, the Baltic States, and Eurasia, also assisted in stimulating interest in Gusinsky's cause in Washington by organizing meetings between the Russian media mogul and congressional leaders. Senator Gordon Smith and Congressman Tom Lantos were particularly active on this issue.

The Clinton administration did respond. Talbott and Sestanovich met periodically with Gusinsky and his Media-Most associates, Igor Malashenko, Andrei Kolossovsky, and Yvgeny Kiselev. The State Department in turn denounced criminal charges trumped up against Gusinsky and issued statements calling for a proper legal process to resolve the ownership disputes between Gusinsky and the other shareholders of Media-Most. After Gusinsky moved to Spain to avoid arrest, the Clinton administration worked with Interpol and the Spanish government to block Gusinsky's extradition back to Russia. While Clinton was visiting Moscow in June 2000, he also made sure to give Ekho Moskvy—a radio station that once belonged to Gusinsky's media empire—an interview in which he stressed the importance of freedom of the press. Clinton administration officials fully understood that Gusinsky was no Andrei Sakharov. Yet they also believed that the legal charges brought against Gusinsky were politically motivated. In his crackdown on oligarchs, Putin was being very selective. The Clinton team worried about the long-term consequences for Russian democracy of this selective application of the rule of law, which in turn produced fewer independent sources of media in Russia.[79]

Beyond fighting successfully for Gusinsky's asylum in Spain and later the United States, the Clinton administration could do little to stop the seizure of NTV and *Itogi* by those hostile to the original mandate of these two media outlets. Again, the most powerful country in the world looked rather powerless as it tried to influence the course of events in Russia.

Conclusion

The Clinton administration was under siege for its Russia policy during the second Chechen war and subsequent other antidemocratic developments in Russia. The Clinton team was playing defense, not offense. Moreover, administration officials were defending a Russia policy that they no longer believed in with the same conviction that they had held on first entering government in 1993. After countless hearings, op-eds, and threats of further actions, however, the policy changed only at the margins. The policy changed only slightly because Clinton officials believed there were no obviously more effective policy alternatives. Most important, Clinton never sympathized with the secessionists in Chechnya given his stake in the relationship with Russia.

Clinton officials' rhetoric about the war did begin to resemble the op eds of some of their greatest detractors. Beyond deploying the right words, however, the Clinton team believed that it had few other policy options that might influence the war in Chechnya or the media battles in Russia in a positive direction. Clinton administration officials rejected full-scale punitive sanctions that in their view might make people in the United States feel better but would not help the plight of the Chechens at all. Russia, in their estimation, was simply too big to be influenced by a set of sanctions from the outside. American tools for transformation were ineffective for a large, strategic country like Russia. When Russia's revolution was moving in the right direction, U.S. officials had tools to prod it along. When Russia's revolution began moving in a negative direction, American policymakers had very few ways to help it get back on track. Yet, even as Russia's democratic trajectory stalled, Clinton administration officials remained proponents of engagement. They were unwilling to return to a confrontational policy on Russia. Clinton was the most vocal advocate of staying the course. By 1999, however, the United States had few carrots left to offer Russia to influence change through incentives rather than punishments. The Clinton team's inability to change Russia's behavior in Chechnya stood as an unfortunate metaphor for how difficult it was to promote internal change from without.

There were potential policy alternatives, at least on Chechnya. Brzezinski, as outlined, offered some. Other decisions might have included cutting all assistance to the state (including Nunn-Lugar) and giving more financial support to human rights activists inside Russia. But cutting off Nunn-Lugar assistance would have been truly damaging to U.S. efforts to stem the proliferation of weapons of mass destruction. And if the United States had adopted all of the alternative measures together—changing aid policy, supporting development in Chechnya, excluding Russia from the G-8—would Russia have adopted a different policy toward Chechnya? Probably not. At the end of the day, Russian leaders believed that they were fighting to defend their national security and preserve their territorial integrity. All other interests, including positive relations with the United States, were vastly subordinate. The United States had the opposite problem: the Chechen war was considered a less important issue in comparison with other items on the agenda of U.S.-Russian relations. These asymmetries of interests, combined with a nearly empty American tool kit for influencing internal politics in Russia, produced policy inertia, with which no one—not the Clinton team, not the Russians, and not the outsiders watching and trying to influence the policy—was satisfied.

12

No Deals

By the end of the Clinton administration, the deal making on bilateral security issues was over. The early pattern of security cooperation was a distant memory. The battle over NATO enlargement had consumed the administration through the first half of 1997. The brief shining moment of U.S.-Russian partnership during the Kosovo campaign—former prime minister Viktor Chernomyrdin's participation in the diplomatic endgame—had been overshadowed by the Russian military backlash, which produced the surprise movement of Russian troops, unauthorized by NATO, to the Pristina airport in Kosovo.

At his bilateral meeting with Bill Clinton during the G-8 summit in Cologne in June 1999, Boris Yeltsin had suggested that an arms control accord—one in which Russian concessions on missile defense would be coupled with a U.S. willingness to cut offensive strategic nuclear warheads—would provide the finishing touch on their legacies in office. But Yeltsin stepped down from office on the last day of the year, and his successor, Vladimir Putin, evinced no interest in dealing with a U.S. administration in its final year in office. When the Russians also failed to cut off conventional arms sales to Iran at the end of 1999 as they had promised, it seemed that any notion of security partnership between the two countries belonged to an idealism of the past.

Amending the ABM Treaty

Discussions on modifying the Anti-Ballistic Missile (ABM) Treaty had begun in the summer of 1992. Twenty years earlier, when President Richard M.

Nixon and General Secretary Leonid Brezhnev signed the treaty, the world was a different place. The superpowers had agreed that stability was created by the possession on each side of nuclear forces that could destroy the other even after one side had struck first. In other words, deterrence would be maintained by mutual assured destruction (MAD). To guarantee MAD, the treaty banned efforts that might give a country the ability to render the other's deterrent worthless and thereby foreclosed an arms race in defensive weapons analogous to the race that continued unabated (despite arms control agreements) on the offensive side. As amended in 1974, the ABM Treaty restricted each side to deployment of an antiballistic system at one site only (the United States had taken down its site in North Dakota many years earlier, but the Russians still had a system deployed around Moscow).

Even with the accord in place, both the United States and the Soviet Union persisted in research on missile defense. Then in 1983, President Ronald Reagan made clear his view that MAD was mad and launched the United States on an effort to build a strategic missile defense system, an initiative dubbed by critics as the Star Wars program. But despite billions spent in the 1980s on various missile defense programs, by the early 1990s the United States had not made much progress in building a system that could defend against incoming strategic missiles.

In early 1991, with the cold war all but over, President George H. W. Bush argued not for Reagan's strategic defense initiative but rather for a more limited system that could defend the country in the event of an accidental launch of Soviet missiles, a program known as Global Protection against Limited Strikes, or GPALS. By the end of the year, as concern grew that the greatest threat was from rogue states, the Bush administration saw GPALS as a system that could involve U.S. and Soviet cooperation against potential strikes from countries like North Korea or Iran.[1]

In late January 1992, with the Soviet Union no longer in existence, Yeltsin proposed his own idea for a global protection system, and the two presidents discussed the possibilities at their Camp David summit. Missile defense proponents at the Pentagon considered the new environment highly promising for a renewed effort to build a shield. There was less enthusiasm for missile defense, however, at the Department of State and at the National Security Council (NSC), and the Bush administration decided to focus first on getting an agreement to reduce further the levels of offensive nuclear warheads. By summer, Yeltsin had agreed to a START II (strategic arms reduction talks) agreement, which was signed by the two presidents in the final weeks of the Bush administration.[2]

At their June 1992 summit announcing the proposed offensive cuts, the two presidents agreed to set up a working group chaired by U.S. State Department official Dennis Ross and Russian deputy foreign minister Georgy

Mamedov to develop the concept of the global protection system and to explore possible cooperation in areas like joint early warning, missile defense technologies, and amendments to existing treaties, namely, the ABM Treaty. Assistant Secretary of Defense Stephen Hadley had proposed that Ross lead the U.S. side both to avoid exacerbating the divisions that existed in the Pentagon about missile defense (the uniformed military was never enamored with diverting resources away from their cherished programs) and to show that Secretary of State James Baker, President Bush's close confidant, was personally committed to the endeavor. Ross came from a traditional arms control background and had been a firm believer in the ABM Treaty, but when the Persian Gulf War demonstrated how close President Saddam Hussein had come to developing nuclear weapons, he became more open to finding a way to cooperate with the Russians on missile defense.[3]

In engaging in these discussions, the Bush administration did not aim to build an elaborate missile defense system that might cause Russia to fear that its deterrent capability had been eviscerated. Rather, the aim was to gain Russian agreement on modifying the ABM Treaty to allow for limited deployments that might be able to thwart an attack coming from Pyongyang or Teheran, or perhaps, from Beijing. National Security Adviser Brent Scowcroft recalls, "I was never a fan of [Reagan's] SDI. GPALS made some sense to me. I thought it was worth exploring with the Russians and Europeans to see if we couldn't take part of SDI and see whether there was something productive that could come of it."[4] In 1991, Defense Department officials also began discussions with their Russian counterparts about a joint research and development program on early warning and missile defense, which later evolved into the Russian American Observation Satellite program (RAMOS). The project, however, was purely scientific and limited in scope.

Ross and his team traveled to Moscow in mid-July 1992. They established working groups on different topics with their counterparts from Mamedov's team. As Ross describes them, "One had to do with the whole idea of developing a common threat assessment. The point here was that there are real threats that face both of us, but the subtext was that they're a lot closer to you than to us. Another objective was to create cooperation in the technology, to look at areas where we might be able to work together. . . . So there was a look at should we have a group that could focus on early warning and even developing a common site where we could sit together to deal with launches. Also a group to begin to focus on regional threats and how you could respond with a theater capability. . . . The third was to deal with space-based advances. . . . We were . . . creating a framework for cooperation divided into different areas and the purpose was to see if we could come up with a joint approach."[5]

U.S. officials told the Russians that they planned to deploy the first land-based ABM site in the United States in 1997–98, and then by the end of the

1990s, hoped to deploy a "space-based sensor for tracking missiles and RVs [reentry vehicles] through the mid-course phase of their flight." But the U.S. briefers took pains to say that the envisioned space-based interceptors would be limited so as not to undermine the Russian nuclear deterrent. The administration was looking specifically for amendments to the ABM Treaty that would remove restrictions on testing and allow for more deployment sites while also limiting the number of interceptors deployed at each site. The Bush team was also proposing to keep the sites far enough apart geographically to make clear that the system was designed against limited strikes only.[6]

The leading advocates of a joint U.S.-Russian effort on missile defense, such as Hadley, believe they were making significant progress, and Hadley calls the Clinton administration decision not to continue the talks a "crime." He cited Mamedov's suggestion that any cooperation be automatically considered outside of the ABM Treaty, thus obviating the need to redo the 1972 deal as evidence of a real opening. But even Hadley acknowledged that Mamedov argued in 1992 that "we are fighting for our lives to have a viable, democratic Russia; if we get it, [cooperation on missile defense] will follow as a matter of course. But if we put this issue up front, you are imperiling our ability to have a democratic Russia."[7]

Ross has remained more skeptical of what was accomplished in the working group, although he asserted that it was much easier to work on the issue with Russia in 1992, when it was eager to be a partner, than late in the 1990s, when Russian officials believed that they needed to show more independence from their American counterparts. The talks had only just gotten under way (Baker describes them as "very rudimentary discussions"), when Ross was pulled over to the White House with Baker in August 1992 to try to prop up the flailing Bush re-election campaign. A second Ross-Mamedov meeting was held in late September in Washington, but by November, Bush had lost, and any movement would have to await the new team.[8]

Shifting the Focus

As Strobe Talbott writes, "The new president had no enthusiasm for strategic defense."[9] The lesson the Clinton team took away from the Persian Gulf War was not that the United States needed to continue to sink billions of dollars into an effort to try to defend the homeland, but rather that the Pentagon should focus on protecting U.S. troops in the field from missiles armed with weapons of mass destruction. Bush had scaled back Reagan's program, but it was still too much for the new Democratic administration. Instead, Les Aspin, the new secretary of defense, decided in the spring of 1993 to focus on building a deployable theater missile defense (TMD).[10]

The new team also believed in traditional arms control regimes. As Leon Fuerth, Gore's national security adviser, says, "Clearly, the administration's attitude toward the ABM Treaty was to preserve it intact; our primary interest was preserving the treaty rather than preparing to dismantle it, and [we] viewed preservation of the treaty as an essential element of an effort to proceed through the ratification of START II and on to a subsequent round of reductions."[11] Thus was born the administration's effort to sign what was called a "demarcation" agreement. The idea was to gain Russian agreement on a U.S. effort to build a theater missile defense whose characteristics still ensured the viability of a treaty designed to prevent the deployment of strategic missile defenses.

The new team had little regard for what was being done in the Ross-Mamedov channel. Talbott argues that the Russians were only involved as a "sop" to Bush and in order to be helpful to the president in his re-election effort, an outcome that Yeltsin's team thought at the time to be in their interests.[12] Clinton's senior director for defense policy at the NSC, Robert Bell, says of the discussions that had been held, "It was never clear to me that they got beyond the conceptual level and that the [Joint] Chiefs [of Staff] were ever going to agree to technology transfer, cooperative development, joint operations, anything that began to pay the bill here that would have gotten the Russians to sign onto GPALS." Ashton Carter, Clinton's assistant secretary of defense for international security policy, adds, "When we talk about cooperation in theater missile defense or national missile defense with the Russians, what are we talking about? We're not going to buy them anything. We don't buy anything for anybody. We don't buy our allies anything!"[13] The Clinton team continued to support the Russian-American research and development project, RAMOS, which one day in the distant future might produce technologies useful for missile defense but nothing else.

Republican critics, who were unhappy that the administration was turning its back on the strategic defense program launched by Ronald Reagan in 1983, were also dismissive of the demarcation exercise. Their view was that theater defenses were not covered by the ABM Treaty to begin with, so what was the rationale for negotiating them with the Russians? But the administration believed firmly that its arms control priorities were linked. If the Russians were confident that strategic defense was not being pursued (being clearly delimited by the new demarcation agreement), then the administration could achieve further reductions in offensive strategic nuclear weapons as well as gain Russian support for other arms control initiatives such as the Comprehensive Test Ban Treaty (which would end nuclear testing) and the extension of the Non-Proliferation Treaty (which was designed to prevent new nuclear states from emerging). Consequently, the first Clinton term was spent

trying to put the demarcation accord together and to urge the Russians to ratify START II (signed by Bush and Yeltsin in 1992), which would allow the
administration to go even further and sign its own START agreement with
Yeltsin.[14]

The administration was heavily constrained in its efforts on the offensive
side by the American Congress and the Russian Duma. The U.S. Senate ratified START II in January 1996, but Congress also passed a law prohibiting the
administration from unilaterally reducing the U.S. arsenal below START I levels until the Duma ratified START II. Secretary of Defense William Perry even
traveled to Moscow in October 1996 to testify before the Duma to urge ratification and argued that the cash-strapped Russians should find the deal in
their interest. Russia's legislators were unenthusiastic. Aleksei Arbatov, deputy
chairman of the Duma's Defense Committee, explained why the Duma would
not budge. "First, there is no money for it. Secondly, the treaty is considered
to be unfair on technical grounds. And thirdly, the general background—the
determination of NATO to expand to the East—is very unfavorable to the
treaty." (START II was forcing Russia to give up its multiple warhead
(MIRVed) weapons in favor of single-warhead missiles. Not only did the military not like this treaty provision, but it was going to cost money to eliminate
the old missiles and build a new generation.)[15] On many security issues in
which American and Russian interests clashed, the Americans could prevail
unilaterally because they had the power to do so. But the Americans could not
get their way on START II without the consent of Russia's parliamentarians.
Of course, many in Russia, including the president, believed that the treaty
served Russia's national security interests. He would not have signed it otherwise. Yet, as U.S.-Russian relations soured over the course of the 1990s, START
II ratification was one of the few tangible outcomes that the Russians could
deny the Americans. Ratification subsequently became linked to every other
issue in U.S.-Russian relations.[16]

Breakthrough at Helsinki

Clinton met with his foreign policy team on January 17, 1997, as he was about
to start his second term. He was upset that his first term went by without any
progress on strategic arms control. Chairman of the Joint Chiefs of Staff Gen.
John Shalikashvili said that he had promised the U.S. Senate during the ratification debate over START II that he would not recommend that the United
States go below 3,500 strategic nuclear warheads without a formal presidential decision that the United States was able to ensure its deterrent capability
with fewer warheads. But he also made clear that a review of the U.S. arsenal
could lead to an assessment that lower numbers would be acceptable. The
Clinton administration, therefore, approached the March 1997 Helsinki

summit with a proposal for a follow-on to START II that envisioned a range of 2,000 to 2,500 warheads.[17]

In Helsinki, Clinton and Yeltsin initially were not able to come to a meeting of the minds, so they sent their experts off to discuss the issues further. According to Talbott, "While Clinton and Yeltsin went back to their rooms to rest, the rest of us stayed in the Finnish presidential residence for one of the wildest negotiating sessions I ever experienced or even heard of. Constantly shifting match-ups of officials occupied every room on the first floor of the building, including the kitchen, and, on several occasions, the men's room. Tempers were frayed. Madeleine [Albright] and [Undersecretary of State] Lynn Davis held at least three meetings with Primakov and his team, and two of those ended with Madeleine throwing up her hands and walking out."[18]

But in the end, the presidents agreed at Helsinki that negotiations on START III would begin as soon as the Duma had ratified START II, and that the goal was a range of 2,000 to 2,500 warheads, one thousand below START II. The presidents also agreed to preserve the ABM Treaty while allowing for theater missile defense. Said Clinton, "Some people have criticized me in my Congress because I do support the ABM treaty. . . . I do support the ABM treaty. I think it's important. I believe in it." NSC senior director Robert Bell argued at the time that Article VI of the 1972 ABM Treaty had stated that restrictions were not to be "circumvented by missiles that were given different functions, but actually had ABM capabilities," and thus the demarcation agreement was needed in order to preserve the ABM Treaty.[19]

The demarcation accord was signed in September 1997. It banned space-based interceptors and allowed land-based interceptors only if their velocity did not exceed 3 kilometers a second, if the target missile's speed did not exceed 5 kilometers a second, and the target's range did not exceed 3,500 kilometers. In other words, any interceptor effective against a strategic missile would still violate the ABM Treaty.[20]

Helsinki seemed like a breakthrough. Arms control expert Jack Mendelsohn noted at the end of the year that in the six months after Helsinki, the two sides had agreed to extend the START II implementation date by four years to give the Russians some financial breathing room; agreed that START III would lower the arsenals by another 1,000 warheads (both provisions were designed to encourage the Duma finally to ratify START II); agreed on differentiating TMD from strategic defense, and kept the ban on space-based interceptors even for theater defense. Perhaps the Clinton administration would get a strategic arms control accord after all.[21]

Alas, it was not meant to be. The goalposts kept moving. The Russian parliament continued to link START II ratification to other contentious issues in U.S.-Russian relations. Secretary of Defense Perry reported that START II during his term in office "was a casualty of NATO expansion."[22] Then in late

1998, the Duma postponed a vote when the United States and Britain launched an air strike against Iraq. In April 1999, the war on Kosovo killed any chance of ratification. As Clinton NSC official Robert Bell recalls of the elusive START III, "We tried to find the right balance. At first we said, get out of here. Deliver what you've already signed up for [that is, START II ratification]. But then we agreed to negotiate a framework, which was Helsinki. And later we agreed to move off that and turn over cards on our START III position. . . . So late in the game [State Department arms control official John] Holum was empowered to go over and start turning over some cards on some specifics that elaborated on Helsinki. And then the Russians wanted to come back and change Helsinki. By the time the administration was over, we'd moved well off the initial position of not even talking about START III until they've ratified START II to showing them an outline and then even details of what an opening U.S. position would look like on START III."[23] Bell argues that Russian domestic politics simply made it impossible to get any traction— every time the Duma was upset about something, it vowed not to ratify START II.[24] The administration thought the Duma was ready to approve the treaty in March 1999, but the onset of the Kosovo campaign quashed yet again its optimism.[25]

American Domestic Politics

Yeltsin was not the only president constrained by domestic politics. If Yeltsin had difficulty gaining parliamentary approval for offensive reductions, Clinton faced Republicans who were pushing hard for U.S. development and deployment of strategic—not just theater—missile defense. Led by Congressman Newt Gingrich (R-Ga.) and his "Contract with America," the Republicans swept both Houses of Congress in November 1994. The contract was thin on foreign policy, but it did include a promise to rejuvenate U.S. missile defense efforts. At the time, though, it was difficult to make a strong case for funding given existing intelligence assessments. A National Intelligence Estimate in 1995 declared that aside from the five major nuclear powers—the United States, Russia, China, the United Kingdom, and France—no other country "will develop or otherwise acquire a ballistic missile in the next 15 years that could threaten the contiguous 48 states and Canada."[26]

In early 1998, however, a bipartisan expert commission under the leadership of former (and future) secretary of defense Donald Rumsfeld set out with a mandate from Congress to canvass broadly the intelligence community in order to gauge the missile threat facing the United States. In July, the commission reported to Congress and declared, "The threat to the United States posed by . . . emerging capabilities is broader, more mature, and evolving more rapidly than has been reported in estimates and reports by the intelligence community." The commission concluded that North Korea and Iran might be able to develop a missile capability to strike U.S. territory within five years, and most disturbingly, that this threat could arise with little or no warning.[27]

The commission report alone would have been unlikely to force the administration's hand; without any confirming events, Republicans and Democrats could simply have debated the different analyses endlessly. But that summer, Iran flew its Shahab 3 medium-range missile for the first time, and then in late August, North Korea tried to launch a satellite. Although the launch failed, the North Koreans had shown the world that they were developing a three-stage rocket, the Taepodong I. The North Korean efforts, coming with no warning, seemed to confirm the prescience of the Rumsfeld Commission. In March of the following year, the Senate overwhelmingly passed legislation that called on the United States to deploy a system that could defend the country as soon as it was "technologically possible" to do so.[28]

Now the Clinton administration had to navigate in more than one arena. Still believing in the importance of the ABM Treaty as a foundation for strategic stability between the United States and Russia, the administration would have to gain Russian agreement on modifying the treaty to allow for limited defense against the rogue threat. The Russians had no desire to give the United States much latitude, but if domestic politics were not an issue, an accord could likely be reached. The administration, however, would have to appease those in Congress who wanted to do more, thus making any negotiation that much more difficult. In addition, of course, a deal would have to be made that could get ratified by the Russian legislature.

The administration had begun to talk in earnest with the Russians in the late summer of 1998, and Deputy Foreign Minister Mamedov suggested using his 1992 conversations with Dennis Ross as a starting point. Ross, who had been serving since early 1993 as the Clinton administration's coordinator for the Middle East Peace Process, soon heard from his colleagues working on Russia. As he recalls, "Next thing I know, I got three calls asking what were the Mamedov-Ross understandings. So I dug out the papers and gave them to them. And then Strobe had me go through them. I said to him that times were different. In '92, you had a window. In '98, it's an entirely different reality. What I said to Strobe was that I'd focus on the cooperative side. I reminded him about the co-located site for early warning that could be more than that. I thought that was the best bet."[29] Talbott adds that, having dropped the discussions in 1993 only to return to them in 1998, "We then reinvented the wheel."[30]

Once the Republican-sponsored legislation passed in 1999, the administration tried to get back in control of the issue by laying out four criteria by which the president would decide whether to proceed with building a missile defense. National Security Adviser Sandy Berger says of the Missile Defense

Act that "the lawyers told us this was not a binding, mandatory statement."[31] Berger had sought to balance the varying demands by laying out criteria the president could use in deciding whether to deploy. As Talbott has written, "The two key variables were whether the technology of the system under development proved itself in tests still to be conducted, and whether proceeding with National Missile Defense [NMD] contributed to the overall security of the U.S., including in its impact on arms control."[32]

In Berger's words, the administration's message to Congress was, "We basically said yes but put a box around it." He adds, "There was a strategic objective. This was not solely political nor solely cynical. What I called the trifecta. If we could get a modification of the ABM Treaty that would enable us to build a limited system and at the same time do START III and send something to the Hill that would have a chance of ratification and put us on the offense, put the anti-arms control people on the defense; that would be a worthwhile accomplishment."[33]

It seemed at the G-8 summit held in Cologne in June 1999, just after the war in Kosovo, that the two sides were headed toward a compromise that would involve modifying the ABM Treaty while pushing for the reductions outlined in the prospective START III. Yeltsin appeared ready to move beyond Kosovo. It helped that he had put in place a new prime minister, Sergei Stepashin, who did not share Primakov's suspicions about the Americans.[34] At Cologne, Berger stated triumphantly, "The two countries are back in business," and he said the two sides planned to discuss START III in the fall as well as revisions to the ABM Treaty. Yeltsin told his fellow leaders, "The most important thing is to mend ties after a fight."[35]

In mid-August, Clinton met with his principal advisers to discuss their proposals on how to proceed with missile defense. Robert Bell laid out the group's view. An initial phase would lead to construction of twenty interceptors in Alaska by 2005, a number that was to grow to one hundred by 2007. A new radar in western Alaska, upgrades to other existing radars, and new satellites were also part of the plan. This would be followed by deployment at a second site, planned for North Dakota, by 2010, with additional radars and satellites for early warning and detection. The United States, said Bell, had six to nine months to negotiate revisions to the ABM Treaty with Russia. Although everyone knew that further offensive reductions were going to have to be offered to Russia to sweeten the deal, the administration was still divided over how low the United States could safely offer to go and still maintain a robust deterrent. Clinton was struck by the absurdity that deterrence was ensured at 2,500 warheads but not 1,500, which was still an extraordinarily destructive arsenal, and he recognized the administration had to come to agreement on this issue in order to get a deal on the ABM Treaty.[36]

In mid-October 1999, Talbott started putting more items on the table in his conversations with Mamedov. He offered Russia assistance in completing a missile-tracking radar station at Mishelevka near Irkutsk, access to early warning data, joint missile defense exercises, greater intelligence sharing on rogue threats, and the possibility of collaboration on satellite systems. He was also arguing in the administration that the United States would have to offer Russia a cap of offensive weapons in the range of 1,500-2,000, rather than the 2,000-2,500 that had been agreed on in March 1997 between the two presidents at Helsinki.[37] Two months later, Col. Gen. Vladimir Yakovlev, commander in chief of the Strategic Missile Troops, went so far as to say, "There is a chance Russia could reach agreement with the USA on modification of the ABM treaty."[38] Optimism about a deal was growing.[39]

Two weeks after Yakovlev's remarks, however, Boris Yeltsin stepped down from the presidency. Clinton quickly tried to establish rapport with Yeltsin's successor, Vladimir Putin, in order to keep momentum on an arms control deal. In January, U.S. officials gave the Russians a draft protocol to cover revisions they were seeking to the treaty; in particular the text would remove restrictions on limited systems banned by Article I of the treaty and would allow the United States to deploy its site in Alaska. Russian officials refused to discuss any text, but Sergei Ivanov, Berger's counterpart in Moscow, arrived in Washington and met with Clinton on February 18, 2000. He brought with him a letter from his president that responded to a Clinton letter that had been sent to Putin several weeks earlier. While in Washington, Ivanov appeared to give in to one of the main U.S. objectives when he implied that Russia could accept that the one system allowed the United States by the ABM Treaty could be deployed somewhere other than North Dakota (that is, in Alaska, the proposed site for the first interceptors that would be arrayed to defend against North Korea). At the same time, he insisted that this agreement did not mean Russian acceptance of a U.S. national missile defense. More good news followed for the American side in April 2000, when the Russian Duma at long last ratified START II. Ratification sailed through because the balance of power in the Duma had shifted dramatically in favor of pro-Kremlin parties after the 1999 parliamentary election.[40] Putin wanted the treaty ratified, so the Duma now loyal to him ratified the treaty, though with the conditions that the U.S. Senate had to approve the changes to the treaty encompassed by the 1997 demarcation agreement, which was unlikely given vigorous Republican opposition.[41]

Despite his positive actions on START II, Putin was not interested in making a deal with an American president in his eighth and final year in office. His advisers urged him to wait for the newly elected president. Clinton traveled to Moscow in June to meet Putin and try to close a deal one last time, but with no success. Talbott stated at a press briefing after the meetings, "President Putin made absolutely clear to President Clinton that Russia continues to oppose the changes to the ABM Treaty that the United States has proposed since last September—that is the changes necessary to permit deployment of phase one of our limited national missile defense plan."[42] As Talbott writes in his memoirs of the Clinton-Putin discussion of missile defense, "Putin had uttered nearly 200 words but they boiled down to one: 'no.'"[43]

In Berger's view, "The main reason [for not reaching agreement] was that Putin wanted to deal with the next administration, which was not an irrational conclusion on his part. I made the argument to them that they should deal with us. They had a 75 percent chance things would be worse and a 25 percent chance they'd be the same. If Bush were elected, it would probably be a more robust system with less commitment to preserve the ABM Treaty. If Gore were elected, he would not do less than we were going to do and given Gore's thinking and history it was conceivable he might do more. The new administration would have been presented with an agreement, both offensive and defensive, a system that in fact dealt with the threat of rogue states, not twenty years from now, but the next decade. [But] number one, they decided not to do a deal with us. Number two, we could not get the Pentagon to agree to go down one bracket [on strategic nuclear warheads down to 1,500, as the Russians had been seeking] which might have been decisive."[44] Presumably, Putin knew from Clinton's statements on the subject that he would not unilaterally abandon the ABM Treaty even if Russia stonewalled on revising it.[45]

Clinton had to make a formal decision about building a missile defense system in the summer of 2000. To have a system ready by 2005 and meet the potential threat from North Korea outlined by the Rumsfeld Commission would mean beginning construction in Alaska for land-based interceptors in spring 2001. To begin construction in 2001 without modification of the ABM Treaty meant that the administration would have to provide formal notification of its intent to withdraw from the treaty in the fall of 2000, since the treaty required a six-month notification of withdrawal. Clinton, who called NMD "a giant banana peel," was not eager to decide that construction should begin. When a test of the NMD system in July 2000 failed, and given that earlier tests had produced mixed results, Clinton had the rationale he needed based on his earlier criteria to decide against construction while he was in office. On September 1, the president announced that a decision on what type of system to build would be left to his successor. Candidate George W. Bush eagerly responded, "I welcome the opportunity to act where they have failed to lead by developing and deploying effective missiles to protect all fifty states and our friends and allies."[46]

Clinton clung to the view that the MAD world that guided U.S.-Soviet relations was still a guarantor of peace even as he sought to reduce the nuclear arsenals possessed by both sides. He made this clear to the Russian people on a Moscow radio program conducted during the June 2000 summit, when he summed up his efforts of the previous seven and one-half years. "I have worked hard to help support Russian democracy, Russian economic reform, and a large role for Russia in the world. I supported Russia coming into the G-8, to the Asian Pacific economic leaders group; having a special partnership with NATO; working on the ground, our troops, Russian troops side by side in the Balkans. And I intend to support Russia's effort to get a program going with the International Monetary Fund, with the World Bank. I believe the world needs a strong and prosperous and democratic Russia that respects the rule of law and the differences among its people. And that's what I've worked for. Believe me, I did not want to scrap the ABM Treaty or the theory of mutual deterrence or strategic stability. Both President Putin and I want to reduce the number of offensive missiles, but keep the theory that has kept us safe all these years."[47] The president did not seem to notice the irony that after all of his talk about integrating Russia, he was arguing at the end of his term that mutual deterrence was still necessary.

Iran

When Putin decided to take his chances with the next administration on questions of strategic nuclear weapons, it was clear that the Clinton Russia team's business was done. But for those officials working on broader security issues, a far greater problem remained: Russia's relationship with Iran. Although Vice President Gore and Prime Minister Chernomyrdin seemed to have struck a deal on limiting Russian assistance back in 1995, Russia did not end its relationship in the nuclear and missile technology spheres, and then at the end of 1999, reneged even on a deal struck for sales of conventional arms.

Similar to its strategy in the early 1990s, the Clinton administration tried early in its second term to find the right carrot to wean Moscow away from its relationship with Iran, and at the same time tried to keep Congress from enacting sanctions against Russia for its trade with Iran. But the pattern that had emerged over Russian-Iranian relations since 1994 continued: U.S. officials made sure the Yeltsin team understood what they knew about the Iranian program and about Russian assistance; Yeltsin and Prime Minister Chernomyrdin continued to deny that Russia was doing anything wrong. At their 1997 summit in Helsinki, for example, when Clinton complained about the transfers from Russia to Iran, Yeltsin replied, "I tell you, Bill, that's categorically not true. That technology could be coming from North Korea or China, but not from Russia. The Israeli Prime Minister Benjamin Netanyahu was recently in Moscow and said something along the same lines. But I've looked into it and there is absolutely nothing to it. We're acutely conscious of

Islamic fundamentalism, and it poses a threat to us as well. . . . I tell you that we'll never be in a position of sending missile technology to Iran."[48]

Talbott writes that soon after the Helsinki summit, "The Ministry of Atomic Energy and other elements in the Russian government seemed to be using NATO enlargement as a pretext for stepping up lethal Russian assistance to Iran." At their June 1997 summit during the G-8 meetings in Denver, Yeltsin tried weakly to explain Russia's behavior by saying to Clinton, "Because of our clumsy democracy, we sometimes allow enterprises to have direct contacts with Iran, and they make agreements on their own."[49] The two presidents then agreed to create a new channel for dealing with the problem; Clinton tapped senior American diplomat Frank Wisner to lead the effort while Yeltsin chose Russian space agency head Yuri Koptev. Back in 1993, Yeltsin had put Koptev in charge of finding a solution to the Indian rocket issue, and that summer, the U.S. offer of space cooperation was sufficient. Once again, the United States was offering Russia more foreign satellite launches, "potentially worth hundreds of millions of dollars," if Russia would stop selling missile technology to Iran.[50]

In the fall of 1997, Yeltsin continued to deny Russia's role in assisting Iran. After meeting with French president Chirac in Moscow, Yeltsin declared, "We are being accused of supplying Iran with nuclear or ballistic technologies. There is nothing further from the truth." In his own meetings in Moscow with Yeltsin, Gore said that "there is no doubt in my mind that Russia is serious about wanting to rein-in any unauthorized missile technology exports" and that the two countries "share the same concern about proliferation of weapons of mass destruction and proliferation of technologies that can assist in the delivery of weapons of mass destruction, such as ballistic missile technologies."[51]

Former NSC senior director for Russia, Ukraine, and Eurasia affairs William Courtney believes that U.S. leaders at the highest levels erred in emerging from meetings with Russian counterparts singing a happy tune about supposed Russian commitments to address Russia-Iran proliferation issues and making it look as though issues were being resolved when, in fact, proliferation activities by Russian entities remained "as bad as ever," and Russian leaders were continuing publicly to allege that U.S. concerns were unfounded and politically motivated. Certainly Prime Minister Chernomyrdin emerged from those September 1997 meetings singing a different tune. On Russian assistance for the nuclear reactor in Bushehr, Iran, Chernomyrdin stated, "We have our obligations and we will fulfill these obligations. Even if someone desires that we change these obligations, we won't do this."[52] And while administration officials were never confident about a cutoff to Bushehr, the problem was that even in areas of Russia's relationship with Iran that seemed to be solved (for example, conventional arms sales), commitments were not in the end fulfilled.

Israeli officials were lobbying Congress to impose sanctions, but the administration was opposed, fearing the effect on Clinton's relationship with Yeltsin. Clinton, however, did write Yeltsin a letter in October that Talbott has described as "one of the longest and toughest to any foreign leader during his presidency," asking Yeltsin to decree that all Russian exports to Iran's ballistic missile program be prohibited. Clinton wrote that special envoy Wisner and CIA chief George Tenet had been sharing intelligence with Russia "in a degree of detail that was without precedent." He also expressed the hope that when Wisner went to Moscow in early November, things would go better.[53] Clinton then followed the letter with a phone call, but Yeltsin again denied a problem existed. Yeltsin's reply came so fast that Talbott surmises it must have been written before the call. [54] The administration desperately hoped that it could find the right incentives to gain Russian cooperation. But it never did. As Deputy National Security Adviser James Steinberg recalls in frustration, "We were heavily into the carrots. Just as we thought with the North Koreans, we'll buy them out, we had no problem with this; we'll buy the Russians out. But they wouldn't be bought. I still don't fully understand why the carrots didn't work. They ignored the carrots."[55] Or as Vice President Gore told Prime Minister Primakov in fall 1998 in an equally frustrated tone, "You can have a piddling trickle of money from Iran or a bonanza with us, but you can't have both. Why do you keep trying to have it both ways?"[56] In fact, Russia could have it both ways because U.S. corporations, which were profiting from joint ventures with the Russians, worked hard to constrain the Clinton administration's ability to tie U.S. carrots such as satellite launch quotas to Russia's behavior on Iran.[57]

In January 1998, Chernomyrdin signed yet another export control measure (a so-called catch-all decree) to help fill in the loopholes in Russian nonproliferation law. But Russian entities continued to deal with Iran; this included the Baltic State Technical University in St. Petersburg, which was training Iranian missile scientists. U.S. envoy Wisner provided the list of American concerns, and the Russians responded as they had before. Said Yuri Koptev in the spring of 1998, "The 13 cases which our American colleagues have so nicely informed us of have been considered, and we have provided detailed explanations. In the cases where we saw some doubtful aspects, these contacts were severed." Meanwhile, any momentum with Prime Minister Chernomydin was halted in March 1998, when he was fired and replaced by Sergei Kiriyenko.[58]

But contacts were not severed. In March, Minister of Atomic Energy Yevgeny Adamov stepped up Russian support for the Iranian nuclear program, in violation of the 1995 deal reached between Gore and Chernomyrdin. At the same time, the Azeri government halted a Russian shipment to Iran that included twenty-two tons of a special alloy of steel that could be used for rocket fuel tanks, a shipment in direct violation of the catch-all decree

Chernomyrdin had issued in January. To make matters worse, the head of the Russian internal security service, Nikolai Kovalyov, summoned U.S. Ambassador to Moscow James Collins to tell him that the steel had originated in Spain or Sweden.[59]

Now the pressure ratcheted up in Congress, and in late May, both houses overwhelmingly passed legislation to sanction Russia for the violations. Clinton vetoed the legislation, but opponents had the votes to override his veto. By now, the main channel for trying to resolve the problem was at a higher level than the Wisner-Koptev one; National Security Adviser Sandy Berger was working with his counterpart, Andrei Kokoshin, to try to get Russia to take enough action to forestall a congressional override. This channel finally seemed to do the trick. Berger came up with what Talbott describes as a "carefully choreographed compromise." In mid-July, the Russian government released a list of nine entities that were assisting the Iranian missile program, and the United States announced that it was imposing "trade restrictions" [that is, sanctions] on seven of them. In return, the Senate did not hold a vote to override, and thus the administration had succeeded in avoiding more drastic sanctions against the Yeltsin government. In particular, Russian participation in the International Space Station could continue.[60]

Al Gore was embarrassed during the 2000 presidential campaign, when it was revealed that the Russians had reneged on the deal signed five years earlier between him and Prime Minister Chernomyrdin in which Russia had agreed to cut off conventional weapons sales to Iran by December 31, 1999. Questions arose over a letter Chernomyrdin wrote Gore in late 1995 in which he again defended Russia's relationship with Iran but also added, "The information that we are passing on to you is not to be conveyed to third parties, including the U.S. Congress."[61]

But what about the role of Congress in overseeing the provisions of the original Gore-McCain sanctions legislation to stem proliferation? Leon Fuerth, Gore's national security adviser, claimed that the legislation did not apply but had been used as leverage privately. "We deliberately used the Gore-McCain law as a fulcrum to negotiate an understanding with Russia to put constraints on their exports to Iran." And that had forced the Russians to agree to the December 1999 deadline. But Russia had not abided by the deal. And in a blistering letter to Foreign Minister Igor Ivanov in January 2000 complaining about Russia's abrogation of the deal, Secretary of State Madeleine Albright said that "without the aide memoire [agreed to by Gore and Chernomyrdin in June 1995], Russia's conventional arms sales to Iran would have been subject to sanctions based on various provisions of our laws."[62] Gore's legislative cosponsor in the Senate, Arizona Republican John McCain, declared that the administration had "violated both the intent and the letter of the law."[63]

The Security Team Disillusioned

Bill Clinton was disappointed that he never achieved a major arms control deal with the Russians. Although he traveled to Russia more times than any president in history (a record unlikely to be broken by future presidents) he was the first president since the era of arms control deals began not to get one. On this score, even his Republican predecessors had done better. Richard Nixon had signed SALT I and the ABM Treaty. Ronald Reagan and Mikhail Gorbachev had reached agreement to eliminate intermediate-range nuclear forces. Bush had signed two START accords.

Clinton had failed to move the START process forward or gain agreement on modification of the ABM Treaty for several reasons. First, Yeltsin remained at loggerheads with the communist-dominated Duma for most of the decade. Only after the communists lost control of the parliament in 1999 was START II finally ratified. Second, many in Russia were piqued about NATO enlargement and the Kosovo campaign and sought retribution somewhere (even if lower arsenals for financially strapped Russia were arguably more in Russia's interest since the United States could afford whatever levels it wanted). Third, by the time Putin ascended to the presidency, it was Bill Clinton's final year in office, and the new Russian president was not persuaded that a deal with a lame duck president would stick. Finally, despite Clinton's desire to have a foreign policy prize, a new treaty did not seem like a real imperative throughout most of the 1990s, since neither side perceived the other as a real threat and other issues—such as the fate of Russian democracy and capitalism—seemed more pressing.

More disturbing for those inside and outside the government was Russia's relationship with Iran. The Russians sold conventional arms. They helped with the construction of the Bushehr reactor. They trained Iranian missile engineers. Nothing the Clinton administration did, even striking a private deal, succeeded. Whether it was the Russian financial stake in Iran, the failure of the Russian government to control public and private actors in their own system, a desire to poke a finger in Uncle Sam's eye, Iranian promises about minimizing support for the Chechens, or some combination of these is difficult to know. Yeltsin had told German chancellor Helmut Kohl back in January 1997 that while he had "no illusions" about the Iranian government, he was wary of giving them any reason to cause trouble in the Caucasus, Central Asia, or most particularly, Chechnya. Talbott believed that for Yevgeny Primakov, the concern was not losing a lucrative market, but rather the fear that if Iran and the United States developed better relations, Russia would lose out in its perceived sphere of influence; if Russia cooperated with Iran, it could perhaps forestall a future geostrategic loss.[64] With respect to Iran, rather than cooperating as partners with shared values, Russian and American officials seemed to be playing a brand of balance of power politics that would have looked very familiar to Nixon and Brezhnev.

When the Russians failed to stop their activity in Iran as promised, they left the Clinton administration security team as disillusioned with them as the economic team had been after the financial meltdown in August 1998 and the democratization crowd had become after the Russian invasion of Chechnya in the fall of 1999. Over and over the Clinton team was promised that the problem had been fixed or that deadlines had been set. And when it was not fixed, and the deadlines were not met, it led many to believe that the Russian government could not control bad actors, or that the Russian government itself was lying, just as the economic team felt in August 1998.[65] At the same time that Russia's economic and political transformation seemed to be faltering, Russian enthusiasm for deal making with the Americans also appeared to wane.

The U.S.-Russian relationship at the end of the Clinton presidency was a far cry from the heady days of 1993. Sestanovich has written of the Iranian issue in the late 1990s that "the assumption that a presidential handshake could stop Russian assistance to Iran proved mistaken and out of date. By the late 1990s, Boris Yeltsin lacked the interest, energy, aptitude, and maybe even the power to meet this complex political and institutional challenge."[66] Certainly the new Russian president, Vladimir Putin, was a much cooler customer around Clinton than Boris Yeltsin had been, and the old bear hug was nowhere to be seen. In 2001, with a new U.S. administration promising a return to realpolitik and stating its intention to avoid what it viewed as undue interference in Russian domestic affairs, tremendous uncertainty filled the air. Even though much would seem to change after September 11, 2001, there never was a U.S.-Russian deal to modify the ABM Treaty. More ominously, the Russians did not budge on their continued assistance to Iran. That issue would frustrate the new Bush administration as much as it had the Clinton team.

13

George W. Bush and Russia

During the 2000 presidential campaign, the group of foreign policy officials that advised Governor George W. Bush declared the Clinton-Gore
approach to Russia a total failure. Their central criticism was not that Clinton
had done too little to promote markets and democracy in Russia and the subsequent integration of Russia into the Western community of democratic
states. Rather, they argued that Clinton and his team had devoted too much
time and too many resources to trying to change Russia internally. In their
view, promoting regime change in a strategic country like Russia was not a
U.S. national security priority. As for integration of Russia into Western international institutions, Bush's foreign policy advisers expressed indifference
during the campaign and instead emphasized the need to strengthen
America's core alliances in Europe and Asia, rather than expanding the core to
peripheral places like Russia.

Bush's team did not advocate neglect of Russia. Headed by Stanford professor Condoleezza Rice, Bush's foreign policy campaign team believed that
the best way to repair U.S.-Russian relations was to treat Russia as realists like
Henry Kissinger, Richard M. Nixon, and George W. Bush's father would—as a
piece on the global chessboard. Russia's power mattered most. How Russia
was governed was a secondary concern. Bush campaign advisers generally
advocated greater attention to the "national interest," which in their view
meant dealing with big countries like Russia and China, and spending less
time on "humanitarian interests" in small places like Haiti, Somalia, Bosnia,
and Kosovo.[1] Bush campaign adviser Robert Blackwill explained that Bush
planned to focus on Russia and China and "not Haiti, not Somalia" because

Russia and China were countries that could threaten American national security interests.[2] Similarly, explaining the necessity of a return to realist thinking, Rice wrote in a *Foreign Affairs* essay during the campaign, "The reality is that a few big powers can radically affect international peace, stability, and prosperity."[3] Rice recognized the importance of promoting American values in foreign affairs, which she described as "universal." But "Their triumph is most assuredly easier when the international balance of power favors those who believe in them. But sometimes that favorable balance of power takes time to achieve, both internationally and within a country, and in the meantime, it is simply not possible to ignore and isolate other powerful states."[4]

Greater attention to great powers with illiberal regimes did not mean a softer line. On the contrary, in reference to both Russia and China, Bush and his campaign officials promised to depart from the Clinton strategy of accommodation and to adhere instead to "tough realism."[5] The Bush team promised to end the romanticism that Clinton's Russia team—and Strobe Talbott in particular—held about Russia. For Bush's advisers, Russia was still a great power but one in decline and thus erratic and dangerous. As Rice wrote, "Moscow is determined to assert itself in the world and often does so in ways that are at once haphazard and threatening to American interests."[6] The American response, according to realists like Rice, might be called neocontainment, that is, to use American power to check Russia's haphazard and threatening behavior.

To deal with Russia, Bush advisers promised to end the "happy talk" and discontinue the overpersonalized approach that Clinton practiced with Yeltsin. As Rice wrote bluntly and stated emphatically throughout the campaign, "The problem for U.S. policy is that the Clinton administration's embrace of Yeltsin and those who were thought to be reformers around him *has failed.*"[7] Clinton's team, in Rice's view, mistakenly let its Russia policy become "synonymous with the agenda of the President of Russia."[8] Bush advisers also threatened sanctions if Russia continued to supply Iran with nuclear and missile technologies and pledged that they would not worry about offending Russian interests in dealing with European security matters or American strategic interests more generally. Rice warned that development of relations between her new government and the Putin team "would depend heavily on [Russia's] record—problematic to date—on the proliferation of ballistic missile and other technologies related to weapons of mass destruction."[9] Candidate Bush also made clear that he would not seek Russian approval for policies he planned to enact unilaterally that he deemed in the American national interest. Most important, he stated categorically that he planned to withdraw from the Anti-Ballistic Missile Treaty no matter what the Russian position on the issue.[10] He also pledged unilaterally to lower the U.S. nuclear arsenal to levels dictated by American interests alone, which meant there was no need to consult the Russians, much less get dragged into lengthy negotiations on a new treaty.

Because the Bush foreign policy advisers were realists, they tended to downplay the importance of regime type and internal politics generally and instead focused on the external behavior of states, which they believed were influenced first and foremost by the balance of power in the international system. According to Rice, "The United States needs to recognize that Russia is a great power, and that we will always have interests that conflict as well as coincide." During the campaign, Rice recommended that the United States could not get bogged down in Russian internal developments but instead "must concentrate on the important security agenda with Russia."[11] In one of the presidential debates, Bush stated even more bluntly, "The only people that are going to reform Russia are Russia [sic]. They're going to have to make the decision themselves."[12]

This said, two internal problems in Russia—corruption and Chechnya—were simply too juicy politically to ignore during the campaign. Candidate Bush and his advisers repeatedly referred to these issues of Russian domestic politics and blamed the Clinton administration for not doing enough in response to these transgressions. In his one major foreign policy speech of the campaign, Bush described Russia as a power "in transition" whose final regime type was still unknown. Echoing Wilsonian themes (after all, he was speaking at the Ronald Reagan Presidential Library), Bush argued that "dealing with Russia on essential issues will be far easier if we are dealing with a democratic and free Russia."[13] Furthermore, assistance for reform should depend on Russian human rights policies. Bush stated emphatically that

> we cannot excuse Russian brutality. When the Russian government attacks civilians—killing women and children, leaving orphans and refugees—it can no longer expect aid from international lending institutions. The Russian government will discover that it cannot build a stable and unified nation on the ruins of human rights. That it cannot learn the lessons of democracy from the textbook of tyranny. We want to cooperate with Russia on its concern with terrorism, but that is impossible unless Moscow operates with civilized restraint.[14]

Four months later, as the following exchange between candidate Bush and PBS news anchor Jim Lehrer demonstrated, Bush promised to do more than the Clinton-Gore team regarding Chechnya.

> Jim Lehrer: On Chechnya and Russia, the U.S. and the rest of the western world had been raising Cain with Russia from the beginning, saying "You are killing innocent civilians." The Russians have said essentially, "We're fighting terrorism, and, by the way, mind your own busi-

ness." What else—what else, if anything, could be done by the United States?

Gov. George W. Bush: Well, we could cut off IMF aid and export/import loans to Russia until they heard the message loud and clear, and we should do that. . . . Putin, who is now the temporary president . . . kind of rode the great wave of popularity as the Russian military looked like they were gaining strength in kind of handling the Chechnya situation in a way that's not acceptable to peaceful nations. . . .

Jim Lehrer: But on Chechnya, specifically, you think . . . —we should hold up International Monetary Fund aid. Anything else we should do?

Gov. George W. Bush: Export/import loans.

Jim Lehrer: And just cut them off?

Gov. George W. Bush: Yes, sir, I think we should.

Jim Lehrer: Until they do what?

Gov. George W. Bush: Until they understand they need to resolve the dispute peacefully and not be bombing women and children and causing huge numbers of refugees to flee Chechnya.

Jim Lehrer: And do you think that would work?

Gov. George W. Bush: Well, it certainly worked better than what the Clinton administration has tried.

Jim Lehrer: You mean, just using words . . . ?

Gov. George W. Bush: Yes.[15]

Candidate Bush, his campaign, and his campaign supporters also tried to make corruption in Russia and Clinton's and Gore's inattention to Russian corruption a campaign issue in the 2000 election. As discussed earlier, Gore and Prime Minister Viktor Chernomyrdin had developed a close personal relationship during their years of service as cochairs of the U.S.-Russian Joint Commission on Economic and Technological Cooperation, often referred to as the Gore-Chernomyrdin Commission. According to Republican critics of Gore, the vice president had allowed his personal relationship with Chernomyrdin to blind him to the allegedly corrupt practices of the Russian prime minister.[16] In his Reagan Library speech, Bush declared, "Our assistance, investments and loans should go directly to the Russian people, not to enrich the bank accounts of corrupt officials."[17] Then in his second debate with the vice president, Bush reminded the American voters of Gore's intimate relationship with Chernomyrdin and the links to corruption: "We went to Russia, we said here is some IMF money, and it ended up in Viktor Chernomyrdin's pocket, and others, and yet we played like there was reform."[18]

Candidate Bush never embraced a causal connection between Russian crime and American foreign policy, but he and his campaign staff did endorse the general characterization of Russia as a lost cause, burdened by imperial proclivities from its past and criminal undertows in its new present. Debate over Russia between Democratic and Republican foreign policy elites, however, was an intramural contest, since the Clinton administration's handling of Russia, like other foreign policy campaign issues, never became a central concern for the American voter, nor was it an issue over which Bush had likely spent much time deliberating. Candidate Bush had no reason to push his anti-Clinton message on Russia because public opinion polls showed that most Americans supported a policy of continued engagement with Russia, despite the allegations of corruption and reform failure.[19] Once elected president, however, Bush eventually had to commit to a course of action—tough realism or renewed engagement. Ironically, Bush eventually gravitated to Clinton's strategy of engagement, even if the objectives sought in pursuing this same strategy were very different.

President Bush: From Confrontation to Reengagement

Early in the administration, President Bush and his new foreign policy team seemed to signal their intent to maintain a tough line on Russia and particularly on Chechnya. After being named national security adviser but before taking office, Condoleezza Rice wrote an opinion piece for the *Chicago Tribune* that restated many of the themes of her *Foreign Affairs* article published a year earlier. In this essay, Rice emphasized again that "the United States needs to recognize that Russia is a great power," and therefore "U.S. policy must concentrate on the important security agenda with Russia."[20] At the same time, she reiterated many of Russia's domestic ills, including weak democratic institutions, half-hearted economic reforms, and corruption. She devoted special attention to the ill effects of the Chechen war and Putin's role in it:

> As prime minister, Vladimir Putin used the Chechnya war to stir nationalism at home while fueling his political fortunes. The Russian military has been uncharacteristically blunt and vocal in asserting its duty to defend the integrity of the Russian Federation—an unwelcome development in civil-military relations. The long-term effect of the war on Russia's political culture should not be underestimated. This war has affected the relations between Russia and its neighbors in the Caucasus, as the Kremlin has been hurling charges of harboring and abetting Chechen terrorists against states as diverse as Saudi Arabia, Georgia, and Azerbaijan. The war is a reminder of the vulnerability of the small, new states around Russia and of America's interest in their independence.[21]

Rice hoped that this blunt statement about Russia's problems and their impact on U.S. interests would stand in contrast to the "sugar-coated" rhetoric of the Clinton years, which, in her opinion, did great damage to U.S.

national security: "There is no longer a consensus in America or Europe on what to do next with Russia. Frustrated expectations and 'Russia fatigue' are direct consequences of the 'happy talk' in which the Clinton administration engaged."[22]

In the spring of 2001, Bush and his foreign policy team did seem determined to end the "happy talk." In March 2001, his administration ordered the expulsion of nearly fifty Russian diplomats from the United States, who were accused of being spies.[23] Bush personally did not make any statements about Chechnya in his first months in power, but his State Department did send a loud signal of support for the Chechen cause by arranging a meeting between the Chechen foreign minister in exile, Ilyas Akhmadov, and the State Department's senior ranking official responsible for Russian affairs, John Beyrle. (Chechen president Maskhadov had met similarly with Beyrle's predecessor Stephen Sestanovich in November 1997, but at that time, Russia and Chechnya were negotiating, so the meeting did not signal an anti-Russian policy.)[24] In this early period, Bush officials also seemed poised to maintain a tough line on Russia's relations with rogue states. Secretary of Defense Donald Rumsfeld called Russia "an active proliferator" while Deputy Secretary of Defense Paul Wolfowitz described the Russians as "willing to sell anything to anyone for money."[25] As Wolfowitz explained, "My view is that they have to be confronted with a choice. You can't have your cake and eat it too. You can't do billions worth of business and aid and all that with the United States and its allies, and then turn around and do small quantities of obnoxious stuff that threatens our people and our pilots and our sailors."[26] (Recall that the Clinton administration policy in 1993–94 was to offer the billions' worth of business and aid to try to steer Russia away from the small quantities of "obnoxious stuff".)

Leaks from the White House suggested that assistance to Russia would be cut, including $100 million from the Nunn-Lugar program, which some Bush officials viewed as subsidies for Russia's military-industrial complex.[27] A new, more confrontational approach to relations with Russia seemed to be emerging. As *New York Times* reporter Jane Perlez concluded in her review of Russia policy at the time, "The Bush administration has not articulated a broad policy toward Russia, but in thoughts and deeds it has taken a sharp departure from the engagement policies of its predecessor, moving toward isolating Russia and its president, Vladimir V. Putin."[28]

In their first months in office, Bush administration officials also did not give Russia a high priority. Despite the statements about the need to treat Russia as a great power during the campaign, what was striking as President Bush and his team entered office was how little interest they showed in the bilateral relationship with Russia (much to the chagrin of Russian Foreign Ministry officials, who were used to being treated by any new team as central to American foreign policy). Engaging and strengthening relations with America's Allies, the new administration argued, was a greater and more immediate concern. Whereas Clinton made a point of meeting Yeltsin first in Vancouver and only went to Europe a year into his presidency, Bush made a point of meeting first with the leaders of America's closest friends and Allies, for example, Mexico, Canada, Japan, and Germany. Only after the insistence of American Allies in Europe did Bush agree to schedule a meeting with Putin as a final stop on his first trip to Europe in the summer of 2001.

Symbolically, the Bush administration also downgraded Russia's place in the foreign policy bureaucracy, by dismantling the Office on the New Independent States (S/NIS) in the State Department that Clinton had created and that Talbott had first headed in 1993. In the new organizational chart at the State Department, Russia was one of fifty-four countries in the new Bureau of Europe and Eurasia Affairs.[29] Rice initiated a parallel reorganization at the National Security Council, folding the directorate on Russia, Ukraine, and Eurasia Affairs into a larger one on Europe and Eurasia Affairs.

This "tough realism" toward Russia did not last long. Like his father in 1989, Bush ordered a major review of U.S. policy toward Russia. Even before the review was completed, however, Bush began to take a different approach than that signaled by his administration's early moves on Russia. Instead of confrontation and neglect, Bush decided to embrace a policy of personal engagement with the president of Russia, Vladimir Putin. Rather than a departure from the Clinton-Yeltsin years, this decision signaled the continuation of the pattern of the relationship established during the previous Bush and Clinton administrations.

As the June 2001 meeting with Putin in Slovenia approached, Bush became personally involved in his Russia policy for the first time.[30] That spring, he made a strategic decision that he was not going to confront Putin with a laundry list of American concerns in their first meeting. Instead, he wanted to establish rapport with the Russian leader as a necessary first step in developing a partnership with his Russian counterpart. It was a businessman's approach to foreign policy.

In making this decision about his approach to the Slovenia summit, Bush was pursuing a strategy similar to Clinton's but for different ends. Clinton had embraced Yeltsin because he believed Yeltsin to be the best hope for Russian reform. In helping his Russian friend, Clinton convinced himself that he was also aiding Russia's internal transformation, which as discussed earlier, he deemed a national security interest. Bush's objective in reaching out to Putin had little to do with Russian regime change. He had a different set of foreign policy goals. The new American president wanted to avoid any long discussion or arguments about Russian internal politics and instead focus on the security issues that animated him the most. In particular, Bush wanted to establish a relationship with Putin to secure Russia's acceptance of American withdrawal from the ABM Treaty so that he could fulfill his campaign pledge to build a defense against ballistic missiles that might be launched by the likes of North Korea or Iraq (or perhaps even China). Early in Bush's presidency, European critics of the administration as well as congressional Democrats warned that U.S. withdrawal from the treaty would produce a cataclysmic break in U.S.-Russian relations. Senator Carl Levin (D-Mich.), who became chairman of the Senate Armed Services Committee in June 2001 when control shifted to the Democrats, even threatened to "try in some way to stop the expenditures of funds for a system that would abrogate the ABM Treaty."[31] Bush and his foreign policy team were determined to abrogate the treaty without derailing U.S.-Russian relations.

Power balancers in the administration who were thinking about China also recommended that Bush seek a cooperative relationship with Putin. In the spring of 2001, the People's Republic of China (PRC) appeared to many in the administration to pose the major threat to U.S. national security in the future, and Russia could be a potential partner in the effort to contain the PRC. The Bush team had cast China as a "strategic competitor" whose attempts to alter Asia's balance of power in its own favor had to be checked.[32] To pursue this strategy of balancing Chinese power required less focus on Russian internal flaws and more focus on the security agenda between the two countries. It was the same strategy that Nixon had pursued in the early 1970s on this strategic triangle, only now Russia and China had traded places. With the presidential campaign over, Bush was returning to the realist proclivities of his closest foreign policy advisers, proclivities also shared by his father. But he was much more radical, saying in a speech at the National Defense University on May 1, 2001, that the ABM Treaty was not the "cornerstone of stability" that it had been called previously but rather epitomized a relationship "based on distrust and mutual vulnerability."[33] Bush could threaten to withdraw unilaterally from the ABM Treaty—one of his top foreign policy objectives before September 11, 2001—because Russia was too weak to do anything about it.

Still, it would be less damaging to U.S.-Russian relations and U.S.-European relations to withdraw from the ABM Treaty with Russian acquiescence. At their first meeting in Slovenia in June 2001, therefore, Bush went out of his way to praise Putin. Instead of depersonalizing relations with Russia, Bush deliberately tried to forge a personal bond with his Russian counterpart during their very first encounter. At this meeting, Bush reported, "I looked the man in the eye. I found him to be very straightforward and trustworthy. . . . I was able to get a sense of his soul." Bush liked what he saw and sensed.[34]

Whatever Putin was doing in Russia was not of major import. According to claims made by White House staffers, Bush and Putin did discuss Chechnya privately, but there was almost no mention of the issue publicly. Nor did Bush mention publicly press freedoms, which Putin had done so much to limit in his first year in office. Instead of a public rebuke on the press issues, the Bush administration decided to work on this matter privately. While in Moscow the following month, Rice took time away from her main agenda—seeking to put an end to the ABM Treaty—to meet with representatives of the Russian press. The roundtable was not a press conference but a frank discussion of the future of the independent media in Russia. According to participants in this meeting, Rice expressed understanding of the issues and sympathy with the "opposition" representatives at the meeting.[35] No concrete policy changes, however, resulted from this meeting or any other meeting of U.S. officials with representatives from the opposition media. Eventually, the Bush administration did establish a media initiative, an exchange between American and Russian press executives whose noble aim was to foster the political independence of the Russian press by securing the financial independence of these independent media outlets. No concrete projects of assistance—rhetorical or otherwise—have resulted yet from this program.

September 11, 2001

American and Russian strategic interests became more aligned with each other after September 11. The bond between Bush and Putin also seemed to deepen.[36] Russian opinion polls indicated that the Russian people also grew fonder of the United States and the American people after September 11.[37] From the ashes of the September 11 tragedy, a new era in U.S.-Russian relations seemed to be blossoming.

Putin moved quickly on his gut feeling. He immediately called Bush after the tragic events occurred to communicate his full support for the United States and the American people. Putin expressed sympathy as a leader of a country that also had suffered from acts of terrorism against civilians in the capital. Putin then followed his words of support with policies of assistance. On September 24, 2001, Putin announced a five-point plan to support the American war against terrorism. He pledged that his Russian government would share intelligence with its American counterparts, open Russian airspace for flights providing humanitarian assistance, cooperate with Russia's central Asian allies to provide similar kinds of airspace access to American flights, participate in international search and rescue efforts, and increase direct assistance—humanitarian as well as military assistance—to the Northern Alliance anti-Taliban force in Afghanistan.

Putin's decision not to try to block an American military presence on the territory of the former Soviet Republics in central Asia represented a historic change in Russian foreign policy. Before September 11, President Putin had vacillated between pro-Western and anti-Western foreign policy stances.

Putin pushed through the Russian parliament ratification of the Comprehensive Test Ban Treaty and START II, expressed a clear desire for Russia to become a fully integrated member of the G-8, the World Trade Organization (WTO), and, more generally, Europe, and stressed in his foreign policy doctrine that Russia would continue to pursue market reforms and foreign investment. At the same time, Putin continued to reach out to North Korea, Cuba, and China and signed a major arms deal with Iran.[38]

In many ways, Putin's dual impulses of seeking at times to integrate into the West while at other times seeking to balance against the West reflect Russia's long-standing love-hate relationship with the West. In the wake of September 11, however, Putin seemed to lean much farther toward the West and the United States. His foreign minister, Igor Ivanov, compared the new situation to the alliance between the United States and the Soviet Union during World War II. Only now, said Ivanov, "We [Russia and the United States] are joined by common democratic values, and it is even more obvious that a struggle against a world threat requires the cooperation of our countries and the entire world community."[39]

Since September 11, Bush has articulated a new strategic doctrine to guide foreign policy. The new defining issue before American foreign policymakers as well as the American public became the "war on terrorism," which came to include a war in Iraq. Bush has stated that this war has divided the world into two groups—those supporting the United States and those not. In this black and white world, Bush repeatedly described Russia as a supporter of the American war on terrorism. In Bush's view, at least until the American war against Iraq that began in March 2003, Russia had become a partner, a friend, and even an ally of the United States in the global struggle against terrorism.[40] U.S. ambassador to Russia Alexander Vershbow even went so far as to declare in February 2002, "The United States and Russia are closer today—politically, economically, and militarily—than at any time in our history."[41]

Selective Wilsonianism

Like all presidents, George W. Bush echoed elements of Wilsonian liberalism and Nixonian realism in articulating his approach to foreign policy during his first months in office. For instance, upon introducing his future secretary of state, Colin Powell, Bush would have made Wilson or Reagan proud when he stated, "Our stand for human freedom is not an empty formality of diplomacy but a founding and guiding principle of this great land. By promoting democracy we lay the foundation for a better and more stable world."[42] These "liberal" statements, however, did not set the tone of Bush's foreign policy before September 11. Instead the president and his foreign policy team deliberately gravitated toward realist themes, in part as a way to distinguish their strategy from Clinton's Wilsonian proclivities. Candidate George W. Bush derided

Clinton and his team for their quixotic missions of exporting democracy and nation building in places like Somalia, Haiti, and Kosovo. After he took office, Bush continued to oppose nation building as a distraction from the more important issues in international politics of managing relations with the great powers. Consistent with a realist approach to international relations, Bush also showed little interest in nurturing multilateral institutions or international treaties. His most ambitious foreign policy initiative during his first months in office was national missile defense, a policy prescription that did not seek to change hostile states internally but to protect the United States from them.

Then came September 11, 2001. The horrific terrorist attacks on that day were seminal, shocking events that compelled every American—including the president of the United States—to rethink basic assumptions about the world we live in. Bush apparently began, almost overnight, to believe that the United States had to go on the offensive and remake the world into a safer place, a mission that sounded more like Wilson's and less like his father's. Bush became a regime transformer.[43] Instead of seeking to preserve the balance of power in the international system, Bush decided to remake the balance of power. To do so required regime change—democratic regime change—in those countries most threatening to American national security interests.

Bush's language about international affairs changed. In June 2002, Bush reminded graduating officers from West Point that "America stands for more than the absence of war. We have a great opportunity to extend a just peace, by replacing poverty, repression and resentment around the world with hope for a better day." In that important speech, Bush also argued that the "twentieth century ended with a single surviving model of human progress, based on non-negotiable demands of human dignity, the rule of law, limits on the power of the state, respect for women and private property and free speech and equal justice and religious tolerance."[44] Bush's National Security Strategy, published in September 2002, made the promotion of liberty around the world an explicit U.S. national security interest. According to his own interpretation, Bush then backed up this rhetoric with concrete actions, including most dramatically the American military campaigns against the Taliban regime in Afghanistan in the fall of 2001 and the dictatorship in Iraq in the spring of 2003. In authorizing the war in Iraq, Bush was deploying a radically new means—preemptive war.[45] But the proclaimed objective—democratic regime change—was one that Wilson, Reagan, and even Clinton would have celebrated.[46]

Russian Regime Change

Promoting regime change in Russia, however, did not figure prominently in Bush's new doctrine for American foreign policy. After September 11,

Wilsonian ideals guided American foreign policy in only a select handful of countries, that is, authoritarian regimes that threatened American national security interests. To destroy these regimes, Bush needed allies and was willing therefore to ignore autocratic practices in countries that assisted in fighting on the frontline of his war on terrorism. Russia was one of those friendly countries.

For immediately embracing the right side in the war on terrorism, Putin was rewarded. Bush changed the way he spoke about Russia's "war against terrorism." On September 26, 2001, White House press secretary Ari Fleischer communicated President Bush's appreciation for Putin's post–September 11 statement. The White House press spokesperson also stated that the "Chechnya leadership, like all responsible political leaders in the world, must immediately and unconditionally cut all contacts with international terrorist groups, such as Osama bin Laden and the Al Qaeda organization."[47] The Clinton administration had previously connected some Chechen fighters to bin Laden's network.[48] But never had the White House spokesperson—the voice of the president—explicitly cast Russia's enemies as one and the same as America's enemies.

Bush radically changed his rhetoric about the Chechen war from his campaigning days and instead eventually accepted Russia's definition of the war on terrorism to include Chechnya. Subsequent meetings between the Bush administration and the Chechen government in exile were downgraded. When visiting Washington in the spring of 2002, on the eve of Bush's trip to Moscow, Chechen foreign minister Akhmadov could not secure a meeting with any senior U.S. government official, as he had a year earlier.[49] The following year, in response to the Chechen terrorist attack against a Moscow theater in October 2002, the Bush administration designated three Chechen groups as "terrorist organizations" and froze their American assets.[50]

President Bush's statement did not give Putin a green light to do what he wanted in Chechnya. Throughout the second war, the Russian armed forces already were doing whatever they wanted in Chechnya with little or no reference to American opinions. The statement of support, however, did underscore the notion that the United States and Russia faced a common enemy. Putin had been pushing this theme for years with his American counterparts. In November 1999, as prime minister, he had published an opinion piece in the *New York Times* in which he said to his American audience, "Imagine ordinary New Yorkers or Washingtonians asleep in their homes. Then, in a flash, hundreds perish at the Watergate or at an apartment on Manhattan's West Side."[51] Putin therefore was pleased to hear that President Bush finally recognized publicly their common cause. In subsequent meetings between Bush and Putin, the war in Chechnya never became a major agenda item. As one journalist summed up, "Bush has shown remarkable discipline in ignoring

Russia's increasingly brutal campaign against separatists in the rebel republic—a campaign dubbed by Yelena Bonner, widow of Nobel Prize–winning
human rights activist Andrei Sakharov, as the 'political genocide' of the
Chechen people."[52]

Before meetings between the Russian and American presidents, Bush
administration officials repeatedly have stressed that the issue of Chechnya is
covered at length behind closed doors.[53] When Bush has alluded to the
Chechen situation publicly, however, he and the senior officials in his government have often adopted Putin's portrayal of the Russian military operation
as part of the war on terrorism. As he reaffirmed at the G-8 meeting in Canada
in the summer of 2002, "President Putin has been a stalwart in the fight
against terror. He understands the threat of terror, because he has lived
through terror. He's seen terror firsthand and he knows the threat of terrorism. . . . He understands what I understand, that there won't be peace if terrorists are allowed to kill and take innocent life. And, therefore, I view
President Putin as an ally, [a] strong ally in the war against terrorism."[54] Even
Secretary of State Colin Powell changed the way in which he described the
Chechen conflict, stating bluntly soon after the May 2002 summit in Moscow
that, "Russia is fighting terrorists in Chechnya, there is no question about that,
and we understand that."[55] Such utterances suggested that the references to
Chechnya behind closed doors may not be as hard hitting as U.S. officials
claimed.

The Bush administration has not always spoken with a unified voice about
Chechnya. Although the president himself has not spoken critically about the
Chechen war since the 2000 presidential campaign, members of his administration have condemned the conduct of the Russian military campaign. When
pressed to talk about Chechnya, Condoleezza Rice has continued to express a
nuanced view of the war:

> We clearly have differences with the Russian government about
> Chechnya. We've said to them that we fully agree that the Chechen lead-
> ership should not involve itself with terrorist elements in the region, and
> there are terrorist elements in the region. But that not every Chechen is
> a terrorist and that the Chechens' legitimate aspiration for political solu-
> tion [sic] should be pursued by the Russian government. And we have
> been very actively pressing the Russian government to move on the
> political front with Chechnya.[56]

U.S. ambassador to Russia Alexander Vershbow has been particularly vocal
in condemning the methods of the campaign, urging a political solution, and
distinguishing between international terrorists fighting in Chechnya and local
Chechen fighters whose aim is independence.[57] In public statements, Deputy
Assistant Secretary for European and Eurasian Affairs Steven Pifer also has

stressed the need to differentiate freedom fighters from international terrorists and has "called on Mr. Maskhadov and other moderate Chechens to dis-
associate themselves with terrorists." Pifer also stated bluntly that "the danger
to civilians in Chechnya remains our greatest concern. The human rights situation is poor, with a history of abuses by all sides."[58] Before September 11,
Secretary of State Powell too emphasized the need for a political solution. As
he noted in his confirmation hearings, "They must achieve a political settlement, the only way to end this terrible conflict and to bring peace to the area.
At the same time, we will hold the Russians to account for internationally recognized norms such as those of the Geneva Convention, and they must allow
humanitarian assistance organizations to have access to the civilians who are
suffering in the region."[59] After September 11, Powell began to describe the
Russian military campaign as an antiterrorist operation but still urged a political settlement.[60]

If the rhetoric of the Bush administration on Chechnya changed considerably over its first two years in office—from the very critical to the very supportive, but with dissident voices continuing to highlight the negative—actual
policy changed very little from the Clinton era. When asked in his confirmation hearings how the Bush approach to Chechnya would differ from the
Clinton policy, Powell answered, "I don't know that I can answer that."[61]
Subsequent statements by Bush administration officials suggest that the actual
policy on Chechnya has changed very little.[62] On the basic issues concerning
Chechnya, State Department spokesperson Richard Boucher said, "To reiter-
ate, our policy has not changed. We recognize Chechnya as part of Russia." He
also added that "they need to take steps to bring the violence to an end, that
there is no military solution to the problem, and they need—both sides need
to find ways to begin a dialogue and reach a political settlement."[63] Under
Bush, the United States has continued to provide humanitarian assistance to
the region. At the same time, Bush administration officials have refrained
from pursuing new policy initiatives regarding Chechnya. They have not
embraced a more activist role in the region such as those proposed by
Zbigniew Brzezinski, nor offered American mediating services to the Russians
and Chechens.

Though little in the conduct of the war has changed since candidate Bush
pledged to sanction Russia until it stops bombing "women and children" and
causing "huge numbers of refugees to flee Chechnya," no sanctions have been
applied.[64] The only significant policy change is rhetorical. If Clinton begrudg-
ingly added statements critical of the Chechen war to his talking points on
Russia, Bush has eliminated them.

The conduct of the war in Chechnya has not been the only sign of democratic backsliding since Putin came to power. On the contrary, nearly every
democratic institution has become weaker, not stronger. On Putin's watch, the

state has muzzled critical media. The two largest national television networks are fully subservient to the Kremlin. Putin's government and its surrogates then wrested control of NTV, Russia's third largest television network and the only station really critical of Putin.[65] The Russian state also has arrested and intimidated print journalists and denied entry to Western journalists planning to report on Chechnya from Russia. Oleg Panfilov, the head of the Center for Journalism in Extreme Situations, has reported that the "the number of criminal cases opened against journalists in three years of Vladimir Putin's rule is more than the number during the entire 10 years of Boris Yeltsin's reign."[66] Putin also put into place a new system for constituting the Federation Council that makes this upper house of parliament subservient to the executive branch.[67] In the lower house, the State Duma, Putin and his allies used state resources to help elect a majority supportive of Kremlin policies. Putin's government has even interfered in the electoral process in a series of regional votes, removing opposition candidates from the ballot and preventing incumbents unfriendly to the Kremlin from running again. Such gross violations of the electoral process raise real questions about Russia's status as an electoral democracy. Putin also seems intent on isolating Russian civil society from the West. In 2003, the Russian government ousted the Organization for Security and Cooperation in Europe from Chechnya, terminated its agreement with the American Peace Corps, and refused reentry to Irene Stevenson, the director of the AFL-CIO's Solidarity Center in Moscow, into Russia. Western journalists and even an American diplomat in transit have also been denied entry into the country.

The Bush administration's response has been difficult to record. At the highest level, President Bush has rarely mentioned the "d" word in public during his meetings with Putin. Instead, U.S. officials have explained that Bush has decided to discuss issues of democracy in private with Putin.[68] Even issues of freedom of the press are not raised publicly.[69] As with the Chechen situation, lower-level American officials have spoken more publicly and critically about the antidemocratic trends in Russia than senior Bush administration officials (although National Security Adviser Rice has made a point of meeting with democratic activists and independent journalists from Russia). In Moscow, Ambassador Vershbow has spoken out against the state's abusive use of power against independent media outlets, human rights activists, and environmentalists.[70] And in its annual report on human rights around the world, the State Department documented in detail the scope and scale of abuses in Russia. To their credit, American embassy officials expressed outrage over the ending of the Peace Corps program in Russia and the ouster of Irene Stevenson. Vershbow noted, "Clearly there is a trend emerging. Forces here that may not be fully convinced of the wisdom of Russia's democratization and its integration with the West . . . are flexing their muscles."[71] Vershbow has very little ability—especially without presidential backing—to help reverse these Russian decisions.

Despite these symbolic gestures and words, democratic erosion in Russia has not been a top agenda issue for Bush in his execution of his Russia policy. He personally has devoted little political capital to the cause, and his administration has recommended deep cuts in funding for democracy assistance programs inside Russia.

According to human rights activists and democratic proponents in Russia, this change in policy has produced very negative consequences for their causes. At the beginning of the Bush administration, these groups were optimistic about the return of a Republican to the White House. Bush said the right things and appeared willing to be tough with the Kremlin authorities. Since September 11, however, Russian democracy activists have noted a real change in tone in Bush's statements about Russia. Tatiana Kasatkina, executive director of the Russian *Memorial* organization, noted that she and her associates "were not satisfied" with Bush's comments about human rights during his first visit to Russia in May 2002. "He spoke about Chechnya and human rights only in passing. There was nothing in the speech like what he said during the election campaign."[72] These same groups now feel abandoned. As Lyudmila Alexeyeva, head of the Moscow Helsinki Group, explained, "The integration of Russia into the anti-terror coalition became a pardon of violations by Western democracies. This ally that we [the Russian human rights movement] had in Western governments, the U.S., the European Union, Canada, is immeasurably less of an ally now."[73] Other Russian human rights activists have complained that Bush's references to the joint American-Russian war on terrorism have given the Russian military officers in Chechnya even more leeway to act as they please. As Valentina Melnikova, an activist with the Soldiers' Mothers Committee, stated in reaction to Bush's comments on Chechnya during the May 2002 Moscow summit, "We know for sure that the way he spoke about it [the war on terrorism] gives more freedom to the Russian military."[74]

Economic Reform

On economic reform, the Bush administration has had to make few policy decisions because Putin's government has proceeded with economic reforms without asking for major external financial or technical assistance. Putin's team has pushed through major tax reforms, produced trade surpluses, maintained balanced budgets, and quelled inflation.[75] In 1999, Russia recovered from the 1998 financial meltdown and recorded 3.2 percent growth in GDP. In 2000, the Russian economy grew 7.7 percent, the highest growth year in decades, but then tapered to 5 percent in 2001 and 2002. Russia's economic success made decisions about aid to Russia easy. The Bush administration did not have to decide whether or not to support new IMF loans to Russia during these years, because the Russian government did not request them. Some analysts called for the forgiveness of Russian debt owed to the United States, but the Russian government never asked for debt forgiveness and so the Bush administration has never offered it. Bilateral economic assistance programs have continued under the Bush administration (though with smaller budgets), but they are not the focus of policy in either capital. The Bush administration dissolved the government-to-government commission headed by former vice president Gore and, for many years, former prime minister Chernomyrdin. In place of this government-to-government arrangement, the Bush administration has given its blessing and support to a set of private bilateral organizations dedicated to these same issues with a focus on stimulating trade and investment.[76] Russian economic reform, however, is not a major issue in U.S.-Russian relations as it was throughout much of the 1990s.

In an essay published in the spring of 2002, Rice's top Russia hand at the National Security Council, Thomas Graham, summarized Russia's attempts at reform in the following way:

> At the dawn of the twenty-first century, Russia remains far short of having fulfilled the grand hopes for its future widely entertained in both Russia and the West at the time of the breakup of the Soviet Union. If there has been a transition at all, it has not been the hoped-for one to a free market democracy, but rather a reincarnation of a traditionally Russian form of rule that in many respects is premodern. Russia has not been integrated into the West in any significant way, contrary to the goals set forth by the Russian and Western governments a decade ago.[77]

The Bush administration in which Graham serves has not seemed troubled by this sober assessment. Especially after September 11, Russia's internal problems disappeared from the U.S.-Russian diplomacy agenda.

A New Russian-American Security Agenda

Bush's focus on cultivating a personal relationship with Putin pushed the reform agenda in Russia, especially the democratic reform agenda, to the periphery of U.S.-Russian relations. In contrast to Yeltsin, Putin also expressed little interest in internationalizing his domestic problems. Instead, Putin and his immediate circle of foreign policy advisers welcome the return of realpolitik as the philosophy guiding U.S.-Russian relations. Even before September 11, this new realism embraced by both presidents helped to reverse the perceived setbacks in U.S.-Russian relations in the second half of the 1990s. The simple fact that both presidents were new also created a sense of optimism in the bilateral relationship. After September 11, the personal bonds between

Putin and Bush and the positive ambience of U.S.-Russian relations more generally seemed to grow even stronger.

The new happy talk between the presidents after summer 2001 seemed to produce concrete cooperation in the war in Afghanistan. Secretary of State Powell praised Russia as "a key member of the antiterrorist coalition," and he asserted that "Russia has played a crucial role in our success in Afghanistan, by providing intelligence, bolstering the Northern alliance, and assisting our entry into central Asia. As a result, we have seriously eroded the capabilities of a terrorist network that posed a direct threat to both of our countries."[78] U.S. and Russian officials continued to echo similar cooperative themes well beyond the efforts established during the military campaign against the Taliban in Afghanistan. At the G-8 meeting in Calgary in 2002, Bush praised Putin as a "man of action when it comes to fighting terror."[79]

But beyond Afghanistan, American and Russian actions in fighting the war on terrorism have occurred in parallel but not together. In the spring of 2002, Russian and American officials discussed a joint operation in Georgia to root out al Qaeda operatives who were allegedly camped in the Pankisi Gorge there.[80] Eventually, American armed forces were deployed in Georgia, but not accompanied by their new Russian allies, who are not perceived as allies by the Georgian government. Instead, the Kremlin escalated threats of military force on Georgian territory in fall 2002. Russian and American officials have maintained different opinions about the desired longevity of American troops in central Asia. Russian parliamentary speaker Gennady Seleznov has warned that "Russia will not approve of permanent U.S. military bases in central Asia."[81] As discussed below, Russia refused to recognize the American invasion of Iraq as part of their shared war on terrorism.

Despite these differences regarding the war on terrorism, Bush and Putin took advantage of their new warm relationship to put to rest two lingering security issues from the previous decade: arms control and the NATO-Russia relationship. On arms control, the Bush administration failed to secure Russian approval for amendments to the ABM Treaty that would have permitted the United States to deploy national missile defense. (It remains unclear whether the Bush administration ever really wanted to maintain any version of the ABM Treaty, though Bush officials claimed even after abrogation that amendment was their preferred outcome.)[82] Instead, on December 13, 2001, Bush officially notified Moscow of his intention to withdraw from the ABM Treaty, which subsequently occurred six months later, so that the United States would have no constraints on its decisions about the construction of a missile defense system.

Putin and many other Russian officials repeatedly stated their disapproval, but the withdrawal announcement had no immediate negative consequence for the bilateral relationship. Putin recognized that an American missile defense effort would have no effect on Russia's security, although he did say that he had hoped that the treaty could be modified, "not because we were afraid, or we feared for our own security. It was simply because we are proponents of a different concept, a different philosophy, of how international security should be built." He added that the Russian position had been "fairly flexible," but he had received no specific parameters to negotiate.[83]

Five months later in May 2002, the two presidents signed the U.S.-Russian Strategic Offensive Reductions Treaty, or Treaty of Moscow, during Bush's first visit to the Russian capital. During the campaign, Bush had proposed that the United States unilaterally reduce its nuclear arsenal to levels dictated by national interest since there was no need to maintain high arsenals now that the cold war was over. But he never presented specifics.[84] Following this logic, Bush originally had not wanted to sign a treaty but instead proposed a handshake or a memorandum of understanding. The signing of an actual treaty that had to be ratified by American and Russian legislators was a concession to Putin. The short treaty committed both countries to reduce their nuclear warheads to a level between 1,700 and 2,200 by December 31, 2012 (the date on which the treaty will expire unless renewed by the two parties). The idea of a range is similar to those embodied in START I and START II, established because Russia for financial reasons wants to go to the lower number, while the Pentagon wants to keep the U.S. floor at the higher number to ensure what it believes are the requirements for deterrence.[85]

The treaty represented the largest proposed reduction in strategic nuclear weapons ever codified in an international agreement. Yet, as critics of the treaty have noted, the agreement does not obligate either country to destroy the nuclear warheads. Rather, the treaty obligates both sides to remove these warheads from their delivery vehicles. The Pentagon intends to keep 2,000 warheads on "active reserve" in the event of new nuclear threats; nearly 5,000 inactive weapons would remain in storage. The accord is thus less groundbreaking than advertised; as Colin Powell has argued, "All previous arms control treaties were of the same type—they didn't deal with the stockpile elimination, they dealt with either launchers or systems. And so this is consistent with those previous treaties—SALT I, SALT II, START I, START II, and the INF Treaty." But defensively he added, "The important point is that warheads are coming off . . . launchers."[86]

As for NATO enlargement, Putin had long realized that blustering about something he could not stop (as Yeltsin did) only made Russia look weaker. Bush made clear in a speech delivered in Warsaw in the summer of 2001 that he would push for a big enlargement that was likely to include the former Soviet republics of Estonia, Latvia, and Lithuania. And he did. But in the fall, after prodding from British prime minister Tony Blair about the need for a new "NATO at 20," the Bush administration also began working to reestablish a special relationship between NATO and Russia. The new NATO-Russia Council was formally signed by the NATO heads of state with Putin in Rome in late May 2002, just after the Bush-Putin summit in Moscow. The new council purportedly improved on its predecessor, the 1997 Permanent Joint Council, by allowing Russia a seat at the table for joint decisionmaking on issues like terrorism. Each NATO member, however, reserves the right to pull an issue out of that forum to a members-only discussion.

The Bush administration also reversed its earlier position on Cooperative Threat Reduction (Nunn-Lugar) assistance. Instead of cutting these programs as discussed in the spring of 2001, Bush and his foreign team requested increased budgets for these programs. After September 11, these programs won even more attention and support. The president's fiscal year 2003 budget requested nearly $1 billion for Nunn-Lugar, the highest annual amount ever earmarked for these programs. In addition, at the G-8 summit in Canada, the United States and the European Commission pledged to spend $20 billion ($10 billion each) over the next ten years "for projects pertaining to disarmament, nonproliferation, counterterrorism, and nuclear safety."[87] Bush and his non-Russian counterparts in the G-8 expanded and internationalized Nunn-Lugar.

Finally, Bush and Putin worked to push the agenda of Russian integration into Western international institutions beyond NATO. The G-8 leaders agreed in Calgary in June 2002 that Russia would host the G-8 summit in 2006. According to the White House, "The decision reflects Russia's economic and democratic transition in recent years under President Putin."[88] President Bush also has stated emphatically that he wants to facilitate the speedy entry of Russia into the World Trade Organization. To help promote membership, his Department of Commerce declared Russia a market economy just after the May 2002 Moscow summit. To facilitate Russian economic integration, Bush also called for Russia's graduation from Jackson-Vanik, although his administration has failed to convince or cajole Congress to change the legislation. (Thirty years ago, Senator Henry "Scoop" Jackson and Congressman Charles Vanik cosponsored an amendment to the 1974 Trade Act, which explicitly linked the Soviet Union's trading status to levels of Jewish emigration. Russia eliminated state controls on Jewish emigration over a decade ago, but the American legislation has not yet been amended, primarily because of concerns not from American Jews but from American farmers. Jackson-Vanik will disappear automatically if Russia joins the WTO.) Bush and Putin also agreed to a new multilateral institutional framework for dealing with the Middle East peace process, which symbolically put the United States and Russia on equal footing together with the United Nations and the European Union. Like the earlier transformation of the G-7 into the G-8, this "quartet" of actors accorded Russia a special status in an important international process.

In some economic sectors such as steel and poultry, Bush policy actions impeding U.S.-Russian trade have trumped rhetorical pledges in support of Russia's integration into the West. But overall, the Bush administration's economic and security policy toward Russia has been framed in terms of integration. Like his father, however, and unlike Bill Clinton, it is an integration without the promotion of internal transformation.

The End of the Honeymoon? Iran, Iraq, and the Future of the World Order

When discussing the war on terrorism in Afghanistan, President Bush and President Putin appeared to be talking from the same script. As Condoleezza Rice reported, "Russia has been an excellent partner in the war on terrorism. Russia, perhaps, understands better than many the impact of terrorism on a society."[89] When discussing the "war on terrorism" in Iran or Iraq, however, the two presidents spoke from different talking points.[90] Eventually, different perceptions of threats and interests regarding Iraq, and to a lesser extent Iran, cooled the alleged special relationship between Bush and Putin and fueled doubts about exactly how close the United States and Russia could or would become in the twenty-first century.

Iran

The Bush administration came to Washington in January 2001 convinced that it could do better than its predecessors in stopping Russian transfers of nuclear and missile technologies to Iran. For the first several months in office, Bush officials had reason to be optimistic. Most generally, Putin seemed interested in revitalizing U.S.-Russian relations by emphasizing mutual strategic interests rather than common values. Well before September 11, Putin wanted terrorism, trade, nuclear weapons, and regional conflicts to form the Russian-American agenda, instead of Chechnya, freedom of the press, or economic reforms. Putin also seemed to be consolidating his control over the foreign policy and security ministries inside Russia, a task in which Yeltsin had failed.[91] In March 2001, Putin seemed to be reining in the renegade Ministry of Atomic Energy (Minatom) when he fired its minister, Yevgeny Adamov, and replaced him with Aleksandr Rumyantsev. Under Adamov, Minatom had developed its own foreign policy, which consisted first and foremost of selling nuclear technologies to paying customers including the Iranians. In contrast with Adamov, Rumyantsev, the former head of the world-renowned Kurchatov Institute, was perceived by U.S. officials as someone more loyal to Putin and potentially more receptive to U.S. worries.[92] Then, of course, September 11 occurred. The goodwill this horrific day sparked between American and Russian leaders (and societies) seemed to create a context in which a deal on Iran could be cut.

Such a deal, however, has yet to materialize. Like Yeltsin, Putin has repeatedly emphasized that the Russian contract to build a nuclear reactor in Bushehr, Iran, in no way contributes to the development of Iran's nuclear weapons capabilities. Instead of shutting down Bushehr, Putin has hinted that Russia's Minatom might help Iran build several more reactors. In the "new" era of U.S.-Russia rapprochement that began during the June 2001 summit in Slovenia and intensified after September 11, Bush has been reluctant to sanction Russia for its transfer of nuclear technologies to this charter member of the "axis of evil." Instead, not unlike the Clinton approach to this issue, Bush has tried to link increased assistance to changed Russian behavior on Iran.[93] The deal was this: stop cooperating with Iran, and the United States would lift restrictions that have blocked Russian efforts to store and reprocess spent nuclear fuel from other parts of the world. Yuri Bespalko, spokesman for the Russian Ministry of Atomic Energy, argued that Russia could not trust the United States to live up to its end of the bargain: "Americans are being rather sly when they offer this kind of swap. It's better to have a bird in the hand than two in the bush."[94] During the summer of 2003, when even more evidence became public that revealed Iran's nuclear weapons aspirations, Russia publicly pressed Iran to allow international inspections of its nuclear sites. Yet, Foreign Minister Ivanov also reiterated Russia's intentions to fulfill the Bushehr contract.[95] To date, Bush's record of success in stopping Russian nuclear technology transfer to Iran looks very similar to Clinton's limited achievements on this issue.

Iraq

During the Clinton-Yeltsin years, unresolved differences over Iran were among the thorniest security issues in U.S.-Russian relations. In the Bush-Putin era, Iraq became the most salient topic of disagreement in the bilateral relationship. In fact, clashes over how to deal with Iraq seemingly ended Bush's romantic embrace of Putin and infused new antagonism into American-Russian relations.

Once success was near in Afghanistan, Bush turned his attention to Iraq. After considerable debate in his administration, Bush decided that the first phase of his campaign against Iraq should be waged at the United Nations. On September 12, 2002, Bush gave a speech at the United Nations in which he urged the body and its Security Council in particular to enforce the dozens of resolutions it had passed about Iraq since the end of the Persian Gulf War a decade earlier. Two months later, the Security Council voted 15-0 to adopt UN Resolution 1441. In the opinion of Bush administration officials, this resolution gave Saddam Hussein one last chance to report on and destroy his weapons of mass destruction or face the "serious consequences" of disarmament being executed by external forces. Russia voted for the resolution.

After the passage of 1441, Saddam Hussein allowed UN weapons inspectors back into Iraq. After months of inspections, however, the Bush administration grew impatient, hinted that Saddam Hussein was in material breach of 1441, and prepared for military action. Putin and his foreign policy team joined the French in interpreting the success of the weapons inspectors much more positively. In February 2003, Bush and his team decided to make one last push to gain renewed UN support for military action as a means of enforcing UN resolution 1441. Bush suggested that he would seek another UN Security Resolution to authorize the use of force. His friend Putin would not go along. Different from the American decisions to withdraw from the ABM Treaty, to push for NATO expansion, or to deploy troops in central Asia, the Bush administration could not secure a new UN vote without Russian approval. American officials tried to offer Russia compensation for its support, including assurances about the $8 billion debt owed to Russia by Iraq, a pledge to allow Russian companies to participate in the reconstruction of Iraq after the war, and a promise to repeal the Jackson-Vanik amendment.[96] In response, however, Putin, like French president Jacques Chirac, claimed he was taking the higher principled ground:

> Russia—and I am profoundly convinced of it—is a reliable partner in international affairs, because we are not being guided by short-term benefits, expediency or any emotions. We have certain principles and we abide by them. We have our own interests there [in Iraq], not only in the oil sphere. But we are not going to bargain, as if we were in an oriental market, selling our position in exchange for some economic benefits.[97]

In a dramatic press conference on March 5, 2003, announcing Russia's decision not to support a new UN resolution, the Russian foreign minister stood next to his French and German colleagues, not the American secretary of state. In issuing a joint statement, Russia, France, and Germany called for more time to allow the inspectors do their job.[98] At least temporarily, Russia was joining forces with Western countries but those opposed to the policy of the United States. In the press briefing, Russian foreign minister Igor Ivanov stated the importance of establishing the "grounds of a new world order, *multi-polar world* based on the principles of international law and respect to the UN resolutions."[99] In an ironic change from the 1990s, a Russian senior official was now lecturing the Americans about norms and the rule of law. Throughout this period, Putin also stated repeatedly, "I am convinced that unilateral action would be a big mistake."[100]

Bush did not listen to his friend's warning. After the joint statement by France, Germany, and Russia, the Bush administration abandoned its campaign for a second resolution and invaded Iraq anyway, without Russia's support. On the first day of the war, Putin harshly denounced the American military campaign as illegal and unwarranted and dangerous to international stability:

> Today the United States started a military action against Iraq . . . contrary to the principles and norms of international law and the Charter of the UN. Nothing can justify this military action. . . . I have already referred to the humanitarian aspect. But the threat of the disintegration of the existing system of international security causes at least as much concern. If we allow international law to be replaced by "the law of the fist," whereby the strong is always right, has the right to do anything, then one of the basic principles of international law will be put into question and that is the principle of immutable sovereignty of a state. And then no one, not a single country in the world, will feel itself secure.[101]

Foreign Minister Ivanov added, "There are no convincing facts to confirm the accusations that Iraq supports international terrorism" and little evidence that Iraq has acquired weapons of mass destruction.[102] During the first week of the war, he warned, "If such massive bombardment continues, a humanitarian, economic and environmental catastrophe will become inevitable in the near future, not only in Iraq but in the whole region."[103] As for one of the stated objectives of the American war, Ivanov replied, "I have serious doubts about a democracy imposed by Tomahawks." More generally, Russian officials have accused the United States of "double standards" for pushing for democracy in Iraq and Iran but not in Saudi Arabia or Egypt.[104]

In a replay of the dramas surrounding START II ratification in the 1990s, the Russian Duma moved to delay ratification of the Treaty of Moscow signed by Putin and Bush in May 2002. The Russian people, who had expressed widespread sympathy toward America after September 11, also soured on the United States as a result of the war in Iraq much as they had during the NATO war on Kosovo in 1999. In polls conducted after the war began, more than 90 percent of Russian respondents expressed a negative view of the American military campaign, even if also showing no particular sympathy for Saddam Hussein.[105]

It was bad enough that Bush's new friend, Vladimir Putin, was not standing at his side in his greatest moment of need. It got worse, when Bush administration officials stated that Russian firms for some time had been delivering global positioning system jamming equipment, antitank missiles, and night-vision binoculars to the Iraqi armed forces.[106] Bush called Putin personally to discuss these alleged violations of UN sanctions—violations that could have direct and negative consequences for American soldiers fighting in Iraq. Publicly, Russian officials vehemently denied the allegations.[107] In response,

U.S. officials threatened sanctions.[108] It began to sound a lot like the Clinton-Yeltsin sparring over Iran.

Conclusion

In May 2002, officials on both sides touted that U.S.-Russian relations had never been better. It did not look that way in the midst of the war on Iraq a year later. Once the war was over, however, the two presidents moved quickly to bring their relationship back to its prewar status. Despite the renewed professions of friendship, the action items in U.S.-Russian relations seemed rather limited by the summer of 2003. Some in the United States continued to worry about democratic backsliding in Russia, but the Bush administration had little interest or energy to engage in Russia's internal affairs. Rhetorically, the American and Russian presidents rededicated their countries to the global war on terrorism but without specifying any joint missions. Neither side seemed to have new ideas for resolving the real, contentious issues in the bilateral relationship, including, most importantly, Iran. Instead, the relationship seemed to move into limbo or equilibrium. No new initiatives for deepening Russia's internal transformation or integrating Russia into the West were on the horizon. Nor, however, were there any looming issues that could change fundamentally the terms of the bilateral relationship.

14

Lessons

In the immediate aftermath of the cold war, there were no issues more important for U.S. national security interests than the transformation of Russia internally and the integration of Russia externally into the West. In the course of three administrations, American foreign policymakers had different understandings of the links between Russia's internal transformation and its external integration and chose different strategies to achieve these two objectives.

Individuals, Ideas, and the Making of American Foreign Policy

The central argument of this book is that individuals working primarily in the executive branch of government made American policy toward Russia in the 1990s. Neither the structure of the international system, nor domestic forces such as economic lobbies, U.S. senators, or American voters, played a determinative role in shaping the particular policies that resulted even if those elements did help configure the playing field. Instead, U.S. policymakers in the executive branch formulated American policy toward Russia, and they were influenced most of all by their ideas about international politics and the place of America and Russia in the world. Some of these decisionmakers embraced "power balancing" as their roadmap for guiding them through the uncertain territory of the post–cold war (dis)order. Others looked at Russian-American relations through the lens of Wilsonian liberalism and emphasized "regime transformation." These worldviews had an identifiable and causal role in the formulation of American foreign policy toward Russia after the collapse of the USSR. The preceding chapters have attempted to show this causal relationship between ideological frameworks held by key decisionmakers on the one hand and American foreign policy toward Russia on the other.

In broad sweep, the story is straightforward. George H. W. Bush embraced realist ideas about international politics. For the forty-first president, the balance of power among states in the international system was the key variable that shaped state behavior. From this analytical framework, the principal U.S. national security interest was decreasing the power capabilities of adversaries and increasing American power. Bush's realist vision also placed a premium on stability or maintaining the status quo, which he believed served American national interests. Regime change inside the USSR and Russia was desirable but not an outcome that Bush believed he could or *should* try to help facilitate.

Bill Clinton was a regime transformer. For the forty-second president, regime type was a key factor in international politics. He believed in the idea that democracies do not fight one another. From this analytical framework, the central objective of American foreign policy in the post–cold war era was to foster regime change in Russia. If democratic and market institutions consolidated inside Russia, then Russia would adopt a more pro-Western, pro-American orientation in its foreign policy. In contrast to his predecessor, Clinton believed that the United States not only should but *could* facilitate Russia's internal transformation.

When dealing with Russia, George W. Bush was a realist. For the forty-third president, promoting regime change became a central feature of his foreign policy after September 11, but not in Russia. Instead, Bush believed that treating Russia as a great power—irrespective of regime type—served the American national interest. In contrast to his father, however, George W. Bush saw gains from cooperation with this power and worried much less about threats emanating from Russia. After September 11, the "war on terrorism" served as the framework for his analysis of the world. Looking through this lens, Russia appeared to be an ally, not because of its internal organization but because of shared threats.

This broad sweep covers up many nuances, paradoxes, and contradictions, while at the same time ignores many factors beyond ideas that intervened to influence the making of American policy toward Russia. Tracing the relationship between ideas and foreign policy is fraught with complexity. In every administration, presidents pursued policies that involved some mix of realpolitik and idealism. Power balancers and regime transformers served in all three administrations. Sorting out the influence of each one has required a careful reconstruction of decisionmaking and an awareness of the ideas not embraced, the decisions not made, and the policies not pursued. This task has been complicated by several intervening factors and by difficult judgments that must be made about the "real" ideological motivations of U.S. foreign policymakers.

First, while the emphasis in a given U.S. administration is shaped by the worldview brought into office by the leading decisionmakers, the nature of global affairs at the time does affect how that worldview gets put into practice. Richard M. Nixon and Henry Kissinger, for example, were power balancers by orientation, but they were also in office at a time when it appeared that the U.S. position in the world was declining owing to the war in Vietnam, the rise of Europe and Japan as economic challengers, and the achievement by Moscow of nuclear parity. Nixon and Kissinger sought to ensure that all of the world's major powers sided with the United States against the Soviet Union, and by maintaining core alliances with Europe and Japan while also reaching out to China, they succeeded in isolating their cold war adversary. Conversely, Bill Clinton and Anthony Lake, who were by inclination regime transformers, came into office after America's major adversary had been defeated, a context more conducive for the exercise of U.S. power to promote multilateral gover-nance and expand the community of market democracies. The change in the global distribution of power enabled the Clinton administration to use America's might in places like Bosnia and Kosovo to promote Wilsonian val-ues. With respect to Russia, the drop in Moscow's relevance to global affairs had changed markedly from 1991, when George H. W. Bush was trying to manage a peaceful end to the cold war, to 2002, when George W. Bush was focused on securing Russian acceptance of his primary foreign policy interests such as the abrogation of the ABM Treaty, further NATO enlargement, and his war on terrorism. If the Russians did not agree, George W. Bush's America had the power to pursue these policies unilaterally.

Second, as was the case in Kosovo, NATO enlargement, or the war against Iraq, it can be difficult to sort out whether a policy is being pursued for real-ist or Wilsonian purposes. As E. H. Carr reminded us more than sixty years ago, idealist international rhetoric is often used to disguise or justify realist policies.[1] NATO enlargement and the NATO war against Serbia did enhance the influence of the United States in a part of Europe formerly under Moscow's domination, even if the effort was undertaken in the name of pro-moting markets and democracy. In the long run, the American war against Saddam Hussein might eventually produce a democratic regime in Iraq. In the short run, the presence of American troops in Iraq has produced greater American influence and less Russian influence over the country and the region. And whenever U.S. administrations espoused Wilsonianism, Russian elites reacted skeptically and assumed that power balancing was the ulterior motivating force.

Third, with respect to Russia, there were often divisions in administrations not just between realists and Wilsonians, but among realists with different pri-orities, and among liberals with different causes. James Baker clashed initially with Brent Scowcroft and Dick Cheney over what to do about nuclear weapons in Ukraine, Kazakhstan, and Belarus, but both sides in this debate invoked realist arguments to support their competing policy recommendations. Wilsonians Lake and Strobe Talbott clashed initially over the timing of NATO enlargement, because Lake considered his liberal mission in central Europe a greater priority than worrying about the reactions of Russian elites, while Talbott thought that his liberal mission of transforming Russia was a more immediate and greater priority than bringing the Czech Republic, Hungary, and Poland into NATO. Realists in and outside the Clinton administration offered different arguments as to why NATO expansion did and did not serve U.S. security interests. More generally, especially during the Clinton years, conflicts also erupted between those who put Russia policy front and center for U.S. interests and those who advocated treating Russia as just another power (and one that for some officials was not particularly worthy of American support). These differences often led to advocacy of more "hawkish" or more "dovish" policies that do not neatly correspond to divisions between power balancers and regime transformers.

Still, the general theme of the book is that the worldviews of key decisionmakers play a central role in the making of American foreign policy. Changes in worldviews between administrations produce changes in policies. The two Bush administrations were much less interested in a U.S. role in Russian internal affairs and focused more exclusively on Russian external behavior, and particularly nuclear weapons policy. The difference, for example, between the Treasury Department under George H. W. Bush in 1992 and the Treasury Department under Bill Clinton in 1993 could not be more stark and can only be explained by examining general philosophical orientations. Similar differences over the use of military force in Kosovo and over missile defense also demonstrate that it mattered which administration holding which worldviews was in power at a given time.

Ideas only matter when forceful policy entrepreneurs embrace them. This book has told the story of individuals working (primarily) in the executive branch competing with one another to define and execute America's Russia policy. The center of gravity in the U.S. executive branch for making Russia policy changed over time and between administrations, depending on the state of the world, presidential proclivities and appointments, and the presence of persuasive policy advocates who were pushing pet projects. In the first Bush administration, everyone from the president on down the chain of command was involved in Russia policy, if only because when they came to office, the Soviet Union was still the primary concern of U.S. foreign policymakers. Everyone, therefore, had an interest in U.S.-Soviet relations, and everyone's policy area was somehow related to this overarching concern. The first Bush administration probably had more balance between bureaucracies of influential people who had input in the making of policy toward the Soviet Union and Russia than its successors would. Secretary of Defense Dick Cheney, Secretary of State James Baker, and National Security Adviser Brent Scowcroft all "played" on Soviet and Russian issues, and all had strong staffs to help them play effectively, even if Baker and his team tended to dominate the direction of policy given both their greater day-to-day involvement and Baker's close personal relationship with the president.

In the Clinton administration, one person—Strobe Talbott—was the dominant bureaucratic actor on Russia. His role stemmed not from his formal position as the State Department's ambassador at large for the new independent states or as deputy secretary of state, but because he was the personal friend of the president, and the president relied on Talbott for advice about how to handle Russia. Even his formal bosses at the State Department realized that this personal bond trumped the bureaucratic pecking order.

Yet Talbott's specific interests and background allowed other policy entrepreneurs to emerge. Talbott had no particular expertise in the issues of economic or political reform, so he assigned these tasks to others. In the Clinton administration, two strong figures, Lawrence Summers and David Lipton at the Treasury Department (and not officials at the State Department, the National Security Council, or the Agency for International Development), armed with concrete ideas, assumed principal responsibility for the economic reform part of the Russia portfolio. Because economic reform was such a crucial part of the Russia policy in the 1990s, the Treasury Department played a more critical role in foreign policy formation during this period than it did before or after. The subject of democracy promotion had no advocate of the same caliber as Summers. Nor, in contrast to those in Treasury or at the IMF, did senior U.S. officials have in hand a blueprint for how to promote democracy in Russia. The absence of policy entrepreneurs and a coherent set of ideas for how to promote democracy meant that democracy promotion often slipped through the cracks until enhanced (though slightly) in the late 1990s by Secretary of State Madeleine Albright, and Ambassador at Large for the New Independent States Stephen Sestanovich, who were more focused on human rights than Warren Christopher and Talbott had been. (To his credit, Talbott had sought to bring in Sestanovich in part because he wanted a strong, independent thinker in that position.)

In the Clinton administration, Secretary of Defense William Perry and his team at the Pentagon were important voices on Russia policy, but only on a particular set of issues related to Cooperative Threat Reduction (the Nunn-Lugar program). On other security topics, such as NATO enlargement, the policy team at the Pentagon was left in the dark. More generally, European security issues trumped Russia policy, especially as it became increasingly obvious that Russia was a declining power. Even Talbott had to make sure his initiatives on Russia did not conflict with but rather complemented American policies in Europe deemed to be of higher priority such as NATO expansion and the NATO war against Serbia.

President George W. Bush also has relied on a trusted friend to guide his Russia policy, but in his administration, that person is located in the White House, not the State Department. National Security Adviser Condoleezza Rice set the agenda and tone of American foreign policy toward Russia. Other policymakers and other bureaucracies have played a secondary role; it is noteworthy when compared to the previous administration how little influence the departments of State and Treasury have exerted on Russia policy since 2001. Of course, on other foreign policy issues, individuals like Vice President Dick Cheney or Secretary of Defense Donald Rumsfeld or even Deputy Secretary of Defense Paul Wolfowitz have assumed leading roles. On Russia, however, Rice has maintained control over the policy to an even larger extent than Talbott enjoyed. During the first Bush administration, all of the principals were involved in Russia policy. During the second Bush administration, two people—the president and Rice— have defined the main features of America's Russia policy.

The Impact of American Power and Purpose

Explaining the formation of American foreign policy toward Russia after the collapse of the Soviet Union is the focus of this book. But how successful were these policies? Did they achieve their objectives? Did some initiatives work better than others? Did the policies cause collateral damage to other American interests? We end this book with some assessments of the effects of these various policies on American national interests, Russia, and U.S.-Russian relations.[2]

In the first decade of America's post-Soviet Russia policy, it often seemed that the administration in question was doing too little or too much. Trying to do things just right proved elusive. Given the speed and complexity of Russia's domestic transformation, it is not surprising that U.S. officials had difficulty in calibrating the "right" policy to react to and at times push along this revolution to ensure that Russia stayed on a pro-Western track. Much of U.S. foreign policy toward Russia in this period suffered from overestimating American power in some areas and underestimating it in others. In particular, for some time, U.S. officials overestimated their capacities to influence change in Russia's domestic affairs and underestimated their power to achieve America's desired outcomes on international issues, regardless of Moscow's objections.

Partly these difficulties stemmed from the challenge of gauging Russia's internal trajectory. Besides overestimating or underestimating U.S. power, American (and many Russian) officials overestimated or underestimated the rate of change in Russia. Policymakers knew that the resources required for transformation would be enormous, but they often underestimated how hard it would be to get rid of entrenched bureaucratic interests. However, they generally overestimated the threat of a communist resurgence through the mid-1990s.

In contrast to America's response to other major social revolutions of the twentieth century—such as in Russia in 1917, China in 1949, or Iran in 1979—American officials wanted this second Russian revolution to succeed. George H. W. Bush expressed his desire to see democratic and market institutions take hold in the Soviet Union and then Russia, even if he was skeptical of the West's role in facilitating these transformations and reluctant to commit scarce (in his view) American resources to the project. Of the three administrations discussed in this book, the Clinton administration demonstrated the greatest commitment to assisting the emergence of market and democratic institutions in Russia, because the Clinton team believed both that a democratic and market-oriented Russia integrated into the West would no longer constitute a threat to American national security and that the United States could play a role in this transformation.

More than a decade later, it is striking how little power the United States exercised over domestic change in Russia. The United States emerged from the cold war as the world's only superpower and has often been described as the most powerful country in history relative to the other countries in the world. Yet, this super-superpower proved unable or unwilling to influence domestic change in Russia. Even Russian integration into Western international institutions proved an elusive goal.

Dramatic change in Russia has occurred, but the U.S. role in facilitating this revolution has been much less important than advertised. U.S. policy did help nudge Russia toward integration with the West, and some American interventions did prod domestic transformation in the intended direction—that is, toward democracy and capitalism. But there was no Marshall Plan to help rebuild Russia's economy. The question is first whether a much greater U.S. effort would have helped Russia avoid economic depression or would have created a firmer basis for the development and consolidation of democratic institutions, and second, whether that effort would have benefited the United States. How much of America's marginal influence stemmed from a lack of ideas, effort and resources, and how much stemmed from the United States' inability to bring about internal change in a country the size and complexity of Russia, no matter how much money was spent or how much attention devoted to it?

The American Role in Promoting Capitalism in Russia

There is no easy way to measure the impact of American foreign policy on the development of Russian capitalism. Even in its most active phase, American involvement in Russia's economic transformation was overshadowed by more fundamental factors, such as the legacy of the Soviet economy, the balance of power among competing economic interest groups in Russia, or swings in the world price of oil. To suggest that the "American factor" was primary—either as a positive or negative force—is ludicrous. At certain critical junctures, nonetheless, American foreign policymakers did make or failed to make important decisions about aiding economic reform that may have pushed Russian economic change in one direction or another.

STABILIZATION. The window of opportunity for influencing reform in Russia opened most widely in the fall of 1991. Boris Yeltsin had just stared down the coup plotters, earning him nearly unanimous approval ratings at home. He then appointed a reformist government headed by economist Yegor Gaidar that was eager to pursue radical reform and welcomed Western assistance. Gaidar knew that his reforms would be unpopular and eventually face serious resistance, but he and his allies believed that sustained and substantial Western assistance could help to keep afloat their government and Russian society through the difficult, initial phase of reform.

Gaidar overestimated Yeltsin's willingness to stay the course of radical economic reform. At the first sign of resistance, Yeltsin diluted his government to include enterprise managers—the so-called red directors—whose aim was not real reform but the preservation of the incredible moneymaking opportunities offered to them and their allies by partial reform. By December 1992, these Soviet-era managers were back in control of the Russian government under the leadership of Viktor Chernomyrdin.

Gaidar's second biggest miscalculation was to overestimate the Western commitment to supporting his economic reforms. His miscalculations are understandable. While Gaidar was in power, the United States and its allies promised a lot but delivered very little. President George H. W. Bush and his administration were slow to embrace Yeltsin, Gaidar, and those responsible for initiating economic reform in Russia. The lack of contact before the Soviet collapse meant that a strategy for economic aid to Russia was not outlined or aired until the process had already begun. Most amazingly, Gaidar was not consulted in any meaningful way before learning about American assistance plans.[3] In the heat of the 1992 presidential campaign, both President Bush and presidential candidate Bill Clinton pledged to deliver billions—$24 billion was the number cited by Bush in April 1992—to Russia. Yet the actual amount of aid delivered was a small fraction of these pledges delivered in an untimely fashion. By the time the International Monetary Fund (IMF) was ready to offer Russia a serious program (though still a small percentage of what was pledged) the reformers had already been ousted from power in Russia.[4]

Consistent with their realpolitik worldview, the Bush foreign policymakers did not define economic assistance to Russia as a top foreign policy objective, except for humanitarian assistance in the winter of 1991–92 to help stave off a potential crisis that might lead to massive unrest and instability. In fact, Treasury officials in the Bush administration were most focused on securing Russian commitments to pay back Soviet debts owed to the United States and much less enthusiastic about finding creative ways to assist Russia's unprecedented transition from communism to capitalism. Most critically, President Bush did not make the *political* decision to provide Russia with the short-term assistance needed to achieve stabilization. The Bush administration exacerbated the damage by raising expectations about what the United States was prepared to do for Russia. The $24 billion figure announced in April 1992 sounded like a tremendous amount of money to Russians. When they never saw any of the cash come their way, they became skeptical that the West was committed to helping Russian reform.

Wilsonians in the Clinton administration, and especially Lawrence Summers and David Lipton at the Department of Treasury, became much more involved in developing strategies of macroeconomic stabilization for Russia. Had they been in office in 1992, they would have been more energetic and sympathetic to the kind of effort that Baker aide Dennis Ross was urging his Treasury counterparts to pursue. Above all else, the Clinton team at the Treasury Department had a theory about how to transform communism into capitalism and a strategy for facilitating the process, complete with real tools and hard indicators of success. Their model and approach were controversial, but the very existence of debate about the program meant that a coherent set of ideas about economic reform could be identified (something lacking in the previous administration and missing in the debate about political reform). From this theory came concrete policy recommendations to their Russian counterparts about inflation rates, budget deficits, and currency exchange and policy innovations such as the new lending instrument for the IMF—the Systemic Transformation Fund (STF)—that allowed the Russian government to receive funds on more favorable terms than offered to other countries seeking loans from the IMF. Others in the Clinton administration, lacking alternative theories or game plans for facilitating reform, generally deferred to the Treasury Department's expertise.

For a time, the new, more aggressive, more engaged strategy seemed to achieve results. Although Gaidar's reformist team fell from power before Summers and Lipton assumed office, the American side seemed to be slowly educating new Russian prime minister Viktor Chernomyrdin about the benefits of low inflation and a stable currency, and to a lesser extent, smaller budget deficits. The IMF in turn signed Russia up to increasingly sophisticated and longer-term agreements, culminating in 1996 with a three-year Extended Fund Facility for $10.2 billion.

Over time, however, the eagerness to support Boris Yeltsin combined with the perceived costs of failure—economic chaos in a country with thousands of nuclear weapons—overrode sound lending practices. The invention of the Systemic Transformation Fund (STF) was an appropriate, creative response to a new challenge: lower the hurdle initially to help bring Russian reform along. In the early 1990s, Russia had no chance of meeting budget deficit caps of 5, let alone 3, percent. The IMF had to adopt a different strategy for achieving stabilization in Russia than it offered to Bolivia or Ghana. Yet once Russian officials became accustomed to special treatment, they began demanding more and more exemptions from IMF conditions. When these demands for special treatment did not produce sympathetic responses from midlevel IMF officials, Yeltsin and other Russian officials would call on their American counterparts to override the bureaucrats and release new money. If politicization of this kind of aid was needed in the early years of Russian reform, politicization in the later years undermined IMF leverage with Russia. In particular, the IMF continued to lend Russia money in 1996 and 1997, even though the Russian government grossly missed targets for budget deficits and other economic indicators negotiated in 1996. Since the big new package was issued in March 1996 during Yeltsin's election campaign, the IMF and Western governments suffered a huge loss of credibility. To cover growing budget deficits, the Russian government issued more and more government debt. Eventually in August 1998, the Russian government had to declare bankruptcy.

The IMF team (working closely with the U.S. Treasury Department) and its Russian counterparts agreed on some bad policy prescriptions during this period. Economists at the IMF and in the Russian government treated a stable ruble exchange rate as sacrosanct. Devaluation, many argued, would trigger hyperinflation again and undermine investor confidence. By 1998, however, the interest rates needed to prop up the ruble became impossible for the Russian government to sustain. The package of prescriptions offered by the IMF, including raising taxes as an alternative way to raise revenues and take pressure off the Russian short-term bond market (GKOs), may have worked over the long term but failed in a crisis. In retrospect, IMF pressure to liberalize Russia's markets also was premature, as the opening of the GKO market to foreigners attracted speculative money that Russia's market could not effectively absorb.

The years of soft conditions for Russia occurred well before the August 1998 meltdown in Russia. In hindsight, it is easy to see that the fragile framework for financial stabilization that allowed Russia to control inflation, steady the ruble exchange rate, and record its first year of growth in 1997 could not endure the Asian financial crisis and consequent fall in world oil prices. But besides a gradual devaluation that may or may not have worked, it is not easy to identify the different policies that could have been initiated by the Russian government and its Western supporters to avoid the August 1998 financial meltdown. In retrospect, devaluation was the logical policy prescription. And well before August 1998, Russian economist Andrei Illarionov had outlined powerful arguments for why a gradual devaluation would succeed. The closer one plays out this counterfactual to the real August 1998 meltdown, however, the more difficult it is to assert plausibly that a devaluation could have been initiated without a restructuring of the government debt.

In retrospect, it all seemed inevitable. Given what we know now, the decision by U.S. Treasury officials and their counterparts at the IMF, World Bank, and in Japan to announce a $22.8 bailout package for Russia, including a first payment of $4.8 billion in July 1998—one month before the crash—looks like a huge miscalculation.

Without knowing for sure what would happen in August 1998, however, a last-minute intervention in July was worth the risk of failure even if the prospects for success were less than 50 percent. The argument that Russia needed support as a strategic country, with thousands of nuclear weapons and the potential for ethnic conflict within its borders, was not unfounded before the events, and from an American standpoint, was always the most important interest. Economic meltdown can breed political instability, as was true in Argentina in 2001 or Russia in 1917. If $5 or $6 billion could have helped Russia avoid that type of calamity with its resulting effect on global stability and U.S. national security interests, it was in America's interests for the IMF to spend it. It was appropriate that even Deputy Secretary of the Treasury Lawrence Summers thought that Russian failure might have security consequences too horrible to contemplate.

Yet, despite the failure, none of the nightmarish scenarios that U.S. officials feared unfolded. Instead, the new government headed by Prime Minister Yevgeny Primakov adhered to basic market tenets and continued to cooperate with IMF and U.S. officials responsible for assisting economic policy in Russia. Though extremely painful to common Russian citizens, August 1998 was the "shock" that produced real results for the Russian economy, including the end of easy money from the government bond market, diminished rents for companies close to the state, and the stimulation of domestic production of real goods.[5] By the summer of 2002, living standards of Russians had returned to precrisis levels.[6]

The record of U.S. success in helping Russia achieve macroeconomic stabilization in the 1990s then is mixed.[7] At two critical moments, the fall of 1991 and the summer of 1998, American foreign policymakers mismanaged opportunities to make critical interventions in the Russian economy. The window for reform was not open long in 1991, and the Bush team's inaction was costly for reformers in Russia. The Clinton team tried to act in the summer of 1998, but it was too late.

Since 1998, Russian successes in achieving macroeconomic stability have been secured in large part without Western assistance, leading one to wonder if the United States would have been better off being out of the game altogether. It is difficult to know. The IMF funding did ease the economic effects of transition in the mid-1990s, which, in turn, probably contributed to the stability of the Russian government and the absence of wild political swings in the Kremlin during this crucial phase. IMF assistance also helped to keep reformers in power within the government, since senior Clinton and IMF officials often implied that the presence of like-minded officials in the Russian government was a precondition for aid. Would a poorer Russian government in the early 1990s with fewer reformers in office have been forced to undertake difficult fiscal reforms? Probably. Would this same government have survived the political backlash of trying to implement these reforms? It is difficult to say. Were the Americans wrong in trying to use multilateral financial assistance to nudge along needed economic reforms? Absolutely not. It is better to have tried and failed than not to have tried to do anything at all.

Whatever the role of capital infusion, U.S. officials did contribute to the transfer of ideas about macroeconomic stabilization. Several years after the collapse of the Soviet Union, some Russian "economists" still asserted that there was no relationship between the expansion of the money supply and inflation. Others, years into the postcommunist period, stressed that the government's first priority must be the stimulation of enterprise production even if the pursuit of this policy meant large government deficits. By contrast, it is striking today how much consensus exists among political and economic elites in Russia about basic macroeconomic principles. Of course, debates still continue (as they should), but the parameters of the debate have narrowed considerably. It would be a stretch for any U.S. Treasury official to claim that she or he taught the Russians macroeconomics 101, but the years of interaction with Western officials who preached these principles did have an important impact on Russian thinking, especially for those officials like Viktor Chernomyrdin and Yevgeny Primakov, who needed an introduction to market economics.

PRIVATIZATION AND OTHER MICROECONOMIC AND INSTITUTIONAL REFORMS. The IMF, supported and encouraged by the United States, spent the big money on aiding Russian economic reform. Although Fund leaders did extend the mandate in Russia beyond the traditional scope of IMF programs, the main focus of this assistance was still macroeconomic policy. On microeconomic issues or institutional reforms, such as enterprise restructuring or banking reform, other international organizations such as the World

Bank, the European Bank for Reconstruction and Development (EBRD), and the European Union's program for technical assistance to the Commonwealth of Independent States (TACIS) played a leading part.

In this realm of reform, direct bilateral assistance from the United States constituted only a small fraction of the total assistance coming from the West. It is true that this program has been comprehensive and diverse. As the following example of fiscal year 2001 funds illustrates, the American effort to assist in Russia's transformation touched on virtually every aspect of Russia's state and society (table 14-1).[8]

Discerning a direct causal impact of this relatively small amount of bilateral economic assistance is next to impossible, since it at best produced just a ripple in an ocean.

As discussed earlier, Americans had very little influence over the design and execution of Russia's two major privatization programs in the 1990s—the 1992–1994 voucher privatization program and the 1995 loans-for-shares program. The first resulted from a compromise between the Yeltsin government and the Russian parliament. Chubais and his allies initiated the second against the advice of their American counterparts.

The footprint of American influence is even harder to see on actual enterprise restructuring. Through the Russian Privatization Center, AID channeled multimillion dollar contracts to American consulting and accounting firms, whose assignment was to turn Soviet enterprises into American-style corporations. The project included only a handful of the 100,000 companies privatized in the 1990s, meaning that even under the best of circumstances, the impact on the Russian economy overall would have been through demonstration effects. To date, however, one cannot discuss demonstration effects systematically, since no one has assessed the results of these technical assistance efforts at the firm level.[9]

Like the American efforts on macroeconomic policy, therefore, it is difficult to identify direct U.S. interventions in the Russian privatization process that produced positive outcomes. Instead, the American contribution to privatization came mostly in the transfer of knowledge about market concepts into the Russian setting. When the Russian State Committee for Property (GKI) was first established with Anatoly Chubais as its head, only a handful of people in Russia could explain concepts like corporatization, the stock market, or a board of directors. By developing close professional relationships with their Russian counterparts, Americans working with the GKI facilitated the transfer of these ideas. Knowledge of these concepts had to come from the West, since such knowledge did not exist in Russia at the time. This form of technical assistance represented a quick and dynamic vehicle for the transfer of this knowledge. The large AID contractors responsible for facilitating postprivatization restructuring made a similar, indirect contribution to the creation of knowledge about markets in Russia. Even if none of these projects produced a profit-making privatized firm, they employed and trained hundreds of Russians in the ways of capitalism to facilitate their work.

The same is true for American contributions to other institutional or structural reforms. Perhaps one of the most successful Russian-American partnerships for facilitating intellectual transfer developed between the Russian Federal Commission on the Securities Market (FCSM) and its American supporters. The FCSM grew out of the State Property Committee (GKI), at which American and Russians had also worked closely together. Under the leadership of Dmitri Vasiliev, first as deputy chairman and then as chairman, the FCSM modeled itself after the American Securities and Exchange Commission (SEC), and not after other European models available. Like the American system, Vasiliev wanted the stock market, not banks, to play the leading role in providing capital to firms. The U.S. Agency for International Development funded consultants to help him design a government agency that might facilitate this kind of capitalism. At times, Vasiliev disagreed with recommendations, especially about the role of banks in the stock market.[10] But he also acknowledges that the creation of the FCSM—even with all its limitations—was greatly facilitated by American technical assistance.[11] An AID-funded project also helped to stimulate the formation of the National Association of Stock Market Participants (NAUFOR), an organization of brokerage firms designed to provide self-regulation of the Russian securities market.[12] As discussed earlier, AID grants to Russian think tanks also facilitated the transfer of knowledge from West to East about taxation that eventually contributed directly to the rewriting of Russia's tax code.[13] More generally at the level of the individual, be it at an AID-sponsored conference on microfinance lending in Nizhny Novgorod or in a microeconomics class at Montana State University attended by Russian exchange students, intellectual transfers are taking place all the time. Measuring their aggregate impact on economic reform in Russia, however, is next to impossible.

Despite years of discussion with their Russian counterparts, American officials at all levels have failed to stimulate banking reform in Russia. On this issue, the problem is no longer knowledge.[14] Rather, powerful financial actors in Russia continue to block serious reforms. Americans also have provided little intellectual assistance to spur welfare reform.[15] More generally, American technical assistance programs devoted too much time and energy to trying to transform Soviet-era enterprises into profit seekers. Instead, these assistance programs should have facilitated the emergence of new, start-up companies as well as the market-supporting institutions that might have stimulated the development of these new companies. Small business development programs

Table 14-1. Funds Budgeted for U.S. Government Assistance
to Russia, Fiscal Year 2001

Freedom Support Act (FSA) and other funds	Millions of dollars[a]
U.S. Agency for International Development (AID)/—	
Bureau for Europe and Eurasia	
Economic restructuring	8.95
Private-sector development	10.36
Environmental management	6.96
Democratic reform	16.10
Social sector reform	14.88
Cross-cutting/special initiatives	4.18
Eurasia Foundation	10.00
Enterprise funds	20.00
Total U.S. AID	91.42
Transfers to other agencies	
U.S. Department of Commerce—SABIT, BISNIS, BDC, CLDP[b]	4.36
U.S. Department of State—Europe/Eurasia (EUR/ACE)–	
humanitarian assistance	
Transportation costs and grants	7.49
Cargo value (Department of Defense excess and privately donated,	
not included in overall total below)	17.77
Total Coordinator's Office of Humanitarian Assistance	25.26
U.S. Department of State	
Bureau for International Narcotics and Law Enforcement—	
Anticrime training and technical assistance	3.04
Export control and related border security	3.50
Bureau of Educational and Cultural Affairs—Public Diplomacy Programs	30.71
Bureau of European Affairs—Public Diplomacy Programs	1.05
International Information Programs	0.20
Total U.S. Department of State	38.50
U.S. Department of Justice	0.90
Environmental Protection Agency	1.14
Civilian R and D Foundation	4.00
U.S. Nuclear Regulatory Commission	0.40
U.S. Department of Agriculture—ARS BW Redirection, Cochran	
Fellowship, Faculty Exchange Program	4.07

Table 14-1. Funds Budgeted for U.S. Government Assistance
to Russia, Fiscal Year 2001 (continued)

Freedom Support Act (FSA) and other funds	Millions of dollars[a]
U.S. Department of the Treasury—technical advisers	1.90
U.S. Department of Health and Human Services—BTEP[c]	5.25
Total transfers to other agencies	68.01
Total FY 2001 Freedom Support Act funds budget	159.43
Other agency funds	
U.S. Agency for International Development—child survival	3.54
U.S. Department of Defense	385.71
U.S. Department of Agriculture—food assistance	60.48
U.S. Department of Energy	335.54
U.S. Department of State	
International Military Exchanges and Training	0.16
NADR/ Export Control and Related Border Security[d]	1.50
NADR/science centers[d]	23.00
Nonproliferation/disarmament	
Warsaw Initiative/foreign military financing	
ECA Bureau – Public Diplomacy Programs (ECE account)[e]	13.86
International Information Programs (ECE account)[e]	0.14
Bureau of Population, Refugees, and Migration	11.63
Total U.S. Department of State	50.29
Library of Congress—Open World Program	10.00
U.S. Department of Transportation	0.65
U.S. Fish and Wildlife Service	0.30
U.S. Department of Education—Fulbright-Hays Exchange Programs	0.54
Peace Corps	3.50
Total FY 2001 agency funds budgeted	850.55
Total FY 2001 U.S. government (FSA + other agencies) funds budgeted	1,009.97

Source: Office of the Coordinator of U.S. Assistance to Europe and Eurasia, *U.S. Government Assistance to and Cooperative Activities with Eurasia, FY 2001 Annual Report* (Department of State, 2002) (www.state.gov/p/eur/ace [July 2003]).

a. Rounded to the nearest $10, 000 as of December 31, 2001.

b. Special American Business Internship Program; Business Information Services for the Newly Independent States; Business Development Council; Commercial Law Development Program.

c. Biotechnology Engagement Program.

d. Nonproliferation, antiterrorism, demining, and related programs.

e. Economic Commission for Europe.

and enterprise funds were part of the overall American aid package to Russia. Earlier in the 1990s, however, the balance of support between postprivatization restructuring programs (which were executed by very expensive American accounting and consulting firms) and new business development was lopsided in favor of the former.[16] Nor, of course, did the United States ever provide direct financial assistance to alleviate the suffering of Russia's poor.[17] This was a big mistake. To be sure, there are huge political obstacles to setting up a program for the poor in Russia given the needs of the poor at home. But it takes much less money to help the poor abroad, and even a token U.S. program administered directly by American government organizations aimed at assisting Russia's most needy would have done wonders to change Russian attitudes about Western aid. Equally important, a program designed to separate the welfare and production functions of Soviet-era enterprises would have assisted the real restructuring of these companies. Without this separation, real labor markets have been slow to emerge.

By the end of the 1990s, many critics charged that American policymakers focused too little on helping to develop the institutions that make markets work.[18] Instead, so the argument went, U.S. officials spent too much time and energy supporting individuals in the Russian government whom they crowned as reformers.[19] While recognizing the serious failures of institutional reform just described, we nonetheless disagree with this more sweeping condemnation of the American strategy for promoting economic reform. If market-supporting institutions do not exist, then they can only be created by individuals committed to fostering their emergence. If institutional reform is needed, it will not be generated by giving assistance to those firmly ensconced in the lingering institutions from the command economy. Reformers are the ones who reform. Especially in a country like Russia at the beginning of the 1990s where old institutions had to be destroyed to create space for new institutions, individuals armed with ideas and leadership skills were the agents of change.

At the same time, outsiders cannot want change more than their counterparts in Russia. Even when U.S. officials found kindred spirits inside Russia, they were often in the minority or surrounded by bureaucracies with other agendas. Throughout the 1990s, the lack of consensus in Russia about the trajectory of economic reform was the real impediment to the consolidation of market-supporting institutions.

TRADE AND INVESTMENT. Starting with the first meeting between presidents Yeltsin and Clinton in April 1993, the promotion of trade and investment has been a staple of all American policy statements about Russia. Clinton and George W. Bush both argued that American foreign investment in Russia, as well as trade between the United States and Russia, was the best mechanism for aiding the development of capitalism in Russia. Their counterparts in the

Kremlin have agreed. It is much easier, after all, to promote trade than it is to accept or provide aid. In Washington, these rhetorical pledges were followed by organizational innovations implemented to help stimulate trade and investment. Most significantly, American and Russian officials established bilateral councils—the Gore-Chernomyrdin Commission in the mid-1990s and the business-to-business commissions established by Bush and Putin—to foster such economic activity.

Like efforts to promote stabilization, privatization, and other market-supporting institutions, the record of success on trade and investment has been mixed. Foreign direct investment (FDI) in Russia is still minuscule. The cumulative figure for the first decade of independence was $18.2 billion, compared with China's $46 billion in 2000 alone. A significant proportion, roughly $7–8 billion dollars, of this foreign direct investment came from the United States, but this figure is still smaller than German investment in Russia.[20] Per capita FDI for Russia is also extremely low ($15) compared with Poland ($84) let alone Hungary ($221).[21] Trade between the United States and Russia is also small and still hampered by barriers left over from the cold war, such as a draconian visa regime, controls on technology transfers, and the Jackson-Vanik Amendment to the 1974 Trade Act linking Russia's trade status to Jewish emigration.[22] Only a decade after the beginning of market reform in Russia did the U.S. Department of Commerce finally declare Russia a market economy. And even if money were truly fungible (and it often was not), it is still diplomatically unhelpful to classify billions of dollars in loan guarantees or even millions in feasibility studies for American firms as "aid to Russia," especially when the Russian people endured one of the most severe economic depressions in modern history.

If the record of achievement in promoting trade and investment is still spotty, the trajectory for the future does look more promising. The Russian economy is finally growing at a steady pace, which in turn has attracted new American portfolio and direct investment. Since the August 1998 crash, the Russian government has managed to pay its debts, refrain from taking new loans from the IMF, balance the budget, and institute some important reforms on tax policy and the rule of law. In 2000, 2001, and 2002 foreign direct investment—including American investment—increased dramatically, prompting some to predict that the number will double by 2005.[23] Portfolio investment and repatriation of Russian capital also spiked in this period.

The American Role in Promoting Democracy in Russia

It is still too early to declare that democratic institutions will permanently replace the old order. In his first term in office, President Putin has done much to undermine Russia's already fragile democratic practices.[24] Nonetheless, it is not too early to say that the autocratic institutions of the Soviet *ancien régime* have collapsed. That every major political leader in postcommunist Russia has come to power through the ballot box is a real accomplishment for a country rich in centuries of autocratic rule. That the constitution adopted in 1993 has remained the highest law in the land is also a good sign. In addition, most polls conducted in Russia in the past five years show that a solid majority of Russian citizens supports democratic ideas and practices.[25]

The American role in facilitating this outcome of partial democracy in Russia is even more difficult to measure than American efforts to promote market institutions, in part because this policy objective received continued rhetorical affirmation but was supported by very few diplomatic initiatives, financial resources, and concrete ideas. Different from the promotion of market reform, American policymakers have underdeveloped theories about how the transition from dictatorship to democracy takes place and a shallow toolbox for promoting such transitions. Without qualification, all three post–cold war American presidents have pledged rhetorically their commitment to facilitating the emergence of democracy in the Soviet Union and Russia. How democracy promotion is defined and how much attention and resources are given to the problem has varied considerably.

President George H. W. Bush embraced a very cautious approach to democracy promotion. He pledged his desire to see the Soviet Union and then Russia governed by a democratic political system but saw little that the United States could do to facilitate this outcome. During the last part of the Soviet era, when many in the Soviet Union believed independence was the first step toward democratization, Bush's policies actually served to impede liberalization. He did not encourage the breakup of the Soviet Union. He did little to reach out to leaders of the anti-Soviet opposition. Instead, he steadfastly supported Mikhail Gorbachev, General Secretary of the Communist Party of the Soviet Union. In 1991, Gorbachev was still the *unelected* leader of the USSR, whereas most leaders of the democratic opposition, including Boris Yeltsin in Russia, had already secured electoral mandates more than once.

The first Bush administration was not unified in its policy toward democracy in Russia in the latter half of 1991, a split that suggests a different policy could have been adopted. Those in the Central Intelligence Agency (CIA) who saw Yeltsin as a prodemocratic force were urging the administration to reach out more vigorously to the Yeltsin team. And the muscular regime transformers at the Pentagon, like Paul Wolfowitz and his staff, were actively supporting Soviet breakup, particularly through their support of Ukrainian independence.

Would a more aggressive policy of encouraging democratization undertaken by the White House have served American interests or helped Russia's democratic consolidation in 1991–92? If Bush could have developed earlier a direct relationship with Yeltsin, would this relationship have helped the transition from communism? Hypothetically, one can wonder if Bush could have persuaded Gorbachev to get rid of the nasty characters in his government who carried out military operations in Latvia and Lithuania in January 1991. If they would have been removed from government in January 1991, then perhaps the coup attempt in August 1991 would not have occurred. Yet had the coup not been attempted and failed so miserably, the Soviet Union might not have collapsed. In the first months of Russia's independence, many believed that Yeltsin should have initiated a series of political reforms that could have important path-dependent consequences for the future consolidation of Russian democracy. Hypothetically, one could imagine that Bush personally could have encouraged Yeltsin to undertake these reforms. In reality, however, both Bush and Yeltsin were focused on so many other issues of seemingly greater priority—such as the peaceful dissolution of the Soviet empire and the control of the strategic nuclear weapons scattered among four newly independent states—that conversations about founding elections and new constitutions seemed premature.

The Clinton team came into office determined to make promoting democracy a bigger part of American foreign policy. They embraced the "democratic peace" dictum that democracies do not go to war with one another. Promoting democracy in a strategic country like Russia, therefore, was in the U.S. national interest. Yet, even when the more Wilsonian Clinton administration was in office, a truism of American foreign policy generally held: when the choice had to be made whether to push democracy over some other traditional security issue in U.S.-Russia relations, security—traditionally defined—always took precedence.[26] As *Washington Post* editorial page editor Fred Hiatt noted, "Clinton cared about democracy in Russia, but other issues—serious, legitimate issues—always seemed to carry greater weight: persuading Russia to remove its troops from the newly independent Baltic states, helping ease nuclear weapons out of Ukraine, winning Russian cooperation in Bosnia or Kosovo or NATO."[27]

Because Clinton saw Yeltsin's hold on power as a necessary condition for market and democratic reforms in Russia, the American president was willing to give his Russian counterpart the benefit of the doubt when Yeltsin seemed to be undermining democracy. Clinton and his team failed to condemn Yeltsin's antidemocratic acts, such as his attack on the parliament in October 1993 and his two invasions of Chechnya in 1994 and again in 1999. During the 1996 Russian presidential election when Yeltsin was flirting with the idea of canceling the vote, Clinton did urge his Russian counterpart to stay the course of electoral democracy. This signal from Washington—different from the signals sent just a few years earlier during the October 1993 showdown or after the 1994 invasion of Chechnya—must have played a role in Yeltsin's calculations, though to what extent we do not know. In response to each of these democratic crises in Russia, Clinton and his team never had good policy options. By the time Clinton became president in January 1993, Yeltsin was already battling the Russian Congress just to stay in office. Throughout 1993, the pace of constitutional reform by the Russian parliament did not serve democratization, and this was a constitution first drafted under General Secretary Leonid Brezhnev. An American policy that supported the actions of Russia's Congress would have been no more democratic than a policy that unequivocally supported Yeltsin as the embodiment of Russian democracy. Between Congress and Yeltsin, Yeltsin had the better credentials as a reformer and as a friend of American interests.

American responses to the first Chechen invasion lacked moral clarity in the Clinton administration, and human rights abuses were ignored to an even greater extent in the Bush administration, particularly after September 11. But again, there was little the United States could do to affect events on the ground. Everyone in the Clinton administration and the entire international community—including most in the Muslim world—recognized Russian sovereignty over the Chechen republic. Particularly after the Chechen rebel invasion of Dagestan in 1999, these same international observers believed that Russia had a right to ensure not only that Chechnya remained part of the Russian Federation but that Russia could defend its territory. At the same time, Clinton could have expressed more outrage at the conduct of the wars and emphasized that members in the club of democratic states do not carry out such campaigns in total disregard for human rights. After all, Clinton knew how much Yeltsin valued this membership, as was evidenced by the impact of the upcoming 1999 Cologne G-8 summit on Russian behavior toward Kosovo in the weeks just before the gathering.

In any of these most extreme cases of democratic backsliding by Yeltsin, would a more passionate denunciation by Clinton have made a difference? Would economic sanctions against Russia for the Chechen invasions have altered the course of the wars? Probably not. U.S. foreign policymakers, when trying to prevent or stop negative internal developments through sanctions, have little leverage in a country as large and complex as Russia.

Nonetheless, words do matter. It is naïve to believe that the United States could have prevented the bombardment of parliament in October 1993 or the invasion of Chechnya in 1994, but American impotence is no excuse for the abandonment of U.S. ideals. Especially for the Wilsonians in the Clinton administration, their failure to at least preserve rhetorical consistency about the importance of democratization undermined their moral authority, especially among the democratic activists in Russia. As Talbott concedes in his memoirs, "We should have focused earlier, more critically and more consistently on the damage that the Russian rampage was inflicting on innocent civilians, and on the damage Russia was doing to its chances of democratization and development as a civil society."[28]

President George W. Bush has followed a policy of indifference about the Kremlin's antidemocratic policies, which have expanded dramatically since Vladimir Putin became acting president and then president in the months following Yeltsin's resignation on December 31, 1999. After September 11, 2001, and the elevation of Putin as trusted friend and ally in the war against terrorism, Bush became even more reluctant to discuss Russian political reform. Bush's silence in turn has weakened democratic forces in Russia.

At the May 2002 Moscow summit, Bush and his team trumpeted that the cold war agenda was finished. Although the cold war had ended a decade earlier, many lingering cold war legacies like U.S.-Russian arms control were finally now a thing of the past. Yet some internal issues that had been of concern during the cold war, including the promotion of human rights and democratic practices in Russia, should have remained on the agenda. As Putin continued his crackdown on freedom at home, Bush should not have remained indifferent. The Wilsonian ideals that Bush embraced in dealing with other parts of the world should have entered his Russia policy. Condemnation of Russia's antidemocratic policies would not have ended the war in Chechnya or restored pluralism on Russia's television airwaves. However, American words in support of democracy would make Bush's grand strategy for foreign policy sound more consistent. More important, a Bush stance on Russian democratic backsliding would embolden those reformers in Russia still fighting for democracy. Over the long run, strengthening these forces will help to democratize Russia.

THE GRASS-ROOTS EXPORT OF DEMOCRATIC IDEAS. Presidential summits are not the only means available for promoting democratization. Throughout the 1990s, the United States has funded hundreds of other programs in the name of promoting democracy. Through exchanges, technical assistance, and financial aid, U.S. programs have facilitated the transfer of democratic ideas into Russia. Given the limited funds for these programs, tracing the flow of these democratic norms from the United States to Russia is even more difficult than following the transfer of ideas about capitalism. For most of the 1990s, economic assistance and denuclearization programs received the lion's share of U.S. assistance budgets. This imbalance was a mistake. The lesson of the 1990s in Russia is that democracy and market promotion assistance must be coordinated and given equal attention. The data on the positive correlation between democracy and economic development in the postcommmunist world are now overwhelming.[29] Aid to stimulate market reforms without accompanying resources to foster democratic development is simply money wasted.

To its credit, AID changed the balance over time between economic and democracy assistance. As budgets declined, AID leaders allowed the economic assistance programs to decline at a faster rate than the democratization programs. The agency also moved more and more money away from the state and into programs that engaged Russian society directly. Over the years, AID also earmarked a greater percentage of resources to those programs outside of Moscow.

It is difficult to claim the direct causal impact of democratic ideas from the outside when the practice of democracy inside Russia is so deeply flawed. Nonetheless, as already mentioned, survey data suggest that Russians have embraced philosophically democratic ideals, even if they are dissatisfied with the practice of democracy in Russia.[30] Although Russian democratic institutions still do not meet the standards of liberal democracies in the West, they are much more democratic today than they were two decades ago (even if they are less democratic than they were a few years ago). In the margins, American influences have helped to contribute to these achievements.

Much of the work done in this sphere came not from the top levels of the U.S. government but from American nongovernmental organizations. At crucial moments in the construction of Russian political institutions—be it the drafting of the constitution, the crafting of parliamentary electoral laws, or the introduction of jury trials into the Russian legal system—American agents provided their Russian counterparts with valuable knowledge about models and experiences in other countries, including of course the United States. More abstractly, all of the institutions of democracy came to Russia from the West. After seventy years of Soviet communism, the ideas of competitive elections, a multiparty system, or civil society had to be imported into Russia.

But while American NGOs may have been helpful in *designing* institutions associated with democratic states, to date they have done little to affect how these institutions *function*. Formally, Russian political rules resemble democratic institutions, but informally, nondemocratic procedures still permeate Russian politics. For instance, elections in Russia occur and do have consequences, but they are not free and fair. U.S. programs to promote the rule of law by working with Russian state agencies have demonstrated little tangible success in making the legal system function better. Finally, ideas about checks and balances and the importance of the separation of powers have been pumped into Russia through a myriad of channels, but the executive at both the national and local level still dominates.

Overestimating American Power in Internal Russian Affairs

The outcome of Russia's revolution so far has been mixed but not disastrous. A decade ago, few predicted that Russia's reformers would be successful in implementing their agenda of *triple* transformation—decolonization, marke-tization, and democratization. A decade later, one has to be impressed with the scale of change already achieved. The Soviet empire is gone and will never be reconstituted. Belarus may join Russia again, but the coercive subjugation of states and people adjacent to Russia's borders seems unlikely. Russian decolonization was remarkably peaceful when compared to the collapse of other empires. Those who believe this transition was inevitable forget how many observers were predicting that the independence of the new states would not last, and that Russia would make every effort to reacquire those lands closest to the Russian Federation on which lived 25 million of its ethnic brethren.[31]

Recognition of the limits of American power in this transformation means that the United States was not responsible for all of Russia's scars. But this recognition of marginality also means that the United States cannot take as much credit for the successes as it would like, even if those successes also hap-pen to be some of the stated goals of U.S. foreign policy. In retrospect, there is no basis for commentators or columnists to blame the Clinton administration for Russian lawlessness, economic depression, or the Chechen war. There is equally no basis, however, when *Time* magazine devotes its cover to celebrating how three U.S. campaign consultants orchestrated Yeltsin's 1996 re-election comeback.[32] At the end of the day when we can finally determine whether Russia's revolution has succeeded or failed, it will be Russians who should be blamed or praised, not Americans.

Does this assessment suggest that it was wrong for U.S. foreign policy offi-cials to try to influence the course of change inside the Soviet Union and Russia in both the political and economic spheres? No. Although we recognize the limits to America's capacity to influence internal developments in a place like Russia, and our limits in assessing these efforts, we also believe that it was in the American national interest to try to push Russia's revolution in a prodemocratic, promarket, and pro-Western direction. In some areas like the promotion of small business development or civil society at the grass-roots level, American leaders should have done more and tried harder. Perhaps the greatest sin of the decade was to fuel expectations in Russia about the size and impact of American economic assistance. U.S. officials, especially early in the 1990s, promised far more than they were prepared to deliver. And as Anthony Lake wrote in 1984, "By promising less, Washington can accomplish more. U.S. influence is diminished only when results fall short of rhetoric."[33]

We will never know for certain if a U.S. push for new elections in the fall of 1991 or a stabilization fund for the Russian ruble in 1992 would have made a fundamental difference in Russia's political and economic transformation. Yet we do know that the United States has benefited tremendously from regime change in Russia, which has in turn enabled Russia's pursuit of integration into the West. Above all else, the specter of nuclear war no longer haunts the American people. Economist Anders Åslund has calculated the American peace dividend resulting from the cold war's end at more than $1.3 trillion.[34] American armed forces also are not engaged in a constant battle to contain communism. Instead of fighting or funding proxy wars in Vietnam and Angola, U.S. and Russian troops have served side-by-side in Bosnia and Kosovo. In part as a consequence of these internal changes, Russia is not pursuing messianic, imperial foreign policies abroad as the Soviet Union once did. Even a weak Russia ruled by a communist, fascist, or imperialist could wreak havoc in the region and threaten U.S. security interests. Imagine the complications of executing the war with Iraq if Saddam Hussein had enjoyed military and technical support from a friendly dictator in the Kremlin. A policy aimed at promoting regime change in Russia, therefore, served U.S. security interests.

Contrary to other analysts who deride the U.S. assistance strategies of the 1990s, we also believe that American assistance efforts did not harm the consolidation of democratic and market institutions in Russia. Nor did these efforts, contrary to conventional wisdom, fundamentally damage the bilateral relationship during this period. The United States was right to try to assist domestic transformation in Russia, but U.S. officials should have done more, promised less, and realized humbly that even their best efforts would not lead to immediate or easily measurable payoffs.

Courting a Security Partner

As with policies on the domestic side, U.S. actions on issues like arms control, NATO enlargement, and the war on Kosovo demonstrate well the mix of power and ideology in explaining policies undertaken by different administrations and why those policy choices would have been made differently had different administrations been in office or different individuals in the various administrations been in charge of the policy.

The first Bush administration, and the Clinton administration even more actively, promoted Russia's integration into the West. Given lingering concerns about Soviet legacies in 1992, Bush the power balancer did not embrace Yeltsin as closely as Yeltsin wanted him to. Bush still worried about a return of bipolar rivalry. At their summit at Camp David in early 1992, Yeltsin was rebuffed in his effort to gain a public declaration from the Americans that the two countries were now allies. As realists, Bush and Baker concentrated on cooperation on strategic nuclear forces and ensuring that a START II Treaty was signed before the administration left office; the Bush team also initiated discussions on cooperation on missile defense, designed to overcome the restraints imposed by the ABM Treaty.

The range of activities related to Russian cooperation with the West visibly increased in the early Clinton years, and their nature reflected the new emphasis on the link between internal transformation and external integration. In some cases, the Clinton administration was resolving issues left over by the previous administration (for example, the withdrawal of Russian troops from the Baltics or ensuring the removal of strategic nuclear weapons from the non-Russian republics), but the way in which those were solved had changed. Even in one of the biggest foreign policy failures of the decade toward Russia (a failure that continued under George W. Bush)—namely, U.S. efforts to stop Russian assistance to the Iranian nuclear weapons program—the Clinton approach remained consistent with that used in a wide variety of areas: offer economic incentives and prospects for joining major Western clubs in exchange for a change in Russian behavior consonant with American policy initiatives. The United States built housing for Russian officers in exchange for Russian withdrawal from the Baltics, promoted space cooperation in exchange for the halt to assisting India's rocket program, and worked to get Russia included as a member of the Group of Eight (G-8) in exchange for the toning down of Russia's rhetoric against NATO enlargement.

But as the decade wore on, the two most significant American policies in Europe involving other U.S. interests—NATO enlargement and the war on Kosovo—highlighted the gaps that remained between U.S. and Russian visions of the world as well as the increasing capacity of the United States to take action regardless of Russian objections. Yet even in these two cases, President Clinton emphasized the need to bring Russia into the game rather than exclude it. The United States had the power to act alone, but Clinton nonetheless decided to act in cooperation with Russia.

European Security

The United States pushed for NATO enlargement and the war on Kosovo because it could and because it had interests in Europe other than Russia's integration. But the primary strategic objective in dealing with Russia and NATO enlargement reflected Clinton's Wilsonian worldview: try to include Russia whenever possible and try to calibrate the timing of expansion so as not to hurt Russian reform (as he defined it). Clinton was sensitive to Yeltsin's electoral concerns; he was keen to ensure that the major Paris signing ceremony on a NATO-Russia accord took place before the new members were invited to join in 1997; and he made sure to promote Russian membership in the G-8 and other international bodies to soften the blow.

Just as one cannot easily measure the positive impact of U.S. efforts on assistance, it is hard to measure the negative impact of NATO enlargement for U.S.-Russian relations on other security concerns. NATO enlargement delayed the Russian Duma's ratification of START II. But did NATO expansion help to foster continued Russian assistance to the Iranian nuclear program? There were domestic interests on the Russian side that were looking to scuttle the START process or to gain financially from the relationship with Iran regardless of what was happening with NATO. But it is true that the cooperative pattern of problem solving on issues like Baltic troop withdrawal and the India rocket deal established in 1993–94 were not repeated after the NATO enlargement process began to move forward for subjects like Iran or START on which the United States needed Russian cooperation.

Similarly on Kosovo, the United States and its allies bombed Serbia despite Russia's vociferous objection. Still, the United States did try to get Russia into the game, and the final diplomacy was worked out by Talbott, Finnish president Martti Ahtisaari, and Russian prime minister Viktor Chernomyrdin. Yeltsin blustered about World War III, but Russia eventually did play a key role in the diplomacy. The dash to Pristina, however, led to fears that retrograde elements in the Russian military were uncontrolled by Yeltsin's civilian authority.

The pro-American lobby in Russia, including Yeltsin, often felt cheated by their American partners. Disappointed expectations—expectations that look unrealistic in retrospect—eventually produced disillusion and even suspicion in both countries about the intentions of the former adversary. American assistance was never as large or as useful as promised. The first wave of NATO enlargement would likely not have had a major impact on its own, but when it was followed by the NATO military campaign against Serbia, Russian foreign policymakers developed serious doubts about the true American intentions in Europe. At the nadir of U.S.-Russian relations in the wake of Kosovo in the spring of 1999, even pro-Western liberals in Russia questioned whether the United States was more concerned with the development of democracy and capitalism in Russia, or with the expansion of American influence in eastern Europe. In polls conducted in December 1999, 55 percent of respondents believed that the United States represented a threat to Russian security.[35] At the end of the 1990s, the goal of Russian integration into the West seemed to have been overshadowed and derailed by other American security objectives in Europe.

Arms Control

Generally, the first post-Soviet decade was marked by missed opportunities. The greatest successes—the signing of START II and the removal of nuclear weapons from Belarus, Kazakhstan, and Ukraine—occurred early. The latter was a major and underappreciated achievement. Nearly a decade passed before START II was ratified by the Russian parliament. The United States should be thankful that a few visionaries—Senator Sam Nunn and Senator Richard Lugar and Secretary of Defense William Perry—understood the need to apply American energy and resources to nuclear dismantlement; otherwise even this program might have been in doubt. But the record of success on this front is mixed and incomplete. More than a decade after the end of the cold war, thousands of American and Russian nuclear warheads remain, and many Russian facilities are dangerously insecure.

In certain respects, George W. Bush's unilateral approach to arms reductions that was most clearly expressed during the 2000 campaign had great appeal. To be sure, there are costs incurred by a unilateral approach, since without a treaty, the United States does not get the verification provisions that allow it to ensure that reductions are carried out. But conceptually, one part of the approach makes sense: the United States could consider its minimal deterrent needs and then eliminate the excess, regardless of what others do. The approach also implied that the United States considered Russia a changed regime with different intentions than its Soviet predecessor. More significant reductions should have and could have occurred. What was disappointing in the Bush approach was the failure to match the reality with the vision of truly lower numbers. The 2002 Treaty of Moscow did presumably end the cold war arms control process begun in 1972. But it did little to rid us of the cold war legacy of oversized nuclear arsenals. The cuts proposed by the treaty simply refer to nuclear warheads operationally deployed. The United States will continue to possess stocks far exceeding any purpose for which they would be needed.[36] Countries opposed to U.S. interests are either rational and will be deterred by a much smaller American nuclear force (would not 1,000 nuclear warheads be more than sufficient to deter any adversary?) or they are not rational, in which case possessing overkill is irrelevant. The main threat to U.S. interests in an age of American hegemony is the proliferation of weapons of mass destruction, including the growth of total numbers of weapons held by other countries as well as the acquisition of such weapons by new states and nonstate actors. A credible policy seeking to reduce the prospects for nuclear developments worldwide will begin at home. After all, if we say we might need thousands for certain contingencies, why should the Chinese and Indians not say the same?

On the other side of the strategic equation, George W. Bush and National Security Adviser Condoleezza Rice could rightly argue that if the United States needed a missile defense against limited nuclear strikes from a rogue state, it should not be hindered by a treaty signed in 1972 with the USSR. Differences across administrations clearly shaped the development of American attitudes toward missile defense and the ABM Treaty during the past decade. The Clinton administration dropped the discussions led by Baker aide Dennis Ross and Russian deputy foreign minister Georgy Mamedov on national missile defense given its lack of interest, the shift in focus to theater defenses, and a firm belief in the importance of treaties like ABM. It is difficult to imagine that a Gore administration would have withdrawn from the ABM accord as the second Bush administration did. The Bush administration showed that given the disparities in power between the two countries, it could withdraw from the treaty regardless of Russian concerns. Even so, Bush made sure to provide a consistent and transparent message to Putin to limit the diplomatic damage. The Clinton administration had similarly proved that it could pursue NATO enlargement because Russia was powerless to stop it, and it seemed to offer enough to Yeltsin to smooth over the problems that arose. What happens, however, when the United States needs the Russian elite's support on a different issue and the residue of Washington's disregard of Russian sensibilities on arms control or other issues hinders progress? Many argued this residue was a serious impediment to U.S. efforts in spring 2003 to convince Russia to support the American position on Iraq.

Post–September 11

The focus on the common threat posed by terrorism helped bring Bush and Putin closer together after September 11. In the first months after the terrorist attacks, Bush managed the personal relationship with Putin in a way that resulted in diplomatic triumphs. In the first year after September 11, the atmosphere of U.S.-Russian relations was much more positive than it was in the spring of 1999 despite the U.S. withdrawal from the ABM Treaty, NATO's 2002 invitation to the Baltic countries to join NATO, and the establishment of U.S. bases in central Asia. Russian integration into the West seemed back on track.

With perspective, however, the spring of 1999 may look like an overly negative aberration, and the euphoria surrounding U.S.-Russian relations and the close personal ties between Putin and Bush immediately after September 11 might look like an overly exuberant moment that cannot be sustained by the long-term factors and dynamics that shape Russian-American relations. During the period since August 1991, long-term continuities in the security arena across administrations are rather striking despite all the differences in approach. George W. Bush achieved a treaty in 2002 on offensive arms control, but the general parameters are what the Clinton team had proposed for START III. Similarly, the G-8 efforts in 2002 to highlight Russian participation follow from the previous administration, as does NATO's "new" relationship with Russia, embodied in a NATO-Russia Council that follows clearly from the earlier Permanent Joint Council of 1997. At the same time, American and Russian officials—be they employees of Clinton, Yeltsin, Bush, or Putin—have continued to disagree about Iran and Iraq. And yet, Russia continues to seek integration with the West, and the United States continues to assist this process. Even at the height of his dissatisfaction with the American war against Iraq, Putin emphasized, "The partnership character of

[our] relations with America will gives [sic] us a basis for continuing our open dialogue."[37]

Russia's Status and American Intentions

In foreign affairs, the main story of the 1990s was the breathtaking speed with which Russia declined as a major power. Once this was finally understood, Russia policy became a secondary concern for many U.S. officials. But this tremendous drop of Russia's international power was not fully appreciated by American officials in real time. Perceptions of Russian power changed more slowly than the velocity of Russian decline. Lingering legacies from the cold war created this distortion.

Making adjustments to a new world in which Russia was marginal to international affairs took time. Lag times are not unusual in history.[38] Moreover, some critical bureaucracies such as the Pentagon and the Central Intelligence Agency had real incentives to remain sensitive to the potential for renewed rivalry with Russia. Many outside pundits, as well as security experts in Russia and the United States, were even slower than government officials to realize that Russia had declined so dramatically and quickly. For instance, critics of administration policy thought Russia was too important to treat badly (for example, by enlarging NATO), and so U.S. policy toward other areas was judged more harshly than often warranted because of a lingering belief that Russia was still a major global power and should not be disrespected. Others argued that U.S. policy toward Russia was failing precisely because the United States did not recognize Russia's great power status. Not surprisingly, Russian officials had an interest in inflating Russia's power and international importance. Boris Yeltsin proved especially adept at selling his Western counterparts on the notion of Russia's great power status.

Ironically, given the criticism, both George H. W. Bush and Bill Clinton appeared to recognize—at least rhetorically—Russia as a great power. For Bush, after all, the Soviet Union had been America's focus of attention, so it was natural for him to treat Russia as if it mattered in world affairs. Clinton pushed his colleagues in the G-7 to accord Russia a special status in this elite economic club even though Russia's GDP was less than that of Portugal because he believed that treating Russia as a great power was the key to gaining Russian acceptance of U.S. policies in other areas.

The belief that Russia was still of special importance in world affairs compelled Western leaders to write special rules for Russia's relations with international institutions, especially, as we have seen, with the IMF. This special great power status accorded to Russia was largely unnecessary to the pursuit of U.S. national security interests. In three critical tests—NATO enlargement, the NATO war over Kosovo, and the American-led war against Iraq—Russia demonstrated that it did not have the power to derail American policies. This circumstance was a radical change from the cold war era. In the run-up to all of these events, U.S. policymakers devoted tremendous time and energy to trying to cooperate with Russia. The major achievement from this strategy of accommodation and cooperation was that Russia did not play a significant spoiler role.

In some areas, the prolonged treatment of Russia as a great power had negative consequences for Russia. The Russia-IMF relationship suffered because of treating Russia as a country with special status. The IMF's Russia team officials lost their credibility before their Russian counterparts when they were trumped by "political considerations," that is, a phone call between Boris and Bill or even a discussion between the leadership of the IMF and the Russian government. From this experience, Russian leaders learned a bad lesson about the malleability of international rules and membership criteria. In Russia today, a freewheeling discussion about how Russia will join NATO and the European Union as soon as these two clubs change their rules to accommodate Russia is illustrative of this bad lesson learned. The offer of a military role for Russia in Kosovo—in deference to its supposed great power status—initially had disastrous consequences that almost produced the first military combat between NATO and Russian troops. American officials also pushed the agenda of democratization with less vigor because they did not want to antagonize this "great" power.

More generally, Western pretending about Russia gave Yeltsin a false sense of his country's place in the world. Though difficult to document, this inflated posture had to contribute to Yeltsin's inability to assess the depth of the crisis in Russia as well as exacerbate his proclivity for bluster in foreign affairs when he believed that Russia was not getting its due. Strikingly, Putin became president of Russia with a much more accurate assessment of Russia's domestic challenges and a more realistic foreign policy. As he stated bluntly in his first address to the nation as acting president on January 1, 2000, "To reach the production level of Portugal and Spain, two countries that are not known as leaders of the world economy, it will take Russia approximately fifteen years if the GDP grows by at least 8 percent a year."[39] Yeltsin never made such an assessment of Russia's place in the world, and his counterparts in Washington did little to compel the first Russian president to understand Russia's real status.

Toward the end of the 1990s, some both inside and outside of government began to argue that American foreign policy would be best served by not treating Russia as an important international actor. Since Russia had been on the "wrong side" of many issues of importance to U.S. policymakers (Kosovo, Iraq, Iran) and had little power to affect these issues anyway, positively or negatively, the policy recommendation was to give Russia much less attention. These voices argued that Russian weakness—that is, its inability to protect its nuclear stockpile or incapacity to secure its borders from Islamic terrorists—was the real problem facing U.S. policymakers.[40]

Of course Russia today is much weaker, militarily, and economically, than the Soviet Union was two decades ago. Even if Russia wanted to underwrite anti-American movements in third countries or construct anti-NATO alliances, it has limited means to do so. Russia's weakness—not its strength—is now the cause of concern when it comes to nuclear weapons. And treating Russia as something it was not did not in the end do Yeltsin any favors. Yet, while a policy that focused less on inflating Russia's sense as a great power could have been pursued, ignoring Russia and its internal transformation would not have served U.S. interests. Russian behavior in the arena of foreign policy, driven by internal reforms, has changed even more substantially than Russian capabilities. If Russia resumed a hostile stance toward the West in the future, its resources, geographic location, advanced military technology, and vast arsenal of nuclear weapons would still allow it to threaten world peace and American security interests. Russia is not going to invade Europe, but a hostile Russia could make life more difficult for U.S. foreign policymakers. If for instance a new anti-Western regime in Moscow sought to sell nuclear weapons to Iran or support North Korea, then the United States would quickly face new security challenges. It is far better to have Russia working with the United States—even in its weakened condition—than to have to face again a new major threat from Eurasia. While being more honest with ourselves and the Russians about Russia's place in the world is a better basis for U.S. foreign policy, this does not mean abandoning a strategy of foreign policy engagement.

Transformation and Integration

It may be hard even for those who lived through the cold war to remember how all-consuming the threat posed by the Soviet Union was for policymakers and the public for nearly a half century. Throughout the 1990s, and especially during the Clinton administration, American foreign policy officials justified policies and programs of domestic transformation in Russia as a way of defending American national interests. If democracy and capitalism took hold in Russia, so the argument went, then Russia would pursue a more pro-Western and pro-American foreign policy. A democratic and market-oriented Russia would seek to join the community of democratic (and Western) states and thereby act in concert with rather than oppose this community and its international security policies. Achieving a range of American foreign policy goals would be far easier if Russia were a partner rather than once again an opponent.

Russia has achieved only partial success in consolidating market and democratic institutions at home. For most of the 1990s, however, the imperative of continuing these domestic changes has compelled Russian foreign policy officials to pursue cooperative relations with the West in general and the United States in particular. Russia stopped pursuing an antagonistic, ideologically motivated foreign policy. When Russia's new leaders succeeded in toppling the Soviet *ancien régime* in 1991, they no longer viewed the United States as an enemy but saw it as an ally in completing their anticommunist revolution. Joining the West replaced promoting communism abroad as the central objective of Russian foreign policy.

It was democratization in the Soviet Union and Russia that allowed Yeltsin to come to power. Once in power, Yeltsin and his first foreign minister, Andrei Kozyrev, played key roles in turning Russia in a pro-American direction. Yeltsin's pro-Western orientation at the beginning of the decade in turn allowed the United States to achieve important strategic objectives throughout Europe and Eurasia. Regime change in Russia served American national security interests.

Yeltsin's lack of imperial ambition permitted the United States and other Western states to move aggressively to recognize all the former Soviet republics as newly independent states. Had Yeltsin allowed sovereignty issues to linger, debates about borders in the former Soviet Union might have erupted into armed conflict, while some states of the former Soviet Union might not be independent states today. Yeltsin's pro-Western orientation also allowed the United States to cooperate with Russia, Ukraine, Belarus, and Kazakhstan in negotiating the dismantling of nuclear arsenals in all of these states but Russia. Yeltsin and Putin also allowed the Nunn-Lugar program to continue to dismantle nuclear weapons in Russia. Such a blatant infringement of domestic sovereignty could not have occurred if Russia's communists or fascists had seized power earlier in the decade.

On nearly all foreign policy issues of primary concern to the first Bush and Clinton administrations, Yeltsin either cooperated or refrained from obstructing U.S. objectives. In part, this change reflected Russia's new decline in power. In part, though, it also reflected changed intentions of those in the Kremlin. Had Russia been ruled by a communist or fascist leader during the 1990s, the United States would have been even less likely to pursue NATO enlargement or the bombing of Yugoslavia because of concerns about the potential for armed conflict with Russia. Had a radical nationalist been in the Kremlin during the NATO war against Serbia or the American-led war in Iraq, Slobodan Milosevic and Saddam Hussein might have received Russian military assistance. In fact, under a communist or fascist dictatorship, Russian troops might still be stationed in Poland or the Baltic states.

New Russian foreign policy preferences generated from domestic transformation have been important in allowing the United States to achieve its security objectives in Europe and elsewhere without risking confrontation with

Russia. Equally important has been the changing balance of power between the two countries during the past decade. Defense spending in Russia declined dramatically in the 1990s, making Russia's military-industrial complex a shadow of its former Soviet self.[41] Even under President Putin, who has placed great emphasis on expanding defense expenditures, the Russian government plans to spend roughly $10 billion annually on national defense in the next decade.[42] In real terms, the United States will spend orders of magnitude more than Russia on defense expenditures in the coming years and may even spend as much on missile defense research and development as Russia will spend on its entire military. Although Russia has projected power in Chechnya, its inability to resolve through military means a conflict at home shows that it does not have the capability to undertake a serious military operation against any ally of the United States. Russia's only real military asset is its diminishing nuclear arsenal, although this is not a military tool Russian leaders can use for purposes other than deterrence.

Given the difficult-to-measure achievements of American efforts to promote democracy and capitalism in Russia and Russia's decline as a major power, it is tempting to conclude that the United States should get out of the missionary business altogether and that Russia's evolution and desire to be a partner with the West would have happened without any U.S. effort to help the country transform itself. This is the wrong conclusion to take away from a reexamination of American policy toward Russia in the 1990s. The changing distribution of power in favor of the United States and the Russian desire to join the West allowed U.S. leaders to pursue and achieve many foreign policy objectives without concern for Russian attitudes. What brought about the new environment, however, was revolution in the Soviet Union and then Russia that radically altered the internal balance of power in the 1990s in favor of liberals, which in turn gave rise to a pro-Western orientation. Cautious realism, as practiced by George H. W. Bush, may have helped to smooth this transformation. In particular, Gorbachev did not feel threatened by his former adversary. Unlike others in his government, Gorbachev did not believe that Bush was trying to take advantage of the Soviet dissolution. The personal rapport between Bush and Gorbachev made the Soviet leader's fall from power more graceful and more peaceful than it might have been had a more hardline, less Western-oriented general secretary occupied the Kremlin during that period who, for example, might have wanted to use the 300,000 troops stationed in eastern Germany.

But ultimately, it was the very regime change feared by Bush that allowed the United States to emerge as the world's only superpower. American policies that aided this revolution in the margins, therefore, also indirectly and eventually facilitated Washington's pursuit of seemingly unrelated policies such as NATO enlargement and the NATO military intervention against Serbia.

Russia still has unique military assets and geostrategic positions despite its decline. Russia still has the second largest nuclear arsenal in the world and could overwhelmingly destroy the United States. Even if President Putin decides to reduce Russia's strategic nuclear weapons to less than a thousand, Russia could still inflict enormous damage to American military and civilian targets. Even those most optimistic about the capabilities of missile defense systems concede that the United States will not be able to defend against a Russian nuclear attack for decades, if ever.

Russia also remains a regional hegemon. Russia may be a weak power, but the states surrounding it are even weaker. Compared to the American military, Russia's armed forces look ill-equipped and ill-prepared. Compared to Georgian or Ukrainian military capabilities, however, the Russian military looks fearsome. These same regional asymmetries are present on economic matters. Compared to any Western corporation, Russian companies look small, poorly managed, and unable to compete. Compared to Moldovan, Uzbek, or even Ukrainian firms, Russian enterprises look powerful if not imperial. The wave of consolidation sweeping most Russian industrial sectors will create even larger firms in search of new markets, and the former Soviet space is the logical place for expansion. If the Russian economy continues to grow over the next several years, Russian economic influence in the region will expand dramatically. These resources in the hands of a Russian dictator or an anti-American regime in Moscow could do serious damage to American security interests. The reorientation of Russia's regime toward the West, therefore, must still figure prominently in any explanation of American security successes in Europe and elsewhere.

Some have asserted that the American liberal impulse to help Russia produced negative results during Russia's transformation. In theory, then, a policy of nonassistance or noninterference might have produced a *more* pro-American foreign policy. As we have documented, some American initiatives did have negative implications for Russian reform. These instances of failure, however, did not trigger reform reversal in Russia. More generally, ideas about the market and democracy, whose transfer was facilitated by the United States, appear in the long run to have had greater staying power than negative Russian attitudes about American intervention. Market and democratic ideas have greater legitimacy in Russia today than they enjoyed a decade earlier. As an example and as the one country in the world most capable of projecting its ideals, the United States played a crucial role in propagating these ideas in Russia.

It is important to note that American assistance in promoting Russian transformation was *the* most important agenda item in U.S.-Russian relations for *Russian* leaders at the beginning of the 1990s. The demand for help in Russia's internal change came from Moscow, not Washington. To ignore in

1992 or 1993 these calls for assistance coming from Yeltsin in the name of *realism* would have impaired the bilateral relationship. As Russian economic and political institutions consolidated and stabilized, the imperative to remain focused on Russian internal change receded for leaders in Washington and Moscow. George W. Bush and his administration have had the luxury of choosing whether to devote attention to Russia's internal problems or not. His father and Clinton throughout most of his first administration did not have the choice of ignoring Russian domestic developments.

History has vindicated those Wilsonians in all three U.S. administrations who believed that Russian transformation was a U.S. national security interest. The United States has greatly benefited from the emergence of a quasi-capitalist, partially democratic Russia in place of the communist Soviet Union. Repeatedly since the end of the cold war, disagreements over security issues undermined harmony in the bilateral relationship. Some listened to the acrimony expressed in Moscow and Washington during NATO expansion, the war over Kosovo, or the war with Iraq and predicted a return to the cold war. Such predictions never came true, however, because of Russia's basic new Western orientation brought about in large measure by internal transformation.

Transformation and integration are inextricably linked. It was true for Germany and Japan after World War II, and it has been true for the USSR and Russia since the late 1980s. The cold war ended because the USSR changed from within and continued doing so under Boris Yeltsin. Many of the difficulties in U.S.-Russian relations in the 1990s were exacerbated by the lack of progress on Russia's internal change. August 1998 was caused in part by the nonmarket practices in the banking and financial sectors that continued unchecked. The dash to Pristina and the continued abuses in Chechnya have been carried out by elements of the Russian military that have resisted reform, and the untransformed elements of the military-industrial complex continue to underwrite Iran's nuclear aspirations and seem to have assisted Iraq in 2002–03.

The Russian revolution remains unfinished, and we should be humble in our assessments of where it is going. Henry Kissinger once asked Zhou Enlai his views on the French Revolution, and the Chinese foreign minister replied that it was too early to tell. And so it is with this second Russian revolution. What we can tell, however, is how dramatically this unfinished revolution has served American foreign policy interests during the previous decade. Geostrategists have long worried about a major military threat emerging from a hostile regime in the heart of Eurasia able to dominate European and Asian affairs. With the collapse of Soviet communism and the emergence of a quasi-democratic, market-oriented Russia, this threat no longer confronts the United States.

Appendix: List of Interviews

This list of individuals interviewed matches the citations in the text. The date of the interview is shown in brackets at the end of each entry.

Ahtisaari, Martti President of Finland (1994–2000) [January 11, 2001].

Albright, Madeleine U.S. Permanent Representative to the United Nations (1993–97); U.S. Secretary of State (1997–2001) [March 1, 2002].

Åslund, Anders Economic Adviser to the Government of the Russian Federation (1991–94) [September 5, 2000].

Atwood, Brian Administrator, U.S. Agency for International Development (1993–99) [January 19, 2001].

Baker, James A., III U.S. Secretary of State (1989–92) [November 6, 2000].

Bass, John NATO-Russia Desk Officer, U.S. Department of State (1997); Special Assistant for European and Eurasian Affairs and then Executive Assistant and Chief of Staff, Office of the Deputy Secretary, U.S. Department of State (1998–2001) [February 1, 2001].

Belanger, Gerard At the time of interview, Deputy Director, European II Department, International Monetary Fund [April 19, 2001].

Bell, Robert Committee on Armed Services, U.S. Senate—Principal Staff Assistant to Chairman Sam Nunn (1984–93); Special Assistant to the President for National Security Affairs and Senior Director for Defense Policy and Arms Control, National Security Council (1993–99); Assistant

Secretary General for Defense Support, NATO (1999– present) [March 20, 2001].

Berger, Samuel R. ("Sandy") Deputy National Security Adviser (1993–97); National Security Adviser (1997–2001) [September 7, 2001].

Beyrle, John Director for Russia, Ukraine, and Eurasia Affairs at the National Security Council (1993–95); Deputy to the Special Adviser to the Secretary of State for the New Independent States (1999–2000); Acting Special Adviser to the Secretary of State for the NIS (2001); Deputy Chief of Mission at the U.S. Embassy in Moscow (2002–present) [October 4, 2001].

Blacker, Coit D. Special Assistant to the President for National Security Affairs and Senior Director for Russia, Ukraine, and Eurasia Affairs, National Security Council (1995–96) [April 3, 2002].

Bourgault, Jeanne Director of the Office of Democratic Initiatives and Human Resources, U.S. Agency for International Development (1994–97) [August 19, 2002].

Brzezinski, Mark Director for Russia, Ukraine, and Eurasia Affairs, National Security Council (1999–2000); Director for Southeast European Affairs, NSC (2000–01) [April 19, 2001].

Burns, R. Nicholas Director for Soviet Affairs and then Special Assistant to the President and Senior Director for Russia, Ukraine, and Eurasia Affairs at the National Security Council (1990–95); U.S. Department of State Spokesman (1995–97); U.S. Ambassador to Greece (1997–2001); U.S. Permanent Representative, at NATO (2001–present) [March 7, 2001, and May 22, 2001].

Carpendale, Andrew Staff member and Deputy Director, Policy Planning, U.S. Department of State (1989–92) [March 15, 2000].

Carter, Ashton Assistant Secretary of Defense for International Security Policy (1993–96) [January 19, 2001].

Chavin, James San Antonio Capital Management (1995–98) [February 16, 2001].

Collins, James Deputy Chief of Mission, U.S. Embassy in Moscow (1990–93); Senior Coordinator, Office of the Ambassador-at-Large for the New Independent States, U.S. Department of State (1994–95); Ambassador-at-Large and Special Adviser to the Secretary of State for the New Independent States (1995–97); U.S. Ambassador to the Russian Federation (1997–2001) [February 28, 2002].

Courtney, William U.S. Ambassador to Kazakhstan (1992–95); U.S. Ambassador to Georgia (1995–98); Special Assistant to the President and Senior Director for Russia, Ukraine, and Eurasia Affairs (1997–98) [September 25, 2000].

Dale, Charles Director, Defense Policy Planning Office, U.S. Mission to NATO (1993–95); Director, Defense Partnership and Cooperation, Office of the Secretary General, NATO (1995–2001) [March 21, 2001].

Diuk, Nadia Director for Central Europe and Eurasia at the National Endowment for Democracy (1987–present) [March 4, 2003].

Donilon, Thomas Assistant Secretary of State for Public Affairs and Chief of Staff for Secretary of State Warren Christopher (1993–96) [March 8, 2001].

Donnelly, Christopher Special Adviser for Central and Eastern European Affairs, NATO (1989–present) [March 22, 2001].

Edelman, Eric Assistant Deputy Undersecretary of Defense for Soviet and East European Affairs (1990–93); Deputy to the Ambassador-at-Large for the NIS (1993); Executive Assistant to the Deputy Secretary of State (1996–98); Ambassador to Finland (1998–2001); Principal Deputy Assistant to the Vice President for National Security Affairs (2001–2003) [August 29, 2001].

Elstein, Adam Managing Director and Head of Bankers Trust Company's Russian Investment and Trading Operations, 1996–99 [March 20, 2003].

Ermarth, Fritz Chairman of the National Intelligence Council (1988–93) [July 6, 2000].

Fischer, Stanley First Deputy Managing Director of the International Monetary Fund (1994–2001) [February 22, 2001].

Fuerth, Leon Senior Legislative Assistant for National Security to Senator Al Gore (1985–93); National Security Adviser to Vice President Gore (1993–2001) [February 9, 2001, February 23, 2001, April 23, 2001, and July 6, 2001].

Fyodorov, Boris Deputy Prime Minister and Finance Minister of Russia (Dec. 1992–Jan. 1994) [April 18, 2001].

Gaidar, Yegor Deputy Prime Minister and then Acting Prime Minister of the Russian Federation (1991–92) [December 11, 2002].

Gati, Toby Special Assistant to the President and Senior Director for Russia, Ukraine, and Eurasia Affairs at the National Security Council (1993),

Assistant Secretary of State for Intelligence and Research (1993–97) [December 7, 2000].

Gottemoeller, Rose Director for Russia, Ukraine, and Eurasia Affairs at the National Security Council (1993–94); Assistant Secretary for Nonproliferation and National Security and then Acting Deputy Administrator for Defense Nuclear Nonproliferation, U.S. Department of Energy (1997–2000) [January 25, 2001].

Graham, Thomas Policy Assistant in the Office of the Undersecretary of Defense for Policy (1990–92); Policy Planning Staff at the U.S. Department of State (1992–94); Head of Political Section, U.S. Embassy in Moscow (1994–97); Deputy Director, Policy Planning Staff, and then Director for Russia Affairs, National Security Council (2001–present) [February 16, 2001].

Grigoryants, Sergei At the time of interview, Chairman of "Glasnost" Foundation [July 2002].

Hadley, Stephen J. Assistant Secretary of Defense for International Security Policy (1989–1993); Deputy National Security Adviser (2001–present) [June 2, 2000].

Hannah, John Member, Policy Planning Staff (1991–93); Special Assistant to the Chief of Staff, U.S. Department of State (1994–96); Deputy Assistant to the Vice President for National Security Affairs (2001–present) [May 15, 2000].

Hauslohner, Peter Member, Policy Planning Staff (1989–91) [October 2, 2000].

Hellman, Joel Senior Political Counselor, Office of the Chief Economist at the European Bank for Reconstruction and Development (1997–2000); Lead Specialist on Governance for the Europe and Central Asia Region, World Bank (2000–present) [October 22, 2000].

Herman, Robert Senior Social Scientist, U.S. Agency for International Development, Bureau for Europe and the Former Soviet Union (1995–99); Member of the Policy Planning Staff (1999–2001) [February 8, 2001].

Igrunov, Vyacheslav Duma Deputy (1993–present); Deputy Chairman of Yabloko (1994–99) [December 19, 1999].

Illarionov, Andrei Manager, Analysis and Planning Group and Adviser to the Prime Minister of the Russian Federation (1993–94); Director of Institute of Economic Analysis (1994–present); Member, Russian Government's

Committee on Economic Reform (1998–2000); Economic Adviser to President of the Russian Federation (2000–present) [July 16, 2002].

Ingram, George Deputy Assistant Administrator, U.S. Agency for International Development (1998–99) [February 15, 2001].

Juster, Kenneth Deputy and Senior Adviser to the Deputy Secretary of State (1989–92); Acting Counselor of the U.S. Department of State (1992–93); Undersecretary of Commerce (2001–present) [May 30, 2000].

Kozyrev, Andrei Russian Minister of Foreign Affairs (1990–96) [July 15, 2002].

Kupchan, Clifford Professional Staff Member Responsible for Russia and Eurasia, House Committee on International Relations (1995–99), Deputy Coordinator of U.S. Assistance to the New Independent States, U.S. Department of State (1999–2000) [September 28, 2000].

Lake, Anthony Assistant to the President for National Security Affairs (1993–97)[June 29, 2000, and July 24, 2001].

Libby, Lewis ("Scooter") Principal Deputy Undersecretary of Defense for Strategy and Resources (1989–92); Deputy Undersecretary of Defense for Policy (1992–93); Chief of Staff and Assistant for National Security Affairs for Vice President Dick Cheney (2001–present) [July 13, 2000].

Lipman, Masha Deputy Editor of *Itogi* (1996–2001) [July 15, 2002].

Lipton, David Deputy Assistant Secretary of Treasury for Eastern Europe and the Former Soviet Union (1993–95); Assistant Secretary of Treasury for International Affairs (1996–97); Undersecretary of Treasury for International Affairs (1998) [February 3, 2001, and April 6, 2001].

Lough, John At the time of interview, Information Officer, Central and Eastern Europe, Office of Information and Press, NATO [March 21, 2001].

Margelov, Mikhail Head, Public Relations Department, Russian Federation Presidential Administration (1996–2001); Chairman, Committee for Foreign Affairs, Russian Federation Council (2001–present) [July 15, 2002].

Markov, Sergei At the time of interview, Editor of International Affairs Division, strana.ru [July 18, 2002].

Mau, Vladimir Adviser to the Prime Minister of the Russian Federation (1992); Adviser to the Deputy Mayor of Moscow (1993); Adviser to the First Deputy Prime Minister of the Russian Federation (1993–94) [April 2, 2002].

McCurry, Michael Spokesman for the U.S. Department of State and Deputy Assistant Secretary for Public Affairs (1993–95); White House Press Secretary (1995–98) [July 5, 2001].

Medish, Mark Special Assistant to the Assistant Administrator for Europe and the Newly Independent States at the U.S. Agency for International Development (1994–96); Senior Adviser to the Administrator of the United Nations Development Program (1996); Deputy Assistant Secretary of the U.S. Treasury for International Affairs (1997–2000); Special Assistant to the President and Senior Director at the National Security Council for Russia, Ukraine, and Eurasia Affairs (2000–01) [April 8, 2001].

Merry, Wayne Head of Political Section at the U.S. Embassy in Moscow (1990–94) [July 5, 2001].

Mizulina, Elena Deputy of the State Duma of the Russian Federation (1995–present) [May 7, 2002].

Moltke, Gebhardt von Assistant Secretary General for Political Affairs, NATO (1991–97); Ambassador of the Federal Republic of Germany to the Court of St. James, London (1997–99); Permanent Representative of the Federal Republic of Germany at NATO (1999–present) [March 20, 2001].

Morningstar, Richard Special Adviser to the President and Secretary of State for the Newly Independent States (1996–98); Special Adviser to the President and Secretary of State for Caspian Basin Energy Diplomacy (1998–99); U.S. Ambassador to the European Union (1999–2001) [March 20, 2001].

Morris, Dick Political Consultant to President Clinton (1994–96) [June 25, 2001].

Mulford, David Assistant Secretary and Undersecretary of the U.S. Treasury for International Affairs (1984–92) [February 16, 2001].

Nacht, Michael Assistant Director for Strategic and Eurasian Affairs at the U.S. Arms Control and Disarmament Agency (1994–97) [October 11, 2000].

Nemtsov, Boris Deputy of the Supreme Soviet of Russia (1990–91); Governor of Nizhny Novgorod, Russian Federation (1991–97); Deputy Prime Minister (1997–98); Deputy of the State Duma of the Russian Federation; Co–Chairman, Union of Right Forces (1999–present) [July 17, 2002].

Norton, Donna Program Officer for the Rule of Law Program, U.S. Agency for International Development, 1994–95 [August 25, 2002].

Nuland, Victoria Political Officer, U.S. Embassy, Moscow (1991–93); Chief of Staff to the Deputy Secretary of State (1994–96); Deputy for Russia and Eurasia, Office of the New Independent States, Department of State (1997–99); Deputy Permanent Representative, U.S. Mission to NATO (1999–2003) [June 26, 2000, and March 20, 2001].

Odling-Smee, John Director, European II Department, International Monetary Fund (1992–present) [April 19, 2001].

Pascual, Carlos Deputy Assistant Administrator for Europe and the New Independent States at the U.S. Agency for International Development and Director of the Office of Program Analysis and Coordination for the New Independent States Task Force (1994–95); Director and then Senior Director for Russia, Ukraine, and Eurasia Affairs at the National Security Council (1995–2000); U.S. Ambassador to Ukraine (2000–2003)[March 14, 2000, May 26, 2000, July 13, 2000, and September 27, 2000].

Peasely, Carol At the time of interview, Mission Director, U.S. Agency for International Development [July 15, 2002].

Perry, William U.S. Deputy Secretary of Defense (1993–94); U.S. Secretary of Defense (1994–1997) [April 3, 2002].

Pifer, Steven K. Director and then Special Assistant to the President and Senior Director for Russia, Ukraine, and Eurasia Affairs at the National Security Council (1994–97); U.S. Ambassador to Ukraine (1998–2000); Deputy Assistant Secretary of State in the Bureau of European and Eurasian Affairs (2000–present) [August 17, 2001].

Poneman, Daniel Director for Defense Policy and Arms Control (1990–92); Special Assistant to the President and Senior Director for Nonproliferation and Export Controls at the National Security Council (1993–96) [April 12, 2001].

Rosner, Jeremy Special Assistant to the President and Senior Director for Legislative Affairs at the National Security Council (1993–94); Special Adviser to the President and Secretary of State for NATO Enlargement Ratification (1997–98) [December 13, 2000].

Ross, Dennis Director, Policy Planning Office, U.S. Department of State (1989–92); Special Middle East Coordinator for the President (1993–2001) [May 26, 2000, and March 2, 2001].

Scowcroft, Brent Assistant to the President for National Security Affairs (1989–93) [July 7, 2000].

Sestanovich, Stephen Ambassador-at-Large and Special Adviser to the Secretary of State for the New Independent States (1997–2001) [March 1, 2001, and March 9, 2001].

Shea, Jamie Assistant to Secretary General for Special Projects, NATO (1988–91); Deputy Head and Senior Planning Officer, Policy Planning Unity and Multilateral Affairs Section of the Political Directorate, NATO (1991–93); Spokesman of NATO and Deputy Director of Information and Press (1993–2000); Director of Information and Press (2000–2003) [March 22, 2001].

Sherwood-Randall, Elizabeth Deputy Assistant Secretary of Defense for Russia, Ukraine, and Eurasia (1994–96) [December 19, 2002].

Steinberg, James Director, Policy Planning Staff, U.S. Department of State (1994–97); Deputy Assistant to the President for National Security Affairs (1997–2001) [August 29, 2001].

Stern, Jessica Director for Russia, Ukraine, and Eurasia Affairs, National Security Council (1994–95) [January 18, 2001].

Stevenson, Irene At the time of interview, Director, AFL-CIO's Solidarity Center in Moscow, Russia [January 3, 2003].

Talbott, Strobe Ambassador-at-Large and Special Adviser to the Secretary of State for the New Independent States (1993–94); Deputy Secretary of State (1994–2001) [October 3, 2000, December 12, 2000, and January 12, 2001].

Tarasyuk, Boris Ukrainian Deputy Foreign Minister (1992–95); Ukrainian Ambassador to Belgium, Netherlands, and Luxembourg, (1995–98); Head of Ukrainian Mission in NATO (1997–98); Minister of Foreign Affairs (1998–2000) [June 21, 2002].

Taylor, William Deputy Coordinator and then Coordinator of U.S. Assistance to the Newly Independent States (1992–2003) [May 2002].

Vasiliev, Dmitri Deputy Head, State Committee for Management of State Property, Russian Federation (1991–94); Deputy Head and Executive Director, Federal Commission for the Securities Market (1994–96); Head, Federal Commission for the Securities Market (1996–99) [July 18, 2002].

Vershbow, Alexander Special Assistant to the President and Senior Director for European Affairs, National Security Council (1994–97); U.S. Ambassador to NATO (1998–2001); U.S. Ambassador to Russia, (2001–present) [March 20 and 22, 2001, and July 16, 2002].

Weil, Christoph At time of interview, Head, East European Partners Section, Political Affairs Division, NATO [March 21, 2001].

Weiss, Andrew Country Director for Russia at the Office of the Secretary of Defense (1992–94); Member of Policy Planning Staff at the U.S. Department of State (1994–98); Director for Russia, Ukraine, and Eurasia Affairs at the National Security Council (1998–2001) [January 11, 2001, and June 25, 2001].

Wethington, Olin Assistant Secretary for International Affairs, U.S. Department of the Treasury (1991–93) [September 11, 2000].

Woolsey, R. James Director of Central Intelligence (1993–94) [April 19, 2001].

Yablokov, Aleksei At the time of interview, President, Center for Russian Environmental Policy, Moscow [March 22, 2003].

Zoellick, Robert Undersecretary of State for Economic and Agricultural Affairs and Counselor to the Department (1989–92); White House Deputy Chief of Staff and Assistant to the President (1992–93); U.S. Trade Representative (2001–present) [May 30, 2000].

Notes

Chapter 1

1. For background on the cold war, see, for example, Adam Ulam, *Expansion and Coexistence: Soviet Foreign Policy 1917–1973,* 2d ed. (Praeger, 1974); Erik Hoffman and Frederic Fleron, eds., *The Conduct of Soviet Foreign Policy* (Aldine, 1971); John Lewis Gaddis, *We Now Know: Rethinking Cold War History* (Oxford: Oxford University Press, 1997); and Raymond Garthoff, *Détente and Confrontation: American-Soviet Relations from Nixon to Reagan,* rev. ed. (Brookings, 1994).

2. The implementation of the grand strategy of containment had many variations over the four decades of the cold war. See John Lewis Gaddis, *Strategies of Containment: A Critical Appraisal of Postwar American National Security Policy* (Oxford: Oxford University Press, 1981).

3. Henry Kissinger, *Does America Need a Foreign Policy? Toward a Diplomacy for the 21st Century* (Simon and Shuster, 2001).

4. It was Franklin D. Roosevelt's idea that the United States, Britain, China, and the Soviet Union would "police" the postwar world.

5. The Americans ready to support state-led assistance and reform in Europe through the Marshall Plan were the same Americans who lived through the Great Depression and therefore appreciated the role of the state and economic assistance in the remaking of the economies. Americans in the 1990s had a very different attitude toward the state and development. On the importance of the "New Deal" for postwar innovations such as the Marshall Plan, see Elizabeth Kopelman Borgwardt, "Imagining the Postwar World: A Cultural Perspective on American Internationalism after the World Wars," paper presented at the American Historical Association, Chicago, January 2000.

6. President Woodrow Wilson's Fourteen Points, delivered to a joint session of Congress, January 8, 1918.

7. On the Wilsonian tradition in American foreign policy, see Alexander George and Juliette George, *Woodrow Wilson and Colonel House* (Dover Publications, 1956); Tony Smith, *America's Mission: The United States and the Worldwide Struggle for Democracy in the Twentieth Century* (Princeton University Press, 1994); and Walter Russell Mead,

Special Providence: American Foreign Policy and How It Changed the World (Alfred Knopf, 2001).

8. On liberalism as a theory of international relations, see Immanuel Kant, "Perpetual Peace" (1795) in Carl Friedrich, ed., *The Philosophy of Kant* (Modern Library, 1949); Joseph S. Nye Jr. and Robert O. Keohane, *Power and Interdependence*, 3d ed. (Addison-Wesley, 2000); Richard Rosecrance, *The Rise of the Trading State: Commerce and Conquest in the Modern World* (Basic Books, 1986); the essays by Michael Doyle, Bruce Russett, and John Owen IV in Michael Brown, Sean Lynn-Jones, and Steven Miller, eds., *Debating the Democratic Peace* (MIT Press 1996); and John Ikenberry, *After Victory: Institutions, Strategic Restraint, and the Rebuilding of Order after Major Wars* (Princeton University Press, 2001). In academia, however, liberal theorists have focused on the liberalizing role of international institutions on domestic policies. They have paid less attention to the role of states in fostering domestic change within other states, our main focus in this book.

9. Classic realist statements include E. H. Carr, *The Twenty Years' Crisis, 1919-1939* (Macmillan and Company, Limited, 1939). Hans Morgenthau, *Politics among Nations: The Struggle for Power and Peace* (Knopf, 1973); Kenneth Waltz, *Theory of International Politics* (Addison-Wesley, 1979); and John Mearsheimer, *The Tragedy of Great Power Politics* (W.W. Norton, 2001).

10. See especially, Gaddis, *We Now Know*; and Smith, *America's Mission*.

11. Patrick Tyler, *A Great Wall: Six Presidents and China* (New York: Public Affairs, 2000).

12. William Burr, ed., *The Kissinger Transcripts: The Top Secret Talks with Beijing and Moscow* (New Press, 1999), p. 64.

13. George Shultz, *Turmoil and Triumph: Diplomacy, Power, and the Victory of the American Ideal* (Simon and Shuster, 1993); and Peter Schweizer, *Reagan's War* (Doubleday, 2002).

14. Anthony Lake, "Do the Doable," *Foreign Policy*, no. 54 (Spring 1984), pp. 102–21. For good discussions of the components of U.S. foreign policy, see Mead, *Special Providence*; and Henry R. Nau, *At Home Abroad: Identity and Power in American Foreign Policy* (Cornell University Press, 2002).

15. In this book, we go beyond the mere identification of ideas and attempt to show their causal weight in the making of policy. Explanation of the origins of these ideas is not a focus of the book, although we do give some attention to these historical roots in passing throughout the narrative.

16. The literature on ideas frequently posits a dichotomy between "material interests" and "ideational interests." We reject this dichotomy and instead argue that the pursuit of alleged "material interests" is also an idea, ideology, or worldview. Since very few U.S. foreign policymakers get personally rich from making foreign policy (at least while in office), their pursuit of so-called material interests is motivated by an *idea* about the national interest. In other words, both realism and idealism/liberalism are ideas/theories/frameworks/worldviews/roadmaps about the nature of the international system and, for our purposes, America's place in it. "Power balancers" and "regime transformers" have different strategies for making foreign policy and pursuing the national interest, but they still share a basic assumption about the broad goals of American foreign policy.

17. Judith Goldstein and Robert Keohane, "Ideas and Foreign Policy: An Analytical Framework," in Goldstein and Keohane, eds., *Ideas and Foreign Policy: Beliefs, Institu-*

tions, and Political Change (Cornell University Press, 1993), p. 17; and G. John Ikenberry, "Creating Yesterday's New World Order," in Goldstein and Keohane, *Ideas and Foreign Policy*, p. 59.

18. On why great powers become ideologically motivated, see Stephen Krasner, *Defending the National Interest: Raw Material Investments and U.S. Foreign Policy* (Princeton University Press, 1978), pp. 337–47.

19. For a discussion among realists, see James Fearon, "Domestic Politics, Foreign Policy, and Theories of International Relations," *Annual Review of Political Science*, vol. 1 (1998), pp. 289–314; Colin Elman, "Horses for Courses: Why *Not* Neorealist Theories of Foreign Policy," *Security Studies*, vol. 6 (Fall 1996) pp. 7–53; and Kenneth Waltz, "International Politics Is Not Foreign Policy," *Security Studies*, vol. 6 (Fall 1996), pp. 54–57.

20. On the unprecedented extent of American hegemony in the post–cold war era, see William Wohlforth, "The Stability of a Unipolar World," *International Security*, vol. 24 (Summer 1999), pp. 5–41.

21. James M. Lindsay, *Congress and the Politics of U.S. Foreign Policy* (Johns Hopkins University Press, 1994); good essays on these internal influences can be found in Eugene R. Wittkopf and James M. McCormick, eds., *The Domestic Sources of American Foreign Policy: Insights and Evidence*, 3d ed. (Rowman and Littlefield, 1998).

22. In the 1990s, American corporations only just began to invest in and trade with Russia. They have an effective lobby organization, the U.S.-Russia Business Council, whose contributions to the policymaking process are discussed in subsequent chapters, but this group did not play a defining role in U.S. foreign policy in this period. Nor is there a large or politically organized Russian ethnic émigré community in the United States. For an assessment of these limited influences, see Sarah Mendelson, *Domestic Politics and America's Russia Policy*, a report by The Century Foundation and the Stanley Foundation (New York, and Muscatine, Iowa, October 2002).

23. Secretary of Defense Dick Cheney, *Defense Strategy for the 1990s: The Regional Defense Strategy* (Department of Defense, January 1993), p. 1. Also Patrick E. Tyler, "U.S. Strategy Plan Calls for Insuring No Rivals Develop," *New York Times*, March 8, 2002, p. 1.

24. See the reference, for example, in George F. Will, "A Dog in That Fight?" *Newsweek*, June 12, 1995, p. 72.

25. See, for example, comments by Brent Scowcroft on the Persian Gulf War policy on PBS *Frontline* (www.pbs.org/wgbh/pages/frontline/shows/gunning [June 25, 2003]).

26. For some in the Bush team, the violent Chinese suppression of the grassroots democratic movement in 1989 offered another example of the dangerous consequences of pushing reform too fast in communist regimes.

27. *A National Security Strategy of Engagement and Enlargement*, White House, July 1994.

28. See in particular his 2002 State of the Union address on January 29, 2002 (www.whitehouse.gov/stateoftheunion/2002/history.html) and *The National Security Strategy of the United States of America* (www.whitehouse.gov/nsc/nssall.html). Websites were accessed June 25, 2003.

29. On this intellectual evolution and the internal battles between the power balancers and the regime transformers within the Bush administration, see PBS *Frontline*, "The War behind Closed Doors," February 20, 2003 www.pbs.org/wgbh/pages/front-

line/shows/iraq; and Nicholas Lemann, "The Next World Order," *New Yorker*, April 1, 2002, pp. 42–28.

30. In earlier periods of world history, the balance of power in the international system had rarely changed without a major war. In 1815, 1919, and 1945, war had made clear who lost and who won, who was less powerful and who was more powerful. See Ikenberry, *After Victory*.

31. On the difficulties of measuring the balance of power in dynamic situations, see Robert Gilpin, *War and Change in World Politics* (Cambridge: Cambridge University Press, 1981), p. 237.

32. For a comprehensive evaluation, see Michael McFaul, *Russia's Unfinished Revolution: Political Change from Gorbachev to Putin* (Cornell University Press, 2001).

Chapter 2

1. See Stephen Kotkin, *Armageddon Averted: The Soviet Collapse 1970-2000* (Oxford: Oxford University Press, 2001); Philip Roeder, *Red Sunset: The Failure of Soviet Politics* (Princeton University Press, 1993); and Steven Solnick, *Stealing the State: Control and Collapse of Soviet Institutions* (Harvard University Press, 1998).

2. On Gorbachev's reform ideas, see George Breslauer, *Gorbachev and Yeltsin as Leaders* (Cambridge University Press, 2002); Archie Brown, *The Gorbachev Factor* (Oxford: Oxford University Press, 1996); Jerry Hough, *Democratization and Revolution in the USSR, 1985-1991* (Brookings, 1997); and Michael McFaul, *Russia's Unfinished Revolution: Political Change from Gorbachev to Putin* (Cornell University Press, 2001); see also Mikhail Gorbachev, *Memoirs* (Doubleday, 1996) and his top national security assistant's memoirs, A. S. Chernayev, *Shest Let s Gorbachym* (Moskva: Progess, 1993).

3. V. A. Kolosov, N.V. Petrov, and L. V. Smirnyagin, eds., *Vesna 89: Geographiya, Parliamentskikh Vyborov* (Moskva: Progess, 1990); Yitzhak Brudny, "The Dynamics of 'Democratic Russia,' 1990-1993," *Post-Soviet Affairs*, vol. 9 (April-June 1993), pp.141–70; and M. Steven Fish, *Democracy from Scratch: Opposition and Regime in the New Russian Revolution* (Princeton University Press, 1995).

4. Stephen Hanson, "Gorbachev: The Last True Leninist Believer?" in Daniel Chirot, *The Crisis of Leninism and the Decline of the Left: The Revolutions of 1989* (University of Washington Press, 1991).

5. Michael McFaul, "The Sovereignty 'Script': The Red Book for Russia's Revolutionaries," in Stephen Krasner, ed., *Problematic Sovereignty: Contested Rules and Political Possibilities* (Columbia University Press, 2001), pp. 194–223; John Dunlop, *The Rise of Russia and the Fall of the Soviet Empire* (Princeton University Press, 1993); and *Gorbachev, Yeltsin: 1500 Dnei Politicheskogo Protivovostoyaniya* (Moskva: "Terra," 1992).

6. *Materiali: II S'ezda Dvizheniya Demokraticheskoi Rossii* (Moskva: DR-Press, November 1991).

7. Gorbachev, *Memoirs*, p. 291. On ethnic mobilization in this period, see Mark Beissinger, *Nationalist Mobilization and the Collapse of the Soviet State* (Cambridge University Press, 2002).

8. Serge Schmemann, "The Tough New Leaders in Moscow Have Kremlinologists Up and Guessing," *New York Times*, January 27, 1991, sec. 4, p. 3; and "The New Soviet

Policymakers," *Economist*, February 9, 1991, pp. 47–48. Bush emphatically writes that he believed Gorbachev. See George Bush and Brent Scowcroft, *A World Transformed* (Alfred A. Knopf, 1998), p. 496.

9. Michael Dobbs, "Yeltsin Snubs Gorbachev's Offer: Russian Leader Later Holds His Own Meeting with Bush," *Washington Post*, July 31, 1991, p. A26.

10. Condoleezza Rice and Philip Zelikow, *Germany Unified and Europe Transformed* (Harvard University Press, 1995).

11. The Esalen Institute, not the U.S. government, sponsored the trip. Speaking fees earned by Yeltsin on the trip were donated for the purchase of syringes to prevent the spread of AIDS in the USSR. See Leon Aron, *Yeltsin: A Revolutionary Life* (St. Martin's Press, 2000), pp. 322–23.

12. Kirsten Lundberg, "CIA and the Fall of the Soviet Empire: The Politics of 'Getting it Right,'" C16-94-1251.0 (Harvard University, Kennedy School of Government Case Program, 1994), p. 39.

13. Bush did eventually drop by Scowcroft's office to meet Yeltsin, for either twelve or sixteen minutes depending on which side was counting. See Aron, *Yeltsin*, p. 336.

14. Interview with Brent Scowcroft. See the appendix for a list of all individuals interviewed, including titles of individuals and dates of interview. See also Elizabeth Drew, "Letter from Washington," *New Yorker*, September 23, 1991, p. 100; Scowcroft's Soviet adviser, Condoleezza Rice, shared his view. Pentagon official Eric Edelman recalled that when Ed A. Hewett replaced Rice in March 1991, "The first thing he saw was, 'This government's got a major Yeltsin problem, and we've got to work our way out of it.'" Quoted in Lundberg, "CIA and the Fall of the Soviet Empire," p. 53.

15. Mark R. Beissinger, "Demise of an Empire-State: Identity, Legitimacy, and the Deconstruction of Soviet Politics," in Crawford Young, ed., *The Rising Tide of Cultural Pluralism: The Nation-State at Bay?* (University of Wisconsin Press, 1993), p. 94.

16. Bush and Scowcroft, *A World Transformed*, p. 499.

17. During this period, Cheney convened Saturday morning seminars to discuss Soviet affairs with outside analysts. Analysts critical of the administration's tendency to support Gorbachev over Yeltsin and the democratic opposition, including Peter Reddaway and Stephen Sestanovich, were active participants in these meetings. For Sestanovich's pro-Yeltsin views at the time, see his "The Hour of the Demagogue," *National Interest*, no. 25 (Fall 1991), pp. 3–15. For Reddaway's skepticism about Gorbachev, see his "The Quality of Gorbachev's Leadership," *Soviet Economy*, vol. 6, no. 2 (1990), pp. 125–40.

18. Interview with Stephen J. Hadley.

19. Interview with Scooter Libby.

20. Jack Matlock, *Autopsy on an Empire: The American Ambassador's Account of the Collapse of the Soviet Union* (Random House, 1995), p. 509.

21. The differences emerge clearly in the discussion in the cabinet on September 5, 1991, just after the coup. Bush and Scowcroft, *A World Transformed*, pp. 541–43; Robert Gates, *From the Shadows: The Ultimate Insider's Story of Five Presidents and How They Won the Cold War* (Touchstone Books, 1997), p. 529; and Michael R. Beschloss and Strobe Talbott, *At the Highest Levels: The Inside Story of the End of the Cold War* (Little, Brown and Company, 1993), p. 445. CIA analyst Grey Hodnett had been arguing since September 1989 that Gorbachev was in trouble; at the top levels, only Cheney and Deputy National Security Adviser Robert Gates were open to this argument. See Lundberg, "CIA and the Fall of the Soviet Empire," p. 36. She also

argues that at the State Department, Soviet desk officer Alexander Vershbow was arguing in the spring of 1991 that the United States should be more supportive of the devolution of power to the republics, but his views were rejected (p. 38).

22. Interview with Dennis Ross.

23. James A. Baker III, with Thomas M. DeFrank, *The Politics of Diplomacy: Revolution, War and Peace 1989-1992* (G. P. Putnam's Sons, 1995), p. 475; and remarks by Kolt during a review of an initial draft of this book, May 23, 2002, Brookings.

24. Bush and Scowcroft, *A World Transformed*, p. 500.

25. George H. W. Bush, "Remarks and an Exchange with Soviet Journalists on the Upcoming Moscow Summit," July 25, 1991 (http://bushlibrary.tamu.edu/papers [June 25, 2003]).

26. Gates, *From the Shadows*, pp. 502, 504. On the CIA analysis, see, for example, the formerly classified CIA report, "Yeltsin's Political Objectives," CIS/SOV91-10026 X (June 1991), declassified and approved for release, April 2000, esp. pp.10–11.

27. Bush and Scowcroft, *A World Transformed*, pp. 493–94.

28. Interview with Scowcroft.

29. Michael Dobbs, "Yeltsin Snubs Gorbachev's Offer: Russian Leader Later Holds His Own Meeting with Bush," *Washington Post*, July 31, 1991, p. A26.

30. George H. W. Bush, "Remarks at the Arrival Ceremony in Moscow," July 30, 1991 (http://bushlibrary.tamu/edu/papers [June 25, 2003]).

31. Bush, in Bush and Scowcroft, *A World Transformed*, p. 501.

32. Thomas L. Friedman, "Arms Talks: A Warm-Up," *New York Times*, June 10, 1991, p. A1.

33. President George H. W. Bush, "Remarks to the Supreme Soviet of the Republic of the Ukraine in Kiev, Soviet Union," August 1, 1991 (http://bushlibrary.tamu.edu/papers [June 25, 2003]).

34. On the role of external actors in hastening the Yugoslav collapse, see Susan Woodward, "Compromised Sovereignty to Create Sovereignty: Is Dayton Bosnia a Futile Exercise or an Emerging Model?" in Stephen Krasner, ed., *Problematic Sovereignty: Contested Rules and Political Possibilities* (Columbia University Press, 2001), pp. 252–300.

35. The Belovezhskaya Accord was signed on December 8, 1991, by the leaders of Russia, Ukraine, and Belarus. The document de jure created the Commonwealth of Independent States and de facto dissolved the Soviet Union.

36. George H. W. Bush, "Remarks at the Moscow State Institute for International Relations," July 30, 1991 (http://bushlibrary.tamu.edu/papers [June 25, 2003]).

37. Bush, in Bush and Scowcroft, *A World Transformed*, p. 502.

38. Don Oberdorfer, "Soviet Pledges to Cut Troops in the Baltics," *Washington Post*, January 30, 1991, p. A24; Francis Clines, "War in the Gulf: Lithuania," *New York Times*, January 31, 1991, p. A15; Helen Dewar, "Senate Hits Soviet Action in the Baltics: Bush Urged to Weigh Economic Pressure," *Washington Post*, January 25, 1991, p. A18; Bush and Scowcroft, *A World Transformed*, p. 497; and James Gerstenzang, "Bush Softens Criticism of Baltics Crackdown," *Los Angeles Times*, January 26, 1991, p. A24.

39. Don Oberdorfer, "Soviet Pledges to Cut Troops in the Baltics," p. A24; Gerstenzang, "Bush Softens Criticism of Baltics Crackdown," p. A24; and Bush and Scowcroft, *A World Transformed*, p. 496.

40. George H. W. Bush, "Remarks and an Exchange with Soviet Journalists on the Upcoming Moscow Summit," July 25, 1991.

41. President George H. W. Bush, "Remarks to the Supreme Soviet of the Republic of the Ukraine in Kiev, Soviet Union," August 1, 1991. On Chicken Kiev, see William Safire, "After the Fall," *New York Times*, August 29, 1991, A29; and "Bush at the UN," *New York Times*, September 16, 1991, A19.

42. John Newhouse, "Diplomatic Round: Shunning the Losers," *New Yorker*, October 26, 1992, p. 46.

43. Scowcroft, in *A World Transformed*, p. 516.

44. Mikhail Gorbachev, *Memoirs* (Doubleday, 1996), p. 621.

45. See Francis Clines, "After the Summit: Bush, in Ukraine, Walks Fine Line on Sovereignty," *New York Times*, August 2, 1991, p. A1.

46. Quoted in Ann Devroy and Michael Dobbs, "Bush Warns Ukraine on Independence," *Washington Post*, August 2, 1991, p. A1.

47. President George H. W. Bush, "Remarks to the Supreme Soviet of the Republic of the Ukraine in Kiev, Soviet Union," August 1, 1991.

48. For an overview, see Linda Cook, *Labor and Liberalization: Trade Unions in the New Russia* (Twentieth Century Fund Press, 1997), chap. 5.

49. At its May 1988 meeting, the NED board adopted a resolution that considered support to national democratic movements crucial for promoting democracy in the Soviet Union. The NED board member, Zbigniew Brzezinski—elected to the board in 1987—played a central role in pushing NED in this direction. (Interview and e-mail exchange with Nadia Diuk, NED program officer for this region since 1987, March 4, 2003).

50. NDI, *Report of the Survey Mission to the Soviet Union: July 29–August 3, 1990* (Washington, 1990), p. 22. For a description of NDI programs in the Soviet Union, see NDI, *The Commonwealth of Independent States: Democratic Developments, Issues, and Options* (Washington, January 1992).

51. Since its inception in 1984, NED has received money directly from the U.S. Congress. In parallel to its own grants programs, NED also gives grants to the NDI, IRI, AFL-CIO, and others. As these nongovernmental organizations (NGOs) expanded their programs in the former Soviet Union, they began to receive the greater share of the funds for the region from the U.S. Agency for International Development. On the business of democracy promotion, see Thomas Carothers, *Aiding Democracy Abroad: The Learning Curve* (Washington: Carnegie Endowment for International Peace, 1999).

52. His engagement is chronicled in Matlock, *Autopsy on an Empire*.

53. On this luncheon with Reagan, see George Shultz, *Turmoil and Triumph: Diplomacy, Power, and the Victory of the American Ideal* (Simon and Shuster, 1993), pp. 1102–03.

54. Some believe that Gorbachev played a role in the coup attempt. In interviews with McFaul in November 1993, both Anatoly Lukyanov and Gennady Yanayev claimed that Gorbachev was fully abreast of their plans from the beginning. According to Lukyanov, Gorbachev was simply waiting to assess the level of domestic opposition before returning. Lukyanov's view is shared by several democratic leaders in Russia, including Elena Bonner. See Dunlop, *The Rise of Russia and the Fall of the Soviet Empire*, pp. 202–03; Amy Knight, *Spies without Cloaks* (Princeton University Press, 1996). For doubts that Gorbachev was a participant in the plan, see Archie Brown, *The Gorbachev Factor*.

55. "Ukaz Prezidenta Rossiiskoi Sovetskoi Federativnoi Sotsialicheskoi Respublika," *Rossiya: Ekstrenyi Vypusk*, August 19, 1991.

56. Interview with Scowcroft.

57. Interview with James Collins.

58. "Excerpts from Bush News Conference on Soviet Coup: Hope and Warning," *New York Times*, August 20, 1991, p. 15; Bush, "Remarks and an Exchange with Reporters in Kennebunkport, Maine, on the Attempted Coup in the Soviet Union," August 19, 1991 (http://bushlibrary.tamu.edu.papers [June 25, 2003]).

59. "Excerpts from Bush News Conference on Soviet Coup: Hope and Warning," *New York Times*, August 20, 1991, p. 15.

60. Bush, "Remarks and an Exchange with Reporters in Kennebunkport, Maine, on the Attempted Coup in the Soviet Union."

61. On Gorbachev's post facto disappointment with the hesitation of Bush and other Western leaders, see Gorbachev, *Memoirs*, p. 663.

62. For details of the standoff, see McFaul, *Russia's Unfinished Revolution*, chap. 3.

63. Interview with Scowcroft.

64. Bush, "The President's News Conference in Kennebunkport, Maine, on the Attempted Coup in the Soviet Union," August 20,1991 (http.//bushlibrary.tamu.edu/papers [June 25, 2003]).

65. Bush, "Exchange with Reporters in Kennebunkport, Maine, on the Attempted Coup in the Soviet Union," August 21, 1991.

66. Boris Yeltsin, *The Struggle for Russia* (Random House, 1994), p. 132.

67. Dick Cheney, address to the American Political Science Association, August 29, 1991.

68. Gates, *From the Shadows*, p. 530.

69. Baker, as quoted in Gates, *From the Shadows*, p. 530.

70. Memorandum of Conversation, NATO Summit, November 7, 1991, Rome, p. 3. Declassified by the Bush library in response to a Freedom of Information Act (FOIA) request from the authors.

71. Bush and Scowcroft, *A World Transformed*, p. 552–53.

72. R. Jeffrey Smith, "U.S. Officials Split over Response to an Independent Ukraine," *Washington Post*, November 25, 1991, p. A18.

73. Smith, "U.S. Officials Split over Response to an Independent Ukraine."

74. Baker, *The Politics of Diplomacy*, pp. 560–61.

75. During this period, Gorbahev's close personal friend, Spanish president Felipe Gonzalez, was warning the Soviet leader that the Americans were less optimistic privately about his prospects to keep the Union together than their public statements seemed to suggest. See excerpts from a letter from Gonzalez to Gorbachev in Anatoly Chernyaev, *My Six Years with Gorbachev* (Pennsylvania State University Press, 2000), p. 394.

76. Baker, *Politics of Diplomacy*, p. 561; Beschloss and Talbott, *At the Highest Levels*, p. 449; and interview with Scowcroft.

77. Interview with James Baker; and Baker, *The Politics of Diplomacy*, p. 562.

78. McFaul, *Russia's Unfinished Revolution*, chap. 4.

79. See Anders Åslund, *How Russian Became a Market Economy* (Brookings, 1995), chap. 2.

80. For details, see McFaul, *Russia's Unfinished Revolution*, chap. 5.

81. Russian president Vladimir Putin is an alumnus of one of these training pro-

grams, organized by the National Democratic Institute (NDI) in St. Petersburg in May 1991.

82. Other experts from around the world provided written commentaries on the different drafts of the Russian electoral law. The NDI never advocated a particular system and actually provided contradictory recommendations from Western experts. Michael McFaul participated in these interactions.

83. As an NDI representative, McFaul participated in two major trips made by NDI officials in October and again in December. During these trips, the NDI delegation did press these issues in most of their meetings with senior Russian officials.

84. Interview with Robert Zoellick; and George Kolt quotation is from the manuscript review session at Brookings, May 23, 2002.

85. Interview with Zoellick.

86. See Lundberg, "CIA and the Fall of the Soviet Empire," p. 44.

87. Interview with Baker.

Chapter 3

1. See Leon V. Sigal, *Hang Separately: Cooperative Security between the United States and Russia, 1985-1994* (New York: Century Foundation, 2000), p. 232.

2. Realist champions of this line of thinking in academia included John Mearsheimer and Kenneth Waltz. See John Mearsheimer, "The Case for a Ukrainian Nuclear Deterrent," *Foreign Affairs*, vol. 72 (Summer 1993), pp. 50–66; and the broader arguments about the benefits of proliferation made by Waltz in Scott Sagan and Kenneth Waltz, *The Spread of Nuclear Weapons: A Debate* (W. W. Norton, 1995).

3. Dimitri Simes, "Russia Reborn," *Foreign Policy*, vol. 85 (Winter 1991–92), pp. 41–62. Concerns about Russian imperialism lingered well beyond the collapse. See Zbigniew Brzezinski, "The Premature Partnership," *Foreign Affairs*, vol. 73 (March-April 1994), pp. 67–82; William Odom and Robert Dujarric, *Commonwealth or Empire? Russia, Central Asia, and the Transcaucasus* (Hudson Institute Press, 1995); and Uri Ra'anan and Kate Martin, eds., *Russia: A Return to Imperialism?* (St. Martin's Press, 1995).

4. Doug Stanglin and Julie Corwin, "The Old Face of Russia," *U.S. News and World Report*, November 11, 1991, p. 48; and "Boris the Great, or the Terrible?" *Economist*, October 5, 1991, pp. 51–52.

5. George Bush and Brent Scowcroft, *A World Transformed* (Alfred A. Knopf, 1998), pp. 543–44.

6. Interview with Brent Scowcroft.

7. Interviews with Stephen Hadley and Scooter Libby.

8. Interview with James Baker.

9. Colin Powell, *My American Journey: An Autobiography* (Random House, 1995), pp. 540–41.

10. "Address to the Nation on Reducing United States and Soviet Nuclear Weapons," September 27, 1991 (www.fas.org [June 25, 2003]). See also Bush and Scowcroft, *A World Transformed*, p. 546–47; and James A. Baker III, with Thomas M. DeFrank, *The Politics of Diplomacy: Revolution, War and Peace 1989–1992* (G. P. Putnam's Sons, 1995), p. 526.

11. Bush and Scowcroft, *A World Transformed*, pp. 546–47; and Baker, *The Politics*

of Diplomacy, p. 526; Sigal, Hang Separately, p. 245; and interview with Stephen Hadley.

12. Interview with Andrew Carpendale. Besides his position in the State Department, Carpendale later assisted Baker with his memoirs.

13. Baker, The Politics of Diplomacy, p. 525; and Bush and Scowcroft, A World Transformed, pp. 543–44, discuss the principles. Derek H. Chollet in "Absent at the Creation? Decision-Making in the Bush Administration and the Transformation of the Soviet Union, August–December 1991," Cornell University, honors thesis, April 1993, provides an excellent discussion, based on interviews with leading officials, whether Bush or Baker would announce the principles. See pp. 30–31.

14. Baker, The Politics of Diplomacy, p. 560. The leak of the U.S. debate appeared in R. Jeffrey Smith, "U.S. Officials Split over Response to an Independent Ukraine," Washington Post, November 25, 1991, p. A18.

15. Interview with Nicholas Burns.

16. Interview with Hadley.

17. Quoted in Chollet, "Absent at the Creation?" p. 74. Chollet's chapter 3 remains the best discussion of the origins of Baker's speech at Princeton in December 1991.

18. Baker, Politics of Diplomacy, p. 563; and David Hoffman, "Baker: U.S. Must Resist Temptation to Move toward Isolationism," Washington Post, December 8, 1991, p. A41.

19. James A. Baker III, "America and the Collapse of the Soviet Union: What Has to Be Done," U.S. Department of State Dispatch, vol. 2 (December 16, 1991), pp. 887–93.

20. Baker, Politics of Diplomacy, pp. 566–67; see also U.S. Department of State (Moscow), "Press Availability by Secretary of State James Baker III and Russian Republic President Boris Yeltsin," Kremlin, December 16, 1991, p. 5.

21. Baker, Politics of Diplomacy, p. 572.

22. Johanna Neuman, "Baker 'Reassured' on Soviet Nukes," USA Today, December 17, 1991, p. A1.

23. That Yeltsin spoke on behalf of these soon-to-be-independent states revealed how difficult the process of securing dissolution and real independence for these new countries would be.

24. "Press Availability by Secretary of State James A. Baker III and Russian Republic President Boris Yeltsin," p. 3.

25. Interview with Carpendale.

26. The "train had left the station" was one of Gorbachev's favorite idiomatic expressions at the time.

27. Baker, Politics of Diplomacy, p. 583.

28. David Hoffman, "Ukraine's Leader Pledges to Destroy Nuclear Arms; Baker Says U.S. Recognition Is Closer," Washington Post, December 19, 1991, p. A1; Thomas L. Friedman, "Soviet Disarray," New York Times, December 19, 1991, p. A1; Johanna Neuman, "Republics Vow Deeper Arms Cuts," USA Today, p. A4; David Hoffman, "Kazakhstan Keeping Nuclear Arms, Republic's President Tells Baker," Washington Post, December 18, 1991, p. A30; and Natalia A. Feduschak, "Former Soviet Union Republics Reassure Baker on Nuclear Arms," Wall Street Journal, December 17, 1991, p. A17.

29. Statement of Chairman Les Aspin of the House Armed Services Committee on Humanitarian Aid to the Soviet Union, August 28, 1991.

30. Dick Cheney, address to the American Political Science Association, August 29, 1991.

31. Ashton Carter and William Perry, *Preventive Defense: A New Security Strategy for America* (Brookings, 1999), pp. 71–72.

32. Sigal, *Hang Separately*, p. 238; and Richard Combs, "U.S. Domestic Politics and the Nunn-Lugar Program," in *Dismantling the Cold War: U.S. and NIS Perspectives on the Nunn-Lugar Cooperative Threat Reduction Program*, edited by John M. Shields and William C. Potter (MIT Press, 1997), pp. 42–44.

33. Interview with Dennis Ross. On the December 12 signing of legislation, see Combs, "U.S. Domestic Politics," p. 44.

34. Interview with Brent Scowcroft; see also Raymond L. Garthoff, "The United States and the New Russia: The First Five Years," *Current History*, vol. 96 (October 1997), pp. 305–12.

35. Sam Nunn, "Changing Threats in the Post–Cold War World," in Shields and Potter, *Dismantling the Cold War*, p. xi. Nunn-Lugar money did not become a regular part of an administration budget request until the Clinton administration's fiscal year 1994 budget. See Combs, "U.S. Domestic Politics and the Nunn-Lugar Program," p. 46.

36. Baker, *Politics of Diplomacy*, p. 617; and interview with Carpendale.

37. On 1989, see Derek H. Chollet and James M. Goldgeier, "Once Burned, Twice Shy? The Pause of 1989," in William C. Wohlforth, ed., *Cold War Endgame* (Pennsylvania State University Press, 2003), pp. 141–73.

38. Baker, *Politics of Diplomacy*, p. 620.

39. Address before a Joint Session of the Congress on the State of the Union, January 28, 1992; Sigal, *Hang Separately*, p. 250; and "Yeltsin-Bush Letter," January 27, 1992, Moscow 02449, American Embassy Moscow to Secretary of State, declassified in response to a Freedom of Information Act request by the authors.

40. Michael Parks and Doyle McManus, "Yeltsin Asks 805 Cut in Warheads for U.S., Russia," *Los Angeles Times*, January 30, 1992, p. A1.

41. See Yeltsin's warm words for Bush's behavior during and immediately after the coup in Yeltsin, *Struggle for Russia*, pp. 131–32.

42. Douglas Jehl and Doyle McManus, "Bush Hoping to Shore Up Yeltsin," *Los Angeles Times*, January 31, 1992, p. A5.

43. Jim Hoagland, "Little Help for Yeltsin," *Washington Post*, February 11, 1992, p. A21.

44. Interview with Burns.

45. A recent Senate delegation to the former Soviet Union had concluded that Yeltsin's chances of success were "50-50 at best." See Press Conference with Senator Jim Exon (D-Neb.), Senator Carl Levin (D-Mich.), Senator Strom Thurmond (R-S.C.), and Senator Connie Mack (R-Fla.), January 21, 1992, p. 2.

46. Baker, *Politics of Diplomacy*, p. 625; statement issued by Presidents Bush and Yeltsin, Camp David, Maryland, February 1, 1992, *U.S. Department of State Dispatch*, vol. 3 (February 3, 1992), pp. 78–79.

47. Baker, *Politics of Diplomacy*, pp. 614ff; and Sigal, *Hang Separately*, p. 236.

48. Senate Armed Services Committee, "Dismantling of the Former Soviet Union's Nuclear Weapons," February 5, 1992, p. 2.

49. John Buntin, "The Decision to Denuclearize: How Ukraine Became a Non-Nuclear Weapons State," C14-98-1425.0 (Harvard University, Kennedy School of Government Case Program, 1997), pp. 4–8; and Sigal, *Hang Separately*, pp. 254–55.

50. Interview with Carpendale.

51. Baker, *Politics of Diplomacy*, pp. 662–63.

52. See Sherman Garnett, *Keystone in the Arch: Ukraine in the Emerging Security Environment of Central and Eastern Europe* (Washington: Carnegie Endowment for International Peace, 1997), pp. 72–76.

53. Baker, *The Politics of Diplomacy*, p. 665. Interview with Stephen Hadley; and Buntin, "Decision to Denuclearize," p. 12.

54. Baker, *Politics of Diplomacy*, pp. 668–69; and Background Press Briefing on U.S.-Russian Summit, June 17, 1992.

55. Interview with Baker.

56. Baker, *Politics of Diplomacy*, p. 669. Emphasis in original.

57. Interview with Carpendale.

58. Background Press Briefing on U.S.-Russian Summit, June 17, 1992; and Martin Sieff, "Baker Pursues Arms Deal on Eve of Yeltsin Visit," *Washington Times*, June 12, 1992, p. A7.

59. At the same time, the costs of implementation of this agreement also helped to stall its ratification in Russia. See Alexei Arbatov, "Start II: Red Ink, and Boris Yeltsin," *Bulletin of Atomic Scientists*, vol. 49 (April 1993), pp. 16–21.

60. Yeltsin remarks of June 16, 1992; and *U.S. Department of State Dispatch*, vol. 3 (June 22, 1992), p. 484.

61. Baker, *Politics of Diplomacy*, pp. 670–71; and see *U.S. Department of State Dispatch*, vol. 3 (June 22, 1992), pp. 492–93.

Chapter 4

1. For the most complete diagnosis of Russia's economic problems at the time, see *Russian Economic Reform: Crossing the Threshold of Structural Change*, a World Bank Country Study (Washington: World Bank, 1992).

2. On this inheritance, see Anders Åslund, *How Russia Became a Market Economy* (Brookings, 1995).

3. Interview with Brent Scowcroft.

4. Sylvia Nasar, "How to Aid Russians Is Debated," *New York Times*, January 20, 1992, p. C1. See also Zbigniew Brezinski, "A Premature Partnership," *Foreign Affairs*, vol. 73 (March–April 1994), pp. 67–82; and Ariel Cohen, *Russian Imperialism: Development and Crisis* (Praeger Press, 1996).

5. Quoted in Thomas Friedman, "Baker, on Hill, Passes Hat for Russia," *New York Times*, May 1, 1992, p. A3.

6. Leslie H. Gelb, "How to Help Russia," *New York Times*, March 14, 1993, p. 17.

7. Mikhail Gorbachev, *Memoirs* (Doubleday 1996), p. 612.

8. Jack Matlock, *Autopsy on an Empire: The American Ambassador's Account of the Collapse of the Soviet Union* (Random House, 1995), pp. 177–78.

9. Åslund, *How Russia Became a Market Economy*, p. 40; and Graham Allison and Robert Blackwill, "America's Stake in the Soviet Future," *Foreign Affairs*, vol. 70 (Summer 1991), pp. 78–79, 95–97.

10. Michael R. Beschloss and Strobe Talbott, *At the Highest Levels: The Inside Story of the End of the Cold War* (Little, Brown and Company, 1993), p. 385; and interview

with Robert Zoellick. See also Henry Kissinger, "No Time for a 'Grand Bargain,'" *Washington Post*, July 9, 1991, p. A19.

11. Some have argued that this situation created a convenient excuse for inaction for U.S. policymakers. Ambassador Jack Matlock expressed this view about the lack of leadership from the Bush administration during the last years of the Soviet Union. See Jack Matlock, *Autopsy on an Empire: The American Ambassador's Account of the Collapse of the Soviet Union* (Random House, 1995), especially chap. 8.

12. Interview with Stanley Fischer; and Martin Feldstein, "A Different Kind of 'Grand Bargain,'" *Wall Street Journal*, July 9, 1991, p. A18. In March 1992, Fischer was quoted as saying of the Russians that they had "done a lot" and "with external support they can go the last few yards." Steven Greenhouse, "U.S. Is Working on Soviet Aid Package," *New York Times*, March 21, 1992, p. A5.

13. The history of these debates is chronicled in Padma Desai, "From the Soviet Union to the Commonwealth of Independent States: The Aid Debate," *Harriman Institute Forum*, vol. 5 (April 1992), pp. 1-16.

14. Chernyaev, *My Six Years with Gorbachev*, pp. 362–63; and Gorbachev, *Memoirs*, pp. 608–17.

15. On the basic strategy of shock therapy, see Anders Åslund, *Post-Communist Economic Revolutions: How Big a Bang?* (Washington: Center for Strategic and International Studies, 1992); Olivier Blanchard, Maxim Boyco, Marek Dobrovski, Rudiger Dornbusch, and Andre Shleifer, *Post-Communist Reform: Pain and Progress* (MIT Press, 1993); and Jeffrey Sachs, *Poland's Jump to a Market Economy* (MIT Press, 1993).

16. Yegor Gaidar, *Days of Defeat and Victory* (University of Washington Press, 1996).

17. Interview with Yegor Gaidar.

18. If Russia had to cover its debt by other means, the printing of money and the issuing of credit would be the most tempting alternative but an alternative that would fuel inflation. Eventually, this is exactly what happened. See Andrei Shleifer and Daniel Treisman, *Without a Map: Political Tactics and Economic Reform in Russia* (MIT Press, 2000), pp. 41–42.

19. Stanley Fischer and Jacob Frenkel, "Macroeconomic Issues of Soviet Reform," *American Economic Review*, vol. 82 (May 1992), p. 41.

20. Interview with Dmitri Vasiliev, who was at the time was a senior adviser to Chubais and later deputy chairman of the GKI.

21. For the blueprint, derived by these experts in large measure from the experience in Poland, see David Lipton and Jeffrey Sachs, "Privatization in Eastern Europe: The Case of Poland," *Brookings Papers on Economic Activity*, no. 2 (1990), pp. 293–333; Anders Åslund, *Post-Communist Economic Revolutions: How Big a Bang?*; and Jeffrey Sachs, *Poland's Jump to the Market Economy*.

22. Jeffrey Sachs, "Life in the Emergency Room," in John Williamson, ed., *The Political Economy of Policy Reform* (Washington: Institute for International Studies, 1994), p. 504; Jeffrey Sachs, "Western Financial Assistance and Russia's Reforms," in Shafiqul Islam and Michael Mandelbaum, eds., *Making Markets: Economic Transformation in Eastern Europe and the Post-Soviet States* (New York: Council on Foreign Relations, 1993), pp.143–75; Jeffrey Sachs, "Helping Russia: Goodwill Is Not Enough," *Economist*, December 21-January 3, 1992, p. 104; and Anders Åslund, "Big Bang in Moscow," *Newsweek*, September 2, 1991, pp. 58–64.

23. *Russian Economic Reform: Crossing the Threshold of Structural Change*, a World Bank Country Study (Washington: World Bank, 1992), p. 49; Richard Nixon, "The Challenge We Face in Russia," *Wall Street Journal*, March 11, 1992, p. 14. See also Richard Nixon, "Save the Peace Dividend," *New York Times*, November 19, 1992, p. A19; Quentin Peel, "Kohl to Ask U.S. to Step Up Assistance for Moscow," *Financial Times*, March 23, 1993, p. 2; and Frances Williams, "Moscow 'Needs Own Marshall Plan'," *Financial Times*, April 14, 1993, p. 8.

24. See Sylvia Nasar, "How to Aid Russians Is Debated," *New York Times*, January 20, 1992, p. C1. See also Mark Kramer, "The Changing Economic Complexion of Eastern Europe and Russia: Results and Lessons of the 1990s," *SAIS Review* (Summer–Fall 1999), pp. 16–46.

25. Steven Greenhouse, "Wrapping Up Big Russian Aid Package," April 27, 1992, p. A7; and Jonas Bernstein, "Aid: The Best Way Up?" *Insight*, March 9, 1992, p. 11.

26. Gaidar talks about the 1917 analogy in his memoir, *Days of Defeat and Victory*, p. 119.

27. Interview with Andrew Carpendale.

28. Interviews with Dennis Ross and Robert Zoellick; and comments by Ross at manuscript review session at Brookings, May 23, 2002.

29. Interviews with David Mulford and Peter Hauslohner.

30. Interview with Mulford; for a discussion of the looming reserve crunch, see Gaidar, *Days of Defeat and Victory*, pp. 91, 112.

31. Interview with Mulford.

32. Ibid.

33. Interviews with Wethington, Mulford, and Hauslohner. See also press conference with David Mulford, October 3, 1991 (Lexis-Nexis); and Mulford's comments on the Russian energy sector at a Hearing before the Subcommittee on International Development, Finance, Trade and Monetary Policy of the House Banking Committee, 102 Cong. 2 sess., April 29, 1992, p. 10. (Throughout this book, the authors cite information on congressional hearings from the Federal News Service (fednews.com) or from lexis-nexis.com/universe.)

34. Interviews with Mulford and Wethington.

35. Gaidar, *Days of Defeat and Victory*, pp. 119–20. See also review of Gaidar book by Jeffrey D. Sachs, "Russia's Tumultuous Decade: An Insider Remembers," *Washington Monthly*, March 2000 (www.washingtonmonthly.com). Brest-Litovsk was the site of the one-sided deal the Germans struck with the Bolsheviks in March 1918 to end their war on the Eastern Front during World War I; the treaty was negated by Germany's subsequent loss in the war.

36. Sachs, "Russia's Tumultuous Decade."

37. Johanna Neuman, "Arms Control Summit 'Relic' of Cold War," *USA Today*, June 16, 1992, p.1A.

38. Hearing on the Russian Application to the World Bank before the House Banking Committee, 102 Cong. 2 sess., February 5, 1992, p. 19.

39. Interviews with Dennis Ross.

40. George Bush and Brent Scowcroft, *A World Transformed* (Alfred A. Knopf, 1998), p. 540.

41. Derek H. Chollet, "Absent at the Creation? Decision-Making in the Bush Administration and the Transformation of the Soviet Union, August–December 1991," Cornell University, honors thesis, April 1993, pp. 37–41.

42. Robert B. Zoellick, "Relations of the United States with the Soviet Union and the Republics," statement before the Subcommittee on Europe and the Middle East of the House Foreign Affairs Committee, 102 Cong. 1 sess., October 2, 1991, in *U.S. Department of State Dispatch*, vol. 2 (October 7, 1991), p. 746.

43. Interview with Victoria Nuland.

44. Interview with Andrei Kozyrev. Bush was still working with Gorbachev on international matters during the fall of 1991, including, most importantly, their collaborative work at the Madrid peace conference in October on the Middle East.

45. Interview with Gaidar.

46. Interview with Zoellick.

47. Derek Chollet, "Absent at the Creation?" pp. 73–74, 76–77, 84; and interview with Andrew Carpendale.

48. James A. Baker III, with Thomas M. DeFrank, *The Politics of Diplomacy: Revolution, War and Peace 1989–1992* (G. P. Putnam's Sons, 1995), p. 524.

49. Ibid., pp. 535–36.

50. Baker, "America and the Collapse of the Soviet Empire: What Has to Be Done."

51. Ibid.

52. Interviews with Carpendale, John Hannah, Kenneth Juster; Chollet, "Absent at the Creation?" p. 92; and Baker, *Politics of Diplomacy*, p. 584.

53. Charles Krauthammer, "Say Goodbye to Gorbachev," *Washington Post*, December 13, 1991, A29; and Leon V. Sigal, *Hang Separately: Cooperative Security between the United States and Russia, 1985–1994* (New York: Century Foundation, 2000), p. 226.

54. Interview with Carpendale.

55. Ibid.

56. Interviews with Robert Zoellick and Dennis Ross.

57. Interview with Ross.

58. Interview with Kenneth Juster.

59. Baker, *Politics of Diplomacy*, p. 619; and Baker, closing statement at Coordinating Conference, U.S. Department of State; and remarks by the president in address to International Conference on Humanitarian Assistance to the Former USSR, January 22, 1992, in *U.S. Department of State Dispatch*, vol. 3 (January 27, 1992), pp. 57–58, 61.

60. William C. Wohlforth, ed., *Cold War Endgame* (Pennsylvania State University Press, 2003), p. 124.

61. William Safire, "Baker's Big Bash," *New York Times*, January 23, 1992, p. A23; and Mary Curtius, "Europeans Voice Reservations over Role of U.S. Aid to Former Soviet Republics," *Boston Globe*, January 21, 1992, p. 6.

62. "Civil Disorder in the Former USSR: Can It Be Managed This Winter?" NIE 11-18.3-91 (November 1991), in Benjamin B. Fischer, *At Cold War's End: US Intelligence on the Soviet Union and Eastern Europe, 1989-1991* (Washington: CIA, 1999), pp. 144, 149. See also pp. 148, 150. See also the National Intelligence Estimates from September 1991, in the same volume, p. 189.

63. Office of the Coordinator of the U.S. Assistance to the NIS, *U.S. Government Assistance to and Cooperative Activities with the New Independent States of the Former Soviet Union: FY 1997 Annual Report* (Department of State, January 1998), p. 158; Baker, *Politics of Diplomacy*, p. 571, 584; David Hoffman, "Pentagon to Airlift Aid to Republics: Ex-Soviets Will Get Food, Medicine," *Washington Post*, January 24, 1992, p.

A1; and Raymond L. Garthoff, "The United States and the New Russia: The First Five Years," *Current History*, vol. 96 (October 1997), p. 308.

64. Baker, *Politics of Diplomacy*, p. 584.

65. Interview with Carpendale.

66. Cable from American embassy in Moscow to the secretary of state, "Info Moscow Political Collective," Moscow 02777, January 29, 1992, and "Secretary's Meeting with Foreign Minister Kozyrev," Secto 00007, January 28, 1992. Both documents were declassified in response to a Freedom of Information Act request by the authors.

67. Gennady Burbulis, "Come, Make Goods and Sell Them," *Washington Post*, January 22, 1992, p. A21; "The President's News Conference with President Boris Yeltsin of Russia," February 1, 1992; Steven Greenhouse with Thomas L. Friedman, "Aid Package for Russia Seems to Be Far from Wrapped Up," *New York Times*, April 9, 1992, p. A1; and "Briefing the Allies on the President's February 1, 1992, Meeting with Russian President Yeltsin," State 037194, February 6, 1992, declassified in response to a Freedom of Information Act request by the authors.

68. Hearing on Russian Application to the World Bank before the House Banking Committee, p. 22.

69. Address by Bill Clinton, April 1, 1992, New York Hilton; and Marvin Kalb, *The Nixon Memo: Political Respectability, Russia, and the Press* (University of Chicago Press, 1994), pp. 130,133–34.

70. See Kalb, *The Nixon Memo*, pp. 217–18, 220; and see also Monica Crowley, *Nixon Off the Record* (Random House, 1996), p. 73.

71. Kalb, *The Nixon Memo*, pp. 220–22.

72. Kalb, *The Nixon Memo*, pp. 52, 56, 59, 80; and Thomas L. Friedman, "Nixon's 'Save Russia' Memo: Bush Feels the Sting," *New York Times*, March 11, 1992, A12.

73. Kalb, *The Nixon Memo*, pp. 105–06; Don Oberdorfer, "Nixon Warns Bush to Aid Russia, Shun 'New Isolationism,'" *Washington Post*, March 12, 1992, p. A1; and Robert W. Stewart, "Nixon Urges U.S. to Assist Commonwealth," *Los Angeles Times*, March 12, 1992, p. A1.

74. Kalb, *The Nixon Memo*, pp. 105, 107.

75. Interview with Scowcroft; Baker, *Politics of Diplomacy*, p. 657; and Don Oberdorfer, "Aid Plan for Russia Was Hurried to Bulwark Yeltsin, Officials Say," *Washington Post*, April 9, 1992, p. A20.

76. Steven Greenhouse, "Bush and Kohl Unveil Plan to 7 Nations to Contribute $24 Billion in Aid for Russia," *New York Times*, April 2, 1992, p. 1.

77. Ibid; "Multilateral Financial Assistance Package for Russia, April 1, 1992," *U.S. Department of State Dispatch*, vol. 3 (April 6, 1992), pp. 265–66; Baker, *Politics of Diplomacy*, p. 657; Garthoff, "The United States and the New Russia," p. 308; Kalb, *The Nixon Memo*, pp. 133–34; and Ann Devroy, "U.S., Allies Set $24 Billion in Aid for Ex-Soviet States," *Washington Post*, April 2, 1992, p. A1.

78. Oberdorfer, "Aid Plan for Russia Was Hurried to Bulwark Yeltsin, Officials Say," p. A20; Greenhouse with Friedman, "Aid Package for Russia Seems to Be Far from Wrapped Up," p. A1; and Kalb, *The Nixon Memo*, pp. 133–34.

79. Baker, *Politics of Diplomacy*, pp. 655–56; interview with Zoellick; and Devroy, "U.S., Allies Set $24 Billion in Aid for Ex-Soviet States," p. A1.

80. Press Conference by the President, Secretary of State James Baker, Secretary of Treasury Nicholas Brady, and Secretary of Agriculture Edward Madigan, April 1, 1992;

interviews with Mulford and Wethington; remarks by the president to the American Society of Newspaper Editors, April 9, 1992, "Aid to the New Independent States: A Peace We Must Not Lose," *U.S. Department of State Dispatch*, vol. 3 (April 13, 1992), pp. 281–83.

81. World Bank loans were designed to stimulate sectoral reforms, such as the restructuring of the coal sector. The consequences of these kinds of reforms, therefore, were not as immediate.

82. In the spring of 1992, Yeltsin added three industrialists to Gaidar's economic team, who in turn responded more sympathetically to enterprises seeking state credits. Stabilization completely unraveled, however, after Viktor Gerashchenko became the head of the Central Bank of Russia in July 1992. He proceeded to issue credits to all sectors of the economy and significantly expanded the money supply, policies that in turn fueled double-digit monthly inflation.

83. Baker, with DeFrank, p. 656.

84. Barbara Crossette, "Bush Is Told of Threat to Soviet Aid Bill," *New York Times*, May 7, 1992, p. A14.

85. A copy of the note was shown to the authors.

86. *Congressional Record*, June 17, 1992, p. H4763.

87. Ibid., p. H4764.

88. Mulford remarks at a Bretton Woods Committee Conference Re: The United States Response to the Economic Future of the Former Soviet Union, June 15, 1992 (Lexis-Nexis).

89. Interviews with Ross, Zoellick, Scowcroft, and Åslund.

90. Peter Reddaway, comments in "Tainted Transactions: An Exchange," *National Interest*, no. 60 (Summer 2000), pp. 102–03.

91. Rudiger Dornbusch, Federico Sturzenegger, and Holger Wolf, "Extreme Inflation: Dynamics and Stabilization," *Brookings Papers on Economic Activity*, vol. 2 (1990), pp. 1–84; Stanley Fischer, "The Role of Macroeconomic Factors in Growth," *Journal of Monetary Economics*, vol. 32 (December 1993), pp. 485–512; and Daniel Treisman, "Fighting Inflation in a Transitional Regime: Russia's Anomalous Stabilization," *World Politics*, vol. 50 (January 1998), pp. 299–335.

Chapter 5

1. On the model, see Anders Åslund, *Post-Communist Economic Revolutions: How Big a Bang?* (Washington: Center for Strategic and International Studies, 1992); and Jeffrey Sachs, *Understanding Shock Therapy* (London: Social Market Foundation, 1994).

2. Importers, trading companies, and commercial banks had been among those that benefited from Gaidar's early reform. But in 1992, none of these beneficiaries of liberalization had organized as political actors. See Aleksei Ulyukaev, *Rossiya na Puti Reform* (Moscow: Evraziya, 1996); Joel Hellman, "Breaking the Bank," Ph.D. dissertation, Columbia University, 1993; and Juliet Johnson, *A Fistful of Rubles: The Rise and Fall of the Russian Banking System* (Cornell University Press, 2000).

3. On the antiliberal majority that had formed within the Congress already by the Sixth Congress, see Thomas Remington, *The Russian Parliament: Institutional Evolution in a Transitional Regime, 1989-1999* (Yale University Press, 2001), chap. 4;

and Mikhail Myagkov and Roderick Kiewiet, "Czar Rule in the Russian Congress of People's Deputies?" *Legislative Studies Quarterly*, vol. 21 (February 1996), p. 34. On Yeltsin's own admission of changing policies and personnel under pressure, see Boris Yeltsin, *The Struggle for Russia* (Times Books, 1995), p. 165; Aleksandr Shokhin, *Moi Golos Budet Vse-taki Uslyshan: Stenogramma Epokhi Peremen* (Moscow: Nash-Dom-L'Age d'Homme, 1995), pp. 30–42, especially p. 34. Gaidar said of another new deputy prime minister, Georgii Khizha, the former director of the giant military enterprise "Svetlana" in St. Petersburg, that "he absolutely was not able to understand fundamental principles of [state] management in market conditions. . . . From May 1992, Khizha became the chief fighter for increasing the budget deficit." Yegor Gaidar, *Dni Porazhenii i Pobed* (Moscow: Vagrius, 1996), p. 206.

4. World Bank, "Subsidies and Directed Credits to Enterprises in Russia: A Strategy for Reform," Report 11782-RU (Washington, April 1993); and Bridget Granville, *The Success of Russian Economic Reforms* (London: Royal Institute of International Affairs, 1995), p. 67.

5. Using the newly acquired emergency powers of the president granted to Yeltsin by the Supreme Soviet in November 1991, Gaidar and his associates attempted to seize control of the bank through a presidential decree. In a compromise, the Supreme Soviet allowed the government to nominate a new chairman, but the candidate had to be approved by the legislative branch. Quickly it became clear that candidates with proven reformist credentials such as Boris Fyodorov or Sergei Ignatiev (then the deputy chairman of the Central Bank) would not be approved. Gaidar, therefore, supported the nomination of Viktor Gerashchenko, the last chairman of the Soviet Central Bank who had a solid reputation as a competent banker. See the interview with Viktor Gerashchenko in *Litsa*, no. 2 (February 1997) p. 27. In retrospect, Gaidar claimed that his decision to support Gerashchenko's candidacy "was the most serious mistake I made in 1992." Gaidar, *Dni Porazhenii i Pobed*, p. 195.

6. Michael McFaul, *Russia's Unfinished Revolution: Political Change from Gorbachev to Putin* (Cornell University Press, 2001); and Boris Yeltsin, "Obrashcheniya Prezidenta na VII S'ezde narodnykh deputatov," December 10, 1992, in *Yeltsin-Khasbulatov: Edinstvo, Kompromis, Bor'ba* (Moskva: Terra-terra 1994), pp. 235–38.

7. "A Personal Account from Moscow, December 1992: Russia after the Congress of People's Deputies," memo from Toby Gati to Mike Mandelbaum, December 16, 1992, p. 4.

8. See, for example, Strobe Talbott, *The Russia Hand: A Memoir of Presidential Diplomacy* (Random House, 2002), pp. 37–38.

9. Thomas L. Friedman with Elaine Sciolino, "Clinton and Foreign Issues: Spasms of Attention," *New York Times*, March 22, 1993, p. A3.

10. Interview with Toby Gati.

11. Immanuel Kant, "To Perpetual Peace: A Philosophical Sketch (1795)," in *Perpetual Peace and Other Essays*, trans. by Ted Humphrey (Indianapolis: Hackett Publishing, 1983), pp. 107–43.

12. The main arguments of this debate in the academic literature are outlined in Michael Brown, Sean Lynn-Jones, and Steven Miller, eds., *Debating the Democratic Peace* (MIT Press, 1996). Strobe Talbott cites this academic literature in his essay, "Democracy and the National Interest," *Foreign Affairs*, vol. 75 (November-December 1996), pp. 47–63.

13. See William J. Clinton, "Liberal Internationalism: America and the Global Economy," speech at American University, February 26, 1993, reprinted in Alvin Rubinstein Albina Shayevich, and Boris Zlotnikov, eds., *The Clinton Foreign Policy Reader: Presidential Speeches with Commentaries* (M. E. Sharpe, 2000), pp. 8–13.

14. Strobe Talbott, "Post-Victory Blues," *Foreign Affairs*, vol. 71 (1991–92), pp. 53–69; and interview with Anthony Lake.

15. Anthony Lake, "From Containment to Enlargement," *U.S. Department of State Dispatch*, vol. 4 (September 27, 1993), pp. 658–64. White House, *A National Security Strategy of Engagement and Enlargement* (Government Printing Office, July 1994); and Thomas Carothers, "The Democracy Nostrum," *World Policy Journal*, vol. 11 (Fall 1994), pp. 47–53.

16. Deputy Secretary of State Strobe Talbott, "Support for Democracy and the U.S. National Interest," remarks before the Carnegie Endowment for International Peace, Washington, March 1, 1996.

17. President Bill Clinton, "A Strategic Alliance with Russian Reform," April 1, 1993, in *U.S. Department of State Dispatch*, vol. 4 (April 5, 1993), pp. 189–94.

18. The phrase is from Talbott, "Democracy and the National Interest."

19. Strobe Talbott, deputy secretary of state, statement before the Subcommittee of the Senate Appropriations Committee, 104 Cong. 1 sess., February 5, 1995 (transcript provided by the Federal News Service, Washington), p. 6; and interview with Talbott.

20. "Statement of Thomas A. Dine before the Senate Foreign Relations Committee," 103 Cong. 2 sess., January 26, 1994, p. 7.

21. Interviews with Nicholas Burns and Gati.

22. Talbott, *The Russia Hand*, p. 58.

23. Jeremy Rosner, *The New Tug of War: Congress, the Executive Branch, and National Security* (Washington: Carnegie Endowment for International Peace, 1995), p. 45.

24. Leyla Boulton, "Russia Lurks in the Shadows of the G7 Feast," *Financial Times*, July 12, 1993, p. 2; Leyla Boulton and Jurek Martin, "G7 Nations Agree to Russia Fund," *Financial Times*, July 9, 1993, p. 1; and Steven Greenhouse, "Russia Aid Plan Promotes Role for U.S. Companies," *New York Times*, July 24, 1993, p. 4.

25. Interview with Talbott.

26. Rosner, *The New Tug-of-War*, p. 46.

27. Interview with Jeremy Rosner.

28. Jeffrey Sachs, "Crash of Nations: Mexico, Si. Russia, Nyet," *New Republic*, February 6, 1995, p. 12.

29. Interviews with Rosner and George Ingram.

30. Clinton first asked Talbott to be his ambassador to Russia. When Talbott turned him down for family reasons, Clinton countered with this idea of creating a "tsar" for the former Soviet Union. Interviews with Talbott, Anthony Lake, and other Clinton administration officials asked in interviews about Talbott's role; and Talbott, *The Russia Hand*, pp. 38–40.

31. William Clinton, "Charter for Special Advisor to the President and to the Secretary of State on Assistance to the New Independent States (NIS) of the Former Soviet Union and Coordinator of NIS Assistance," memorandum for the heads of executive departments and agencies, White House, April 4, 1995; and interview with Morningstar.

32. The U.S. Agency for International Development (AID) funded several types of training and exchange programs for Russian students, teachers, entrepreneurs, parliamentarians, journalists, agricultural specialists, and women leaders. Reports on these programs appeared annually in the coordinator's report to Congress on the Freedom Support Act. On think tanks, see Raymond Struyk, *Reconstructive Critics: Think Tanks in Post-Soviet Bloc Democracies* (Washington: Urban Institute, 1999), chap. 5. On the activities of the Eurasia Foundation, see Richard Blue and others, *Final Report Eurasia Foundation Evaluation*, conducted for USAID by Nathan Associates Inc. and Pangaea Partners, PCE-I-00-98-00016-00 (U.S. Agency for International Development, January 2001).

33. Interview with Brian Atwood.

34. Interview with Jeanne Bourgault, director of the Office of Democratic Initiatives and Human Resources, U.S. Agency for International Development (1994–97).

35. Interview with Atwood.

36. Interview with Morningstar.

37. See Julie Corwin, "Playing the AID Game," *U.S. News and World Report*, October 3, 1994, pp. 35–36.

38. Interview with Bourgault.

39. Quoted in Fred Hiatt and Daniel Sutherland, "Grass-Roots Aid Works Best in Russia," *Washington Post*, February 12, 1995, p. A1.

40. Interview with Mark Medish. Morningstar made similar observations.

41. Interviews with Carlos Pascual, Atwood, and Morningstar.

42. General Accounting Office, *Foreign Assistance: International Efforts to Aid Russia's Transition Have Had Mixed Results*, GAO-01-8 (November 2000) p. 57. Interview with Ingram. Having a coordinator who acted like the GAO did not make Morningstar popular with AID officials working in Moscow. Relations between Morningstar and James Norris, AID mission director, were particularly tense.

43. Interview with David Lipton.

44. Writing with Jeffrey Sachs, Lipton had authored several influential articles and papers on the reforms necessary to dismantle command systems and create market economies. See, in particular, Jeffrey Sachs and David Lipton, "Prospects for Russia's Economic Reforms," *Brookings Papers on Economic Activity*, vol. 2 (1992), pp. 213–65; and Jeffrey Sachs and David Lipton, "Remaining Steps to a Market-Based Monetary System," in Anders Åslund and Richard Layard, eds., *Changing the Economic System in Russia* (St. Martin's Press, 1992), pp. 163–82. On Summers's ideas about postcommunist transition, see Lawrence Summers, "The Next Decade in Central and Eastern Europe," in Christopher Clague and Gordon Rausser, eds., *The Emergence of Market Economics in Eastern Europe* (Oxford: Blackwell Publishers, 1992), pp. 25–34.

45. Interview with Talbott; also interviews with Lipton, Morningstar, and Atwood.

46. In retrospect, it is often forgotten how difficult the achievement of this first goal actually was. See Gaidar's recollection of the difficulties, in Yegor Gaidar, *Days of Defeat and Victory* (University of Washington Press, 1999), chap. 6.

47. The IMF's managing director, Michel Camdessus, did claim that "*In part because of IMF support*, Russia now has a professional central bank." Emphasis added. See Michel Camdessus, "Russia and the IMF: Meeting the Challenges of an Emerging Market in a Transition Economy," address to the U.S.-Russian Business Council, Washington, April 1, 1998, p. 2.

48. The team was not completely new. The Clinton National Security Council staffer responsible for economic assistance, Nicholas Burns, was a holdover from the Bush administration.

49. Interview with Lipton. On these three "tions" of reform, see Anders Åslund, *How Russia Became a Market Economy* (Brookings, 1995).

50. Interview with Lipton.

51. Interview with Yegor Gaidar. Gaidar was particularly annoyed at the IMF's insistence on a common ruble zone within the Commonwealth of Independent States. The difficult relationship in this period is also acknowledged by Augusto Lopez-Claros, who was the resident representative for the IMF in Moscow during the period 1992–95. See Augusto Lopez-Claros, "The Fund's Role in Russia," unpublished manuscript, June 19, 1996, p. 7, note 7.

52. On the Memorandum on the Economic Policy of the Russian Federation, see Åslund, *How Russia Became a Market Economy*, p. 64.

53. Fyodorov, as quoted in Leyla Boulton, "Fyodorov Hopes Aid Will Be Disbursed Quickly," *Financial Times*, April 13, 1993, p. 3. On missing the 1992 window, see Anders Åslund, "Ruble-shooters," *New Republic*, May 4, 1992, p. 13. On what was promised in 1992 versus what was delivered, see Steven Greenhouse, "U.S. Maps an Aid Plan for Russia Though Roadblocks May Remain," *New York Times*, April 1, 1993, pp. A1, 10.

54. Lopez-Claros, "The Role of International Financial Institutions during the Transition in Russia."

55. See Thomas Schelling, "The Marshall Plan: A Model for Eastern Europe?" p. 24.

56. Randall W. Stone, *Lending Credibility: The International Monetary Fund and the Post-Communist Transition* (Princeton University Press, 2002), p. 124.

57. Stone, *Lending Credibility,* p. 124; and Lopez-Claros, "The Role of International Financial Institutions during the Transition in Russia."

58. Interview with Lipton.

59. See Stone, *Lending Credibility.*

60. For summaries of the activities of these other multilateral lending institutions, see the appendixes in General Accounting Office, *Foreign Assistance* (November 2000). While the United States is a shareholder in both the European Bank for Reconstruction and Development and the World Bank, the United States devotes less attention to the projects of these institutions. The European Union also established the Technical Assistance for the Commonwealth of Independent States (TACIS), which committed $2.7 billion and disbursed $1.6 billion in assistance to Russia between 1992 and 2000. Again, however, the United States had nothing to do with this program.

61. World Bank, "Russia's Economy: World Bank Says Growth May Begin in 1998 but Reforms Are Key," press backgrounder, the World Bank, Europe, and Central Europe Region, Washington, March 1997, p. 5; Chrystia Freeland, "World Bank Lends $6bn to Russia," *Financial Times*, April 15, 1997, p. 2; Michael Carter, World Bank country director for Russia, made this admission in a talk at the Center for Strategic and International Studies, Washington, April 8, 1998. Altogether, since the first World Bank loan to Russia in August 1992 until the spring of 1998, the World Bank had started thirty-nine operations in Russia totaling $10.0 billion before the August 1998 financial crash, making Russia the Bank's third largest borrower after China and India. World Bank, "World Bank President James Wolfensohn Addresses U.S.-Russia Business Council," press release, Washington, April 1, 1998.

62. Thomas Friedman, "U.S. Planning Aid to Shore Up Yeltsin's Position," *New York Times*, March 6, 1993, p. 1.

63. See Yeltsin's remarks during a state visit to France, as reported in John Lloyd, "Call by Yeltsin for Immediate Western Support," *Financial Times*, March 17, 1993, p. 16.

64. United Press International, "Russian Parliament Leader Lashes Out at 'Foreign Interference,'" April 2, 1993.

65. Olivier Blanchard, Maksim Boyco, Marek Dabrowski, Rudiger Dornbusch, Richard Layard, and Andrei Shleifer, *Post-Communist Reform: Pain and Progress* (MIT Press, 1993), p. 54.

66. Michael McFaul, "State Power, Institutional Change, and the Politics of Privatization in Russia," *World Politics*, vol. 47 (January 1995), pp. 210–43; for details, see Joseph Blasi, Maya Kroumova, and Douglas Kruse, *Kremlin Capitalism: Privatizing the Russian Economy* (Cornell University Press, 1997).

67. Interview with Dmitri Vasiliev, deputy chairman of the State Property Committee at the time.

68. Tragically, as discussed in chap. 9, this success story eventually ended in scandal when the two American advisers to the GKI funded by AID, Jonathan Hay and Andrei Shleifer, were accused of improper use of AID funds for private gain.

69. See Matt Bivens and Jonas Bernstein, "The Russia You Never Met," *Demokratizatsiya*, vol. 6 (Fall 1998), pp. 613–47; and Janine Wedel, "The Harvard Boys Do Russia," *Nation*, June 1, 1998, pp. 11–16; and Janine Wedel, *Collision and Collusion: The Strange Case of Western Aid to Eastern Europe, 1988–1998* (St. Martin's Press, 1998).

70. Interview with Atwood.

71. Interview with Morningstar.

72. Interview with Ingram.

73. Interview with James Steinberg.

74. Interviews with Wayne Merry and Thomas Graham.

75. Interview with Anders Åslund.

76. Interview with Talbott.

77. Steven Greenhouse, "Russia Aid Plan Promotes Role for U.S. Companies," *New York Times*, July 24, 1993, p. 4; and David Kramer, "Russian Aid (II)," *National Interest*, no. 39 (Spring 1995), pp. 78–82.

78. General Accounting Office (GAO), *Overseas Investment: Issues Related to the Overseas Private Investment Corporation's Reauthorization*, GAO/NSIAD-97-230 (September 1997), pp. 18–19.

79. Quoted in David Kramer, "Russian Aid (II)," *National Interest*, no. 39 (Spring 1995), p. 79.

80. GAO, *Overseas Investment*, p. 20.

81. Interviews with Andrei Kozyrev and Talbott. Talbott, *The Russia Hand*, pp. 64–65.

82. Interview with Rose Gottemoeller.

83. Interview with David Lipton.

84. Office of the Coordinator of the U.S. Assistance to the NIS, *U.S. Government Assistance to and Cooperative Activities with the New Independent States of the Former Soviet Union: FY 1997 Annual Report* (Department of State, January 1998), p. 75.

85. Sachs, "Western Financial Assistance and Russia's Reforms," p. 159.

86. See Åslund, *How Russia Became a Market Economy*, p. 69; and John Lloyd, "Moscow Seeks Active G7 Backing for Reforms," *Financial Times*, March 20-21, 1993, p. 2.

87. Freeland, "World Bank Lends $6bn to Russia," p. 2; Private foundations, such as George Soros's Open Society Institute, were more active than the U.S. government. See Irina Dezhina and Loren Graham, *Russian Basic Science after Ten Years of Transition and Foreign Support*, Working Papers, no. 24 (Washington: Carnegie Endowment for International Peace, February 2002); see Rosner, *The New Tug of War*, p. 52, for the political problems associated with proposing social safety net funds.

88. Janine Wedel's book on aid to Russia does not even mention Cooperative Threat Reduction or democracy assistance. See Wedel, *Collision and Collusion*.

89. Office of the Coordinator of the U.S. Assistance to the NIS, *U.S. Government Assistance to and Cooperative Activities with the New Independent States of the Former Soviet Union* (Department of State, April 1996), pp. 2–3.

90. Defense Secretary William Perry, "Forging Realistic, Pragmatic Relations with Russia," address at George Washington University, March 14, 1994, in *Defense News*, vol. 9, no. 19 (1994), pp. 1–6; and interview with Elizabeth Sherwood-Randall.

91. Ashton Carter and William Perry, *Preventive Defense: A New Security Strategy for America* (Brookings, 1999), especially chap. 2.

92. On these budgetary debates in the House and Senate, see Amy Woolf, "Nuclear Weapons in Russia: Safety, Security, and Control Issues," *CRS Issue Brief for Congress* (Washington: Congressional Research Service, November 5, 2001).

93. Woolf, "Nuclear Weapons in Russia," p. 8.

94. Office of the Coordinator of the U.S. Assistance to the NIS, *U.S. Government Assistance to and Cooperative Activities with Eurasia, Fiscal Year 2001* (Department of State, March 2002), p. 153.

95. Office of the Coordinator of the U.S. Assistance to the NIS, *U.S. Government Assistance to and Cooperative Activities with the New Independent States of the Former Soviet Union*, p. 3. The benefits of offering this employment, of course, are very difficult to measure.

96. Interview with Daniel Poneman.

97. The MPC&A budgets were as follows: 1993, 3 million; 1994, 11 million; 1995, 73 million; 1996, 99 million; 1997, 115 million; 1998, 137 million; 1999, 152 million; 2000, 145 million; and 2001, 145 million.

98. Woolf, "Nuclear Weapons in Russia," p. 12.

99. Office of the Coordinator of the U.S. Assistance to the NIS, *U.S. Government Assistance to and Cooperative Activities with Eurasia, Fiscal Year 2001*, p. 153.

100. Interview with William Perry.

101. Interview with Ashton Carter.

102. Perry, "Forging Realistic, Pragmatic Relations with Russia."

103. Interview with James Collins.

104. Interviews with Morningstar, William Taylor, Perry, and Carter.

105. Laurie Morse, "Thumbs Down from Grain Traders," *Financial Times*, April 6, 1993, p. 4.; White House press release, "Vancouver Summit Assistance Package," March 31, 1993; "Background Briefing by Senior Administration Officials, April 4, 1993, "Canada Place, Vancouver, British Columbia; Office of the Coordinator of the U.S. Assistance to the NIS, *U.S. Government Assistance to and Cooperative Activities with Eurasia, Fiscal Year 2001*, p. 153.

106. Interview with Atwood.

107. Rosner, *The New Tug-of-War*, pp. 49–50.

108. Interview with Atwood. Talbott's lack of involvement in their issues was also a theme of interviews with Lipton and Morningstar.

109. Yegor Gaidar, *Days of Defeat and Victory* (University of Washington Press, 1999), p. 152.

110. Interview with Lipton.

111. Seymour Martin Lipset, "Some Social Requisites of Democracy: Economic Development and Political Legitimacy," *American Political Science Review*, vol. 53, no. 1 (1959), pp. 69–105. See also Seymour Martin Lipset, *Political Man: The Social Bases of Politics* (Doubleday, 1960); and more recently, Adam Przeworski, Michael Alvarez, Jose Antonio Cheibub, and Fernando Limongi, *Democracy and Development: Political Institutions and Well-Being in the World, 1950-1990* (Cambridge University Press, 2000).

112. This observation is based on McFaul's interactions with dozens of AID and State Department officials during this period.

113. Discussions with senior officials in AID, the Eurasia Foundation, and others in Washington and Moscow. This idea also came from one of the classic texts of social science widely popular when most senior Clinton officials were students. The phrase, "no middle class, no democracy," comes from Barrington Moore, *Social Origins of Dictatorship and Democracy: Lord and Peasant in the Making of the Modern World* (Beacon Press, 1966).

114. Yevgeny Yasin, "A Normal Economy Is the Main Condition for Democracy," *Izvestiya*, August 27, 1991, reprinted in *Current Digest of the Soviet Press*, vol. 43 (October 9, 1991), p. 15. In the early 1990s, McFaul participated in many discussions about assistance to Russia with U.S. government officials in which this argument was frequently made.

115. Yasin, "A Normal Economy Is the Main Condition for Democracy," p. 15. For the analytical underpinnings of this fear, see Adam Przeworski, *Democracy and the Market: Political and Economics Reforms in Eastern Europe and Latin America* (Cambridge: Cambridge University Press, 1991).

116. On these debates, see Vladimir Mau, *Ekonomiki i Vlast'* (Moskva: Delo, 1995).

117. Yeltsin's address to the Fifth Congress, October 28, 1991, in *Yeltsin-Khasbulatov*, p. 96.

118. Mau, *Ekonomika i Vlast'*, p. 43. Yeltsin then blamed Gaidar for not being politically astute, even though Yeltsin himself was president and should have shouldered at least some of the political responsibility for selling economic reform. As he wrote in his memoirs, "Still, by sophisticatedly refusing to 'dirty their hands with politics' and leaving all political initiative to their chief [Burbulis], the Gaidar team made a tactical error that cost us all a great deal." Boris Yeltsin, *The Struggle for Russia* (Times Books, 1995), p. 159.

119. See McFaul, *Russia's Unfinished Revolution*, chap. 4.

120. McFaul's interview with Yegor Gaidar, October 8, 1997.

121. Yeltsin's close aide, Anatoly Chubais, emphasized this point in recounting the initial strategies for economic reform during an address at the Carnegie Endowment for International Peace, May 17, 1999.

122. Interview with Jeanne Bourgault, at the time, director of the Office of Democratic Initiatives and Human Resources (DIHR).

123. Between 1992 and 1999, the IMF loaned $22 billion to Russia, which was roughly three-quarters of all multilateral lending to Russia in the 1990s. See Augusto Lopez-Claros, "The Role of International Financial Institutions during the Transition in Russia," unpublished manuscript, September 2002.

124. We use 1995 figures here because 1994 was the peak of AID funds to Russia. As the overall budget decreases, the imbalance between economic and political reform narrows because spending on economic assistance declines.

125. Authors' calculations based on analyses of budgets described in the annual reports of the aid compiled by the Office of the Coordinator of U.S. Assistance to the NIS, called *U.S. Government Assistance to and Cooperative Activities with the New Independent States of the Former Soviet Union* (Department of State, various years).

126. Joseph Stiglitz, "Whither Reform? Ten Years of Transition," paper delivered at Annual World Bank Conference on Development Economics, Washington, 1999; and Jerry Hough, *The Logic of Economic Reform in Russia* (Brookings, 2001).

127. Interview with Stanley Fischer.

128. See, for instance, Michael McFaul, "Why Russia's Politics Matter," *Foreign Affairs*, vol. 74 (January–February 1995), pp. 87–99; and Michael McFaul, *When Capitalism and Democracy Collide in Transition*, Working Paper 1 (Harvard University, Davis Center for Russian Studies, 1997), pp. 1–37.

129. National Democratic Institute, "Submission of the National Democratic Institute to the Congressionally Authorized Study on U.S. Government-Funded Democracy Programs" (Washington, July 1994), p. 2.

130. Joel Hellman, "Winners Take All: The Politics of Partial Reform in Post-Communist Transitions," *World Politics*, vol. 50 (January 1998), pp. 203–34; Jean-Jacques Dethier, Hafez Ghanem, and Edda Zoli, "Does Democracy Facilitate the Economic Transition? An Empirical Study of Central and Eastern Europe and the Former Soviet Union," unpublished manuscript, World Bank, June 1999; European Bank for Reconstruction and Development, *Transition Report 1999: Ten Years of Transition* (London, 1999), chap. 5; and Anders Åslund, *Building Capitalism: The Transformation of the Former Soviet Bloc* (Cambridge: Cambridge University Press, 2001).

131. Stiglitz worked for the Clinton administration at the time but was not part of the team advising on aid strategy. It was only from his position at the World Bank as chief economist that he began to speak and write about these issues. See, in particular, his "Whither Reform?" and "The Insider: What I Learned at the World Economic Crisis," *New Republic,* April 17 and 24, 2000, pp. 56–60.

132. Interview with Gati.

133. Regrettably, no comprehensive history or assessment of these programs in Russia has been written. On some individual sectors, see James Richter, "Evaluating Western Assistance to Russian Women's Organizations," and Leslie Powell, "Western and Russian Environmental NGOs: A Greener Russia?" in Sarah Mendelson and John Glenn, eds., *The Power and Limits of NGOs: A Critical Look at Building Democracy in Eastern Europe and Eurasia* (Columbia University Press, 2002); Lisa McIntosh Sundstrom, "Strength from Without? Transnational Influences on NGO Development in Russia," Ph.D. dissertation, Stanford University, December 2001; and Sarah Mendelson, "Democracy Assistance and Political Transition in Russia: Between Success and Failure," *International Security*, vol. 25 (Spring 2001), pp. 68–106.

134. See Office of the Coordinator of the U.S. Assistance to the NIS, *U.S. Government Assistance to and Cooperative Activities with Eurasia, Fiscal Year 2001* (Department of State, March 2002), p. 153.

135. On the difficulties, see Thomas Carothers, *Aiding Democracy Abroad: The Learning Curve* (Washington: Carnegie Endowment for International Peace, 1999); and Diamond, *Promoting Democracy in the 1990s.*

136. Interview with Atwood.

137. Interview with Bourgault.

138. On why smaller states are usually more effective than larger ones, see Moises Naim, "Latin America: The Second Stage of Reform," *Journal of Democracy*, vol. 5 (October 1994), pp. 32–48.

139. *The Eurasia Foundation: 1996-1997 Report* (Washington, 1997), p. 9.

140. See David Kramer, "Russian Aid (II)," *National Interest*, no. 39 (Spring 1995), p. 78.

141. Strobe Talbott, deputy secretary of state, statement before the Subcommittee of the Senate Appropriations Committee, 104 Cong. 1 sess., February 5, 1995, p. 5.

142. Elizabeth Sherwood-Randall, "U.S. Policy and the Caucasus," *Contemporary Caucasus Newsletter* (Spring 1998), pp. 3–4, University of California, Berkeley, Program in Soviet and Post-Soviet Studies.

143. Section 907 states, "United States assistance under this or any other Act . . . may not be provided to the Government of Azerbaijan until the President determines, and so reports to the Congress that the Government of Azerbaijan is taking demonstrable steps to cease all blockades and other offensive uses of force against Armenia and Nagorno-Karabakh."

144. Stuart Goldman, "IB92089: Russia," *CRS Report for Congress* (Congressional Research Service, June 15, 2000), p. 25.

145. Elaine Sciolino, "Clinton Adds Visit from Russian Official on Aid," *New York Times*, March 19, 1993, p. A5.

146. Interview with Talbott.

147. Yeltsin, television address, December 30, 1991, reprinted in *Yeltsin-Khasbulatov*, p. 111.

148. Quoted in Ronald D. Asmus, *Opening NATO's Door: How the Alliance Remade Itself for a New Era* (Columbia University Press, 2002), p. 112.

Chapter 6

1. "A Personal Account from Moscow, December 1992: Russia after the Congress of People's Deputies," memo from Toby Gati to Mike Mandelbaum, December 16, 1992, p. 4.

2. Interview with Brian Atwood.

3. Interviews with Anthony Lake and Coit D. Blacker.

4. Interviews with Sandy Berger, Leon Fuerth, Strobe Talbott, and James Steinberg.

5. Anthony Lake, *Six Nightmares: Real Threats in a Dangerous World and How America Can Meet Them* (Little, Brown, 2000), p. 194.

6. Interviews with Lake and Talbott; and Lake, *Six Nightmares*, p. 194.

7. TASS, February 13, 1992, in Foreign Broadcast Information Service (FBIS)-SOV-92-031, February 14, 1992, p. 45; and "Rezolyutsii II Chrezvychainogo S'ezda CPRF," *Sovetskaya Rossiya*, February 25, 1993, p. 2.

8. Joel Hellman, "Winners Take All: The Politics of Partial Reform in Post-Communist Transitions," *World Politics*, vol. 50, no. 1 (January 1998), pp. 203–34; A self-styled centrist political coalition, Civic Union, was composed of several important leaders, parties, and interest groups. Dismayed with democratic Russia's support for Soviet disintegration but reluctant to join forces with more militant nationalists, Nikolai Travkin and his Democratic Party of Russia found a kindred organization in Vice President Rutskoi's People's Party for Free Russia, a post-Soviet outgrowth of the Communist Party of the Soviet Union. These two parties then united with Arkady Volsky and his Russian Union of Industrialists and Entrepreneurs, a political lobby that claimed to represent the interests of Russia's enterprise directors. On June 21, 1992, these three organizations joined forces with the influential parliamentary fraction, *Smena*, and a host of smaller organizations to form Civic Union. In the fall of 1992, the Federation of Independent Russian Trade Unions (FNPR), the renamed Soviet trade union organization, which claimed more than 60 million members at the time, also sided with Civic Union.

9. See Grazhdanskii Soyuz, "Programma antikrizisnogo uregulirovaniya" (Moskva, 1992), pp. 13–23; and *Izvestiya*, August 5, 1992, p. 2.

10. John Lloyd, "Yeltsin Suffers Setback as Congress Rejects Gaidar," *Financial Times*, December 10, 1992, p. 16.

11. See Boris Yeltsin, "Obrashcheniya Prezidenta na VII S'ezde narodnykh deputatov," December 10, 1992, in *Yeltsin-Khasbulatov: Edinstvo, Kompromis, Bor'ba* (Moskva: Terra-terra, 1994), pp. 235–38.

12. United Press International, March 16, 1993.

13. John Lowenhardt, *The Reincarnation of Russia: Struggling with the Legacy of Communism, 1990-1994* (Duke University Press, 1995), pp. 134–35; and Vyacheslav Kostikov, *Roman s Prezidentom: Zapiski Press-Sekretaria* (Moskva: Vagrius, 1997), p. 169.

14. Interviews with Wayne Merry and Thomas Graham.

15. Columbia University professor Robert Legvold, who attended the dinner, shared this observation with the authors.

16. George Stephanopoulos, *All Too Human: A Political Education* (Little, Brown and Co., 1999), p. 138.

17. Strobe Talbott, *The Russia Hand: A Memoir of Presidential Diplomacy* (Random House, 2002), p. 68.

18. Serge Schmemann, "Summit in Vancouver: The Overview," *New York Times*, April 5, 1993, p. A1.

19. Interview with Graham.

20. Talbott, *The Russia Hand*, p. 70.

21. Anatoly Sobchak, "Dostup k vechnozelneyuchshemu delu," *Moskovskie Novosti*, March 21, 1993, p. 7a; and Boris Yeltsin, *The Struggle for Russia*, translated by Catherine A. Fitzpatrick (Times Books, 1994), p. 247.

22. Ruslan Khasbulatov, *Velikaya Rossiiskaya Tragediya*, II (Moscow: SIMS, 1994).

23. Dimitri Simes, "Reform Reaffirmed," *Foreign Policy*, no. 90 (Spring 1993), pp. 38–56.

24. Interview with Nicholas Burns.

25. "Clinton Sends Yeltsin His Full Support," *Associated Press*, September 23, 1993.

26. Fred Kaplan, "Yeltsin Suspends Legislature, Faces Impeachment Bid," *Boston Globe*, September 22, 1993, p. 1; Elaine Sciolino, "U.S. Supports Move by Russian

Leader," *New York Times*, September 22, 1993; Saul Friedman, "U.S. Giving Boris Its Grudging Support," *Newsday*, September 22, 1993, p. 4; and Thomas Friedman, "U.S. to Speed Money to Bolster Yeltsin," *New York Times*, September 23, 1993.

27. Douglas Jehl, "Clinton Repeats Support for Yeltsin," *New York Times*, September 30, 1993, p. A14; and Clinton, quoted in Saul Friedman, "A Minefield in Moscow," *Newsday*, September 23, 1993, p. 114.

28. Louis D. Sell, "Embassy under Siege: An Eyewitness Account of Yeltsin's 1993 Attack on Parliament," *Problems of Post-Communism*, vol. 50 (July-August 2003), p. 64.

29. Clinton, "Remarks and an Exchange with Reporters on Russia," October 3, 1993, reprinted in *Public Papers of the President: William J. Clinton—1993*, vol. 2 (Government Printing Office, 1994), pp. 1647–48; and Douglas Jehl, "Showdown in Moscow: Clinton Reaffirming Support for Yeltsin, Blames Rutskoi's Faction for the Violence," *New York Times*, October 4, 1993, p. A11.

30. Douglas Jehl, "Showdown in Moscow: U.S. Reaction: Clinton Is 'Foursquare' behind Yeltsin but Expects Elections Soon," *New York Times*, October 5 1993, p. A19.

31. Ibid.

32. Interviews with Nicholas Burns and Thomas Donilon.

33. Peter Gosselin and Michael Putzel, "U.S. Reaffirms Full Support for Russian Leader," *Boston Globe*, October 5, 1993, p. 12.

34. Jeremy Rosner, *The New Tug of War: Congress, the Executive Branch, and National Security* (Washington: Carnegie Endowment for International Peace, 1995), pp. 55, 59.

35. Other leading members of Congress made similar statements. Thomas Friedman, "Showdown in Moscow: U.S. to Speed Money to Bolster Yeltsin," *New York Times*, September 22, 1993, p. A13.

36. Steven Holmes, "$2.5 Billion in Aid for Russia Backed in Key Senate Vote," *New York Times*, September 24, 1993, p. A6. The headline in this article erroneously implied that the entire package was devoted to Russia.

37. Speaker's Advisory Group on Russia, Christopher Cox, Chairman, *Russia's Road to Corruption: How the Clinton Administration Exported Government Instead of Free Enterprise and Failed the Russian People* (U.S. House of Representatives, September 2000), especially chap. 4.

38. After October 4, Senator Robert Dole (R-Kans.) adopted a more skeptical view of Yeltsin and his "shock therapy" reforms. Gosselin and Putzel, "U.S. Reaffirms Full Support for Russian Leader," p. 12.

39. Quoted in Mary Curtius, "U.S. Banking on Win for Russia Reforms," *Boston Globe*, December 12, 1993, p. 20.

40. Elaine Sciolino, "U.S. Offers Help to Russians to Insure Election Are Fair," *New York Times*, October 24, 1993, p. A12; McFaul was one of the international election observers.

41. Interview with Boris Fyodorov; Anders Åslund, *How Russia Became a Market Economy* (Brookings, 1995), p. 199.

42. Interview with Merry.

43. Michael McFaul, "Russian Electoral Trends," in Zoltan Borany, ed., *Russian Politics: Challenges of Democratization* (Cambridge University Press, 2001), pp. 19–63.

44. Alexander Yanov, *Weimar Russia* (New York: Slovo-Word, 1995); Michael McFaul "Nut 'n' Honey: Why Zhirinovsky Can Win," *New Republic*, February 14, 1994,

pp. 23–24; and McFaul, "Spektr Russkogo Fashizma," *Nezavisimaya Gazeta*, November 2, 1994.

45. Charles Fairbanks, "The Politics of Resentment," *Journal of Democracy*, vol. 5 (April 1994), p. 41.

46. Yegor Gaidar raised the specter of institutional standoff at a press conference on December 14, 1993, that McFaul attended. See also Vladimir Lysenko, "Toward Presidential Rule," *Journal of Democracy*, vol. 5 (April 1994), pp. 9–13; Fred Hiatt, "Democrat Looks Back in Anger," *Moscow Times*, September 23, 1994, p. 4; and Paul Norton, "Yavlinsky Offers Grim Assessment of Russian Reform," *Moscow Tribune*, January 27, 1995, p. 6.

47. Daniel Williams and R. Jeffrey Smith, "U.S. Now Gloomy on Russia Vote; Dazed Delegation in Moscow Rules Out Meeting Zhirinovsky," *Washington Post*, December 15, 1993, p. A1; and interview with Talbott.

48. McFaul's impressions from a dinner meeting in Moscow with Talbott, Nuland, Ambassador Thomas Pickering, and Leon Fuerth, December 14, 1993. See also Thomas Friedman, "On Russian Vote, Clinton Accentuates the Positive," *New York Times*, December 14, 1993, p. A16.

49. Hellman, "Winners Take All."

50. For details, see Michael McFaul, *Understanding Russia's 1993 Parliamentary Elections: Implications for American Foreign Policy*, Essays in Public Policy (Palo Alto: Hoover Institution Press, 1994).

51. Peter Passell, "Russia's Political Turmoil Follows Half Steps, Not Shock Therapy," *New York Times*, December 30, 1993, p. D2.

52. Interview with David Lipton. Amy Kaslow, "World Lenders Move to Ease Terms for Russia," *Christian Science Monitor*, December 24, 1993, p. 1. For negative reactions to Gore's remarks from the economists who had been advising the Russian government, see Peter Passell, "Russia's Political Turmoil Follows Half Steps, Not Shock Therapy," *New York Times*, December 30, 1993, sec. D, p. 2.

53. Elaine Sciolino, "U.S. Is Abandoning 'Shock Therapy' for the Russians," *New York Times*, December 21, 1993, p. A1.

54. Interview with Lipton.

55. Andrew Nagorski, "Trying to Keep Russia on Track," *Newsweek International*, January 29, 2001.

56. Interview with Talbott.

57. Interview with Boris Fyodorov.

58. R.W. Apple, "The Russia Vote: Results in Russia Shake Washington," *New York Times*, December 15, 1993, p. A16.

59. Interviews with James Steinberg and Donilon.

60. Appearing on ABC's *Nightline* on December 14, 1993, former secretary of state James Baker suggested that the president's national security adviser, Anthony Lake, might try to meet with Zhirinovsky. McFaul attended several meetings with government officials at this time at which the idea of engagement with Zhirinovsky was floated.

61. Apple, "The Russia Vote: Results in Russia Shake Washington," p. A16.

62. John King, "A Rebuke for Zhirinovsky: Gore Blasts Harsh Views, Urges Greater Aid for Russia," *Record*, December 16, 1993, p. A21; and Elaine Sciolino, "Clinton Reaffirms Policy on Russia," *New York Times*, December 16, 1993, p. A11.

63. Vladimir Mau, *Ekonomiskaya reforma: skvoz' prizmu konstitutsii i politiki* (Izd-vo Ad Marginem, 1999); Jeffrey Sachs, "Betrayal," *New Republic*, January 31, 1994, p. 15; and the interview with Jeffrey Sachs, "They Are Going to Pursue Dangerous Policies," in *Time*, January 31, 1994, p. 90; and Leyla Boulton, "Chubais Sounds Inflation Warning," *Financial Times*, February 3, 1994, p. 2. Until resigning on January 24, 1994, Sachs and Aslund were formally affiliated with the Ministry of Finance. Interview with Anders Åslund.

64. Lilia Shevtsova, *Yeltsin's Russia: Myths and Reality* (Washington: Carnegie Endowment for International Peace, 1999), p. 111.

65. Emil' Pain and Arkady Popov, "Vlast' i obshchestvo na barrikadakh" [State and society at the barricades], *Izvestiya*, February 10, 1995, p. 4. In interviews with McFaul during the summer of 1995, liberal presidential advisers Giorgy Satarov, Mark Urnov, and Leonid Smirnyagin claimed to play a marginal role in these deliberations. Similar accounts of the liberals' marginalization can be found in Yegor Gaidar, *Dni Porazhenii i Poded* [*Days of Defeat and Victory*] (Moscow: Vagrius, 1996), chap. 13; and David Remnick, *Resurrection: The Struggle for Russia* (Random House, 1997), chap. 9.

66. On the formation of this coalition, see Aleksandr Minkin, "Advokat shefa KGB Kriuchkova zashchishchaet Prezidenta Yeltsina" [The Lawyer of KGB chief Kryuchkov defends President Yeltsin], *Moskovskii Komsomolets*, January 14, 1995, pp. 1–2.

67. John Dunlop dates their domination over decisionmaking to be between October 1994 and February 1995. See his "Five Months That Shook Russia," *Hoover Digest*, no. 2 (1996), pp. 90–94. Zhirinovsky and his Liberal Democratic Party had captured almost a quarter of the popular vote, demonstrating to Yeltsin's inner circle of advisers that Yeltsin had to change his liberal image, rhetoric, and allies in order to win the next presidential election. See Vladimir Lysenko, "Avtoritarnyi Rezhim Neizbezhen," *Nezavisimaya Gazeta*, December 22, 1994; Emil Payin and Arkady Popov, "Chechnya," in Jeremy Azrael and Emil Payin, eds., *U.S. and Russian Policymaking with Respect to the Use of Force* (Santa Monica: Rand, 1996), pp. 25–27; and Shevtsova, *Yeltsin's Russia*, pp. 113–14.

68. Gaidar, *Dni Porazhenii i Poded*, p. 329. These motivations are precisely one of the causes of war outlined in Edward Mansfield and Jack Snyder, "Democratization and the Danger of War," *International Security*, vol. 20 (Summer 1995), pp. 5–38.

69. John B. Dunlop, *Russia Confronts Chechnya: Roots of a Separatist Conflict* (Cambridge University Press, 1998), p. 124; On the near anarchic condition of Chechnya under Dudayev during the period of de facto independence, see Anatol Lieven, *Chechnya: Tombstone of Russian Power* (Yale University Press, 1998), pp. 74–84.

70. After his 1996 re-election, Yeltsin appointed General Alexander Lebed to negotiate a formal peace settlement with Chechnya, as Lebed placed a strong third in the first round of the presidential election as an antiwar candidate. Although Lebed eventually clashed with Yeltsin and was removed from office, he successfully completed his negotiations with the Chechens on August 31, 1996, buoyed by his electoral mandate of 11 million voters to end the war. In his careful counting of combatants and noncombatants on both sides, John Dunlop came up with a "conservative total" of 46,500. See John Dunlop, "How Many Soldiers and Civilians Died during the Russo-Chechen War of 1994-1996?" *Central Asian Survey*, vol. 19, nos. 3 and 4 (2000), p. 338. Russian politician Grigory Yavlinsky put the number at 100,000. See Grigory Yavlinsky, "Where Is Russia Headed? An Uncertain Prognosis," *Journal of Democracy*, vol. 8 (January 1997), p. 4.

71. Interview with Talbott.

72. Interview with Talbott. Dudayev allegedly sent a letter to Clinton on November 10, 1994, warning of the impending invasion, but no senior official in the Clinton administration remembers seeing the note. On the letter, see Dunlop, *Russia Confronts Chechnya*, p. 178, note 41.

73. Interviews with Talbott and James Woolsey, then director of Central Intelligence.

74. Talbott, *The Russia Hand*, p. 148; and interview with Nicholas Burns.

75. Interviews with Talbott and Steinberg.

76. Interview with Victoria Nuland.

77. Interviews with Steinberg, Coit D. Blacker, Lake, and Fuerth.

78. Interview with Ashton Carter.

79. Warren Christopher, *In the Stream of History*, p. 266.

80. Interview with Carter.

81. Interview with Lake.

82. Anthony Lake, "The Challenge of Change in Russia," remarks before the U.S.-Russia Business Council, April 1, 1996, White House, Office of the Press Secretary, April 3, 1996, p. 2; President Clinton, final press conference at the Summit of the Americas, Florida, December 11, 1994; and CNN, May 11, 1995, transcript 1020-3.

83. Interview with Burns.

84. Interview with Talbott; Jeffrey Smith, "U.S. Interests Seen Allied with Russian in Chechnya," *Washington Post*, December 25, 1994, p. A27; and interview with Warren Christopher on *MacNeil/Lehrer Newshour*, December 13, 1994. For an alternative perspective that dismissed this domino metaphor, see Michael McFaul, "Russian Politics after Chechnya," *Foreign Policy*, no. 99 (Summer 1995), pp. 149–65.

85. On this point, Talbott and his greatest critics seemed to agree. See Thomas E. Graham, *Russia's Decline and Uncertain Recovery* (Washington: Carnegie Endowment for International Peace, 2002).

86. U.S. Department of State, Office of the Spokesman, daily press briefing, January 3, 1995. In an interview, McCurry said emphatically that Clinton himself formulated this analogy and senior officials had signed off on it.

87. David Hoffman and John Harris, "Clinton, Yeltsin Gloss Over Chechen War," *Washington Post*, April 22, 1996, p. A1.

88. Interviews with Nuland and Talbott; and Talbott, *The Russia Hand*, p. 205.

89. Anthony Lake, "The Challenge of Change in Russia," p. 2; see Strobe Talbott, deputy secretary of state, statement before the Subcommittee of the Senate Appropriations Committee, February 5, 1995, 104 Cong. 1 sess., p. 3; Warren Christopher, *In the Stream of History: Shaping Foreign Policy for a New Era* (Stanford University Press), p. 249.

90. Deputy Secretary of State Strobe Talbott, "Supporting Democracy and Economic Reform in the New Independent States," statement before the Subcommittee on Foreign Operations of the Senate Appropriations Committee, February 9, 1995, 104 Cong. 1 sess., in *U.S. Department of State Dispatch*, vol. 6 (February 20, 1995), p. 121; and interview with Christopher on *MacNeil/Lehrer Newshour*.

91. Mike McCurry, State Department briefing, January 3, 1995.

92. Interview with Christopher on *MacNeil/Lehrer Newshour*; and interview with Fuerth.

93. Christopher, *In the Stream of History*, p. 268.

94. Interview with Talbott.

95. *NPR's Morning Edition*, March 30, 1995, transcript 1574-5, p. 2.

96. Wendy Ross, "The Role of Foreign Policy Advisors in Dole, Clinton Campaigns, U.S. Foreign Policy Agenda," *USIA Electronic Journals*, vol. 1 (October 1996). Dole also called the May 1995 summit a failure because Clinton failed to secure any concessions on Chechnya. See CNN, May 11, 1995, transcript 1020-3; and American Foreign Policy Council, *Russian Reform Monitor*, no. 8 (May 10, 1995).

97. Brzezinski, on *CNN International*, June 15, 1996, transcript 1549-3.

98. Grigory Yavlinsky, "Shortsighted," *New York Times Magazine*, January 8, 1995, p. 66.

99. For details, see Michael McFaul, "Russian Politics after Chechnya," *Foreign Policy*, no. 99 (Summer 1995), pp. 149–65.

100. Interview with Burns.

101. The phrase is dreadful because the process of marketization and the process of democratization are related but separate phenomena. One, therefore, should not modify the other. Curiously, Clinton officials never used the phrase "democratic capitalism." On the tensions between these reform processes, see Michael McFaul, *When Capitalism and Democracy Collide in Transition*, Working Paper 1 (Harvard University, Davis Center for Russian Studies, 1997), pp. 1–37.

102. See David Hoffman, *The Oligarchs: Wealth and Power in the New Russia* (Public Affairs, 2002).

103. Interviews with Steinberg, Fuerth, and other U.S. government officials.

104. On why Yavlinsky could not win in 1996, see Michael McFaul, "Russia between Elections: The Vanishing Center," *Journal of Democracy*, vol. 7 (April 1996), pp. 90–104.

105. Veliko Vujacic, "Gennady Zyuganov and the 'Third Road,'" *Post-Soviet Affairs*, vol. 12 (April–June 1996), pp. 118–54; Yuri Nevezhin, "Novyi gost' u shakhterov," *Nezavisimaya Gazeta*, March 30, 1996, p. 2; and Eugene Lawson and Blake Marshall, "Russia on Election Eve: A U.S.-Russia Business Council Report to the Board of Directors" (Washington: U.S.-Russia Business Council, May 17, 1996), pp. 4–5, 15.

106. Daniel Singer, "The Burden of Boris," *Nation*, April 1, 1996, p. 23; and Jerry Hough, Evelyn Davidheiser, and Susan Goodrich Lehmann, *The 1996 Russian Presidential Election* (Brookings, 1996), p. 86; and Lawson and Marshall, "Russia on Election Eve," p. 15.

107. Yeltsin had requested that Clinton not meet with Zyuganov one-on-one and Clinton obliged. See Alessandra Stanley, "Clinton Is Served Watered-Down Communism," *New York Times*, April 22, 1996, p. A7.

108. Interview with Gaidar.

109. Korzhakov quoted in Boris Yeltsin, *Midnight Diaries*, translated by Catherine A. Fitzpatrick (Public Affairs, 1999), p. 23; and David Remnick, *Resurrection: The Struggle for Russia* (Random House, 1997), chap. 11. Those working for Korzhakov at the time expressed similar pessimism about Yeltsin's prospects to McFaul.

110. On the NATO issue, see chap. 8 in this volume.

111. Vladimir Potanin, the head of Interros at the time, cooperated with Anatoly Chubais to draw up the plans for the program. For details of the loans for shares program, see Hoffman, *The Oligarchs*, chap. 12; and Chrystia Freeland, *Sale of the Century: Russia's Wild Ride from Communism to Capitalism* (Crown Business, 2000), chap. 8.

112. Interviews with David Lipton, Lake, and other U.S. government officials.

113. Interviews with Lipton, Atwood, and Talbott.

114. Interview with Talbott. Collins quoted in Elaine Sciolino, "Who'll Win Russia? For America, Uncertainty Wraps the Riddle," *New York Times*, May 19, 1996, sec. 4, p. 1.

115. Interviews with Talbott and Blacker. A photograph of the meeting is in Christopher, *In the Stream of History*.

116. Interviews with Blacker and Fuerth. Only Yavlinsky's friend, William Safire, believed that Yavlinsky was a competitive candidate and wrote often in support of him in his *New York Times* columns. Yavlinsky won only 7 percent of the vote in the first round.

117. Talbott, *The Russia Hand*, p. 195.

118. Dick Morris, *Behind the Oval Office: Getting Reelected against All Odds* (Los Angeles: Renaissance Books, 1999), p. 250; and interviews with Dick Morris and Sandy Berger.

119. *PBS Frontline*, "Return of the Czar," 2000 (www.pbs.org.).

120. Alison Mitchell, "Clinton Tiptoes around Russian Vote Except to Say He's for It," *New York Times*, April 21, 1996, sec. 1, p. 10; and Stewart Powell, "Clinton Cautious as Russian Vote Nears," *Times Union* (Albany, N.Y.), June 9, 1996, p. A9.

121. "Backing Boris: Summiteering, Electioneering, and Debt Relief," *Prism: A Bi-Weekly on Post-Soviet States*, vol. 11 (May 3, 1996), part I.

122. Interview with Morris.

123. Aleksandr Bekker, "Zapad idet na vyruchku rossiiskim vlastyam," *Segodnya*, March 28, 1996, p. 1; and OECD, *Russian Federation 1997* (Paris, 1997) p. 69.

124. Interviews with Carlos Pascual and Lipton. Alison Mitchell, "Pulling for Yeltsin, but Gingerly," *New York Times*, April 14, 1996, sec. 4, p. 4; and Steven Erlanger, "Chicken Parts and Politics on Agenda at Sinai Talks," *New York Times*, March 28, 1996. Talbott credits Dick Morris for the Saudi debt scheme. See Talbott, *The Russia Hand*, p. 447, note 6.

125. Interviews with Fyodorov and Lipton; and Anders Åslund, *Building Capitalism: The Transformation of the Former Soviet Bloc* (Cambridge University Press, 2001), p. 427.

126. Augusto Lopez-Claros, "The Role of International Financial Institutions during the Transition in Russia," unpublished manuscript, September 2002, p. 18.

127. Lawson and Marshall, "Russia on Election Eve," p. 1; and interview with Stanley Fischer.

128. Press conference by Vice President Gore and Prime Minister Chernomyrdin of Russia, Old Executive Office Building, Room 450, White House, Office of the Press Secretary, January 30, 1996.

129. Interviews with Lipton, Berger, and other U.S. government officials.

130. Paul Quinn-Judge, "Clinton Gives Yeltsin a Vote of Confidence; Declares Support for $9 Billion Loan," *Boston Globe*, January 31, 1996, p. 2; and Barry Schweid, "Clinton, Gore Back Huge Loan to Russia," *Associated Press*, January 31, 1996; Michael Gordon, "Russia and I.M.F. Agree on Loan for $10.2 Billion," *New York Times*, February 23, 1996, p. 2; and interviews with Lipton, Pascual, and other U.S. officials.

131. Gordon, "Russia and I.M.F. Agree on Loan for $10.2 Billion," p. 1.

132. Fyodorov, quoted in Gordon, "Russia and I.M.F. Agree on Loan for $10.2 Billion," p. 2.

133. See interviews with Lipton and Fischer.

134. Anders Åslund, *Building Capitalism: The Transformation of the Former Soviet Bloc* (Cambridge University Press, 2001); and Daniel Treisman, "Fighting Inflation in a Transitional Regime: Russia's Anomalous Stabilization," *World Politics*, vol. 50 (January 1998), pp. 235–65; and Stanley Fischer, "The Russian Economy: Prospects and Retrospect," address to the Higher School of Economics, Moscow, Russia, June 19, 2001 (http://www.imf.org/external/np/speeches/2001/061901.htm [July 2003]). The IMF has used this tactic of trying to "tie the king's hands" in other countries such as Brazil before a critical election.

135. Gaidar, upon hearing of the cancellation plan that morning, rushed to Spaso House, Pickering's residence, to urge the Americans to intervene with Yeltsin while his colleague, Anatoly Chubais, went to meet directly with Yeltsin to urge against cancellation. Gaidar recalls the day as one of the most pivotal in Russia's revolution. Interview with Gaidar.

136. Interviews with Talbott, Blacker, and Berger; and Talbott, *The Russia Hand*, p. 195.

137. Interviews with Talbott, Blacker, and others; and Talbott, *The Russia Hand*, p. 195.

138. On the divides and changes of control in Yeltsin's 1996 presidential campaign team, see Michael McFaul, *Russia's 1996 Presidential Election: The End of Polarized Politics* (Hoover Institution Press, 1997), chap. 3.

139. McFaul's interviews in 1996 with Yeltsin campaign officials Anatoly Chubais, Igor Malashenko, Vyacheslav Nikonov, and Giorgy Satarov. See also Michael Kramer, "Rescuing Boris," *Time*, July 15, 1996. Kramer's piece grossly overstates the role played by the American advisers, but it does provide an accurate account of their activities.

140. According to Talbott, he and others learned of Clinton's contacts, via Morris, with the American consultants in Moscow on March 29. Interviews with Talbott, Lake, Mike McCurry, and Dick Morris. See also Talbott, *The Russia Hand*, p. 447, n. 6.

141. Interview with Morris.

142. In one famous incident, the U.S. embassy requested that AID dismiss the head of the International Foundation for Electoral Systems office in Moscow, Michael Caputo, because Caputo had spoken out too publicly in support of his client, the Central Election Commission. At the time, the CEC was taking actions to prevent parties (including one pro-Western party, Yabloko) from participating in the 1995 parliamentary election. Caputo supported their actions. U.S. embassy officials also recommended that NDI and IRI curtail their party programming activities six months before the parliamentary vote and keep inactive their campaign training programs until after the 1996 presidential vote, a "recommendation" that infuriated NDI and IRI staffs in Moscow and Washington.

143. In collaboration with NDI, a Russian think tank, INDEM, published a six-volume series on *How to Win Elections*. NDI and IRI programs also introduced their Russian counterparts to American campaign techniques such as direct mail, negative ads, door-to-door voter mobilization, the use of focus groups, and "Rock the Vote."

144. As one example, NDI brought sixteen people from Russia to witness the 1992 presidential campaign in the United States. Roughly half of the alumni of this program were working for Yeltsin's campaign in 1996. Many senior staff members in the Yeltsin campaign also had close and long-standing ties to IRI.

145. For a serious and thoughtful effort, see Sarah Mendelson, "Democracy Assistance and Political Transition in Russia," *International Security*, vol. 25 (Spring 2001), pp. 68–106.

146. Richard Rose and Evgeny Tikhomirov, "Russia's Forced-Choice Presidential Election," *Post-Soviet Affairs*, vol. 12 (October–December 1996) pp. 351–79; Timothy Colton, *Transitional Citizens: Voters and What Influences Them in the New Russia* (Harvard University Press, 2000); and McFaul, *Russia's 1996 Presidential Election*.

147. Aleksei Zudin, "Biznes i politika v prezidentskoi kampanii 1996 goda," *Pro et Contra*, vol. 1 (October 1996), pp. 46–60. Some analysts have stressed the importance of pork to Yeltsin's re-election victory. See Yitzhak Brudny, "In Pursuit of the Russian Presidency: Why and How Yeltsin Won the 1996 Presidential Election," *Communist and Post-Communist Studies*, vol. 3 (Fall 1997), pp. 255–75; and Dan Treisman, "Deciphering Russia's Federal Finance: Fiscal Appeasement in 1995 and 1996," *Europe-Asia Studies*, vol. 50 (July 1998), pp. 893–906; Andrei Zapelkii, Aleksei Mukhin, and Nikita Tyukov, *Rossiya: Prezidentskaya kampaniya–1996* (Moscow: SPIK-Tsentr, 1996); and more skeptically, Frank Thames, "Did Yeltsin Buy Elections? The Russian Political Business Cycle, 1993-1999," *Communist and Post-Communist Studies*, vol. 34 (March 2001), pp. 63–76; and David Hoffman, *The Oligarchs*, chap. 13.

148. To the best of our knowledge, opinion polls conducted at the time did not ask this question.

149. Yeltsin, *Midnight Diaries*, p. 25.

150. Asmus, *Opening NATO's Door*, p. 166.

Chapter 7

1. The framing of the problem in terms of eating spinach is attributed to Talbott's chief assistant, Victoria Nuland. See Strobe Talbott, *The Russia Hand: A Memoir of Presidential Diplomacy* (Random House, 2002), chap. 3.

2. Fiona Hill, "The Caucasus and Central Asia," *Policy Brief*, no. 80 (Brookings, May 2001).

3. Interview with Elizabeth Sherwood-Randall.

4. Interview with Victoria Nuland.

5. For a good overview of the Missile Technology Control Regime (MTCR) process, see Deborah A. Ozga, "A Chronology of the Missile Technology Control Regime," *Nonproliferation Review*, vol. 1 (Winter 1994), pp. 66–93.

6. Gore-McCain Missile and Proliferation Control Act, *Congressional Record*, August 4, 1989, p. S10230.

7. Ozga, "Chronology," pp. 82–83.

8. Richard Armitage, "Russia's Eligibility for Assistance under the FREEDOM Support Act," unclassified action memorandum from EUR Thomas M. T. Niles and D/CISA, released in full by the Department of State, June 27, 2001, in response to a Freedom of Information Act (FOIA) request from the authors.

9. Interviews with Leon Fuerth, Rose Gottemoeller, and Daniel Poneman. Gottemoellor was directing the Clinton transition team for the Arms Control and Disarmament Agency at the time she was appointed to the National Security Council (NSC).

10. Ibid.

11. Interviews with Gottemoeller and Poneman. Reporters covering the issue understood the quid pro quo; for example, see R. Jeffrey Smith, "U.S., Russia Near Accord on Technology for India," *Washington Post*, July 14, 1993, p. A17.

12. Interviews with Fuerth and Andrei Kozyrev; Talbott, *The Russia Hand*, pp. 59–60.

13. Interviews with Fuerth and Gottemoeller.

14. Michael R. Gordon, "U.S. Sets Penalty for Russian Firms," *New York Times*, June 25, 1993; and R. Jeffrey Smith, "U.S., Russia Near Accord on Technology for India."

15. Interview with Strobe Talbott; Talbott, *The Russia Hand*, pp. 81–82; and Smith, "U.S., Russia Near Accord on Technology for India."

16. Interview with Talbott; and Talbott, *The Russia Hand*, pp. 81–82.

17. Smith, "U.S., Russia Near Accord on Technology for India"; interview with Talbott; and Talbott, *The Russia Hand*, p. 441, note 6.

18. Ozga, "Chronology," p. 88.

19. Barbara Rosewicz, "Technology: Former Space-Race Rivals Poised to Launch Greater Cooperation; First U.S. Commercial Use of Russia's Mir Station to Be Pact's Centerpiece," *Wall Street Journal*, September 2, 1993, p. B6; Barbara Rosewicz, "Technology: U.S. and Russia May Join Forces on Space Station," *Wall Street Journal*, September 3, 1993, p. B3; William E. Clayton Jr. and Mark Carreau, "U.S., Russia Agree to Joint Space Venture," *Houston Chronicle*, September 3, 1993, p. A1; Ralph Vartabedian and Doyle McManus, "U.S., Russia to Jointly Build Space Station," *Los Angeles Times*, September 3, 1993, p. A8; and Steven A. Holmes, "U.S. and Russians Join in New Plan for Space Station," *New York Times*, September 3, 1993, A1.

20. Carla Anne Robbins and Barbara Rosewicz, "Reaching Out: U.S. Hopes to Move Moscow into the West through Deeper Ties; but Courting Russia's Elites in Military and Industry Entails Significant Risks—Helping Future Imperialists?" *Wall Street Journal*, December 13, 1993, p. A1. Interviews with Fuerth and Gottemoeller.

21. Interview with Boris Tarasyuk.

22. For elaboration, see Sherman Garnett, *Keystone in the Arch: Ukraine in the Emerging Security Environment of Central and Eastern Europe* (Washington: Carnegie Endowment for International Peace, 1997), chap. 5.

23. Interview with Talbott; and John Buntin, "The Decision to Denuclearize: How Ukraine Became a Non-Nuclear Weapons State," Kennedy School of Government Case Program, C14-98-1425.0, 1997, p. 13.

24. Interview with Gottemoeller.

25. During the review process, there were divisions within the administration as to whether carrots or sticks should be deployed. Those pushing for carrots won out. See Garnett, *Keystone in the Arch*, p. 118. Garnett at the time was deputy assistant secretary of defense for Russia, Ukraine, and Eurasia.

26. Leon Sigal, *Hang Separately: Cooperative Security between the United States and Russia, 1985–1994* (Century Foundation Press, 2000), pp. 251–62; Buntin, "Decision to Denuclearize," pp. 16–17; and interviews with Gottemoeller and Ashton Carter. The administration began publicly to emphasize it was changing the tone from sticks to carrots. See Michael R. Gordon, "With Aid, U.S. Seeks to Sway Ukraine on A-Arms," *New York Times*, June 4, 1993, p. A7.

27. (Eventually, as discussed in chapter 5 in this volume, Carter and his team were able to get direct appropriations for the Nunn-Lugar program.) Ashton B. Carter and William J. Perry, *Preventive Defense: A New Security Strategy for America* (Brookings,

1999), pp. 73–75; Carter was criticized during his confirmation hearings for starting work in these areas before his confirmation at the end of June. See "Nomination of Ashton B. Carter, of Massachusetts, to be an Assistant Secretary of Defense," *Congressional Record*, May 25, 1993, p. S8209-8211.

28. Tarasyuk asserted in retrospect that the United States focused too much on the nuclear question and too little on broader issues of Ukrainian democracy and integration into the West at this critical moment in Ukraine's development as an independent and democratic state. In his view, opportunities for a close partnership between Ukraine and the United States were lost. Interview with Tarasyuk.

29. Interview with Carter.

30. James Goodby, *Europe Divided: The New Logic of Peace in U.S.-Russian Relations* (Washington: U.S. Institute of Peace, 1998), p. 80.

31. Interview with Talbott; and Talbott, *The Russia Hand*, p. 80.

32. Interview with Talbott; on the Garmisch meetings, see Melissa Healy, "Aspin Proposes U.S.-Russian Joint Maneuvers," *Los Angeles Times*, June 6, 1993, p. A1; see also Michael R. Gordon, "Aspin Meets Russian in Bid to Take Ukraine's A-Arms," *New York Times*, June 6, 1993, p. 16; and Michael R. Gordon, "Russians Fault U.S. on Shifting Ukraine's Arms," *New York Times*, June 7, 1993, p. A1. For a discussion of Grachev's unhappiness with U.S. involvement in what he saw as a Ukraine-Russia issue, see Chrystyna Lapychak, "U.S. Changes Its Strategy to Help Ukraine Disarm," *Christian Science Monitor*, June 9, 1993, p. 2.

33. Talbott, *The Russia Hand*, p. 83.

34. At this summit meeting in Massandra, Crimea, Yeltsin had proposed debt relief for Ukraine in return for Ukraine's share of the Black Sea fleet. Different reactions within the Ukrainian government to the deal severely divided the Ukrainian delegation and sparked a major public debate about Russian coercive diplomacy within Ukraine. See Garnett, *Keystone in the Arch*, p. 117; and Goodby, *Europe Divided*, p. 82.

35. Sigal, *Hang Separately*, p. 264.

36. The United States, the Soviet Union, and the United Kingdom declared after formal submission of the Non-Proliferation Treaty to the UN General Assembly twenty-five years earlier that the United Nations Security Council would be appealed to for assistance to support any non-nuclear state party to the NPT that was threatened by a nuclear state.

37. Secto 17049, Secretary's Meeting with Ukrainian President Kravchuk, October 25, 1993, Kiev, declassified on May 11, 2000, in response to a Freedom of Information Act request by the authors.

38. Secto 17049; also Secto 17045, Secretary's Meeting with Ukrainian Rada Leaders, October 25, 1993, Kiev, declassified May 11, 2000, in response to a Freedom of Information Act request by the authors.

39. Sigal, *Hang Separately*, p. 264; and Buntin, "Decision to Denuclearize," p. 20.

40. Interview with Talbott.

41. Talbott, *The Russia Hand*, p. 109.

42. Article V of the North Atlantic Treaty states in part that "an armed attack against one or more of them in Europe or North America shall be considered an attack against them all."

43. Interview with Talbott; and Talbott, *The Russia Hand*, p. 109.

44. Buntin, "Decision to Denuclearize," pp. 24–26; and Sigal, *Hang Separately*, p. 264.

45. John Buntin, "Epilogue: To Budapest and Beyond," KSG Case Program, C14-98-1425.1, 1997, p. 4; Ashton Carter recalls of June 1996, "I was there on that date, and believe me, I wasn't even sure the last warheads were going to cross the border that morning. They were still arguing about it. It was a complicated dynamic." Interview with Carter.

46. For background, see John R. Beyrle, "The Long Good-Bye: The Withdrawal of Russian Military Forces from the Baltic States," Pew Case Studies in International Affairs, case 371 (Georgetown University, Institute for the Study of Diplomacy, 1996). Beyrle served on the NSC staff from 1993 through 1995.

47. Beyrle, "The Long Good-Bye," pp. 2–3.

48. Beyrle, "The Long Good-Bye," pp. 6–7; and Beyrle's NSC colleague, Nicholas Burns, discussed Lake's interest in the Baltics in an interview with the authors. For a brief overview of some of the issues, see Lee Hockstader, "Russia to Remove Troops from Estonia by Aug. 31," *Washington Post*, July 27, 1994, p. A22.

49. Talbott, *The Russia Hand*, p. 63; and Beyrle, "The Long Good-Bye," p. 7.

50. Interviews with Talbott and Burns.

51. Beyrle, "The Long Good-Bye," p. 7.

52. Talbott, *The Russia Hand*, p. 443, note 3; interview with Talbott; and Beyrle, "The Long Good-Bye," pp. 7–9.

53. Beyrle, "The Long Good-Bye," p. 8; and Talbott, *The Russia Hand*, p. 126.

54. Talbott, *The Russia Hand*, p. 126.

55. Burns is quoted in Beyrle, "The Long Good-Bye," p. 9. For Clinton's statements on the issue while in Latvia, see Press Conference by President Clinton, President Ulmanis of Latvia, and President Meri of Estonia, Press Availability, State Room, Riga Castle, Riga, Latvia, White House, Office of the Press Secretary (Warsaw, Poland), July 6, 1994.

56. Talbott, *The Russia Hand*, p. 127.

57. Talbott, *The Russia Hand*, p. 128; interview with Talbott; John Aloysius Farrell, "Yeltsin Makes Concessions on Baltic Security," *Boston Globe*, July 11, 1994, p. 8; and Beyrle, "The Long Good-Bye," p. 9.

58. Talbott, *The Russia Hand*, pp. 126, 130.

59. Talbott, *The Russia Hand*, p. 128. Many U.S. government officials in interviews cite this general process of letters, calls, and summits as ways of getting Yeltsin to follow through, often on things that were only vague commitments in the private meetings. On the Estonia issue, see Beyrle, "The Long Good-Bye," p. 10.

60. Talbott, *The Russia Hand*, p. 128.

61. Ibid., p. 129; and interview with Talbott.

62. Interview with Nuland.

63. For representative comments, see Foreign Minister Kozyrev's comments as reported by Talbott in *The Russia Hand*, pp. 158–59.

64. For more on the deal, see Steven Greenhouse, "Russia and China Pressed Not to Sell A-Plants to Iran," *New York Times*, January 25, 1995, p. A6; and Robert J. Einhorn and Gary Samore, "Ending Russian Assistance to Iran's Nuclear Bomb," *Survival*, vol. 44 (Summer 2002), pp. 51–70; and Talbott, *The Russia Hand*, p. 158.

65. Interview with Talbott.

66. David Lauter, "Yeltsin Pledges to End Arms Sales to Iran," *Los Angeles Times*, September 29, 1994, p. A12.

67. Fred Kaplan, "Reactor Sale Adds to U.S.-Russia Strain," *Boston Globe*, February 26, 1995, p. 22.

68. Warren Christopher, *In the Stream of History: Shaping Foreign Policy for a New Era* (Stanford University Press, 1998), p. 253; and Daniel Williams and Thomas W. Lippman, "Christopher Charges Iran Continues Nuclear Program," *Washington Post*, January 21, 1995, p. A11.

69. See Elaine Sciolino, "Congress Presses Russia, and Clinton, over Iran Deal," *New York Times*, February 22, 1995, p. A8; and Steven Greenhouse, "Russia Insists Reactor Sale to Iran Is Firm," *New York Times*, February 24, 1995, p. 5. Talbott in an interview said Gingrich later apologized for his remarks.

70. Talbott, *The Russia Hand*, pp. 152–54; and interview with Coit D. Blacker.

71. Stephanopoulos, *All Too Human*, pp. 329–30.

72. Interview with Dick Morris. See also Dick Morris, *Behind the Oval Office: Getting Reelected against All Odds* (Los Angeles: Renaissance, 1999), pp. 250–51.

73. Interview with Dick Morris; and Morris, *Behind the Oval Office*, pp. 250–51. Even after more setbacks inside Russia in the second half of the 1990s, the vast majority of the American people remained committed to assisting Russia's transformation because Russia was considered too important to be allowed to fail. See the polling results reported in Mark Penn, "People to Government: Stay Engaged," *Blueprint*, vol. 5 (Winter 2000), p. 82.

74. Interview with Poneman.

75. Steven Greenhouse, "U.S. Gives Russia Secret Data on Iran to Discourage Atom Deal," *New York Times*, April 3, 1995, p. A9; and Steven Erlanger, "Russia Says Sale of Atom Reactors to Iran Is Still On," *New York Times*, April 4, 1995, p. A1.

76. Christopher, *In the Stream of History*, p. 267.

77. Talbott, *The Russia Hand*, pp. 159–60. Since Morris was under strict instructions only to discuss foreign policy with the president alone, Talbott and other foreign policy advisers likely did not know the details of the polling Morris was doing.

78. Elaine Sciolino, "Clinton and Yeltsin Seeking Common Ground for Talks," *New York Times*, April 28, 1995, p. A8.

79. Steven Erlanger, "Summit in Moscow: The Overview," *New York Times*, May 11, 1995, p. A1; Talbott, *The Russia Hand*, pp. 161 and 445, n. 7; and remarks by President Clinton and President Yeltsin in a Joint Press Conference, Moscow, May 10, 1995.

80. Michael Dobbs, "Summit Seen as 'Failure' by Republicans on Hill," *Washington Post*, May 11, 1995, p. A32; and John M. Broder and Carol J. Williams, "Yeltsin Offers Minor Concessions to U.S.," *Los Angeles Times*, May 11, 1995, p. A1.

81. Steven Erlanger, "Facing Threat in Parliament, Yeltsin Removes 3 Ministers," *New York Times*, July 1, 1995, p. 1; and Richard Boudreaux, "Russia Agrees to Stop Selling Arms to Iran," *Los Angeles Times*, July 1, 1995, p. A1.

82. Einhorn and Samore, "Ending Russian Assistance to Iran's Nuclear Bomb," p. 53; and John M. Broder, "Despite a Secret Pact by Gore in '95, Russian Arms Sales to Iran Go On," *New York Times*, October 13, 2000, A1. For other details, see "Contracts Suspended with Iran That Could Be Renewed Outlined," Foreign Broadcast Information Service (FBIS)-SOV-2000-1123, November 23, 2000.

83. John M. Broder, "Despite a Secret Pact by Gore in '95, Russian Arms Sales to Iran Go On," *New York Times*, October 13, 2000, p. A1.

Chapter 8

1. Founding Act on Mutual Relations, Cooperation and Security between the Russian Federation and the North Atlantic Treaty Organization, May 1997 (www.nato.int).

2. "Russia and the 'Threat' of NATO" (interview with Anatoly Chubais), *Time*, February 17, 1997, p. 40.

3. On the attacks on the Partnership for Peace (PFP), see the interview with Kozyrev in *Time*, July 1994, pp. 44–45. On the attacks on the charter, see Leon Aron, "The Foreign Policy Doctrine of Postcommunist Russia and Its Domestic Context," in Michael Mandlebaum, ed., *The New Russian Foreign Policy* (New York: Council on Foreign Relations, 1998), p. 47.

4. Michael McFaul, "A Precarious Peace: Domestic Politics in the Making of Russian Foreign Policy," *International Security*, vol. 22 (Winter 1997–98), pp. 5–35.

5. Andrei Kozyrev, "Don't Threaten Us," *New York Times*, March 18, 1994, p. A11.

6. See James M. Goldgeier, *Not Whether but When: The U.S. Decision to Enlarge NATO* (Brookings, 1999), pp. 14–17. The Genscher quote is in Stephen F. Szabo, *The Diplomacy of German Unification* (St. Martin's Press, 1992), pp. 57–58.

7. Philip Zelikow and Condoleezza Rice, *Germany Unified and Europe Transformed: A Study in Statecraft* (Harvard University Press, 1995), p. 176.

8. Zelikow and Rice, *Germany Unified and Europe Transformed*, pp. 180–83.

9. On this point, see Robert L. Hutchings, *American Diplomacy and the End of the Cold War: An Insider's Account of U.S. Policy in Europe, 1989-1992* (Woodrow Wilson Center Press, 1997), pp. 290ff; see also Ronald D. Asmus, *Opening NATO's Door: How the Alliance Remade Itself for a New Era* (Columbia University Press, 2002), p. 5. A 1997 report from Moscow had Soviet documents showing that British prime minister John Major and foreign minister Douglas Hurd had said to the Soviets in March 1991 that NATO had "no plans" for enlargement and could foresee "no conditions" under which this would happen. See Aleksey Konstantinovich Pushkov, "The West's Leaders Have Not Kept Their Promises," *Nezavisimaya Gazeta*, March 19, 1997, in Foreign Broadcast Information Service (FBIS)-Sov-97-059.

10. For a discussion of the debate within the administration during this period, see Goldgeier, *Not Whether but When*, chap. 2; and Asmus, *Opening NATO's Door*.

11. Interview with Anthony Lake.

12. Interview with William Perry.

13. Asmus, *Opening NATO's Door*, p. 50; and Strobe Talbott, *The Russia Hand: A Memoir of Presidential Diplomacy* (Random House, 2002), pp. 99–100.

14. Secretary Christopher's meeting with President Yeltsin, October 22, 1993, Moscow. October 25, 1993. Declassified in response to a Freedom of Information Act (FOIA) request by the authors, May 8, 2000; and Talbott, *The Russia Hand*, p. 115.

15. Grachev, quoted in Alessandra Stanley, "Russia Seeks Link to NATO but Nationalists Are Bitter," *New York Times*, March 18, 1994, p A4. See also Bruce Clark, "Russian Warms to Nato Partnership," *Financial Times*, April 28, 1994, p. 2.

16. Some Russian foreign policy experts even recommended active participation in PFP as a strategy for stalling NATO expansion. See "Rossiya i NATO: Tezisi Soveta po vneshnei i oboronnoi politike," *Nezavisimaya Gazeta*, June 21, 1995, p. 3.

17. William Clinton, "The President's News Conference with Visegrad Leaders in Prague," January 12, 1994, *Public Papers of the Presidents of the United States*, Book 1

(Government Printing Office, 1994), p. 40. The Kozyrev statement to a group of Russian ambassadors was referred to in an interview with Strobe Talbott.

18. William Clinton, "Interview with Tomasz Lis of Polish Television," July 1, 1994, *Public Papers*, Book 1, p. 1187; William Clinton, "Remarks following Discussions with President Lech Walesa of Poland and an Exchange with Reporters in Warsaw," July 16, 1994, *Public Papers*, Book 1,1994, pp. 1250–06.

19. Interview with Talbott; and see also Talbott, *The Russia Hand*, p. 131.

20. "U.S.-German Relations and the Challenge of a New Europe," *U.S. Department of State Dispatch*, vol. 5 (September 12, 1994), pp. 597–98; and James Goldgeier's interviews with Wesley Clark and John Shalikashvili in 1998 and 1999.

21. Interview with Talbott.

22. On domestic constraints on Yeltsin in foreign policy matters, see Pavel Fel'gengauer, "Rossiiskoe obshchestvo prokhodit k konsenssusu po voprosu o natsional'nikh interesakh," *Segodnya*, May 26, 1995, p. 9; and on the Yeltsin-Walesa communiqué, see Asmus, *Opening NATO's Door*, p. 37.

23. Talbott, *The Russia Hand*, p. 136; and Asmus, *Opening NATO's Door*, p. 90.

24. Talbott, *The Russia Hand*, p. 137.

25. Daniel Thomas, *The Helsinki Effect: International Norms, Human Rights, and the Demise of Communism* (Princeton University Press, 2001).

26. Interview with Talbott.

27. Talbott, *The Russia Hand*, pp. 138–39; and interview with Talbott.

28. Willy Claes, "NATO and the Evolving Euro-Atlantic Security Architecture," *NATO Review*, no. 6 (December 1994)—no. 1 (January 1995) (www.nato.int); and Warren Christopher, "North Atlantic Council Final Communique," *Department of State Dispatch*, vol. 5 (December 19, 1994), p. 833

29. ITAR-TASS, December 4, 1994, in FBIS, *Daily Report: Soviet Union*, December 5, 1994, p. 4.

30. Interview with Thomas Donilon.

31. William Clinton, "The President's News Conference with President Kuchma of Ukraine," November 22, 1994, *Public Papers of the Presidents of the United States*, Book 2 (1994), p. 2115.

32. Interview with Talbott; and Talbott, *The Russia Hand*, p. 141; "Remarks by the President at the Plenary Session of 1994 Summit of the Council [sic] on Security and Cooperation in Europe," Office of the Press Secretary (Budapest), December 5, 1994.

33. FBIS, *Daily Report: Soviet Union*, December 5, 1994, p. 4; and Asmus, *Opening NATO's Door*, p. 95.

34. Interviews with Burns and Talbott.

35. Interview with Ross. Talbott confirms the essence of the call in *The Russia Hand*, p. 41.

36. Interview with Victoria Nuland.

37. Interview with Talbott.

38. Interview with Perry.

39. Russian liberals interested in the same goals for Russia asked why membership should not be extended to Russia.

40. Goldgeier, *Not Whether but When*, chap. 4.

41. Interview with Talbott.

42. Interview with Fuerth.

43. Interview with Talbott; Talbott, *The Russia Hand*, pp. 144–45; and Steven

Erlanger, "Gore Upbeat after Talks with Top Russian Leaders," *New York Times*, December 17, 1994, p. 7.

44. Talbott, *The Russia Hand*, p. 444, n. 11.

45. Ashton B. Carter and William J. Perry, *Preventive Defense: A New Security Strategy for America* (Brookings, 1999), pp. 29–31; Talbott, *The Russia Hand*, pp. 145–46; and interview with Perry.

46. Interview with Perry.

47. See Goldgeier, *Not Whether but When*, pp. 75–76; and Talbott's version of events is in *The Russia Hand*, pp. 145–46.

48. Talbott, *The Russia Hand*, p. 154.

49. Interview with Talbott; and see also Talbott, *The Russia Hand*, p. 156.

50. R. Jeffrey Smith and Daniel Williams, "U.S. Plans New Tack on Russia-NATO Tie," *Washington Post*, January 16, 1995, p. A1; and R. Jeffrey Smith, "Russia Intends to Pursue Guarantees from NATO," *Washington Post*, March 11, 1995, p. A21.

51. Alexei Pushkov, "Reacting to NATO Expansion, Russia Should Take Its Time," *Moscow News*, March 24, 1995.

52. Interview with Talbott; and Talbott, *The Russia Hand*, pp. 161–62.

53. Interview with Talbott.

54. On the treaty, see Richard A. Falkenrath, *Shaping Europe's New Military Order: The Origins and Consequences of the CFE Treaty* (MIT Press, 1995); and Joseph Harahan and John Kuhn III, *On-Site Inspections under the CFE Treaty* (Washington: On-Site Inspection Agency, 1996).

55. Remarks by President Clinton and President Yeltsin in a Joint Press Conference, Moscow, May 10, 1995.

56. Interview with Perry. Even a year earlier, when he was dealing with the siege of Sarajevo, Perry implied that Russia assisted in persuading the Serbs to withdraw their artillery from the outskirts of Sarajevo. Perry now soberly recognized that "Russia can be both our partner and our rival and both at the same time." His focus, however, was in trying to make Russia a better partner. See William Perry, "Forge Realistic, Pragmatic Relations with Russia," speech delivered at George Washington University, March 14, 1994, in *Defense Issues*, vol. 9, no. 19 (1994).

57. Interview with Ashton Carter.

58. On the October 8 meeting, see Perry and Carter, *Preventive Defense*, pp. 35–39; and Talbott, *The Russia Hand*, p. 175; for public comments at the time on a Russian nonmilitary role, see remarks by Anthony Lake in John Aloysius Farrell, "Clinton, Yeltsin Split on NATO, Planning for New Bosnia Force," *Boston Globe*, October 23, 1995, p. 1.

59. Interview with Carter.

60. Carter and Perry, *Preventive Defense*, p. 44; interview with Carter; and Talbott, *The Russia Hand*, pp. 176, 186.

61. Interview with Talbott.

62. This same debate would erupt again in 2002 concerning cuts in Russian and American nuclear arsenals, but that time, Russia would get a treaty. See chap. 13.

63. Thomas W. Lippman, "Russia Offered Ties with NATO; U.S. Hopes to Ease Moscow's Opposition to Alliance's Expansion," *Washington Post*, September 7, 1996, p. A15.

64. Yeltsin brought in Primakov at the beginning of his 1996 presidential campaign when he was seeking to strengthen his appeal to nationalist voters. See Michael

McFaul, *Russia's 1996 Presidential Election: The End of Polarized Politics* (Hoover Institution Press, 1997), p. 18.

65. Talbott, *The Russia Hand*, p. 228; and interview with Eric Edelman.

66. On Primakov's return to a more realpolitik approach to foreign affairs in contrast to Kozyrev's liberal strategy, see Michael McFaul, "Revolutionary Ideas, State Interests, and Russian Foreign Policy," in Vladimir Tismaneanu, ed., *Political Culture and Civil Society in Russia and the New States of Eurasia* (M. E. Sharpe, 1995), pp. 27–52.

67. Goldgeier, *Not Whether but When*, p. 105.

68. Ibid., pp. 105–06.

69. "Remarks by the President to the People of Detroit," White House, Office of the Press Secretary, October 22, 1996; and John F. Harris, "Campaign '96—Clinton Vows Wider NATO in 3 Years," *Washington Post*, October 23, 1996, p. A1.

70. Interview with Eric Edelman; William Drozdiak, "Europeans Approve Arms Cuts; Russia Still Opposes an Expanded NATO," *Washington Post*, December 3, 1996, p. A20. Talbott describes Chernormyrdin's tone on the subject as one of "abject desperation." See Talbott, *The Russia Hand*, p. 222.

71. Warren Christopher, "Fulfilling the Founding Vision of NATO," *U.S. Department of State Dispatch*, vol. 7 (December 9, 1996), p. 601; and William Drozdiak, "NATO Pledges Not to Put Nuclear Arms in New Member States," *Washington Post*, December 11, 1996, p. A16.

72. Talbott, *The Russia Hand*, p. 229; and Drozdiak, "NATO Pledges Not to Put Nuclear Arms in New Member States," p. A16; Drozdiak, "Russia Accepts NATO's Offer of Negotiations on New Ties," *Washington Post*, December 12, 1996, p. A1; and Norman Kempster, "Russia, NATO to Hammer Out a New Treaty," *Los Angeles Times*, December 12, 1996, p. A1.

73. Interviews with Talbott and other U.S. officials who were in the larger meeting, including NSC staffer Carlos Pascual, Treasury official David Lipton, and Arms Control and Disarmament Agency (ACDA) official Michael Nacht; and Talbott, *The Russia Hand*, pp. 230–31. See also "Russia and the 'Threat' of NATO" (interview with Anatoly Chubais), *Time*, February 17, 1997, p. 40. NATO press secretary Jamie Shea recalls Chubais saying to Solana that his father had told him that he and his generation could never accept NATO enlargement. Interview with Jamie Shea.

74. Talbott, *The Russia Hand*, p. 225.

75. Interview with Talbott.

76. Talbott, *The Russia Hand*, pp. 226–27.

77. Interview with Talbott.

78. Interviews with Bass and Talbott.

79. Talbott makes an interesting comparison between the security and economic agendas. See *The Russia Hand*, p. 284.

80. Goldgeier, *Not Whether but When*, p. 113; and Craig R. Whitney, "NATO Says It Won't Base New Forces in the East," *New York Times*, March 15, 1997, p. A6.

81. Quoted in William Drozdiak, "Poland Urges NATO Not to Appease Russia: The Smell of Yalta Is Always with Us," *Washington Post*, March 17, 1997, p. A13.

82. Talbott, *The Russia Hand*, p. 237.

83. On MIRVs, ibid., p. 438, note 14.

84. Ibid., p. 238.

85. "Clinton and Yeltsin and How They Failed 'Three Fundamental Challenges,'" *New York Times*, March 22, 1997, p. A6. On Yeltsin, see Alessandra Stanley, "Yeltsin Tells Russians That Bending on the NATO Issue Paid Off," *New York Times*, March 27, 1997, p. A5. On Denver, see "Remarks by President Clinton and President Yeltsin in Photo Opportunity," Brown Palace Hotel, White House, Office of the Press Secretary (Denver), June 20, 1997; "Press Briefing by Press Secretary Mike McCurry, Deputy Director of the NSC Jim Steinberg, and Deputy Secretary Larry Summers," White House, Office of the Press Secretary, June 20, 1997; and Peter Baker, "Industrial Powers Gather; in Transition, Russia Attends Denver Summit," *Washington Post*, June 21, 1997, p. A1. Russia formally joined the Paris Club on September 17, 1997. See "Russia Joins the Paris Club of Creditors," *Washington Post*, September 18, 1997, p. A26.

86. Boris Yeltsin, *Midnight Diaries*, translated by Catherine A. Fitzpatrick (Public Affairs, 1999), p. 130.

87. Ibid., p. 131.

88. Interviews with Sandy Berger, Lake, and Lipton.

89. For Clinton public statements, see "Press Conference of President Clinton and President Yeltsin," Kalastaja Torppa, White House, Office of the Press Secretary (Helsinki, Finland), March 21, 1997; on the Baltic issue, see Talbott, *The Russia Hand*, pp. 239–41.

90. Interview with John Bass.

91. Interviews with Jamie Shea and Talbott. On Primakov-Yeltsin and positions on military equipment, see also Michael Dobbs, "For Clinton, Sticking with Yeltsin Sealed Agreement on NATO," *Washington Post*, May 27, 1997, p. A11.

92. The Founding Act is posted on the NATO website (www.nato.int).

93. Remarks by the President in Live Telecast to Russian People, Ostankino TV Station, Moscow, Russia, White House, Office of the Press Secretary (Moscow, Russia), January 14, 1994; "Remarks by President Clinton, French President Chirac, Russian President Yeltsin, and NATO Secretary-General Solana at NATO-Russia Founding Act Signing Ceremony," White House, Office of the Press Secretary (Paris, France), May 27, 1997.

94. For a survey, see Angela Stent, *Russia and Germany Reborn: Unification, the Soviet Collapse, and the New Europe* (Princeton University Press, 1999), pp. 226–29; the Gaidar quote is on p. 227.

Chapter 9

1. For a similar view, see Michael McFaul remarks and prepared statement in *Russia's Election: What Does It Mean?* Hearing before the Commission on Security and Cooperation in Europe, 104 Cong. 2 sess., July 10, 1996, pp. 19–21 and 57–67. Others did not. See Peter Reddaway, "Russia Heads for Trouble," *New York Times*, July 2, 1996, p. A15. Richard Layard and John Parker in *The Coming Russian Boom: A Guide to New Markets and Politics* (Free Press, 1996) were well ahead of the pack in predicting Russia's economic growth.

2. Strobe Talbott, "The End of the Beginning: The Emergence of a New Russia," address delivered at Stanford University, September 19, 1997; and Strobe Talbott, "The Struggle for Russia's Future," *Wall Street Journal*, September 25, 1997, p. A22.

3. Talbott, "The End of the Beginning."

4. On how the constitution took root, see Michael McFaul, *Russia's Unfinished Revolution: Political Change from Gorbachev to Putin* (Cornell University Press, 2001), chap. 7; Clinton's remarks were posted at www.g7.utoronto.

5. American Foreign Policy Council, *Russia Reform Monitor*, no. 308 (Washington, September 1997); and Michael Gordon, "Russia Resists IMF's Strategy for Reducing Budget Deficit," *New York Times*, May 16, 1998, p. 3. Leon Fuerth was one top official who held a dissenting view about the "dream team." Interview with Fuerth.

6. Homi Khara, Brian Pinto, and Sergei Ulatov, "An Analysis of Russia's 1998 Meltdown: Fundamentals and Market Signals," *Brookings Papers on Economic Activity*, vol. 1 (2001), p. 14.

7. Daniel Treisman, "Fighting Inflation in a Transitional Regime: Russia's Anomalous Stabilization," *World Politics*, vol. 50 (January 1998), pp. 235–65; and General Accounting Office, "Foreign Assistance: International Efforts to Aid Russia's Transition Have Had Mixed Results," report to the House Committee on Banking and Financial Services, GAO-01-8 (November 2000), p. 46.

8. "Joint Statement on U.S.-Russia Economic Initiative," March 21, 1997. *Public Papers of the President, 1997*, vol. 1 (Government Printing Office, 1997), p. 345.

9. Gore-Chernomyrdin press conference, September 23, 1997, U.S. Information Agency transcript.

10. "U.S. to Push for Russia's Integration into the WTO," *Wall Street Journal*, April 1, 1997, p. A5.

11. Stanley Fischer, "The Russian Economy: Prospects and Retrospect," address to the Higher School of Economics, Moscow, Russia, June 19, 2001 (www.imf.org/external/np/speeches/2001/061901.htm [July 2003]).

12. Stanley Fischer, "What Went Wrong in Russia," *Financial Times*, September 27, 1999, p. 26.

13. Lawrence H. Summers, "The Global Stake in Russian Economic Reform," speech to the U.S.-Russia Business Council, April 1, 1997 (www.ustreas.gov/press/release/rr1578 [July 2003]).

14. See Fischer, "What Went Wrong in Russia."

15. Michael McFaul, "Russia's 'Privatized' State as an Impediment to Democratic Consolidation," part 2, *Security Dialogue*, vol. 29 (Summer 1998), pp. 219–36; and David Hoffman, *The Oligarchs: Wealth and Power in the New Russia* (Public Affairs, 2002), p. 419.

16. Hoffman, *The Oligarchs*, p. 433.

17. Ibid., p.437.

18. The book's chapters were in fact boilerplate overviews of privatization, hardly worth the honoraria paid. See Anatoly Chubais, ed., *Privatizatsiya po-rossiiski* (Moskva: Vagrius, 1999).

19. Andrei Illarionov, "Inflatsiya i antiinflatsiya politika," in L. Krasavina, ed., *Inflatsiya i antiinflatsiya politika v Rossii* (Moscow: Finansy i Statistika, 2000), pp. 81–87; and Andrei Kounov; Sergei Aleksashenko, *Bitva za rubl'* (Moskva: AlmaMater, 1999), p. 236.

20. "World Bank/IMF Agenda," *World Bank Transition Newsletter*, Washington, December 1997.

21. Khara, Pinto, and Ulatov, "An Analysis of Russia's 1998 Meltdown."

22. David Woodruff, *Money Unmade: Barter and the Fate of Russian Capitalism* (Cornell University Press, 1999).

23. *Rossiiskii statisticheskii ezhegodnik: 1997*, p. 535; and Clifford Gaddy, "Statement to the House Committee on International Relations," Hearings on U.S.-Russian Relations before the House Committee on International Relations, 105 Cong. 2 sess., July 16, 1998.

24. Joseph Blasi, Maya Kroumova, and Douglas Kruse, *Kremlin Capitalism: Privatizing the Russian Economy* (Cornell University Press, 1997).

25. Elaine Buckberg and Brian Pinto, "How Russia Is Becoming a Market Economy," unpublished manuscript, September 1997.

26. "After the Fall Was Over," *Business Russia*, June 1998, p. 1 (Economist Intelligence Unit) (eiu.com); and Debra Javeline, *Protest and the Politics of Blame: The Russian Response to Unpaid Wages* (University of Michigan Press, 2002).

27. Joseph Kahn and Timothy L. O'Brien, "Easy Money: A Special Report: For Russia and Its U.S. Bankers, Match Wasn't Made in Heaven," *New York Times*, October 18, 1998, p. 1; and Khara, Pinto, and Ulatov, "An Analysis of Russia's 1998 Meltdown," p. 4. This number does not include the new Eurobonds that came into the Russian market as the result of a GKO-Eurobond swap undertaken in July 1998 to help (unsuccessfully) stave off the crash.

28. In the end, the GKOs were not guaranteed by the government, but it was the perception at the time that they were safer investments than loans to private actors. We thank Pavel Khokhryakov, vice president of Promsvyazbank, for this observation.

29. Hoffman, *The Oligarchs*, p. 470; Anders Åslund, *Building Capitalism: The Transformation of the Former Soviet Bloc* (Cambridge: Cambridge University Press, 2001), p. 409; and *Dengi i Kredit*. no. 10 (1998), p. 43.

30. Hoffman, *The Oligarchs*, p. 469.

31. Andrei Illarionov, "The Roots of the Economic Crisis," *Journal of Democracy*, vol. 10 (Spring 1999), p. 75.

32. Randall Stone, *Lending Credibility: The International Monetary Fund and the Post-Communist Transition* (Princeton University Press, 2002), pp. 153–58; *Dengi i Kredit*. no. 10 (1998), p. 43; Aleksashenko, *Bitva za rubl'* p. 109; and "Russia's Challenges in the 1990s: An Interview with Martin Gilman of the IMF," December 3, 2002 (www.washprofile.org).

33. U. A. Konstantinov and A. I. Il'inskii, *Finansovii krizis: prichini i preodolenie* (Moskva: ZAO "Finstatinform," 1999), p. 44; Vladimir Popov, "Uroki valutnogo krizisa v Rossii i v drugikh stranakh," *Voprosi Ekonomiki*, no. 6 (June 1999), p. 101. On the worldwide crisis, see Paul Blustein, *The Chastening: Inside the Crisis That Rocked the Global Financial System and Humbled the IMF* (Public Affairs, 2001).

34. Chrystia Freeland, *Sale of the Century*, p. 297; Aleksashenko. *Bitva za rubl'*, pp. 108–10; General Accounting Office, "Foreign Assistance: International Efforts to Aid Russia's Transition Have Had Mixed Results," p.46; and John Thornhill, "IMF and Russia in a New Loan Accord," *Financial Times*, July 8, 1998, p. 2.

35. When the value of their collateral fell, Russian banks faced two choices. They could pay their Western creditors the difference between the new value of the Eurobonds (that is, the collateral) and the amount of liabilities outstanding, or they could provide Western banks with new collateral.

36. The causal effect of falling oil prices is disputed. Russian government officials placed great weight on this factor after the crash, but others are more skeptical. For the skeptical view, see Khara, Pinto, and Ulatov, "An Analysis of Russia's 1998 Meltdown," pp. 20–21.

37. Joseph Stiglitz, *Globalization and Its Discontents* (Basic Books, 2002) p. 145.

38. William Cooper, "The Russian Financial Crisis: An Analysis of Trends, Causes, and Implications," report for Congress 98-578, February 18, 1999 (ncseonline.org/NLE/CRSreports/international/inter-16.cfm [July 2003]).

39. See Andrei Illarionov, "Udalos' li Chubaisu obmanut' prezidenta Rossii?" *Izvestiya*, March 21, 1998, p. 2; Andrei Illarionov, "Effektivnost' byudzhetnoi politiki v Rossi 1994–1997 godakh," *Voprosy Ekonomiki*, no. 2 (February 1998), pp. 22–36; and Andrei Illarionov, "Financial Crisis in Russia," presentation to Aspen Institute Conference, Budapest, August 21, 1998. In retrospect, Stiglitz has asserted that the World Bank was pushing for devaluation at the time since, "It was clear that the ruble was overvalued." See Stiglitz, *Globalization and Its Discontents*, p. 145. Public statements to this effect *before* the crisis, however, are hard to find.

40. Some in the IMF questioned the singular focus on fighting inflation as a goal of the Fund's programs with Russia. In 1996, for instance, Augusto Lopez-Claros asserted provocatively, "The relationship between inflation and growth is probably highly non-linear; that very high inflation is very harmful and every effort should be made to eradicate it. Nevertheless, there is a threshold below which what the actual rate of inflation is probably does not matter much for growth." Augusto Lopez-Claros, "The Fund's Role in Russia," unpublished manuscript, June 19, 1996, p. 6. This position, however, was not shared in the Russian government at the time, which believed that slaying inflation was its biggest achievement in the 1990s.

41. Interview with Mark Medish. Supporters of Russia's reformers in the West staked out a similar position during the crisis. See, for instance, Anders Åslund, "Don't Devalue Ruble," *Moscow Times*, July 7, 1998.

42. Interview with Dmitri Vasiliev. Of course, whether these reforms—and mass privatization in particular—should be considered "successful" is another issue. For skeptical views, see Michael McFaul, "State Power, Institutional Change, and the Politics of Privatization in Russia," *World Politics*, vol. 47 (January 1995), pp. 210–43; and Bernard Black, Reiner Kraakman, and Anna Tarassova, "Russian Privatization and Corporate Governance: What Went Wrong?" *Stanford Law Review*, vol. 52 (July 2002), pp. 1731–1808.

43. Carla Anne Robbins and Steve Liesman, "How an Aid Program Vital to New Economy of Russia Collapsed," *Wall Street Journal*, August 13, 1997, pp. 1, 6.

44. Cited in David Marcus, "U.S. Halts Harvard Contracts in Russia," *Boston Globe*, May 21, 1997, p. A1.

45. Excerpt from Chubais's letter to AID administrator Brian Atwood, May 19, 1997, in Peter Reddaway, "Beware the Russian Reformer: While the U.S. Depends on Chubais, Accusations Fly in Moscow," *Washington Post*, August 24, 1997, p. C1. At the time, the Harvard Institute for International Development (HIID) was working especially closely with Dmitri Vasiliev, the head of the Federal Securities Commission, a stock market watchdog agency modeled after the U.S. Securities and Exchange Commission. Although Vasiliev was a deputy to Chubais at the State Property Committee earlier in the decade, the two radically disagreed at the time about the future of the Russian stock market. Chubais favored a German model, in which banks played a leading role in holding securities, while Vasiliev favored the American model in which the stock market played a leading role in channeling investment. Some, therefore, assert that Chubais undercut the HIID as a way to weaken Vasiliev and the SEC.

46. Interview with Brian Atwood.

47. Interview with David Lipton.

48. Hoffman writes that the turning point from net asset to net liability occurred on April 1, 1998. See Hoffman, *The Oligarchs*, p. 472.

49. Interview with Lipton.

50. Lopez-Claros, "The Role of International Financial Institutions during the Transition in Russia," p. 18; Blustein, *The Chastening*, p. 243; and Stone, *Lending Credibility*.

51. Incoherency within the Russian government was a major reason for this intimate engagement. In fact, Martin Gilman, the IMF's senior resident adviser in Moscow from 1997 to 2002, asserts that "one of the key contributions of IMF was not the money, and not even necessarily the specific advice on budgetary policy, but it was advice on how governments works." ("Russia's Challenges in the 1990s: An Interview with Gilman of the IMF," *Washington Profile News Agency*, December 12, 2002.) Such an assignment did not fall in the traditional portfolio of services offered by the IMF.

52. Interview with Boris Fyodorov.

53. This was an argument of a number of Western officials interviewed by the authors. None, however, wanted to be quoted directly for sharing this observation.

54. Joseph Stiglitz, *Globalization and Its Discontents* (Norton and Company, 2002), p. 149.

55. On the Fund's limited resources at the time, see Paul Blustein, "IMF Battens Down for More Ill Wind: Fund Keeps Weather Eye on Risk Spots," *Washington Post*, July 29, 1998, p. A16; Senator Lauch Faircloth, "Unwise Bailouts: The Clinton administration has effectively privatized the lenders' profits and socialized their losses," *Washington Post*, December 12, 1997, p. A29; and George Shultz, William Simon, and Walter Wriston, "Who Needs the IMF," *Wall Street Journal*, February 3, 1998, p. A22.

56. Interview with Stephen Sestanovich.

57. Interview with Medish.

58. Interviews with Sestanovich and Fuerth, Madeleine Albright, Medish, and others.

59. Interview with Fuerth.

60. Interview with Albright.

61. Freeland, *Sale of the Century*, p. 304. See also "Russia's Challenges in the 1990s: An Interview with Martin Gilman of the IMF."

62. General Accounting Office, "International Monetary Fund: Approach Used to Establish and Monitor Conditions for Financial Assistance," GAO-GGD-NSIAD-99-168 (Letter Report [June 1999]).

63. Michael Gordon, "Russia Resists IMF's Strategy for Reducing Budget Deficit," *New York Times*, May 15, 1998, p. 3.

64. "World Bank/IMF Agenda," *World Bank Transition Newsletter*, December 1997 (www.worldbank.org/html/prddr/trans/dec97/pgs29-31.htm [July 2003]); and Timothy Frye, *Brokers and Bureaucrats: Building Market Institutions in Russia* (University of Michigan Press, 2000), p. 200. Frye cites Margot Jacobs, "Russian Banks: Sailing Ahead or Sinking Fast," research report (Moscow: United Financial Group, August 1998), pp. 1–71. One loan, $800 million, was a second structural adjustment loan (SAL II) earmarked to stimulate the reform of "natural" monopolies, private sector development, fiscal management, banking reform, and trade policy reform. The other, also $800 million, was a second infusion of capital to assist in the restructuring of the Russian coal industry.

65. Christian Caryl, "Crisis? What Crisis?" *U.S. News and World Report*, June 22, 1998, p. 44.

66. Anders Åslund, "Russia's Financial Crisis: Causes and Possible Remedies," *Post-Soviet Geography and Economics*, vol. 39 (June 1998), pp. 309–28.

67. Freeland, *Sale of the Century*, p. 307.

68. *Public Papers of the President: William Jefferson Clinton, 1998*, vol. 1 (GPO, 1998), p. 853. See also the positive spin that American and Russian government officials gave to the Clinton statement in Steven Fidler, "Russian Financial Turmoil Poses Dilemma for IMF," *Financial Times*, June 1, 1998, p. 3.

69. Freeland, *Sale of the Century*, p. 307.

70. Matthew Brzezinski, "IMF Doubts Whether It Can Afford Russian Aid," *Wall Street Journal*, June 22, 1998, p A17.

71. Minna Nikitin, "Bank of Finland: Russian and Baltic Economies, the Week in Review," June 26, 1998; John Thornhill, "IMF and Russia in a New Loan Accord," *Financial Times*, July 8, 1998, p. 2; Art Pine, "IMF, Russia Open Talks on Large Loan," *Los Angeles Times*, June 27, 1998, p 3; and "Finance and Economics: To the Rescue," *Economist*, July 18, 1998, pp. 65–66.

72. Blustein, *The Chastening*, p. 254.

73. Strobe Talbott, *The Russia Hand: A Memoir of Presidential Diplomacy* (Random House, 2002), p. 275.

74. Interview with James Steinberg.

75. Interviews with Medish and Lipton.

76. "IMF Sets $22.6 Billion Loan Accord with Russia—Aid Plan Depends on Nation's Ability to Deliver Reforms," *Wall Street Journal*, July 14, 1998, p. A12; and David Wessel and Carla Anne Robbins in D.C., with Mark Whitehouse in Moscow, "Russia Vows Reforms after IMF Cuts Funds," *Wall Street Journal*, July 22, 1998, p. A10.

77. Matthew Brzezinski, "Yeltsin Sets Tax to Meet IMF Pledge," *Wall Street Journal*, July 20, 1998, p. A15; and Patricia Kranz, "And Now, the Pain: Can Yeltsin Meet IMF Terms While Curbing the Backlash?" *Business Week*, July 27, 1998, p. 43; and Kahn and O'Brien, "Easy Money: A Special Report."

78. Stanley Fischer, "Press Briefing on Russia," July 13, 1998, Washington (www.imf.org/external/np/tr/1998/tr980713.htm [July 2003]).

79. Both are quoted in Wessel and Robbins, with Whitehouse, "Russia Vows Reforms after IMF Cuts Funds," p. A10.

80. "Finance and Economics: To the Rescue," *Economist*, July 18, 1998, pp. 65–66.

81. "Camdessus Sees Improvement in Russian Finances," *Agence France-Presse*, July 13, 1998.

82. Rubin, quoted in "Rubin Warns about Delay of IMF Funds to Russia," *Wall Street Journal*, July 29, 1998, p. A4. On the same day, Fischer made similar upbeat remarks. See Blustein, "IMF Battens Down for More Ill Wind," p. A16.

83. "Russia Can Expect 2 Portions of IMF Credit in September," *Interfax*, August 7, 1998.

84. "Russian Financial Crisis: Confidential Interim Assessment, no. 1," Institute for EastWest Studies (iews.org), August 20, 1998.

85. Freeland, *Sale of the Century*, p. 312.

86. Interview with Lipton.

87. George Soros, letter to the editor, "Soros Sees G7-Backed, $50bn Currency Board for Russia as Only Way out of Crisis," *Financial Times*, August 13, 1998, p. 18.

Subsequently, Russian officials claimed that Soros made hundreds of millions of dollars from his letter by speculating against the German mark, which also fell sharply in reaction to the collapsing Russian economy. Whether true or not, overall, Soros is estimated to have lost roughly $2 billion in Russia.

88. The expectation in the market was that the government would not default on its ruble-denominated debt (that is, GKOs), since in the extreme case it always had the ability to generate funds to repay such debt by printing money. Defaulting on internal debt was entirely unprecedented in the experience of all "emerging market" creditor countries at the time and was perceived as a crazy option by most foreign investors since such a move would completely and unnecessarily undermine government credibility. Interview with Adam Elstein.

89. Freeland, *Sale of the Century*, p. 323. Formally, Kiriyenko announced that the government was going to restructure the debt by rolling the short-term GKOs into new ruble-denominated bonds with longer maturities. The promised plan, however, was never implemented.

90. As a consequence of pressure from Russia's banks, the Russian government reclassified these forward contracts as gambling contracts, which made them unenforceable under Russian law.

91. Lawrence H. Summers, testimony before the House International Relations Committee on Russia, September 17, 1998, 105 Cong. 2 sess. (www.treas.gov/press/releases/rr2686.htm [July 2003]); and Hoffman, *The Oligarchs*, p. 493.

92. IMF News Brief 98/30, Washington, August 17, 1998 (www.imf.org/external/np/sec/nb/1998/nb9830.htm [July 2003]); and interview with Lipton.

93. IMF News Brief 98/30.

94. Interviews with James Chavin and Elstein.

95. David E. Sanger, "U.S. Official Questions How Russia Used Loan," *New York Times*, March 19, 1999, p. A8. Western investors at the time used much stronger words to describe the theft of these funds for the well-connected Russian banks.

96. Elstein, as quoted in John Thornhill, "Communists Attack Yeltsin and Foreign Investors: Zyuganov Demands President's Resignation over Monetary Policy U-turn," *Financial Times* (August 15, 1999). See also Konstantinov and Il'inskii *Finansovii krizis: prichini i preodolenie*; Kahn and O'Brien, "Easy Money," p. 1; and George Matlock, "Russian Worries Overwhelm Stock Markets," *Wall Street Journal Europe*, August 28–29, 1998, p. 13.

97. Thomas Lippman, "Turmoil, Drift in Russia Prompt U.S. Policy Shift; Flexibility, Recognition of Limits Mark New Approach," *Washington Post*, November 1, 1998, p. A27.

98. Illarionov, "The Roots of the Economic Crisis," pp. 68–69. Emphasis in original. Ironically, a year after writing these words, Illarionov became President Putin's chief economic adviser and helped to revive many of these liberal ideas that seemed so discredited in 1999.

99. "20 naibolee vliyatel'nykh politikov rossii v yanvare," *Nezavisimaya Gazeta*, January 30, 1999.

100. Mark Whitehouse, "Politics Silence Russian Markets: Yeltsin's Leadership Might Face End," *Wall Street Journal*, August 28–29, 1998, p. 7.

101. "Democratic Choice Warns of Threat of Dictatorship," *Itar-Tass*, January 30, 1999; Stephen Hanson and Jeffrey Kopstein, "The Weimar/Russia Comparison," *Post-Soviet Affairs*, vol. 13 (July-September 1997), pp. 252–83; and Stephen Shenfield, "The

Weimar/Russia Comparison: Reflections on Hanson and Kopstein," in *Post-Soviet Affairs*, vol.14 (October-December 1998), pp. 355–68.

102. Bill Powell and Evgeniya Albats, "Summer of Discontent," *Newsweek* (international edition), January 19, 1999, p. 28.

103. "Primakov's 'Non-Aggression' Initiative Gets Mixed Reviews," *Monitor—A Daily Briefing on the Post-Soviet States*, January 27, 1999 (Washington: Jamestown Foundation).

104. The most comprehensive and thoughtful plan for reform can be found in Viktor Sheinis, "Konstitutsiya I Zhizn" *Nezavisimaya Gazeta*, January 27, 1999. Even the head of the propresidential faction, Our Home Is Russia, supported constitutional amendments to limit the powers of the presidency. See Timothy Heritage, "Russia Faces Obstacles to Political Truce," *Reuters*, February 11, 1999.

105. Keith Bush, *The Russian Economy in June 1999* (Washington: Center for Strategic and International Studies, June 1999) p. 5; John Thornhill, "Primakov Defies IMF Advice," *Financial Times*, September 17, 1998, p. 2; and John Thornhill, "Luzhkov Lays Blame on IMF for Woes," *Financial Times*, September 24, 1998, p. 2.

106. See Primakov's detailed recollections of his negotiations with the IMF in Yevgeny Primakov, *Vosem' Mesyatsev Plyus* (Moskva: "Mysl", 2001), pp. 109–29.

107. Talbott writes of the effects of Lewinsky and the ensuing impeachment process. See *The Russia Hand*, p. 276.

108. David Kramer, "It May Be a Summit of Embarrassment," *Boston Globe*, August 30, 1998, p. E2.

109. Talbott, *The Russia Hand*, p. 281; and "President Clinton Announces Summit Meeting with Russian Federation President Boris Yeltsin," White House, Office of the Press Secretary, July 6, 1998.

110. Interview with Medish, also confirmed by other interviews.

111. See Peter Baker, *The Breach: Inside the Impeachment Trial of William Jefferson Clinton* (Scribner, 2000), p. 59.

112. John Lloyd, "Who Lost Russia? The Devolution of Russia," *New York Times Magazine*, August 15, 1999, pp. 34–41, 52, 61, 64.

113. For complete details of the Bank of New York scandal, see (www.russian-law.org/bonynews.htm [July 2003]).

114. Catherine Belton, "Was the July '98 IMF Aid Diverted?" *Moscow Times*, July 27, 2000.

115. Peter Reddaway, "Is Chernomyrdin a Crook?" *Post-Soviet Prospects*, vol. 3 (August 1995), pp. 1-4; and Anders Åslund, "Russia's Sleaze Sector," *New York Times*, July 11, 1995, p. A17.

116. James Risen, "Gore Rejected CIA Evidence of Russian Corruption," *New York Times*, November 23, 1998, p. A8. See Talbott, *The Russia Hand*, p. 448, note 11, on the lack of concrete evidence about the memo.

117. Speaker's Advisory Group on Russia, Christopher Cox, chairman, *Russia's Road to Corruption: How the Clinton Administration Exported Government Instead of Free Enterprise and Failed the Russian People* (House of Representatives, September 2000 (policy.house.gov/Russia [July 7, 2003]). Chapter 6 of this study is called "Bull****: Gore and Other Administration Policy Makers Systematically Ignore Evidence of Corruption of Their 'Partners."

118. Besides Lloyd's essay, a sampling of pieces with the exact same title include Jonathan Broder, "Who Lost Russia?" *Salon*, September 1, 1998 (salon.com); "Who

Lost Russia?" *Socialism Today*, no. 32 (October 1998); a special symposium of several authors under the title, "What Went Wrong in Russia," *Journal of Democracy*, vol. 10 (April 1999) pp. 3–86; George Soros, "Who Lost Russia?" *New York Review of Books*, April 13, 2000, p. 10; "Who Lost Russia?" *New York Post*, September 24, 2000, p. 56; Mark Gage, *Looking behind Potemkin's Wall: How American Policy Has Failed Russia*, Washington, Nixon Center Working Paper, October 2000; a book review by Robert Kaplan, called "Who Lost Russia?" *New York Times*, October 8, 2000, sec. 7, p. 29.

119. "Who Lost Russia?" *New York Post*, September 24, 2000.

120. David Ignatius, "Who Robbed Russia?" *Washington Post*, August 25, 1999, p. A17.

121. Caspar Weinberger, "Historical Solutions Would Have Worked Better," remarks in "Who Lost Russia?" *Heritage Lectures*, no. 629 (January 8, 1999).

122. Gail Lapidus, "Transforming Russia: American Policy in the 1990s," in Robert Lieber, *Eagle Adrift: American Foreign Policy at the End of the Century* (Longman, 1997), p. 130.

123. *U.S.-Russian Relations at the Turn of the Century* (Washington: Carnegie Endowment for International Peace, 2000), pp. 19–20.

124. Thomas E. Graham, "A World with Russia?" paper presented at Jamestown Foundation Conference, June 9, 1999, p. 1.

125. Boris Fyodorov and Andrei Illarionov were two of the loudest voices making the argument that the IMF was too lenient. As Fyodorov said soon after the crash, "The IMF should learn a lesson from the past five years. The IMF was pretending that it was seeing a lot of reforms in Russia. Russsia was pretending to conduct reforms." (Fyodorov, as quoted in Stefan Hedlund, "Russia and the IMF," *Demokratizatsiya*, vol. 9 (Winter 2001), p. 134.) See also Andrei Illarionov, "How the Russian Financial Crisis Was Organized," *Voprosy Ekonomiki*, no. 11 (November 1998), pp. 20–35, translated by Foreign Broadcast Information Service (FBIS), FTS19990225001481; and Andrei Illarionov, "Russia and the IMF," statements prepared for the General Oversight and Investigation Subcommittee of the U.S. House Committee on Banking and Financial Services, *Hearing to Examine the Russian Economic Crisis and the International Monetary Fund (IMF) Aid Package*, September 10, 1998, 105 Cong. 2 sess. Westerners making similar arguments included Ben Slay, "Russia and the IMF: Economic Choices and Political Will," *Russian Business Watch*, vol. 7 (Summer 1999) pp. 1, 16–20; and Michael McFaul, "Getting Russia Right," *Foreign Policy*, no. 117 (Winter 1999-2000) (www.foreignpolicy.com).

126. Hedlund, "Russia and the IMF," pp. 104–36.

127. Dimitri K. Simes, "Russia's Crisis, America's Complicity," *National Interest*, no. 54 (Winter 1998–99), pp. 12–22; and Peter Reddaway and Dmitri Glinski, *The Tragedy of Russia's Reforms: Market Bolshevism against Democracy* (Washington: U.S. Institute of Peace, 2001).

128. On the first school, see Stone, *Lending Credibility*. On the second school, see Åslund, *Building Capitalism*. On the third school, see Illarionov, "Inflatsiya i antiinflatsiya politika."

129. The FDI figures were reported in Kahn and O'Brien, "Easy Money: A Special Report."

130. Lapidus, "Transforming Russia: American Policy in the 1990s," p. 130.

131. Dimitri Simes, *After the Collapse: Russia Seeks Its Place as a Great Power* (Simon and Shuster, 1999); and Stephen Cohen, *Failed Crusade: America and the Tragedy of*

Post-Communist Russia (W.W. Norton, 2000). Both Simes and Cohen stress the very negative consequences of American intervention in the internal affairs of Russia.

132. Simes, "Russia's Crisis, America's Complicity," pp. 12–22.

133. Stephen Blank, "Partners in Discord Only," *Orbis*, vol. 44 (Fall 2000), pp. 557–70. Advocates of less engagement in Russia's domestic affairs include Cohen, *Failed Crusade*, Simes, *After the Collapse*, and both American contributions to the Carnegie Endowment report, *U.S.-Russian Relations at the Turn of the Century* (Washington: Carnegie Endowment for International Peace, 2000). Advocates of a new version of containment included Condoleezza Rice, Zbigniew Brzezinski, and Henry Kissinger. For arguments for renewed engagement, see *An Agenda for Renewal: U.S-Russian Relations*, a report by the Russian and Eurasian Program of the Carnegie Endowment for International Peace (Washington: Carnegie Endowment for International Peace, December 2000).

134. David Lipton, testimony before the House Banking General Oversight Committee and Investigations Subcommittee on Russia," 105 Cong. 2 sess., September 10, 1998.

135. Strobe Talbott, "Gogol's Troika: The Case for Strategic Patience in a Time of Troubles," address at Stanford University, November 6, 1998.

136. Lipton, testimony before the House Banking General Oversight Committee and Investigations Subcommittee on Russia.

137. "U.S. Policy toward Russia: Foundations, Achievements, and Continuing Agenda," document sent to McFaul from David Leavy, National Security Council, Office of Public Affairs and Communications, September 17, 1999, p. 2.

138. Lawrence Summers, testimony before the House International Relations Committee on Russia, 105 Cong. 2 sess., September 17, 1998.

139. Interview with Atwood.

140. Madeleine Albright, address to the U.S.-Russia Business Council, Chicago Illinois, October 2, 1998; and Lippman, "Turmoil, Drift in Russia Prompt U.S. Policy Shift. Flexibility, Recognition of Limits Mark New Approach," p. A27.

141. Lawrence H. Summers, "The Global Stake in Russian Economic Reform," speech to the U.S.-Russia Business Council, April 1, 1997.

142. Lippman, "Turmoil, Drift in Russia Prompt U.S. Policy Shift. Flexibility, Recognition of Limits Mark New Approach," p. A27.

143. Madeleine Albright, address to the U.S.-Russia Business Council.

144. Talbott, "Gogol's Troika: The Case for Strategic Patience in a Time of Troubles."

145. Talbott, *The Russia Hand*, p. 286.

146. Curt Tarnoff, "U.S. Bilateral Assistance to Russia, 1992-2001," in *Russia's Uncertain Economic Future*, compendium of papers submitted to the Joint Economic Committee, Congress of the United States (Government Printing Office, December 2001), p. 381.

147. Interview with George Ingram.

148. "U.S. Policy toward Russia: Foundations, Achievements, and Continuing Agenda," p. 2.

149. Madeleine Albright, address to the U.S.-Russia Business Council; and Albright, address to Carnegie Endowment.

150. Strobe Talbott, deputy secretary of state, "Russia: Its Current Troubles and Its

Ongoing Transformation," prepared testimony before the House International Relations Committee, 106 Cong. 1 sess., October 19, 1999, p. 5.

151. Stanley Fischer, "What Went Wrong in Russia," *Financial Times*, September 27, 1999, p. 26.

152. Albright, address to the U.S.-Russia Business Council.

153. Talbott, *The Russia Hand*, p. 287.

154. "Excerpts from Clinton's Remarks: 'You Have to Play by the Rules,'" *New York Times*, September 2, 1998, p. A10.

155. Talbott, *The Russia Hand*, p. 286.

156. Albright, address to the U.S.-Russia Business Council; and interview with Lipton.

157. See Primakov, *Vosem' Mesyatsev Plyus . . .* , pp. 129–44. In discussing the American position, Primakov singled out a particularly tense and unpleasant meeting with Strobe Talbott on February 23, 1999 (p. 135).

158. Interview with Talbott.

159. Talbott, *The Russia Hand*, p. 296.

160. "IMF Says Russia Managing Well without IMF Loans," *Reuters*, September 8, 2000.

161. Anders Åslund, "Go Long on Russia," *International Economy*, July-August 2000, pp. 38–39. For a more skeptical view of the long-term lessons learned from August 1998, see Clifford Gaddy and Barry Ickes, *Russia's Virtual Economy* (Brookings, 2002), chap. 9.

162. See Putin's summary of their achievements in his remarks to the World Economic Forum, "Meeting in Russia 2001," October 30, 2001, translated and distributed by the Federal News Service. Eventually, farm land ownership was permitted as well.

163. Again, estimates of Russian GDP figures vary considerably among analysts and sources. The 1999 figure comes from Brunswick UBS Warburg, *Russia Equity Guide 2000/2001* (Moscow, 2000), p. 21. This figure of 7.7 percent is quoted from German Gref, Russian minister of economic development and trade, in *Russian Business Watch*, vol. 9 (Summer 2001), p. 8. Others have estimated the growth in GDP in 2000 to be as high as 8.5 percent.

164. Anders Åslund and Peter Boone, "Russia's Surprise Economic Success," *Financial Times*, October 9, 2002, p. 13. On specific sectors, see "Further Expansion of Manufacturing Economy Recorded in April as Demand Rises Sharply," *Moscow Narodny Purchasing Manager's Index*, May 1, 2001, p. 1.

165. Brunswick UBS Warburg, *Russia Equity Guide 2000/2001*, p. 21.

166. See, for instance, the shared assessments from very different analyses in Jacques Sapir, "The Russian Economy: From Rebound to Rebuilding," *Post-Soviet Affairs*, vol. 17 (January-March 2002), pp. 1–22; James Millar, "The Russian Economy: Putin's Pause," *Current History* (October 2001), pp. 336–42; Gaddy and Ickes, *Russia's Virtual Economy*; and Åslund, *Building Capitalism*.

167. Remarks by Stephen Sestanovich, Carnegie Endowment for International Peace, February 21, 2001.

168. Russia has continued to interact with the IMF because "a valid agreement with the Fund is a condition for restructuring Paris Cub debt." Deputy Finance Minster Aleksei Ulyukaev, as quoted in Svetlana Kovalyova, "Russian Government Upbeat on Economy, but Still Needs IMF," *Reuters*, September 14, 2000.

169. *RFE/RL Newsline*, vol. 5, no. 229, part I, December 5, 2001.

Chapter 10

1. David Halberstam, *War in a Time of Peace: Bush, Clinton and the Generals* (Scribner, 2001).

2. Interview with Strobe Talbott.

3. Michael McFaul, "Russia's Many Foreign Policies," *Demokratizatsiya*, vol. 7 (Summer 1999), pp. 393–412.

4. Supporters and critics agreed with this analysis of the administration's purpose. Michael Mandelbaum, "A Perfect Failure," *Foreign Affairs*, vol. 78 (September-October 1999), pp. 2–8; and Joseph Nye, "Redefining the National Interest," *Foreign Affairs*, vol. 78 (July-August 1999), pp. 22–35.

5. Boris Yeltsin, *Midnight Diaries*, translated by Catherine Fitzpatrick (Public Affairs, 2000), p. 255. Though there was general criticism of the NATO-led campaign, Russian responses did differ. See Andrei Tsygankov, "The Final Triumph of Pax Americana? Western Intervention in Yugoslavia and Russia's Debate on the Post–Cold War Order," *Communist and Post-Communist Studies*, vol. 33 (June 2001), pp. 133–56.

6. Yeltsin, *Midnight Diaries*, p. 255.

7. This recognition of weakness is reflected in a report on U.S.-Russian relations written after the war by some of Russia's foreign policy elites. See Council on Foreign and Defense Policy Working Group, "A Crisis in Relations," in *U.S.-Russian Relations at the Turn of Century* (Washington: Carnegie Endowment for International Peace, 2000), especially pp. 58–59.

8. For more on the background to the war, see Ivo H. Daalder and Michael E. O'Hanlon, *Winning Ugly: NATO's War to Save Kosovo* (Brookings, 2000).

9. Strobe Talbott, *The Russia Hand: A Memoir of Presidential Diplomacy* (Random House, 2002), p. 300.

10. See Daalder and O'Hanlon, *Winning Ugly*, pp. 45–49.

11. Ibid.; and Halberstam, *War in a Time of Peace*.

12. Interviews with a number of U.S. and Western officials, including Al Gore's national security adviser, Leon Fuerth, and NATO press spokesman Jamie Shea.

13. Interviews with James Steinberg and Leon Fuerth.

14. Interview with Alexander Vershbow; Daalder and O'Hanlon, *Winning Ugly*, p. 91; Thomas W. Lippman, "Albright Misjudged Milosevic on Kosovo," *Washington Post*, April 7, 1999, p. A1; and Dana Priest, "Tension Grew with Divide over Strategy," *Washington Post*, September 21, 1999, pp. A1, 16. Talbott writes that Supreme Allied Commander Wesley Clark was one of those who said if it started, they would be in for a "long haul." See Talbott, *The Russia Hand*, p. 304.

15. Interview with Talbott aide John Bass.

16. Interview with Madeleine Albright, *Newshour* transcript (www.pbs.org/newshour/bb/europe/jan-june99/albright_3-24.html [July 2003]). For the view that Albright did misjudge how long war would last, see Lippman, "Albright Misjudged Milosevic on Kosovo," p. A1.

17. Yeltsin, *Midnight Diaries*, p. 257.

18. On length of call, see press briefing by Joe Lockhart, The Briefing Room, White House, March 24, 1999; recollection comes from interview with Andrew Weiss. His recollection mirrors Talbott's in *The Russia Hand*, p. 305.

19. Yevgeny Primakov, *Vosem' Mesyatsev Plyus* (Moscow: "Mysl'", 2001), p. 148.

20. Interview with Fuerth.

21. Primakov made the decision to turnaround, and Yeltsin confirmed it. See Primakov, *Vosem' Mesyatsev Plyus,* p. 152; and Talbott, *The Russia Hand,* p. 310.

22. "Remarks by President Clinton, French President Chirac, Russian President Yeltsin, and NATO Secretary-General Solana at NATO-Russia Founding Act Signing Ceremony," White House, Office of the Press Secretary (Paris, France), May 27, 1997.

23. Interview with Jamie Shea.

24. Polls taken by the Foundation for Public Opinion, April 3–4, 1999 (www.fom.ru.).

25. Talbott, *The Russia Hand,* p. 307.

26. Press conference with Arbatov, National Press Institute, March 26, 1999, translation and transcript provided by Federal News Service.

27. Interview with Andrew Weiss.

28. Clark, *Waging Modern War,* pp. 212–13; and David Filipov, "Russia's Military Sees a Balkan Opportunity," *Boston Globe,* April 8, 1999, p. A1.

29. Daalder and O'Hanlon, *Winning Ugly,* p. 127; Judith Matloff, "Russia's Tough Talk Unsettles West," *Christian Science Monitor,* April 12, 1999, p. 1; interview with Steinberg; and Thomas L. Friedman, "Our Buddy Boris," *New York Times,* April 16, 1999, p. A25.

30. Statement on Kosovo, issued by the Heads of State and Government participating in the meeting of the North Atlantic Council in Washington, April 1999. Available at NATO website (www.nato.int.).

31. Daalder and O'Hanlon, *Winning Ugly,* pp. 139–40.

32. Interviews with Steinberg and Sandy Berger.

33. In his memoirs, Yeltsin claims that Gaidar was also considered a serious candidate, suggesting that Yeltsin wanted to appoint someone with good standing in the West. The foreign policy credentials of the emissary appear to have been a lesser concern. See Yeltsin, *Midnight Diaries,* p. 261.

34. Talbott, *The Russia Hand,* p. 310.

35. Ibid., p. 311.

36. Talbott, *The Russia Hand,* pp. 311.

37. Press briefing by senior administration officials, the Briefing Room, White House, May 3, 1999; and Talbott, *The Russia Hand,* p. 311, 313–14.

38. Interviews with Eric Edelman, Carlos Pascual, and Martti Ahtisaari; and Talbott *The Russia Hand,* p. 314.

39. Interview with Edelman.

40. Interview with Ahtisaari; and Talbott, *The Russia Hand,* p. 314.

41. Interview with Ahtisaari.

42. Quoted in Martti Ahtisaari, *Tehtava Belgradissa* (Mission in Belgrade), which was translated by the U.S. embassy in Helsinki; the embassy provided a copy of the translated manuscript to the authors. Our cites are to that unofficial translation of the manuscript.

43. Daalder and O'Hanlon, *Winning Ugly,* pp. 170–71; and Ahtisaari, *Mission in Belgrade.*

44. Talbott, *The Russia Hand,* pp. 316–17.

45. Interview with Edelman; Talbott confirms outlines of this story in *The Russia Hand,* pp. 317–18.

46. Ahtisaari, *Mission in Belgrade;* Talbott, *The Russia Hand;* and interview with Edelman.

47. Interview with Talbott.

48. Talbott, *The Russia Hand*, pp. 318–19.

49. Ahtisaari, *Mission in Belgrade*.

50. Daalder and O'Hanlon, *Winning Ugly*, p. 171.

51. Yeltsin, *Midnight Diaries*, p. 130.

52. Daalder and O'Hanlon, *Winning Ugly*, p. 172. On the importance of Cologne, see Talbott, *The Russia Hand*, pp. 317, 322–23.

53. Talbott, *The Russia Hand*, pp. 324–25; and interviews with members of Talbott's team.

54. Talbott, *The Russia Hand*, p. 324.

55. Clark, *Waging Modern War*, pp. 345–46.

56. Talbott, *The Russia Hand*, p. 326.

57. Interview with Ahtisaari. On the U.S. doubts, information comes from interviews with members of the team.

58. Clark, *Waging Modern War*, pp. 351–54.

59. Ibid., p. 373.

60. Ibid., pp. 371–73.

61. Interview with John Bass; and Talbott, *The Russia Hand*, pp. 324ff.

62. Interviews with Bass and Andrew Weiss; and Talbott, *The Russia Hand*, p. 337.

63. Subsequent analyses confirmed this perception. See Allen Lynch, "The Realism of Russia's Foreign Policy," *Europe-Asia Studies*, vol. 53 (January 2001), p. 20.

64. Eric Schmitt, "Crisis in the Balkans: NATO Bars Russia from Reinforcing Troops in Kosovo," *New York Times*, July 3, 1999, p. A1; Clark, *Waging Modern War*; and Talbott, *The Russia Hand*, pp. 346–47.

65. Clark, *Waging Modern War*, pp. 390–92.

66. Ibid., p. 392.

67. Ibid., p. 395.

68. Ahtisaari, *Mission in Belgrade*; and interview with Vershbow.

69. Interview with Carlos Pascual.

70. Talbott, *The Russia Hand*, p. 351.

71. Igor Ivanov, "Russia in a Changing World: The President and the Foreign Ministry Will Seek to Build a Multipolar World," *Nezavisimaya Gazeta*, June 25, 1999, pp. 1, 6, translated and distributed by *Federal News Service*.

72. Talbott, *The Russia Hand*, p. 352; and remarks by the president on agreement from Helsinki, in front of Cologne Cathedral, White House, Office of the Press Secretary (Cologne), June 18, 1999.

73. Lynch, "The Realism of Russia's Foreign Policy," pp. 7–31.

74. Public attitudes toward the NATO war and NATO expansion, however, are complex. Opinion polls did show a noticeable increase in anti-NATO and anti-American sentiment after the NATO bombing campaign against Yugoslavia, but the staying power of this anti-Western sentiment is harder to measure. See William Zimmerman, *The Russian People and Foreign Policy: Russian Elite and Mass Perspectives, 1993–2000* (Princeton University Press, 2002), chap. 6; and Institut Fonda, "Obshchestvennoe mnenie," *Amerika: vzglyad iz Rossii. Do i posle 11 sentyabrya* (Moskva: FOM, 2001).

75. Ahtisaari, *Mission in Belgrade*; and interview with Ahtisaari. Zbigniew Brzezinski agrees. See his testimony in "The War in Kosovo and a Postwar Analysis,"

Hearings before the Senate Committee on Foreign Relations, 106 Cong. 1 sess., October 6, 1999 (Government Printing Office, 2000), pp. 77ff.

76. Yeltsin, as quoted in George Breslauer, *Gorbachev and Yeltsin as Leaders* (Cambridge: Cambridge University Press, 2002), p. 226. Breslauer builds the case for why focusing on domestic development, especially economic growth, was the logical Russian response to the exposure of Russian weakness after Kosovo.

77. Interview with Leon Fuerth.

78. Alexander Timofeev, "Almost Relatives: Russia and China to Develop Military-Technical Cooperation and Strategic Military Partnership," *Vremya MN*, June 10, 1999, p. 6, translated and distributed by *ISI Emerging Markets*; Yevgeniy Dezhin, "A Strategic Partnership between Russia and China May Become a Counterbalance to Ties with NATO," *Nezavisimaya Voyennoye Obozreniye*, no. 13, April 9–15, 1999, translated and posted on *Johnson's Russia List*, May 7, 1999 (cdi.org). Of course, the viability of such an anti-American alliance is questionable, given the security interests of China and Russia. But the rhetorical attention to such a partnership spiked considerably at the end of the 1990s.

79. Ivanov, "Russia in a Changing World." See also the Russian government's "Concept of National Security," which took effect at the beginning of 2000, stressing, at least rhetorically, this reorientation. For explanations of the changes in this doctrinal statement see, Mark Kramer, *What is Driving Russia's New Strategic Concept?* PONARS Policy Memo Series, no. 113 (Harvard University, January 2000); Sergey Rogov, *The New Russian National Security Concept* (Alexandria, Va.: Center for Strategic Studies, November 2000); and Celeste Wallander, "Wary of the West: Russian Security Policy at the Millennium," *Arms Control Today*, vol. 30 (March 2000), pp. 7–12.

Chapter 11

1. Shamil Basayev first became famous for leading a raid on Budyonnovsk, Russia, during the first Chechen war. During the raid, Basayev forces killed dozens of Russian civilians and held hundreds more hostage in a hospital in the small Russian town, from which he eventually escaped. He became a popular figure in Chechnya but eventually had a falling out with the president of Chechnya, Aslan Maskhadov. Most believe that he was acting on his own and not on behalf of the Chechen government when he invaded Dagestan.

2. The details of this invasion are murky. An excellent reconstruction can be found in John Dunlop, "Two Incursions into Dagestan and Their Extraordinary Consequences," *Contemporary Caucasus Newsletter*, no. 9 (Spring 2000), pp. 20–24.

3. Jamie Rubin, U.S. Department of State Noon Briefing, Tuesday, August 10; see also "Amerika obsuzhdaet deystvia bandformirovanii na Severnom Kavkaze," *Rossiiskaya Gazeta*, August 13, 1999, p. 1.

4. Jamie Rubin, U.S. Department of State Daily Press Briefing, August 16, 1999.

5. ITAR-TASS, "Operatsiya nachalas, Goriachaya Chronika," *Rossiiskaya Gazeta*, August 14, 1999, p. 3.

6. Vladimir Zainetdinov, Aleksei Siviv, and Maria Belocklova, "Vchera v schkolakh ot Chokhotki do Kaliningrada prozvenel pervii zvonok. A v Ohotnom riyadu poslednii zvonok," *Rossiiskaya Gazeta*, September 2, 1999, p.1; "Terrakt in Buynaksk,"

Rossiiskaya Gazeta, September 6, 1999, p. 2; Aleksandr Babakin, "V boi idut odni pat-sani," *Rossiiskaya Gazeta,* September 7, 1999, p. 1; and Aleksandr Shapovalov, "Buynaksk, dva raza Moskva, teper' Volgodonsk: gde dal'she?" *Nezavisimaya Gazeta,* September 17, 1999, p.1.

7. We have not investigated the full body of evidence to draw any definitive conclusions. For supporters of this thesis, see Aleksandr Litvinenko and Yurii Fel'shtinskii, *Kuda Edet 'Krysha' Rossii pod nazvaniem FSB?* a book published in serial form in *Novaya Gazeta* and in English, in a slightly different form, in Aleksandr Litvinenko and Yurii Fel'shtinskii, *Blowing Up Russia: Terror from Within* (S.P.I. Books, 2002). Boris Berezovsky also produced a short documentary film on the subject. Anatol Lieven, however, writes, "The suggestion that a force largely composed of Arab Muslim extremists would lack the motive, the expertise, or the ruthlessness to carry out a terrorist bombing campaign against Russia is absolutely ridiculous." Anatol Lieven, "Through a Distorted Lens: Chechnya and the Western Media," *Current History,* vol. 99 (October 2000), p. 324.

8. David Hoffman, "Russian Premier Pins Bombing on Chechens," *Washington Post,* September 16, 1999, p. A26; and Putin, as quoted in "Na voine kak na voine," *Rossiiskaya Gazeta,* September 25, 1999, p. 1.

9. "Goriachia Chronoka: Konechnaya tsel unichtozhit banditov," *Rossiiskaya Gazeta,* October 6, 1999, p. 1.

10. Mark Kramer, "Civil-Military Relations in Russia and the Chechnya Conflict," *Policy Memo Series,* no. 99 (Harvard University, Program on New Approaches to Russian Security, December 1999); and Dmitri Trenin, "Chechnya: Effects of the War and Prospects for Peace," unpublished manuscript, 2000.

11. Human Rights Watch doggedly documented human atrocities carried out in the second Chechen war, including summary executions, bombings of villages, and rape of Chechen women. See, for instance, their publications, "Now Happiness Remains: Civilian Killings, Pillage, and Rape in Alkhan-Yurt," Chechnya, *Russia/Chechnya,* vol. 12, no. 5 (D) (April 2000), pp. 1–33; "February 5: A Day of Slaughter in Novye Aldi," *Russia/Chechnya,* vol. 12, no. 9 (D) (June 2000), pp. 1–43; "The 'Dirty War' in Chechnya: Forced Disappearances, Torture, and Summary Executions," *Russia,* vol. 13, no. 1 (D) (March 2001), pp. 1–42; and "Burying the Evidence: The Botched Investigation into a Mass Grave in Chechnya," *Russia/Chechnya,* vol. 13, no. 3 (D) (May 2001), pp. 1–26. The *Chechnya Weekly,* published by the Jamestown Foundation, also provides comprehensive coverage of events related to the war, including extensive reporting on human rights violations. Amnesty International, Physicians for Human Rights, Doctors of the World, and Doctors without Borders have also contributed to the documentation of human rights abuses. In Russia, *Memorial* has provided the most comprehensive coverage of human rights abuses inside Chechnya and serves as the primary material for many Western publications on the subject. The Glasnost Foundation is another important source of primary material. See also Matthew Evangelista, *The Chechen Wars: Will Russia Go the Way of the Soviet Union?* (Brookings, 2003); Anne Nivat, *Chienne de Guerre: A Woman Reporter behind the Lines of the War in Chechnya* (Public Affairs, 2000); and Anna Politkovskaya, *A Dirty War: A Russian Reporter in Chechnya* (London: Harvill Press, 2001); and Department of State, Bureau of Democracy, Human Rights, and Labor, *Country Reports on Human Rights Practices, Russia, 1995-2001* (various years).

12. This figure is cited in Sarah E. Mendelson, "Russia, Chechnya, and International Norms: The Power and Paucity of Human Rights," Working Paper (Washington: National Council for Eurasian and East European Research, July 17, 2001), p. 11.

13. Evangelista, *The Chechen Wars: Will Russia Go the Way of the Soviet Union?* p. 155. Evangelista devotes an entire chapter of his book to assessing Russia's violations of the Geneva Conventions.

14. Interview with Irene Stevenson, Aleksei Yablokov, and Sergei Grigoryants. Stevenson, the head of the AFL-CIO's Solidarity Center in Russia, was denied reentry to Russia in December 2002. For details on democratic erosion under Putin, see Sarah Mendelson, "The Putin Path: Civil Liberties and Human Rights in Retreat," *Problems of Post-Communism*, vol. 47 (September-October 2000) pp. 3–12; and Timothy Colton and Michael McFaul, *Popular Choice and Managed Democracy in Russia: The 1999-2000 Electoral Cycle* (Brookings, 2003), chap. 8.

15. The successful of appeal of treason charges against the environmental activist, Aleksandr Nikitin, fueled hope that the courts were becoming more autonomous. Nikitin was optimistic. Nikitin's release, however, was followed by the conviction of Grigory Pas'ko, a journalist accused of treason for publishing in the Japanese press information about the dangerous dumping of nuclear waste by Russian nuclear submarines.

16. Timothy J. Colton and Michael McFaul, "Reinventing Russia's Party of Power: Unity and the 1999 Duma Election," *Post-Soviet Affairs*, vol. 16 (Summer 2000), pp. 201–24.

17. On the battles between these parties, see Michael McFaul, Nikolai Petrov, and Andrei Ryabov, eds., *Rossiya v izbiratel'nom tsikle 1999–2000 godov* (Moscow: Moscow Carnegie Center, 2000).

18. Eugene Huskey, "Political Leadership and the Center–Periphery Struggle: Putin's Administrative Reforms," in Archie Brown and Lilia Shevtsova, eds., *Gorbachev, Yeltsin and Putin: Political Leadership in Russia's Transition* (Washington: Carnegie Endowment for International Peace, 2001), pp. 113–42.

19. For details, see Masha Lipman and Michael McFaul, "'Managed Democracy' in Russia: Putin and the Press," *Harvard International Journal of Press/Politics*, vol. 6 (Summer 2001), pp. 117–28; and Hoffman, *The Oligarchs*, pp. 476–85.

20. Interview with John Beyrle.

21. Strobe Talbott, *The Russia Hand: A Memoir of Presidential Diplomacy* (Random House, 2002), pp. 276–77.

22. Interview with Strobe Talbott.

23. Interview with James Steinberg.

24. Interview with Talbott.

25. See the final chapter of Michael McFaul, *Russia's 1996 Presidential Election: The End of Polarized Politics* (Stanford, Calif.: Hoover Institution Press, 1997).

26. Over time, support for the war has declined considerably. By August 2002, according to VTsIOM (All-Russian Center on Research of Public Opinion) the number of citizens who approved of the Russian military campaign in Chechnya had fallen to 30 percent. See "Public Support for Chechnya Operation Declining," *RFE/RL Newsline*, vol. 6, September 9, 2002 (www.rferl.org/newsline/ [July 2003]).

27. See the chapter on SPS in Michael McFaul, Andrei Ryabov, and Nikolai Petrov, *Primer on Russia's 1999 Duma Elections* (Washington: Carnegie Endowment for International Peace, 1999).

28. This is the assessment of Yabloko's campaign director for the 1999 elections, Vyacheslav Igrunov. Interview with Igrunov. The actual impact of Yavlinsky's stance on Yabloko electoral performance is difficult to trace. See Colton and McFaul, *Popular Choice and Managed Democracy in Russia*, chap. 6.

29. Strobe Talbott, deputy secretary of state, "Russia: Its Current Troubles and Its Ongoing Transformation," prepared testimony before the House International Relations Committee, 106 Cong. 1 sess., October 19, 1999, p. 1.

30. Strobe Talbott, deputy secretary of state, "Pursuing U.S. Interests with Russia and with President-Elect Putin," prepared testimony before the Subcommittee on Foreign Operations of the Senate Appropriations Committee, 106 Cong. 2 sess., April 4, 2000, p. 6.

31. Aleksandr Koretskii, "Chechnya ob'yavila voinu SSHA," *Segodnya*, August 24, 1999, p. 1.

32. Ambassador-at-Large Stephen Sestanovich, special adviser to the secretary of state for the new independent states, "The Conflict in Chechnya and Its Implications for U.S. Relations with Russia," testimony before the Senate Foreign Relations Committee, 106 Cong. 1 sess., November 4, 1999, p. 2.

33. Bill Powell, "Boris to Bill: Butt Out," *Newsweek*, November 29, 1999, p. 60; and Talbott, *The Russia Hand*, pp. 361–62.

34. Madeleine Albright, "Clear on Chechnya," *Washington Post*, March 8, 2000, p. A31.

35. "Remarks by Secretary of State Madeleine K. Albright following statement by acting president Vladimir Putin at Multilateral Steering Committee Group Meeting," Moscow, Russia, *State Department Briefing*, February 1, 2000, reprinted by *Federal News Service*.

36. Talbott, *The Russia Hand*, pp. 359–60.

37. Pavel Baev, "Will Russia Go for a Military Victory in Chechnya?" *Policy Memo Series*, no. 107 (Harvard University, Program on New Approaches to Russian Security, February 2000), p. 1.

38. Sestanovich, "The Conflict in Chechnya and its Implications for U.S. Relations with Russia," pp. 2–3.

39. Talbott, "Pursuing U.S. Interests with Russia and with President-Elect Putin," p. 6.

40. Madeleine Albright, "Clear on Chechnya," *Washington Post*, March 8, 2000, p. A31.

41. Talbott, "Russia: Its Current Troubles and Its Ongoing Transformation," p. 2; and Strobe Talbott, acting secretary of state, "Statement on Russian Attack on Grozny, Chechnya," as released by the Office of the Spokesman, Department of State, October 22, 1999.

42. Talbott, "Russia: Its Current Troubles and Its Ongoing Transformation," p. 2.

43. Talbott, deputy secretary of state, "Pursuing U.S. Interests with Russia and with President-Elect Putin," pp. 7–8.

44. "Albright Warns against Remaking Russia a U.S. Enemy," *Agence France-Presse*, November 25, 1999.

45. Bill Clinton, "Remembering Yeltsin," *Time*, January 1, 2001, p. 94. Clinton's attitude is discussed at length in Talbott, *The Russia Hand*.

46. Interviews with Leon Fuerth and Stephen Sestanovich. See also Stephen Sestanovich, "Where Does Russia Belong?" *National Interest*, no. 62 (Winter 2000–2001), p. 15.

47. Interview with John Beyrle. In April 2000, the Parliamentary Assembly of the Council of Europe (PACE) did issue criticism of Russia's conduct in carrying out military operations in Chechnya and suspended Russia's voting rights in PACE. Voting rights were renewed the following year, however, even though Russian military tactics and abuses in Chechnya had not changed. See Evangelista, *The Chechen Wars*, pp. 149–50. More generally on Western inaction and inattention, see Sarah E. Mendelson, "Russians' Rights Imperiled: Has Anybody Noticed?" *International Security*, vol. 26 (Spring 2002), pp. 36–68.

48. Office of the Coordinator of the U.S. Assistance to the NIS, *U.S. Government Assistance to and Cooperative Activities with the New Independent States of the Former Soviet Union: FY 2000 Annual Report* (Department of State, January 2001), pp. 73–92.

49. McFaul's conversations with Stephen Sestanovich and William Taylor, various interactions (Fall 1999).

50. The IMF did not actually send any real money to Moscow but used this new loan money to pay back old Russian debts to the IMF.

51. Interviews with a number of U.S. officials.

52. Interviews with a number of U.S. officials.

53. Sestanovich, "Where Does Russia Belong?" p. 15.

54. David Briscoe, "U.S. Gov't Bank to Nix Russia Loans," *Associated Press*, December 21, 1999.

55. Interview with Madeleine Albright.

56. Talbott, T*he Russia Hand,* p. 359; and press statement by Jamie Rubin, November 12, 1999.

57. Ambassador-at-Large Stephen Sestanovich, special adviser to the secretary of state for the new independent states, "Russia's Elections and American Policy," testimony before the Senate Foreign Relations Committee, 106 Cong. 2 sess., April 12, 2000, p. 3.

58. Interview with Talbott; and Sestanovich, "Where Does Russia Belong?" p. 15.

59. Talbott, *The Russia Hand,* p. 357.

60. Interview with Beyrle.

61. Prepared statement of Senator Mitch McConnell before the Foreign Operations Subcommittee of the Senate Appropriations Committee, 106 Cong. 2 sess. April 4, 2000.

62. *Russia's Road to Corruption,* pp. 57–59.

63. Senate Resolution 262, 106 Cong. 2 sess., February 24, 2000.

64. Talbott, "Russia: Its Current Troubles and Its Ongoing Transformation," p. 5.

65. The legislation, H.R. 2121, was passed by both the House and Senate (though without funding) during the Bush administration. The idea for and drafting of the bill, however, took place in 2000.

66. Briscoe, "U.S. Gov't Bank to Nix Russia Loans."

67. Interview with George W. Bush on the *Newshour with Jim Lehrer*, February 16, 2000 (www.pbs.org/newshour/bb/election/jan-june00/bush_2-16.html). See chap. 13.

68. Zbigniew Brzezinski, "Why the West Should Care about Chechnya," *Wall Street Journal*, November 10, 1999, p. A22. He made a similar argument in Zbigniew Brzezinski, testimony before Panel II of a Hearing of the Subcommittee on European Affairs of the Senate Foreign Relations Committee, 106 Cong. 2 sess., April 12, 2000.

69. Brzezinski, testimony before Panel II of the Subcommittee on European Affairs.

70. American Committee for Peace in Chechnya, "Founding Declaration," sent to Michael McFaul, February 10, 2000.

71. Brzezinski, testimony before Panel II of the Subcommittee on European Affairs.

72. American Committee for Peace in Chechnya, "Founding Declaration."

73. Brzezinski, "Why the West Should Care about Chechnya."

74. See, for instance, Michael McFaul, "Indifference to Democracy," *Washington Post*, March 3, 2000, and the response by Albright, "Clear on Chechnya."

75. Interview with Talbott.

76. Anatol Lieven, "It Is Hypocrisy to Condemn Russia over Chechnya," *Independent* (London), December 13, 1999, p. 5 ; and Anatol Lieven, "Through a Distorted Lens: Chechnya and the Western Media," *Current History*, vol. 99 (October 2000), pp. 321–28.

77. Dimitri Simes, from transcript of Jim Lehrer's *Newshour*, November 18, 1999 (www.pbs.org/newshour/bb/international/july-dec99/chechnya_11-18.html [July 2003]).

78. Robert Bruce Ware, "The West's Failure to Understand Chechnya," *Boston Globe*, October 26, 1999.

79. Interview with Sestanovich.

Chapter 12

1. For background, see Bradley Graham, *Hit to Kill: The New Battle over Shielding America from Missile Attack* (New York: Public Affairs, 2001), pp. 18–19.

2. Interviews with Brent Scowcroft, James Baker, Stephen Hadley, and Dennis Ross; and Graham, *Hit to Kill*, pp. 20–21.

3. Interviews with Dennis Ross and Stephen Hadley; background briefing by senior administration officials, the Briefing Room, White House, Office of the Press Secretary, June 16, 1992; and Joint U.S.-Russian Statement on a Global Protection System, June 17, 1992, *U.S. Department of State Dispatch*, vol. 3 (June 22, 1992), pp. 493–94.

4. Interview with Scowcroft. On combating the China threat, see Stephen J. Hadley, "A Call to Deploy," *Washington Quarterly*, vol. 23 (Summer 2000), pp. 95–108.

5. Interview with Ross.

6. The information in this paragraph comes from an unclassified draft of the U.S. talking points shown to the authors.

7. Interview with Hadley. For another view that Ross-Mamedov was making real headway and should have been continued in the Clinton administration, see R. James Woolsey, "Rethinking Russia and Missile Defense Debate," *San Diego Union-Tribune*, June 25, 2000, p. G1.

8. Interviews with Ross and Baker.

9. Strobe Talbott, *The Russia Hand: A Memoir of Presidential Diplomacy* (Random House, 2002), p. 375.

10. Interviews with Sandy Berger, Leon Fuerth, Ashton Carter, Robert Bell, and Michael Nacht. See also Graham, *Hit to Kill*.

11. Interview with Leon Fuerth.

12. Talbott, *The Russia Hand*, p. 375; and interview with Kozyrev.

13. Interviews with Bell and Carter; and Talbott, *The Russia Hand*, p. 375.

14. Interview with Bell.

15. David Hoffman, "Perry Seeks Russian Vote on Arms Pact," *Washington Post*, October 16, 1996, p. A17; "Russians Resist Perry on Arms Pact," *Washington Post*, October 18, 1996, p. A44; "A START Chronology," *Current History*, October 1999, p. 342; and Talbott, *The Russia Hand*, p. 376.

16. Alexei Arbatov, "As NATO Grows, Start 2 Shudders," *New York Times*, August 26, 1997, p. A15; and Alexander Pikaev, *The Rise and Fall of START II: The Russian View*, Working Papers, no. 6 (Washington: Carnegie Endowment for International Peace, September 1999).

17. Interview with Strobe Talbott.

18. Ibid.

19. Press conference of President Clinton and President Yeltsin, *Kalastaja Torppa*, White House, Office of the Press Secretary (Helsinki, Finland), March 21, 1997; press briefing by Robert Bell, senior director for the National Security Council for Defense Policy and Arms Control, Briefing Room, White House, Office of the Press Secretary, March 24, 1997. A joint statement issued at the summit said, "The United States and Russia are each committed to the ABM Treaty, a cornerstone of strategic stability." See Joint Statement concerning the Anti-Ballistic Missile Treaty, White House, Office of the Press Secretary (Helsinki, Finland), March 21, 1997.

20. For the agreement, see Standing Consultative Commission Agreed Statement, September 26, 1997 (www.fas.org/nuke/control/abm/text/abm_scc1.htm).

21. Jack Mendelsohn, "The U.S.-Russian Strategic Arms Control Agenda," *Arms Control Today*, vol. 27 (November-December 1997), pp. 12–16.

22. Interview with William Perry. See also Primakov's remarks linking enlargement with arms control in Ronald D. Asmus, *Opening NATO's Door: How the Alliance Remade Itself for a New Era* (Columbia University Press, 2002), p. 144.

23. Interview with Bell.

24. He was right. See Pikaev, *The Rise and Fall of START II*.

25. Interview with Bell; for a chronology of the delays, see "A START Chronology," p. 342.

26. Cited in Graham, *Hit to Kill*, pp. 32–33.

27. Ibid., p. 44.

28. See "National Missile Defense Act of 1999," *Congressional Record*, March 15, 1999, p. S2625; and Talbott, *The Russia Hand*, p. 379.

29. Interview with Ross.

30. Interview with Talbott.

31. Interview with Berger.

32. Talbott, *The Russia Hand*, p. 380; the other two criteria were cost and the nature of the threat. For the development of the criteria, see Graham, *Hit to Kill*, p. 106.

33. Interview with Berger.

34. Steve Mufson, "U.S.-Russia to Resume Arms Control Negotiations," *Washington Post*, July 28, 1999, p. 1.

35. Gerard Baker and David Buchan, "Yeltsin and Clinton End Chill," *Financial Times*, June 21, 1999, p. 1; and press briefing by National Security Adviser Sandy Berger, Hotel Mondial am Dom, White House, Office of the Press Secretary (Cologne, Germany), June 20, 1999.

36. Graham, *Hit to Kill*, pp. 143–44.

37. Art Pine, "U.S. Offers Russia Proposal to Renegotiate Missile Pact," *Los Angeles*

Times, October 17, 1999, p. A1; Steven Mufson and Bradley Graham, "U.S. Offers Aid to Russia on Radar Site," *Washington Post*, October 17, 1999, p. A1; and Graham, *Hit to Kill*, p. 170.

38. ITAR-TASS, December 17, 1999, in Foreign Broadcast Information Service (FBIS)-SOV-1999-1217 (wnc.fedoworld.gov.).

39. Alexander Pikaev, "Moscow's Matrix," *Washington Quarterly*, vol. 23 (Summer 2000), pp. 187–94.

40. Thomas Remington, "Putin, the Duma, and Political Parties," in Dale Herspring, ed., *Putin's Russia: Past Imperfect, Future Uncertain* (Lanham, Md.: Rowman and Littlefield, 2003), pp. 39–62.

41. "Russian Security Adviser Flies Home after Washington Talks," *Agence France-Presse*, February 20, 2000; and Jane Perlez, "Russian Aide Opens Door a Bit to U.S. Bid for Missile Defense," *New York Times*, February 19, 2000, p. A3.

42. Press briefing by Deputy Secretary of State Strobe Talbott, National Hotel, White House, Office of the Press Secretary (Moscow, Russia), June 4, 2000. See also Igor Ivanov, "Missile Defense Madness," *Foreign Affairs*, vol. 79 (September-October 2000), pp. 15–21.

43. Talbott, *The Russia Hand*, p. 394.

44. Interview with Berger.

45. See Graham, *Hit to Kill*, p. 120.

46. Ibid., pp. 126–28, 326–32.

47. Interview of the president on Live National Radio Program with Ekho Moskvy, White House, Office of the Press Secretary (Moscow, Russia), June 4, 2000.

48. Interview with Talbott; and Talbott, *The Russia Hand*, p. 255. See also Robin Wright, "Russia Warned on Helping Iran Missile Program," *Los Angeles Times*, February 12, 1997, p. A1; and Robert J. Einhorn and Gary Samore, "Ending Russian Assistance to Iran's Nuclear Bomb," *Survival*, vol. 44 (Summer 2002), p. 54.

49. Talbott, *The Russia* Hand, pp. 256–57.

50. Ibid. See also Einhorn and Samore, "Ending Russian Assistance," p. 54; and Michael R. Gordon, "U.S. Is Pressing Moscow on Iran and Missile Aid," *New York Times*, March 9, 1998, p. A1.

51. Thomas W. Lippman, "Israel Presses U.S. to Sanction Russian Missile Firms Aiding Iran," *Washington Post*, September 25, 1997, p. A31; David Hoffman, "Gore Says Probe Shows Iran Seeks Technology to Build Nuclear Arms," *Washington Post*, September 24, 1997, p. A26; and Chrystia Freeland, "Yeltsin Denies That Russia Aided Iran N-weapons Effort," *Financial Times*, September 27, 1997, p. 2.

52. Interview with William Courtney; and Freeland, "Yeltsin Denies That Russia Aided Iran N-weapons Effort."

53. Talbott, *The Russia Hand*, p. 259; and interview with Talbott.

54. Interview with Talbott.

55. Lippman, "Israel Presses U.S. to Sanction Russia Missile Firms"; and interview with James Steinberg.

56. Interview with Talbott.

57. Stephen Sestanovich, "At Odds with Iran and Iraq: Can the United States and Russia Resolve Their Differences?" A Century Foundation and Stanley Foundation Paper (New York and Muscatine, Iowa, February 2003), p. 22.

58. Gordon, "U.S. Is Pressing Moscow on Iran and Missile Aid," p. A1; David Hoffman, "Russia Was Lab for Theories on Foreign Policy," *Washington Post*, June 4,

2000, pp. A1, 9; "U.S. Praises Russian Step on Arms Materials," *New York Times*, January 23, 1998, p. A6; Einhorn and Samore, "Ending Russian Assistance," p. 54; and Talbott, *The Russia Hand*, pp. 260–65.

59. Talbott, *The Russia Hand*, p. 265; and interview with Talbott.

60. See Einhorn and Samore, "Ending Russian Assistance," p. 54; interview with Steinberg; Talbott, *The Russia Hand*, pp. 272–73; and interview with Talbott.

61. Bill Gertz, "Letter Shows Gore Made Deal," *Washington Times*, October 17, 2000, p. 1.

62. Ibid.

63. John M. Broder, "Despite a Secret Pact by Gore in '95, Russian Arms Sales to Iran Go On," *New York Times*, October 13, 2000, p. A1; Gertz, "Letter Shows Gore Made Deal"; and Jim Hoagland, "From Russia with Chutzpah," *Washington Post*, November 22, 2000, p. A27.

64. Interview with Talbott. On the Chechen issue, see also Einhorn and Samore, "Ending Russian Assistance," p. 62.

65. Interview with Steinberg.

66. Sestanovich, "At Odds with Iran and Iraq," p. 22.

Chapter 13

1. Condoleezza Rice, "Promoting the National Interest," *Foreign Affairs*, vol. 79 (January–February 2000), pp. 45–62.

2. Blackwill, as quoted in R.W. Apple, "Bush Questions Aid to Moscow in a Policy Talk," *New York Times*, November 20, 1999, p. A1.

3. Rice, "Promoting the National Interest," p. 49.

4. Condoleezza Rice, "Exercising Power without Arrogance," *Chicago Tribune*, December 31, 2000. On Rice's view of the importance of values in American foreign policy, see also her remarks at the U.S. Institute of Peace on January 17, 2001, published in "Passing the Baton: Challenges of Statecraft for the New Administration," *Peaceworks*, no. 41 (Washington: U.S. Institute of Peace, May 2001), pp. 57–62.

5. Governor George W. Bush, "A Period of Consequences," address at the Citadel, South Carolina, September 23, 1999 (citadel.edu/pao/presbush [July 2003]).

6. Rice, "Promoting the National Interest," p. 57. Rice used the same language to describe Russia a year later, after the U.S. election was over, in "Exercising Power without Arrogance."

7. Rice, "Promoting the National Interest," *Foreign Affairs*, p. 57. Emphasis added.

8. Rice, quoted in Romesh Ratnesar, "Condi Rice Can't Lose," *CNN.com*, September 20, 1999.

9. Condoleezza Rice, "Redefining U.S.-Russia Relations," *San Francisco Chronicle*, January 3, 2001, p. A19.

10. Bush, "A Period of Consequences;" and George W. Bush, "New Leadership on National Security," press conference, Washington, May 23, 2000.

11. Rice, "Promoting the National Interest," p. 58. The emphatic plea to tell the truth is on the same page.

12. The Second 2000 Gore-Bush Presidential Debate, October 11, 2000 (www.debates.org/pages/trans2000b.html [July 2003]).

13. Governor George W. Bush, "A Distinctly American Internationalism," Ronald Reagan Presidential Library, Simi Valley, California, November 19, 1999.

14. Bush, "A Distinctly American Internationalism."

15. Interview with George W. Bush on the *Newshour with Jim Lehrer*, February 16, 2000 (www.pbs.org/newshour/bb/election/jan-june00/bush_2-16.html [July 2003]).

16. Speaker's Advisory Group on Russia, Christopher Cox, chairman, *Russia's Road to Corruption: How the Clinton Administration Exported Government Instead of Free Enterprise and Failed the Russian People* (U.S. House of Representatives, September 2000), chap. 6. On Chernomyrdin's alleged corrupt practices, see especially Peter Reddaway, "Is Chernomyrdin a Crook?" *Post-Soviet Prospects*, vol. 3 (August 1995), and Anders Åslund, "Russia's Sleaze Sector," *New York Times*, July 11, 1995, p. A19.

17. Bush, "A Distinctly American Internationalism."

18. Bush, "A Distinctly American Internationalism." Chernomyrdin was so outraged by the statement that he threatened to sue Bush for defamation of character. See "Chernomyrdin Demands Apology," *Reuters*, October 16, 2000. See also note 12.

19. Mark J. Penn, "People to Government: Stay Engaged," *Blueprint*, vol. 5 (Winter 2000), pp. 72–82.

20. Rice, "Exercising Power without Arrogance."

21. Ibid.

22. Ibid.

23. Vernon Loeb and Susan Glaser, "Bush Backs Expulsion of 50 Russians," *Washington Post*, March 23, 2001, p. A1.

24. Beyrle, as acting head of the Office on the New Independent States (S/NIS), was at the time equal in status to an assistant secretary of state. This meeting and subsequent meetings between U.S. and Chechen officials were labeled unofficial and held outside of the State Department. Interview with John Beyrle. On Sestanovich's meeting, see U.S. Department of State daily press briefing, November 13, 1997.

25. Rumsfeld, interviewed by Winston Churchill, March 18, 2001 (www.telegraph.co.uk [July 2003]). Paul Wolfowitz quoted in James Risen and Jane Perlez, "Russian Diplomats Ordered Expelled in a Countermove," *New York Times*, March 21, 2001, p. A1.

26. Wolfowitz, interviewed by Winston Churchill, March 18, 2001 (www.telegraph.co.uk [July 2003]).

27. Michel McFaul, "A Step Backward on Nuclear Cooperation," *New York Times*, April 11, 2001, p. A23.

28. Jane Perlez, "Tougher on Russia," *New York Times*, March 23, 2001, p. A4.

29. The first head of the new bureau, Elizabeth Jones, was a career foreign service officer, not a political appointee. For an argument about why a reorganization of the State Department along these lines could help bring Europe and Russia policy in greater sync, see James M. Goldgeier, *Not Whether but When: The U.S. Decision to Enlarge NATO* (Brookings, 1999), p. 163.

30. Among other preparatory meetings, Bush held a two-and-one-half-hour seminar with five outside experts on Europe and Russia that McFaul attended. Evan Thomas and Roy Gutman, "See George. See George Learn Foreign Policy," *Newsweek*, June 18, 2001, p. 20.

31. Bradley Graham, *Hit to Kill: The New Battle over Shielding America from Missile Attack* (New York: Public Affairs, 2001), p. 368.

32. Rice, "Promoting the National Interest," p. 56. The downed American spy plane in China in April 2001 created the first foreign policy crisis of the Bush administration. Although defused eventually, the crisis further emboldened those in the Bush

administration who wanted to cast China as the principal strategic rival of the United States. Only September 11, 2001, diverted the administration's focus of attention away from China.

33. Graham, *Hit to Kill*, p. 358.

34. "Press Conference by President Bush and Russian President Putin," Brdo Castle, Brdo Pri Kranju, White House, Office of the Press Secretary (Slovenia), June 16, 2001.

35. Interview with Masha Lipman, a Russian journalist who participated in this meeting.

36. After September 11, Bush repeatedly referred to Putin as his personal friend. Putin, however, has shown less emotion when speaking about his American counterpart.

37. Institut Fonda, "Obshchestvennoe mnenie," *Amerika: vzglyad iz Rossii. Do i posle 11 sentyabrya* (Moskva: FOM, 2001).

38. Some described Putin's pursuit of this set of policies as astute and strategic, while others assessed the same policies with an opposite conclusion. On the former, see Celeste Wallander, "Russian Foreign Policy: The Implications of Pragmatism for U.S. Policy," testimony before the Subcommittee on Europe of the House Committee on International Relations, 107 Cong., 2 sess., February 27, 2002. On the latter, see Robert Legvold, "Russia's Unformed Foreign Policy," *Foreign Affairs*, vol. 80 (September–October 2001), pp. 62–75, and Legvold, "All the Way: Crafting a U.S.-Russian Alliance," *National Interest*, no. 70 (Winter 2002–03), pp. 21–31.

39. Igor Ivanov, "Organizing the World to Fight Terror," *New York Times*, January 27, 2002, p. A13. For a more skeptical view of this comparison, see James M. Goldgeier, "The United States and Russia," *Policy Review*, no. 109 (October–November 2001), pp. 47–56.

40. "President Bush, President Putin Discuss Joint Efforts against Terrorism: Remarks by President Bush and President Putin in Photo Opportunity," Calgary Kananaskis, Canada, June 27, 2002 (www.whitehouse.gov/news/releases/2002/06/20020627-3.html [July 2003]).

41. Ambassador Vershbow, "NATO and Russia: Redefining Relations for the 21st Century," address at St. Petersburg State University," February 22, 2002 (http://usinfo.state.gov/topical/pol/nato/02022201.htm [July 2003]).

42. President-elect Bush News Conference nominating Colin L. Powell as secretary of state, December 16, 2000.

43. Bush could make this transformation so easily in part because he, as a novice, was not deeply committed to his previous foreign policy strategy, and in part because "regime transformers" in his administration and their neoconservative allies outside of government offered up this new grand strategy to fill the void left after September 11. For a sampling of their views, see Robert Kagan and William Kristol, ed., *Present Dangers: Crisis and Opportunity in American Foreign and Defense Policy* (Encounter Books, 2000). On the ideological contest in the administration which eventually produced this Wilsonian turn, see Bob Woodword, *Bush at War* (Simon and Shuster, 2002); PBS *Frontline*, "The War behind Closed Doors," February 20, 2003 (www.pbs.org/wgbh/pages/frontline/shows/iraq); and Nicholas Lemann, "The Next World Order," *New Yorker*, April 1, 2002, pp. 42–48.

44. Remarks by the president at 2002 graduation exercise of the United States Military Academy, West Point, New York (www.whitehouse.gov).

45. On the novelty and danger of this new strategy, see Ivo Daalder, James Lindsay, and James Steinberg, "The Bush National Security Strategy: An Evaluation," *Policy Brief* (Brookings, October 4, 2002).

46. In 1998, Clinton, in fact, did make regime change in Iraq the stated goal of American foreign policy. Clinton, however, was not willing to use massive military force to achieve this objective.

47. White House press secretary Ari Fleischer, White House briefing, September 26, 2001.

48. According to Clinton's ambassador-at-large for the NIS Stephen Sestanovich, "Chechen rebels are receiving help from radical groups in other countries, including Usama Bin Laden's network and others who have attacked or threatened Americans and American interests." See his "The Conflict in Chechnya and Its Implications for U.S. Relations with Russia," testimony before the Senate Foreign Relations Committee, 106 Cong. 1 sess., November 4, 1999, p. 2.

49. *Chechnya Weekly*, vol. 3 (June 4, 2002), p. 2. Akhmadov met with lower-level State Department officials in Washington in January 2002, again in an unofficial capacity. See Fred Hiatt, "Tiptoe Diplomacy," *Washington Post*, January 28, 2002, p. A21.

50. Steven Wiesman, "U.S. Lists 3 Chechen Groups as Terrorist and Freezes Assets," *New York Times*, March 1, 2003, p. A10.

51. Vladimir Putin, "Why We Must Act," *New York Times*, November 14, 1999, sec. 4, p. 15.

52. Jamie Dettmer, "Bush Woos Putin but Ignores Chechnya," *Insight on the News*, August 27, 2001 (www.insightmag.com).

53. Dana Milbank and Peter Baker, "Bush Wary of Confronting Putin," *Washington Post*, May 26, 2002, p. A22.

54. "President Bush, President Putin Discuss Joint Efforts against Terrorism: Remarks by President Bush and President Putin in Photo Opportunity," p. 3.

55. *Chechnya Weekly*, vol. 3 (June 4, 2002), p. 1.

56. Rice, in answer to a question after her remarks to the Conservative Political Action Conference, Arlington, Virginia, February 1, 2002 (www.whitehouse.gov/news/releases/2002/02/20020201-6.html [July 2003]), p. 50.

57. "U.S. Envoy Hails Ties, Chides Russia on Chechnya," *Reuters*, December 28, 2001; "Vershbow Cites Some Progress," *Chechnya Weekly*, vol. 3 (January 4, 2002), p. 2; and Francesca Mereu, "Russia: U.S. Ambassador Discusses Bilateral Ties, Press Freedom, Chechnya," *RFE/RL*, May 31, 2002 (rferl.org. [July 2003]).

58. Steven Pifer, deputy assistant secretary for European and Eurasian Affairs, statement, Hearing: Developments in the Chechen Conflict, Commission on Security and Cooperation in Europe, May 9, 2002 (www.csce.gov/briefings.cfm?briefing_id=216 [July 2003]). Pifer also stressed that "Contrary to some media reporting, we have not seen evidence of extensive ties between Chechens and Al-Qaida in Chechnya" (pp. 2–3).

59. Colin Powell, confirmation hearing, January 17, 2001.

60. *Chechnya Weekly*, vol. 3 (June 4, 2002), p. 1.

61. Colin Powell, "U.S. Security Interests in Europe," hearing before the Senate Foreign Relations Committee, 107 Cong. 1 sess., June 20, 2001,

62. Pifer, deputy assistant secretary for European and Eurasian Affairs, statement, Hearing: Developments in the Chechen Conflict, p.1.

63. Richard Boucher, spokesperson, Department of State daily briefing, March 21, 2001, pp. 4, 7.

64. Interview with George Bush on *Newshour with Jim Lehrer*, February 16, 2000; and Bush, "A Distinctly American Internationalism."

65. The new Kremlin-friendly NTV fired most of its critically minded journalists and hired an American, Boris Jordan, to run the place more like a business. Then even Jordan was deemed to be too fond of independent reporting and was fired.

66. Andrei Zolotov Jr., "Report: Russia Is Not Safe for Press," *Moscow Times*, January 10, 2003, on *Johnson's Russia List* (www.cdi.org/russia/johnson/7012-1.cfm [July 2003]).

67. Under earlier formulas, the members of the Federation Council were elected. Now they are appointed, making the body much less legitimate and much less of a check on presidential power.

68. See the remarks by the U.S. ambassador to Russia, Alexander Vershbow, in Mereu, "Russia: U.S. Ambassador Discusses Bilateral Ties."

69. Milbank and Baker, "Bush Wary of Confronting Putin," p. A22.

70. "U.S. Envoy Hails Ties, Chides Russia on Chechnya."

71. Sharon LaFraniere, "Anti-Western Sentiment Grows in Russia: Putin Gives Security Service More Leeway as Disputes Rise over Outside Influence," *Washington Post*, January 19, 2003, p. A24.

72. Quoted in Milbank and Baker, "Bush Wary of Confronting Putin," p. A22.

73. "West Accused of Ignoring Russian Human Rights Abuses," *Associated Press*, July 9, 2002.

74. Quoted in Milbank and Baker, "Bush Wary of Confronting Putin."

75. For an overview of positive and negative trends in the Russian economy, see especially the set of articles published in *Russia's Uncertain Economic Future: Compendium of Papers*, Joint Economic Committee, Congress of the United States (Government Printing Office, December 2001).

76. After meeting in Genoa, Italy, in July 2001 on the sidelines of a G-8 meeting, Bush and Putin called for the formation of the Russian-American Business Dialogue (RABD). The RABD is composed of four private organizations—the U.S.-Russia Business Council, the Russian-American Business Council, the American Chamber of Commerce in Russia, and the Union of Industrialists and Entrepreneurs—which in effect have worked together to replace the old state-to-state commission chaired by Gore and Chernomyrdin. At the May 2002 summit in Moscow, the RABD submitted its initial report to Putin and Bush.

77. Thomas E. Graham, *Russia's Decline and Uncertain Recovery* (Washington: Carnegie Endowment for International Peace, 2002), p. 73.

78. Secretary Colin Powell, testimony before the House Appropriations Subcommittee on Foreign Operations, Export Financing, and Related Programs, 107 Cong. 2 sess., February 13, 2002.

79. "President Bush, President Putin Discuss Joint Efforts against Terrorism: Remarks by President Bush and President Putin in Photo Opportunity," p. 3.

80. Patrick Tyler, "Russia's Leader Says He Supports American Leader Aid for Georgia," *New York Times*, March 2, 2002, p. A7.

81. Seleznov, quoted in *Izvestiya*, no. 12, quoted from *RIA Novosti*, January 2002.

82. See, for instance, Secretary of State Powell's remarks before the Senate Foreign Relations Committee, 107 Cong. 2 sess., July 9, 2002.

83. "Interview with Vladimir Putin," *Financial Times,* December 15, 2001 (ft.com).

84. Graham, *Hit to Kill,* pp. 346–48.

85. The full text of the treaty is at www.whitehouse.gov/news/releases/2002/05/print/20020524-3.html (July 2003).

86. "Press briefing by Secretary of State Colin Powell on President's Trip to Russia," Grand Europa Hotel, St. Petersburg, Russia, May 25, 2002; on the Pentagon's plans, see James Dao, "U.S.-Russia Atomic Arms Pact Wins Senate Panel's Backing," *New York Times,* February 6, 2003, p. 10; a good critique of the treaty is Ivo H. Daalder and James M. Lindsay, "One-Day Wonder: The Dangerous Absurdity of the Bush-Putin Arms Treaty," *American Prospect,* August 26, 2002 (www.prospect.org).

87. "Fact Sheet G-7/8 Kananaskis Summit Day Two—U.S. Accomplishments," White House, Office of the Press Secretary, June 27, 2002 (www.whitehouse.gov/news/releases/2002/06/20020627-8.html [July 2003]), p.1.

88. "Fact Sheet G-7/8 Kananaskis Summit Day One—U.S. Accomplishments," White House, Office of the Press Secretary, June 26, 2002 (www.whitehouse.gov/news/releases/2002/06/20020626-11.html [July 2003]), p. 1.

89. "Interview of the National Security Advisor by ITAR-TASS," circulated on *Johnson's Russia List,* no. 7064, February 16, 2003 (www.cdi.org/russia/johnson [July 2003]).

90. James Gerstenzang and Edwin Chen, "U.S., Russian Disagree on 'Axis of Evil' Direction of Terror War," *Los Angeles Times,* February 5, 2002, p. A1.

91. "Putin Still Popular with Majority of Russians on Third Anniversary of Election," *Interfax,* March 26, 2003. On the idea that Putin's popularity at home made him less vulnerable to attacks from dissatisfied interest groups, see Stephen Sestanovich, *At Odds with Iran and Iraq: Can the United States and Russia Resolve Differences?* A Century Foundation and Stanley Foundation Paper (New York and Muscatine, Iowa, February 2003).

92. Sestanovich, *At Odds with Iran and Iraq,* pp. 32–33.

93. The assistance in question has been the new $20 billion package for Cooperative Threat Reduction proposed at the G-8 summit in Canada. See Sestanovich, *At Odds with Iran and Iraq,* p. 35.

94. Peter Baker, "Russia Resists Ending Iran Project: Moscow Balks at U.S. Offer for Curtailing Work on Reactor," *Washington Post,* October 22, 2002, p. A19; Robert Einhorn and Gary Samore, "Heading Off Iran's Bomb: The Need for Renewed U.S.-Russian Cooperation," *Yaderny Kontrol Digest,* vol. 7 (Summer 2002) pp. 9–23; and Mark Katz, "Russian-Iranian Relations in the Putin Era," *Demokratizatsiya,* vol. 10 (Winter 2002), pp. 69–82.

95. Sabrina Tavernise, "Russia Presses Iran to Accept Scrutiny of the Nuclear Sites," *New York Times,* July 1, 2003, p. A9.

96. Robin Shepherd, "U.S. Tempts Russia with Profits of Ousting Saddam," *Times* (London), September 13, 2002, p. 17; Michael Wines, "Putin Again Rejects U.S. Calls for Support of a War, Fearing Effect on the Mideast," *New York Times,* March 1, 2003, p. A8; and "Lugar Introduces Bill to Improve Trade with Russia," press release, March 10, 2003.

97. "Interview Granted by President Vladimir Putin to France-3 Television," February 10, 2003, transcript and translation provided by Federal News Service (fed-news.com).

98. John Leicester, "France, Russia, Germany Will 'Not Allow' Passage of U.N. Resolution," *Associated Press*, March 5, 2003.

99. "News Conference with the Foreign Ministers of Germany, France, and Russia," March 5, 2003 (fednews.com).

100. "Interview Granted by President Vladimir Putin to France-3 Television."

101. "Statement by President Putin on Iraq at a Kremlin Meeting," broadcast on RTR, March 20, 2003, transcript and translation provided by Federal News Service (fednews.com).

102. "Speech by Russian Foreign Minister Igor Ivanov at the State Duma Session," March 21, 2003, transcript and translation provided by Federal News Service (fednews.com.).

103. Ivanov, as quoted in Vladimir Isachenkov, "Russia" U.S. Trying to Destroy Iraq," *Associated Press*, March 26, 2003.

104. John Chalmers, "U.S., Russia at Odds over War on Terrorism," *Reuters*, February 3, 2002.

105. Andrei Ryabov, "Putin as the Mirror of Russians' Attitude to the Iraqi War," *Profil*, no. 12 (March 2003), translated by *RIA Novosti*.

106. Arshad Mohammed, "U.S. Believes Russian in Baghdad Aiding Iraq," *Reuters*, March 24, 2003. The United States had made claims of this nature and threatened sanctions well before the war began. See "Russia Angered by Sanctions Moves," *United Press International*, September 13, 2002.

107. "Igor' Ivanov: Rossiya ne postavlyalal v Irak vooruzheniya," *strana.ru*, March 24, 2003; and "MP Denies Russia Delivers Arms to Iraq," *Interfax*, March 24, 2003.

108. "U.S. Threatened Sanctions against Russian Firms," *RFE/RL Newsline*, March 27, 2003.

Chapter 14

1. Edward Hallett Carr, *The Twenty Years' Crisis 1919–1939: An Introduction to the Study of International Relations* (Macmillan & Co., Limited, 1939).

2. In the language of political science, the next section treats the dependent variable of this book—American foreign policy—as the independent variable in the transformation of Russia internally and the integration of Russia into the West. Of course, we recognize that the conclusions that follow are tentative and speculative. Further research is needed to confirm or disconfirm these claims.

3. Interview with Yegor Gaidar.

4. As discussed in chapter 4, the biggest unfulfilled pledge was a $6 billion stabilization fund that Bush announced in April 1992 but *never* provided.

5. As discussed in chapter 9, the causes and sustainability of Russia's economic recovery are debated, especially since one exogenous variable—rising oil prices—might be the real driver of growth.

6. *RIA* (Russian Information Agency) *Novosti*, July 31, 2002 (en.rian.ru/rian/index.cfm [July 2003]).

7. For a more comprehensive discussion of programs, see General Accounting Office, *Foreign Assistance: International Efforts to Aid Russia's Transition Have Had Mixed Results* (November 2000).

8. Over the years, the categories of assistance have changed. The basic breadth represented in the 2001 budget, however, remained expansive throughout the 1990s.

9. National surveys of enterprise restructuring in general are numerous, but few have tried to isolate the influence of foreign-provided technical assistance on the process. See, for instance, Joseph Blasi, Maya Kroumova, and Douglas Kruse, *Kremlin Capitalism: Privatizing the Russian Economy* (Cornell University Press, 1997).

10. Interview with Dmitri Vasiliev. See also Timothy Frye, *Brokers and Bureaucrats: Building Market Institutions in Russia* (University of Michigan Press, 2000), pp. 187–88.

11. Interview with Vasiliev.

12. Frye, *Brokers and Bureaucrats,* p. 181.

13. AID sponsored multiyear contacts between American tax experts such as Duke professor Robert Conrad and Russian tax experts based at Yegor Gaidar's Institute for the Economy in Transition. Much of this work was conceptual or academic in the 1990s since the political context was not conducive for tax reform. When this political environment changed after Putin's election as president in 2000, a fully revamped tax code could be taken off the shelf and pushed quickly into law.

14. For instance, the ideas outlined in *Fixing Russia's Banks: A Proposal for Growth* by Michael Bernstam and Alvin Rabushka (Hoover Institution Press, 1998) are now well known in Russia.

15. If ideas from Americans have been limited (and overshadowed by advisers from Chile), transfers provided by international financial institutions have been substantial. For an early accounting, see Scott Thomas, "Social Policy in the Economics of Transition: The Role of the West," in Ethan Kapstein and Michael Mandelbaum, eds., *Sustaining the Transition: The Social Safety Net in Postcommunist Europe* (New York: Council on Foreign Relations, 1997), pp. 147–72.

16. The Agency for International Development has redressed this imbalance. See U.S.AID, *USAID/Russia Strategy Amendment (1999-2005)* (Moscow, February 2002).

17. The United States did provide food assistance, but there is little evidence to suggest that this kind of aid helped to alleviate poverty in Russia.

18. Joseph Stiglitz, *Globalization and Its Discontents* (Norton and Company, 2002).

19. Janine R. Wedel, *Collision and Collusion: The Strange Case of Western Aid to Eastern Europe* (St. Martin's, 2001). Cohen, *Failed Crusade*; and Reddaway and Glinski, *The Tragedy of Russia's Reforms.*

20. Whether Germany or the United States is ranked higher depends on the accounting procedures for measuring direct investment. For a method that ranks the United States higher, see Inga Livitsky, Matt London, and Tanya Shuster, "U.S.-Russian Trade and Investment: Policy and Performances," in *Russia's Uncertain Economic Future,* Compendium of papers submitted the Joint Economic Committee, Congress of the United States (Government Printing Office, December 2001), pp. 411–24.

21. Figures quoted from Mehmet Ogutcu, "Attracting Foreign Direct Investment for Russia's Modernization: Battling against the Odds," paper presented at OECD-Russian Investment Roundtable, St. Petersburg, Russia, 2000, pp. 3–4.

22. Jackson-Vanik is a symbolic issue rather than a real trade barrier, but symbols do matter.

23. Blake Marshall, executive vice president, U.S.-Russia Business Council, testimony before the European Subcommittee of the House Committee of International

Relations, 107 Cong. 2 sess., February 27, 2002; V. G. Kur'erov, "Inostrannyie investitsii v ekonomiku rossii v 2002 g" (http://econom.nsc.ru.).

24. For an account of these backward steps, see Timothy J. Colton and Michael McFaul, "Russian Democracy under Putin," *Problems of Post-Communism*, vol. 50 (July–August 2003), pp. 12–21.

25. James Gibson, "The Struggle between Order and Liberty in Contemporary Russian Political Culture," *Australian Journal of Political Science*, vol. 32 (July 1997), pp. 271–90; James Gibson, "The Russian Dance with Democracy," *Post-Soviet Affairs*, vol. 17 (April–June 2001), pp. 101–28; Timothy J. Colton and Michael McFaul, "Are Russians Undemocratic?" *Post-Soviet Affairs*, vol. 18 (April–June 2002), pp. 91–121; and Vserossiiskii Tsentr Izucheniya Obshchestvennogo Mneniya (VTsIOM), *Ot mennii – k ponimaniyu: Obshchestvennoe mnenie – 2000* (VTsIOM, December 2000). For more skeptical findings that focus on respect for human rights, see Theodore Gerber and Sarah Mendelson, "Russian Public Opinion on Human Rights and the War in Chechnya," *Post-Soviet Affairs*, vol. 18 (October–December 2002), pp. 271–305.

26. We emphasize "traditional" security issue to suggest that democracy promotion could also be considered a security interest of the United States. See Michael McFaul and Sarah Mendelson, "Russian Democracy—A U.S. National Security Interest," *Demokratizatsiya*, vol. 8 (Summer 2000), pp. 330–53. Moreover, some of the issues that trumped democracy promotion were policies pursued based on liberal motivations.

27. Fred Hiatt, "Chicken before Chechnya," *Washington Post*, June 17, 2002, p. A17.

28. Strobe Talbott, *The Russia Hand: A Memoir of Presidential Diplomacy* (Random House, 2002), p. 211.

29. See Joel Hellman, "Winners Take All: The Politics of Partial Reform in Post-Communist Transitions," *World Politics*, 50, no. 1 (1998); Jean-Jacques Dethier, Hafez Ghanem, and Edda Zoli, "Does Democracy Facilitate the Economic Transition? An Empirical Study of Central and Eastern Europe and the Former Soviet Union," unpublished manuscript, World Bank (June 1999); *Transition Report 1999: Ten Years of Transition* (London: European Bank for Reconstruction and Development, 1999), chap. 5; and Anders Åslund, *Building Capitalism: The Transformation of the Former Soviet Bloc* (Cambridge: Cambridge University Press, 2001). The causal relationship between democracy and economic growth is less well understood.

30. Colton and McFaul, "Are Russians Undemocratic?"

31. William Odom and Robert Dujarric, *Commonwealth or Empire? Russia, Central Asia, and the Transcaucasus* (Hudson Institute Press, 1995); and Uri Ra'anan and Kate Martin, eds., *Russia: A Return to Imperialism?* (St. Martin's Press, 1995). For theoretical arguments that make clear how likely conflict is in these types of situations, see Stephen Walt, *Revolution and War* (Cornell University Press, 1996); and Jack Snyder, *From Voting to Violence: Democratization and Nationalist Conflict* (W. W. Norton, 2000).

32. "Yanks to the Rescue," *Time*, July 15, 1996.

33. Anthony Lake, "Do the Doable," *Foreign Policy*, no. 54 (Spring 1984), p. 121.

34. Åslund, *Building Capitalism: The Transformation of the Former Soviet Bloc*, p. 401.

35. The poll was conducted by Timothy Colton and Michael McFaul. A total of 1,919 voters were interviewed between November 13 and December 13, 1999. They were selected in a multistage area-probability sample of the voting-age population, with sampling units in thirty-three regions of the Russian Federation. The work was

carried out by the Demoscope group at the Institute of Sociology of the Russian Academy of Sciences (Moscow).

36. For a similar argument, see Ivo H. Daalder and James M. Lindsay, "One-Day Wonder: The Dangerous Absurdity of the Bush-Putin Arms Treaty," *American Prospect*, August 26, 2002 (www.prospect.org [July 2003]).

37. Putin, quoted in "Putin: Iraq War Most Serious Crisis since Cold War's End," *Dow Jones Newswires*, March 28, 2003.

38. See, for example, Robert Jervis, *Perception and Misperception in International Politics* (Princeton University Press, 1974).

39. Vladimir Putin, "Rossiya na rubezhe tysyacheletnii," January 1, 2000 (government.gov.ru. [July 2003]).

40. Thomas E. Graham, Jr., "A World without Russia?" Jamestown Foundation Conference, Washington, 1999, published in *Johnson's Russia List*, no. 3336, June 11, 1999 (www.cdi.org/russia/johnson [July 2003]).

41. Christopher Hill, "Russia's Defense Spending," in *Russia's Uncertain Economic Future*, Compendium of papers submitted the Joint Economic Committee, Congress of the United States (GPO, December 2001), pp. 161–82.

42. According to Finance Minister Alexei Kudrin, defense spending will increase dramatically in the 2003 budget, jumping to 346.1 billion rubles (roughly 11 billion dollars), or 14.9 percent of the national budget. *RIA Novosti*, August 15, 2002 (en.rian.ru/rian/index.cfm [July 2003]).

Index